Discovering
Business Statistics

by James S. Hawkes and Quinton J. Nottingham

HAWKES
LEARNING
SYSTEMS

HAWKES
LEARNING
SYSTEMS

A division of Quant Systems, Inc.
546 Long Point Road, Mt. Pleasant, SC 29464

Printed in the United States of America

ISBN:

Student Textbook: 978-1-932628-69-2

Student Textbook and Software Bundle: 978-1-932628-70-8

Table of Contents

CH3   Organizing, Displaying, and Interpreting Data

CH4   Numerical Descriptive Statistics

 Probability, Randomness, and Uncertainty

CH6   Discrete Probability Distributions: Information about the Future

CH7 Continuous Random Variables

CH8 Samples and Sampling Distributions

CH9 Estimating Means and Proportions

 Hypothesis Testing: Single Samples

CH11 Inferences about Means and Proportions: Two Samples

Appendix A: Statistical Tables

Decision Making Using Statistics

 **Discovering the Real World**

The Centers for Disease Control and Prevention estimates that 500,000 people die in the United States each year from smoking and related diseases. That is considerably more deaths than those attributed to alcohol, heroin, murders, suicide, car accidents, and AIDS combined. Surprisingly, the evidence relating smoking to cancer is largely statistical, most of which could be digested after an introductory statistics course.

Cigarettes did not always carry warnings such as "Smoking causes lung cancer, heart disease, emphysema, and may complicate pregnancy" or "Quitting smoking now greatly reduces serious risks to your health." In the early 1960's Congress debated the Surgeon General's plan to label all packages of cigarettes with a warning that smoking could be hazardous to your health. Hearings were held and testimonies were gathered from interested parties. The tobacco companies did not want a health notice placed on their product, so they sponsored a significant amount of investigation into the health effects of smoking. On the other side of the issue was a large group of medical researchers who had analyzed the effects of smoking on animals and had collected considerable data on the health of both smoking and nonsmoking populations. The evidence presented seemed unquestionable: heavy smokers had a much higher incidence of lung cancer, about thirty times higher than nonsmokers. Furthermore, researchers found smoking is associated with cancers of the mouth, pharynx, larynx, esophagus, pancreas, uterus, cervix, kidney, and bladder. Even suicide rates were at higher levels for smokers.

The tobacco companies countered with their own experts who pointed out that the underlying cause of both disease and smoking could be attributed to heredity. That is, whatever caused people to have higher rates of lung cancer, heart disease, and so forth, could also cause them to smoke. If this were the case, then the proposed warning on packages of cigarettes would be untruthful. So, the pivotal problem was how could someone know whether smoking or heredity caused cancer?

One method of attacking this problem is to perform a **controlled experiment**. In a controlled experiment the researcher collects data that will hopefully clarify the relationship between variables. A simple method of accomplishing this task would be to create two groups, smokers and nonsmokers, and compare them. The nonsmokers would be the **control group** and the smokers the **treatment group**. Each subject is randomly assigned to one of two groups, in this case smokers and nonsmokers, to avoid bias. The smoking group would be required to smoke a pack of cigarettes per day (for say 15 years) and at the end of the time period their health would be compared to the health of the nonsmokers. By randomly choosing members of the population, the hereditary pool of both groups should be similarly mixed and thus any subsequent differences in health between the two groups could be attributed to the **treatment** (smoking) that was applied to one group. This method of experimentation has one drawback; it is impossible to get human beings to volunteer for the experiment. As a result, the experiment has never been done.

However, researchers have performed controlled statistical experiments on many different kinds of animals, and have discovered that smoking does cause problems similar to those observed in human beings. In 1964, the Surgeon General produced a historic report linking tobacco smoking to cancer. Since January 1, 1966, all cigarette packages sold in the United States have been required to carry the health warning. Since January 1, 1971, all cigarette television advertising has been banned. The percentage of adults who smoke in the United States has decreased significantly. The prevalence of smoking has diminished in the United States since the exposure of the statistical evidence, from about 40% in 1965 to about 29% in 1987, 23% in 2002, and 21% in 2008. However, this is not the case in many parts of the world.

Statistics made a difference. They helped people make informed decisions about their choice to smoke or not. Fortunately, it was not speculation, opinion, or special interest that decided the issue. Research on the effects of smoking continues and of the 4,000 substances found in tobacco smoke, about 60 are now believed to be associated with cancer or tumor formation.

So does smoking cause cancer? There is no absolute proof, but the evidence overwhelmingly suggests that it does. In 1998, tobacco companies reached a $206 billion agreement with 46 states to settle a lawsuit on the health damage done by cigarette smoking.

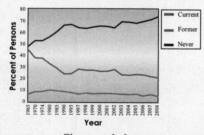

Percent of Young Adults (Ages 18-24) Who Were Current, Former, or Never Smokers

Figure 1.1

Source: National Center for Health Statistics

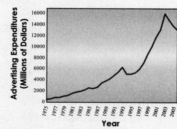

U.S. Advertising and Promotional Expenditures (Millions of Dollars)

Figure 1.2

Source: Federal Trade Commission

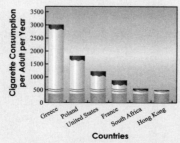

World Tobacco Use in 2007

Figure 1.3

Source: ERC Group Plc.

Introduction

How we conduct business and make business decisions in the real world is intensely data driven. In business today, almost all decisions are made based on the analysis of data. In fact, decisions in all aspects of our lives are based on the diverse and ubiquitous data that are available to us.

CEOs, CFOs, Presidents, Vice Presidents, and many leaders and executives of multinational corporations need to justify their decisions. Almost all of the time, these decisions are supported by statistical models, summary statistics (graphs and tables), and other statistical tools and concepts that we will discuss in this text.

Decision makers use statistics to collect data, analyze the data, and make interpretations – all relevant to their profession. They build models with data and then make decisions using those models. They describe data using graphs and summary measurements. They develop methods of designing experiments and gathering data that are cost effective and diminish bias.

Business and Statistics

Simply put, statistics will help managers make better business decisions. Managers use data to help them oversee multiple divisions of their company, countless products, and thousands of employees. Even for small businesses, understanding data via the use of statistics is critical in today's competitive environment. Even though many business decisions are made based on expert intuition and experience, ignoring all relevant information available (such as the use of statistical techniques) would be senseless.

Thus, the use of statistical techniques must be viewed as an important part of the decision-making process. Combining intuition, experience, and statistical analysis arms the manager with a wealth of information giving him or her an advantage over the competition. If not an advantage, then this combination of tools certainly allows the manager, company, or corporation to maintain its competitive status in its respective industry.

For example, the development of Six Sigma can be traced back to the eighteenth century when Carl Frederick Gauss introduced it as a metric for the normal curve. Later Walter Shewhart began showing how three sigma deviations from the mean required a process correction. In the 1980s, a Motorola engineer coined the term Six Sigma (and copyrighted it) for improving quality management. Today Six Sigma is viewed as a concept that incorporates many statistical techniques to improve processes and make business decisions.

 # Who Will Be Our Next President?

Once every four years the media extravaganza known as the American presidential election is intensely carried over the airwaves and newspapers for a period of at least six months. We speculate on who the candidates will be, watch the primary campaigns, see the conventions, look at the debates, put up with slick image-making commercials, and endure negative advertisements. Finally we cast our votes and watch the results on the evening news.

Often times, the results of the election are known well in advance. How can this be the case? With statistics! By sampling registered voters prior to the election, one can get an estimate of the outcome and thus, who will win the election. Of course, even though there is a chance that the candidate receiving the highest percentage of votes may not win, it is expected that if the sample is large enough, then the estimate of votes that each candidate receives will be close to the outcome of the actual election.

Recent evidence indicates the statistical forecasts based on sample estimates are becoming increasingly accurate. Table 1.1 provides a list of the predicted percentages of popular vote for the winning candidate the day prior to the election and the actual vote received by the candidate.

Table 1.1 – Presidential Polls			
Year	Candidates	Winner's Predicted %	Actual Winning %
1976	**Carter** Ford	48%	50.1%
1980	**Reagan** Carter	47%	50.8%
1984	**Reagan** Mondale	59%	59.2%
1988	**Bush** Dukakis	56%	53.0%
1992	**Clinton** Bush, Perot	49%	43.3%
1996	**Clinton** Dole, Perot	52%	50.1%
2000	**Bush** Gore, Nader	47%	47.9%
2004	**Bush** Kerry	49%	50.7%
2008	**Obama** McCain	55%	52.8%

Source: Gallup.com

What methods do statisticians use to make predictions? The most difficult part of the process is finding a sample that accurately reflects those people who plan to vote in the election. Those who will vote on Election Day define a group of people that we are interested in studying. In statistics the group we wish to study is called the **population**.

Population

Definition

A **population** is the total set of subjects or things we are interested in studying.

Populations are defined by what a researcher is studying and can come in all shapes and sizes. If someone is studying houses foreclosed upon in 2008, then all the houses foreclosed upon in 2008 would constitute the population. If someone is studying banks in the United States, then all banks in the United States would represent the population. Citizens who are registered to vote in a presidential election constitute a population of considerable interest to presidential candidates. The parties spend hundreds of millions of dollars finding out what people think (sampling) and adopt or reject political positions consistent with the preponderance of the data. In the world of political science this "data-driven" approach to politics is called populism.

Frame

Definition

A list containing all members of the population is referred to as a **frame**.

According to the Census Bureau there are about 309 million people in the United States and about 6.8 billion people around the world. The **frame** for the population of the U.S. would be a rather long list containing about 309 million names. Although a previous census would be a good start in developing a frame for the U.S. population, it is doubtful that an exact frame could ever be developed at a given point in time since there is one new birth every 8 seconds, one death every 12 seconds, and one new immigrant every 36 seconds. There are just too many people being born, dying, and immigrating over a 10-year period to get an exact frame for the U.S. population. But for problems that deal with smaller populations, frames are easily developed. For example, if your business statistics class were the population under consideration, the class roll would be the frame for the population.

Note: A strict definition of a **census** is a survey that includes all the elements or units in the **frame**.

Population Parameter

Definition

Population parameters are facts about the population. Since parameters are descriptions of the population, a population can have many parameters.

For a presidential election, some population parameters in which candidates and pollsters will be interested are:

- The percentage of eligible voters who will vote on Election Day.
- The percentage of voters who will vote for a specific candidate.
- The percentage of men who favor a candidate.
- The percentage of women who favor a candidate.
- The percentage of people in the 18-25 age group who favor a candidate.
- The average income of voters who favor a candidate.

The parameters mentioned in the example are either averages or percentages. However, other measures such as the maximum or minimum value of the population measurement as well as other characteristics would also be considered population parameters. For a specific population at a specific point in time, population parameters do not change; they are fixed numbers. But seldom will the value of a population parameter be known since the value involves all the population measurements which are usually too expensive or time consuming to collect. It is the statistician's job to discover these values. This is done by taking a sample and using the sample measurements to estimate the desired population measurement.

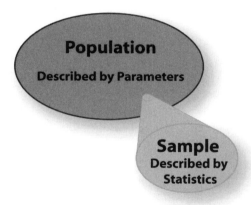

Population
Described by Parameters

Sample
Described by Statistics

The percentage of votes a presidential candidate receives on Election Day is a parameter presidential candidates spend enormous amounts of money trying to estimate. Sample data are used to estimate this population parameter. Sample estimates and population parameters for the percentage of votes the winning candidate received in an election appear in Table 1.1.

Populations in the NYSE

As a student studying business (whether it be management, marketing, finance, or management science), your ultimate goal is to make money by making good business decisions. What makes up the New York Stock Exchange? The NYSE is made up of many companies and organizations, large and small. As someone attempting to make money on the NYSE, there are many populations to study. One can study the daily closing price of a particular stock; the stocks valued at less than a certain dollar amount, say $10; or the number of profitable companies on the NYSE. As you can see, since there are more than 2,700 companies valued at more than 28.5 trillion dollars, one needs to make informed decisions in order to be profitable.

Definition

A **sample** is a subset of the population which is used to gain insight about the population. Samples are used to represent a larger group, the population.

Sample

Definition

A **statistic** is a fact or characteristic about a sample.

In Table 1.1 the winner's predicted percentage is a statistic since it is computed from a sample. The elected president's actual percentage is a parameter, since it is computed using the votes of all who participated in the election (the population in this instance).

For any given sample a statistic is a fixed number. Because there are lots of different samples that could be drawn from a population, statistics will vary depending on the sample selected. Statistics are used as estimates of the population parameters. See Figure 1.4.

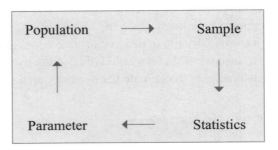

Figure 1.4

Studying an entire population can be an expensive proposition. In 2000 the census cost the government $39.98 per household. Total expenditure during the 2000 census cycle was approximately 4.5 billion dollars. The estimated cost of the 2010 census was around 14.5 billion dollars, or $117.33 per household. Because of the enormous expense, even the United States government with all its resources does not undertake a census of its citizens but once every ten years. Yet amazingly accurate information about the population, even large populations like the United States, can be found by using a small sample. If the sample is a good representation of the population, then the conclusions reached using sample data will likely be reasonable for the population as a whole. A statistician faces the interesting problem of developing a representative sample without spending an inordinate amount of time or money.

Political pollsters spend much of their resources developing a representative sample of Americans who will cast their votes on Election Day. After the sample is identified, the problem becomes one of obtaining candidate preferences from the selected voters. Tallying the votes and computing the actual percentages will take a computer at most a few seconds. After the estimates of the population parameters are calculated, one of the interesting statistical questions is, *how good are the estimates?* As Table 1.1 demonstrates, none of the estimates of the percentage of votes each candidate would receive were exactly correct, but most were very close. If we cannot determine how much faith we should place in our estimates, it will be difficult to use the estimates to make decisions. The process of selecting samples and determining the reliability of our estimates is a large part of what statistics is about.

1.2 Statistics and Quality

"Statistical thinking is critical to improvement of a system."

-Mary Walton, *The Deming Management Method.*

Definition

A **process** is a series of actions that changes inputs to outputs.

Process

The idea of a process is closely tied to quality control. For a physician a process is a treatment performed in a series of steps designed to improve a patient's condition. In a business context a process is a series of steps that produces a product or service. Closely monitoring and continuously improving processes produce high quality products. Monitoring the process means taking measurements of key variables over time. Improving processes means reducing process variation by finding the causes of variation and eliminating them.

In order to improve a process there must be an understanding of how the process is currently performing. This requires definition and monitoring of the process. Statistics helps with decisions about how the data will be collected, what data will be needed, and the analysis of the data. In addition to ferreting out production problems, **Statistical Process Control** (SPC) is a group of statistical methods designed to monitor and control processes. SPC is helpful in detecting problems in a process before they create a defective product or service. We will study this subject more extensively in Chapter 17.

Where Did the Term *Statistics* Come From?

LATIN
The evolution of the word statistics comes from the modern Latin phrase *statisticum collegium* (lecture about state affairs).

GERMAN
The German term *Statistik* was first used by Gottfried Achenwall in 1749.

ENGLISH
The anglicized form of the German term was introduced by John Sinclair (a Presbyterian pastor) who published the *Statistical Account of Scotland*, a 21 volume compilation. This work was published at various periods during the 1790s.

1.3 Descriptive Versus Inferential Statistics

The science of statistics is divided into two categories, **descriptive** and **inferential**. Descriptive methods describe and summarize data, while inferential methods aid in drawing conclusions and making decisions and predictions about populations and processes for which it is impractical to obtain measurements on each member.

Descriptive Statistics

Examples of Descriptive Statistics

- Frequency Distribution
- Measures of Central Tendency:
  - Mean
  - Median
  - Mode
- Measures of Dispersion:
  - Range
  - Variance
  - Standard Deviation

Descriptive Statistics

The emphasis in **descriptive statistics** is analyzing observed measurements, usually from a sample. With descriptive statistics we try to answer questions such as:

- What is a typical value for the measurements?
- How much variation do the measurements possess?
- What is the shape or distribution of the measurements?
- Are there any extreme values in the measurements and, if so, what does that tell us?
- What is the relative position of a particular measurement in the group of data?
- What kind of relationship exists, if any, when there are two variables and how strong is the relationship?

Definition

Descriptive statistics is the collection, organization, analysis, and presentation of data.

The application of descriptive statistical tools is usually *ad hoc*, that is, the exact method of analysis changes from one problem to the next. Sometimes the application of descriptive statistics can raise as many questions as it answers. And when that happens, statistics is working at its best as a problem-solving or process-improvement tool.

The importance of descriptive statistics as an information-producing tool relates to the amount of data to be comprehended. If there are only two observations, say 6 and 4, then comprehending the data in its entirety is not difficult and descriptive statistical aids are of little value. However, the 100 observations of the revenues of the top 100 U.S. companies in Table 1.2 suggest a different story. Individually inspecting 100 revenues would produce very little useful knowledge. To comprehend a large set of data, it must be summarized. That is the function of descriptive statistical techniques. Descriptive techniques are the most common statistical applications.

Table 1.2 – Profits of the Top 100 Companies by Revenues in the Fortune 500 (Millions of Dollars)

14,335	1,707	−1,098	1,054
19,280	1,312	3,021	−329
10,483	2,661	−21,553	740
11,025	2,488	1,056	202
6,276	4,745	5,704	−71,969
4,858	2,006	3,307	2,468
12,535	12,266	6,134	−338
2,717	767	3,638	−1,237
11,728	1,280	98	12,901
7,660	14,569	1,686	1,755
8,055	3,829	4,369	−537
−1,606	1,433	1,277	2,130
3,651	13,385	683	−2,915
823	8,635	3,124	−459
−10,949	1,463	895	381
1,151	1,783	−2,436	204
3,696	2,152	854	−115
12,275	3,024	2,394	6,342
13,425	1,003	1,346	1,935
3,822	648	1,023	828
13,436	−2,855	6,824	−887
70	235	1,040	3,622
503	28	2,153	1,161
1,086	5,946	5,746	902
−1,982	−2,246	−3,378	−30,860

Source: CNNMoney.com

Inferential Statistics

It would be preferable to have measurements of the entire population, but in most cases these data are either not obtainable or would be much too costly to obtain. For example, to be absolutely certain that all car air bags will inflate in head-on collisions would require each new car to be crash tested in a head-on crash. If 100 percent inspection were a requirement, cars would be a scarce commodity. Fortunately for automobile manufacturers, statistical sampling techniques can reliably estimate, with a relatively small sample, the fraction of air bags that will inflate.

Use Sample Data to Make Inferences about Unknown Population Characteristics

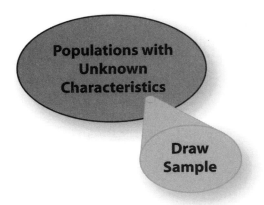

Definition
The objective of **inferential statistics** is to make reasonable estimates about population characteristics using sample data.

The Consequences of Statistical Illiteracy

Part of being an intelligent human being is the desire to learn the truth about the world we live in. But as Oscar Wilde said:

"The truth is rarely pure and never simple."

-Oscar Wilde, *The Importance of Being Earnest.*

Being statistically illiterate puts one (or one's organization) at a competitive disadvantage compared to companies that possess and use statistical knowledge and analytical tools. Statistics and its uses cannot be avoided. Therefore, learning and using statistical tools will give you and your organization more flexibility when making decisions.

To intelligently appreciate or produce statistical information, you must be statistically literate to defend yourself from a persuasive but fallacious statistical argument, to decrease your vulnerability to pseudo-sciences, and to diminish the chances of making poor and sometimes injurious business decisions.

A statistically literate person understands the language of statistics and understands statistical concepts and reasoning. To become statistically literate one should be able to think "statistically". This will involve asking questions like:

- Where did the data come from?
- How was the sample taken and is the sample large enough?
- How reliable or accurate were the measures used to generate the reported data?
- Are the reported statistics appropriate for this kind of data?
- Is a graph drawn appropriately?
- How was this probabilistic statement calculated?
- Do the claims make sense?
- Should there be additional information?
- Are there alternative interpretations?

Liar or Statistician?

In his book *How to Tell the Liars from the Statisticians*, Robert Hooke sheds light on our exposure to misleading statistics in everyday life. In the preface he writes, "The science of statistics has made great progress in this century, but progress has been accompanied by a corresponding increase in the misuse of statistics. The public, whether it gets its information from television, newspapers, or news magazines, is not well prepared to defend itself against those who would manipulate it with statistical arguments. Many people either believe everything they hear or come to believe in nothing statistical, which is even worse." Throughout the remaining chapters, Hooke uses examples from politics, economics, entertainment, and the medical community to illustrate the dangers of being statistically illiterate. You might be surprised to learn the ways in which the misuse of statistics affects you every day. In order to digest the plethora of statistical information you encounter, you must first become statistically literate.

Source: Hooke, Robert. *How to Tell the Liars from the Statisticians.* New York, New York: Marcel Dekker Inc., 1983. Print.

R Chapter 1 Review

Key Terms and Ideas

- Controlled Experiment
- Population
- Frame
- Census
- Population Parameters
- Sample
- Statistic
- Process
- Statistical Process Control
- Descriptive Statistics
- Inferential Statistics
- Statistical Literacy

1 Exercises

Basic Concepts

1. What are three objectives of statistical methods?

2. Briefly describe the role of statistics in managerial decision making.

3. What is a controlled experiment?

4. Explain the purpose of a control group.

5. Explain the purpose of a treatment.

6. How is it possible to know the results of a presidential election before Election Day?

7. What is a population?

8. What is a frame?

9. What is a population parameter?

10. Why is it often difficult to determine the exact value of a population parameter?

11. What is a sample?

12. What is a statistic?

13. Describe the relationships between populations, samples, parameters, and statistics.

14. Define statistical inference.

15. Describe the role of statistics in the quality movement.

16. What is a process. How are processes improved?

17. What is the difference between descriptive and inferential statistics?

18. What are the consequences of being statistically illiterate? How could this put you at a disadvantage in business?

Exercises

1. Jakob Nielsen, a website consultant, recently conducted an eye-tracking survey to determine whether people ignore purely decorative images when viewing web pages. An aspect of the study compared a set of products on Pottery Barn's furniture website and a page of televisions on Amazon.com. The study found that consumers tended to ignore the televisions on Amazon.com because they were generic, making the product image less inviting. When consumers viewed Pottery Barn's website, they were more inclined to view the photos of the bookcases for longer periods of time because they were images of the actual products for sale. **Source**: New York Times

   a. Identify the population of interest.

   b. What characteristic of the population is being measured?

   c. Is the purpose of the data collection to perform descriptive or inferential statistics?

2. A recent study at Britain's Oxford and Exeter Universities explored whether a woman's diet before conception affects the gender of her child. Researchers studied the eating habits of 740 women during their first-time pregnancies and found that higher caloric intake prior to conception can significantly increase the chances of having a son while more restricted diets are more likely to produce daughters. They found that high potassium diets (eating bananas) and calcium rich diets (cereal and milk) were associated with having a baby boy. Researchers concluded that eating a bowl of cereal for breakfast can increase the chances of a male birth. "Of women eating cereals daily, 59 percent had boys, compared with only 43 percent who bore boys in the group eating less than a bowlful per week."
Source: CNNHealth.com

   a. Identify the population of interest.

   b. What characteristic of the population is being measured?

   c. Identify the sample.

   d. Is the purpose of the data collection to perform descriptive or inferential statistics?

   e. What are some problems that could be associated with collecting data in this study?

3. Researchers at The Ohio State University and Zeppelin University Friedrichshafen, in Germany, recently conducted a study regarding the elderly and negative news coverage. The researchers presented 276 subjects with several stories (with photos) about either old or young people. Participants were presented with one of two versions of each story. In one version the main character was painted in a positive light and in the other the same character was described negatively. After the participants finished reading their self-esteem was measured. The study found that older readers were more inclined to read the negative stories about youth. In addition, they found that the more negative stories older people read about younger individuals, the higher their self-esteem tended to be. This could explain the prominence of negative media coverage on networks with an older audience such as Fox News and MSNBC. **Source**: Huffpost Media

   a. Identify the population of interest.

   b. What characteristics of the population are being measured?

   c. Identify the sample.

   d. What are some problems that could be associated with this study?

   e. Is the purpose of this study to perform descriptive or inferential statistics?

4. Researchers at Pepperdine University's Graziadio School of Business and Management recently conducted a study to determine whether the capital crunch is affecting small businesses' ability to expand. The companies studied included alternative lenders, venture capitalists, and private equity firms, among others. The project surveyed 559 privately held businesses and 1,430 lenders and investors nationwide. The study found that 78 percent of businesses had solid growth strategies but only 40 percent had access to the resources needed to grow. Lenders and investors rejected 90 percent of loan applications or investment proposals that would be secured by a business's real estate holdings and 73 percent of loan applications or investment proposals that are based on a business's cash flow. According to the survey author John Paglia, "The study shows private business owners feel they are being constrained by access to financial capital. Owners currently expect a 10 percent revenue growth over the next 12 months. If they were to receive additional capital, they estimate their revenue growth rate to jump to 25 percent." **Source**: smallbiztrends.com

   a. Identify the population of interest.

   b. What characteristics of the population are being measured?

   c. Identify the sample.

   d. Is the purpose of this study to perform descriptive or inferential statistics?

5. Ruder Finn, one of the world's largest independent public relations agencies, recently announced the *Mobile Intent Index* which studies mobile phone user habits and explores the underlying reasons that people have for accessing the internet on mobile devices. The *Mobile Intent Index* asked 500 American adults 18 years of age and older how often they use their mobile phones to access the internet for 295 reasons. The study found that 91% of mobile phone users go online to socialize compared to 79% of desktop users. In addition, 60% of mobile internet users go online to manage finances compared to only 45% of desktop users. They also found that mobile users were less likely to use the internet for educational purposes, only 42% compared to 92% of desktop users. Finally, unsurprisingly, mobile phones are not used for creative purposes; only 42% of mobile users personally express themselves online compared to 54% of desktop users. **Source**: PR Newswire

   a. Identify the population of interest.

   b. What characteristic of the population is being measured?

   c. Identify the sample.

   d. What are some problems that could be associated with this study?

   e. Is the purpose of this study to perform descriptive or inferential statistics?

6. A personnel director is interested in determining how effective a new reading course will be in improving the reading comprehension of her company's employees. The director randomly selects twenty employees and determines the average reading comprehension both before and after instruction in the reading course.

    a. Identify the population.

    b. What characteristic of the population is being measured?

    c. Identify the sample.

    d. Is the purpose of the data collection to perform descriptive or inferential statistics?

7. In 2009 and 2010 the market research firm Chadwick Martin Bailey conducted several studies to provide insights into recent dating behavior in the United States. The data were collected through research via an online Consumer Research Panel. In the "Marriage Survey" (a survey of recently married people), 7,000 adults 18 years of age and older who were married in the past 5 years were polled. The study found that 17% of couples married within the last 3 years met each other on an online dating site. This is compared to 26% that met their significant other through a friend or family member, 36% who met through work or school, 4% who met through a church or place of worship, 11% who met through bars, clubs, or social events, and 7% who met in some other manner. **Source**: Chadwick Martin Bailey/Match.com

    a. Identify the population of interest.

    b. What characteristics of the population are being measured?

    c. Identify the sample.

    d. What are some problems that could be associated with this study?

8. In a recent study, seat belt users were found to have 20% fewer fatalities than those who do not wear seat belts. Do these results prove that seat belts reduce the chances of a fatality?

9. States having an abundance of coastline have an obvious advantage over landlocked states, or states with little coastline, in that their economies may profit from an extensive fishing industry, tourism, shipping, or other water related activities. Alaska, the leader by far in miles of coastline, has a total of 6,640 miles, of which 5,580 miles border the Pacific Ocean and 1,060 miles border the Arctic. Florida, the leader in the continental United States, has a total of 1,350 miles with 580 miles on the Atlantic Ocean and 770 miles on the Gulf of Mexico. Of all states with some coastline, New Hampshire, with 13 miles of coastline, is in last place.

    a. Identify the population.

    b. What characteristic is being measured?

10. A young actuary (statistician usually working in the insurance industry) has been asked to summarize the number of automobile accident claims by region for his company. He randomly selects 50 automobile accident claims which his company has settled in the last year and counts the number of accidents in each region: North, South, East, and West. He summarizes the counts by region in a chart and gives the results to his supervisor.

    a. Identify the population.

    b. What characteristic of the population is being measured?

    c. Identify the sample.

    d. Is the purpose of the data collection to perform descriptive or inferential statistics?

 # Discovery Project

On February 13, 2009, Congress passed the American Recovery and Reinvestment Act of 2009 at the urging of President Obama, who signed it into law four days later. A direct response to the economic crisis, the Recovery Act has three immediate goals:

1. Create new jobs and save existing ones.

2. Spur economic activity and invest in long-term growth.

3. Foster unprecedented levels of accountability and transparency in government spending.

The Recovery Act intends to achieve these goals by:

1. Providing $288 billion in tax cuts and benefits for millions of working families and businesses.

2. Increasing federal funds for education and healthcare as well as entitlement programs (such as extending unemployment benefits) by $224 billion.

3. Making $275 billion available for federal contracts, grants, and loans.

4. Requiring recipients of recovery funds to report quarterly on how they are using the money.

Data are posted online (www.recovery.gov) so the public can track the recovery funds. In addition to offering financial aid directly to local school districts, expanding the Child Tax Credit, and underwriting a process to computerize health records to reduce medical errors and save on healthcare costs, the Recovery Act is targeted at infrastructure development and enhancement. For instance, the act plans investment in the domestic renewable energy industry and the weatherizing of 75 percent of federal buildings as well as more than one million private homes around the country. Construction and repair of roads and bridges as well as scientific research and expansion of broadband and wireless service are also included among the many projects that the Recovery Act will fund. While many projects are focused more immediately on jumpstarting the economy, others, especially those involving infrastructure improvements, are expected to contribute to economic growth for many years.

There are (and were) many skeptics of the act. However, before the act was passed, specific reporting requirements were set for recipients of recovery funds, as well as agency reporting requirements. With that said, opponents to the act want to check on the progress and statistics of recovery. How will the opponents, as well as its supporters, carry out such checks?

Go to the website www.recovery.gov and discuss the following:

1. What would you define as the population of recipients for the recovery funds?

2. What variable(s) is/are of interest for those seeking information about the Recovery Act? Support your response with data from the website.

3. Do you think the Recovery Act served its purpose? Support your response with data from the website or other sources (news articles, tables, etc.).

Data, Reality, and Problem Solving

2

 # Discovering the Real World

The main objective of any business is to earn a profit and consequently companies depend heavily on measurement, data, and statistical thinking. In fact, there is an old management adage, *You can't manage what you can't measure.* Perhaps this adage would be better stated as *You can't manage unless you know what "reality" is.* That is why there are so many important measurement systems in a business. The accounting system is designed to measure profitability and to inform management of potential problems. The inventory system is a measurement tool designed to measure the status of inventory, indicate when orders should be placed, and spot potential inventory theft. The cash flow system is a forecasting system that measures the company's need for cash.

Your career will essentially be a choice of the kinds of problems you desire to solve. The more difficult the problems you decide to solve, the more you will depend upon data and measurement to solve them.

Introduction

For most people, the words "data" and "measurement" are words that generate about as much enthusiasm as watching dust settle. So why should you be interested in measurement and data?

The poem *Under Ben Bulben*, written in 1939, is one of the last poems of the Irish poet W. B. Yeats. The poem contains the insightful line "*Measurement began our might*." Long ago, our species learned that if you do not know what "reality" is, it is difficult to predictably change it to a more desirable state. Measurement is the first step in understanding the "reality" of any circumstance you wish to change in a predictable way. Thus, measurement is a fundamentally important link in controlling our environment. That is why measurement is so pervasive in our culture. We seem to want to measure just about everything in the physical world: temperature, weight, distance, pressure, hardness (Moh's scale of hardness), wind speed (Beaufort wind scale), earthquakes (Richter scale), and so on. We even try to measure feelings, like love.

W.B. Yeats
1865-1939

Type "measurement" into an Internet search engine and you will be surprised by the number of organizations that are devoted to measurement. One of those groups, The International Society for Measurement and Control (ISA), plays a prominent role in setting worldwide standards. Without measurement, standards would not be possible. Without complex measurements and standards, just about all of the conveniences that we take for granted (telephones, automobiles, refrigerators, televisions, and computers) would not exist.

Measurements can be quite costly. A company looking for oil invests substantial sums of money to obtain seismic measurements, the principal discovery tool in the hunt for oil. For companies that do oil exploration, seismic data are the company's crown jewels. Data can be just as important on the personal level.

2.1 Quality of Measurements

Measurement and selling the resulting data is big business. Did you know…

- …that most prescriptions are recorded in a database at the local pharmacy and then sold (without names attached) to firms that collect and summarize this information? The data is then resold to pharmaceutical companies, enabling them to measure how often specific doctors prescribe their drugs. As a consequence, they are able to measure the effectiveness of their salespersons.

- ...that when you are late on a car payment, house payment, or credit card payment, the information may wind up in a national credit database? This database is used by companies in the credit business to assess credit worthiness. It is also used by many businesses in employment screening.

- ...that banks and other institutions that issue credit cards keep data on your spending habits? This data is used to build models to help prevent credit card fraud. If the bank's model determines that you have used your credit card to make "unusual" purchases, it's possible that someone from the credit card company will call and confirm that you did make the purchases. This proactive use of data has prevented an enormous amount of credit card fraud.

- ...that when you order something from a mail order company, your name and what you ordered are recorded and frequently sold to other businesses? Even your grocery store gives you a card so it can collect and sell data on what and how often you buy grocery items.

Measurement

A large part of using statistics to make good business decisions is developing an ability to appraise the quality of measurements. For many problems, what you measure and how you measure it is more important than how you analyze the data. Thus, it is not surprising that the science of statistics is just as concerned with producing good data as it is with interpreting it.

When you encounter data, ask yourself the following questions:

Procedure

Do we have good measurements?

1. Is the concept under study adequately reflected by the proposed measurements?

2. Is the data measured accurately?

3. Is there a sufficient quantity of the data to draw a reasonable conclusion?

If each of these questions can be answered affirmatively, the data possess good properties.

The development of a suitable measurement involves two essential questions: *What should be measured?* and *How should the concept be measured?* Measures (sometimes called metrics) are developed from the field of study, not statistics. Suppose you decide to measure the speed of an object. The concept of speed is well-defined. It is measured in distance per unit of time (for example, 60 miles per hour). Therefore, determining the speed of an object will require two variables to be measured, one distance and the other time. There are well-defined standard measures (such as feet, yards, miles) to use for distance traveled, as well as time, so the measurement is relatively easy to obtain. However, measuring someone's intelligence is another story. How do you define intelligence? Are there standard measures that can be applied? While IQ tests exist, what do they really measure? The more well-defined a concept, the easier it is to develop measurements for it. Our ability to comprehend the world we live in is rooted in good measurement.

2.1 Exercises

Basic Concepts

1. What are the two fundamental problems of measurement?

2. When measurements are used to help solve a problem, what desirable characteristics should the measurements possess?

3. Name and briefly describe three measurement systems commonly used in business.

4. When you encounter any type of data, what three questions should you ask to determine the quality of the measurements?

Exercises

1. Specify whether the following variables are well-defined or not. Justify your answer.

   a. Height

   b. Weight

   c. Hot

   d. Temperature

   e. Beauty

2. A researcher has developed a test that reportedly measures intelligence. The test includes questions such as:

   What is the lowest common denominator of the fractions $\frac{5}{32}$ and $\frac{6}{9}$?

   Who invented the digital computer?

   Is it reasonable to measure intelligence with these questions? Discuss.

3. A hotel manager is interested in getting feedback from guests. Two variables of interest to the manager are cleanliness and aesthetics of the rooms. Discuss what problems you would encounter when measuring those variables.

2.2 Science and Data

Measurement and data are an integral part of science. Methods for exploring research problems have been developed over a long period of time and have become standards in the scientific community. These methods are collectively known as the **scientific method**.

Procedure

The Scientific Method

1. Gather information about the phenomenon being studied.
2. On the basis of the data, formulate a preliminary generalization or hypothesis.
3. Collect further data to test the hypothesis.
4. If the data and other subsequent experiments support the hypothesis, it becomes a law.

Statistics and data are fundamental to the scientific method. Data from carefully designed experiments are the ultimate evidence that support or discredit new theories.

The data collection process in steps one and three of the scientific method can be quite different. The first step of the scientific method is exploratory, finding out what "reality" is about the subject under consideration. Since the data in this phase need not produce convincing evidence, whatever data are available are used to generate ideas. However, the third step begins the validation of a hypothesis. Scientists are trained to be critical thinkers. If a new idea is to be accepted by the scientific community, convincing evidence must be developed at the third stage. The manner in which the data are collected is an important part of that evidence. If the evidence is to be persuasive, a data gathering strategy (an experimental design) that will produce data without the unwelcome influences of **confounding variables** (i.e., an uncontrollable or unaccounted for variable that damages the integrity of the experiment or the other data) is required.

Definition

Confounding Variable

A **confounding variable** is a variable that was not controlled or accounted for by the researcher and thus damaged the integrity of the experiment.

Because of science's emphasis on data, statistics has become inextricably linked with the scientific method. Experiments are designed to yield data with maximum information. There are two branches of statistics: descriptive and inferential. The branch of **descriptive statistics** focuses on exploratory methods for examining data that yield the hypothesis mentioned in step two. The branch of **inferential statistics** develops theories to test the hypothesis using data collected from an experiment to make formal conclusions about a population or parameter.

2.2 Exercises

Basic Concepts

1. What is the scientific method?

2. What is a confounding variable?

3. How does statistics interact with the steps in the scientific method?

4. Name and briefly describe the two main branches of statistics.

Exercises

1. Suppose you want to determine the proportion of college students in the state of Virginia that pays more than $500 per year on textbooks. Using the scientific method, how would you conduct the experiment?

2. The manager of an electronics company was interested in determining the reason for the increase in sales volume over the last three years. The manager randomly selected data on the advertising budget, number of salespeople, and average product costs. When examining the data, the manager found that her average product costs were fairly stable but the advertising budget steadily increased over the last two years along with the number of salespeople. Are there any confounding variables in this study? If so, what are they and why do you consider them confounding?

3. A company that produces bulbs for projectors wanted to conduct an experiment to determine the length of life of its bulbs. The company's leading competitor's bulbs have an average life of 1000 hours. The company sampled its bulbs and found that the average life of the bulbs was 1200 hours. Thus, the company has concluded and advertises that their bulbs last longer than their competition by at least 100 hours. Were the results of this experiment an example of descriptive or inferential statistics? Explain your answer.

Decision Making and Data

Collecting data is a natural part of our lives. For example, consider the everyday question, *What will I have for dinner?* Although virtually no one formally applies the scientific method to such a problem, most people perform experiments and collect data (by eating). This leads to generalizations such as *I hate asparagus* or *I like ice cream.* After sufficient experimentation, these generalizations become personal preference laws.

Selecting the evening meal does not have incredible consequences, yet important problems, by definition, do.

Procedure

The Decision-Making Method

1. Clearly define the problem and any influential variables.
2. Decide upon objectives and decision criteria for choosing a solution.
3. Create alternative solutions.
4. Compare alternatives using the criteria established in the second step.
5. Implement the chosen alternative.
6. Check the results to make sure the desired results are achieved.

Notice the first step in the decision-making method is to define the problem. This is important because almost *any solution to the right problem is better than the best solution to the wrong problem.*

Measurement, Data, and Problem Definition

When you go to a physician what is the first thing the physician does? Most physicians measure your weight, temperature, and blood pressure before he or she meets with you. During the examination the doctor will elicit more data. If there are insufficient data to make a diagnosis, more data (perhaps the dreaded blood test) will be ordered. In the medical world it is extremely important to know what reality is. That is why medical professionals gather so much data. Data is just as important in solving business problems.

Consider a trucking company manager who is beginning to hear a few complaints about freight being delivered late. If the operations manager of the trucking company keeps data on the number of shipments delivered late each week, then statistics can be used to help assess the magnitude of the problem. For example, if the number of late deliveries is plotted (see Figure 2.1), the data in the graph confirms a disturbing trend. Late deliveries are on the rise. Left unsolved, this problem can jeopardize jobs and the existence of the business.

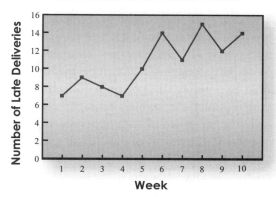

Figure 2.1

Suppose a nurse working on the late shift takes a patient's temperature once each hour. After recording the measurements in the patient's chart, the data are plotted (see Figure 2.2). The data reveal a potential problem. Undoubtedly, more data will be needed.

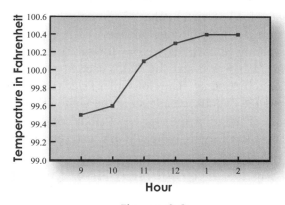

Figure 2.2

Graphical and numerical summaries are frequently useful in discovering the existence of a problem as well as in shedding light on what some of the potential causes may be. In many instances, problems are caused by systems that do not operate as they are designed. Collecting data (finding out system "reality") and using simple statistical tools to monitor a system are the most common ways of insuring a system performs properly.

Problems are not always the result of a diagnosis of some complaint or system malfunction. A "problem" may well be the result of an inquiry into unexpectedly good system performance. That is, often times, improving a process does not imply that something was wrong with the process. In this context, a problem presents itself as an opportunity for improvement. Suppose, for example, a finance instructor develops a new method for teaching introductory finance. Measurements are kept on his students as well as students taking subsequent finance courses. Using statistical methods to compare students using the new method to those using the old method can be valuable in pointing out potential educational improvements that may be used at other institutions. As another example, consider the development of the Intel chip. Improving the speed of its processors/chipsets is a constant goal for research and development, regardless of the current speed of the chip. It is not a matter of the chips being too slow, but as technology and hardware advance, the chipsets need to "keep up" so that computers using the chips maintain (or improve) their processing speeds.

Statistics as Criteria

The second step in the decision-making method suggests defining objectives and developing criteria in order to evaluate various alternative decisions. Not all statistics are simple means, proportions, or standard deviations. Managers and researchers often develop their own statistical measures for summarizing some aspect of a phenomenon. In baseball, for example, teams regularly compute the Earned Run Average (ERA) of each pitcher. This statistic summarizes the average number of earned runs per nine innings pitched. ERA is used as a criterion for comparing and evaluating pitchers as well as for salary negotiations. The Mean Time Before Failure (MTBF) is a statistic that is used to compare the reliability of various equipment or components. The Consumer Price Index (CPI) is a summary statistic that describes the overall price level in the United States. This statistic is an economic measure of inflation and is used in labor contracts to escalate wages as well as to calculate cost of living increases in social security payments.

What Should Be Measured and How Should It Be Measured?

What should be measured depends on the problem to be solved. Sometimes what should be measured is obvious and relatively easy. If the problem is to maintain or improve a system, key variables are monitored and decisions are made based on the level of these variables. For example, if you are responsible for a machine manufacturing pistons, then some of the variables that should be measured and controlled are: the diameter of the piston, the length of the piston, the width of the piston wall, and the number of defects on the piston's surface. However, if you are trying to design a system to perform automated stock trading, deciding what variables are important could take years to discover.

A precisely defined concept is usually easy to measure. The less precise (the fuzzier) the concept the more difficult the measurement becomes. There is a vast difference in measuring the height of a person and measuring his or her intelligence. Defining height is relatively simple. It is nothing more than the vertical length of an object. There are standard scales, such as inches and feet, that everyone agrees upon, that can be used to measure height. The National Institute of Standards and Technology maintains rods which define a government standard for distance measures (feet and inches). Because these standards are widely accepted, if ten different people measure a person's height, there should not be large differences in their measurements. This is not true when measuring intelligence. The National Institute of Standards and Technology does not have a measuring rod for intelligence. It is unlikely that ten randomly selected people could agree on a definition of intelligence, much less on how it should be measured. Intelligence is a fuzzy concept because there is no universally accepted definition and hence there can be no universally accepted standard of measure. If a concept cannot be precisely defined, it cannot be precisely measured. How do you measure fuzzy concepts?

Measuring Fuzzy Concepts

Fuzzy concept definitions produce fuzzy measurements. One could devote an enormous amount of time developing measuring instruments for fuzzy concepts such as love, rivalry, and prejudice, and still have a poor measurement. These concepts are fuzzy because they are perceptions. No person can be sure that their perception of love, rivalry, or prejudice is the same as someone else's. Science that relies on fuzzy measurements usually makes the assumption that everyone's interpretation of the concept is more or less alike.

Often when measuring fuzzy concepts, the instrument used to measure the concept ends up defining the concept. The Wechsler Adult Intelligence Scale (WAIS) is a test that is often used to measure intelligence – an IQ test. There could be a long debate over what constitutes intelligence. For most researchers studying intelligence, developing a new instrument to measure intelligence, however it is defined, is simply not a practical alternative. If a measuring device is needed for a fuzzy concept, using an established instrument like the WAIS is usually the method of choice. However, the necessity for using a measuring instrument does not validate the instrument.

There has been a great deal of controversy in recent years over whether the SAT Reasoning Test accurately measures scholastic aptitude. Still the SAT is an important part of the college admission process. Why? Because college admission committees apparently believe there is no better alternative. When measurements purport to represent what you believe is a fuzzy concept, it is important to think critically about the measurements. Are they valid measures of the intended concept? This issue is important and will again be addressed later in the chapter in the levels of measurement section.

2.3 Exercises

Basic Concepts

1. What is the decision-making method?

2. What is different between the scientific method and the decision-making method?

3. Are problems that can be solved by collecting data always the result of a system malfunction? Explain.

4. Give an example of how statistics can be used to improve a process.

5. What are fuzzy concepts? What are the measurement problems associated with fuzzy concepts?

6. Give an example of a tool that has been widely accepted as an instrument used to measure a fuzzy concept.

2.4 Collecting Data

Essentially there are two ways to obtain data: **observation** and **controlled experiments**. The data collection method is related to the nature of the problem to be solved and the ethical and practical constraints of collecting data in some particular environment. There are many instances in which controlled experiments that would produce particularly appropriate data are not practical or would be unethical. For example, scientists cannot exclude data in an analysis for the purpose of validating their theory or viewpoint.

There are many instances in which data that have been collected provide either no information or misleading information about the effect under study.

Suppose a high school physics teacher wants to determine if there is any beneficial effect of studying calculus before taking physics. He obtains the records of his physics students and compares the group of students that had calculus or are taking it concurrently with those who have not. The average physics grade for those having had calculus is a great deal higher than those that had not. The conclusion reached from this data is: The study of calculus improves one's understanding of physics. Does the data and the manner in which it was collected support such a conclusion?

Students who elect to take calculus generally have above average skills in mathematics. Are the higher physics grades of the calculus students due to their average mathematical skills or to the content of the calculus course? Because of the data collection method, the data is not of sufficient quality to reach a conclusion as to the benefits of taking calculus prior to taking the physics course. A confounding variable (the exceptional mathematical ability of students electing to take calculus) makes it impossible to distinguish the effects we wish to study.

Fuzzy Data May Produce Misleading Conclusions

In a statistical analysis, it is usually not possible to recover from poorly measured concepts or badly collected measurements. Unfortunately, during your lifetime you will be bombarded with statistics derived from poorly measured concepts, confounded measurements, and simply fictitious data. When confronted with statistical evidence of any kind, regardless of whether or not the statistical analysis is done in good faith, it is ultimately up to you to ask reasonable questions about the data. The conclusions suggested by statistics can be no stronger than the quality of the measurements which produced the statistical evidence. Fuzzy or confounded measurements must produce fragile conclusions.

Controlled Experiments: Data by Design

Suppose you wanted to know whether an agricultural crop would have higher yields if a different amount of fertilizer was used. This kind of question would be ideal for a **controlled experiment**. The purpose of controlled experiments is to reveal the response of one variable (crop yield, the response variable) to changes in another variable (level of fertilization, the explanatory variable). In a controlled experiment the researcher attempts to control the environment of the experiment so that the effect of one variable on another can be isolated and measured. In these studies there is a **control group** and an **experimental group**. Ideally there is no initial difference between the two groups. During the experiment a **treatment** is applied to the experimental group. The exact form of the treatment will depend on the particular experiment. If the experimental group were an agricultural crop, a treatment might be applying a given level of fertilizer. The treatment changes the level of the **explanatory variable** in the experiment. The effect of the treatment can be measured by comparing the **response variable** in the control and experimental groups.

Response Variable

> ### Definition
> The **response variable** is the variable of interest in an experiment.

Explanatory Variable

> ### Definition
> An **explanatory variable** is a variable that affects the variable of interest (response variable) in an experiment.

Comparative Experiments

Isolating the effects of one variable on another means anticipating potentially confounding variables and designing a controlled experiment to produce data in which the values of the confounding variables are regulated. In the physics example in the previous section, the confounding variable is the mathematical ability of those students taking calculus before physics. To control for this *bias*, students could be randomly assigned to take the calculus course. By randomly assigning students to take the calculus course before the physics course, the mathematical ability of the two groups should be equalized. Since mathematical ability is controlled, any difference in physics scores could be attributed to a beneficial effect of the calculus course. An experimental design in which experimental units (students in this case) are randomly assigned to two different treatments is called a **completely randomized design**.

For this example of a completely randomized design:

Response Variable: Students' grades in the physics course.

Explanatory Variable: Whether students take calculus before physics.

Randomization is often used as a method of controlling bias and is an important principle in the design of experiments.

Flowchart for the Calculus before Physics Experiment

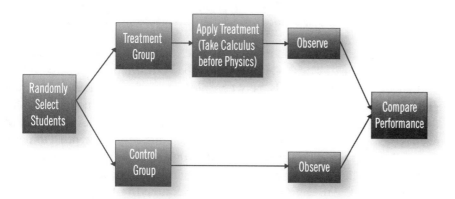

Example 2.1

Suppose a new species of tomato has been genetically engineered to increase yields. The question: Is there a relationship between the use of the new species and yield?

Solution

In this experimental design, the plots of tomatoes will be divided into two groups, one that contains the new species and another that contains the unaltered variety. The plots containing the genetically engineered variety will be called the **treatment group**, and the plots containing the standard variety are called the **control group**. If the experiment is properly performed, any change in the response variable (yield) can be attributed to the explanatory variable (genetic engineering) and not to other variables that are controlled. The untangling of variables at the data-gathering stage makes the analysis of the data much easier. There is no better way to establish a causal relationship.

Plot 1	Plot 2	Plot 3	Plot 4
Plot 5	Plot 6	Plot 7	Plot 8
Plot 9	Plot 10	Plot 11	Plot 12
Plot 13	Plot 14	Plot 15	Plot 16

Variables like rainfall, amount of sunshine, or type of soil can affect the yield of tomatoes. These variables must be controlled in the experiment so that differences in yields between plots can be attributed just to the genetically engineered species. One possible method of controlling for these variables is to create small plots in the same field. Several plots of each type of tomato are planted. Each plot contains only one type of tomato. Rainfall is measured and supplemented with irrigation to assure that each plot has the same amount of water. By controlling for these variables in this manner, we can say that any differences noted in the yield (response variable) between the genetically engineered variety (treatment group) and the unaltered variety (control group) is due to genetic improvements (explanatory variable).

The Before and After Study

The before and after study also contains a comparative experiment. The control group and the experimental group are initially identical. The response variable is measured in the control group at the beginning of the study, and then a treatment is applied to the control group. After the treatment is applied, the control group becomes the experimental group. The response variable is again measured after the treatment has been applied. If the treatment affects the response variable then there should be a difference between the value of the response variable for the control and experimental groups, presumably caused by the treatment. An example of a before and after study is given in Example 2.2.

Example 2.2

Does an SAT preparation course improve performance on the SAT Reasoning Test?

Solution

A group of high school students take the SAT. Then they are given an SAT preparation course. They retake the SAT. If the group's second SAT performance improves, then it may be related to the SAT preparation course.

For this example of a before and after study:

Explanatory variable: SAT preparation course.

Response variable: SAT scores.

In this experiment there is only one group of students. Suppose there were two groups of students, one that had taken the course (treatment group) and one that had not (the control group). Could you assign any difference in results solely to the SAT preparation course? Because of potential differences in the cognitive abilities of the two groups of students, this experiment would be much more vulnerable to the justifiable criticism that the differences in student cognitive ability caused the difference in the group's SAT performance rather than the SAT preparation course. However, by using a before and after study we have only one group of students and cognitive ability is controlled.

The Placebo Effect

A difficult problem arises in experiments involving people. In clinical trials of some drug or medical treatment, patients often respond favorably to any treatment, including a "dummy" or "fake" treatment. These fake treatments are called **placebos**. In medical research, a placebo is a pill that contains none of the drug that is being tested. It has been shown in several pain studies that placebos relieve pain in 30 to 40 percent of patients, even though the placebo has no active ingredients. The placebo effect is not confined to medicine. Similar effects have been noticed in psychological research in which the subjects seem to try to help the researcher prove some conclusion.

One of the more interesting experiments contaminated by this effect was the Hawthorne Study conducted at the Western Electric Company's Hawthorne Works in Chicago between 1927 and 1932. The studies were initiated to determine the effect of lighting on worker productivity. Lighting was increased in stages, and the investigators found that each time lighting increased worker output increased. The investigators were suspicious that another effect might be causing worker productivity to improve. So, workers were told lighting was to be increased when, in fact, it was decreased. Despite the decrease, worker output increased again. Clearly there was some other variable affecting worker output.

Placebos

One might think that the effectiveness of placebos should be close to zero; this, however, is not the case. Studies have shown that up to 62% of headache sufferers, 58% of those suffering from sea sickness, and even 39% of those suffering from postoperative wound pain showed symptom relief given a placebo. This is a stunning revelation of the effect of psychology on our mind and body.

An intriguing but ethical question for you to ponder is this: *If placebos can be 62% effective for curing headaches, would or should a physician treat a headache with a placebo only?*

The workers wanted the study to be successful, and their desire was confounding the experiment. Instead of discovering the expected relationship between worker output and lighting, the investigators found that the social system and the employees' roles within that system had a great deal more to do with worker productivity than lighting. The Hawthorne Study has been credited with introducing psychology to the workplace. It also points out the hazards of measurement, even in a controlled experiment.

Double Blind Studies

The placebo effect is prevalent in medical studies. **Double blind studies** are used to counteract this effect. In a double blind study the subjects are not told whether they are members of the treatment group or the control group. The evaluators (the persons that measure the response variable) are also not told whether their subjects are members of the control or experimental group. An example of a double blind study is given in Example 2.3.

Example 2.3

Until recently, ulcers in the upper intestine were a rather common illness. A new treatment for ulcers was proposed. This treatment involved gastric freezing and required the patient to swallow a deflated balloon with tubes attached. A refrigerated solution was then pumped through the balloon for an hour. The idea behind this therapy was to cool the stomach wall and reduce the amount of acid produced. Initially, the results looked promising and the treatment was used for several years. However, none of the initial studies were double blind.

In the double blind study half of the patients were given the procedure and the other half were given a placebo treatment, which included swallowing the balloon, but no cooling solution was injected into the balloon. Patients that received the placebo treatment actually did better than the ones receiving the refrigerated solution. Gastric freezing was eventually abandoned as a treatment for upper-intestinal ulcers.

Observational Studies

Observational data comes about by measuring "what is." If you are trading stocks, the market data you receive are observational. The data show simply what is happening in the marketplace at the time. Census data are observational; they are a measure of how things are in a specific geographic area at a given point in time. There is no experimentation to see how manipulating one variable will affect another variable or variables. Virtually all of the data we routinely encounter is observational. Examples regularly appearing in the newspaper include:

- Stock, commodity, bond, option, and currency market data
- Almost all federal government data, including census, economic, and educational data
- Virtually all local and state government data
- Sports data (scores, outcomes, etc.)

The data described above are often collected to satisfy state and government regulation as well as for business purposes, such as to examine trends in a particular stock price or interest rates. These data values are not the result of a designed experiment.

Observational studies can be extremely valuable. For example, the effect of vitamin C has been the subject of controversy for some time. Numerous claims of beneficial health effects from regularly consuming vitamin C have been made. However, Enstrom, Kemin, and Klein ("Vitamin C Intake and Mortality," *Epidemiology*, May 1992) in an observational study with 10,000 participants noted that males in their study who supplemented their diets with 500 milligrams of vitamin C each day (on average) lived approximately six years longer than those who did not take the vitamin. Females taking this dosage of vitamin C (on average) lived approximately one year longer. Although this study was quite large, it does not prove that vitamin C causes increased longevity. If the data had come from a controlled experiment the strength of the study's conclusion would be much more powerful. The vitamin C study is an observational study because the subjects were not chosen randomly for the control and treatment groups. If the experiment were conducted as a controlled experiment, the control group would be given a placebo and the treatment group would be given vitamin C.

Untangling Variables in an Observational Study

In 1973, the Graduate Division at the University of California, Berkeley, carried out an observational study on gender bias in admissions to the Graduate School. There were 8442 men and 4321 women who applied for admission. Of the men that applied, 3714 were subsequently accepted, and 1512 of the women were accepted. Given that almost twice as many men applied to the graduate program, it is reasonable to expect that more men would be accepted. To make a reasonable comparison, the first thing that is needed is to adjust for the difference in application rates between men and women. This is achieved by comparing the percentage of each group that was accepted. Nearly 44% of the men and 35% of the women were admitted. These admission statistics suggested there was rather substantial support for the idea of discrimination against women.

The admission process at Berkeley was done by major. If there was discrimination against women, those departments that were discriminating would stand out when the admissions data were examined separately. But when the data were examined, the investigator did not find what was expected.

Table 2.1 – College Acceptance Rates				
	Men		Women	
Major	Number of Applicants	Percent Admitted	Number of Applicants	Percent Admitted
I	825	62	108	82
II	560	63	25	68
III	325	37	593	34
IV	417	33	375	35
V	191	28	393	24
VI	373	6	341	7

Source: P.J. Bickel, E.A. Hammel, and J.W. O'Connell. Sex Bias in Graduate Admissions: Data from Berkeley. Science, 187:398-404, 1975.

Suppose the data in Table 2.1 represent the six largest majors on the Berkeley campus.

In four of the six majors, women were admitted more frequently than men. Not only were women not being discriminated against, but there appears to be potential discrimination against men in Major I. How could this completely opposite conclusion be true? A close examination of the data shows that in the majors with the largest percentage admitted (the easiest to get into) there were a large number of male applicants and very few female applicants. The majors that had very low acceptance rates (difficult to be admitted) had relatively very few men and a large number of women applying. Thus the variable, major field of study, was **confounding** the variable gender in the original analysis and **biasing** the original conclusion.

The original conclusion was the result of the fact that women were applying to the most difficult departments for admission, not because of sex discrimination. By separating the data by major, the analyst was able to **control** for the confounding variable, choice of major, and remove the bias. When it is possible to remove the effect of one variable, we are said to be **controlling for** that variable. The Berkeley data illustrates a subtle problem in the comparison of two or more proportions.

In this instance the analyst was able to untangle the two variables, but this is not always the case. Unless the data is gathered with a controlled experiment, it may not be possible to untangle the effects of the causal factors. This is an example of **Simpson's Paradox** where the results are counterintuitive. This paradox is often seen with reports based on frequency data when making inferences about relationships between two or more variables.

Surveys

A great deal of the statistical information presented to us is the result of surveys. Often we will see in the news that one of the major polling organizations, Gallup, Harris, ABC-Washington Post, or NBC-New York Times, is reporting findings on various topics, from the approval rating of the President to the popularity of gun control.

In some instances, the purpose of a survey is purely descriptive, as those described above. However, in many cases the researcher is interested in discovering a relationship. Because virtually all surveys produce observational data, survey research belongs to steps one and two of the scientific method. Sometimes a plausible relationship is discovered and a designed experiment is undertaken to more convincingly demonstrate the relationship.

A famous observational study, known as the Framingham Study, recorded various data on 4500 middle-aged men. The men were followed for many years with the hope of uncovering what factors relate to the development of heart disease. It was discovered that the development of heart disease seemed to be associated with obesity, heavy smoking, and high blood pressure. Because of the large number of participants and the researcher's ability to control for potentially confounding variables after the data were collected, this research influenced many physicians to work with their patients to control the three **causal factors** found in the study.

Even Hollywood studios do survey research. The survey shown in Figure 2.3 is used by a major studio. Looking at the questions that are posed, you can see they want data on *why you came to the movie and what you liked about it.* Collecting this data on a wide variety of movies gives the studio insight into what makes a movie successful, the importance of stars, and what other factors have universal appeal.

Steps to Consider When Conducting a Survey

1. Have specific goals.
2. Consider alternatives for collecting data.
3. Select samples to represent the population.
4. Match question wording to the concepts being measured.
5. Pretest questionnaires.
6. Construct quality checks.
7. Use statistical analysis and reporting techniques.
8. Disclose all methods used to conduct the survey.

Source: American Association for Public Opinion Research

SAMPLE MOVIE SURVEY

Please complete the first 9 questions of this survey before the movie begins and questions 10 through 14 after the movie.
Please give the completed questionnaire to the persons collecting them at the exits.

1. Indicate the <u>one item</u> in the list below that was most influential in your decision to see the movie. (Check one)

Newspaper:
Ad..........................( )1
Review......................( )2
Article.....................( )3

Magazine:
Ad..........................( )4
Review......................( )5
Article.....................( )6

Television:
Commercial..................( )7
Review......................( )8
MTV or other Music Videos...( )9
Other cable.................( )0
Talk Show, other............( )x

Radio:
Ad..........................( )1
Review......................( )2

Around Town:
Received a Complimentary Pass..........( )3
Coming Attractions.....................( )4
Poster or Billboard....................( )5
The soundtrack album...................( )6
Recommended from a friend or relative..( )7
Computer on-line service...............( )8
Internet...............................( )9
Other:.................................( )0

2. Which of the following were important to you in deciding to come to this movie? (Mark as many as apply)

Tony Curtis ....( )1
Marilyn Monroe ....( )2
Jack Lemmon ....( )3

Billy Wilder, the producer...............( )4
The story................................( )5
The drama................................( )6

The visual effects...............( )7
The reviews ....( )8
Other _____ ( )9

3. What is your age? (Check one)

Under 12 ....( )1
12 to 14 ....( )2
15 to 17 ....( )3
18 to 20 ....( )4
21 to 24 ....( )5
25 to 29 ....( )6

30 to 34..............( )7
35 to 39..............( )8
40 to 44..............( )9
45 to 49..............( )0
50 to 59..............( )x
60 & over.............( )y

4. What is the last grade of school you completed?

Some high school or less................( )1
Completed high school...................( )2
Some college/currently in college...( )3
Completed 2 year college................( )4
Completed 4 year college................( )5
Currently in/completed post-grad.....( )6

5. Are you...(Check One)
Male...................( )1
Female.................( )2

6. What is your ethnic background? (Check One)
African-American ....( )1
Asian ....( )2
Latino ....( )3
Caucasian ....( )4
Native American ....( )5

7. What is your marital status? (Check one)
Single...........................( )1
Married..........................( )2
Divorced/Separated...............( )3
Widowed ....( )4

8. Before today, how familiar were you with the storyline? Very familiar...( )1   Somewhat familiar...( )2   Not at all familiar...( )3

9. How many times before today have you seen the movie?
None.................( )1   Once....................( )2   Twice..........( )3   Three or more times...............( )4

XXXXXXXXXX COMPLETE QUESTIONS 10 THROUGH 14 AFTER THE MOVIE XXXXXXXXXX

10. How would you rate the movie?
Excellent ....( )1
Very Good ....( )2
Good...............( )3
Fair................( )4
Poor...............( )5

11. Would you recommend the movie?
Definitely..........( )1
Probably............( )2
Probably Not.....( )3
Definitely Not...( )4

12. How did the movie measure up to your expectations?
Better than expected..........( )1
About what I expected.......( )2
Not as good as expected.....( )3

13. Which of the following words or phrases best describe the movie you just saw? (Mark as many as apply)

Entertaining........................( )1
Boring/dull.........................( )2
Dramatic............................( )3
Interesting settings ....( )4
Too slow in parts ....( )5
Offensive...........................( )6
Confusing...........................( )7
Interesting characters ....( )8
Too silly/stupid....................( )9
Action packed.......................( )0

Worn-out theme ....( )1
Surprising................................( )2
Too long ....( )3
Different/original ....( )4
Not my kind of movie......................( )5
Controversial.............................( )6
Moved just right..........................( )7
Humorous ....( )8
Good cast ....( )9
In bad taste ....( )0

Well acted...............................( )1
Not enough drama.................( )2
Has a good story.................( )3
Unrealistic......................( )4
Educational......................( )5
Nothing new/done before.......( )6
Thought provoking................( )7
Too predictable..................( )8
Believable.......................( )9
Depressing.......................( )0

14. Would you pay to see this movie again?   Yes.........................( )1   No...........................( )2

Figure 2.3

2.4 Exercises

Basic Concepts

1. What are the two ways of obtaining data?

2. What are the dangers of making conclusions based on poorly collected data?

3. How do you treat the problem of a confounding variable?

4. Explain the difference between the control group and the experimental group in a controlled experiment.

5. What is an explanatory variable?

6. What is a response variable?

7. What is bias? How can it be controlled?

8. What is a completely randomized design? What are the advantages of using a completely randomized design?

9. What is a before and after study?

10. What is the placebo effect? Give an example.

11. What is a double blind study?

12. How do observational studies differ from controlled experiments?

13. What kinds of problems can be associated with an observational study?

14. Researchers use surveys for two main purposes. Name and give an example of each.

Exercises

1. The health and social problems associated with obesity can be a severe hindrance in attaining many of life's goals. Methods for treating obesity were compared in "One Year Behavioral Treatment of Obesity: Comparison of Moderate and Severe Caloric Restriction and the Effect of Weight Maintenance Therapy," in the *Journal of Consulting and Clinical Psychology*. In the study, a group of 25 women, each of whom was at least 25 kilograms (kg) overweight, were randomly split into two groups. The first group received behavior therapy and was placed on a 1200 calorie per day diet for a period of one year. The second group received behavior therapy and was placed on a 420 calorie per day diet for the first 17 weeks of the year. Then they returned to a 1200 calorie per day diet for the remainder of the year. At the end of a 26-week period, the average weight lost was 11.86 kg for the first group and 21.45 kg for the second group. But after 52 weeks, the average weight lost was 10.94 kg for the first group and 12.18 kg for the second group.

   a. Why is this study an example of a controlled experiment?

   b. What is the explanatory variable?

   c. What is the response variable?

   d. Is there a control group in the study? Explain.

   e. Suppose that the data were gathered from an observational study instead of from a controlled experiment. How would this affect the conclusions that might be made from the study?

2. An article appearing in the *New England Journal of Medicine* investigated whether the academic performance of asthmatic children being treated with the drug Theophylline was inferior to a non-asthmatic group. In one part of the study, 72 children were identified as being treated for asthma. For each child with asthma, a non-asthmatic sibling was also identified. (The use of sibling controls allows for control of family environment and certain genetic factors on academic achievement.) All 144 children were then given a test to measure academic achievement. There were no significant differences on the test between the two groups.

   a. Why is this study an example of a controlled experiment?

   b. What is the explanatory variable?

   c. What is the response variable?

   d. Is there a control group in the study? Explain.

   e. Suppose that the data were gathered from an observational study instead of from a controlled experiment. How would this affect the conclusions that might be made from the study?

3. A small clinical pilot study was conducted by a research team from Harvard Medical School and the School of Public Health. Fifteen individuals in the early stages of Multiple Sclerosis were fed bovine myelin, a substance containing two antigens thought to be the target of the immune system's attack in Multiple Sclerosis. Another 15 were given a placebo. In the study, fewer members of the group fed bovine myelin had major attacks of the disease. **Source:** *Science,* Vol. 259, No. 5099

    a. Which phase of the Scientific Method best describes this study?

    b. Is this an observational study or a controlled experiment?

    c. What is the response variable?

    d. What is the explanatory variable?

    e. Which group is the treatment group?

    f. Which group is the control group?

4. London scientists conducted a study to determine if chocolate can trigger migraines. Twelve migraine-prone subjects were given a peppermint-laced chocolate candy and eight migraine-prone subjects were given a peppermint-laced placebo made of carob, peppermint, and vegetable fat. Five subjects from the group given chocolate developed a migraine headache within one day. No one from the group given the placebo developed a migraine in the same time period. **Source:** *Self* magazine

    a. Which phase of the Scientific Method best describes this study?

    b. Is this an observational study or a controlled experiment?

    c. What is the response variable?

    d. What is the explanatory variable?

    e. Which group is the treatment group?

    f. Which group is the control group?

5. The Nurse's Health Study conducted on 87,245 women at Boston's Brigham and Women's Hospital revealed that women who eat a cup of beta carotene-rich food a day have 40 percent fewer strokes and 22 percent fewer heart attacks than those who consume a quarter of a cupful per day. **Source:** *Self* magazine

    a. Which phase of the Scientific Method best describes this study?

    b. Is this an observational study or a controlled experiment?

    c. What is the response variable?

    d. What is the explanatory variable?

    e. Which group is the treatment group?

    f. Which group is the control group?

6. In May, 2011, Internet Explorer reversed its trend in the United States and gained usage share (the percentage of users using a particular Internet browser). In June of 2011, the trend reversal became global. Internet Explorer gained 0.57% in June across all operating systems with Internet Explorer 8.0 gaining 0.86% globally. The gains for Internet Explorer came primarily at the expense of Mozilla Firefox (−0.51%). Google Chrome's pace of usage share gains slowed to +0.2% for June. The gains for IE were the largest in Europe and Asia:

   Internet Explorer in Europe: +0.88%

   Internet Explorer in Asia: +0.81%

   This increase may be the result of a marketing campaign. In early June, Microsoft launched their "Confidence" campaign aimed at showing the security features of Internet Explorer 8. **Source**: netmarketshare.com

   a. Are the results stated above likely to have come from an observational study?

   b. How can Microsoft (and other companies) benefit from this information?

 **Levels of Measurement**

Like most things in life, data come in different qualities. Some measurements are purely numerical and are based on well-defined standards, such as pounds, inches, dollars, and percentages. On the other hand, some measurements are exceedingly "fuzzy" and the standard of measure is ill-defined, if defined at all. For example, consider the response to the following evaluation:

What is your opinion of the President's performance?

1. Extremely disappointing

2. Disappointing

3. Satisfactory

4. Good

5. Extraordinary

Someone's *good* response may be equal to someone else's *extraordinary*. There can be no guarantee of a common scale and thus the level of consistency between measurements is unreliable. This type of data is much lower quality than measurements on some standard scale, such as pounds or inches.

Definition

The quality of data is referred to as the **level of measurement**.

Level of Measurement

The terms used to describe the quality of data are **nominal**, **ordinal**, **interval**, and **ratio**. When analyzing data you must be exceedingly conscious of the data's level of measurement because many statistical analyses can only be applied to data that possess a certain level of measurement.

Because of different levels of measurement, not all data are created equally. Unfortunately, once data are in numerical form, many believe that a number is a number. Everyone knows that you can add, subtract, multiply, and divide numbers. But for some measurements, adding, subtracting, multiplying, and dividing are simply meaningless.

Standard mathematical operations (such as addition and subtraction) are not defined for nominal and ordinal data, and, consequently, many forms of statistical analysis (descriptive and inferential) are not appropriate.

Nominal Data

Sex (male or female) and hair color (blond, brunette, or redhead) are examples of nominal variables. If the gender variable is coded numerically, say female = 1, male = 0, then what do the numbers mean?

Nominal Data

Definition

Data that represent whether a variable possesses some characteristic are called **nominal**.

Is it meaningful to add, subtract, multiply, or divide these numbers? Let's try addition:

1	+	0	=	1	**?**
female	+	male	=	female	

Is it meaningful to add a female and a male and get a female? If it is, it is certainly a bizarre interpretation.

Let's try subtraction.

1	−	0	=	1	**?**
female	−	male	=	female	

Is it meaningful to subtract a male from a female and get a female? If this kind of mathematics works, it doesn't say a lot for males!

Similarly absurd conclusions can be reached for multiplication and division. For strictly nominal data, none of the arithmetic operators can be applied. Statistically speaking, only some graphical and a very few numerical statistical procedures can be applied to nominal data. Keep in mind that the nominal level of measurement identifies the variable in name only.

Ordinal Data

Consider a response to the fill in the blank question.

Frosty Pops taste _____ .

1. Very bad   **2.** Bad   **3.** Fair   **4.** Good   **5.** Very good

Ordinal Data

Definition

Ordinal data represent categories that have some associated order.

The response to this question is often referred to as being measured on the Likert Scale, in which one rates the taste of Frosty Pops on a scale from 1 to 5. These responses are ordered on the basis of an individual's impression of the goodness of Frosty Pops. The response *bad* is perceived to be better than *very bad*, *good* better than *fair*, and so forth. If numerical codes are used to represent the responses, should the properties of addition, subtraction, multiplication, and division be applied to them? Let's try addition.

1	+	1	+	1	+	1	+	1	=	5	
Very bad	+	Very bad	+	Very bad	+	Very bad	+	Very bad	=	Very good	**?**

This means that if you thought that a Frosty Pop tasted *very bad* (1) you should eat five of them and doing so would be equivalent to eating something that you thought was *very good* (5). Addition of ordinal values is not reasonable. And for that matter, neither are subtraction, division, and multiplication. So the only difference between ordinal and nominal data is that ordinal data possess order. Here again, like nominal data, only a very limited number of statistical analyses can be performed.

Note that ordinal data are also nominal, but they possess the additional property of ordinality (or ranking).

Interval Data

Definition

If the data can be ordered and the arithmetic difference is meaningful, the data are **interval**.

Interval Data

One example of interval data is temperature (measured on the Fahrenheit scale).

48 degrees	–	45 degrees	=	3 degrees
72 degrees	–	69 degrees	=	3 degrees

In the case above, the difference between the temperatures is three degrees, and it is true that the difference in kinetic energy between 48 and 45 degrees is the same as the difference between 72 and 69 degrees.

Interval data also have another interesting property, an arbitrary zero value. You don't have to be a mathematician to appreciate the usual meaning of the zero concept, having zero dollars means that you do not have any money. However, a temperature of zero degrees on the Celsius or Fahrenheit scale does not mean there is no kinetic energy, and thus in the case of temperature, zero has been arbitrarily selected. In fact, the Celsius temperature scale places the value of zero at a temperature equivalent to 32 degrees Fahrenheit.

2

Get Out of Here Aristotle

"Aristotle maintained that women have fewer teeth than men; although he was twice married it never occurred to him to verify this statement by examining his wives' mouths."

—Bertrand Russell

One implication of an arbitrary zero point is that the ratio of two variables has no meaning. For example, the kinetic energy associated with a temperature of four degrees on the Fahrenheit scale is not twice as great as the kinetic energy associated with a temperature of two degrees. The property that distinguishes interval data is the notion that equal intervals represent equal amounts. For example, the interval between four degrees and one degree represents the same difference in kinetic energy as the difference between 71 degrees and 74 degrees.

Interval data are numerical data that possess both the property of ordinality (ranking) and the interval property. However, interval data do not possess a meaningful origin (zero value).

Ratio Data

Ratio Data

Definition

Ratio data are similar to interval data, except that they have a meaningful zero point and the ratio of two data points is meaningful.

The Greek philosopher Aristotle held that one could develop all the laws that govern the universe by pure thought and that it was unnecessary to obtain measurements that would confirm the validity of these laws. Perhaps this explains why he never bothered to count his wife's teeth. The goal of Aristotelian science was to explain *why* things happen. Galileo's approach originated the method of controlled experiments which form the basis of scientific investigation. Controlled experiments yield data. Statistics allows people to think with data. If Aristotle had been right, there wouldn't be a very large demand for statistics.

The operations of addition, subtraction, multiplication, and division are reasonable on ratio data. Many of the variables we commonly encounter are ratio variables: volumes, heights, weights, pressure. Being aware of the data's level of measurement is an extremely important part of any statistical analysis, since many statistical measures that are meaningful for interval and ratio data are not meaningful for ordinal and nominal measurements. Ratio data are the most desired and meaningful type of data for decision makers. We will explore analytical techniques for each type of data in subsequent chapters of this text.

Example 2.4

Is money a ratio variable?

Solution

Say a friend has $40 and you have $20.

$$\frac{\$40}{\$20} = 2$$

According to the ratio we just computed your friend has twice as much money as you. Is this really true? Money is a ratio variable because ratios (quotients) are meaningful. If someone does have $40 and you have $20, they do have twice as much money as you.

2.5 Exercises

Basic Concepts

1. What is a level of measurement?

2. What are the four levels of measurement? Give an example of each.

3. For which level(s) of measurement is arithmetic appropriate?

4. What is the primary difference between nominal and ordinal data?

5. What is an arbitrary zero value? Which level of measurement has this property?

6. What is the fundamental difference between interval and ratio data?

7. Decision makers usually prefer to consider data that possess which level of measurement?

Exercises

1. Determine the level of measurement (nominal, ordinal, interval, or ratio) for each of the following variables.

    a. The temperature (in degrees Fahrenheit) of patients with pneumonia.

    b. The age at which the average male marries.

    c. Client satisfaction survey responses: Poor, Average, Good, and Excellent.

    d. The region of the U.S. in which an individual lives: North, South, East, or West.

    e. The number of people with a Type A personality.

2. Determine the level of measurement (nominal, ordinal, interval, or ratio) for each of the following variables.

    a. The time it takes for a student to complete an exam.

    b. Majors of randomly selected students at a university.

    c. The category which best describes how frequently a person eats chocolate: Frequently, Occasionally, Seldom, Never.

    d. The number of pounds of snack food eaten by an individual in his or her lifetime.

3. Give examples of nominal, ordinal, interval, and ratio data. Justify your classification for each example.

4. Given the table below on browser usage (see Exercise 6 in Section 2.4), what is the highest level of measurement that this data could have? Justify your answer.

Table for Exercise 4 – Browser Usage Share (%)				
Month	Microsoft Internet Explorer	Mozilla Firefox	Google Chrome	Apple Safari
July, 2010	60.74	22.91	7.16	5.09
August, 2010	60.48	22.90	7.50	5.15
September, 2010	59.62	22.97	7.99	5.27
October, 2010	59.18	22.83	8.50	5.36
November, 2010	58.44	22.76	9.26	5.55
December, 2010	57.08	22.81	9.98	5.89
January, 2011	56.00	22.75	10.70	6.30
February, 2011	56.77	21.74	10.93	6.36
March, 2011	55.92	21.80	11.57	6.61
April, 2011	55.11	21.63	11.94	7.15
May, 2011	54.27	21.71	12.52	7.28
June, 2011	54.84	21.20	12.72	7.41

 **Data Classifications**

Data or variables can be classified as **qualitative** or **quantitative**. If data or variables are quantitative, they can be further identified as **discrete** or **continuous**. Since the kind of data available affects the kind of analyses that can be performed, it is important to recognize data attributes.

Qualitative and Quantitative Data

Definition

Qualitative data are measurements that can change in kind, but not in degree. Qualitative measurements often consist of labels or descriptions and do not have naturally occurring numerical values.

Qualitative Data

Qualitative data are measured on the nominal and ordinal scales. Some examples of qualitative data are gender (M/F), occupation (doctor, lawyer, professor, etc.) and eye color (brown, blue, and green). As discussed earlier, regardless of how the measurements are coded, arithmetic operations cannot be performed with qualitative data.

Definition

Quantitative data are measurements that change in magnitude from trial to trial such that some order or ranking can be applied. Quantitative variables can be measured using a naturally occurring numerical scale.

Quantitative Data

Quantitative data are measured on the interval or ratio scale and we can perform arithmetic operations with quantitative variables. Some examples of quantitative data are the number of students in class today, the number of dependents claimed on a tax return, and the number of fans at a sporting event.

Discrete and Continuous Data

Quantitative data or variables can be categorized as either discrete or continuous. To illustrate, suppose that observations are taken on two variables: the number of stocks and bonds in a mutual fund and the annual yield for the fund. In looking at the data, one difference is that the number of stocks and bonds is a whole number, whereas the annual yield is decimal-valued. Since it is impossible for a mutual fund to have 10.167 stocks and bonds, or any fractional number for that matter, there are gaps in the values that the variable "Number of Stocks" can assume.

Number of Stocks	10	20	30	40	50
Annual Yield (%)	4.25	3.86	13.52	15.00	9.62

The stock data given above are **discrete**. While the data representing stocks and bonds can only assume integer values, it would be misleading to create the impression that a discrete variable can only assume integer values. Discrete data may assume decimal values. For example, a variable that takes only the values 1, 1.5, 2, 2.5 is discrete.

Definition

Discrete Data

Data in which the observations are restricted to a set of values (such as 1, 2, 3, 4) that possesses gaps are **discrete**.

The annual yield data given above are **continuous**. It may appear that the annual yields are discrete, since values appear to only take on values up to the second decimal place. However, it is only the inadequacy of the measuring instrument that creates this illusion. The first annual yield is listed as 4.25%, but the actual annual yield of the first mutual fund may be 4.2531642%. If the measuring device can only detect differences in the hundredths place, then all measurements will be given to the hundredths place. Any digits beyond the hundredths place will be ignored. However, just because these digits are ignored doesn't mean they don't exist.

Definition

Continuous Data

Data that can take on any value within some interval are **continuous**.

Example 2.5

State whether each of the following variables is qualitative or quantitative. If the variable is quantitative, indicate whether it is discrete or continuous.

a. Political party affiliation

b. Amount of time spent on the computer

c. Marital status

d. Number of online orders made per month

Solution

a. Examples of political party affiliation are Republican, Democrat, Independent, etc. These are qualitative measurements because they identify the party by name only and we are unable to perform any arithmetic operations or establish distances between parties. Thus, political party affiliation is a qualitative variable.

b. Examples of time spent on the computer could be any value from a few seconds to a large number of hours. Also, depending on the quality of the measurement, time could be recorded (or reported) in any number of significant digits. With that said, time spent on the computer is a quantitative, continuous random variable.

c. For marital status, examples could be single, married, or divorced. These are qualitative measurements since one classification cannot be considered to be more than another and we also cannot perform any arithmetic operations on this variable.

d. The number of online orders is countable, starting at 0. Thus, this is a quantitative, discrete random variable.

2.6   Exercises

Basic Concepts

1. What are qualitative data? Give an example.

2. What are quantitative data? Give an example.

3. Which levels of measurement are associated with qualitative data? Which levels are associated with quantitative data?

4. If data are quantitative, they can be further classified into two categories. Name and briefly describe these categories.

5. What is the difference between discrete and continuous data?

Exercises

1. Identify the following variables as discrete or continuous.

   a. The number of doctors who wash their hands between patient visits.

   b. The amount of liquid consumed by the average American each day.

   c. The weight of newborn babies at a local hospital.

    d. The time it takes a person to react to a stimulus.

    e. The number of voters who favor a particular candidate.

2. Identify the following variables as discrete or continuous.

    a. The number of on-time flights at the Hartsfield International Airport in Atlanta.

    b. The height of skyscrapers in New York City.

    c. The price of General Electric's common stock.

    d. The temperature of U.S. cities.

    e. The number of alcoholics who are men.

3. The results of a study investigating the nutritional status of mid-nineteenth century Americans were reported in "The Height and Weight of West Point Cadets: Dietary Changes in Antebellum America," in the *Journal of Economic History*. The data are based upon physical examination lists for West Point applicants from 1843 to 1894. Some of the information obtained from each cadet were his height, weight, the state from which the cadet was appointed, the occupation of the father, the income of the parents, and the type of home residence (city, town, or rural) of the cadet.

    a. List the different variables measured on the cadets.

    b. Which variables are quantitative and which are qualitative?

    c. Give the levels of measurement for these variables.

    d. Why is some method of data summary necessary here?

4. The major television networks regularly conduct polls in order to ascertain the feelings of Americans on current political issues. In May of 1993, such a poll was conducted by ABC concerning United States involvement in Bosnia. The respondent's gender, political affiliation, and opinion (approve, disapprove, or no opinion) on how President Clinton was handling the situation in Bosnia represented some of the information supplied by the respondent on the survey. Each respondent was also asked to rate the job that the news media had done (excellent, good, not so good, poor) in covering the situation in Bosnia.

    a. List the different variables measured on the respondents.

    b. Which variables are quantitative and which are qualitative?

    c. Give the levels of measurement for these variables.

    d. What are some problems associated with collecting data in polls such as the one described in this exercise?

5. Under most states' auto lemon laws, dealers or car makers must replace defective autos that aren't successfully repaired after three attempts or that remain in the shop for 30 days. The table below shows data for Hawaii for the year 2010, weighing car makers' lemons against statewide market share. Assume the "lemon index" is the share of the complaints divided by the total market share for each manufacturer. **Source:** Hawaii.gov

Table for Exercise 5 – Lemon Index: Hawaii, 2010			
Best	**Lemon Index**	**Worst**	**Lemon Index**
Toyota (includes Lexus)	0.212	Chrysler (includes Dodge and Jeep)	6.512
Honda	0.462	Kia	2.750
Ford (includes Lincoln)	0.868	GM (includes Chevrolet, GMC, Buick)	2.375
Nissan (includes Infinity)	1.056	BMW	2.129
Mazda	1.833	Hyundai	2.000

Answer the following questions for the variable "lemon index".

a. Is the data quantitative or qualitative? Why?

b. What is the highest level of measurement which this data could have?

2.7 Time Series Data

Recall from Chapter 1, the science of statistics is divided into two categories: descriptive statistics and inferential statistics. Fundamental to the concept of statistical inference is the notion of population – the total collection of measurements. *Time series data originate as measurements usually taken from some process over equally spaced intervals of time.* Because measurements are taken over time, the concept of a population gets a little blurry. Suppose we want to examine the divorce rate in the United States since 1900. What is the population we are studying?

Presumably the members of the population under study would be the residents of the United States. But in 1900 there were only about 76 million people in this country. Now there are over 317 million. Moreover, none of the 76 million that were around in 1900 are alive today, so the population from which the divorce data is drawn is certainly not fixed. In addition, cultural and sociological conditions prevailing in 1900 are substantially different from those in the 2011s. Why is this important? If a population doesn't contain a fixed set of members or subjects, how can inferences be made about it? The concept of population is not sufficiently broad to cope with time series measurements.

Table 2.2 – Divorce Rate in the United States 1900–2008 (Per 1,000 People)			
Year	**Number of Divorces**	**Year**	**Number of Divorces**
1900	0.7	1985	5.0
1905	0.8	1990	4.7
1910	0.9	1995	4.4
1915	1.0	1996	4.3
1920	1.6	1997	4.3
1925	1.5	1998	4.2
1930	1.6	1999	4.1
1935	1.7	2000	4.1
1940	2.0	2001	4.0
1945	3.5	2002	3.9
1950	2.6	2003	3.8
1955	2.3	2004	3.7
1960	2.2	2005	3.6
1965	2.5	2006	3.7
1970	3.5	2007	3.6
1975	4.8	2008	3.5
1980	5.2		

Source: Centers for Disease Control and Prevention

Time series data originate from processes. Processes can be divided into two categories: stationary and nonstationary. All time series that are interesting vary, and the nature of the variability determines how the process is characterized. In a **stationary process** the time series varies around some central value and has approximately the same variation over the series. In a **nonstationary process** the time series possesses a trend – the tendency for the series to either increase or decrease over time.

Example 2.6

A company's cash operations are defined as its revenues minus all operating expenses, but calculated through a series of adjustments to net income. Table 2.3 contains cash operations data for Applied Materials, a technology manufacturing company. The company's cash operations range from approximately −$185 million to more than $850 million.

Table 2.3 – Applied Materials (AMAT) Cash Operations October 1999 – October 2009 (Millions of Dollars)			
Period	**Cash Operations**	**Period**	**Cash Operations**
Oct. 1999	413.85	Jan. 2005	236.98
Jan. 2000	184.05	Apr. 2005	475.97
Apr. 2000	369.18	Jul. 2005	336.41
Jul. 2000	405.36	Oct. 2005	197.78
Oct. 2000	693.22	Jan. 2006	411.73
Jan. 2001	−4.32	Apr. 2006	502.96
Apr. 2001	838.62	Jul. 2006	361.94
Jul. 2001	294.02	Oct. 2006	659.09
Oct. 2001	451.98	Jan. 2007	419.18
Jan. 2002	101.10	Apr. 2007	475.15
Apr. 2002	20.40	Jul. 2007	637.56
Jul. 2002	182.30	Oct. 2007	677.40
Oct. 2002	188.33	Jan. 2008	389.73
Jan. 2003	87.45	Apr. 2008	874.00
Apr. 2003	313.41	Jul. 2008	320.42
Jul. 2003	−97.06	Oct. 2008	126.31
Oct. 2003	497.95	Jan. 2009	−185.21
Jan. 2004	217.29	Apr. 2009	84.30
Apr. 2004	220.27	Jul. 2009	193.70
Jul. 2004	682.63	Oct. 2009	239.87
Oct. 2004	507.08		

The cash operations data are plotted in Figure 2.4. Notice that the time series seems to fluctuate around some central value and the dispersion around the central value is reasonably constant throughout this time frame. Thus, the time series appears to be stationary.

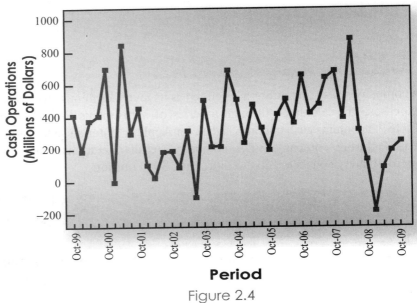

Figure 2.4

Example 2.7

Figure 2.5 shows the divorce data from Table 2.2. There is strong evidence of an upward trend. Thus, the time series is nonstationary. (Note these data are not affected by population increases over the years since it is given in divorces per 1000 people.)

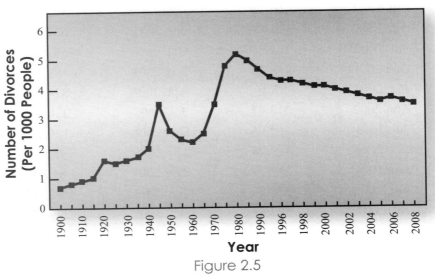

Figure 2.5

Example 2.8

As can be seen in Figure 2.6, hourly compensation for manufacturing durable goods has been on a steady increase since 1990. Given that the time series increases from year to year, this is obviously not a stationary series. The data for this plot is shown in Table 2.4.

Table 2.4 – Hourly Compensation of Manufacturing Durable Goods 1990 – 2010 (U.S. Dollars)	
Year	**Hourly Compensation**
1990	89.12
1991	94.83
1992	100.00
1993	101.96
1994	104.52
1995	105.27
1996	106.42
1997	108.27
1998	115.27
1999	120.33
2000	129.81
2001	133.57
2002	140.10
2003	153.01
2004	152.52
2005	157.24
2006	160.72
2007	168.19
2008	173.10
2009	182.34
2010	182.35

Source: Bureau of Labor Statistics

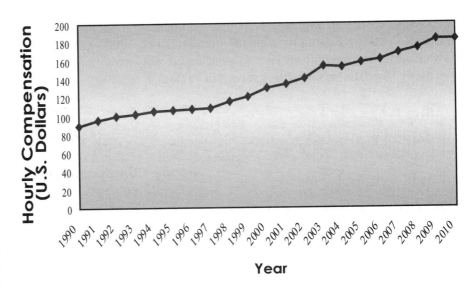

Figure 2.6

2.7 Exercises

Basic Concepts

1. What are time series measurements?

2. What problems are associated with the concept of population when studying time series data?

3. What is a stationary process?

4. What is a non-stationary process?

5. What is a trend? If a time series has an 'upward trend' what does this mean?

Exercises

1. Consider the following graph of long-term interest rates (10-year treasury notes) and inflation rates. **Source:** Federal Reserve Bank of Saint Louis

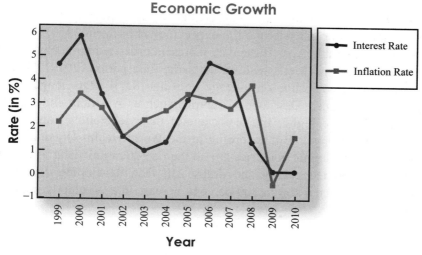

Economic Growth

a. Are the interest rate data presented above time series data?

b. Are the inflation rate data presented above time series data?

c. For each of parts (a) and (b) if the data is time series data, does the series appear to be stationary or non-stationary?

2. Consider the following graph of total exports. **Source:** Federal Reserve Bank of Saint Louis

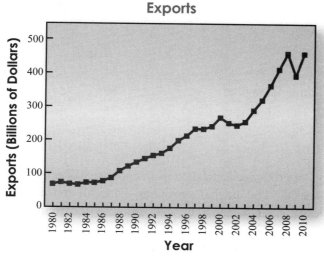

Exports

a. Are these data time series data?

b. If the data are time series data, does the series appear to be stationary or non-stationary?

3. Using a newspaper, journal, or website as your source, give an example of time series data. Be sure to reference your source and give a brief description of the data.

2.8 Cross-Sectional Data

Cross-sectional data are measurements created at approximately the same period of time. For example, consider the life expectancy at birth (in 2010) for selected countries given in Table 2.5. These data represent cross-sectional measurements since the measurements were made in the same time period (2010). People in Andorra are expected to live on average until age 82, 4 years longer than the average for Americans. Developed countries such as Australia and the United States generally have higher life expectancies than developing countries such as Botswana and Kenya. But according to the World Health Organization, life expectancies in developing countries are on the rise due to medical interventions based on advanced technology and drugs. In fact, developing countries are expected to experience a 200 to 300 percent increase in their elderly populations in the next 35 years.

Table 2.5 – Life Expectancy at Birth: 2010	
Country	Life Expectancy (Years)
Afghanistan	45
Andorra	82
Australia	82
Botswana	61
Egypt	72
Guatemala	71
Kenya	59
Sri Lanka	75
Sweden	81
United Kingdom	80
United States	78

Source: CIA World Fact Book

Another example of cross-sectional data is greenhouse gas emissions of each state on a per capita basis. The air that surrounds the earth consists of a mixture of oxygen and nitrogen, interspersed with small amounts of carbon dioxide, methane, and other trace gases. The trace gases capture heat as the sun warms the earth and holds part of that heat in the atmosphere in what is known as the "greenhouse effect."

These gases prevent the sun's heat from simply hitting the ground and being rechanneled back into space. For most of the last several thousand years, the earth's greenhouse gases have been stable. The most abundant trace gas, carbon dioxide, was processed by plants and maritime organisms at approximately the same rate as it was given off by other organisms, until about the time of the Industrial Revolution. The natural world's ability to absorb carbon dioxide has been unable to keep up, and consequently the level of carbon dioxide in the atmosphere has been rising. A time series of the atmospheric carbon dioxide concentrations at Mauna Loa Observatory reveals a disturbing trend, as seen in Figure 2.7.

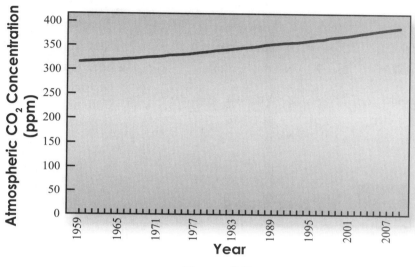

Figure 2.7

Source: Carbon Dioxide Research Group, Scripps Institution of Oceanography, University of California

The U.S. produces 19.9% of the world's carbon dioxide. It would be interesting to examine the greenhouse emissions of each state on a per capita basis.

Table 2.6 – Per Capita Carbon Dioxide Emissions by State in 2007 (Metric Tons)					
State	**Emissions**	**State**	**Emissions**	**State**	**Emissions**
Wyoming	126.67	Ohio	23.39	Nevada	16.20
North Dakota	82.26	Mississippi	23.07	Arizona	16.03
West Virginia	64.76	Arkansas	22.62	Maine	15.64
Alaska	64.63	Pennsylvania	22.21	New Jersey	15.37
Louisiana	42.46	Tennessee	20.53	New Hampshire	14.50
Montana	39.38	Colorado	20.42	Florida	14.12

Indiana	37.09	Delaware	20.00	Maryland	12.32
Kentucky	37.07	South Carolina	19.85	Washington	12.64
Alabama	31.48	Georgia	19.47	Massachusetts	12.32
Oklahoma	30.54	Minnesota	19.38	Oregon	11.65
New Mexico	30.07	Illinois	19.05	Connecticut	11.55
Kansas	29.04	Hawaii	19.03	California	11.10
Iowa	28.84	Wisconsin	18.74	Idaho	10.81
Texas	26.83	Michigan	18.24	Vermont	10.48
Utah	26.43	South Dakota	17.31	New York	10.31
Nebraska	25.09	North Carolina	17.10	Rhode Island	10.24
Missouri	23.79	Virginia	16.71	District of Columbia	4.26

Source: Environmental Protection Agency

2.8 Exercises

Basic Concepts

1. What are cross-sectional data?

2. What is the difference between cross-sectional data and time series data?

Exercises

1. The following table shows the annual average crude oil price from 1946 through 2011. Prices are adjusted for inflation to April, 2011 prices using the Consumer Price Index (CPI-U) as presented by the Bureau of Labor Statistics. Inflation adjusted prices were at an all-time high in 1980, reaching $102.26 dollars per barrel. Crude oil prices reached an all-time low in 1998 (lower than the price in 1946!) when the price per barrel dipped to $16.44. (**Source:** www.inflationdata.com) Using the data in the table, discuss if the data set contains time series or cross sectional data. Also, discuss the data and make some inferences. That is, can you explain some of the fluctuations in the oil prices?

Table for Exercise 1 – Annual Average Domestic Crude Oil Prices ($ per Barrel)

Year	Nominal	Inflation Adjusted (April, 2011)	Year	Nominal	Inflation Adjusted (April, 2011)
1946	1.63	18.49	1979	25.10	77.05
1947	2.16	21.73	1980	37.42	102.26
1948	2.77	25.92	1981	35.75	88.55
1949	2.77	26.17	1982	31.83	74.24
1950	2.77	25.90	1983	29.08	65.69
1951	2.77	24.00	1984	28.75	62.26
1952	2.77	23.47	1985	26.92	56.28
1953	2.92	24.50	1986	14.44	29.62
1954	2.99	25.04	1987	17.75	35.13
1955	2.93	24.57	1988	14.87	28.32
1956	2.94	24.35	1989	18.33	33.24
1957	3.14	25.12	1990	23.19	39.80
1958	3.00	23.38	1991	20.20	33.36
1959	3.00	23.15	1992	19.25	30.85
1960	2.91	22.15	1993	16.75	26.09
1961	2.85	21.44	1994	15.66	23.76
1962	2.85	21.19	1995	16.75	24.73
1963	2.91	21.39	1996	20.46	29.32
1964	3.00	21.75	1997	18.64	26.12
1965	3.01	21.47	1998	11.91	16.44
1966	3.10	21.48	1999	16.56	22.30
1967	3.12	21.04	2000	27.39	35.76
1968	3.18	20.53	2001	23.00	29.23
1969	3.32	20.36	2002	22.81	28.50
1970	3.39	19.65	2003	27.69	33.86
1971	3.60	20.00	2004	37.66	44.81
1972	3.60	21.44	2005	50.04	57.57
1973	4.75	23.87	2006	58.30	65.03
1974	9.35	42.58	2007	64.20	69.51
1975	12.21	51.00	2008	91.48	95.25
1976	13.10	51.78	2009	53.48	55.96
1977	14.40	53.41	2010	71.21	73.44
1978	14.95	51.58	2011 (Partial)	86.84	–

2. Do you think the pay of executives working for digital companies increases/ decreases as the company's stock price increases/decreases? Examine the following table. **Source**: paidContent.org

Exec	Salary/ Bonus ($)	Stock/ Options ($)	Other Non-Equity Compensa- tion ($)	Total 2007 Compensa- tion ($)	Change from 2006 Compensa- tion (%)	2007 Stock Perfor- mance (%)
Tom Rogers (Tivo)	800,000	6,200,000	495,075	7,495,075	+102	+32
Mel Karmazin (Sirius)	5,250,000	–	18,743	5,268,743	+23	−23
Paul Sagan (Akamai)	403,651	3,554,264	497,362	4,455,277	−40	−48
Reed Hastings (Netflix)	850,000	1,568,307	270	2,418,577	+5	−6
Rob Glaser (RealNetworks)	1,169,384	643,400	354,200	2,166,984	−26	−45
Bobby Kotick (Activision Blizzard)	899,560	1,188,467	–	2,088,027	+6	+49
Magid M. Abraham (comScore)	421,952	1,125,000	–	1,546,952	+185	−16
Barry Diller (IAC)	500,000	–	927,429	1,427,429	+270	+21
John S. Riccitiello (Electronic Arts)	750,000	–	625,350	1,375,350	−37	−38
Steve Ballmer (Microsoft)	1,340,833	–	10,001	1,350,834	N/A	0
Wayne T. Gattinella (WebMD)	830,000	–	9,214	839,214	+6	+10

Table for Exercise 2 – CEO Compensation and Stock Performance

What type of data is in the Salary/Bonus column? What do you think about executive salaries as a function of the company's stock performance? Justify your responses.

 **Data Resources**

We live in a data rich society. Anyone with access to a personal computer can access thousands of different databases throughout the Internet. These databases are full of observational data.

Here are some interesting sites that you might wish to explore:

- Data Interchange Standards Association – www.disa.org
- The World Bank – data.worldbank.org
- The Population Reference Bureau – www.prb.org/DataFinder.aspx
- The World Health Organization – www.who.int

The United States government is one of the more prolific producers of data in the world.

Check out a few of the many U.S. government's websites which publish a wide array of national statistics:

- Federal Statistics – www.fedstats.gov
- The National Center for Education Statistics – www.nces.ed.gov
- Centers for Disease Control and Prevention – www.cdc.gov/nchs
- The Whitehouse – www.whitehouse.gov
- The United States Census Bureau – www.census.gov/compendia/statab
- The Bureau of Labor Statistics – www.bls.gov

Discovering Technology

Note: If you are not familiar with Excel, Appendix C is a tutorial section that will familiarize you with the controls in Excel.

USING EXCEL

Line Chart

For this exercise, use the information from Example 2.6.

1. Enter the time period data into Column A – label as "Period".

2. Enter the data for the cash operations into Column B – label as "Cash Operations".

3. Highlight the data in Column A and Column B and under the "Insert" tab click on the **Line** button. Select **Line with Markers** (the first graph in the second row under 2-D lines) so that you can see each data point that is plotted.

4. Excel has created a line chart. Under the "Design" tab, click on **Select Data**.

5. In the "Select Data Source" box, click on the **Edit** button on the right hand side under the heading "Horizontal (Category) Axis Labels". You are prompted to select the axis label range. Highlight all of the values in the "Period" column and click **OK**.

6. In the "Select Data Source" box on the left hand side under the heading "Legend Entries (Series)", highlight the title "Period" and click **Remove**. Click **OK**.

7. You now see a time series plot of the cash operations data. To change the interval of the *x*-axis, select the values on the *x*-axis, right click and select **Format Axis**. In the "Axis Options" dialog box, next to "Major unit" select the radio button for **Fixed**. Enter **6** in the dialog box and make sure that **Months** is selected. Select Inside from the drop down menu next to "Minor tick mark type". Click **Close**.

8. To format the *y*-axis, select the values on the *y*-axis, right click and select **Format Axis**. Since there are negative values in this data set, the chart may be easier to read if the horizontal axis crosses at a negative value, say –400.0 rather than 0. Under the heading "Horizontal axis crosses" select the radio button next to "Axis value" and enter **–400.0** in the dialog box. Click **Close**. Now the entire line chart is above the *x*-axis.

9. Under the "Layout" tab you can change the chart title, axis titles, and legend. Click on the **Legend** button and select **none**. The legend is now removed and the chart is easier to read. There are numerous ways to format your chart in Microsoft Excel.

Excel Line Chart

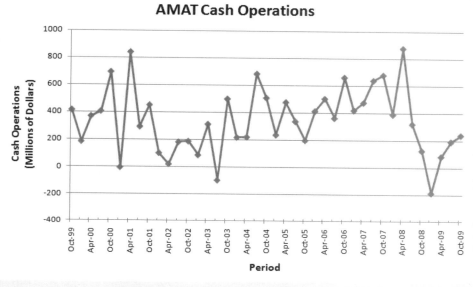

Figure 2.8

USING MINITAB

Time Series Plot

For this exercise, use the information from Example 2.8.

1. Enter the data for the years in Column C1 – label as "Year".

2. Enter the corresponding data for the annual hourly compensation in Column C2 – label as "Hourly Compensation".

3. Click **Graph** and select **Time Series Plot**.

4. Select the "Simple" time series plot. Click **OK**.

5. In the "Time Series Plot – Simple" dialog box, highlight "Hourly Compensation" in the box on the left hand side and click **Select**. This moves "Hourly Compensation" into the "Series" box on the right hand side.

6. Now click **Time/Scale**. This will bring up the "Time Series Plot – Time/Scale" dialog box.

7. On the right hand side under the heading "Time Scale", select **Calendar**. In the drop down menu next to "Calendar" select **Year**.

8. Under the heading "Start Values", select **One set for all variables**. In the white box below the heading "Year" enter **1990**. This tells Minitab that time on the *x*-axis should begin at the year 1990.

9. In the box next to "Data Increment" enter **1**. This tells Minitab that the labels on the *x*-axis should be in increments of 1 year. Click **OK**.

10. Now in the "Time Series Plot – Simple" dialog box, click **OK** to display the graph.

Minitab Time Series Plot

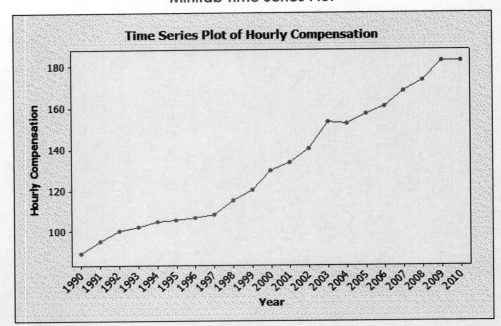

Figure 2.9

R   Chapter 2 Review

Key Terms and Ideas

- The Scientific Method
- Confounding Variable
- The Decision-Making Method
- Fuzzy Concepts
- Controlled Experiment
- Control Group
- Experimental Group
- Treatment
- Explanatory Variable
- Response Variable
- Before and After Study
- The Placebo Effect
- Double Blind Study
- Observational Study
- Bias

- Surveys
- Level Of Measurement
- Nominal Data
- Ordinal Data
- Interval Data
- Ratio Data
- Qualitative Data
- Quantitative Data
- Discrete Data
- Continuous Data
- Time Series Data
- Stationary Process
- Nonstationary Process
- Trend
- Cross-Sectional Data

2

AE   Additional Exercises

1. Suppose you were the administrator of a public school system. What kinds of variables would you measure and how would you collect the measurements on the following subjects:

   a. Student learning

   b. School discipline

   c. Teacher preparation

   d. Absenteeism (pupil and teacher)

   e. Cafeteria food quality

2. The head of the Veterans Administration has been receiving complaints from a Vietnam Veterans organization concerning disability checks. The organization claims that checks are continually late. The checks are to arrive no later than the tenth of each month.

   a. What variables would you measure to explore this problem?

   b. How would you collect measurements on these variables?

3. A family member has unexpectedly bequeathed you a sizable sum of money.

   a. What criteria might you wish to evaluate in deciding how to invest the money?

   b. What data might be useful in your considerations?

4. Flying Eagle Airlines advertises that it surpasses all other airlines in flights that arrive on time. A competitor states that it has a better on–time record than any other airline. Can they both be correct? Explain.

5. Two local grocery stores both claim to have the lowest prices in town. Develop a measurement that you believe could be used as a criterion to determine which store actually has the lowest prices.

6. At the end of 2001, the United States had 32.9 million people living in poverty according to the Census Bureau (www.census.gov). This was an increase of 1.3 million from the previous year. Poverty is defined by the Census Bureau as having a cash income less than $14,255 a year. The Census Bureau does not include in their income measurement any part of $167 billion spend on Medicaid, a federal program by which medical care is provided to the poor. The Census Bureau only includes $34.9 billion out of the $205 billion spent annually on public welfare. Forty percent of those classified as impoverished own their own homes. How should poverty be defined?

7. The quality movement has compelled American businesses to address the problem of measuring customer satisfaction. How would you measure customer satisfaction if you owned a car dealership?

8. Identify the following variables as discrete or continuous.

    a. Average test score on a test ranging from 0 to 100

    b. Number of boot errors on a computer

    c. Investment ratios for earnings per share

    d. Energy usage in a production process

9. Determine the level of measurement for each of the following variables.

    a. Golf score in relation to par

    b. SAT score

    c. Rating from 1 to 5 of quality of service in a restaurant

    d. Make and model of a vehicle

    e. The number of students with a business major

10. According to a Danish researcher, if you drop your average daily activity level by taking elevators instead of stairs, by parking your car in the closest space, or by never walking to run errands, you increase your risk of diabetes, heart disease, and premature death. The researcher studied two groups of healthy men (eight in the first group with an average age of 27 and an average body mass index (BMI) of 22.9, which is well within the normal range; and ten in the second group with an average age of 23.8 years and a BMI of 22.1). In addition to age and BMI, researchers also collected information such as number of steps per day (each group of men was fitted with pedometers), height, weight, and race. With the first group of men, the researchers asked that they reduce their daily activity (steps) by taking cars on short trips and elevators instead of stairs. The insulin levels were also measured for each group and the researchers found that with the reduced activity, insulin levels rose by nearly 60 percent after two weeks of inactivity, thus increasing the risk of diabetes and heart disease. However, the good news is that by increasing activity over a two-week period of time, one can begin to reduce their risk of diabetes and heart disease. (**Source**: U.S. News and World Report)

    a. List the different variables measured in this study.

    b. Which variables are quantitative and which are qualitative?

    c. Of the variables that are quantitative, are they discrete or continuous?

    d. Give the levels of measurement for these variables.

    e. Why is some method of data summary necessary here?

11. Consider the world production of crude oil given in millions of barrels per day. **Source**: Energy Information Administration

Table for Exercise 11 – World Production of Crude Oil			
Year	Total World Production (Millions of Barrels per Day)	Year	Total World Production (Millions of Barrels per Day)
1980	63.987	1995	70.274
1981	60.602	1996	71.919
1982	58.098	1997	74.160
1983	57.934	1998	75.656
1984	59.568	1999	74.853
1985	59.172	2000	77.768
1986	61.407	2001	77.686
1987	62.086	2002	76.994
1988	64.380	2003	79.598
1989	65.508	2004	83.105
1990	66.426	2005	84.595
1991	66.399	2006	84.661
1992	66.564	2007	84.543
1993	67.091	2008	85.507
1994	68.590	2009	84.389

a. What is the level of measurement of the data?

b. Are the data time series or cross-sectional? If the data are time series is the series stationary or non-stationary?

12. Consider the graph of the number of respondents (in percentages) who think things in the U.S. are now on the wrong track versus those that think the economy is going in the right direction. The data were collected using a survey asking the question, *In general, are you satisfied or dissatisfied with the way things are going in the United States at this time?* Source: Gallup Poll

Right Direction or Wrong Track?

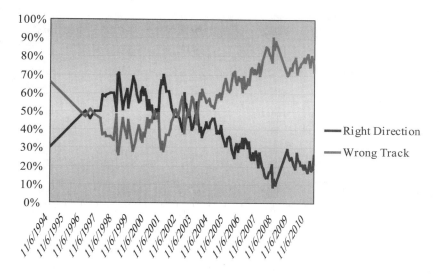

a. Are the opinions on the outlook of the economy presented in time series or cross-sectional data? Justify your answer.

b. If the data are time series data, does the series appear to be stationary or non-stationary? Explain your answer.

13. Can you think of a process that would yield measurements that did not have any variability? Would studying such a process be very interesting?

14. One of the measurements that population experts use in predicting trends in population growth is the fertility rate. The total fertility rate is sometimes defined as the number of likely births one woman will have in her lifetime. The accompanying table gives the fertility rate from 1934 to 2005. How would you describe these measurements? **Source:** U.S. National Center for Health Statistics

Table for Exercise 14 – Fertility Rates					
Year	Fertility Rate	Year	Fertility Rate	Year	Fertility Rate
1934	2.294	1958	3.693	1982	1.829
1935	2.250	1959	3.705	1983	1.803
1936	2.207	1960	3.654	1984	1.806
1937	2.236	1961	3.629	1985	1.843
1938	2.288	1962	3.474	1986	1.836
1939	2.238	1963	3.333	1987	1.871
1940	2.301	1964	3.208	1988	1.933
1941	2.399	1965	2.928	1989	1.977
1942	2.628	1966	2.736	1990	2.081
1943	2.718	1967	2.573	1991	2.073
1944	2.568	1968	2.477	1992	2.065
1945	2.491	1969	2.465	1993	2.046
1946	2.943	1970	2.480	1994	2.036
1947	3.274	1971	2.267	1995	2.019
1948	3.109	1972	2.010	1996	2.040
1949	3.110	1973	1.879	1997	2.000
1950	3.091	1974	1.835	1998	2.030
1951	3.267	1975	1.774	1999	2.070
1952	3.355	1976	1.738	2000	2.056
1953	3.418	1977	1.790	2001	2.034
1954	3.537	1978	1.760	2002	2.013
1955	3.574	1979	1.808	2003	2.043
1956	3.682	1980	1.840	2004	2.046
1957	3.760	1981	1.815	2005	2.054

15. One of the problems associated with the management of solid waste is the NIMBY (not in my backyard) syndrome. In separate surveys taken in 1988, 1989, and 1990 the National Solid Waste Management Association asked, Would you object to a new landfill in your community? The percentage response is given in the table below.

Table for Exercise 15 – Survey Results			
Survey Date	Don't Object	Object	Not Sure
March 1990	36	59	5
February 1989	23	65	12
February 1988	30	62	8

   a. What is the level of measurement of the survey data?

   b. Are the data time series or cross-sectional?

   c. What other information would be useful in evaluating the results of the study?

16. In a recent study of four leading anesthetics, three hundred patients were randomly selected and assigned to be given one of the four products during a surgery. One of the products performed significantly better than the rest. Is this an observational study or a controlled experiment?

Cases

1. Consider the data for Case One in Appendix B.

   a. List the variables of interest for this case.

   b. For each of the variables listed in part (a), determine

      i. if the data are qualitative or quantitative.

      ii. if the data are discrete or continuous.

      iii. the highest level of measurement of the data.

      iv. if the data are time series or cross-sectional.

2. Consider the data for Case Three in Appendix B.

   a. List the variables of interest for this case.

   b. For each of the variables listed in part (a), determine

      i. if the data are qualitative or quantitative.

      ii. if the data are discrete or continuous.

      iii. the highest level of measurement of the data.

      iv. if the data are time series or cross-sectional.

3. Consider the data for Case Six in Appendix B.

   a. List the variables of interest for this case.

   b. For each of the variables listed in part (a), determine

      i. if the data are qualitative or quantitative.

      ii. if the data are discrete or continuous.

      iii. the highest level of measurement of the data.

      iv. if the data are time series or cross-sectional.

Discovery Project

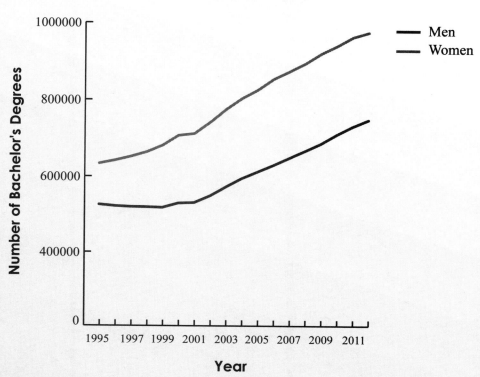

Bachelor's Degrees by Gender

Number of Bachelor's Degrees

1000000

800000

600000

400000

0

1995 1997 1999 2001 2003 2005 2007 2009 2011

Year

— Men
— Women

Source: National Center for Educational Statistics

1. What is the level of measurement of the data displayed in the graph above?

2. Are the data above time series or cross-sectional data?

3. Are the data in the graph above part of a stationary or nonstationary process? Why?

4. According to the graph, is the difference between the number of women and men earning bachelor's degrees increasing, decreasing, or remaining constant? Try to think of some reasons why this is true.

5. Do you believe the data? Elaborate.

3

Organizing, Displaying, and Interpreting Data

Discovering Technology

Creating a histogram using Microsoft Excel

Creating a line graph using Microsoft Excel

Creating a stem-and-leaf display using Minitab

Creating a histogram using Minitab

Introduction

Statistics is about understanding data. Graphical images are universally regarded as a powerful form of communicating data because the eyes and brain process visual data with amazing speed. The processing of a visual image begins in the retina of the eye where a thin layer containing a few hundred million neurons pass their output to about a million ganglion cells which in turn pass the visual data into the brain. This system enables the equivalent of approximately 90 million bytes per second of data to be transmitted to the brain from the eyes. The brain creates three-dimensional color models (our visual reality) from this data. The brain's ability to process an enormous quantity of data and to create and interpret images in their totality is an astonishing processing feat.

Although the eyes, in conjunction with our visual processing system, are a fabulous sensory system, they digest text or numbers slowly in comparison to the comprehension of a visual image. Reading is a tremendously complex transformation. When we read words or numbers, the brain must recognize the letters, decide what word they form, and think about the definition and how it relates to previous words. Recognizing letters and words is such an integral part of our lives that it is performed without conscious thought. Nevertheless, this process is slow (perhaps 50 bytes a second) compared to absorbing a picture or graphical display. Therefore, graphical displays are used daily in business meetings and presentations to communicate data quickly and effectively. For example, an advertising agency may use a chart showing an upward trend in sales to convince a potential client that their services are beneficial.

In financial markets, technical analysts (sometimes called technicians) use graphs, tables, and other tools to identify price patterns, trends, and relationships in an effort to forecast price movements over certain periods of time.

3.1   Frequency Distributions

Statistics exists because of variation. The statistician's job is to comprehend variation by looking for structure. Frequency distributions are one method of examining a data set's structure. To examine structural characteristics, ask questions such as, *Where are most of the observations located? Do the data cluster around one central point or are there several points that data seem to cluster around? Do the data seem to be uniformly spread out over some interval or bunched in some range?* These questions all relate to the concept of "distribution".

Definition

A **frequency distribution** summarizes data into classes and provides in tabular form a list of the classes along with the number of observations in each class.

Frequency Distribution

The process of refining information is interesting. The analyst begins with raw data, then organizes that data by counting the number of observations in each classification. In Table 3.1, (shown on the following page) the raw data consist of population counts in each state for the years 2000 and 2008. By comparing the populations in 2008 with the populations in 2000, a percentage population growth can be computed for each state over the 8-year period.

When the growth rate data is classified in the frequency distribution (see Table 3.2), the actual magnitudes of the data values disappear. Losing information may not seem to be a desirable result, but without some lumping together it is difficult to comprehend large amounts of data.

Table 3.2 – Frequency Distribution State 8-Year Population Growth Rates	
Percentage Population Growth 2000–2008	**Frequency**
Less than or equal to 0	2
0.01 to 5	21
5.01 to 10	15
10.01 to 15	7
15.01 to 20	3
20.01 to 25	1
25.01 to 30	1
Greater than 30	1

Source: U.S. Census Bureau

3

Table 3.1 – Population Count of Individual States in 2000 and 2008 (Rounded to the nearest 100,000)

State	2000 Population	2008 Population	Growth	Percent Growth	State	2000 Population	2008 Population	Growth	Percent Growth
Alabama	4447	4662	215	4.83	Montana	902	967	65	7.21
Alaska	627	686	59	9.41	Nebraska	1711	1783	72	4.21
Arizona	5131	6500	1369	26.68	Nevada	1998	2600	602	30.13
Arkansas	2673	2855	182	6.81	New Hampshire	1236	1316	80	6.47
California	33872	36757	2885	8.52	New Jersey	8414	8683	269	3.20
Colorado	4302	4939	637	14.81	New Mexico	1819	1984	165	9.07
Connecticut	3406	3501	95	2.79	New York	18977	19490	513	2.70
Delaware	784	873	89	11.35	North Carolina	8047	9222	1175	14.60
D.C.	572	592	20	3.50	North Dakota	642	641	-1	-0.16
Florida	15983	18328	2345	14.67	Ohio	11353	11486	133	1.17
Georgia	8187	9686	1499	18.31	Oklahoma	3451	3642	191	5.53
Hawaii	1212	1228	16	1.32	Oregon	3421	3790	369	10.79
Idaho	1294	1524	230	17.77	Pennsylvania	12281	12448	167	1.36
Illinois	12420	12902	482	3.88	Rhode Island	1048	1051	3	0.29
Indiana	6081	6377	296	4.87	South Carolina	4012	4480	468	11.67
Iowa	2926	3003	77	2.63	South Dakota	755	804	49	6.49
Kansas	2689	2802	113	4.20	Tennessee	5689	6215	526	9.25
Kentucky	4042	4269	227	5.62	Texas	20852	24327	3475	16.67
Louisiana	4469	4411	-58	-1.30	Utah	2233	2736	503	22.53
Maine	1275	1316	41	3.22	Vermont	609	621	12	1.97
Maryland	5297	5634	337	6.36	Virginia	7079	7769	690	9.75
Massachusetts	6349	6498	149	2.35	Washington	5894	6549	655	11.11
Michigan	9938	10003	65	0.65	West Virginia	1808	1814	6	0.33
Minnesota	4919	5220	301	6.12	Wisconsin	5364	5628	264	4.92
Mississippi	2845	2939	94	3.30	Wyoming	494	533	39	7.89
Missouri	5597	5912	315	5.63					

With the frequency distribution, we are able to see the broader structure of the data. It is now easy to see that most state population 8-year growth rates are between 0 and 15 percent. Further, growth rates above 20% are uncommon. Without the organization that a frequency distribution provides, these conclusions would be more difficult to establish. If there were 10,000 data values instead of 51, it would be much more difficult to make similar conclusions.

There are only two steps in the construction of a frequency distribution:

- choosing the classifications, and
- counting the number in each class.

For simple data, such as the results from tossing a coin (H, T), the choice of classifications is easy. Heads is one category and tails the other. However, for continuous data, such as weights, heights, and volumes, the choice of classification scheme becomes less obvious, since there are an enormous number of possibilities. There are two requirements that should be met when setting up the categories for classification: the categories must be both mutually exclusive and exhaustive. Essentially, this means categories should not overlap and should cover all possible values.

Since choosing the classification depends on whether the data are qualitative (nominal or ordinal) or quantitative (interval or ratio), the discussion of frequency distributions and the associated graphs will be presented on the basis of these data types.

Constructing Frequency Distributions for Qualitative Data

To construct a frequency distribution for qualitative data, choose the categories to classify the data. In many instances, the problem at hand will suggest the classification scheme. For instance, in the coin-tossing example there are only two classes, heads and tails. If we are classifying students by gender, again there are only two classes, male and female. For qualitative data, it would be unusual if a reasonable set of categories is *not* relatively obvious.

After the categories have been chosen, count the items belonging to each class in order to construct the frequency distribution.

Example 3.1

A Model to Determine Virtual Security Practices

Our increased reliance on digital information and our expansive use of the internet for a steadily rising number of tasks requires that more emphasis be placed on digital information security. The importance of securing digital information is apparent but the success in persuading individual users to adopt and utilize tools to improve security has been arguably more difficult. In a recent study conducted by Information Security Associates, they wanted to determine security measures that students use on their computers to protect personal information. One of the survey items was, "I am aware that there are measures that I can take to help protect my personal information on my personal computer." The frequency of each response category is shown in Table 3.3. The summary tables are much more informative than looking at more than a thousand observations for each question (note that the number of observations for each question are different because every student did not answer every question on the survey). The frequency distribution for the second item, "I am aware that I can reduce exposure to system compromise by restricting who uses my personal computer," is given in Table 3.4.

Table 3.3 – Frequency Distribution of Response "I am aware that there are measures that I can take to help protect my personal information on my personal computer."	
Strongly Agree	419
Slightly Agree	327
Neutral	250
Slightly Disagree	124
Strongly Disagree	85

Table 3.4 – Frequency Distribution of Response "I am aware that I can reduce exposure to system compromise by restricting who uses my personal computer."	
Strongly Agree	520
Slightly Agree	435
Neutral	310
Slightly Disagree	115
Strongly Disagree	90

In Table 3.5 and Table 3.6, relative frequency distributions are calculated. In those tables, the frequencies are converted into percentages. (See Section 3.4 for an additional discussion of relative frequency distributions.)

Table 3.5 – Relative Frequency Distribution of Response	
"I am aware that there are measures that I can take to help protect my personal information on my personal computer."	
Strongly Agree	35%
Slightly Agree	27%
Neutral	21%
Slightly Disagree	10%
Strongly Disagree	7%

Table 3.6 – Relative Frequency Distribution of Response	
"I am aware that I can reduce exposure to system compromise by restricting who uses my personal computer."	
Strongly Agree	35%
Slightly Agree	30%
Neutral	21%
Slightly Disagree	8%
Strongly Disagree	6%

As one can see in Tables 3.3–3.6, the majority of students are aware that there are measures that they can take to protect the information on their personal computers. However, what has been found (through further research and analysis), is that many students don't take the time to actually perform these measures to protect their information. Summarizing the qualitative data (via a frequency distribution table or relative frequency distribution table) allows the researcher to make conclusions about the data without having to view each observation.

Exercises

Basic Concepts

1. From a comprehension standpoint, what are the advantages of visual images over the written word?

2. Describe two situations in which graphical displays are used in business.

3. Describe the purpose of a frequency distribution.

4. What are the three basic questions to ask when examining the structure of a data set?

5. What are the two steps to constructing a frequency distribution?

6. In the construction of a frequency distribution, what are the two requirements that the classification categories must meet?

Exercises

1. In order to help him decide when and where to advertise, a local repairman decided to pull his invoices for the month of June and tally what type of machines he had worked on. There were forty-eight items repaired that month:

Office copier	Washing machine	Air conditioner
Air conditioner	Fan	Lawn mower
Lawn mower	Air conditioner	Fan
DVD Player	Fan	Air conditioner
Air conditioner	Lawn mower	Washing machine
Lawn mower	Air conditioner	Stereo
Exercise bike	DVD Player	Air conditioner
Air conditioner	Lawn mower	Lawn mower
Lawn mower	Air conditioner	Fan
Radio	Washing machine	Air conditioner
Air conditioner	Radio	Stereo
Fan	Air conditioner	Lawn mower
Washing machine	Lawn mower	Air conditioner
Air conditioner	Fan	Fan
Lawn mower	Air conditioner	DVD player
Washing machine	Washing machine	Air conditioner

    a. What level of measurement does the data possess?

    b. Construct a frequency distribution for the data. Any machine types worked on three or less times are classified as miscellaneous.

2. Parkinsonism is an affliction of the aged and is frequently caused by Parkinson's disease, Alzheimer's disease, or other illnesses. The results from a recent study on parkinsonism were reported in "Prevalence of Parkinsonian Signs and Associated Mortality in a Community Population of Older People", *New England Journal of Medicine*. A sample of 467 people, all 65 years of age or older, was selected from East Boston, Massachusetts. Each person was clinically evaluated and various signs of parkinsonism, if any, were noted. The table below is a frequency distribution for some of the signs of parkinsonism:

Table for Exercise 2 – Signs of Parkinsonism	
Sign	**Frequency**
Reduced arm swing	210
Prolonged turning	153
Right leg rigidity	141
Left leg rigidity	154
Slow finger taps	197
Shuffling gait	83

a. What level of measurement does the data possess?

b. What percent of the sample suffered from left leg rigidity?

c. Add up the frequencies. Why does the sum of the frequencies exceed the total sample size of 467?

d. Suppose 30 people suffer from both left leg rigidity and right leg rigidity. How many people in the sample suffer from rigidity in at least one of their legs?

3. A small commuter airline in the West keeps records on complaints received from its customers. Complains for March and July are listed below:

Table for Exercise 3 – Customer Complaints		
Type of Complaint	March	July
Tickets cost too much	11	15
Stewardess did not provide blankets	8	3
Schedules not convenient	12	17
Plane often late	17	16
Seats too stiff	3	3
Airplane too hot	6	20
Airplane too cold	8	5
Poor reservation system	5	5
Plane interior looks shabby	5	6

a. Classify the items by the following categories: comfort, price, service, and schedule, and develop a qualitative frequency distribution.

b. Classify the items by the following categories: plane, personnel, building equipment, and other, and develop a qualitative frequency distribution.

c. Would another person necessarily assign the same items to the same categories as you have? Discuss the implications of this when reviewing data collected and distributed by someone else for open answer questions.

d. Do the categories chosen in parts (a) and (b) meet the requirement that categories be mutually exclusive and exhaustive? Discuss.

3

3.2 The Value of Graphs

Graphical analysis is a tradeoff. We lose sight of the individual observations (the raw data). In return we are able to see a representation of the totality of observations. The trade is almost always beneficial since a well-designed graph gives our visual processing system the kind of image it processes best, a picture.

Because a set of data can be graphically represented in many different ways, selecting and creating graphical displays requires a certain amount of artistic judgment. Fortunately, the development of graphics software has made the creation of sophisticated graphs quite easy.

Several types of graphs and tabular displays will be discussed in this chapter: bar charts (2-D and 3-D), pie charts, line charts, stem-and-leaf diagrams, several types of frequency distributions, and histograms. A quick look at publications such as *Time, USA Today, The Wall Street Journal, Scientific American*, or *Forbes* provides convincing evidence of the frequent and beneficial usage of these graphical display techniques.

3.2 Exercises

Basic Concepts

1. What are some benefits of graphing?

2. What is the major disadvantage of graphing?

3.3 Displaying Qualitative Data Graphically

Bar charts, stacked bar charts, 3-D bar charts, and pie charts are effective, visually appealing methods of graphically displaying qualitative data. These tools will help us visually describe the distribution of the data.

Bar Charts

Bar charts are used to illustrate a frequency distribution for qualitative data.

> ### Definition
>
> The **bar chart** is a simple graphical display in which the length of each bar corresponds to the number of observations in a category.

Bar Chart

Bar charts are valuable as presentation tools and are especially effective at reinforcing differentials in magnitudes, since they permit the visual comparison of data by displaying the magnitude of each category by a vertical or horizontal bar. Figure 3.1 is a bar chart constructed from majors in a business statistics course.

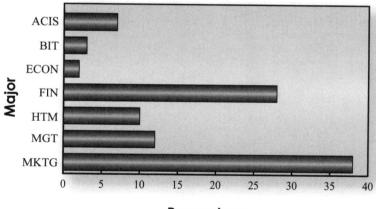

ACIS (Accounting and Information Systems)

BIT (Business Information Technology)   MKTG (Marketing)

ECON (Economics)   FIN (Finance)   MGT (Management)

HTM (Hospitality and Tourism Management)

Figure 3.1

3

The Aesthetics of Bar Chart Construction

Bar chart construction requires numerous arbitrary layout decisions such as size, use of color, and labeling locations. These decisions are frequently made on a trial and error basis. However, certain conventions have been developed that improve the quality and effectiveness of charts. They are presented below as suggestions, not rules. Actually, several of the points are general in nature and would serve as useful guidelines in the construction of any graph.

- Bar charts can be constructed horizontally or vertically. Customarily horizontal orientation is used for categories that are descriptively labeled, and vertical (or columnar) orientation is used for categories that are numerical. It is important to remember that this idea is only a suggestion. If you believe that a vertical bar chart is more appealing, use it.

- If the categories have some associated order, they maintain that order in the bar chart. Otherwise, the categories may be listed alphabetically, in either ascending or descending order, or in some other pattern related to the nature of the data.

- Miscellaneous or "other" categories should be listed at the bottom of the chart (if oriented horizontally) or at the far right (if oriented vertically).

- The difference in bar length is the principal visual feature in comparing differences in category amounts. Consequently, scales for the axes should be chosen that will most effectively allow for the desired comparisons. **Unless there is a good reason, the axis used to measure the bars should start at zero. Otherwise the axis can be stretched to exaggerate differences in the bar lengths.** For example, suppose the following data were plotted:

Table 3.7 – Sales Performance	
Sales Person	**Total Dollars in Sales (in Thousands)**
Susan	187
William	201
Beth	207
Rob	193

Figures 3.2 and 3.3 are plots of the same data (Table 3.7). What a difference axis selection can make on perception! Figure 3.3 begins the y-axis at 180 instead of zero. If you want to emphasize similarity, use Figure 3.2 to do the job. If you want to emphasize differences, use Figure 3.3. However, it is difficult to imagine any legitimate reason for using Figure 3.3 to represent the data. Axis stretching is often employed to mislead. **When you see an axis that does not start at zero, you should be a bit skeptical as to the conclusions the author intends for you to make.**

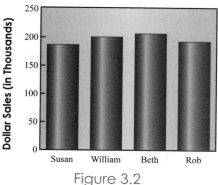

Figure 3.2

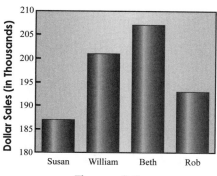

Figure 3.3

- Bar widths should be chosen that are visually pleasing and should not be allowed to vary within a particular chart.

- Appropriate shading, crosshatching, and coloring of the bars can help in presenting data. Many spreadsheet programs incorporate sophisticated graphing programs which make changes in shading, color, and crosshatching patterns extremely easy.

- The spacing between bars can dramatically affect the perception of the graph. Spacing should be set at approximately one-half the width of a bar. This, however, is not a rigid rule. Artistic judgment is needed.

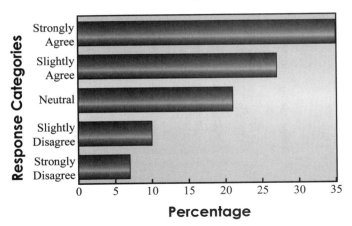

Figure 3.4

- Gridlines extended into the body of the chart are often useful and may be included if deemed helpful. Study Figure 3.4 and Figure 3.5. Both bar charts illustrate the same data. Notice that the readability of the graph in Figure 3.5 below is improved by adding gridlines.

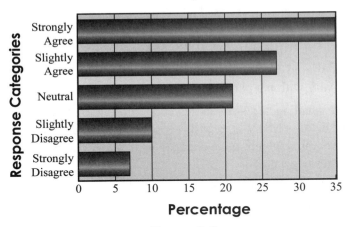

Figure 3.5

- If there is sufficient room on the graphs, labels should be provided for each bar (category) and for each axis.

- Notes on sources of data or other footnotes should be given below the chart.

Bar charts used to be flat and simple. Now, computer graphics packages offer three-dimensional, stacked, side-by-side, colored, and other variations of bars. These capabilities offer the user the chance to create spectacular, multi-dimensional, eye catching graphics.

3-D Bar Graph

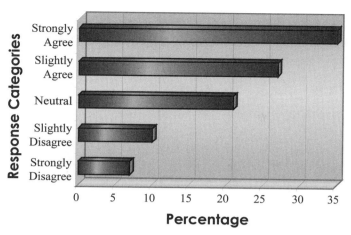

Figure 3.6

Rotating the axes on a bar chart can create a very different graphical perspective. Figures 3.6 and 3.7 are identical graphs with a slight difference in perspective. If you are using a large number of graphics in a document, even 3-D graphs can be burdensome. It would be more visually interesting to change the perspective of the graphic from time to time. Making the changes from 2-D to 3-D and performing the rotation are simple operations in most graphics programs.

3-D Bar Graph

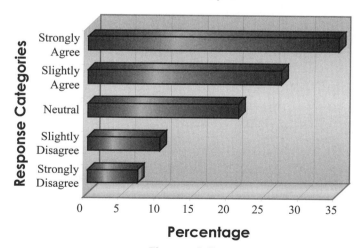

Figure 3.7

One of the themes of this chapter is that a graph can be an analytical device and a presentation tool. Simple graphics are fine for analytical purposes, but if you are trying to make a point, then a higher standard is required to create visual impact. Designing effective graphics is not just about making things look better; graphics can help the reader comprehend information. Using graphics well can emphasize meaning and organize content.

Stacked Bar Charts

Stacked bar charts are an interesting variation on the standard bar chart. The number of medals (gold, silver, bronze) won during the 2010 Winter Olympics for selected countries is given in Figure 3.8.

Using the stacked bar chart enables the reader to compare the total number of medals for each country as well as observe the number of each type of medal won.

Without the stacked bar chart, the reader would have to view either three different charts tallying medal counts for the 2010 Winter Olympics or a much "busier" chart plotting each medal on the horizontal axis above each country.

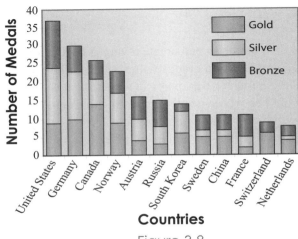

Figure 3.8

Figure 3.9 is a stacked bar chart displaying the number of grandchildren by age group living with their grandparents based on which parent is in the household.

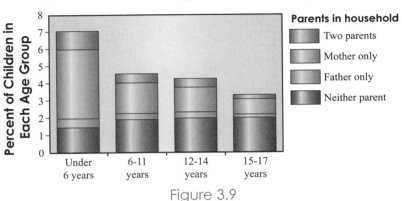

Figure 3.9

3-D Bar Charts

Another interesting way of looking at the Olympic medal data is to plot a three-dimensional bar chart. If the purpose of the graph is to compare the number of medals of each type between countries, the 3-D bar chart is a better choice than the stacked bar chart. Using this graph, the totals for each type of medal are graphed for each country.

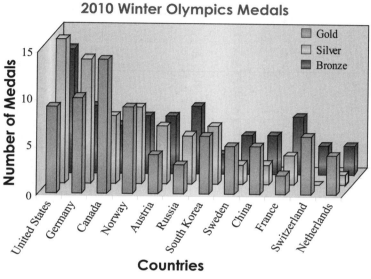

Figure 3.10

When constructing a 3-D graph, as in Figure 3.10, there are a number of perspective issues that affect the visual quality of the graph. For example, in this graph we are barely able to see the number of bronze medals won by Germany. All the major graphics programs permit you to spin and tilt the graph until you find a perspective you like.

Pie Charts

We have just seen how bar charts are used as a means of expressing frequency distributions. Pie charts can perform the same function.

The circle represents the total "pie" available, and the slices are proportional to the amount in each category. Each slice of the pie represents the proportion of total observations belonging to the category. One of the advantages of the pie chart is the ability to easily compare the total in each of the classifications to the total number of observations.

One common use of pie charts is to display how some set of assets is spent. The biggest asset pie in the world is the budget of the United States government. In 2009 government outlays were in the neighborhood of 3.52 trillion dollars. If the budget is split into six categories, the percentages spent in 2009 in each category are provided in Table 3.8. While the table provides the information, it is not visually interesting. A pie chart will enable you to improve the presentation of the information in Table 3.8.

| Table 3.8 – Percentage Spent by the Federal Government in 2009 ||
Category	Percentage Spent
Social Security	20%
Non-Defense Discretionary	12%
National Defense	23%
Other Entitlements	21%
Medicare and Medicaid	19%
Net Interest	5%

The pie chart in Figure 3.11 tells an interesting story about how our tax dollars are spent. In a glance at the pie chart, your eyes are drawn to the biggest slice of the pie, the 23% spent on National Defense. If you would like to look at current information on how government monies are spent go to www.whitehouse.gov/omb/budget.

Federal Government Spending, Fiscal Year 2009

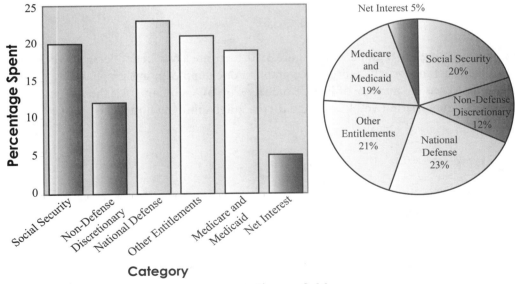

Figure 3.11

A three-dimensional version of the pie chart (see Figure 3.12) adds some spice to any presentation. If you are working with a computer application that can perform graphics, changing the image from a two-dimensional pie chart to a three-dimensional chart takes only a few mouse clicks.

A 3-D pie chart showing where government revenues originate is given below.

To learn how to make these charts in Excel, go to Appendix C.

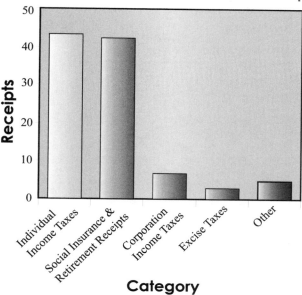

Figure 3.12

3.3 Exercises

Basic Concepts

1. Describe in general terms the types of data that a bar chart would be useful in displaying.

2. Generally, where should miscellaneous categories be displayed in a bar chart?

3. Explain how axis scales on bar charts can be misleading.

4. What is a stacked bar chart?

5. Why would a stacked bar chart be preferred over a normal bar chart?

6. What is one disadvantage of using a 3-D chart?

7. What is a pie chart?

8. What is the main advantage of using a pie chart?

Exercises

1. A consumer magazine uses bar charts to compare four popular brands of automobiles. This particular bar chart represents a comparison of the miles per gallon (mpg) for the four brands.

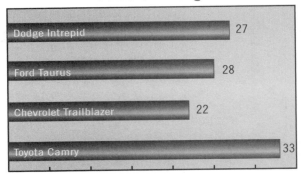

Vehicle Mileage

a. What is wrong with this picture?

b. Evaluate the bar chart using the guidelines suggested in the section on the aesthetics of bar chart construction.

2. The following bar chart presents the median income of U.S. employees by education level.

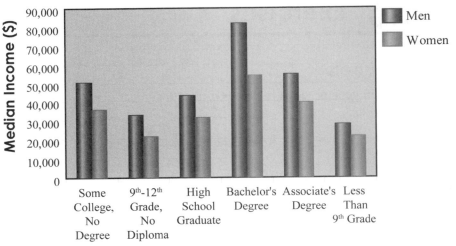

Median Income by Education, 2008

Evaluate the bar chart using the guidelines suggested in the section on the aesthetics of bar chart construction.

3. Consider the following data regarding the number of wildfires in the U.S. categorized by the size class in acres and the cause of the fire.

Table for Exercise 3 – Number of Wildfires in the U.S.		
Size Class (Acres)	Lightning-Caused	Person-Caused
.25 or less	4637	2367
.26 – 9	1940	1904
10 – 99	219	571
100 – 299	44	103
300 – 999	26	52
1000 – 4999	43	17
5000 +	21	9
Total	6930	5023

a. Construct a bar chart for the number of wildfires caused by lightning.

b. Construct a bar chart for the number of wildfires caused by people.

c. Construct a stacked bar chart for the number of wildfires caused by lightning and the number of wildfires caused by people.

d. Construct a pie chart for the number of wildfires caused by lightning.

e. Construct a pie chart for the number of wildfires caused by people.

f. What did you learn from the charts created in parts (a) through (e)?

4. Consider the following data regarding the average spending on healthcare per person for various countries. **Source**: www.creditloan.com

Table for Exercise 4 – Healthcare Costs Around the World per Capita, 2009	
Country	Average Cost ($)
Australia	2886
Canada	2998
Denmark	2743
Finland	2104
France	3048
Germany	2983
Iceland	3159
Ireland	2455
Japan	2249
Sweden	2745
Switzerland	3847
United Kingdom	2317
United States	5711

3

a. Construct a bar chart for the average healthcare cost per person for the various countries.

b. What did you learn from the chart?

5. Consider the following data regarding professions with high projected growth rates for the years 2008 through 2018. **Source:** Bureau of Labor Statistics

Table for Exercise 5 – Occupation Growth Rates	
Occupation	Projected Increase 2008 – 2018
Biomedical engineers	72%
Network systems and data communications analysts	53%
Home health aides	50%
Personal and home care aides	46%
Financial examiners	41%
Medical scientists, except epidemiologists	40%
Physician assistants	39%
Skin care specialists	38%

a. Construct a bar chart for the projected growth rates of the various occupations.

b. What did you learn from the chart?

6. Consider the following data regarding the methods which consumers use to pay for items purchased a particular store.

Table for Exercise 6 – Payment Methods	
Method of Payment	Relative Frequency
Cash	81.1%
Checks	7.6%
General – Purpose Credit Cards	5.5%
Proprietary Credit Cards	5.3%
Debit Cards	0.5%

a. Construct a bar chart for the relative frequencies of the various methods of payment.

b. Construct a pie chart for the relative frequencies of the various methods of payment.

c. Comment on any information about the relative frequencies of the various methods which you were able to ascertain by examining the charts.

Constructing Frequency Distributions for Quantitative Data

When data are qualitative (nominal or ordinal), selecting the categories for display is relatively easy. However, selecting categories for quantitative data is not particularly obvious, since using different schemes can dramatically affect the perception of the data. The fundamental decision in constructing the frequency distribution is selecting the number of classes.

Example 3.2

A data set containing the revenues (in millions) of the top 100 companies on the Fortune 500 is listed below. Of course, looking at the raw numbers is not very revealing. Given the number of observations, it is difficult to get a good idea of the measurements. Instead of trying to consume all 100 values, a frequency distribution is given in Table 3.10. Examining the frequency distribution, an analyst can look at a table divided into ten categories and ten frequencies, thus reducing its complexity.

Table 3.9 – Revenues of the Top 100 Companies on the Fortune 500 (Millions of Dollars)

116	408	31	26	25
29	77	99	118	35
72	66	45	36	71
37	32	49	53	100
25	105	45	31	30
36	25	38	44	96
45	115	27	50	27
41	43	87	80	99
140	107	61	65	31
47	28	108	45	44
25	164	62	157	41
26	70	1	35	109
112	26	63	35	58
103	32	285	30	31
69	30	33	27	65

3

36	30	32	35	31
37	32	30	52	123
29	32	25	27	25
45	60	28	68	26
25	150	40	53	34

Table 3.10 – Frequency Distribution	
Revenue (Millions of Dollars)	Number of Companies
0 to 41	50
41 to 82	29
82 to 123	15
123 to 164	4
164 to 205	0
205 to 246	0
246 to 287	1
287 to 328	0
328 to 369	0
369 to 410	1

With the frequency distribution, we are able to see the broader structure of the data. It is now easy to see that the overwhelming majority of revenues are between $1 million and $180 million. Further, revenues above $164 million are uncommon. These conclusions would be considerably more difficult to establish without the organization that the frequency distribution provides.

The purpose of the frequency distribution is to condense the set of data into a meaningful summary form. There are only two steps in the construction of a frequency distribution:

1. choosing the classifications, and

2. counting the number in each class.

Selecting the Number of Classes

Choosing the number of classes is arbitrary and should depend on the amount of data available. In general, the more observations one has in a data set, the more classes or intervals that can be used in the frequency table or histogram. Consequently, only very general guidelines exist. Generally, fewer than four classes would be too much compression of the data and greater than 20 classes provides too little summary information. To start, a good rule of thumb for the number of classes to create is to round $\sqrt{n}$ or $\sqrt[3]{2n}$ to the nearest whole number.

Determining Class Width

After deciding on the desired number of classes, the next step is to specify the width of each class. Using classes that are of equal widths makes the histogram easier to interpret. There is really no perfect formula for class width that will work for every data set. However, a good starting point for determining class width is:

$$\text{class width} = \frac{\text{largest value} - \text{smallest value}}{\text{number of classes}}.$$

Suppose we wanted to create a frequency distribution from the revenue data in Example 3.2. If there are to be 10 classes, determine a class width.

$$\text{class width} = \frac{\text{largest value} - \text{smallest value}}{\text{number of classes}} = \frac{408 - 1}{10} = \frac{407}{10} = 40.7$$

Class endpoints with fractional values will make the graph slightly harder to digest. If possible, try to keep the width to an integer value (i.e. round up). If the calculated class width is 40.7, you might try a class width of 41. An interval width of 41 is used throughout the revenue example.

Generally, class widths should be equal. We want the lower limit of the first interval to be 0 or a multiple of the class width. In the example, we have selected the starting point as 0 because our smallest value is 1, and obviously we want the first interval to contain the smallest observation. If 0 is selected as the beginning point for the first interval, then the first category will span the interval (0,41]. An observation is counted in an interval if it is greater than the lower limit and less than or equal to the upper limit. Adding the class width to the lower class limit creates the next interval. That is, we want the lower limit of each subsequent interval to be a multiple of the class width. If this pattern is followed, the result will be intervals that will not overlap and will capture all the data. The frequency distribution given in Table 3.10 is just one way of organizing the data. There are three other distributions that can be calculated from the frequency distribution: relative frequency, cumulative frequency, and cumulative relative frequency. Each gives a slightly different perspective on the data.

Relative Frequency Distribution

Relative frequency represents the proportion of the total observations in a given class. The **relative frequency distribution** enables the reader to view the number in each category in relation to the total number of observations. Relative frequency is a standardizing technique. Converting the frequency in each class to a proportion in each class enables us to compare data sets with different numbers of observations.

Relative Frequency

Formula

The **relative frequency** of any class is the number of observations in the class divided by the total number of observations.

$$\text{relative frequency} = \frac{\text{number in class}}{\text{total number of observations}}$$

Table 3.11 – Relative Frequency Distribution of Revenue Data

Revenue (Millions of Dollars)	Relative Frequency
0 to 41	$\frac{50}{100} = .50$
41 to 82	$\frac{29}{100} = .29$
82 to 123	$\frac{15}{100} = .15$
123 to 164	$\frac{4}{100} = .04$
164 to 205	$\frac{0}{100} = .00$
205 to 246	$\frac{0}{100} = .00$
246 to 287	$\frac{1}{100} = .01$
287 to 328	$\frac{0}{100} = .00$
328 to 369	$\frac{0}{100} = .00$
369 to 410	$\frac{1}{100} = .01$

Cumulative Frequency Distribution

The cumulative frequency distribution gives the reader an opportunity to look at any category and determine immediately the number of observations that are smaller than or belong to that category.

Definition

The **cumulative frequency** is the sum of the frequency of a particular class and all preceding classes.

Cumulative Frequency

Table 3.12 – Revenue Data Cumulative Frequency Distribution		
Revenue (Millions of Dollars)	Frequency	Cumulative Frequency
0 to 41	50	50
41 to 82	29	79
82 to 123	15	94
123 to 164	4	98
164 to 205	0	98
205 to 246	0	98
246 to 287	1	99
287 to 328	0	99
328 to 369	0	99
369 to 410	1	100

In this example, the reader can easily see in Table 3.12 that virtually all the revenues are less than or equal to $164 million.

Cumulative Relative Frequency

To obtain the cumulative relative frequency, add the relative frequencies of all preceding classes to the relative frequency of the current class.

Definition

The **cumulative relative frequency** is the proportion of observations in a particular class and all preceding classes.

Cumulative Relative Frequency

3

Table 3.13 – Revenue Data Cumulative Relative Frequency Distribution			
Revenue (Millions of Dollars)	Frequency	Relative Frequency	Cumulative Relative Frequency
0 to 41	50	.50	.50
41 to 82	29	.29	.79
82 to 123	15	.15	.94
123 to 164	4	.04	.98
164 to 205	0	.00	.98
205 to 246	0	.00	.98
246 to 287	1	.01	.99
287 to 328	0	.00	.99
328 to 369	0	.00	.99
369 to 410	1	.01	1.00

From the cumulative relative frequency in Table 3.13 it is easy to see that 98% of the revenues are less than or equal to $164 million.

3.4 Exercises

Basic Concepts

1. What is the fundamental decision in constructing frequency distributions for quantitative data?

2. Describe the general guidelines for selecting the number of classes for a quantitative frequency distribution.

3. What is a good starting point for determining the class width?

4. What is a relative frequency distribution? How do you calculate relative frequencies from raw frequencies?

5. What is a cumulative frequency distribution?

6. What is a cumulative relative frequency distribution?

Exercises

1. A business magazine was conducting a study into the amount of travel required for mid-level managers across the U.S. Seventy-five managers were surveyed for the number of days they spent traveling each year.

Table for Exercise 1 – Mid-Level Manager Travel

Days Traveling	Frequency
0 – 6	15
7 – 13	21
14 – 20	27
21 – 27	9
28 – 34	2
35 and above	1

    a. Construct a relative frequency distribution.

    b. Construct a cumulative frequency distribution.

2. The closing prices (in pence) for selected stocks trading on the London Stock Exchange were:

Table for Exercise 2 – Closing Prices

Stock	Closing Price (Pence)
Allied Lyons	439
Babcock	208
Barclays Bank	543
Bass Ltd	992
British GE	238
Cadbury Sch	257
Guinness	379
Hanson Trust	169
Lucas Indus	655
Reed Int'l	467
STC	318
Tate & Lyle	833
Thorm EMI	741
Utd. Biscuit	326

Construct a frequency distribution for the stock prices.

3

3. Every year the average temperatures of 100 selected U.S. cities are published by the National Oceanic and Atmospheric Administration. The average temperature (°F) for the month of October for 15 randomly selected cities from the list of 100 are listed below:

68.5	50.9	67.5	57.5	56.0
47.1	50.1	65.8	51.5	49.5
75.2	56.0	62.3	53.0	46.1

   a. Construct a frequency distribution for the average temperatures for the month of October.

   b. Construct a relative frequency distribution for the average temperatures for the month of October.

   c. Construct a cumulative frequency distribution for the average temperatures for the month of October.

4. Consider the assets (in billions of dollars) of the 10 largest life insurance companies listed below:

$148.4	$110.8	$55.6	$52.4	$50.4
$42.7	$41.7	$36.2	$35.7	$35.7

   a. Construct a frequency distribution for the assets (in billions of dollars) of the 10 largest life insurance companies.

   b. Construct a relative frequency distribution for the assets (in billions of dollars) of the 10 largest life insurance companies.

   c. Construct a cumulative frequency distribution for the assets (in billions of dollars) of the 10 largest life insurance companies.

3.5 Histograms

A histogram is a common graphical method that reveals the **distribution of the data**.

Definition

> A **histogram** is a bar graph of a frequency or relative frequency distribution in which the height of each bar corresponds to the frequency or relative frequency of each class.

Histogram

Each of the classes in the frequency distribution is represented by a vertical bar whose height is proportional to the frequency of the interval. The horizontal boundaries of each vertical bar correspond to the class endpoints. Once the frequency distribution has been calculated, all the information necessary for plotting a histogram is available. In Figure 3.13, the histogram is created from the frequency distribution of the revenue data.

Histogram of Revenue Data

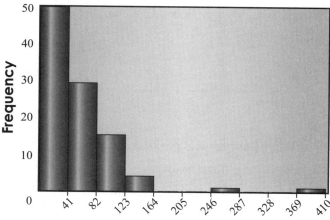

Revenue (Millions of Dollars)

Figure 3.13

Histograms are one of the more frequently used statistical tools. A histogram is not only easy to interpret; it also reveals a great deal about the structure of the data. You can quickly see that most of the revenues are in the first and second categories (0 to 41 and 41 to 82). The center of the data appears to be near 41 and the data appears to be skewed to the right. You will see many histograms throughout this text. Figure 3.14 represents a 3-D histogram of the revenue data.

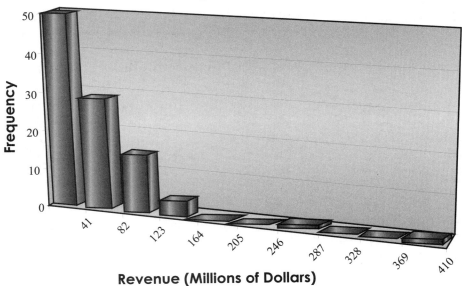

Figure 3.14

When we look at a histogram, what features are important?

1. Is the distribution symmetric or skewed (one tail is longer than the other)?

2. Is it bell shaped?

3. Does the distribution have several peaks or modes?

4. Where is the center of the distribution?

5. Are there outliers (data values that are very different from the others)?

3.5 Exercises

Basic Concepts

1. What is the main characteristic of data that a histogram reveals?

2. Describe the type of data that could be usefully described with a histogram.

3. True or false: A frequency distribution contains all of the information needed to construct a histogram.

4. List the important features to look for when studying a histogram.

Exercises

1. The closing prices (in dollars) for selected stocks trading on the New York Stock Exchange were:

Table for Exercise 1 – Closing Prices	
Stock	Closing Price ($)
Citigroup (C)	4.50
Pfizer (PFE)	20.42
Herbalife (HLF)	102.48
JP Morgan Chase (JPM)	45.86
Intel (INTC)	23.27
WalMart (WMT)	55.50
Microsoft (MSFT)	25.82
PepsiCo (PEP)	69.58
General Motors (GM)	33.00
Verizon Communications (VZ)	37.77
Southwest Airlines (LUV)	11.54
Sprint Nextel (S)	5.12
Yahoo! Inc (YHOO)	17.92
International Business Machines (IBM)	172.87

a. Construct a frequency distribution for the stock prices.

b. Construct a histogram for the stock prices.

2. A sample of 80 laborers is selected from a large city and their annual salaries are determined. The histogram below summarizes the data.

Histogram of Annual Salaries

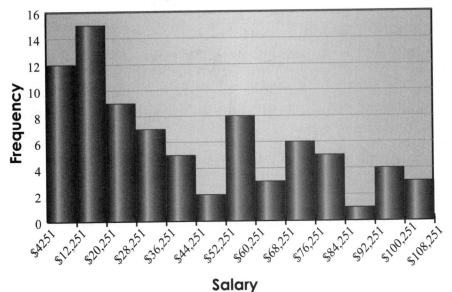

a. What is the level of measurement of the variable?

b. How many of the laborers earn at least $36,251?

c. What percent of the laborers earn at most $28,251?

d. What percent of the laborers earn at least $84,251?

3. A nutritionist is interested in knowing the percent of calories from fat which Americans consume on a daily basis. To study this, the nutritionist randomly selects 25 Americans and evaluates the percent of calories from fat consumed in a typical day. The results of the study are as follows:

34%	18%	33%	25%	30%
42%	40%	33%	39%	40%
45%	35%	45%	25%	27%
23%	32%	33%	47%	23%
27%	32%	30%	28%	36%

a. Construct a frequency distribution for the percent of calories from fat.

b. Construct a relative frequency distribution for the percent of calories from fat.

c. Construct a histogram of the relative frequency distribution.

d. Comment on any information about the percent of calories from fat consumed by the participants in the study which you were able to ascertain by examining the distributions and the histogram.

4. Consider the assets (in billions of dollars) of the 10 largest commercial banks listed below:

$216.9	$138.9	$115.5	$110.3	$103.5
$98.2	$76.4	$64.0	$53.5	$49.0

a. Construct a frequency distribution for the assets (in billions of dollars) of the 10 largest commercial banks.

b. Construct a relative frequency distribution for the assets (in billions of dollars) of the 10 largest commercial banks.

c. Construct a histogram of the relative frequency distribution.

d. Comment on any information about the assets (in billions of dollars) of the 10 largest commercial banks which you were able to ascertain by examining the distributions and the histogram.

3.6 The Stem-and-Leaf Display

The **stem-and-leaf display** is a hybrid graphical method. The display is similar to a histogram, but the data remains visible to the user. Like all graphical displays, the stem-and-leaf display is useful for both ordering and detecting patterns in the data. It is one of the few graphical methods in which the raw data is not lost in the construction of the graph. As the name implies, there is a "stem" to which "leaves" will be attached in some pattern.

Consider the following data: 97, 99, 108, 110, and 111. If we are interested in the variation of the last digit, the stem and leaves are as shown in Table 3.14 and displayed in Figure 3.15. The leaves in this case are the *ones* digit and the stem is the *tens* digit. All of the data values that have common stems are grouped together, and their leaves branch out from the common stem.

Table 3.14 – Data, Stems, and Leaves		
Data	**Stem**	**Leaf**
97	09	7
99	09	9
108	10	8
110	11	0
111	11	1

Stem-and-Leaf Display

Stem	Leaves
09	7 9
10	8
11	0 1

Figure 3.15

If we are interested in the variation of the last two digits, the stem and leaves are shown in Table 3.15 and displayed in Figure 3.16. The leaves in this case are the *last two* digits and the stem is the *hundreds* digit. Again all of the data values that have common stems are grouped together, and their leaves branch out from the common stem.

Table 3.15 – Data, Stems, and Leaves

Data	Stem	Leaf
97	0	97
99	0	99
108	1	08
110	1	10
111	1	11

Stem-and-Leaf Display

Stem	Leaves
0	97 99
1	08 10 11

Figure 3.16

Let's look at the historical closing stock price of Microsoft Corporation from December 1990 through December 2006 (rounded to the nearest dollar). The histogram of the data is given in Figure 3.17 along with the stem-and-leaf display (Figure 3.18). Here the *tens* digit is the stem and the *ones* digit is the leaf.

MSFT Closing Prices December 1990-December 2006

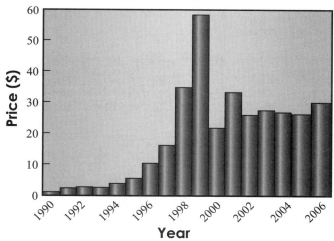

Figure 3.17

Stem-and-Leaf Display (MSFT)

```
0 | 1 2 3 3 4 5
1 | 0 6
2 | 2 6 6 7 7
3 | 5 3 0
4 |
5 | 8
```

Figure 3.18

The stem-and-leaf display is similar to a histogram with one important difference: The data remains visible. Another advantage of the stem-and-leaf display is that it makes it easy to sort a fairly small set of data. Deciding which part to make the stem and which part to make the leaf depends on the focus of the analysis. Sometimes the choice of stem and leaf is easy. With the stock price data, using a stem of the *tens* unit will break the data into five classes.

Example 3.3

The closing stock prices for Apple Computer from December 1990 through December 2006 are given in Table 3.16. Construct a stem-and-leaf display to compare the closing stock price of Apple Computer (rounded to the nearest dollar) to the closing price of Microsoft Corporation over the 16 year period (split adjusted).

Table 3.16 – Closing Price of AAPL December 1990 through December 2006	
Period	**Closing Price (Dollars)**
December 1990	11
December 1991	14
December 1992	15
December 1993	7
December 1994	10
December 1995	8
December 1996	5
December 1997	3
December 1998	10
December 1999	26
December 2000	7
December 2001	11

December 2002	7
December 2003	11
December 2004	32
December 2005	72
December 2006	85

Solution

In order to compare the closing price of Apple to the closing price of Microsoft, we need to construct a stem-and-leaf display using the tens digit as the stem and the ones digit as the leaf.

Stem-and-Leaf Display (AAPL)

```
0   357778
1   0011145
2   6
3   2
4
5
6
7   2
8   5
```

From the stem-and-leaf display we can see that the closing prices for APPL appear to be more clustered than those of MSFT. For Apple Computer, there are six prices corresponding to the 0 stem and seven prices corresponding to the 1 stem. All remaining stems have either zero or one corresponding leaf. Microsoft, however, has only two leaves corresponding to the 1 stem, five leaves corresponding to the 2 stem, and three leaves corresponding to the 3 stem. This would lead us to believe that on average closing prices of Microsoft were greater than the closing prices of Apple Computer over this 16 year period.

3.6 Exercises

Basic Concepts

1. Explain why the stem-and-leaf display is sometimes called a "hybrid graphical method".

2. Identify the advantages of a stem-and-leaf display.

3. Consider the following data value: 39. What would be the stem and leaf for this value if we identified the stem as the tens digit? What would be the steam and leaf if we identified the stem as the hundreds digit?

4. When constructing a stem-and-leaf display, how do you determine which part to make the stem and which part to make the leaf?

Exercises

1. Fifty hospitals in a western state were polled as to their basic daily charges for a semi-private room. The results are listed below, rounded to the nearest dollar.

125	135	148	156	248	215	156	148	135	149
178	156	135	125	214	256	258	265	156	148
123	147	189	199	189	248	215	259	158	235
268	269	158	198	147	258	269	239	288	199
179	179	189	169	258	178	257	249	259	259

a. What level of measurement does the data possess?

b. Construct a stem-and-leaf display for the data.

c. Comment on the shape of the distribution.

2. Consider the top 10 states in toxic emissions (in thousands of tons).
Source: Toxics in the Community, U.S. Environmental Protection Agency

| 206 | 147 | 441 | 128 | 127 | 133 | 422 | 152 | 114 | 134 |

a. Construct a stem-and-leaf display for the data.

b. Comment on any information about the toxic emissions (in thousands of tons) of the top 10 states which you were able to ascertain by examining the stem-and-leaf display.

3. Consider the following highway miles per gallon for 19 selected models of mini-compact, sub-compact, and compact cars.

| 26 | 46 | 36 | 31 | 28 | 28 | 27 | 38 | 42 | 36 |
| 37 | 33 | 23 | 29 | 37 | 34 | 29 | 40 | 28 | |

a. Construct a stem-and-leaf display for the data.

b. Comment on any information about the highway mpg of the selected models which you were able to ascertain by examining the stem-and-leaf display.

4. An instructor is interested in comparing exam scores for fraternity and non-fraternity males in her class. Meaningful comparisons between two sets of data can be made using a side-by-side stem-and-leaf display. To illustrate this, note the following display summarizing the scores:

Leaves (Non-Fraternity)	Stem	Leaves (Fraternity)
	0	9
2	1	4 0 8
	2	5 7 9 4 5 5 1
3 9	3	2 6 6 9 7 7 3 2 1 6 0
	4	2 7 5
5 6 4 8 9 9 0 2	5	4 7 6 7
4 4 7 8 1 0 3 2 2 6 8 9	6	6 8 9 9 5
5 4 7 8 4 3 8 8 9 1	7	3 4 2 7 8 6 7 4 3
2 9 7 4	8	4 5 3 8 9 9 6 4 2 1 1 4 5
4 2	9	4 3 5 1 6 7 7 0 3

Table for Exercise 4 – Student Grades

a. What level of measurement does the data possess?

b. Based upon the stem-and-leaf display, compare the two groups. Think of the several ways in which this can be done.

c. Suppose that 60% is considered a passing score on the exam. What percent of the fraternity students passed the exam? Non-fraternity students?

d. If someone scores 90 or higher on the exam, they will be exempt from taking the next exam. What percent of the fraternity students will be exempt from taking the next exam? Non-fraternity students?

3.7 The Ordered Array

An **ordered array** is a listing of all the data in either increasing or decreasing magnitude. Data listed in increasing order are said to be listed in rank order. If listed in decreasing order, they are listed in reverse rank order. Listing the data in an ordered way can be very helpful. It allows you to scan the data quickly for the largest and smallest values, for large gaps in the data, and for concentrations or clusters of values.

Example 3.4

The personnel records for a clothing department store located in the local mall are examined, and the current ages for all employees are noted. There are 25 employees, and their ages are listed below. It is desired that their ages be placed in rank order.

Ages (raw)												
32	21	24	19	61	18	18	16	16	35	39	17	22
21	60	18	53	18	57	63	28	20	29	35	45	

Solution

Ages (ordered)												
16	16	17	18	18	18	18	19	20	21	21	22	24
28	29	32	35	35	39	45	53	57	60	61	63	

It is always a good idea to get a look at the ordered array of the data early in your analysis. Examining the ranked data produces a good intuitive sense for the data. Looking at the ordered array, it is evident that over half of the employees are younger than 25 and only three employees are within 5 years of retirement. Ordered arrays are easy to create. Virtually all statistics, spreadsheet and database programs enable the user to quickly sort the data in ascending or descending order. If a spreadsheet or database program is not available, a stem-and-leaf display can be helpful in sorting the data.

3.7 Exercises

Basic Concepts

1. What is an ordered array?

2. What are some advantages of the ordered array?

Exercises

1. Microsoft's consumer PC sales growth for the last 16 quarters is listed below. Examine the data (sales growth, in percentages) below and answer the following questions. **Source:** Citi Investment Research and Analysis IDC, Company Reports, May 2011

Table for Exercise 1 – PC Sales Growth			
Quarter	Sales Growth (%)	Quarter	Sales Growth (%)
1	20	9	20
2	24	10	19
3	22	11	33
4	19	12	37
5	23	13	24
6	27	14	10
7	16	15	0
8	10	16	−4

   a. Construct an ordered array of the data.

   b. What conclusions can you make based on the ordered array?

2. *Fortune* magazine publishes a list of the top 100 best companies to work for. For the top 10 companies on this list, the average annual employee salaries are given below (in thousands of dollars).

121	122	136	74	118	101	114	61	95	132

   a. Construct a stem-and-leaf display for the data.

   b. Comment on any information about the average annual salaries (in thousands of dollars) of the top 10 companies which you were able to ascertain by examining the stem-and-leaf display.

   c. Construct an ordered array of the average annual salaries.

   d. Does the ordered array provide any additional insight into the nature of the data?

3.8   Dot Plots

A **dot plot** is a graph where each data value is plotted as a point (or a dot) above a horizontal axis. If there are multiple entries of the same data value, they are plotted one above another.

Example 3.5

Construct dot plots of the closing stock price on December 1ˢᵗ for Microsoft Corporation and Apple Computer from data in the presented in Section 3.6.

Solution

We plot each data value on the horizontal axis. For values where there are multiple entries, such as $3, we stack the points on top of one another.

Microsoft Corporation

Apple Computer

As we can see, most prices for both companies are less than $30. For Microsoft Corporation, the values that occur most often are $3, $26, and $27. For Apple Computer, the values that occur most frequently are $7 and $11.

3.8   Exercises

Basic Concepts

1. What is a dot plot?

2. What are some advantages of using a dot plot?

3. How can the most frequently occurring value be identified by studying a dot plot?

Exercises

1. Construct a dot plot for the following set of data.

Table for Exercise 1				
23	19	15	20	17
16	18	14	23	22
19	23	19	16	25
17	20	21	23	24

2. Listed below is the number of passing attempts per game by super bowl champion Aaron Rodgers in the 2010 NFL season. Construct a dot plot for the data set. **Source**: ESPN

Table for Exercise 2 – Passing Attempts by Aaron Rodgers				
31	29	45	17	46
33	34	34	34	31
35	30	11	37	28

3. Below is a table of the average monthly energy consumption (in kilowatt hours) by households for nine South Atlantic states in 2007. Construct a dot plot for the data set. **Source:** U.S. Energy information Administration

Table for Exercise 3 – Monthly Energy Consumption (Kilowatt Hours)
773
960
1163
1171
1086
1143
1210
1207
1138

3.9   Plotting Time Series Data

A **time series plot** graphs data using time as the horizontal axis. A good example of time series data is the census measurements taken every decade since 1790. The population of the United States has been growing steadily since the first census (as shown in Table 3.17). Interestingly, the change in population between 2000 and 2010 was 27.3 million, which is greater than the entire population of the United States in 1850. In Figure 3.19, each of the observations in the graph is represented with a bar. However, there are other ways of representing the data values. In Figure 3.20, a line graph connects consecutive points in the time series with a line. Although the two graphs represent exactly the same data, they look different. Using the bars to represent the observations creates a more dramatic image.

Table 3.17 – U.S. Census Data	
Year	**Population (in Millions)**
1790	3.9
1800	5.3
1810	7.2
1820	9.6
1830	12.9
1840	17.1
1850	23.2
1860	31.4
1870	38.6
1880	50.2
1890	63.0
1900	76.2
1910	92.2
1920	106.0
1930	123.2
1940	132.2
1950	151.3
1960	179.3
1970	203.3
1980	226.5
1990	248.7
2000	281.4
2010	308.7

For a quick look at the current population of the U.S. and the world go to www.census.gov. **Source:** U.S. Census Bureau; 2010

Bar Graph – Population of the United States (in Millions)

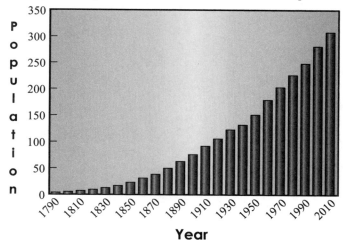

Figure 3.19

Line Graph – Population of the United States (in Millions)

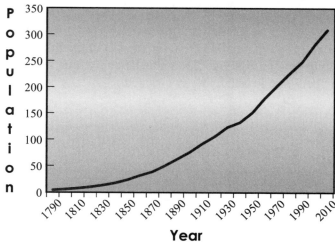

Figure 3.20

Another plot, called a 3-D line plot or a ribbon plot, is a three-dimensional version of a time series plot (see Figure 3.21). Although it is difficult to determine the population size in any one year, the three dimensional graph makes an interesting visual statement about population in the United States.

3

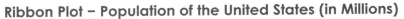

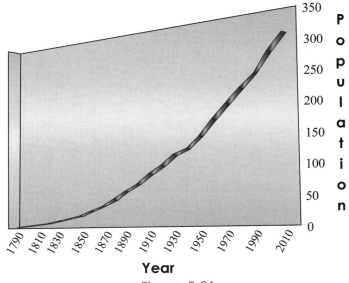

Ribbon Plot – Population of the United States (in Millions)

Year

Figure 3.21

Does it make sense to draw a histogram for a nonstationary time series? We could create a histogram of the population data we have been examining, but it would not reveal anything very interesting. For a nonstationary time series (a time series with a trend), a histogram is usually not warranted.

3.9   Exercises

Basic Concepts

1. Why is it important to plot time series data?

2. The time variable is always graphed on which axis?

3. Identify a variation on a time series plot that can make the data more visually interesting.

4. Are histograms appropriate for time series data? Why or why not?

Exercises

1. Below is a chart of the total (in billions of dollars) IRA and Keogh accounts in the U.S., charted from 1990 to June, 2011. Source: www.economagic.com

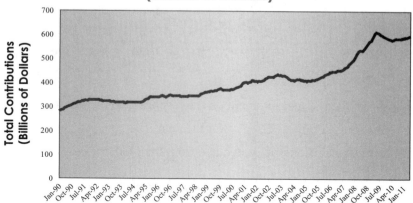

Total Contributions to IRA and Keogh Accounts
(Billions of Dollars)

a. What conclusions can you make regarding the total contributed to the accounts?

b. Are the data time series data?

c. If the data are time series data, is the series stationary or nonstationary?

2. The following chart contains LIBOR (which stands for London Interbank Offered Rate) data for January, 2011 through June, 2011. Source: www.economagic.com

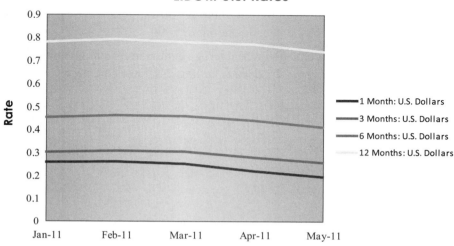

LIBOR: U.S. Rates

a. Examine the chart and discuss the data. What conclusions can you make?

b. If the data are time series data, is it a stationary or nonstationary time series? Explain your reasoning.

3. The Gallup Poll frequently obtains responses to the question, *At the present time, do you think religion as a whole is increasing its influence on American life or losing its influence?* The percent of the respondents who answered "increasing" is given below for various polls.

Table for Exercise 3 – Survey Responses										
Date	2001	1995	1992	1991	1990	1988	1986	1984	1982	1980
Percent	71	38	27	27	33	36	48	42	41	35
Date	1978	1977	1975	1974	1970	1969	1968	1965	1962	1957
Percent	37	37	39	31	14	14	19	33	45	69

 a. What level of measurement do the responses to the question possess?

 b. Construct a time series plot for the data.

 c. What conclusions can you make from the plot?

4. The table below gives the number of immigrants (in thousands) and the average annual immigration rate per 1000 U.S. population for the decade ending in the year given.

Table for Exercise 4 – Annual Immigration										
Year	1900	1910	1920	1930	1940	1950	1960	1970	1980	1990	2000
Number	3688	8795	5736	4107	528	1035	2515	3322	4493	7338	9095
Rate	5.3	10.4	5.7	3.5	0.4	0.7	1.5	1.7	2.1	2.9	3.2

 a. What levels of measurement do the three variables in this exercise possess?

 b. Construct a time series plot of the number of immigrants per decade.

 c. Find the percent change in the number of immigrants from the decade ending in 1900 to the decade ending in 1990.

 d. Find the percent change in the average annual immigration rate per 1000 U.S. population from the decade ending in 1900 to the decade ending in 1990.

3.10 A Look at Unemployment Rate

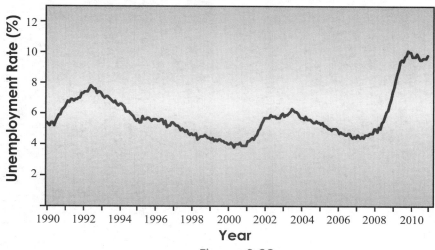

Line Graph of Unemployment Rate 1990-2010

Figure 3.22

Source: Federal Reserve Bank of St. Louis; 2010

Figure 3.22 contains a time series plot of the civilian unemployment rate from January, 1990 through November, 2010. Civilian unemployment rate is defined as the number of unemployed people divided by the total size of the labor force. People who are jobless, looking for jobs, and available for work are considered unemployed. The labor force is made up of people that are either employed or unemployed. As can be seen in the figure, over the last 20 years, there was quite a bit of fluctuation in the unemployment rate. There was a steady decline in the unemployment rate from 1991-2001. In 2001, the unemployment rate began to rise. At this same time, the U.S. economy was entering into a recession along with the events of September 11, 2001. Post 9/11, the unemployment rate rose to 6.3% in June of 2003 and then declined to 4.4% in December of 2006. The unemployment rate was fairly stable in 2007 but then began to rise steadily each month to a high of 10.1% in October 2009. It is also interesting to note that during the steady increase in unemployment rate from 2008 through 2009, the U.S. economy was also in a recession. The figure only shows overall unemployment rates. If one wanted to further explore the unemployment rates, data could be collected (and displayed) by worker groups, gender, and race, for example.

Graphs and Art

Graphs don't always have to be just bars and lines. The following graphs present data in an artistic as well as functional manner. We show these graphs to give some alternative ideas on how data can be presented.

Number of Home Runs per Game Throughout the Decades

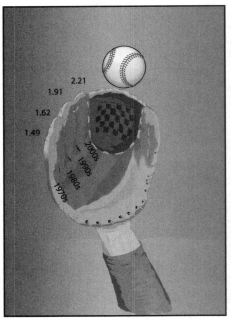

Source: www.mlb.com; 2003

Most Expensive Cities for Business Travel per Day

New York $622
Washington $564
Paris $526
Oslo $508
Tokyo $492
Amsterdam $488

Source: Business Travel News Corporate Travel Index; 2010

Percentage Composition of Receipts by Source

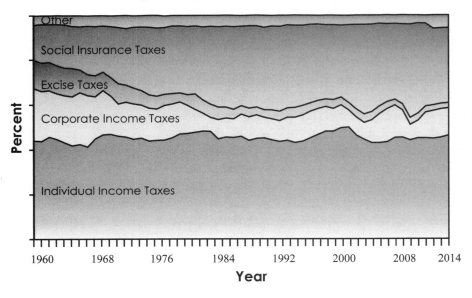

Source: U.S. Government Printing Office; 2010

Discovering Technology

USING EXCEL

Histogram

A histogram is a graphical image of a frequency distribution.

Use the data in Example 3.2 on company revenues for this exercise.

1. Enter the data from the example into Column A of a new worksheet.

2. In Column B, you will enter the upper class limits (Excel calls these "Bins"). For the frequency distribution in Table 3.10, these are 41, 82, 123, 164, 205, 246, 287, 328, 369, and 410. However, you can experiment with different class widths if you wish.

3. To create a histogram, you will need the Data Analysis ToolPak add-in. If the add-in is installed, it will be found under the "Data" tab, and will be a button labeled "Data Analysis." If the add-in is already installed, proceed to step 8. If it is not installed, follow steps 4 through 7.

4. Click on the Microsoft button in the top left hand corner of Excel. At the bottom of the menu, select **Excel Options**.

5. In the Excel Options window, select **Add-ins** from the menu on the left hand side. In the Add-ins window, click **Go**.

6. In the Add-ins dialog box, place a check mark next to "Analysis ToolPak" and click **OK**.

7. A box may appear that says the feature is not currently installed would you like to install it now? Click **Yes**. This will install the add-in.

8. Under the "Data" tab, click on **Data Analysis**, and choose **Histogram**.

9. The Histogram dialog box will appear. Set the "Input Range" to **A1:A100**. You can click on the box in the address window to drag a selection rather than typing in cell addresses if you like.

10. Set the "Bin Range" to **B1:B10**.

11. Click on the Output Options radio button next to New Worksheet Ply.

12. Check the box next to Chart Output to get a visual representation of the histogram.

13. Click **OK**.

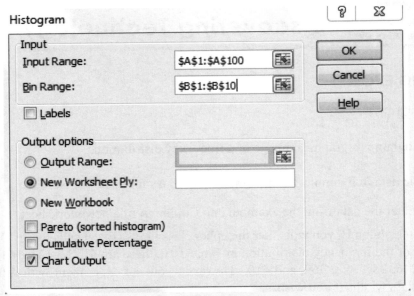

Figure 3.23

You should now have a new worksheet appear that looks like this.

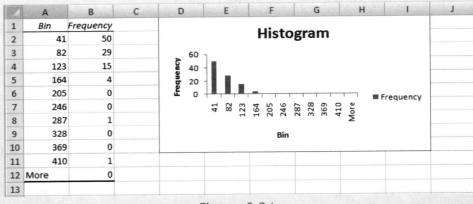

Figure 3.24

You can adjust your histogram by changing the number of bins and the values associated with them.

Line Graph

Use the data in Table 3.17 for this exercise.

1. Enter the data from Table 3.17 into columns A and B in Microsoft Excel. Enter the years in Column A and the population in Column B.

2. Highlight all of the data values, and under the "Insert" tab, select **Line**.

3. You can choose to make a 2-D or 3-D line graph here. Select the line graph in the top left hand corner of the graphs given.

4. A line graph is now displayed. Under the "Design" tab, choose **Select Data**.

5. On the right hand side under "Horizontal (Category) Axis Labels" click **Edit**.

6. This prompts you to enter an axis label range. Select the data values in column A. Click **OK**. This makes time the horizontal axis.

7. In the left box under "Legend Entries (Series)" highlight **Series1** and click **Remove**.

8. Click **OK**.

You should now have a line graph that appears something like this.

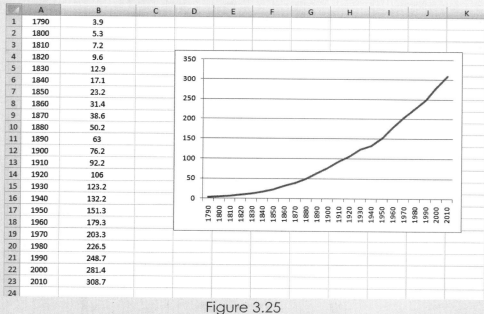

Figure 3.25

You can adjust the look of the graph using the Chart Tools.

USING MINITAB

Stem-and-Leaf Display

Use the information from Example 3.3 for this exercise.

1. Enter the data into Column C1.

2. Choose **Graph**, and select **Stem-and-Leaf**.

3. Select **C1** for the "Graph Variables". Enter **10** for the "Increment" and select **OK**. This will create the Stem-and-Leaf display.

Histogram

Use the information from Example 3.2 for this exercise.

1. Enter the data into Column C1.

2. Choose **Graph**, and select **Histogram**.

3. Select the **Simple Histogram**, and click **OK**.

4. Select **C1** as the "Graph Variables". Click **OK**. A histogram of the data will be displayed.

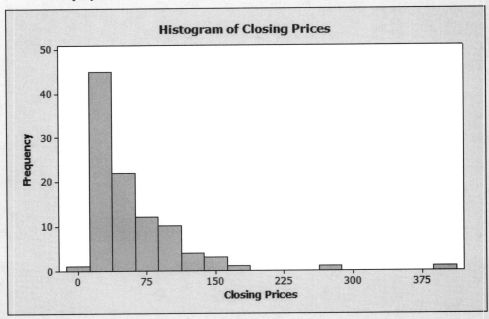

Figure 3.26

Chapter 3 Review

Key Terms and Ideas

- Frequency Distribution
- Bar Chart
- 3-D Bar Chart
- Stacked Bar Chart
- Pie Chart
- Relative Frequency
- Cumulative Frequency
- Cumulative Relative Frequency
- Histogram
- Stem-and-Leaf Display
- Ordered Array
- Dot Plot
- Time Series Plot
- Ribbon Plot

Key Formulas

Concept	Formula	Section
Number of Classes	Round $\sqrt{n}$ or $\sqrt{2n}$ to the nearest whole number.	3.4
Class Width	$\dfrac{\text{largest value} - \text{smallest value}}{\text{number of classes}}$	3.4
Relative Frequency	$\dfrac{\text{number in class}}{\text{total number of observations}}$	3.4

3

AE | Additional Exercises

1. Median family income has grown substantially in recent years. The table below contains median household incomes in the United States for the years 1990 through 2009. **Source**: U.S. Census Bureau

Table for Exercise 1 – Median Family Income

Year	Income ($)	Percent Change	Year	Income ($)	Percent Change
1990	29,943	–	2000	41,990	3.2
1991	30,126	0.6	2001	42,228	0.6
1992	30,636	1.7	2002	42,409	0.4
1993	31,241	2.0	2003	43,318	2.1
1994	32,264	3.3	2004	44,334	2.3
1995	34,076	5.6	2005	46,326	4.5
1996	35,492	4.2	2006	48,201	4.0
1997	37,005	4.3	2007	50,233	4.2
1998	38,885	5.1	2008	50,303	0.1
1999	40,696	4.7	2009	49,777	– 1.0

a. What graphical methods would be useful in displaying the data?

b. Graph the data.

c. Write a short paragraph describing the data.

2. The following data represent mean earnings by age group and educational attainment. **Source**: U.S. Census Bureau; 2005

Table for Exercise 2 – Income, Age, and Educational Attainment – 2005

Educational Attainment	Under $5000	$5000 – $9999	$10,000 – 14,999	$15,000 – 24,999	$25,000 – 34,999	$35,000 – 49,999	$50,000 – 74,999	$75,000 & over	Median Income
Elementary	16.3%	26.7%	17.2%	19.7%	9.9%	6.4%	2.9%	0.8%	$11,730
< 8 years	18.4	27.9	17.3	18.1	8.9	5.9	2.7	0.7	10,884
8 years	13.7	25.2	17.1	21.7	11.0	7.0	3.1	1.0	12,999
High School	6.8	12.4	12.0	21.8	17.8	17.0	9.5	2.8	23,382
1 – 3 years	10.9	19.4	14.9	22.2	14.2	11.2	5.6	1.6	16,727
4 years	5.4	10.0	11.0	21.6	19.0	18.9	10.8	3.2	25,910
College	2.6	4.3	5.8	15.1	16.3	22.7	20.1	13.2	38,337
1 – 3 years	3.6	6.6	8.1	18.7	18.1	22.6	16.1	6.1	31,865
4 years +	1.8	2.5	4.1	124	14.9	22.8	23.0	18.5	43,952

a. What graphical methods would be useful in displaying the data?

b. Use a graphics program to display the data.

c. Discuss any conclusions you made from your graph(s).

3. Where do business school students most want to work? A CNNMoney list ranks companies that MBA students want to work for most after getting their degree. It can be seen that men and women have different desires when it comes to employment after business school. The table below shows seven of the top companies students want to work for and the percentage of students that ranked the particular company in their top 5. **Source**: CNNMoney.com

Table for Exercise 3 – Most Desired Companies		
Company	Percent of Men	Percent of Women
Google	22.36	21.72
Goldman Sachs	17.76	5.81
Johnson & Johnson	5.68	11.41
Bain & Company	12.89	7.88
Apple Computer	12.80	11.01
Nike	8.06	9.04
J.P. Morgan	12.08	4.44

a. What graphical method would be useful in summarizing where business school students most want to work?

b. What graphical method would be useful in comparing the most desirable companies for men and women?

c. Graph the data.

d. Write a short paragraph describing the data.

4. Many people have more than one job. The data below give the percentage of people in the U.S. holding more than one job. **Source**: Bureau of Labor Statistics Graph the data using a method that would contrast the difference between men and women in this situation.

Table for Exercise 4 – Percentage Holding More Than One Job		
Year	Men	Women
1970	7.0%	2.2%
1979	5.9%	3.5%
1989	6.4%	5.9%
1999	5.7%	5.6%
2003	5.2%	5.4%

5. *Billboard* magazine, in cooperation with Arbitron, produces a national radio format rating. The data below was gathered from radio listeners.

Table for Exercise 5 – Radio Formats						
	Persons 12+ Mon – Fri 6 – 10am	Persons 12+ Mon – Fri 10am – 3pm	Persons 12+ Mon – Fri 3 – 7pm	Persons 12+ Mon – Fri 7pm – 12am	Persons 12+ Mon – Sun 12am – 6am	Persons 12+ Mon – Sun 6am – 12am
Adult Contemporary	17.2%	19.7%	17.7%	15.0%	16.2%	21.0%
News/Talk	17.9	13.1	12.5	14.3	5.3	16.6
Country	13.0	13.2	13.2	10.3	11.7	15.3
Album Rock	10.0	10.4	10.9	9.8	18.7	10.2
Top 40	8.9	9.7	10.9	12.9	14.3	4.7
Urban	7.5	7.6	8.9	14.1	11.8	7.1
Oldies	6.0	6.8	6.9	5.5	4.3	10.2
Classic Rock	4.7	3.6	3.7	2.9	6.1	2.9
Spanish	4.5	4.2	3.7	–	4.9	4.2
Adult Standards	3.4	4.2	3.7	2.7	0.3	3.8
Religious	2.1	1.7	1.8	1.8	1.3	2.5
Classical	1.4	1.7	1.7	1.9	0.5	2.3
Easy Listening	0.9	1.1	0.9	0.8	0.2	1.2
Modern Rock	1.0	1.1	1.3	1.6	2.4	0.4
Adult Alternative	1.5	1.9	2.1	2.2	1.8	2.6

a. What kinds of graphs would be appropriate for displaying the data?

b. Graph a column of the data.

c. Create a graph that would be useful in visually comparing two columns of the data.

6. The Caribbean has been a favorite vacation spot for affluent North Americans and Europeans, especially during the winter months. The table below lists the number of tourists during the first six months of the year for a number of countries.

Table for Exercise 6 – Number of Tourists			
	USA	Canada	Europe
Antigua & Barbuda	53,811	10,709	18,591
Aruba	94,028	1320	4681
Barbados	105,236	51,830	34,562
Bermuda	250,390	21,241	11,715
Bonaire	12,210	352	2266
Cayman Islands	81,180	3791	3025
Curacao	15,186	572	6543
Guadeloupe	15,596	10,654	25,409
Trinidad & Tobago	29,110	12,470	11,820

a. Develop graphs to display where each of the countries' tourists do their Caribbean travel.

b. Develop graphs to compare the tourists' destinations of each country.

7. Below is a list of the top 20 global corporations, ranked by amount spent on research and development in 2009. **Source:** Booz & Company

Rank	Company	R&D Spending (Millions of $)	Spending as a % of Sales	Headquarters Location	Industry
1	Roche Holding	9120	20.1	Europe	Healthcare
2	Microsoft	9010	15.4	N. America	Software and Internet
3	Nokia	8240	14.4	Europe	Computing and Electronics
4	Toyota	7822	3.8	Japan	Auto
5	Pfizer	7739	15.5	N. America	Healthcare
6	Novartis	7469	16.9	Europe	Healthcare
7	Johnson & Johnson	6986	11.3	N. America	Healthcare
8	Sanofi-Aventis	6391	15.6	Europe	Healthcare
9	GlaxoSmithKline	6187	13.9	Europe	Healthcare
10	Samsung	6002	5.5	S. Korea	Computing and Electronics
11	General Motors	6000	5.7	N. America	Auto
12	IBM	5820	6.1	N. America	Computing and Electronics
13	Intel	5653	16.1	N. America	Computing and Electronics
14	Merck	5613	20.5	N. America	Healthcare
15	Volkswagen	5359	3.7	Europe	Auto
16	Siemens	5285	5.1	Europe	Industrials
17	Cisco Systems	5208	14.4	N. America	Computing and Electronics
18	Panasonic	5143	6.4	Japan	Computing and Electronics
19	Honda	4996	5.4	Japan	Auto
20	Ford	4900	4.1	N. America	Auto

Table for Exercise 7 – Amount Spent on Research and Development (R&D) in 2009

a. For comparative purposes, which of the two columns reporting R&D spending is more useful, and why?

b. What types of graphs would be useful in presenting these data?

c. Develop a histogram for the percent of sales.

d. Use computer software to develop pie charts for the headquarters location and industry categories of the top 20 global R&D spenders.

8. In New York, a group of women challenged the state's ban on topless sunbathing. The legal issue was whether the ban was discriminatory. During the controversy, the Gallup poll conducted a survey asking the following question: *Do you think women should be permitted to sunbathe topless on public beaches, if they choose to, or do you think topless sunbathing on public beaches should be banned?*

Table for Exercise 8 – Response to Survey Question				
	Permitted	Banned	No Opinion	Number of Interviews
National	33%	63%	4%	1001
Sex				
Male	50	45	5	500
Female	18	79	3	501
Age				
18 – 29	47	51	2	219
30 – 49	39	58	3	411
50 – 64	18	76	6	206
65 +	18	77	5	357
Region				
East	39	59	2	247
Midwest	34	62	4	254
South	25	71	4	301
West	38	57	5	199
Community				
Urban	42	55	3	345
Suburban	35	62	3	351
Rural	23	72	5	298
Race				
White	33	64	3	871
Non-white	39	57	4	121
Education				
College Grads	46	48	6	288
Some College	35	62	3	233
No College	28	69	3	475
Sex/Education				
Male/College	56	40	4	238
Male/No College	45	49	6	238
Female/College	26	70	4	264
Female/No College	13	85	2	237

a. Suggest two different types of graphs that might be useful in graphing the data.

b. Create two different graphs using the data.

c. Write a short paragraph describing the data.

9. The nation's political identification (Republican, Democrat, or Independent) changes over time. The data in the following table represents Harris poll results on political identification from 1977 to 2008. **Source**: Harris Interactive

Year	Republican	Democrat	Independent	Year	Republican	Democrat	Independent
Table for Exercise 9 – Nation's Political Identification (Percent of the Population) 1977 – 2008							
2008	26	36	31	1992	30	36	29
2007	26	35	23	1991	32	37	26
2006	27	36	24	1990	33	38	25
2005	30	36	22	1989	33	40	23
2004	31	34	24	1988	31	39	25
2003	28	33	24	1987	29	38	28
2002	31	34	24	1986	30	39	25
2001	31	36	22	1985	30	39	26
2000	29	37	23	1984	27	40	24
1999	29	36	26	1983	26	41	27
1998	28	37	27	1982	26	40	28
1997	29	37	26	1981	28	39	28
1996	30	38	26	1980	24	41	29
1995	31	36	28	1979	22	41	31
1994	32	37	26	1978	22	43	30
1993	29	38	27	1977	21	48	25

a. What types of graphs would be useful in visualizing this data?

b. Construct two different types of graphs from the data.

c. Examine the data and write a short paragraph on your conclusions.

10. Monaco is noted for having one of the highest population densities in the world, approximately 16,923 persons per square kilometer. Usually, dense urban areas have relatively high crime rates. This is not the case in Monaco. The following table gives crime data per 100,000 population for the year 2000 in Monaco as well as other urban areas. **Source**: U.S. Department of Justice, CIA, BBC

Table for Exercise 10 – Crime Data per 100,000 Population					
	Monaco	London	Chicago	New York	San Francisco
Homicide	1.0	4.7	23.0	43.4	8.6
Forcible Rape	7.9	34.7	–	19.1	26.7
Robbery	–	625	635.6	352.5	409.9
Aggravated Assault	–	847.4	880.4	473.7	327.2
Burglary	–	938.9	895.4	394.6	764.8
Larceny/Theft	333.0	2675.3	3361.9	1674.2	803.0

a. What types of graphs would be useful in visualizing this data?

b. Construct two different types of graphs from the data.

c. Examine the data and write a short paragraph on your conclusions.

Numerical Descriptive Statistics

4

Discovering Technology

Finding the sample mean and standard deviation using a TI-84 Plus calculator

Calculating the correlation coefficient r using a TI-84 Plus calculator

Finding the sample mean and standard deviation using Microsoft Excel

Finding percentiles and quartiles using Microsoft Excel

Calculating the correlation coefficient r using Microsoft Excel

Finding the sample mean and standard deviation using Minitab

Calculating the correlation coefficient r using Minitab

Discovery Project

Describing Everyday Data

Introduction

In almost all data analysis, frequency distributions, bar charts, pie charts, and histograms (all of which were discussed in Chapter 3) can be informative visual tools for examining the big picture. But there is a lack of exactness in the language that we use to describe these graphs. Suppose we say that one data set is more compact than another. This only leads to the question, *How much more compact is it?* Graphical analysis is ill-equipped to answer that question precisely.

Doctor's Office Waiting Times

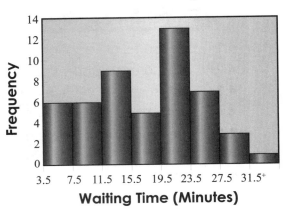

Figure 4.1

ER Waiting Times

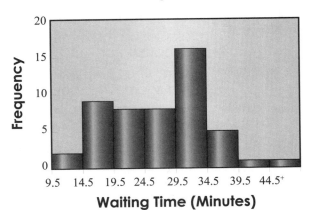

Figure 4.2

If we examine Figure 4.1 and Figure 4.2, we notice the two histograms are somewhat similar, but there is a clear difference in the underlying data. To precisely describe the differences, we need summary measures to characterize specific data attributes:

- Location: Where is the center of the data?

- Dispersion: Are the data widely scattered or tightly grouped around the central value?

- Shape: Are the data spread symmetrically about the central value? Are the data unbalanced or skewed (e.g. are the values much larger than the mean, but not much smaller)?

- Are there outliers (values that are drastically different from the mean) in the data?

- Do the data tend to cluster in several groups?

Different types of measurements will be developed for each of the attributes listed above. For example, the mean (average) and the median measure the location or central tendency of a data set. Both of these statistical measures are trying to tell us something about the location of the middle of the data, but they use different ideas for defining that notion of middle.

From the morning paper to the evening news, general concepts are translated into specific statistical measures such as:

- The proportion of United States residents earning below the poverty level was 14.3% in 2009. **Source**: U.S. Census Bureau

- The median price of new homes sold in 2009 was $216,700. **Source**: U.S. Census Bureau

- The average hourly manufacturing wage in the U.S. in 2010 was $18.90. **Source**: U.S. Department of labor

Such measures are examples of **numerical descriptive statistics**.

Definition

Numerical descriptive statistics are numerical summaries of data.

Numerical Descriptive Statistics

There is a distinction between measures that are applied to populations and measures that are applied to samples.

Definition

Measures that apply to population data are called **parameters**.

Parameters

Definition

Measures that apply to sample data are called **statistics**.

Statistics

In most instances a data analyst will not know what the population parameters are, since the cost and/or feasibility of obtaining all the population's data is usually prohibitive.

Definition

Inferential statistics is concerned with making conclusions about population parameters using sample statistics.

There are many formulas in this chapter that you will have to spend some time examining to appreciate. In most cases, the concepts which motivate these formulas are simple. Yet if these concepts are either ignored or forgotten, statistics becomes a meaningless assortment of symbols, instead of a useful problem-solving and decision-making tool.

The data in Table 4.1 are costs (rounded to the nearest dollar) of fill-ups at a local gasoline station in December 2010 for 400 transactions. Looking at the 400 observations without using a graphical representation would be confusing. (It seems 400 measurements would contain a great deal of information, yet the sheer volume of the data obscures comprehension.) It is the old problem of not being able to see the forest for the trees.

Table 4.1 – Costs of Fill-ups – December 2010								
$22	$39	$25	$35	$43	$36	$52	$44
32	32	35	44	33	51	44	28
37	45	44	28	51	38	47	34
33	45	28	54	38	40	37	42
30	40	36	38	32	38	28	23
43	43	25	24	47	36	22	24
39	45	36	36	38	32	43	32
45	58	49	23	55	43	29	11
48	36	22	34	18	27	37	50
57	48	36	64	62	33	33	58
36	38	33	41	26	43	28	42
50	32	47	22	42	35	21	56
50	23	52	46	31	41	35	33
54	43	43	44	51	49	31	56
34	51	38	34	28	36	43	35
31	32	37	22	44	34	19	42
29	48	32	30	25	61	30	21
41	24	42	39	25	45	36	43
31	46	55	27	57	32	56	45

30	33	37	33	41	59	33	24
44	58	53	47	50	46	30	36
17	54	59	54	41	39	60	40
41	45	43	50	53	28	49	45
51	35	67	49	38	38	41	30
11	48	37	27	32	42	34	31
36	41	30	31	44	34	39	38
32	45	55	20	48	46	35	36
48	41	31	31	54	52	35	34
28	14	41	50	43	44	47	40
43	53	28	32	47	50	38	53
34	44	40	42	37	51	39	46
19	40	72	40	37	20	43	38
45	45	33	53	46	39	42	49
43	50	26	41	36	45	27	43
47	42	55	48	54	24	30	52
35	49	25	42	38	55	47	49
37	38	34	35	48	45	43	53
45	46	21	56	35	37	46	24
37	50	45	36	31	36	60	40
29	30	45	39	49	36	25	42
52	27	31	21	47	42	23	51
38	29	39	37	25	41	41	29
51	47	52	43	49	47	32	40
42	33	42	43	43	47	54	43
34	49	46	28	50	30	55	34
34	66	44	19	44	42	37	25
39	29	44	36	28	51	35	35
31	47	26	25	55	32	46	43
43	36	33	43	54	50	32	24
46	43	37	41	30	37	31	51

Looking at a graph of the data (see Figure 4.3) is always a good first step. But, we need to learn more. To do this, we use statistical tools designed to reveal the data's fundamental characteristics. These statistical tools answer important questions such as, *Where is the center of the data?* and *How can the dispersion of the data be measured?*

4.1 Measures of Location

Statistically speaking, the idea of location is similar to knowing the whereabouts of a person. If we think of a data set as a group of data values that cluster around some central value, then this central value provides a focal point for the data set – a location of sorts. Unfortunately, the notion of central value is a vague concept, which is as much defined by the way it is measured as by the notion itself. There are several statistical measures that can be used to define the notion of center: the arithmetic mean, trimmed mean, median, and mode.

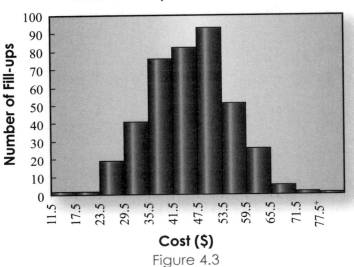

Costs of Fill-ups – December 2010

Figure 4.3

The Arithmetic Mean

The arithmetic mean is one of the more commonly used statistical measures. It appears every day in newspapers, business publications, and frequently in conversation. For example, when your instructor returns an assessment, after viewing your grade, one of the first questions asked is, *What is the average?*

Arithmetic Mean

> **Formula**
>
> Suppose there are n observations in a data set, consisting of the observations $x_1, x_2, ..., x_n$; then the **arithmetic mean** is defined to be
>
> $$\frac{1}{n}\left(x_1 + x_2 + ... + x_n\right).$$

If we use some common mathematical notation (summation notation, represented by Σ), the formula can be simplified to

$$\frac{\sum x_i}{n},$$

where x_i is the ith data value in the data set and Σ (pronounced sigma) is a mathematical notation for adding values. There are two symbols that are associated with the expression given above:

$$\mu = \frac{1}{N}\left(x_1 + x_2 + \ldots + x_N\right)$$ the **population mean**, and

$$\bar{x} = \frac{1}{n}\left(x_1 + x_2 + \ldots + x_n\right)$$ the **sample mean**.

Here N refers to the size of the population and n refers to the size of the sample. Otherwise, the calculations are made in precisely the same way. The Greek letter μ representing the population mean is pronounced *mu* and the symbol $\bar{x}$ representing the sample mean is pronounced *x-bar*.

Example 4.1

Calculate the sample mean of the following sample data values: 4, 10, 7, 15.

Solution

Note that $x_1 = 4$, $x_2 = 10$, $x_3 = 7$, $x_4 = 15$, and $n = 4$.

$$\bar{x} = \frac{1}{4}\left(4 + 10 + 7 + 15\right) = 9$$

$$= \frac{\sum\limits_{i=1}^{4} x_i}{n} = \frac{4 + 10 + 7 + 15}{4} = \frac{36}{4} = 9.$$

The sample mean is 9. But why does adding up a group of numbers and dividing by the number of observations measure central tendency? As unlikely as it sounds, the answer is related to balancing a scale.

Definition

Given some point A and a data point x, then $x - A$ represents how far x **deviates** from A. This difference is also called a **deviation**.

Deviation

Let's calculate the deviations from the mean for the data in Example 4.1. Examining the deviations from the mean in Table 4.2, we can see the deviations on the left side (−5 and −2) and right side (1 and 6) are in balance. In fact, the mean is considered a point of centrality because the deviations from the mean on the positive side and the negative side are equal (See Figure 4.4). The sample mean can be interpreted as a center of gravity.

Table 4.2 – Deviations from the Mean	
Data (x_i)	Deviations from the Mean $(x_i - 9)$
4	−5
10	1
7	−2
15	6
	$\sum(x_i - 9) = 0$

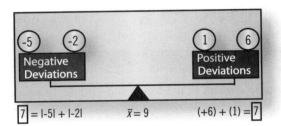

Figure 4.4

On the other hand, if we calculate the deviations about any other value the deviations do not balance. For example, if we calculate the deviation about $x = 8$ we get the deviation found in Table 4.3. Assume the central value is 8. The deviations from the alleged central value, 8, for each data value are calculated in Table 4.3 and shown in Figure 4.5.

The positive deviations (2 and 7) are not counterbalanced by the negative deviations (−4 and −1). A desirable characteristic of a central value would be to have the positive and negative deviations equal to each other in absolute value.

Table 4.3 – Deviations from Some Other Value	
Data (x_i)	Deviations from 8 $(x_i - 8)$
4	−4
10	2
7	−1
15	7
	$\sum(x_i - 8) = 4$

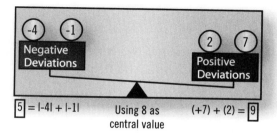

Figure 4.5

Although the arithmetic mean is frequently used, there are times when it should not be employed. Since the mean requires that the data values be added, it should only be used for quantitative data. Furthermore, if one of the data values is extremely large or small relative to others, this could be considered an **outlier**. An outlier is a data value that can have a dramatic impact on the value of the mean.

Definition

Statistical measures which are not affected by outliers are said to be **resistant**.

Resistant

The arithmetic mean is not a **resistant measure**.

The Weighted Mean

The weighted mean is similar to the mean except it allows you to give different weights (or importance) to each data value. The weighted mean gives you the flexibility to assign weights where you find it inappropriate to treat each observation the same. The weights are usually positive numbers that sum to one, with the largest weight being applied to the observation with the greatest importance. The weights can be determined in a variety of ways, such as the number of employees, market value of a company, or some other objective or subjective method. There are occasions in which it is easier to assign the weights without worrying that they will sum to one. If you are concerned about your weights summing to one, you can make your weights sum to one by dividing each weight by the sum of all the weights.

Formula

The **weighted mean** of a data set with values x_1, x_2, x_3,..., x_n is given by

Weighted Mean

$$\bar{x} = \frac{w_1 x_1 + w_2 x_2 + ... + w_n x_n}{w_1 + w_2 + ... + w_n} = \frac{\sum \left(w_i x_i \right)}{\sum w_i}$$

where w_i is the weight of observation x_i.

Example 4.2

The following table consists of the November 2010 unemployment rates and civilian labor force sizes for the Mid-Atlantic states.

State	Size of Civilian Labor Force (Thousands)	Unemployment Rate (%)
Delaware	422.4	8.4
Maryland	2972.7	7.4
New Jersey	4490.6	9.2
New York	9658.4	8.3
Pennsylvania	6362.0	8.6
Virginia	4177.7	6.8
District of Columbia	331.6	9.8
West Virginia	777.6	9.3

Table 4.4 – Unemployment Rates

Source: U.S. Department of Labor, Bureau of Labor Statistics

Using the weighted mean, calculate the average unemployment rate for the Mid-Atlantic states.

Solution

The average unemployment rate is calculated by

$$\overline{x} = \frac{\sum(w_i x_i)}{w_i}$$

$$\sum(w_i x_i) = 422.4(8.4) + 2972.7(7.4) + 4490.6(9.2) + 9658.4(8.3) + 6362.0(8.6)$$
$$+ 4177.7(6.8) + 331.6(9.8) + 777.6(9.3)$$
$$= 240627.3$$

$$\sum w_i = 422.4 + 2972.7 + 4490.6 + 9658.4 + 6362.0 + 4177.7 + 331.6 + 777.6$$
$$= 29193$$

$$\text{so, } \overline{x} = \frac{\sum(w_i x_i)}{\sum w_i} = \frac{240627.3}{29193} \approx 8.24\%.$$

Thus, the average unemployment rate, calculated by the weighted mean, is 8.24%. It is appropriate to use the weighted mean to calculate the average unemployment rate since the size of the civilian labor force (the weight) is different for each state.

The Trimmed Mean

Since outliers can have an enormous effect on the value of the mean, the mean's usefulness as a typical measure of data is diminished if the data contain outliers.

Definition

The **trimmed mean** is a modification of the arithmetic mean which ignores an equal percentage of the highest and lowest data values in calculating the mean.

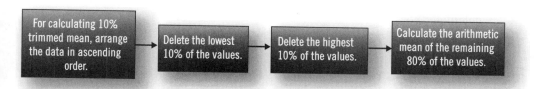

For calculating 10% trimmed mean, arrange the data in ascending order. → Delete the lowest 10% of the values. → Delete the highest 10% of the values. → Calculate the arithmetic mean of the remaining 80% of the values.

Finding the 10% Trimmed Mean

Before calculating the trimmed mean, the data is arranged in ascending order of magnitude. A 10% trimmed mean uses the middle 80% of the values. It is calculated by chopping off the top 10% and the bottom 10% of the data values, and finding the arithmetic average of the remaining values. If the data set does not contain any outliers, the mean and the trimmed mean will be similar.

Example 4.3

Consider the following data.

$$15, 21, 25, 31, 35, 42, 48, 51, 54, 60$$

Find the 10% trimmed mean.

Solution

Since there are 10 observations, removing the highest 10% and the lowest 10% means removing only one observation from each end of the data.

That is,

$$10\% \text{ of } 10 = 0.1 \cdot 10 = 1.$$

Trimmed Mean
Measuring Figure Skating Performances

Almost every figure skating competition has some scoring controversy. The Winter Olympics of 2002 were no exception. French judge, Marie-Reine Le Gougne, said she was "pressured to vote a certain way" when she scored the Russian couple, Elena Berezhnaya and Anton Sikharulidze, over the Canadian pair, Jamie Sale and David Pelletier. In addition, very few people understood exactly how Sarah Hughes won the gold medal and how Michelle Kwan dropped to third after leading the event.

For almost a century figure skating has used a scoring method that is similar to the methodology of the trimmed mean in order to remove bias. Skaters are scored on a 0 to 6 scale. The highest and lowest scores are discarded (the data is trimmed) and the resulting score is computed.

Continued...

4

... Continued

The intent of trimming the data is to avoid bias caused by judges with nationalistic or political agendas.

Since the controversy, the International Skating Union has replaced this scoring method with a new system which, though it is different, still utilizes trimmed data to eliminate bias.

Note that the data are already sorted. If the mean is calculated without including the values of 15 and 60, the resulting measure is called the 10% trimmed mean.

$$\cancel{15}, \; 21, \; 25, \; 31, \; 35, \; 42, \; 48, \; 51, \; 54, \; \cancel{60}$$

$$10\% \text{ trimmed mean} = \frac{21+25+31+35+42+48+51+54}{8} = \frac{307}{8} = 38.375.$$

If there had been 100 observations, the largest 10% and the smallest 10% (a total of 20 data values) would have been removed before the mean was calculated.

The Median

The median of a set of data provides another measure of center. It is a simple idea. To find the median, place the data in ascending order and then find the observation that has an equal number of data values on either side. That is, half of the observations are less than the median and half of the observations are greater than the median. The median is the middle value.

Median

Definition

The **median** of a set of observations is the data value in the middle of an ordered array. The same number of data values is on either side of the median value.

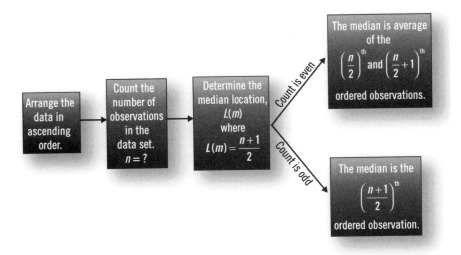

Finding the Median

Example 4.4

Given the following eleven observations, find the median.

$$2, 4, 0, 3, 0, 1, 8, 5, 1, 5, 9$$

Solution

First, the data set must be ordered.

$$0, 0, 1, 1, 2, 3, 4, 5, 5, 8, 9$$

The number of observations, $n = 11$.

Next, calculate the median location, $L(m) = \dfrac{n+1}{2} = \dfrac{11+1}{2} = 6.$ Therefore, the median is the 6th ordered observation, 3.

$$\underbrace{0,\ 0,\ 1,\ 1,\ 2,}_{\text{5 data values}}\ \boxed{3},\ \underbrace{4,\ 5,\ 5,\ 8,\ 9}_{\text{5 data values}}$$

Example 4.5

Consider the following ten test scores:

$$65, 98, 76, 83, 94, 79, 88, 72, 90, 85.$$

Find the median.

Solution

The number of observations, $n = 10$.

The median location, $L(m) = \dfrac{10+1}{2} = \dfrac{11}{2} = 5.5.$

If there is an even number of observations, average the two center values in the ordered array. The median is the average of the $\dfrac{10}{2} = 5^{th}$ and 6th ordered observations.

$$\underbrace{65,\ 72,\ 76,\ 79,}_{\text{4 data values}}\ \boxed{83},\ \boxed{85},\ \underbrace{88,\ 90,\ 94,\ 98}_{\text{4 data values}}$$

To find the median, average the fifth and sixth observations.

$$\frac{85+83}{2} = 84 \text{ (the median)}.$$

The median possesses a rather obvious notion of centrality, since it is defined as the central value in an ordered list. It is not affected by outliers and is thus a resistant measure. For example, if we replaced 98 with 200,000,000 in the data set from Example 4.5 then the median would not change at all. The median does possess one limitation: it cannot be applied to nominal data. In order to calculate the median, the data must be placed in order. To accomplish this task meaningfully, the level of measurement must be at least **ordinal**.

Unless the data set is skewed or contains outliers, the median and the mean usually have similar values.

Example 4.6

a. Consider the following data.

$$16, 18, 20, 21, 23, 23, 24, 32, 36, 42$$

$$\text{mean} = 25.5$$

Find the median and 10% trimmed mean.

Solution

First, find the median.

The number of observations, $n = 10$.

The median location, $L(m) = \dfrac{10+1}{2} = \dfrac{11}{2} = 5.5$.

If there is an even number of observations, average the two center values in the ordered array. The median is the average of the $\dfrac{10}{2} = 5^{th}$ and 6th ordered observations.

$$\underbrace{16,\ 18,\ 20,\ 21,}_{\text{4 data values}}\ \boxed{23},\ \boxed{23},\ \underbrace{24,\ 32,\ 36,\ 42}_{\text{4 data values}}$$

To find the median, average the fifth and sixth observations.

$$\frac{23 + 23}{2} = 23 \text{ (the median).}$$

Now find the 10% trimmed mean.

Since there are 10 observations, removing the highest 10% and the lowest 10% means removing only one observation from each end of the data.

$$10\% \text{ of } 10 = 0.1 \cdot 10 = 1$$

If the mean is calculated without including the values 16 and 42 in the data, the resultant measure is the 10% trimmed mean.

$$\cancel{16},\ 18,\ 20,\ 21,\ 23,\ 23,\ 24,\ 32,\ 36,\ \cancel{42}$$

$$10\% \text{ trimmed mean} = \frac{18+20+21+23+23+24+32+36}{8} = 24.625$$

b. Consider the same data set, except the last data value is replaced with an outlier (490). Compare the mean, median, and 10% trimmed mean for this data set to the mean, median, and 10% trimmed mean of the original data set.

$$16, 18, 20, 21, 23, 23, 24, 32, 36, 490$$

mean = 70.3   median = 23   10% trimmed mean = 24.625

Solution

The median and 10% trimmed mean are not affected by the addition of the outlier, while the mean increases dramatically. This illustrates why the median and 10% trimmed mean are said to be resistant measures while the arithmetic mean is not.

The Mode

The mode is another measure of location. It is not used as frequently as the mean or the median, and its relation to these values is not so predictable. The mode is the only measure of location that can be used for nominal (or qualitative) data. Of the three measures of location, the mode is used the least due to the limited information it provides. Sometimes sorting the data (in ascending or descending order) makes it easier to find the mode.

Definition

The **mode** of a data set is the most frequently occurring value.

Mode

Example 4.7

Find the mode in the following data set.

$$0, 1, 4, 3, 9, 8, 10, 0, 1, 3, 0$$

Solution

Since the value of 0 occurs more than any other value, it is the mode. In this instance, as a measure of location, the modal value is not a particularly appealing choice. However, the mode does possess one very favorable property – it is the only measure of location that can be applied to nominal data. Thus, for nominal measurements like color preferences, it would be perfectly reasonable to discuss the modal color.

Kiwi Eggs are Outliers!

Both plant and animal kingdoms offer spectacularly odd and beautiful sights. A kiwi bird (one of the many interesting life forms from New Zealand) lays eggs that are close to 25% of its body weight and sometimes lays two or three such eggs at a time. For most species of birds, eggs usually correspond to about 5% of the bird's body weight.

If you draw a graph relating (log) egg weight to (log) body weight you get a so-called hummingbird-moa curve (Moa is an extinct ostrich-like bird of the New Zealand area). In this curve, the kiwi bird is an outlier. Using the kiwi body weight (about 5 lbs) one expects an egg weight of about 55 to 100 grams while the actual weight of kiwi eggs is about 400 to 435 grams. This egg weight matches an expected body weight of about 40 lbs according to the hummingbird-moa curve. Why is this the case, and what accounts for such an anomaly?

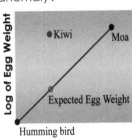

Continued ...

Suppose we added one more value to the data set in Example 4.7. If this value were a 1, then both 0 and 1 would be repeated three times and there would be two modes. When this occurs, the data is said to be **bimodal**. Any time data has more than two modes it is said to be **multimodal**.

The Relationship between the Mean, Median, and Mode

Often times, the shape of the data determines how the mean, median, and mode are related. For a bell-shaped distribution, the mean, median, and mode are identical.

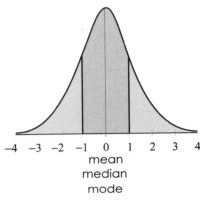

mean
median
mode

Figure 4.6

Certainly, not all data produce distributions which follow a bell-shaped curve. If the distribution of the data has a long tail on the right, it is said to be skewed to the right, or positively skewed. Conversely, if the distribution has a long tail on the left, it is said to be skewed to the left, or negatively skewed.

Positively Skewed Curve

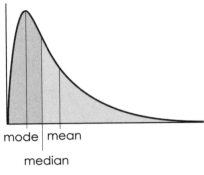

mode | mean
median

Figure 4.7

If the data are **positively skewed**, the median will be smaller than the mean.

Negatively Skewed Curve

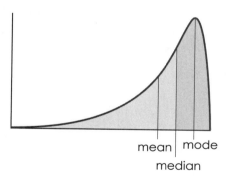

Figure 4.8

... Continued

The most reasonable explanation provided by biologists is that kiwis and moa birds are members of the same species except the kiwis have dwarfed through their evolutionary history. A sub-area of biology called "allometry" states that as body size decreases the internal organs decrease relatively slowly which supports the dwarfism hypothesis. The kiwis have lost body weight but not their internal womb structure which still holds large eggs. Outliers are important because they force you to think about data more seriously.

If the data are **negatively skewed**, the mean will be smaller than the median.

Where does the mode fall on these graphs? The area containing the greatest number of observations contains the mode. That area is represented by the large "humps" in the curve. In Figure 4.7 and Figure 4.8 the highlighted "humps" in the curve are the portions of the distributions that will contain the mode. The highest point on the curve will be the mode of the distribution. Notice that in a symmetrical distribution (Figure 4.6), the mode is equal to the mean and median. If the distribution is positively skewed (Figure 4.7), the mode is less than the mean and median. If the distribution is negatively skewed (Figure 4.8), the mode is greater than the mean and median.

Selecting a Measure of Location

The objective of using descriptive statistics is to provide measures which convey useful summary information about the data. When selecting a statistic to represent the central value of a data set, the first thing to consider is the type of data being analyzed.

The arithmetic mean is used so frequently that its computation is almost a knee-jerk reaction to analyzing data. Unfortunately it is not always a reasonable measure of location. Table 4.5 defines the applicable levels of measurement for each measure of location. Table 4.6 defines the sensitivity to outliers for each measure of location. When the data are qualitative (nominal or ordinal), the mean should not be calculated and, if the data are quantitative and contain outliers, the mean does not convey the notion of typical value as well as some other measures. The only time in which the mean should be used without any explanation is when the distribution of the data is symmetrical or nearly so. In that event, the mean and median should be about the same value.

Table 4.5 – Applicable Levels of Measurement				
	Applicable Level of Measurement			
	Qualitative		Quantitative	
	Nominal	Ordinal	Interval	Ratio
Mean			✓	✓
Median		✓	✓	✓
Mode	✓	✓	✓	✓
Trimmed Mean			✓	✓

Table 4.6 – Sensitivity to Outliers		
Measure of Location	Not Sensitive	Very Sensitive
Mean		✓
Median	✓	
Mode	✓	
Trimmed Mean	✓	

The median is also a good measure of central tendency. It is not sensitive to outliers and can be applied to data gathered from all levels of measurement, except nominal.

If the data's level of measurement is at least interval and there are no outliers, the mean is a reasonable choice. If the data appears to have any unusual values, then the trimmed mean or the median would be more appropriate.

If the data's level of measurement is nominal or ordinal (the data is qualitative), appropriate measures of center are limited. If the data is ordinal, then the median is the best choice. If the data is nominal, there is only one choice, the mode. The mode is applicable to any level of data, although it is usually not very useful for quantitative data.

Time Series Data and Measures of Location

We discussed two types of time series data in Chapter 3, stationary and non-stationary. Stationary time series wobbled around some central value, so calculating a central value is perfectly reasonable, and the methods we previously discussed are applicable. A non-stationary time series is another story. Non-stationary time series possess trend. That means there is no central value for the time series. Instead, the series trends in one direction or another. Computing a central value using the methods discussed earlier would be inappropriate for such data.

Table 4.7 shows the average U.S. gas price over a 20 year period. In this non-stationary time series, the central value of the process is trending upward as shown in Figure 4.9. One way to capture this movement is with a moving average.

Time Series Plot

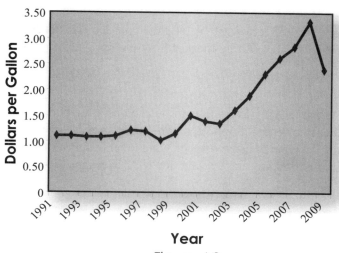

Figure 4.9

Table 4.7 – Average U.S. Gas Price 1991-2010 (Dollars per Gallon)			
Year	Average U.S. Gas Price	2 Period Moving Average	3 Period Moving Average
1991	1.14		
1992	1.13	1.135	
1993	1.11	1.120	1.127
1994	1.11	1.110	1.117
1995	1.15	1.130	1.123
1996	1.23	1.190	1.163
1997	1.23	1.230	1.203
1998	1.06	1.145	1.173
1999	1.17	1.115	1.153
2000	1.51	1.340	1.247
2001	1.46	1.485	1.380
2002	1.36	1.410	1.443
2003	1.59	1.475	1.470
2004	1.88	1.735	1.610
2005	2.30	2.090	1.923
2006	2.59	2.445	2.257
2007	2.80	2.695	2.563
2008	3.27	3.035	2.887
2009	2.35	2.810	2.807
2010	2.79	2.570	2.803

Source: Bureau of Labor Statistics

> ## Definition
>
> A **moving average** is obtained by adding consecutive observations for a number of periods and dividing the result by the number of periods included in the average.

We will assume the moving average is to be used as a method of forecasting the next level of the time series. Suppose a two-period moving average is calculated for the gas price data and is used to specify the level of the series at a given point in time. The two-period moving average for 1992 averages the values of the time series in 1991 and 1992.

$$\frac{1.14 + 1.13}{2} = 1.135$$

Similarly, the two-period moving average for 1993 would be the average of the time series values in 1992 and 1993.

$$\frac{1.13 + 1.11}{2} = 1.120$$

Since data are not available for 1989 or 1990, the three-period moving average for 1991 cannot be calculated. The three-period moving average associated with 1993 is the average of the time series values in 1991, 1992, and 1993.

$$\frac{1.14 + 1.13 + 1.11}{3} = 1.127$$

The three-period moving average for 1994 would be the average of the time series values in 1992, 1993, and 1994.

$$\frac{1.13 + 1.11 + 1.11}{3} = 1.117$$

The chart in Figure 4.10 displays the time series and the two and three-period moving averages. Both of the averages follow the time series quite closely. However, notice that the two-period moving average (the red line) follows the actual data values (the blue line) more closely than the three-period moving average (the green line).

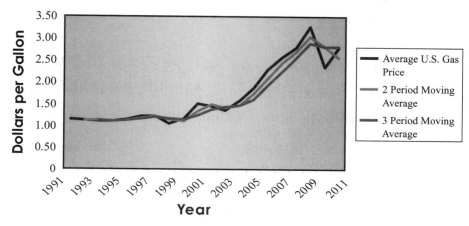

Average U.S. Gas Price with Moving Averages

Figure 4.10

4.1 Exercises

Basic Concepts

1. Describe the difference between statistics and parameters.

2. Discuss three major attributes used in summarizing a data set.

3. What are numerical descriptive statistics and why are they important?

4. Identify and describe five measures of location. List the advantages and disadvantages of each.

5. List the types of data that are appropriate for each of the measures of location discussed in the previous question.

6. Why is the mean a measure of central tendency?

7. What is a resistant measure?

8. Describe a situation in which using the weighted mean as a measure of location would be appropriate.

9. What does it mean if we say that a data set is positively skewed? Negatively skewed?

10. Explain why the mean should not be calculated for a non-stationary time series.

11. What is a moving average? When is it useful?

Exercises

1. Calculate the mean, median, 10% trimmed mean, and mode for the following data.

90.25	93.83	91.41	92.27	90.89	99.12	92.88	97.74	96.28	95.33
91.16	94.30	95.51	92.27	97.63	95.94	90.95	94.76	92.27	92.88

2. Calculate the mean, median, 20% trimmed mean, and mode for the following data.

19	14	11	11	18
20	10	19	11	18
20	18	10	11	15

3. Calculate the mean, median, 20% trimmed mean, and mode for the following data.

0.5380	0.8856	0.2738	0.4895	0.8422

4. Calculate the mean, median, 10% trimmed mean, and mode for the following data.

2	22	6	18	10	14	12	12	16	8

5. Discuss the usefulness of each of the measures of central tendency with respect to the following situations.

   a. A company is considering a move into a regional market for specialty soft drinks. In analyzing the size containers that his competitors are currently offering, would the company be more interested in the mean, median, or mode of their containers?

   b. The creative director for an advertising agency is trying to target an ad campaign that will be shown in one city only. Would he be more interested in the mean or median family income in the city?

   c. A young economist was assigned the task of comparing the interest rates of ninety day certificates of deposit (CD's) in three major cities. Should she compare the mean, median, or modal interest for the banks in the three cities?

   d. A telephone company is interested in knowing how customers rate their service: excellent, good, average, or poor. Would the company be more interested in studying the mean, median, or mode of the customer service ratings?

6. Discuss the usefulness of each of the measures of central tendency with respect to the following situations.

   a. A doctor is interested in analyzing the increase in systolic blood pressure caused by a certain antibiotic. Would the manufacturer be more interested in the mean, median, or mode of the ratings?

   b. A car manufacturer is trying to decide in what colors it should offer its new sports coupe. In analyzing the preferred colors of other sports coupes, would the manufacturer be more interested in the mean, median, or mode of the colors?

   c. The maker of Lindor chocolate bars is interested in knowing how people rate their chocolate: the best, above average, average, below average, or the worst. Would the company be more interested in the mean, median, or mode of the ratings?

   d. A realtor is interested in studying the prices of recent home sales in an area which has many diverse neighborhoods. Would the mean, median, or mode of the prices of recent home sales be the best measure of central tendency?

7. The following are the daily high temperatures for a southern city in July (measured in degrees Fahrenheit).

84	85	84	88	94	100	97	102	97	89
89	90	88	95	91	95	99	93	97	99
90	94	90	88	91	88	106	99	102	85

   a. Calculate the mean of the daily high temperatures.

   b. Calculate the median of the daily high temperatures.

   c. Calculate the mode of the daily high temperatures.

   d. Calculate the 10% trimmed mean of the daily high temperatures.

   e. Which measure of central tendency do you think best describes the center of the data set? Why?

8. A tour guide informs his group that the "average" temperature at their destination is 60 degrees Fahrenheit. Once they arrive, they discover that the daytime highs are about 120 degrees Fahrenheit and the nighttime lows are about 0 degrees Fahrenheit. Do you feel the tour guide accurately described the temperatures to the group? Discuss.

9. A worker is participating in a test on a new machine. Her daily production, measured in numbers of units, for the twenty day test is listed in the following table. On days 4 and 5, the worker was ill and went home shortly after coming to work.

Table for Exercise 9 – Daily Production									
Day	1	2	3	4	5	6	7	8	9	10
Units	100	104	117	20	20	111	105	106	115	101
Day	11	12	13	14	15	16	17	18	19	20
Units	101	102	115	116	113	103	104	119	118	108

a. What level of measurement does the data possess?

b. Compute the 10% trimmed mean and the 20% trimmed mean.

c. Considering the worker's illness, which measure computed in part (b) best describes the production capability of the machine? Discuss.

10. Consider the following per capita greenhouse emissions (tons of carbon dioxide equivalent per capita) for 10 randomly selected states:

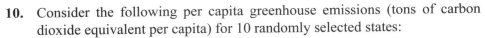

11.76	15.65	22.93	24.75	21.22
18.72	22.55	27.99	12.23	114.40

a. What level of measurement does the data possess?

b. Compute the 10% trimmed mean and the 20% trimmed mean.

c. Considering the data, which measure computed in part (b) best describes the per capita greenhouse emissions? Discuss.

11. Consider the following monthly sales for a small clothing store in a resort community.

Table for Exercise 11 – Sales	
Month	Sales ($)
January	100,500
February	120,000
March	133,000
April	145,000
May	160,000
June	180,000
July	200,000
August	185,000
September	175,000
October	120,000
November	180,000
December	330,000

a. Draw a line graph of the data.

b. Calculate the two-period moving averages for the data.

c. Calculate the three-period moving averages for the data.

d. Add line graphs for the two-period moving averages and three-period moving averages to the graph which you constructed in part (a).

e. Which series of data (the original sales data, the two-period moving averages, or the three-period moving averages) do you think best represents sales for the year? Why?

12. Late in the summer of 1996, Tiger Woods became a professional golfer. This highly publicized event followed a sensational college career at Stanford University, where Tiger won three United States Amateur championships. Tiger was not a professional very long before he had his first win on the pro tour, the Las Vegas Invitational. He received a total of $297,000 for his accomplishment. The prize money (in thousands of dollars) for the top 40 finishers in the tournament are given below.

Table for Exercise 12 – Tournament Prize Money (Thousands of Dollars)							
297.0	60.2	46.2	31.3	21.4	14.5	10.7	8.5
178.2	60.2	31.3	31.3	14.5	14.5	10.7	8.5
95.7	46.2	31.3	24.7	14.5	14.5	8.5	8.5
95.7	46.2	31.3	21.4	14.5	14.5	8.5	8.5
60.2	46.2	31.3	21.4	14.5	10.7	8.5	8.5

a. Find the mean.

b. Find the median.

c. Find the mode.

d. Find the 10% trimmed mean and compare it to the mean and the median.

e. Comment on the skewness of the distribution.

4.2   Measures of Dispersion

Suppose all people looked alike, all cars looked alike, everyone wore the same kind of clothes, and there was only one kind of hamburger (plain). Without diversity it would be a boring world and a world in which statistics would be of little value. Since much of statistics is devoted to describing, analyzing, and explaining variability, understanding how variability is measured is essential to understanding statistics.

The concept of variability (also referred to as dispersion or spread) is as vague as the concept of central tendency. And vague concepts lead to different measurement ideas. The same issues that are important in evaluating measures of location are meaningful in evaluating measures of dispersion.

Many of the good measures of dispersion use the concept of deviation from the mean. If the mean is a focal point of base, use it as a common basis from which to measure variation. The distance that a point is from its mean is called a **deviation from the mean**. A data set and its deviations from the mean are calculated in Table 4.8.

Table 4.8 – Calculating Deviations from the Mean		
Data Set: 3, 12, 20, 15, 0 Mean = 10		
Data Values	Deviations from the Mean (Data – Mean = Deviation)	
3	3 – 10	–7
12	12 – 10	2
20	20 – 10	10
15	15 – 10	5
0	0 – 10	–10

Because the mean is the point at which the sum of the positive deviations equals the sum of the absolute values of the negative deviations, the deviations will always sum to zero. Many of the variability measures average the deviations in some form.

The Range

The range is the simplest measure of dispersion. It does not provide much depth or understanding of the measure of spread and does not use the deviation concept.

Definition

The **range** is the difference between the largest and smallest data values.

Range

Example 4.8

Calculate the range of the following data set: 4, 6, 16, 9, 24, 8, 0, 12, 1.

Solution

The largest value equals 24 and the smallest value equals 0. Thus, the range is calculated as

$$\text{Range} = 24 - 0 = 24.$$

The problem with the range is that it is also affected by outliers, and it does not bring all the information in the data directly to bear on the problem of measuring variation. That is, the range only uses two values (the largest and smallest) to measure spread rather than all of the observations. The other measures of dispersion discussed in this chapter are generally more appropriate measures of spread.

Mean Absolute Deviation

One of the ways of obtaining information about the spread of the data is to analyze the deviations from the mean. Instead of adding the raw deviations, suppose the absolute values of the deviations (which can be interpreted as distance from the mean) are summed and divided by the number of deviations. This new measure computes the average distance from the mean for the data set. This measure is called the **mean absolute deviation**. If data set A has a larger average deviation than B, then it is reasonable to believe that data set A has more variability than data set B.

Formula

The sample mean absolute deviation (MAD) is

$$\text{MAD} = \frac{\sum |x_i - \bar{x}|}{n}.$$

Mean Absolute Deviation

Example 4.9

Suppose six people participated in a 1000 meter run. Their times, measured in minutes, are given below.

$$4, 10, 9, 11, 9, 7$$

The mean time is 8.333 minutes. Find the mean absolute deviation.

Solution

In Table 4.9 we do the basic calculations needed to compute the mean absolute deviation.

Table 4.9 – Calculating Mean Absolute Deviation			
Time (Minutes)	Deviation $x_i - \bar{x}$	Absolute Deviation $\|x_i - \bar{x}\|$	% of Total
4	4 – 8.33	4.33	38.18
10	10 – 8.33	1.66	14.73
9	9 – 8.33	0.66	5.91
11	11 – 8.33	2.66	23.54
9	9 – 8.33	0.66	5.91
7	7 – 8.33	1.33	11.73
Total		11.33	100.00

$$\text{Mean Absolute Deviation } = \frac{11.34}{6} = 1.89 \text{ minutes}$$

Thus, on average, the points are 1.89 units from the mean. Note that the contribution to the sum of the deviations is proportional to the size of the deviation. That is, if one absolute deviation is twice as large as another, it contributes twice as much to the value of the statistic. For example, compare the data point 7, which is 1.33 units from the mean, to the data point 11, which is 2.67 units from the mean. The percentage contribution to the total deviation is 11.73% for 7 and 23.54% for 11, which is in proportion to their respective distances from the mean. A variability measure in which each data value contributes proportionally to its distance from the mean seems reasonable.

Example 4.10

Suppose the value 200 is added to the data set given in Example 4.9.

The mean is drastically affected, increasing from 8.33 to 35.71. In Table 4.10 we redo the basic calculations for the mean absolute deviation. What effect, if any, does the value of 200 have on the MAD?

Solution

Table 4.10 – Calculating Mean Absolute Deviation

Data	Deviation $x_i - \bar{x}$	Absolute Deviation $\lvert x_i - \bar{x} \rvert$
4	4 – 35.71	31.71
10	10 – 35.71	25.71
9	9 – 35.71	26.71
11	11 – 35.71	24.71
9	9 – 35.71	26.71
7	7 – 35.71	28.71
200	200 – 35.71	164.29
Total		328.55

The mean absolute deviation changes dramatically, increasing to 46.9 $\left(\dfrac{328.55}{7}\right)$. Therefore, the mean absolute deviation is sensitive to outliers and is not a resistant measure. The mean absolute deviation is a very intuitive measure of variation.

Variance and Standard Deviation

The **variance** and **standard deviation** are the most common measures of variability. Since the standard deviation is computed directly from the variance, our discussion will center on the variance. Like the MAD, the variance and standard deviation provide numerical measures of how the data vary around the mean. If the data are tightly packed around the mean, the variance and standard deviation will be relatively small. On the other hand, if the data are widely dispersed about the mean, the variance and standard deviation will be relatively large.

Variance

Formula

The **variance** of a data set containing the complete set of *population* data is given by

$$\sigma^2 = \frac{\sum (x_i - \mu)^2}{N},$$

where μ is the population mean of the data set, N is the size of the population, and x_i, is a particular value in the data set. σ^2 is pronounced *sigma squared*, and is called the **population variance**.

The **variance** of a data set containing *sample* data is given by

$$s^2 = \frac{\sum (x_i - \bar{x})^2}{n-1},$$

where $\bar{x}$ is the mean of the sample data, n is the size of the sample, and x_i is a particular value in the sample. s^2 is called the **sample variance**.

Both these definitions can be construed to be averages, although at first glance it may not be readily apparent. That is, for the population variance, we are adding up the sum of the squared deviations and dividing by the number of items that are added. Thus, the population variance is the average squared deviation from the mean. For the sample variance, we are dividing by $n-1$ because it gives us an unbiased estimate of the population variance.

It is usually not necessary to compute a variance by manual methods, except to become familiar with the definition.

Example 4.11

Given the following times in minutes of six persons running a 1000 meter course, compute the sample variance.

$$4, 10, 9, 11, 9, 7$$

Solution

We previously computed the mean of this sample as 8.33. In Table 4.11 we do the basic calculations needed to compute the sample variance.

Data	Deviation $x_i - \bar{x}$	Squared Deviation $(x_i - \bar{x})^2$	% of Total
	Table 4.11 – Calculating the Sample Variance		
4	$4 - 8.33 = -4.33$	18.7489	59.84
10	$10 - 8.33 = 1.67$	2.7889	8.90
9	$9 - 8.33 = 0.67$	0.4489	1.43
11	$11 - 8.33 = 2.67$	7.1289	22.75
9	$9 - 8.33 = 0.67$	0.4489	1.43
7	$7 - 8.33 = 1.33$	1.7689	5.65
Total		31.3334	100%

$$s^2 = \frac{\sum (x_i - \bar{x})^2}{n-1} = \frac{31.3334}{5} \approx 6.267 \text{ minutes squared}$$

Thus the average squared deviation of the data is 6.267 minutes squared. The phrase "minutes squared" in the last sentence may seem a bit odd. No one carries out transactions in square minutes, or square dollars, or square tons, so it is difficult to interpret the significance of the measurement in this form. That is why the standard deviation exists. It converts the measure into the original units by taking the square root of the variance.

Definition

The **standard deviation** is the square root of the variance.

Standard Deviation

But since there are two measures of variance, there will be two standard deviations, one for population data and one for sample data.

$$\sigma = \sqrt{\sigma^2} \text{ the \textbf{population standard deviation}}$$

$$s = \sqrt{s^2} \text{ the \textbf{sample standard deviation}}$$

For Example 4.11,

$$s = \sqrt{6.267 \text{ minutes}^2} \approx 2.50 \text{ minutes}.$$

It is important to remember these symbols $(\sigma \text{ and } s)$, since the standard deviation is a fundamental statistical concept.

Describing the standard deviation in an intuitive way is not easy. It is not the average deviation from the mean (which always equals 0), although in most cases it will be reasonably close to the mean absolute deviation. The fact is that the standard deviation is the square root of the average squared deviation. It is not an intuitive concept! Certainly a reasonable question at this juncture is, if the standard deviation is not very intuitive, why use it to measure deviation? Part of the answer lies in the fact that it is expressed in the same unit as the data. The variance is an important theoretical measure of variability because it has "nice" mathematical properties (in contrast to the more intuitive MAD).

The standard deviation can be used to measure how far data values are from their mean. You will often see the majority of data values within one standard deviation of the mean. Further, relatively few data values will be more than two standard deviations from the mean.

The variance and standard deviation both suffer from the same problem as the mean: they are very sensitive to outliers. Suppose the value 200 was added to the data in Example 4.11. The sample variance would increase from 6.267 to 5253.238. The new sample variance (which includes the outlier 200) then is 838 times as large as the original variance. The standard deviation increases from 2.50 to 72.50. The presence of the outlier tarnishes the interpretation of the standard deviation as a measure of variability.

Another interesting property of the variance is that values further from the mean contribute a disproportionate amount to the value of the statistic. In Example 4.11, one data point, 4, which is 4.33 units from the mean, contributes almost 60% of the variation in the data (see the column labeled "% of Total" in Table 4.11). Compare this to the data point 7, which is 1.33 units from the mean yet only contributes to 5.65% of the total variation. The reason that 4 contributes so heavily to the total variation is because the deviations are squared. By squaring the deviations, values further from the mean have disproportionate affects on the sum of the squared deviations.

While there are a number of descriptive tools available for summarizing variability, the variance and standard deviation are the most frequently used statistics.

Dispersion and Time Series Data

If the time series is stationary, then the methods discussed in this section can be used to measure dispersion. However, if the series is non-stationary, the dispersion measures we have discussed are not applicable. Measuring variation in a non-stationary time series is beyond the scope of this text.

Using the Standard Deviation

Although the standard deviation is not an especially intuitive concept, knowing the mean and standard deviation of a data set provides a great deal of information about the data. If the histogram of the measurements is bell-shaped, the empirical rule describes the variability of a set of measurements. **Chebyshev's Theorem** is a more general rule describing the variability of **any** set of data regardless of the shape of its distribution.

Empirical Rule

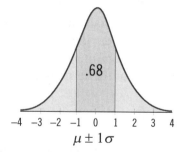

Figure 4.11 – One Sigma

One sigma rule: If the distribution of the data is bell-shaped, about 68% of the data should lie within one standard deviation of the mean.

A deviation of more than one sigma from the mean is to be expected about once in every three observations.

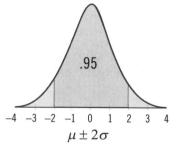

Figure 4.12 – Two Sigma

Two sigma rule: If the distribution of data is bell-shaped, about 95% of the data should lie within two standard deviations of the mean.

A deviation of more than two sigma from the mean is to be expected about once in every twenty observations.

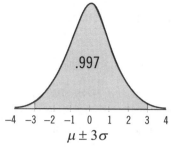

Figure 4.13 – Three Sigma

Three sigma rule: If the distribution of the data is bell-shaped, about 99.7% of the observations should lie within three standard deviations of the mean.

A deviation of more than three sigma from the mean is to be expected about once in every 333 observations, slightly less than 0.3% of the time.

Example 4.12

Who is King of the Hill?

In 1961, Wilt Chamberlain was the National Basketball Association (NBA) rebounding leader with 27 rebounds per game. In 1992, the colorful Dennis Rodman won the same honor with 18.7 rebounds per game. Common sense suggests that professional basketball in the 1990's is played at a much higher level than in the 1960's. So why have the rebounding leader's number fallen? Is it another case of "less is more"?

Researchers investigating this interesting puzzle considered two other variables: the number of rebounding opportunities (this had gone down since the field goal percentage has increased historically) and the average number of minutes played per game, which has also fallen.

Continued...

Suppose a group of high technology stocks has an average earnings per share of $6.26, with a standard deviation of $1.37. If the data possesses a bell-shaped distribution, which interval contains 68% of the earnings? Which interval contains 95% of the earnings?

Solution

Using the one sigma rule, we will capture 68% of the observations.

$$\mu \pm 1 \cdot \sigma = \$6.26 \pm \$1.37$$

Using the one sigma rule results in an interval from $6.26 - $1.37 to $6.26 + $1.37. Doing the arithmetic produces an interval from $4.89 to $7.63.

To capture 95% of the earnings, use the two sigma rule, $6.26 \pm 2 \cdot $1.37. Doing the arithmetic results in an interval from $3.52 to $9.00.

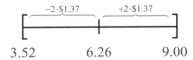

Note that to increase the percentage of data captured from 68% to 95% requires an interval that is twice as large.

Chebyshev's Theorem

It is important to remember that *the empirical rule applies only to bell-shaped distributions*. For **any** distribution, regardless of shape, Chebyshev's Theorem may be used, although its results are much more approximate.

Theorem

Chebyshev's Theorem

The proportion of any data set lying within k standard deviations of the mean is at least

$$1 - \frac{1}{k^2}, \text{for } k > 1.$$

For example, if $k = 2$ at least $1 - \frac{1}{2^2} = \frac{3}{4}$ (or 75%) of the data values lie within 2 standard deviations of the mean, for any data set.

Similarly, if $k = 3$ at least $1 - \frac{1}{3^2} = \frac{8}{9}$ (or 88.9%) of the data values lie within 3 standard deviations of the mean, for any data set.

Also note that k does not have to be an integer value. If $k = 1.5$, at least $1 - \frac{1}{1.5^2} = \frac{5}{9}$ (or 55.6%) of the data values will lie within 1.5 standard deviations of the mean, for any data set.

... Continued
Thus, when we adjust the actual rebounds obtained by the rebounding leaders to the number of minutes played and the total number of rebounding opportunities, we see a completely different picture. The adjusted rebound numbers for Chamberlain and Rodman are 35.42 and 51.06 respectively.

Example 4.13

The tuition and fees of colleges and universities distribution histogram for the United States in 2009-2010 is shown below. The mean of the data is $16,442, while the standard deviation is $10,014. What can we conclude from Chebyshev's Theorem using $k = 2$?

Histogram of Tuition and Fees at U.S. Colleges and Universities 2009–2010

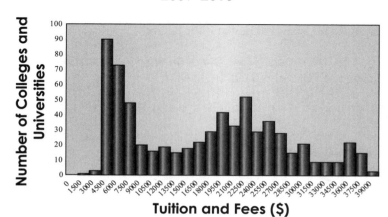

Figure 4.14

Solution

Because we are interested in $k = 2$, we will look at the values two standard deviations above and below the mean.

Two standard deviations above the mean is

$$\mu + 2\sigma = 16422 + 2(10014) = \$36,450$$

and two standard deviations below the mean is

$$\mu - 2\sigma = 16422 - 2(10014) = -\$3,606.$$

Because costs (in this case) cannot be negative, we have a natural boundary, so we will consider this as zero.

Therefore, by Chebyshev's Theorem, we can say that at least 75% of the tuition and fees of colleges and universities in the United States are between $0 and $36,450 for 2009-2010.

4.2 Exercises

Basic Concepts

1. Describe three measures of variation. Discuss the strengths and weaknesses of each.

2. What does the standard deviation measure?

3. Why are the variance and standard deviation more commonly used as measures of variability than the MAD?

4. Explain how the variance can be construed as an average.

5. True or false: The variance and standard deviation are resistant measures.

6. When is it appropriate to calculate the variance of a time series?

7. What is the empirical rule?

8. What is Chebyshev's Theorem?

Exercises

1. Find the missing age in the following set of four student ages.

Table for Exercise 1 – Student Ages		
Student	Age	Deviation from the Mean
A	19	−4
B	20	−3
C	?	+1
D	29	+6

2. Find the missing weight in the following data set.

Table for Exercise 2 – Weights		
Person	Weight	Deviation from the Mean
A	144	−20
B	156	−8
C	?	+1
D	176	+12

3. Consider the following time until failure for 10 randomly selected car batteries (measured in years):

5	3	4	6	2	5	7	10	8	4

   a. Calculate the sample variance of the time until failure.

   b. Calculate the sample standard deviation of the time until failure.

   c. Calculate the range of the time until failure.

   d. What are some of the factors which might contribute to the variation in the observations?

4. Consider the following distances jumped (in feet) by 8 randomly selected long jumpers:

21	15	12	18	10	14	17	11

   a. Calculate the sample variance of the distances jumped.

   b. Calculate the sample standard deviation of the distances jumped.

   c. Calculate the range of the distances jumped.

   d. What are some of the factors which might contribute to the variation in the observations?

5. The interest rates on 30 year mortgages offered by seven randomly selected banks in a large metropolitan area are recorded below.

7.5%	8.0%	7.0%	7.25%	8.5%	8.25%	7.75%

    a. Calculate the sample variance of the interest rates.

    b. Calculate the sample standard deviation of the interest rates.

    c. Calculate the range of the interest rates.

    d. What are some of the factors which might contribute to the variation in the observations?

6. A researcher has hypothesized that female college students are more disciplined than male college students. The researcher believes that a reasonable measure of discipline is performance on a statistics test in terms of both absolute scores and consistency of scores. Seven male statistics students and seven female statistics students are randomly selected and their scores on a statistics test are observed.

Table for Exercise 6 – Test Scores							
Males	65	100	75	45	85	73	95
Females	75	80	95	85	82	72	49

    a. Calculate the average test score for male students and female students separately.

    b. Calculate the variance of the test scores for male students and female students separately.

    c. Calculate the standard deviation of the test scores for male students and female students separately.

    d. Do you think that the data tend to support the hypothesis that female college students are more disciplined than male college students based on the researcher's measurement?

    e. What do you think about this particular measurement of discipline?

7. Consider the following market values of two portfolios of stocks at five randomly selected times during a year.

Table for Exercise 7 – Market Values ($)					
Portfolio A	150,000	155,000	145,000	160,000	140,000
Portfolio B	130,000	175,000	100,000	150,000	195,000

    a. What statistical criteria might you use to select the better portfolio? Justify your answer.

    b. Calculate the statistics you proposed in part (a).

    c. Which portfolio has the least amount of risk? Why?

8. Add 20 to each of the following data values.

81	99	97	81	85	86
99	93	96	83	82	91

    a. Compute the mean and standard deviation for both the original data and adjusted data.

    b. Compare the mean and standard deviation of the adjusted data to the mean and standard deviation of the original data.

    c. Describe the effect on the mean and standard deviation of adding a constant to a data set.

9. Adjust the following data values by subtracting 20 from each data value.

745	789	712	764	736
758	722	773	751	741

    a. Calculate the mean and variance for the original and adjusted data.

    b. Compare the mean and variance of the adjusted data to the mean and the variance of the original data.

    c. Describe the effect of subtracting a constant value from each member of a data set on the mean and variance of the data.

10. The average score on a pre-employment test is 26 with a standard deviation of 7. Using Chebyshev's Theorem, state the range in which at least 88.89% of the data will reside.

11. The daily average number of phone calls to a call center is 972 with a standard deviation of 127. Using Chebyshev's Theorem, state the range in which at least 75% of the data will reside.

12. There is an annual chowder eating contest in a small New England town. The average amount of chowder eaten at the contest was 32 ounces with a variance of 64 ounces. Given that one hundred people participated in the contest, find:

    a. the approximate number of people who ate between 24 and 40 ounces of chowder.

    b. the approximate number of people who ate between 16 and 48 ounces of chowder.

    c. What assumptions did you make about the amount of chowder eaten by each contestant in answering parts (a) and (b)?

13. The manager of a local diner has calculated his average daily sales to be $4500 with a standard deviation of $750.

   a. In what range can the manager expect his daily sales to be 68% of the time?

   b. In what range can the manager expect his daily sales to be 95% of the time?

   c. In what range can the manager expect his daily sales to be 99.7% of the time?

   d. What assumption did you make about daily sales when answering parts (a), (b), and (c)?

14. A management consulting firm is evaluating the salary structure for a large insurance company. The goal of the study is to develop salary ranges for each of the possible job grades within the company. The company and the firm have agreed that a reasonable salary range for each job grade can be determined by finding the salary range in which 95% of the current salaries for that job grade fall. The average salary and the standard deviation of the salaries are listed in the table below for three of the job grades.

Table for Exercise 14 – Salaries			
Job Grade	**25**	**33**	**40**
$\overline{x}$	$22,000	$35,000	$45,000
s	$1500	$2000	$5000

   a. Determine the appropriate salary ranges for the three job grades.

   b. What assumption did you make about the salaries in each of the job grades in answering part (a)?

Measures of Relative Position

Suppose you want to know where an observation stands in relation to other values in a data set. For example, on many standardized tests such as the SAT, GMAT, and ACT, the test scores themselves are rather meaningless unless they are associated with some measure that tells you how well you did relative to others taking the same test. There are two principal methods of communicating relative position: percentiles and z-scores. Both of these methods are data transformations which change the scale of the data in some way.

Percentiles

The most commonly used measure of relative position is the percentile. In fact, we have already discussed the 50th percentile; it is the median. For example, in data sets that do not contain significant quantities of identical data, the 30th percentile is a value such that about 30 percent of the values are below it, and around 70 percent are above it.

Definition

Given a set of data $x_1, x_2, ..., x_n$, the Pth **percentile** is a value, say X, such that approximately P percent of the data is less than or equal to X and approximately $(100 - P)$ percent of the data is greater than or equal to X.

P^{th} Percentile

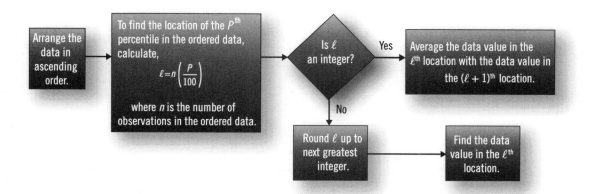

Finding the Pth Percentile

To determine the Pth percentile, perform the following steps.

Procedure

Calculating the Pth Percentile

1. Form an ordered array by placing the data in order from smallest to largest.

2. To find the location of the Pth percentile in the ordered array, let

$$\ell = n\left(\frac{P}{100}\right)$$

where n is the number of observations in the ordered data.

3. If ℓ is not an integer, then round ℓ up to the next greatest integer. For example, if $\ell = 7.1$, then round ℓ up to 8 and find the data value in the ℓth location. If ℓ is an integer value, then average the data value in the ℓth location with the data value in the $(\ell + 1)^{th}$ location.

Interpreting Percentiles

When students take the SAT Reasoning Test, they receive a copy of their scores as well as the percentile they fall into. This percentile can sometimes be confusing. If a student receives a score of 620 on the verbal section, they might fall into the 84th percentile. This means that they received a higher score than 84 percent of the students. The same score on the math section might place the student into the 80th percentile. Receiving a score of 800 on verbal or math will put the student in the 99th percentile. This means that less than 1 percent of the students taking the SAT had the same score.

It is important to remember that when you find the value of ℓ, this result is <u>not</u> the percentile. It is the location of the percentile in the ordered array. Thus, if the result of calculating (and rounding up) ℓ is 15, then the desired percentile would be the fifteenth value in the ordered list.

Example 4.14

Find the 50th percentile for the following data set.

$$3, 5, 0, 1, 9, 2, 7$$

Solution

Number of observations, $n = 7$.

The percentile, $P = 50$.

The location of the percentile, $\ell = 7 \cdot \left(\frac{50}{100}\right) = 3.5$.

Since the location of the percentile is not an integer, the value is rounded up to 4.

Thus, the fourth observation in the ordered array is the 50th percentile.

$$0, \quad 1, \quad 2, \quad \boxed{3}, \quad 5, \quad 7, \quad 9$$
$$\underbrace{}_{\text{fourth observation}}$$

Therefore, the median value (which is the 50th percentile) is 3.

Example 4.15

Suppose the 40 members of your company are given a screening test for a new position. These scores are reported in Table 4.12. To inform potential employees of their screening test performance you may wish to report various percentiles for the test scores. Find the 10th and 88th percentiles for the test.

Table 4.12 – Test Scores			
67	45	18	82
45	54	61	55
63	47	21	31
58	46	43	49
35	71	69	56
54	80	73	77
27	70	41	29
66	32	44	33
21	64	52	81
48	55	57	62

Table 4.13 – Ordered Test Scores			
18	43	54	66
21	44	55	67
21	45	55	69
27	45	56	70
29	46	57	71
31	47	58	73
32	48	61	77
33	49	62	80
34	52	63	81
41	54	64	82

Solution

In order to calculate the percentiles, the data must be placed in an ordered array (Table 4.13). To compute the 10th percentile, its position in the ordered array must be determined.

The number of observations, $n = 40$.

The percentile, $P = 10$.

The location of the percentile, $\ell = 40 \cdot \left(\dfrac{10}{100} \right) = 4$. Since ℓ is an integer, the 4th and 5th observations in the array must be averaged. Since the fourth data value is 27 and the fifth data value is 29, then the

$$10^{th} \text{ percentile} = \frac{27 + 29}{2} = 28.$$

To determine the 88th percentile, first calculate its location in the ordered array:

$$\ell = 40 \cdot \left(\frac{88}{100} \right) = 35.2.$$

Since the location is not an integer, its value is rounded up to 36. The 36th observation in the ordered array will correspond to the 88th percentile. The 36th value is 73 in Table 4.13, so 73 is the 88th percentile.

A slightly different problem connected with percentiles involves taking a raw score and determining its corresponding percentile. Raw scores are usually not very meaningful. If someone scores a 56 on the screening test in the previous example, is that substantially less or about the same as someone who scored a 67 on the same test? To compare these two scores find the percentile of each.

Formula

The **percentile** of some data value x is given by:

$$\text{percentile of } x = \frac{\text{number of data values less than or equal to } x}{\text{total number of data values}} \cdot 100$$

Note that when finding the percentile of a specific value, if there are multiple occurrences of that value in the data, they all need to be counted in the numerator in order to calculate the percentile. To determine the percentile for a score of 56, the number of data values less than or equal to 56 must be counted. Since there are 24 data values less than or equal to 56, the resulting percentile would be

$$\text{percentile of a score of } 56 = \frac{24}{40} \cdot 100 = 60.$$

Hence a score of 56 on the screening test corresponds to the 60th percentile. Thus, 60 percent of the scores are less than or equal to 56. Next, compute the percentile for a score of 67:

$$\text{percentile of a score of } 67 = \frac{32}{40} \cdot 100 = 80.$$

A score of 67 on the screening test corresponds to the 80th percentile. The score was better than or equal to 80 percent of all other scores on the test. By computing percentiles, we have changed the data's scaling. We see the data from a new perspective. Using percentiles, it is clear that a score of 67 is significantly better than a score of 56. The 11 point difference in raw score is translated into a 20 percent differential on the percentile scale.

Quartiles

The 25th, 50th, and 75th percentiles are known as **quartiles** and are denoted as Q_1, Q_2, and Q_3. They serve as markers that divide the data into four equal parts. Q_1 separates the lowest 25 percent, Q_2 represents the median (50th percentile), and Q_3 marks the beginning of the top 25 percent of the data.

Since quartiles are nothing more than percentiles (25th, 50th, and 75th), the same methods used to calculate percentiles will also produce quartiles. For the screening test data in the previous example, the location of the 25th percentile would be

$$\ell = 40 \cdot \left(\frac{25}{100}\right) = 10.$$

Since the location is an integer, we average the 10th and 11th observations in the ordered data to find the 25th percentile.

$$Q_1 = 25^{th} \text{ percentile} = \frac{41+43}{2} = 42.$$

Therefore, we would expect 25 percent of the data to be less than or equal to 42.

The location of the 50th percentile is given by

$$\ell = 40 \cdot \left(\frac{50}{100}\right) = 20.$$

Since the location is an integer, we must average the 20th and 21st observations in order to calculate the percentile.

$$Q_2 = 50^{th} \text{ percentile} = \frac{54+54}{2} = 54,$$

which means approximately half the data is at or below 54.

The location of the 75th percentile is given by

$$\ell = 40 \cdot \left(\frac{75}{100}\right) = 30.$$

Since the location is an integer, average the 30th and 31st observations in the ordered array.

$$Q_3 = 75^{th} \text{ percentile} = \frac{64+66}{2} = 65$$

The quartiles are useful descriptions of data. They provide a good idea of how the data varies.

The Zen of Statistics

Douglas Hofstadter in his book *Gödel, Escher, Bach* describes Zen as an attitude in which words and truth are incompatible, or at least that no words can capture truth. If we think of the collected data as truth, statistics is a language whose "words" are pictures and numerical measures which seek to describe that "truth." Despite our best efforts, the statistical language suffers from the same inadequacies as our own language. We ignore the totality of the data in order to summarize it. There is a trade off – the loss of the "truth" for a better understanding.

Definition

The **interquartile range** is a measure of dispersion which describes the range of the middle fifty percent of the data.

Interquartile Range

For the screening test data, the interquartile range is $65 - 42 = 23$, indicating that the middle 50 percent of the data spans a 23 unit range.

Box Plots – Graphing with Quartiles

A very important use of quartiles is in the construction of box plots. As the name implies, box plots are graphical summaries of the data which, when constructed, have a box-like shape. They provide an alternative method to the histogram for displaying data. A **box plot** is a graphical summary of the central tendency, the spread, the skewness, and the potential existence of outliers in the data. Figure 4.15 displays a box plot of the screening data from Example 4.15.

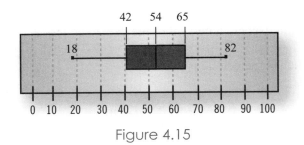

Figure 4.15

The box plot is constructed from five summary measures: the largest data value, the smallest data value, the 25th percentile, the 75th percentile, and the median.

The lower boundary of the box is the 25th percentile, which is 42 for the screening test data. The upper boundary of the box is the 75th percentile, which is 65 for the screening test data. The median is marked with a line through the box. The median of the test scores data is 54. Notice that the box itself represents the middle 50% of the data, and the length of the box is the interquartile range.

In Figure 4.15, a line is drawn from the 25th percentile to the smallest test score of 18, and another line is drawn from the 75th percentile to the largest score of 82. These lines are often referred to as whiskers and the box plot is often referred to as the box and whisker plot. The box plot for the screening test scores shows that the test score data are slightly skewed to the left. Why? Because the whisker extending from Q_1 appears to be longer than the whisker that extends from Q_3.

Although the box plot can be used to display data for a single data set, the histogram is probably more useful for this purpose. The real power of the box plot is the ease with which it allows the comparison of several data sets. Consider the number of wins per season for the New York Yankees, Los Angeles Dodgers, Atlanta Braves, and Chicago Cubs. The four data sets are displayed by box plots in Figure 4.16. It is easy to see from the box plots that the center of the Yankees' number of wins is higher than that for the Dodgers which has a higher center than the center of Braves, and finally the Cubs. Also it appears that the spread of the data or the variation within the observed values is not the same for all four data sets. This type of comparison will be used in later chapters to help confirm assumptions which must be made about the data in order to perform statistical inference.

Box Plots of the Number of Franchise Wins per Season 1961–2010

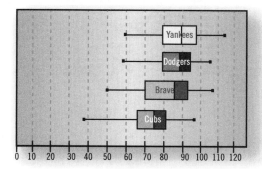

Figure 4.16

Detecting Outliers

The concept of an outlier is an arbitrary concept. What you consider an outlier and what someone else considers an outlier may not be the same thing. However, one definition of an outlier which has gained some acceptance is developed in the context of a box plot.

Definition

A data point is considered an **outlier** if it is 1.5 times the interquartile range above the 75th percentile or 1.5 times the interquartile range below the 25th percentile.

Outlier

If there is an outlier in the data set, the whiskers are drawn to the largest or smallest data point which is within 1.5 times the interquartile range from the box, and the outliers are marked with an open circle. For example, suppose test scores of 110 and 2 were added to the screening test data.

Table 4.14 – New Test Scores			
67	45	18	82
45	54	61	55
63	47	21	31
58	46	43	49
35	71	69	56
54	80	73	77
27	70	41	29
66	32	44	33
21	64	52	81
48	55	57	62
110	2		

Table 4.15 – Ordered New Test Scores			
2	43	55	67
18	44	55	69
21	45	56	70
21	45	57	71
27	46	58	73
29	47	61	77
31	48	62	80
32	49	63	81
33	52	64	82
34	54	66	110
41	54		

Baseball Players, Better or Worse?

In the history of Major League Baseball (MLB), the last time someone had a batting average above .400 was Ted Williams in 1941. Before that, Ty Cobb had hit .420 in 1911.

Finally, in 1980 George Brett came close but hit only .390. From this it appears that with time hitting for high averages is becoming more difficult. Is this then evidence of progress or lack of progress? The late evolutionary biologist Stephen Jay Gould, himself an avid baseball fan, had an interesting statistical angle to this riddle. He computed and observed: (1) The yearly batting averages have remained more or less stable (around .267) over the history of the league.

Continued ...

z-Score

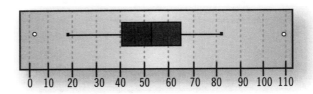

Figure 4.17

Since 110 is larger than 103.5, it is considered an outlier. Since 2 is smaller than 3.5, it is also considered an outlier. Figure 4.17 shows the box plot of the screening test data with the outliers incorporated. Notice that the whiskers did not change because 82 and 18 are still the largest and smallest observations within 1.5 times the interquartile range from the box.

For the new screening test data, a point is considered an outlier if the data point is

- Larger than the 75th percentile + 1.5 times the interquartile range

$$= 66 + 1.5 \cdot 25 = 103.5$$

- Smaller than the 25th percentile + 1.5 times the interquartile range

$$= 41 - 1.5 \cdot 25 = 3.5$$

z-Scores

The **z-score** is a standardized measure of relative position, with respect to the mean and variability (as measured by the standard deviation) of the data set.

Formula

The **z-score** transforms a data value into the number of standard deviations that value is from the mean.

$$z = \frac{x - \mu}{\sigma}$$

Describing a data value by its number of standard deviations from the mean is a fundamental concept in statistics that is found throughout this book. It is used as a standardization technique to describe properties of data sets and to compare the relative values of data from different data sets.

Example 4.16

Suppose you scored an 86 on your marketing test and a 94 on your management test. The mean and standard deviations of the two tests are given below:

Table 4.16 – Test Scores

Course	Mean	Standard Deviation
Marketing	74	10
Management	82	11

What are the z-scores for your two tests? On which of the tests did you perform relatively better?

Solution

The z-score for the marketing test is $z = \dfrac{86 - 74}{10} = 1.2$.

The z-score for the management test is $z = \dfrac{94 - 82}{11} = 1.09$.

On the marketing test you scored 1.2 standard deviations above the mean, compared to only 1.09 standard deviations above the mean for the management test. Even though the raw score on the management test is larger than the raw score on the marketing test, relative to the mean of the data sets, the performance on the marketing test was slightly better. Once again, changing the scale of the data has beneficial effects. It enables the comparison of two measurements that are drawn from different populations.

If a z-score is negative, the data value is less than the mean. Conversely, if the z-score is positive, the data value is greater than the mean. The z-score is also a unit free measure. That is, regardless of the original units of measurement (whether the data are measured in centimeters, meters, or kilometers), an observation's z-score will be the same.

... Continued

(2) The annual standard deviations have declined steadily over the same period. (3) Finally, the yearly batting averages are all normally distributed. Gould then computed the z-scores for all three players and observed they were all well above 4.0. His conclusion: Hitting has improved since the standard deviations of the averages are getting smaller.

The best hitters are still at the fence of the normal distribution and are the best of their times. Therefore, as a result of the decline in standard deviation, the apparent decrease in batting average (disappearance of .400 hitters) is actually a sign of improvement! Less can actually be more in some situations!

Exercises

Basic Concepts

1. What are two methods for describing relative position?

2. If a data value is calculated to be the 72nd percentile, what does this mean?

3. Describe how to find the percentile of a particular data value.

4. What are quartiles? Are they equivalent to percentiles? If so, how?

5. What is the interquartile range? What does it measure?

6. What are the advantages of using a box plot to display a data set?

7. What are the key calculations needed in order to construct a box plot?

8. What is an outlier? How can they be identified?

9. What is a z-score? Why is it useful?

Exercises

1. The following test scores were recorded for an economics final examination.

60	81	100	44	90	56	71	42	64	100	69	80	90	87	94
41	78	100	50	96	77	61	38	41	68	50	69	85	47	86

   a. Calculate the 20th percentile.
   b. Calculate the 95th percentile.
   c. Interpret the meaning of each of these percentiles.
   d. Determine the percentile rank for the student who scored 56.
   e. Determine the percentile rank for the student who scored 80.

2. Copiers Etc. collects data on the number of copiers sold each day by each salesperson. The number of copiers sold for each salesperson for a small office on a randomly selected day is listed below.

1	5	2	3	7	6	1	0	0	3	4	5

   a. What level of measurement does the data possess?
   b. Calculate the 25th percentile.
   c. Calculate the 90th percentile.
   d. Interpret the meaning of each of these percentiles.
   e. Determine the percentile rank for the salesperson who sold 5 copiers.
   f. Determine the percentile rank for the salesperson who sold 1 copier.

3. Subjects in a marketing study were shown a film and at the end of the film were given a test to measure their recall. The scores are listed below.

97	31	61	49	61	85	35	57	31	26	27	40	86	78	28
61	87	62	92	58	38	95	81	68	64	72	45	57	84	100

   a. Calculate Q_1, the first quartile.

   b. Calculate Q_2, the second quartile.

   c. Calculate Q_3, the third quartile.

   d. Explain the meaning of these quartiles in the context of the marketing study.

   e. Calculate the interquartile range.

   f. Construct a box plot for the test scores. Are there any outliers?

   g. Compute the z-score for a test score of 81.

   h. Compute the z-score for a test score of 62.

   i. Explain what the z-scores in parts (g) and (h) are measuring.

4. A baseball recruiter is interested in 20 perspective players. He goes to several games and determines the batting average for each player. The batting averages are displayed below.

.330	.260	.180	.150	.200	.400	.020	.190	.290	.200
.170	.150	.250	.270	.320	.280	.270	.220	.270	.300

   a. Calculate Q_1, the first quartile.

   b. Calculate Q_2, the second quartile.

   c. Calculate Q_3, the third quartile.

   d. Explain the meaning of these quartiles in the context of the batting averages.

   e. Calculate the interquartile range.

   f. Construct a box plot for the batting averages. Are there any outliers? (Guess which player is the pitcher.)

   g. Compute the z-score for a batting average of .020.

   h. Compute the z-score for a batting average of .330.

   i. Explain what the z-scores in parts (g) and (h) are measuring.

   j. Determine the percentile rank for a player who had a batting average of .270.

   k. Determine the percentile rank for a player who had a batting average of .150.

5. Consider a set of data in which the sample mean is 64 and the sample standard deviation is 21. For the following specific values, calculate the z-score and interpret the results.

    a. $x = 80$

    b. $x = 64$

    c. $x = 40$

6. A statistics student scored a 75 on the first exam of the semester and an 82 on the second exam of the semester. The average score and standard deviation of scores for the two exams are given below. On which exam did the student perform relatively better?

Table for Exercise 6 – Test Scores		
	First Exam	Second Exam
$\bar{x}$	74	85
s	10	7

7. A hospital measures babies' heights when they are born in both inches and centimeters. Eight baby girls are randomly selected and the following heights are recorded in both inches and centimeters.

Table for Exercise 7 – Newborn Heights								
Baby	1	2	3	4	5	6	7	8
Inches	17.75	18.50	19.25	19.75	20.25	20.50	20.50	20.75
Centimeters	45.09	46.99	48.90	50.17	51.44	52.07	52.07	52.71

    a. Calculate the average height in inches and centimeters for the baby girls.

    b. Calculate the standard deviation of the heights of baby girls in both inches and centimeters.

    c. Calculate the z-score for the height of Baby Girl 3 measured in inches.

    d. For Baby Girl 3, calculate the z-score for the height measured in centimeters.

    e. Consider the z-scores calculated in parts (c) and (d). Are the z-scores as you expected them to be? Explain.

4.4 Data Subsetting

Looking at the tuition data presented in Example 4.13 with a histogram using fewer intervals gives a slightly different picture. Figure 4.18 provides some idea about **location** and **dispersion** of the data, but nothing specific. Histograms are outstanding at defining the **shape** of the data.

Where is the Central Value of the Tuition Data?

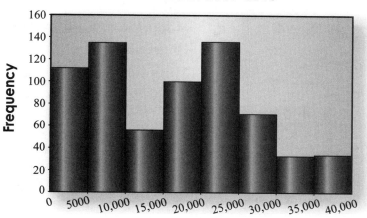

Tuition Data in 2009-2010

Cost of a Year's Tuition ($)

Figure 4.18

There are several measurements that can be used to describe the location or central value of the tuition data. The mode is not considered because the data are quantitative and because there are a large number of observations. Moreover, the mode is not a very informative measure of central tendency. Since the median of the data ($17,468) is substantially larger than the mean ($16,442) or trimmed mean ($16,087), the choice will make a difference. The graph suggests a somewhat multi-modal distribution given the large chunks of data between $0 and $10,000 and from $15,000 to $25,000.

Since the trimmed mean is roughly the same as the mean, the lack of outliers seems to be confirmed. Which one of the three candidate measurements should be considered as the central value of the data?

The choice is not easy. You are justified in selecting any of the three statistical measures. However, because of the difference between the median and the other two measures, reporting two measures (the mean and median) would not be a bad idea. If only one measure is reported, identify the measure as the mean or the median rather than the average. The term "average" is a bit too ambiguous in current usage.

Describing Dispersion of the Tuition Data

Several measurements which assess variation have been discussed, including variance, standard deviation, mean absolute deviation, and percentiles. Since the variance and standard deviation are different forms of the same measurement, usually only the standard deviation is reported. For the tuition data, a reasonable description of dispersion for the 677 values would be given by the following statistics.

Table 4.17 – Tuition Data	
Location Measurement	Value
Mean	$16,442
Median	$17,468
10% Trimmed Mean	$16,087

Standard Deviation: $10,014

Minimum: $790

First Quartile (Q_1): $6,049

Median (Second Quartile, Q_2): $17,468

Third Quartile (Q_3): $23,800

Maximum: $38,140

Table 4.18 – Tuition Data Percentiles	
Percentile	Value
100th	$38,140
95th	$35,015
90th	$29,982
75th	$23,800
50th	$17,468
25th	$6,049
10th	$4,166
5th	$3,558
0	$790

The histogram in Figure 4.18 reveals an interesting characteristic of the data. There appear to be two distinct groups of values: a bundle of data between $0 and $10,000, and another bundle of data between $15,000 and $25,000. What might be responsible for the clustering? We could be looking at the difference between state supported institutions and private institutions. This supposition could be checked rather easily if the data are divided (subsetted) into private and state supported schools.

The original data contained the annual tuition costs of private and state funded institutions. In-state tuition was used for the state supported schools. The structure of a batch of data is often exposed by using another variable to break the data in smaller groups. This is called **subsetting**. A natural structuring of the tuition data is a grouping of private and state supported institutions.

**State Supported Institutions
(*n* = 231):**

Mean Tuition: $5,396

Median Tuition: $5,177

Trimmed Mean Tuition: $5,232

Standard Deviation: $1,864

Q_1 = $3,995

Q_3 = $6,162

Minimum: $2,685

Maximum: $12,844

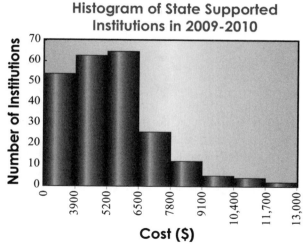

Figure 4.19

**Private Institutions
(*n* = 446):**

Mean Tuition: $22,163

Median Tuition: $21,630

Trimmed Mean Tuition:
$22,174

Standard Deviation: $7,376

Q_1 = $17,650

Q_3 = $26,468

Minimum: $790

Maximum: $38,140

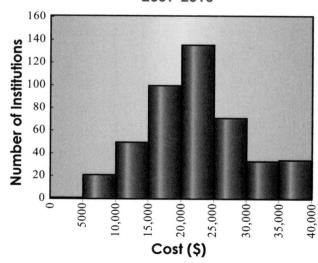

Figure 4.20

The data subsetting suggests that the data clustering revealed in the histogram in Figure 4.18 is the result of merging data from different kinds of educational institutions. Once the data are subsetted, the strong bimodal nature of the data disappears. For private institutions the majority of the values tend to cluster in the middle. However, for state supported institutions, it appears that the data are positively skewed with many values clustered to the left of the mean tuition and fees. The data tells quite an interesting story. From a tuition point of view, state supported schools are substantially less expensive than private schools. There is roughly a $17,000 average annual tuition difference between private colleges and in-state tuition at state supported schools.

Another data characteristic should stimulate our interest. One of the data points for private school tuition is $790. Is this a mistake? The z-score for this data point is

$$z = \frac{790 - 22163}{7376} = -2.90$$

which would indicate the point may be an outlier. Any point 2.90 standard deviations from the mean is worth investigating. In this case the school is Berea College in Berea, KY, which awards every student a 4-year tuition scholarship.

 **Exercises**

Basic Concepts

1. Describe the purpose of data subsetting.

2. Describe a data set where data subsetting should be implemented. What are the disadvantages of not subsetting the data?

 **The Coefficient of Variation**

The **coefficient of variation**, another statistical measure, compares the variation in data sets. For population data, the measure is defined as

$$CV = \left(\frac{\sigma}{\mu} \cdot 100\right) \%,$$

and for a sample,

$$CV = \left(\frac{s}{\bar{x}} \cdot 100\right) \%.$$

When comparing the variation of data sets, many times the units of measure will be different. The coefficient of variation standardizes the variation measure by dividing it by the mean. The division has one interesting side effect: the unit of measure is removed from the statistic.

$$CV_{private} = \frac{\$7376}{\$22163} \cdot 100\% = 33.28\%$$

$$CV_{public} = \frac{\$1864}{\$5396} \cdot 100\% = 34.54\%$$

The coefficient of variation for the private tuition data is 33.28% of the mean value. The group with the largest variation relative to the mean is the in-state tuitions. Their variation is 34.54% of the mean. Using the criterion of variation relative to the mean, the data set with the smallest absolute variation $(s = \$1864)$ has the largest relative variation.

 **Exercises**

Basic Concepts

1. Discuss the purpose of the coefficient of variation.

2. How is the coefficient of variation calculated?

3. Why is the coefficient of variation important?

Exercises

1. A consumer interest group is interested in comparing two brands of vitamin C. One brand of vitamin C advertises that its tablets contain 500mg of vitamin C. The other brand advertises that its tablets contain 250 mg of vitamin C. Tablets for each brand are randomly selected and the milligrams of vitamin C for each tablet are measured with the following results.

Table for Exercise 1 – Vitamin C Content		
	Brand A (500mg)	Brand B (250mg)
$\bar{x}$	500 mg	250 mg
s	10 mg	7 mg

   a. Calculate the coefficient of variation for Brand A.

   b. Calculate the coefficient of variation for Brand B.

   c. Which brand more consistently produces tablets as advertised? Explain.

2. A manufacturer of bolts has two different machines. One machine is used to produce $\frac{1}{4}$ inch bolts; the other machine is used to produce $\frac{1}{2}$ inch bolts. It is very important that the machines consistently produce bolts of the correct diameters, or the bolts will not fit on the corresponding nuts. In order to compare the two machines, management randomly selects bolts produced from each machine and computes the average diameter of the bolts and the standard deviation of the bolts. The results of the study are shown in the table below.

Table for Exercise 2 – Bolt Diameter		
	Machine X $\left(\frac{1"}{4}\right)$	Machine Y $\left(\frac{1"}{2}\right)$
$\bar{x}$	.25"	.50"
s	.03"	.05"

   a. Calculate the coefficient of variation for Machine X.

   b. Calculate the coefficient of variation for Machine Y.

   c. Which machine more consistently produces bolts of the correct diameter? Explain.

4.6 Analyzing Grouped Data

All of the statistical measurements we have discussed so far presume that raw data measurements are readily available. However, there may be instances in which only a frequency distribution of the data is available. When data is presented in that form, it is called **grouped data**. It is important to be able to compute measures such as the mean and variance for this type of data. Because the raw data observations are not available, the measures will be approximate.

Finding the Mean and Variance of Grouped Data

The strategy for finding the mean of grouped data involves finding the midpoint of each of the classes in the frequency distribution and then weighting each of these midpoints by the number of observations in the class. To develop the measure, several symbols must be defined. Let

f_i = number of observations in the ith class and

N = the total number of observations in all classes, $N = \sum f_i$, and

M_i = midpoint of the ith class.

The mean of the grouped data is given by

$$\mu = \frac{\sum (f_i M_i)}{N}.$$

If the grouped data represent sample observations, then the symbol changes for the mean but the measure is the same. The sample mean of grouped data is given by the expression

$$\bar{x} = \frac{\sum (f_i M_i)}{n},$$

where n is the number of observations in the sample.

The variance of grouped data is given by the expression

$$\sigma^2 = \frac{\sum (f_i M_i^2) - \dfrac{\left(\sum (f_i M_i)\right)^2}{N}}{N} = \frac{\sum (f_i M_i^2)}{N} - \left(\frac{\sum (f_i M_i)}{N}\right)^2.$$

The corresponding formula for the sample variance is:

$$s^2 = \frac{\sum\left(f_i M_i^2\right) - \dfrac{\left(\sum\left(f_i M_i\right)\right)^2}{n}}{n-1}$$

where n equals the total number of observations in the sample.

Example 4.17

Table 4.19 presents, in grouped form, the amount of cash on hand for 45 technology companies in the business software and services industry. To compute the mean and variance, the midpoints of each interval must be calculated. The class midpoint is given by

$$\text{midpoint} = \frac{\text{lower class boundary} + \text{upper class boundary}}{2}.$$

The midpoints as well as the other required calculations are presented in Table 4.20.

Table 4.19 – Cash on Hand for Technology Companies	
Cash on Hand (Millions of Dollars)	Frequency
0 – 10	10
10 – 20	7
20 – 30	7
30 – 40	7
40 – 50	1
50 – 60	4
60 – 70	2
70 – 80	2
80 – 90	2
90 – 100	3

Table 4.20 – Midpoints and Other Required Calculations					
Cash on Hand (Millions of Dollars)	Midpoint M_i	Frequency f_i	$f_i \cdot M_i$	M_i^2	$f_i \cdot M_i^2$
0 – 10	5	10	50	25	250
10 – 20	15	7	105	225	1575
20 – 30	25	7	175	625	4375
30 – 40	35	7	245	1225	8575
40 – 50	45	1	45	2025	2025
50 – 60	55	4	220	3025	12100
60 – 70	65	2	130	4225	8450
70 – 80	75	2	150	5625	11250
80 – 90	85	2	170	7225	14450
90 – 100	95	3	285	9025	27075
Totals		45	1575	33250	90125

Assuming the data in Table 4.19 are population data, the mean cash on hand for the 45 companies is:

$$\mu = \frac{\sum (f_i M_i)}{N} = \frac{1575}{45} = \$35 \text{ million.}$$

The variance of the grouped data is:

$$\sigma^2 = \frac{\sum (f_i M_i^2) - \dfrac{\left(\sum (f_i M_i)\right)^2}{N}}{N}$$

$$= \frac{90125 - \dfrac{1575^2}{45}}{45} = 777.78.$$

If the data are sample data, then the variance is:

$$s^2 = \frac{\sum (f_i M_i^2) - \dfrac{\left(\sum (f_i M_i)\right)^2}{n}}{n-1}$$

$$= \frac{90125 - \dfrac{1575^2}{45}}{44} = 795.45.$$

It is important to remember that the calculations of the mean and variance are approximate. That is, if the raw data are available, the actual mean and variance would differ from the measures calculated using the grouped data.

4.6   Exercises

Basic Concepts

1. When analyzing grouped data, are the measurements exact? Why or why not?

2. What calculations are required in order to analyze grouped data?

Exercises

1. A client of a commercial rose grower has been keeping records on the shelf-life of a rose. The client sent the frequency distribution to the grower. Calculate the mean and variance for the shelf-life given the following frequency distribution.

Table for Exercise 1 – Rose Shelf-Life	
Days of Shelf-Life	Frequency
1 – 6	2
7 – 12	3
13 – 18	9
19 – 24	6
25 – 30	3
31 – 36	1

2. An article in *Business Week* discussed the large spread between the federal funds rate and the average credit card rate. The table below is a frequency distribution of the credit card rate charged by the top 100 issuers. Note that at the time these figures were published the average federal funds rate was well below 5%.

Table for Exercise 2 – Credit Card Rates	
Credit Card Rate	**Frequency**
19% – 24%	36
18% – 18.9%	8
17% – 17.9%	15
16% – 16.9%	12
15% – 15.9%	29

a. Calculate the average credit card rate charged by the top 100 issuers based on the frequency distribution.

b. Calculate the variance of the credit card rate charged by the top 100 issuers based on the frequency distribution.

c. Calculate the standard deviation of the credit card rate charged by the top 100 issuers based on the frequency distribution.

4.7 Proportions

The **proportion** is one of the more common summary measures.

Proportion

Definition

A **proportion** measures the fraction of a group that possesses some characteristic.

To calculate a proportion, simply count the number in the group that possess the characteristic and divide the count by the total number in the group. Let

X = number of observations that possess the characteristic,

N = number of observations in the population,

n = number of observations in the sample, then

$$p = \frac{X}{N} = \text{ the population proportion, and}$$

$$\hat{p} = \frac{X}{n} = \text{ the sample proportion.}$$

The symbol $\hat{p}$ is pronounced *p-hat*.

Example 4.18

Suppose your statistics class is composed of 48 students of which 4 are left-handed. What proportion of the class is left-handed?

Solution

There are 48 pieces of data in the class. Think of data as composed of 0s and 1s. Any left-handed person will be a 1, and any right-handed person will be a 0. In our data set, there will be four 1s and forty-four 0s.

$$\text{Assuming } x = \begin{cases} 1 \text{ if person is left-handed} \\ 0 \text{ if person is right-handed} \end{cases}$$

$$\text{then } \sum x = 1+1+1+1+0+0+...+0 = 4.$$

In the notation we used earlier, X equals the number of observations that possess the characteristic. Therefore,

$$X = \sum x = 4, \text{ and}$$

$$p = \frac{X}{N} = \frac{4}{48} = .083.$$

Thus 8.3% of people in the class are left-handed.

Note that we are using p, the population proportion in this case because we are considering the population of students in your statistics class. If we were using the data from your statistics class to estimate the proportion of all statistics students that are left-handed, we would use the symbol $\hat{p}$, the sample proportion, since we would then be computing the proportion from sample data.

Example 4.19

Suppose you have been playing softball and have kept records on each plate appearance. According to your records you have batted 216 times. Of these 216 plate appearances, you have walked 24 times, gotten on base by a fielding error 7 times, and reached base on a hit 64 times. Let's compute your batting average, which is a proportion. The batting average is the proportion of times you reached base on a hit, excluding walks and errors. In this case the number in the group of at bats we will consider is

$$N = \text{Plate appearances} - \text{Walks} - \text{Bases by fielding errors}$$
$$= 216 - 24 - 7$$
$$= 185 \text{ at bats.}$$

The proportion of times you got a hit (excluding walks and errors) is

$$p = \frac{64}{185} = .346.$$

Hence your batting average is .346.

This chapter has been devoted to summarizing data. Yet, with the exception of the mode, none of the summary methods discussed should be applied to nominal data. Using proportions is one of the few summary methods available for analyzing qualitative data.

4.7 Exercises

Basic Concepts

1. What is a proportion?

2. What is the difference in notation between a population proportion and a sample proportion?

3. Other than the mode, proportions are one of the few summary methods available to analyze what type of data?

Exercises

1. A survey of shoppers at the Tech Mall was taken to study the shopping habits of consumers. The mall contains a variety of specialty stores, especially stores that specialize in electronics and gadgets. One question in particular asked, "Do you enjoy shopping for electronics?" Of the 300 men surveyed, 175 answered "Yes." Of the 200 women surveyed, 55 answered "Yes."

   a. What proportion of men enjoy shopping for electronics?

   b. What proportion of women enjoy shopping for electronics?

   c. What is the overall proportion of consumers at the Tech Mall that enjoy shopping for electronics?

2. A survey released in April, 2011 conducted by the consulting firm Booz & Company regarding the automobile industry found that U.S. automotive executives were skeptical about the industry's economic recovery. Suppose that 118 original equipment manufacturers (OEM) and 82 supplier executives participated in the study. When asked whether the overall state of the industry is fairly similar to, or only somewhat better than, its low point in January 2009, 59 OEMs and 28 supplier executives answered that the current state of the industry was "about the same", and 55 OEMs and 52 supplier executives answered that the current state of the industry was "somewhat better". **Source:** Booz & Company; 2011

   a. Calculate the sample proportion of original equipment manufacturers that believe the state of the automobile industry is "about the same" as in January 2009.

   b. Calculate the sample proportion of supplier executives that believe the state of the automobile industry is "about the same" as in January 2009.

   c. Calculate the sample proportion of original equipment manufacturers that believe the state of the automobile industry is "somewhat better" than in January 2009.

d. Calculate the sample proportion of supplier executives that believe the state of the automobile industry is "somewhat better" than that in January 2009.

e. Do these responses seem to support Booz & Company's conclusion that automotive executives are skeptical about the industry's economic recovery? Discuss.

3. An experiment was conducted to study how investors selected mutual funds. Two groups of investors were selected. Group 1 consisted of investors that used online brokerages and Group 2 was made up of investors that used full-service brokerages. Of the 150 investors in Group 1, 120 indicated that they selected mutual funds on their own, while 30 stated that they selected mutual funds using recommendations of the brokerage, family, and friends. Of the 200 investors in Group 2, 25 indicated that they selected their funds on their own, while 175 indicated that they selected the mutual funds using recommendations of the brokerage, family, and friends.

a. What proportion of Group 1 investors selected mutual funds on their own?

b. What proportion of investors in Group 2 selected mutual funds on the recommendation of others?

c. What does this tell you about investors that use online brokerages versus those using full-service brokerages?

4. According to a study administered by the National Bureau of Economic Research, half of Americans would struggle to come up with $2000 in the event of a financial emergency. The majority of the 1900 Americans surveyed said they would rely on more than one method to come up with emergency funds if required. In the survey, 532 people said that they "certainly" would not be able to cope with an unexpected $2000 bill if they had to come up with the money in 30 days, and 418 people said they "probably" would not be able to cope. **Source**: CNNMoney.com; 2011

a. What percentage of Americans "certainly" would not be able to produce $2000 in the event of an emergency according to the study?

b. What percentage of Americans would "probably" not be able to pay a $2000 bill in 30 days if required?

c. What does this say about the savings habits of Americans?

5. What college football conference has the right to brag about putting players in the NFL? A random sample of 100 current NFL players was surveyed to determine the conference in which they played college football. The table below displays the results of the survey.

Table for Exercise 5 – NFL Players and College Football Conferences	
Conference	**Number of Players**
SEC	20
Big 12	16
Big 10	12
Pac 10	6
ACC	6
MAC	2
Big East	2
Other	36

a. What proportion of players are from the SEC?

b. What proportion of players are from a conference other than the first 6 listed?

c. Is it true that a player in the SEC has a better chance of being drafted in the NFL than a player from any other conference? Explain.

6. According to a survey administered by the market research group ChangeWave in February 2011, 27% of respondents reported that they plan on buying a tablet device in the future. This result was 2 percentage points higher than in a similar survey administered in November of 2010. In the February study, 3091 customers were surveyed on tablet demand and future buying trends. Suppose that in the November study, 721 people said they planned on buying a tablet device in the future. **Source:** InvestorPlace; 2011

a. In the February study, how many people said that they planned on buying a tablet device in the future?

b. In the November study, how many total customers were surveyed?

7. It is no secret that Wall Street firms compete aggressively to lure their clients. Having more high-end clients translates into fees and revenues that turn into profits. A survey of 150 high-end clients asked what lured them to their respective Wall Street firm. The table below shows the results.

Table for Exercise 7 – High-End Client Response	
Perk Received	**Client Response**
Pay a Kick-Back	25
Lucrative Golf Outings	12
Lavish Dinners	8
Free Private Jet Use	33
Prime Seats at Sports Events	20
Other	22
No Perk Received	30

a. Which type of perk appears to be most successful in luring clients?

b. What proportion of clients were lured to a Wall Street firm by the perk identified in part (a)?

c. What proportion of clients did not receive a perk at all?

d. Given that these perks aren't inexpensive, what conclusion can you make about providing perks to clients? Explain.

4.8

Measures of Association between Two Variables

Often times a manager or decision maker is interested in the relationship between two variables. Such relationships could be the amount of sales and advertising expenditures, education level and income, number of contacts made and sales, sales and earnings, number of real estate foreclosures and home prices, and so on. In the earlier chapters, we discussed methods used to study each of these measurements individually. Now we want to study the measurements of two different variables at the same time to see if there is a relationship between them. The purpose of studying the relationship between two variables is three-fold: to describe and understand the relationship, to forecast and predict a new observation, and if one is working with a process, not understanding the relationship could be detrimental to making necessary adjustments. There are statistical tools that can aid in the discovery of relationships.

Thinking about relationships is something that everyone does. Why, for example, does an admissions counselor want to know the relationship between SAT scores and college performance? The admissions counselor's task is to select students who will be successful at that college. If college performance is related to SAT scores and the relationship can be specified explicitly, then SAT scores can be used to *predict* performance. Consequently, the relationship would be helpful in selecting students for admission. On the other hand, if SAT scores are not useful in predicting college performance, then they should not be considered very important in making admissions decisions. Discovering whether SAT scores are related to college performance could improve the admissions process. Accurate predictions of a variable often suggest methods for process improvement.

Most students view grades as important and work to make good grades for self-satisfaction and to enhance career opportunities. Because grades are perceived as important, students often wonder about the relationship between the amount of time spent studying and the resulting exam grade. If study time is related to the grade received, a student could use the relationship to predict a grade based on study time. In addition, if the student is able to predict the grade this way, the student could adjust study time to obtain whatever grade is desired. Being able to predict a low grade could lead to corrective action and an improvement in grade point average. The ability to predict often leads to the ability to control.

Bivariate Data

In earlier sections, all of the statistical summary measurements, like the mean, variance, and proportions, were concerned with describing **univariate** data (measurements of one variable). To understand the relationship between two variables, data on both variables need to be collected. This type of data is called **bivariate** data. With bivariate data, two observations are recorded from some entity.

Table 4.21 contains 60 bivariate data points of monthly rent and vacancy rates for various locations in the southeastern part of the United States.

Table 4.21 – Monthly Rent by Vacancy Rate for Various Locations					
Location	Monthly Rent	Vacancy Rate (%)	Location	Monthly Rent	Vacancy Rate (%)
Accomack	$639.00	9.0	Hanover	$587.00	10.9
Airport	$752.00	17.3	Hickory	$604.00	9.1
Albermarle	$717.00	11.7	Highland	$611.00	15.0
Anson	$589.00	9.4	Iredell	$693.00	11.2
Appomattox	$605.00	14.5	Kannapolis	$606.83	11.3
Avery	$698.00	7.8	Kernersville	$609.00	14.9
Bloomsburg	$600.00	7.0	Lancaster	$761.00	9.1
Botetourt	$645.17	14.3	Louisa	$624.00	9.2
Buchanan	$613.00	11.3	Macon	$614.00	6.7
Cabarrus	$632.00	7.1	Mecklenburg	$648.00	8.4
Caldwell	$701.00	7.3	Montgomery	$620.00	8.6
Catawba	$643.83	12.4	Mooresville	$579.00	5.1
Charlotte	$612.00	6.8	Nash	$597.00	12.1
Charlottesville	$655.00	14.5	Nelson	$658.00	8.3
Chester	$623.00	6.2	Newton	$589.00	5.1
Cleveland	$607.50	8.9	New Castle	$602.00	5.7
Clover	$780.00	22.3	Norfolk	$630.17	7.6
Conover	$634.00	4.4	Northampton	$614.00	5.7
Danville	$604.00	9.2	Orange	$643.00	7.5
Davidson	$725.00	9.3	Pamlico	$666.00	9.6
Fort Mill	$658.00	7.9	Pittsylvania	$662.00	7.0
Franklin	$661.00	15.3	Rock Hill	$569.00	8.6
Frederick	$681.00	11.5	Rockingham	$636.50	10.3
Gaston	$585.00	9.1	Rowan	$617.67	7.7
Gates	$622.00	8.4	Rutherford	$677.17	9.1
Giles	$678.00	11.6	Salisbury	$577.00	8.6
Gloucester	$740.00	11.6	Stokes	$624.00	6.7
Granville	$622.00	8.9	Surry	$624.00	9.2
Grayson	$605.00	11.3	Union	$582.00	4.1
Greene	$746.00	20.1	York	$672.00	7.2

Looking for Patterns in the Data

Detecting a relationship between two variables often begins with a graph. In the case of bivariate data, a **scatterplot** is the traditional graphical method used to display the relationship between two variables. In a **scatterplot**, measurements are plotted in pairs with one variable plotted on each axis. When examining a scatterplot we are trying to draw conclusions concerning the overall pattern of the data. Does the pattern roughly follow a straight line? Is the pattern upward sloping or downward sloping? Are the data values tightly clustered in the pattern or widely dispersed? Are there significant deviations from the pattern?

A number of different scatterplots are shown below. In the first two scatterplots (Figures 4.21 and 4.22) the data are strongly related and, in fact, falls on a straight line. In Figure 4.21 the slope of the relationship is positive, that is, as the x variable increases the y variable also increases.

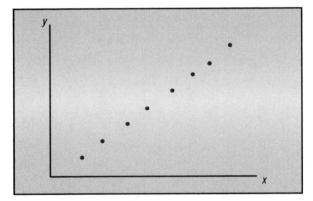

Figure 4.21 – Scatterplot 1

In Figure 4.22 the relationship is negative; as the x variable increases, the y variable decreases. This is also called an **inverse relationship**.

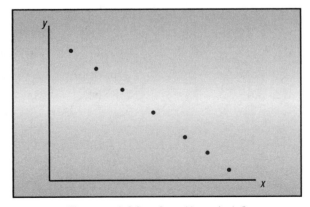

Figure 4.22 – Scatterplot 2

Figures 4.23 and 4.24 show less obvious relationships between the data. Figure 4.23 reveals a very imprecise relationship between x and y, although as x increases, y tends to increase. The relationship between x and y is much more apparent in Figure 4.24 than in Figure 4.23.

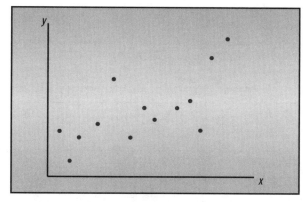

Figure 4.23 – Scatterplot 3

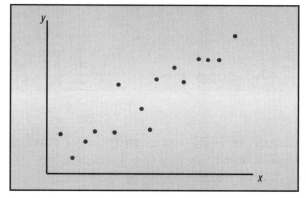

Figure 4.24 – Scatterplot 4

Figure 4.25 reveals a downward sloping relationship between x and y. That is, as x increases, y tends to decrease. The relationship is not as exact as the relationship in Figure 4.22. In Figure 4.26, there is no apparent relationship between the x and y. That is, there is no tendency for y to increase or decrease as x increases.

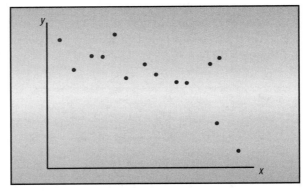

Figure 4.25 – Scatterplot 5

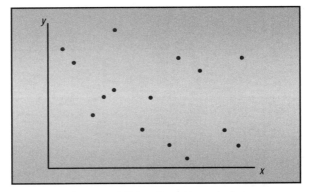

Figure 4.26 – Scatterplot 6

Let's explore the data in Table 4.21 with a scatterplot (see Figure 4.27). Examining the scatterplot reveals a slightly upward sloping relationship. That is, as monthly rent increases, the vacancy rate also increases.

Monthly Rent and Vacancy Rate

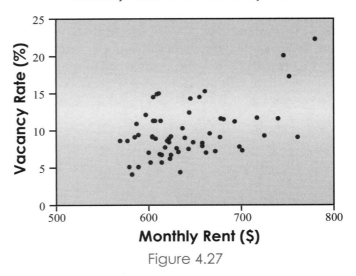

Figure 4.27

While the relationship between monthly rent and vacancy rate is apparent, the relationship is not very strong. Interestingly, the law of supply and demand for rental space suggests that higher rents are a result of an increase in demand, contributing to higher prices. Thus, one would expect to see lower vacancy rates as rents rise, which could result in the development of more apartment units. However, that doesn't appear to be the case with these data. The fact that there appears to be a positive relationship between monthly rent and vacancy rate does not prove that high rent causes high vacancy rates even though such a conclusion may seem reasonable. One of the temptations that must be avoided is equating association with causation. There are many potential confounding variables in this observational data. However, we can quantify the strength of this relationship using the correlation coefficient, which is a measure of the linear association between two variables.

Measuring the Degree of Linear Relationship: The Correlation Coefficient

A scatter diagram is a useful exploratory tool for detecting relationships between two variables. Eventually, however, a researcher will want to know the strength of the relationship between the two variables. Karl Pearson in 1896 developed a measure called the **correlation coefficient**, r, to measure the degree of linear relationship.

Formula

The correlation coefficient is an index number used to summarize the strength of a linear relationship.

$$r = \frac{1}{n-1}\left\{\sum_{i=1}^{n}\left(\frac{x_i - \overline{x}}{s_x}\right)\left(\frac{y_i - \overline{y}}{s_y}\right)\right\} \quad -1 \le r \le 1$$

Correlation Coefficient

Within the parentheses, there are two familiar expressions:

$$\frac{y_i - \overline{y}}{s_y},$$

which is a z-score that shows how far y deviates from its mean measured in standard deviation units (s_y is the standard deviation of y), and

$$\frac{x_i - \overline{x}}{s_x},$$

which is a z-score that shows how far x deviates from its mean measured in standard deviation units (s_x is the standard deviation of x).

Francis Galton
1822 – 1911

Galton was the ninth child of a wealthy English family in Birmingham, England. He did extensive traveling early in his life and became interested in heritability of human traits. He was also greatly influenced by his first cousin, Charles Darwin. He believed that physical characteristics such as weight, height, and intelligence, as well as some personality traits were inherited. He collected data on these traits from mothers, fathers, and their children and found some interesting results. Tall fathers, for example, tended to have shorter children than themselves. Short fathers tended to have children that were taller than themselves. He also found this same property in seeds of wheat. He named this phenomena regression toward the mean. This is how the term regression entered statistics.

Galton was partially responsible for the development of the correlation coefficient. He needed some method of assessing the strength of the physical relationships between parents and their children.

Continued...

Summing the products of these **deviation measures** for each data pair determines the sign of the correlation coefficient.

Positive Relationships

When r is positive, there is a tendency for y to increase as x increases. If both of the deviations are positive, then each of the observations is above its mean. If both are negative, then each is below its mean. In a positive linear relationship, when one of the variables is above its mean, the other variable tends to be above its mean.

Positive Relationship between x and y

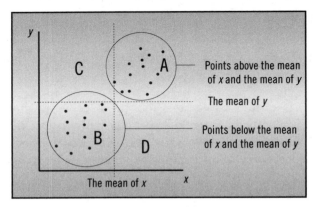

Figure 4.28

Similarly, if one variable is below its mean, the other tends to be below its mean. Such is the case in Figure 4.28. The points in the group labeled **A** are points whose x values are greater than the mean of x and whose y values are greater than the mean of y. Since for each point in group **A**, the deviations $x_i - \bar{x}$ and $y_i - \bar{y}$ will be positive numbers, the expression $\left(\dfrac{x_i - \bar{x}}{s_x} \right) \left(\dfrac{y_i - \bar{y}}{s_y} \right)$ will be the product of two positive numbers, which will be *positive*.

The points in the group labeled **B** are points whose x values are below the mean of x and whose y values are below the mean of y. Since $x_i - \bar{x}$ and $y_i - \bar{y}$ will both be negative numbers for members of this group, the expression $\left(\dfrac{x_i - \bar{x}}{s_x} \right) \left(\dfrac{y_i - \bar{y}}{s_y} \right)$ will be the product of two negative numbers, which will be *positive*.

Since all the points fall into either group **A** or **B**, all the products in the summation are positive. Thus, the correlation coefficient (r) will have a positive value for an upward sloping (positive) relationship. Now, let's look at a downward sloping relationship.

Negative Relationships

Negative Relationship between x and y

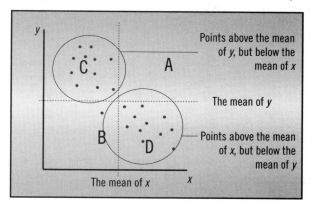

Figure 4.29

... Continued

He enlisted a young English statistician named Karl Pearson to work on a measure that could be used to determine association. It was Pearson that developed the correlation coefficient for this purpose. It is unclear exactly what role Galton played in the development of the correlation coefficient, however in the social science literature Galton is recognized as a co-developer of the statistic.

In downward sloping (negative) relationships, a value above the mean for one variable will tend to be associated with a value below the mean for the other variable. For every point in group **C** the value of y is above y's mean, but the value of x is below x's mean. In group **D** the reverse is true. This kind of relationship is often called an **inverse relationship**. You see this kind of relationship quite often. For example, consider the relationship between price and quantity sold. For virtually all *normal* goods, as the price increases, the quantity sold will decrease. Examining the correlation measure for negative relationships reveals that the product in the summation $\left(\dfrac{x_i - \bar{x}}{s_x}\right)\left(\dfrac{y_i - \bar{y}}{s_y}\right)$ will be negative for points in groups **C** and **D**. Since all but one of the points belong to groups **C** and **D**, then the summation will consist of mostly negative values for $\left(\dfrac{x_i - \bar{x}}{s_x}\right)\left(\dfrac{y_i - \bar{y}}{s_y}\right)$;

therefore, the value of the correlation coefficient will be negative.

Example 4.20

Table 4.22 contains the age and the annual maintenance costs of a certain model compact vehicle. Calculate the correlation coefficient to determine if a relationship exists between the age and annual maintenance cost of that model.

Table 4.22 – Vehicle Age and Maintenance Cost		
Observation	Age	Annual Maintenance Cost (Dollars)
1	2	225
2	4	400
3	5	475
4	7	650
5	9	800
6	12	1175

Solution

To calculate the correlation coefficient, we need to use

$$r = \frac{1}{n-1}\left\{\sum_{i=1}^{n}\left(\frac{x_i - \bar{x}}{s_x}\right)\left(\frac{y_i - \bar{y}}{s_y}\right)\right\}.$$

Some useful summary statistics needed to calculate r are:

$$\bar{x} = 6.5, \; \bar{y} = 620.83, \; s_x = 3.62, \text{ and } s_y = 336.68.$$

Using the summary statistics, we get

$$r = \frac{1}{6-1}\left\{\left(\frac{2-6.5}{3.62}\right)\left(\frac{225-620.83}{336.68}\right) + \ldots + \left(\frac{12-6.5}{3.62}\right)\left(\frac{1175-620.83}{336.68}\right)\right\}$$

$$= .9950.$$

Given the large magnitude of r, one can say that there is a strong, positive, linear relationship between the age of the vehicle and the annual maintenance cost. That is, as the vehicle gets older, one can expect to spend more money on annual maintenance.

Many calculators and virtually all statistics programs will compute the correlation coefficient, r, so it is unlikely that you will need to manually compute the measure.

Some Properties of the Correlation Coefficient

This leads to the following properties of the correlation coefficient:

Properties

- The correlation coefficient, r, measures the degree of linear relationship – how well the data cluster around a line.
- The value of r is always between -1 and $+1$.
- A value of r near -1 or $+1$ means the data are tightly bundled around a line.
- A value of r near -1 or $+1$ means that it would be very easy to predict one of the variables by using the other.
- Positive association is indicated by $r > 0$ and an upward sloping relationship.
- Negative association is indicated by $r < 0$ and a downward sloping relationship.
- A value of r near zero means there is no linear relationship between x and y.
- It does not matter whether you correlate y with x or x with y; you will still get the same value for r.

Properties of the Correlation Coefficient

Correlation Coefficients

$r = .95$

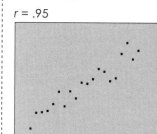

$r = -.86$

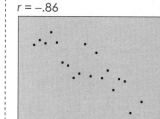

$r = -.05$

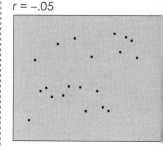

Avoiding Some Correlation Pitfalls

A high correlation does not imply causation. Suppose that a high correlation has been observed between the weekly sales of ice cream and the number of snake bites each week. It seems unlikely that ice cream sales would cause snakes to bite people or that more snake bites would cause higher ice cream sales. Yet when the data is correlated, you may find an unexpectedly high correlation. If the two variables aren't actually related, what could explain such an observed relationship?

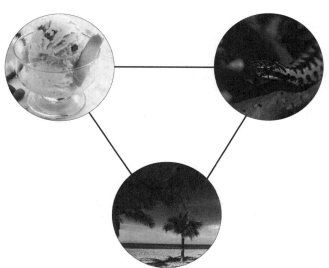

Baldness and Heart Attacks

Newsweek magazine reported the results of a medical study that identified increased risk of heart attack with male pattern baldness. This kind of information based on correlation can be useful in the sense that men with pattern baldness can be extra vigilant about possible cardiac arrest. On the surface, this increased risk is hard to explain. What do you think is a reasonable explanation? The medical researchers that studied this problem came to the conclusion that there may be a third variable, often called a lurking variable, which is a male hormone that induces both pattern baldness and propensity to increased heart attack. This finding opened new research questions that centered around finding such a male hormone.

The apparent relationship is an illusion caused by a phenomenon called **common response**. That is, both variables are related to a third variable. In this case the high temperatures in the summer cause increases in both ice cream sales and reptile activity.

Correlating summary measures (such as means) will tend to provide an inflated correlation measurement. Ignoring the variation of the individual values magnifies the correlation measure and gives a somewhat distorted view of the underlying relationship.

Suppose there is good reason to believe that a causal relationship exists between two variables, but when a correlation is performed the value of the correlation is near zero, indicating no association. Does the lack of correlation between the two variables prove no relationship exists? There are several reasons two related variables might not have a high correlation.

Quadratic Relationship

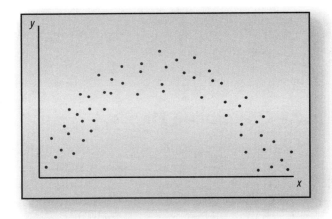

Figure 4.30

A low correlation could mean that no linear relationship exists.

In Figure 4.30 the relationship between x and y is not a straight line. The correlation measure for these points is going to be very close to zero. Yet, there does appear to be a very strong relationship between x and y. The kind of relationship exhibited by this data is called a **quadratic relationship**.

Another problem that can produce low correlations is **confounding**. Confounding occurs when more than one variable affects the dependent variable, and the effects of the variables cannot be distinguished from each other. Suppose that the variable y is dependent on x. Thus, as x changes, it produces changes in y. Such a relationship should produce a significant correlation measure between the two variables. But suppose there is another variable z, which also affects y. As z changes so does y. It is certainly possible that changes in z will mask the changes caused by x.

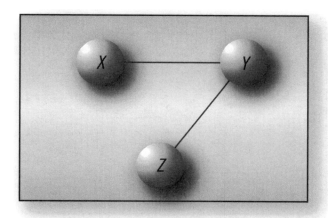

Figure 4.31

The range of x values selected for correlation can also significantly affect the value of the correlation coefficient. If the range of the x data is large, the correlation will usually be greater than if the range of the x values is small, as shown in Figure 4.32.

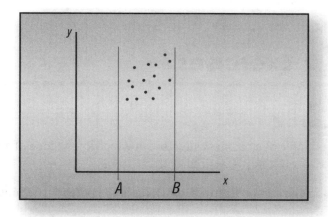

Figure 4.32

If the points below A in Figure 4.33 were removed and the points above B were removed from the data, (as shown in Figure 4.32), the correlation between x and y will be considerably weaker. Thus, when looking at correlation data, you should ask if the data are complete.

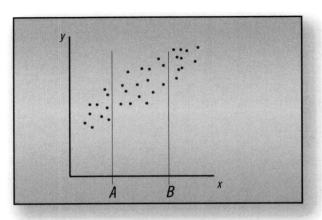

Figure 4.33

Sometimes unrelated variables are highly correlated. When this occurs the variables are said to have a **spurious** correlation. For example, over a short period of time daily car sales and the number of penguins in Antarctica might be related. However, it is doubtful that a significant change in the penguin population will cause a change in car sales, or vice versa.

4.8 Exercises

Basic Concepts

1. Give an example of a business situation in which knowledge of a relationship between two variables is desired.

2. If a relationship can be uncovered, what are the potential benefits?

3. What are bivariate data? How is this different from univariate data?

4. What graphical tool is often used in the discovery of relationships?

5. What are four common questions you should ask when studying a graphical representation of bivariate data?

6. If bivariate data exhibit an inverse relationship, what does that mean?

7. How do you construct exact relationships between two variables?

8. In what range is the value of r when bivariate data exhibit a positive relationship? A negative relationship?

9. If the value of r is small, does this always mean that no relationship exists? Explain.

10. What is confounding? Why is confounding a problem?

Exercises

1. Consider the following scatterplots and answer the following questions regarding the overall pattern of the data for each of the graphs.

   - Does the pattern roughly follow a straight line?
   - Is the pattern upward sloping or downward sloping?
   - Are the data values tightly clustered in the pattern or widely dispersed?
   - Are there significant deviations from the pattern?

   a.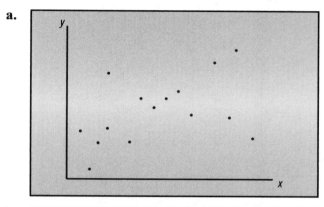

   b.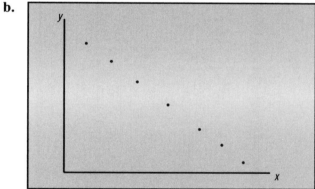

2. Consider the following scatterplots and answer the following questions regarding the overall pattern of the data for each of the graphs.

- Does the pattern roughly follow a straight line?
- Is the pattern upward sloping or downward sloping?
- Are the data values tightly clustered in the pattern or widely dispersed?
- Are there significant deviations from the pattern?

a.

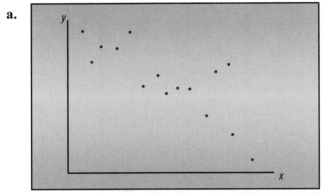

b.

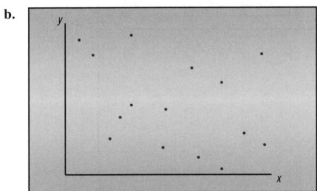

3. A manufacturing company which produces laminate for countertops is interested in studying the relationship between the number of hours of training which an employee receives and the number of defects per countertop produced. Ten employees are randomly selected. The number of hours of training which each employee has received is recorded and the number of defects on the most recent countertop produced is determined. The results are as follows.

Table for Exercise 3 – Employee Training	
Hours of Training	**Defects per Countertop**
1	1
4	4
7	0
3	3
2	5
2	4
5	3
5	2
1	5
6	1

  a. Analyze the data collected for the study by answering the following questions.

      i. Do the variables selected for measurement seem appropriate for answering the question?

      ii. What biases or errors might be present in the data?

      iii. How are the data collected – through observation or controlled experiment?

  b. Plot the data points on a scatterplot.

  c. Based on the scatterplot in part (b), answer the following questions regarding the overall pattern of the data.

      i. Does the pattern roughly follow a straight line?

      ii. Is the pattern upward sloping or downward sloping? Are the data values tightly clustered in the pattern or widely dispersed?

      iii. Are there significant deviations from the pattern?

4. Illustrate, using a scatterplot, a data set that would have a correlation coefficient of 1.

5. Illustrate, using a scatterplot, a data set that would have a correlation coefficient of −1.

6. Describe the relationships indicated by the correlation coefficients as tightly clustered in a positive linear fashion, tightly clustered in a negative linear fashion, loosely clustered in a positive linear fashion, loosely clustered in a negative linear fashion, or no linear relationship.

   a. $r = .9$

   b. $r = .5$

   c. $r = -.9$

   d. $r = -.5$

   e. $r = 0$

   f. What assumption did you make about the scatterplots in answering (a) through (e)?

7. Describe the relationships indicated by the correlation coefficients as tightly clustered in a positive linear fashion, tightly clustered in a negative linear fashion, loosely clustered in a positive linear fashion, loosely clustered in a negative linear fashion, or no linear relationship.

   a. $r = .8$

   b. $r = .4$

   c. $r = -.8$

   d. $r = -.4$

   e. $r = .1$

   f. What assumption did you make about the scatterplots in answering (a) through (e)?

8. A sample of 10 female swimmers, all 17 years old, is selected from a local swim league. Each swimmer's best time (in seconds) in the 50-yard freestyle and in the 100-yard individual medley are obtained. The 100-yard individual medley consists of swimming 25 yards with each of the four major strokes. The data are given in the following table.

Table for Exercise 8 – Best Times									
Freestyle	27.4	27.0	26.8	30.7	28.5	28.6	29.6	30.8	31.5	29.8
Medley	66.3	66.4	66.7	78.7	69.4	72.0	73.5	81.1	78.6	73.5

   a. Make a scatterplot of the data.

   b. Does there appear to be a negative or positive relationship between the variables?

   c. Compute the correlation coefficient.

9. A personnel director is interested in studying the relationship (if any) between age and salary. Sixteen employees are randomly selected and their age and salary are recorded.

Table for Exercise 9 – Ages and Salaries			
Age	Salary ($)	Age	Salary ($)
25	22,000	49	39,000
55	45,000	37	45,000
27	43,000	62	60,000
30	30,000	40	35,000
22	24,000	35	34,000
33	53,000	29	30,000
19	18,000	58	73,000
45	38,000	52	42,000

a. Plot the data points on a scatterplot.

b. Determine the correlation coefficient.

c. Describe the relationship indicated by the correlation coefficient and the scatterplot.

10. The following variables have high positive linear correlations. Is it reasonable to conclude that an increase in one variable causes an increase in the other variable? Explain what could be causing this apparent relationship.

a. Height and vocabulary

b. Absenteeism from school and sale of cough syrup

c. Sale of turkey and sale of toys

11. The following variables have high positive linear correlations. Is it reasonable to conclude that an increase in one variable causes an increase in the other variable? Explain what could be causing this apparent relationship.

a. Sale of air conditioners and sale of tomatoes

b. Sale of greeting cards and sale of chocolates

c. The number of wrecks on a local highway and absenteeism from work

Discovering Technology

USING THE TI-84 PLUS CALCULATOR

Sample Mean and Standard Deviation

Use the data from Example 4.9 (4, 10, 9, 11, 9, 7).

1. Press **STAT**, select "EDIT", "Edit", and **ENTER**. Then input the data into list L1.

2. Press STAT and select "CALC", then choose "1: 1-Var Stats" and press ENTER. Press **L1** (2^(nd) and 1) and press ENTER.

3. Observe the Output Screen for the sample mean and sample standard deviation.

Calculating the Correlation Coefficient *r*

For this exercise, use the data from Example 4.20.

1. Press STAT and select 1: Edit.

2. Enter the *x* data values in **L1** and the *y* data values in **L2**.

3. Access the catalog by pressing **2^(nd)** then **0**.

4. Press the down arrow and find **DiagnosticOn**. Press **ENTER**, then **ENTER** again.

5. Press **STAT**, press the right arrow key so that **CALC** is highlighted.

6. Highlight 4: **LinReg (ax + b)**. Press **ENTER**.

7. Press **ENTER** again. The calculator will display values for *a* and *b* in the equation $y = ax + b$ for the data entered in the lists.

8. The last value listed will be the correlation coefficient for the two sets of data, *r*.

USING EXCEL

Sample Mean and Standard Deviation

Use the data from Example 4.9 (4, 10, 9, 11, 9, 7).

1. Enter the data into Column A.

2. Under the "Data" tab, choose **Data Analysis**, then **Descriptive Statistics**. Select **OK**.

3. Enter the Input Range **A1:A6**, select the radio button next to "Output Range" and enter **A8**. Check the box next to "Summary Statistics". Select **OK**.

4. Observe the Output Screen for the summary statistics.

Percentiles and Quartiles

Use the data from Example 4.15.

Microsoft Excel has a function (PERCENTILE) to calculate the kth percentile of a data set and a function (QUARTILE) to calculate the quartiles of a data set. The method that Excel uses to calculate percentiles and quartiles is different from that which was shown in this chapter. The method is beyond the scope of this text, but it is important to realize that this method results in percentiles that are not always members of the data set. For example, as you will see, Excel identifies the 10th percentile of the data set as 28.8, which is not found in the list of test scores. Excel also equates the first quartile with the 25th percentile, the 2nd quartile with the 50th percentile, and the third quartile with the 75th percentile.

1. In cell A1 type the label **Data**.

2. Enter the data values in Column A, beginning in cell A2.

3. In cell B1 type the label **Percentile**.

4. In Column B, enter the following percentiles, beginning in cell B2. **10, 25, 40, 50, 60, 75, 90**.

5. In cell D1 type the label **Quartile**.

6. In Column D, enter the following quartiles, beginning in cell D2. **1, 2, 3, 4**.

7. The percentile function is **PERCENTILE(array,k)** where *array* corresponds to the data set you are interested in and k is the kth percentile, expressed as a number between 0 and 1.

8. Now calculate the 10th percentile by entering the following function in cell C2:

$$=PERCENTILE(A2:A41,0.10).$$

As calculated by Excel, the 10th percentile is 28.8. Calculate the 25th, 40th, 50th, 60th, 75th, and 90th percentiles using the appropriate function in cells C3 through C8, respectively.

	A	B	C	D	E
1	Data	Percentile		Quartile	
2	67	10	28.8	1	
3	45	25	42.5	2	
4	63	40	47.6	3	
5	58	50	54	4	
6	35	60	56.4		
7	54	75	64.5		
8	27	90	73.4		
9	66				
10	21				

Figure 4.34

9. The quartile function is **QUARTILE(array,quart)** where *array* corresponds to the data set you are interested in and *quart* is the quartile (1 through 4).

10. Now calculate the first quartile by entering the following function in cell E2:

$$=QUARTILE(A2:A41,1).$$

As calculated by Excel, the first quartile is 42.5. Notice this value is the same as the 25th percentile. Calculate the second, third, and fourth quartiles using the appropriate function in cells E3 through E5, respectively. Notice that the second and third quartiles are equal to the 50th and 75th percentile, respectively, and that the fourth quartile is the maximum value in the data set (corresponding to the 100th percentile).

	A	B	C	D	E
1	Data	Percentile		Quartile	
2	67	10	28.8	1	42.5
3	45	25	42.5	2	54
4	63	40	47.6	3	64.5
5	58	50	54	4	82
6	35	60	56.4		
7	54	75	64.5		
8	27	90	73.4		
9	66				
10	21				

Figure 4.35

Calculating the Correlation Coefficient *r*

For this exercise, use the data from Example 4.20.

1. Enter the *x* data values in Column A.

2. Enter the *y* data values in Column B.

3. Under the "data" tab select **data analysis**.

4. Select "Correlation" and press **OK**.

5. Enter **A1:B7** in the "Input Range".

6. Select the radio button next to "Output Range" and enter **E1**. Press **OK**.

7. In the summary output, the correlation coefficient, *r*, is displayed.

USING MINITAB

Sample Mean and Standard Deviation

Use the data from Example 4.9 (4, 10, 9, 11, 9, 7).

1. Enter the data into Column C1.

2. Under "Stat", choose "Basic Statistics", then **Display Descriptive Statistics**.

3. In the "Display Descriptive Statistics" dialog box, input **C1** under Variables. Select **OK**.

4. Observe the Output Screen for the summary statistics.

Descriptive Statistics: C1

Variable	N	N*	Mean	SE Mean	StDev	Minimum	Q1	Median	Q3	Maximum
C1	6	0	8.33	1.02	2.50	4.00	6.25	9.00	10.25	11.00

Figure 4.36

Calculating the Correlation Coefficient *r*

For this exercise, use the data from Example 4.20.

1. Enter the *x* data values in Column C1.

2. Enter the *y* data values in Column C2.

3. Under "Stat", highlight "Basic Statistics", and select **Correlation**.

4. Enter **C1** and **C2** in the box for "Variables". Press **OK**.

5. The correlation coefficient *r* is displayed in the summary output.

Correlations: C1, C2

```
Pearson correlation of C1 and C2 = 0.995
P-Value = 0.000
```

Figure 4.37

 **Chapter 4 Review**

Key Terms and Ideas

- Numerical Descriptive Statistics
- Parameters
- Statistics
- Inferential Statistics
- Arithmetic Mean
- Sample Mean
- Population Mean
- Deviation
- Weighted Mean
- Trimmed Mean
- Median
- Resistant Measure
- Mode
- Bimodal
- Multimodal
- Positively Skewed
- Negatively Skewed
- Moving Average
- Deviation from the Mean
- Range
- Mean Absolute Deviation
- Population Variance
- Sample Variance
- Standard Deviation

- Empirical Rule
- Chebyshev's Theorem
- P^{th} Percentile
- Percentile
- Quartile
- Interquartile Range
- Outlier
- z-Score
- Shape
- Subsetting
- Coefficient of Variation
- Mean of Grouped Data
- Variance of Grouped Data
- Population Proportion
- Sample Proportion
- Univariate Data
- Bivariate Data
- Scatterplot
- Linear Relationship
- Inverse Relationship
- Correlation Coefficient
- Quadratic Relationship
- Common Response
- Confounding

Key Formulas

Concept	Formula	Section
Arithmetic Mean	$\dfrac{1}{n}\left(x_1 + x_2 + \ldots + x_n\right)$	4.1
Population Mean	$\mu = \dfrac{1}{N}\left(x_1 + x_2 + \ldots + x_n\right)$	4.1
Sample Mean	$\bar{x} = \dfrac{1}{n}\left(x_1 + x_2 + \ldots + x_n\right)$	4.1
Weighted Mean	$\bar{x} = \dfrac{w_1 x_1 + w_2 x_2 + \ldots + w_n x_n}{w_1 + w_2 + \ldots + w_n} = \dfrac{\sum\left(w_i x_i\right)}{\sum w_i}$	4.1
Median Location	$L(m) = \dfrac{n+1}{2}$	4.1
Range	largest value − smallest value	4.2
Mean Absolute Deviation	$\text{MAD} = \dfrac{\sum\left|x_i - \bar{x}\right|}{n}$	4.2
Population Variance	$\sigma^2 = \dfrac{\sum\left(x_i - \mu\right)^2}{N}$	4.2
Sample Variance	$s^2 = \dfrac{\sum\left(x_i - \bar{x}\right)^2}{n-1}$	4.2
Population Standard Deviation	$\sigma = \sqrt{\sigma^2}$	4.2
Sample Standard Deviation	$s = \sqrt{s^2}$	4.2
Empirical Rule	One Sigma Rule: $\mu \pm 1\sigma$ contains about 68% of the data Two Sigma Rule: $\mu \pm 2\sigma$ contains about 95% of the data Three Sigma Rule: $\mu \pm 3\sigma$ contains about 99.7% of the data	4.2
Chebyshev's Theorem	The proportion of any data set lying within k standard deviations of the mean is at least $1 - \dfrac{1}{k^2}$ for $k > 1$	4.2
Location of the Pth Percentile	$\ell = n\left(\dfrac{P}{100}\right)$	4.3

Percentile	The percentile of x is given by: $\dfrac{\text{number of data values less than or equal to } x}{\text{total number of data values}} \cdot 100$	4.3
Location of Q_1	$\ell = n\left(\dfrac{25}{100}\right)$	4.3
Location of Q_2	$\ell = n\left(\dfrac{50}{100}\right)$	4.3
Location of Q_3	$\ell = n\left(\dfrac{75}{100}\right)$	4.3
Interquartile Range	$Q_3 - Q_1$	4.3
Outlier	Data value greater than $Q_3 + 1.5 \cdot$ Interquartile Range Or Data value less than $Q_1 - 1.5 \cdot$ Interquartile Range	4.3
z-Score	$z = \dfrac{x - \mu}{\sigma}$	4.3
Coefficient of Variation	Population data: $CV = \left(\dfrac{\sigma}{\mu} \cdot 100\right)\%$ Sample data: $CV = \left(\dfrac{s}{\bar{x}} \cdot 100\right)\%$	4.5
Mean of Grouped Data	Population data: $\mu = \dfrac{\sum(f_i M_i)}{N}$ Sample data: $\bar{x} = \dfrac{\sum(f_i M_i)}{n}$	4.6
Variance of Grouped Data	Population data: $\sigma^2 = \dfrac{\sum(f_i M_i^2) - \dfrac{\left(\sum(f_i M_i)\right)^2}{N}}{N}$ $= \dfrac{\sum(f_i M_i^2)}{N} - \left(\dfrac{\sum(f_i M_i)}{N}\right)^2$ Sample data: $s^2 = \dfrac{\sum(f_i M_i^2) - \dfrac{\left(\sum(f_i M_i)\right)^2}{n}}{n-1}$	4.6

Class Midpoint	$M_i = \dfrac{\text{lower class boundary} + \text{upper class boundary}}{2}$	4.6
Population Proportion	$p = \dfrac{X}{N}$	4.7
Sample Proportion	$\hat{p} = \dfrac{X}{n}$	4.7
Correlation Coefficient	$r = \dfrac{1}{n-1}\left\{\sum\limits_{i=1}^{n}\left(\dfrac{x_i - \bar{x}}{s_x}\right)\left(\dfrac{y_i - \bar{y}}{s_y}\right)\right\}$	4.8

 Additional Exercises

1. A carpenter is attempting to repair a porch and needs twenty boards which are eight feet long. The salesman at the hardware store says he has twenty boards that "average" eight feet long. When the carpenter checks what he has bought, there are ten boards at six feet and ten boards at ten feet. Do you feel the salesman accurately represented the lengths? Discuss.

2. The maximum heart rates achieved while performing a particular aerobic exercise routine are measured (in beats per minute) for 9 randomly selected individuals.

145	155	130	185	170	165	150	160	125

    a. Calculate the sample variance of the maximum heart rate achieved.

    b. Calculate the sample standard deviation of the maximum heart rate achieved.

    c. Calculate the range of the maximum heart rate achieved.

    d. What are some of the factors which might contribute to the variation in the observations?

3. A sample of teenagers was asked how many times they went to the movies in the past 3 months. The frequency table summarizes the results.

Table for Exercise 3 – Teenager Movie Visits	
Number of Visits	**Frequency**
0	13
1	18
2	11
3	7
4	4
5	3
6	0
7	3
8	3
9	0
10	2

    a. What proportion of the sample visited the movies at least 3 times in the previous 3 months?

    b. Find the mean and standard deviation of the number of visits using the formulas for grouped data.

    c. Compute the interval one standard deviation about the mean.

d. Find the percent of data falling in the interval one standard deviation about the mean.

e. Is the percent of the data falling in the interval one standard deviation about the mean close to what the Empirical Rule predicts? What is the reason for the discrepancy, if any?

4. A high school math teacher summarized the 35 math SAT scores for the students in her calculus class. The mean for the class was 521 and the median was 535. The range of the scores was 235 and the highest score in the entire class was 675. Approximately 40% of the class scored higher than 562. State whether each of the following is true or false.

a. The 45th percentile exceeds 540.

b. The lowest score in the class was 440.

c. The z-score for a score of 510 is a negative number.

d. The third quartile exceeds 562.

e. The percentile rank of 562 is 40.

5. Consider the following number of defective circuit boards produced by two different machines on seven randomly selected days.

Table for Exercise 5 – Defective Circuit Boards							
Machine A	2	3	7	4	5	1	0
Machine B	2	3	4	3	4	2	4

a. Calculate the average number of defective circuit boards produced by each machine.

b. Calculate the variance of the number of defective circuit boards produced by each machine.

c. Calculate the standard deviation of the number of defective circuit boards produced by each machine.

d. Which machine do you think is better? Why?

6. A basketball coach has one remaining scholarship to offer and has narrowed his choice to two players. Listed below are the points scored per game over the last season for each player.

Table for Exercise 6 – Points Scored		
Game Number	Braudrick	Douglas
1	27	35
2	34	21
3	29	50
4	25	28
5	28	missed
6	35	32
7	31	29
8	33	missed
9	33	23
10	25	35
11	28	31
12	32	36
Total	360	320

a. What level of measurement do the data possess?

b. What statistical criteria might you use to select the better player? Justify your answer.

c. Calculate the statistics you proposed in (b).

d. Which player is more consistent? Why?

7. Consider the literacy data given below. **Source**: United Nations Development Programme Report, 2009

Table for Exercise 7 – Literacy Rates			
Country	Literacy Rate (%)	Country	Literacy Rate (%)
Australia	99.0	Luxembourg	99.0
Bolivia	90.7	Mexico	92.8
Canada	99.0	Netherlands	99.0
Denmark	99.0	Peru	89.6
France	99.0	Saudi Arabia	85.0
India	74.0	United States of America	99.0
Kenya	73.0	Zimbabwe	91.2

a. What is the mean literacy rate for these selected countries?

b. What is the standard deviation of these literacy rates?

c. How many countries in this group would we expect to have literacy rates between one standard deviation below the mean and one standard deviation above the mean?

d. How many countries in this group actually have literacy rates between one standard deviation below the mean and one standard deviation above the mean?

e. What assumption did you make in answering part (c) above?

8. A manufacturer considers her production process to be "in control" if the proportion of defective items is less than 3%. She randomly selects 200 items and determines that 9 of the items are defective.

a. Calculate the sample proportion of defective items.

b. Based on the sample, do you think it is reasonable for the manufacturer to conclude that the production process is "out of control"? Why or why not?

9. A pharmacist is interested in studying the relationship between the amount of a particular drug in the bloodstream (in mg) and reaction time (in seconds) of subjects taking the drug. Ten subjects are randomly selected and administered various doses of the drug. The reaction times (in seconds) are measured 15 minutes after the drug is administered with the following results.

Table for Exercise 9 – Reaction Times	
Amount of Drug (mg)	Reaction Time (Seconds)
1	0.5
2	0.7
3	0.6
4	0.7
5	0.8
6	0.8
7	0.9
8	0.6
9	0.9
10	1.0

a. Analyze the data collected for the study by answering the following questions:

   i. Do the variables selected for measurement seem appropriate for answering the question?

   ii. What biases or errors might be present in the data?

   iii. What level of measurement (nominal, ordinal, interval, ratio) does the data possess?

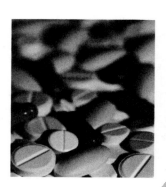

b. Plot the data points on a scatterplot.

c. Based on the scatterplot in part (b), answer the following questions regarding the overall pattern of the data.

   i. Does the pattern roughly follow a straight line?

   ii. Is the pattern upward sloping or downward sloping? Are the data values tightly clustered in the pattern or widely dispersed?

   iii. Are there significant deviations from the pattern?

10. Sometimes the following descriptions are assigned to the correlation coefficient:

$$r = 0 \quad \text{no linear relationship}$$
$$-.5 < r < 0 \quad \text{weak negative linear relationship}$$
$$0 < r < .5 \quad \text{weak positive linear relationship}$$
$$-.8 < r \leq -.5 \quad \text{moderate negative linear relationship}$$
$$.5 \leq r < .8 \quad \text{moderate positive linear relationship}$$
$$-1.0 < r \leq -.8 \quad \text{strong negative linear relationship}$$
$$.8 \leq r < 1.0 \quad \text{strong positive linear relationship}$$
$$r = 1 \quad \text{exact positive linear relationship}$$
$$r = -1 \quad \text{exact negative linear relationship}$$

Describe the relationships indicated by the correlation coefficients below using the descriptions defined above.

a. $r = .9$

b. $r = .5$

c. $r = -.9$

d. $r = -.5$

e. $r = 0$

f. What assumption did you make about the scatterplots in answering (a) through (e)?

11. Describe the relationships indicated by the correlation coefficients below using the descriptions defined in problem 10 above.

a. $r = .8$

b. $r = .4$

c. $r = -.8$

d. $r = -.4$

e. $r = .1$

f. What assumption did you make about the scatterplots in answering (a) through (e)?

12. Consider the following data.

x	1	2	3	4	5	6	7
y	1	4	9	16	25	36	49

Table for Exercise 12

  a. Plot the data points on a scatterplot.

  b. Determine the correlation coefficient.

  c. Describe the relationship between x and y.

13. Consider the following data.

x	1	2	3	4	5	6	7
y	1	1.41	1.73	2	2.24	2.45	2.65

Table for Exercise 13

  a. Plot the data points on a scatterplot.

  b. Determine the correlation coefficient.

  c. Describe the relationship between x and y.

Discovery Project

1. Consult the Farmer's Almanac and determine the Almanac's weather prediction for your area during the last three months. Evaluate the accuracy of the Almanac's predictions. How accurate is the Almanac's forecast? What does it mean to be accurate? Is the almanac forecast a better predictor than simply guessing? Describe your findings in a report.

2. Determine the average length of a rock and roll single. *Billboard* magazine would be an excellent source for the data.

3. Suppose there were 20 quizzes during your statistics course. What would be the advantages and disadvantages of using the trimmed mean to compute your quiz average?

Probability, Randomness, and Uncertainty

5

Discovering the Real World

The Credit Card Industry

Discovering Technology

Calculating probabilities using Microsoft Excel

Calculating the number of combinations using Microsoft Excel

Calculating the number of permutations using Microsoft Excel

253

 **Discovering the Real World**

The majority of students on college campuses are approached by vendors representing credit card companies soliciting students to apply for credit cards. The solicitors preach to the students the importance of establishing a credit history before graduating. Having this credit history will make it easier for the students to obtain financing for cars, homes, and even apartment leases upon graduation. Below is a list of facts about credit cards and the credit card industry that may surprise you.

- 84% of the student population overall have credit cards. **Source**: Sallie Mae, "How Undergraduate Students Use Credit Cards," April, 2009

- 50% of college undergraduates had four or more credit cards in 2008. **Source**: Sallie Mae, "How Undergraduate Students Use Credit Cards," April, 2009

- 76% of undergraduates have credit cards with an average debt of $2,200. **Source**: Nellie Mae, "Undergraduate Students and Credit Cards in 2004: An Analysis of Usage Rates and Trends"

- Seniors graduated with an average credit card debt of more than $4,100. Close to one fifth of seniors carried balances greater than $7,000. **Source**: Sallie Mae, "How Undergraduate Students Use Credit Cards," April, 2009

- 609.8 million credit cards are held by U.S. consumers. **Source**: "The Survey of Consumer Payment Choice," Federal Reserve Bank of Boston, January 2010

- The average credit card debt per household with credit card debt: $15,788. **Source**: www.creditcards.com

- There are 576.4 million total credit cards in circulation in U.S. as of year-end 2009. **Source**: Nilson Report, February 2010

- 3.5 is the average number of credit cards held by cardholders as of year-end 2008. **Source**: "The Survey of Consumer Payment Choice," Federal Reserve Bank of Boston, January 2010

- 78 percent of American households (about 91.1 million) had one or more credit cards at the end of 2008. **Source**: Nilson Report, April 2009

- 14.67% is the average APR on a credit card with a balance on it as of February, 2010. **Source**: Federal Reserve's G.19 report on consumer credit, May 2010

- $852.6 billion is the amount of total U.S. revolving debt (98 percent of which is made up of credit card debt) as of March 2010. **Source**: Federal Reserve's G.19 report on consumer credit, March 2010

- $2.45 trillion is the amount of total U.S. consumer debt as of March 2010. **Source**: Federal Reserve's G.19 report on consumer credit, May 2010

- The top 10 U.S. credit card issuers held an 87.55 percent market share of $972.73 billion in general purpose card outstandings in 2008. That includes Visa, MasterCard, American Express, and Discover. **Source**: Nilson Report, April 2009

- 13.01% is the U.S. credit card default rate. **Source**: Fitch Ratings, April 2010)

- 4.27% is the U.S. credit card 60-day delinquency rate. **Source**: Fitch Ratings, April 2010

Like any other industry, banks take profit maximization as their ultimate goal. Given the above statistics, it is clear that over the past several years, competition in the U.S. credit card industry has been fierce because there is a great deal of money to be made. However, maximizing profit doesn't come without risk. This competition has led many banks, including large, full-service institutions, to lose customers to issuers that are aggressively expanding their card portfolios. Some of the more visible winners of this competition are Capital One Bank, Citibank, First USA Bank N.A., Fleet Bank, Household Bank N.A., MBNA America Bank N.A., and Universal Card. The tremendous volume of card loans generated has created an equally immense need for inexpensive, reliable funding. To be competitive and successful in this industry, credit card issuers must have sophisticated risk-based and risk-controlling technology models to determine not only who is issued a credit card but also the rate it can offer to a particular customer based on that customer's risk profile.

The traditional approach of assessing a customer's risk is by examining their credit score. By comparing the applicant's/borrower's credit history to all other borrowers' information, banks check whether the applicant's credit history is the same as those who regularly default and even declare bankruptcy to determine their credit worthiness. There are also other factors that are examined such as income, lengths of continuous employment at current (and past) jobs, number of credit cards, and whether one owns or rents their home. Rather than simply seeking to minimize the loss or zero risk of a card, examining these factors allows the banks to determine an acceptable level of risk. Thus, when issuing a card to a customer, banks attempt to find the best balance or combination of risks and revenue. The capacity and the technology of controlling risks are the key to a bank's profitability.

Once the accounts are acquired (i.e., a customer has been approved for a credit card), banks begin managing the customer's account, which includes authorization of repeated credit purchases, credit line management, fraud detection, sales promotion, cross-selling, and collections. Risk management closely monitors the delinquency and utilization patterns along with charge-offs, bankruptcies and fraud occurrences. Based on the aforementioned items, authorization and credit line policies are modified to reduce loss or improve profitability. Behavioral score cards, vintage performance dashboards, and reports are developed to support the decision process. Marketing analyzes activation and sales patterns and prompts the customers to buy more through rewards and other offers. Cross-selling of financial products like personal loans and mortgages to existing customers is another area marketing analytics focuses on. The collections analytics team identifies the likely defaulters using behavioral score cards and, based on the risk profiles, devises strategies for collections. They use the past experiences to improve the collection efficiency and work closely with the operations team to implement data driven strategies. The operations analytics team, typically aligned with customer service operations, forecasts the call volumes and analyzes call logs to improve the call routing and support processes. Collection efficiency of the analysts in terms of number of calls and amount collected are some of the metrics monitored by this department.

In summary, card issuers use a variety of tools and utilities in consumer lending to perform an array of analytics activities ranging from simple reporting to complex statistical modeling. Assessing customers' risk is the foundation during the whole process of risk control including risk identification, risk estimation and risk assessment. Only by assessing customers' risk and issuing cards to the applicants can bank card business begin. Accurately assessing customers' risk is an important basis for credit. It can play a role of early warning. Based on it, banks can develop appropriate risk control policies to improve their revenues and profit levels.

Introduction

We all have to cope with uncertainty. Uncertainty is that uneasy feeling we get when our gas tank is nearly empty a few miles from the closest gas station. You remember in the past your car continued to run when the gauge was even lower, but you are not quite sure it will this time. In everyday usage, the word *probably* describes an event or circumstance the speaker believes will occur. At the same time the speaker reserves the possibility that it may not occur. In this sense, *probably* reflects a strong but nonspecific degree of belief.

Probability is used to quantify uncertainty. If a person says he believes there is a .95 probability that his car will make it to a gas station before it runs out of gas, he has made a precise statement which, no doubt, reflects his past experiences and indicates a strong belief in his chances of finding a gas station. This statement is vastly different from the statement that there is a .40 probability the car will make it to a gas station, which casts considerably more doubt on his prospects. The probability statement provides more precise information than phrases like *maybe I'll make it, I might make it*, or *I should make it*. Therein lies its value.

Uncertainty doesn't necessarily have to be associated with events in the future. There can be plenty of uncertainty about the past. What was the Native American population of the continental United States in the year 1492? Nobody knows, so ascribing a probability to the statement *the population of Native Americans in 1492 was between 1.1 and 1.8 million* attaches someone's degree of belief to the statement.

The word **randomness** suggests a certain haphazardness or unpredictability.

Randomness and uncertainty are vague concepts that deal with variation. And even though these words are not synonyms, their discussion leads to the concept of probability.

A simple example of randomness involves a coin toss. Unless the person tossing the coin possesses magical powers, the outcome of the toss (heads or tails) is uncertain. Since the coin tossing experiment is unpredictable, the outcome is said to exhibit randomness. There are many different kinds of randomness. Some are easily described, like the toss of a coin, and others are extraordinarily complex, like molecular motion or changes in stock prices.

Even though individual flips of a coin are unpredictable, if we flip the coin a large number of times, a pattern will emerge. For almost all coins, roughly half of the flips will be heads and half will be tails. This long-run regularity of a random event is described with probability. Our discussions of randomness will be limited to phenomena that in the short run are not exactly predictable but do exhibit long-run regularity.

5.1 Probability Concepts

Games of chance, such as tossing a coin, provide a way to demonstrate some of the fundamental laws (rules) of probability. Statistically speaking, the playing of the game is called an **experiment**.

Definition

Random Experiment

A **random experiment** is defined as any activity or phenomenon that meets the following conditions:

i.   There is one distinct outcome for each trial of the experiment.

ii. The outcome of the experiment is uncertain.

iii. The set of all distinct outcomes of the experiment can be specified and is called the **sample space**, denoted by S.

Definition

Outcome

An **outcome** is any member of the sample space.

If you were to toss a single coin there are only 2 outcomes {Head, Tail} in the experiment. The sample space of an experiment contains every potential outcome that could occur in one trial of the experiment. For a coin tossing experiment, the sample space would be S = {Head, Tail}. The sample space may be called the **outcome set**, since it contains all possible outcomes of an experiment.

The result of a random experiment must be an outcome.

Definition

An **event** is a set of outcomes.

Event

Examples of random experiments, events, and outcomes follow. These experiments will be used throughout the chapter to illustrate the laws of probability.

Experiment Number 1: Toss a coin and observe the outcome. Have we met the three conditions of a random experiment?

i. There will only be one outcome for each trial of the experiment since it is not possible to observe both a head and a tail on the same toss.

ii. The outcome is unknown before the toss.

iii. The sample space can be specified and contains two outcomes, S = {Head, Tail}.

Because each of the three conditions is satisfied, for all practical purposes, this experiment meets the conditions of a random experiment.

It is possible for a coin to land on its edge and thus neither be heads nor tails. Any theory, however, involves a certain degree of idealization, which means, in this case, that landing on an edge will not be considered a possible outcome.

Experiment Number 2: Toss a coin three times and observe the number of heads. Have we met the three conditions of a random experiment?

i. There will be only one outcome since it is not possible to have **exactly** one and **exactly** two heads on the same trial.

ii. The outcome will be unknown before tossing the three coins.

iii. The sample space can be specified and is composed of eight outcomes,
S = {TTT, TTH, THT, THH, HTT, HTH, HHT, HHH}.

This experiment meets the conditions of a random experiment.

An **event** could be obtaining more than one head, which involves the following set of outcomes, {THH, HTH, HHT, HHH}.

5

Experiment Number 3: Roll a die and observe the number of dots on the uppermost surface. Have we met the three conditions of a random experiment?

i. There will only be one outcome.

ii. The value of the outcome is not known.

iii. The sample space can be specified and is composed of simple events,

S = {1, 2, 3, 4, 5, 6}.

This experiment meets the conditions of a random experiment.

An example of an **event** could be rolling an even number, which would be given by the set of outcomes, {2, 4, 6}.

Experiment Number 4: Assume we have a deck of playing cards consisting of 13 hearts, 13 clubs, 13 spades, and 13 diamonds. Draw a card from a well shuffled deck and observe the suit of the card. Have we met the three conditions of a random experiment?

i. There will be only one outcome.

ii. The suit will be unknown since the card will be drawn at random.

iii. The sample space consists of the set of outcomes,

S = {heart, club, spade, diamond}.

This experiment meets the conditions of a random experiment.

If the random experiment involves drawing a card and observing a spade or a club, then the **event** would be given by the set of outcomes, {spade, club}.

Experiment Number 5: Inspect a transistor to determine if it meets quality control standards. Have we met the three conditions of a random experiment?

i. There will only be one outcome.

ii. The outcome of the experiment will be unknown if the transistor is selected from a manufacturing process that occasionally produces defective parts.

iii. The sample space consists of the set of outcomes, S = {meets standards, does not meet standards}.

This experiment meets the conditions of a random experiment.

5.1 Exercises

Basic Concepts

1. Describe randomness.

2. What is probability?

3. What are the conditions of a random experiment?

4. Consider the random experiment of flipping a fair coin twice. What is the sample space for this experiment?

5. What is an event?

6. Consider the random experiment of rolling a fair die once. Give an example of an event for this experiment and list the outcomes associated with that particular event.

Exercises

1. Consider the following random experiment: A potato chip manufacturer is interested in determining if the brand of potato chip which it manufactures is preferred over three of its major competitors. Several customers are randomly selected and asked which brand of potato chip they prefer: Brand A, Brand B, Brand C, or Brand D.

   a. Determine the sample space for the above experiment.

   b. If the manufacturer makes Brand A, list the outcomes in the event M = {customer does not prefer the manufacturer's brand}.

2. Consider the following random experiment: A doctor is interested in determining whether or not his patients think that he listens attentively to what they are saying. He randomly selects several patients and asks which of the following categories best describes his attentiveness: Very Attentive, Somewhat Attentive, Not Attentive.

   a. Determine the sample space for the above experiment.

   b. Determine all possible outcomes for the event A = {the doctor is not described as very attentive}.

5

5.2   Interpreting Probability

What is Probability?

If someone is asked, *What is probability?*, they are likely to respond correctly with *It is the chance of something happening.* A more formal definition of probability is the likelihood of the occurrence of a particular event. However, there are many ideas of what probability is and how it should be calculated. There is **subjective probability**, which is one's personal belief about the occurrence of a specific event. With subjective probability, there is no specific calculation, and the probability simply reflects a person's opinion and/or past experiences. On the other hand, **objective probability** is the likelihood of the occurrence of a particular event that is based on recorded outcomes. Objective probabilities are more accurate than subjective probabilities. In this section we will discuss two types of objective probability, relative frequency and the classical approach, as well as subjective probability.

Relative Frequency

Someone who wanted to determine the probability of getting a head on the toss of a coin could toss a coin a large number of times and observe the number of times that a head appeared. The probability could be computed as the number of times a head was observed divided by the number of times the coin was flipped. This is the relative frequency interpretation of probability.

Formula

Relative Frequency

If an experiment is performed n times, under identical conditions, and the event A happens k times, the **relative frequency** of A is

$$\text{Relative Frequency of } A = \frac{k}{n}.$$

Let's flip a coin 42 times and observe the relative frequency of a head during those tosses.

1	2	3	4	5	6	7
100%	50%	67%	75%	60%	50%	43%

8	9	10	11	12	13	14
38%	44%	40%	36%	42%	38%	36%

15	16	17	18	19	20	21
33%	38%	41%	39%	37%	35%	38%

22	23	24	25	26	27	28
36%	35%	38%	36%	35%	33%	32%

29	30	31	32	33	34	35
34%	33%	35%	38%	36%	35%	34%

36	37	38	39	40	41	42
36%	35%	34%	36%	35%	34%	36%

In Figure 5.1, you can see that the percentage of heads is very unstable during the first 15 flips. The percentage of heads begins to stabilize at around flip 20, although there is still some fluctuation in its value. Looking at the first 42 flips makes you wonder whether this is a "fair" coin, since heads is occurring only 36% of the time. In Figure 5.2, which starts at about 200 flips, the percentage of heads becomes very stable. By flip number 296, there are 141 heads and 155 tails which equate to a .4764 probability (or relative frequency) of heads. Although this is slightly less than expected, such a percentage is reasonable considering the randomness of the coin toss.

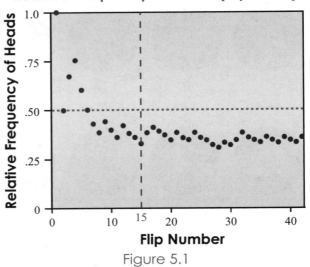

Figure 5.1

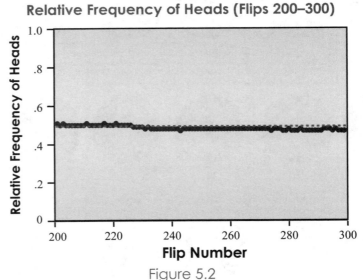

Figure 5.2

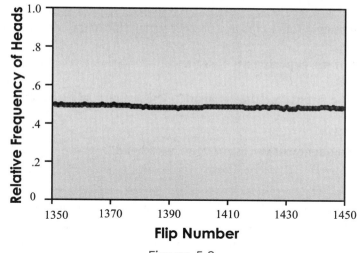

Figure 5.3

As can be seen in Figure 5.2 and Figure 5.3, the percentage of heads converges on some point which is close to .5. Figure 5.3 starts at about 1350 flips. As you can see, the percentage of heads remains very stable. At flip number 1450 there are 718 heads and 732 tails which equate to a .4952 probability (or relative frequency) of heads.

What is the Relative Frequency of a Head on Our Coin?

Our best available guess is .4952, since it is the observed relative frequency of heads using all 1450 tosses.

$$\text{Relative Frequency of } A = \frac{k}{n} = \frac{718}{1450} = .4952$$

How good is this guess for the relative frequency of heads? Since the coin has been tossed a large number of times and the observed frequency is very stable, the guess should be very good.

Will the Observed Relative Frequency Ever Reach .5?

No mathematical or physical law requires the observed relative frequency to ever reach some predetermined level. But if the probability of observing a head was really .5, the observed relative frequency should closely approach this value after a large number of flips.

A Summary

The experiment: Toss a coin and observe which side of the coin appears on top.

Duration of the experiment: Toss the coin 1450 times. $n = 1450$.

Observe the event "getting a head": The event was observed 718 times. $k = 718$.

Relative frequency of the event "getting a head": $\dfrac{k}{n} = \dfrac{718}{1450} = .4952$.

The relative frequency of a head seems to converge to the expected relative frequency of .5. This kind of convergence is sometimes called **statistical regularity**. Although the outcomes of the experiment may vary, in the long run the relative frequency of an outcome tends to some value, its probability.

Problems with the Relative Frequency Idea

The problem with the relative frequency approach to defining probability is that probability only exists for events that can be repeated under the same conditions. Coin, dice, and card experiments can easily be repeated. However, because of the strict requirements of identical and repeatable experiments, many events in which it would be desirable to have relative frequency probabilities do not satisfy the requirement of repetition. Whether the next launch of the space shuttle will be successful, or whether you will make an "A" in your statistics course are examples of experiments that are not repeatable under the exact same conditions. Thus, they are not appropriate for the application of the relative frequency idea. This perspective greatly limits the application of the relative frequency interpretation of probability. Despite its limitations, the relative frequency approach is a widely held interpretation of probability.

Example 5.1

Suppose we perform an experiment drawing three numbers, without replacement, from an urn containing 64 numbers. Have we met the conditions of a random experiment?

Solution

No! This does not meet the conditions of a random experiment because it cannot be repeated under the same conditions. That is, as each number is selected, it is not returned to the urn prior to the subsequent selection, thus decreasing the number remaining in the urn which changes the experiment.

Classical Approach

The second objective approach commonly used in probability is the classical approach. Classical probability can be measured as a simple proportion: the number of outcomes that compose the event divided by the number of outcomes in the sample space, when it can be assumed that all of the outcomes are equally likely. Namely, the probability of an event A, denoted $P(A)$, is given by

$$P(A) = \frac{\text{number of outcomes in } A}{\text{total number of outcomes in the sample space}}.$$

Example 5.2

In experiment number 2, a coin was tossed three times and the number of heads was observed. The sample space consists of 8 outcomes {TTT, TTH, THT, THH, HTT, HTH, HHT, HHH}. Let A be the event of getting at least one head. What is $P(A)$?

Solution

Since the event A consists of 7 outcomes, {TTH, THT, THH, HTT, HTH, HHT, HHH}, and there are 8 equally likely outcomes in the sample space,

$$P(A) = \frac{7}{8}.$$

5

Example 5.3

In experiment number 3, let A be the event of observing an even number. What is $P(A)$?

Solution

Since there are 3 outcomes in A and 6 outcomes in the sample space,

$$P(A) = \frac{3}{6} \text{ or } \frac{1}{2}.$$

If the sample space is composed of equally-likely outcomes, then once the set of outcomes is determined, computing a probability is simply a matter of counting the members in each set and dividing by the total number of outcomes.

It is very important to remember that the classical approach rests on the assumption of equally-likely outcomes. If the assumption is not reasonable, some other method of determining the probability must be used.

Example 5.4

In experiment number 2, a coin was tossed three times and the number of heads was observed. The outcomes in the sample space were

$$S = \{TTT, TTH, THT, THH, HTT, HTH, HHT, HHH\}.$$

Could the sample space in this experiment have been formulated differently? Could, for example, the outcomes be defined as the number of heads in three tosses, $S = \{0, 1, 2, 3\}$?

Solution

Using the classical definition of probability requires that the outcomes be equally likely. Since the sample space $S = \{0, 1, 2, 3\}$ does not contain equally likely events, the classical definition of probability is not applicable.

Subjective Approach

The subjective viewpoint regards the probability of an event as a measure of the degree of belief that the event has occurred or will occur. Someone's degree of belief in some event will depend on his or her life experiences. Different life experiences produce different degrees of belief. Hence, the subjective approach must allow for differences in the degree of belief among reasonable people examining the same evidence. One of the significant advantages of this view is the ability to discuss the probability of events that cannot be repeated. Thus, a subjectivist would be willing to assign the probability of making an "A" in your statistics course. Someone who adopts the subjective view could use the frequency interpretation to influence the determination of a subjective probability. For example, suppose that a coin had been tossed 20,000 times and had come up heads 63% of the time. It would certainly be reasonable for a subjectivist to use this information in the formulation of a statement of probability about the outcome of the next toss.

Criticism of the Subjective View

If science is defined as finding out what is probably true, there should be a probability criterion on which all reasonable persons could agree. But if probability is subjective, how can it be used as a universally accepted criterion? Two reasonable persons might examine the same data and reach different conclusions about their degree of belief about some proposition.

 **Exercises**

Basic Concepts

1. What are the two main branches of probability?

2. What are the two approaches to objective probability?

3. What are some of the problems associated with the relative frequency approach?

4. True or false: According to mathematical law of probability, the observed relative frequency of heads when flipping a coin will eventually reach .5 since the probability of heads is .5.

5. What is statistical regularity?

6. Describe the classical approach to probability.

7. Using the classical approach, describe how you would determine the probability of event A.

8. What is the subjective approach to probability? Discuss the problems of applying the subjective interpretation.

Exercises

1. A gambler has made a weighted die. In order to decide which of the six sides is most likely to turn up, he tosses the die 33 times and notes the number of dots on the upper-most surface. The results of the experiment are shown below:

Table for Exercise 1 – Rolls of a Weighted Die										
1	2	1	3	1	4	1	5	6	3	1
3	1	5	1	2	1	3	1	2	1	2
2	1	3	5	1	2	1	2	1	4	6

   a. Using the relative frequency approach, what is the probability of observing each side?

   b. Which side do you think the gambler will bet on when the die is tossed?

2. Assume there are two red, two yellow, and two blue buttons in a hat. A button is drawn out of the hat, the color is noted, and the button is returned. This is repeated fifty times. The results are listed in the following table.

Table for Exercise 2 – Button Drawing				
Yellow	Yellow	Red	Yellow	Red
Red	Red	Blue	Red	Blue
Blue	Red	Red	Yellow	Red
Red	Blue	Yellow	Red	Yellow
Yellow	Blue	Red	Blue	Red
Red	Red	Red	Red	Yellow
Blue	Yellow	Yellow	Blue	Red
Yellow	Red	Red	Red	Yellow
Red	Yellow	Yellow	Yellow	Red
Red	Red	Blue	Red	Blue

   Using the relative frequency approach, what is the probability of drawing each color?

3. Twenty-five insurance agents are randomly selected and asked if they own a handgun. Twenty-two of those surveyed said that they do own a handgun. If an insurance agent is randomly selected, estimate the probability that the agent will own a handgun.

4. Thirty elementary school teachers are randomly selected and asked if they favor standardized testing of elementary school children. Twenty of those surveyed said that they did favor standardized testing of elementary school children. If an elementary school teacher is randomly selected, estimate the probability that the teacher will favor standardized testing for elementary school children.

5. Fifty chief executive officers (CEOs) of publicly traded companies are randomly selected and their salaries are determined. Forty-five of the CEOs selected have salaries in excess of $500,000. If a CEO from one of the selected publically traded companies is randomly selected, find the probability that the CEO will have a salary in excess of $500,000.

6. Forty emergency calls to which a local police department responded were randomly selected. Of the forty emergency calls 15 were categorized as domestic arguments. Estimate the probability that the next emergency call to which the local police department responds will be a domestic argument.

7. For the following situations, decide which probability interpretation is most reasonable to use: relative frequency, subjective, or classical.

   a. Whether or not you will have a wreck on your next trip to the mall.

   b. Whether or not a car coming off the Ford assembly line will have a defect.

   c. The probability that you will graduate from college in four calendar years.

   d. Whether a person will be in an automobile accident during the next year.

   e. The probability that you will be dealt a full house from a well-shuffled deck of cards.

8. For the following situations, decide which probability interpretation is most reasonable to use: relative frequency, subjective, or classical.

   a. Suppose you have purchased a lottery ticket. Describe your chances of winning the lottery.

   b. The probability you will enjoy a vacation trip to Mexico.

   c. The probability your company's sales will exceed seven million dollars this year.

   d. One hundred people receive keys to a new car in a radio contest. Only one key actually fits the car. The probability that key number 25 will open the car door.

   e. The probability that you will get a ticket if you drive 70 mph on the interstate between work and home this coming Tuesday.

   f. The probability that the S&P 500 will increase or decrease by at least 25 points in one day.

5

9. A couple plans to have two children.

   a. List all possible outcomes for the sexes of the two children.

   b. Find the probability that the couple will have 2 boys.

   c. Find the probability that the couple will have at least 1 girl.

10. Consider a student who is taking a multiple choice examination where there are five possible answers for each question. Since the student has not studied or attended any of the classes, the student decides to randomly guess at each question.

    a. Find the probability that the student will answer the first question correctly.

    b. Find the probability that the student will answer the first question incorrectly.

11. A game show contestant has to choose one of three doors to win a prize. Behind one door the prize is a trip to Hawaii; behind another door, the prize is a color TV; behind the final door, the prize is a bag of potatoes. If a contestant randomly selects a door,

    a. Find the probability that the contestant will win a trip to Hawaii.

    b. Find the probability that the contestant will not win a trip to Hawaii.

5.3 Probability, Statistics, and Business

Most of the time, when working with samples, statisticians try to deduce from the samples the population parameters (means, proportions, variances, etc.) of certain variables. This process of making judgments about population parameters is called **statistical inference**. Because samples are random, there is no guarantee that the sample will be representative of the population. If the sample is not representative, then using the sample mean as an estimate (inference) of the population mean would not be very wise. Probability is used to assess the quality of our inference. All statistical conclusions must be endowed with a degree of uncertainty. Because probability is used to assess the reliability of sample inferences, it is the foundation of all inferential statistics.

The probability concept also has many direct applications in business. When a manager wonders whether dropping a bid price by 5% will increase the probability of winning the bid, he or she is thinking about chance. Probability is also used as a criterion in designing and evaluating product reliability, evaluating insurance, inventory management, project management, and in the study of queuing theory (a probabilistic analysis of waiting lines).

Probability theory emerged from the need to better understand a game of chance. Business decisions, like games, have uncertain outcomes. In an effort to make better decisions, businesses spend considerable monies trying to quantify uncertainty. This means trying to turn uncertainty into a probability. Insurance companies have historically done a good job of quantifying uncertainty. In fact, a special kind of statistician called an actuary has emerged to assist in the development of insurance models which quantify uncertainty and aid in business decisions.

For example the next time you watch a 30-second commercial during the Super Bowl, consider that some company has just spent roughly $3 million for the air time plus a substantial amount of money developing the advertisement. Without knowing the effect of the advertisement in advance, extensive amounts of money are put at risk with an uncertain outcome. The manager making the decision uses subjective probability to assess the risk and reward.

5.3 Exercises

Basic Concepts

1. What is statistical inference?

2. Discuss the relationship between probability and statistics.

3. Give three applications of probability in business.

4. Describe the importance of probability in the insurance industry.

5. What type of probability does the manager of a company use when purchasing a commercial spot during the Super Bowl? Explain why.

5.4 Laws of Probability

Interpreting probability via the classical approach is a good way of thinking about the basic probability principles.

Probabilities must obey certain laws, no matter how probability is defined.

Probability Law 1

A probability of zero means the event cannot happen.

For example, the probability of observing three heads in two tosses of a coin is zero.

Probability Law 2

A probability of one means the event must happen.

If we toss a coin, the probability of getting either a head or tail is one.

Probability Law 3

All probabilities must be between zero and one inclusively. That is, $0 \leq P(A) \leq 1$.

The closer the probability is to 1, the more likely the event. The closer the probability is to 0, the less likely the event.

Probability Law 4

The sum of the probabilities of all outcomes must equal one. That is, if $P(A_i)$ is the probability of event A_i, and there are n such outcomes, then
$$P(A_1) + P(A_2) + \ldots + P(A_n) = 1.$$

There are a number of rules concerning the relationships between events that are useful in determining probabilities.

Struck by Lightning

Many people have a greater chance of meeting someone who survived a lightning strike than someone who won the lottery. There are an estimated 1,800 new thunderstorms being created around the world every minute and the odds against someone being struck by lightning are 606,944 to one. That is unless you are Roy C. Sullivan. Mr. Sullivan was a former U.S. park ranger who was struck by lightning over seven times in 41 years.

Origins of Probability

Galileo performed one of the earliest probability analyses. Galileo was approached by an Italian nobleman who had observed that three dice were more likely to obtain a sum of 10 than a sum of 9 when thrown. Galileo became interested in the uncertainties of throwing dice and wrote a short work outlining his findings. Galileo's work set forth some of the theory of probability. The next step in the birth of probability came from the French.
Continued ...

Compound Event

... Continued

A French nobleman, Chevalier de Mere, won quite a few francs by getting unwitting souls to bet him that he would not roll at least one six in a sequence of four tosses of a die. He then lost his profits by wagering that he would get at least one double 6 in a sequence of 24 tosses of two dice. Chevalier de Mere asked two of the leading mathematicians of the time, Pierre de Fermet (1601–1622) and Blaise Pascal (1623–1662), to consider his problem. The exchange of letters between Fermat and Pascal led to some of the first analysis of random phenomena, and development of the first principles of probability theory.

Union

Definition

A **compound event** is an event that is defined by combining two or more events.

Suppose that the marketing director of *Sports Illustrated* believed that anyone who possessed an income greater than $50,000 and/or subscribed to more than one other sports magazine could potentially be a good prospect for a direct mail marketing campaign.

Let the events

A = {annual income is greater than $50,000}

and

B = {subscribes to more than one other sports magazine}.

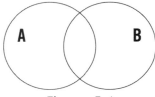

Figure 5.4

There are several different types of compound events. To illustrate the concepts consider the two events A and B in Figure 5.4. The set of outcomes in which either or both of these events occurs is called the **union** of the two sets.

Definition

The **union** of the events A and B is the set of outcomes that are included in A or B or both, and is denoted $A \cup B$.

Figure 5.5

Notice in Figure 5.5 that the union includes all points in both A and/or B.

Definition

The **intersection** of the events A and B is the set of all outcomes that are included in both A and B.

Intersection

Suppose the marketing director was interested in persons who possessed an annual income of $50,000 and subscribed to more than one other sports magazine, that set would be called the intersection of A and B.

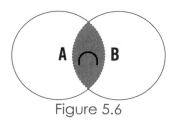

Figure 5.6

The symbol for the intersection is $\cap$. Symbolically, the intersection of A and B would be denoted $A \cap B$ and is read "A intersect B". Notice in Figure 5.6 that the intersection includes only those points in both A **and** B.

Two other useful concepts are the notions of the **complement** of an event and events which are **mutually exclusive**.

Definition

The **complement** of an event A is the set of all outcomes in the sample space that are not in A.

Complement

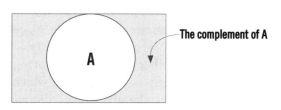

Figure 5.7

The complement of the set A is written as A^c. Notice in Figure 5.7 that the complement of event A includes all points which are not in A. For the event $A = \{$annual income is greater than $50,000$\}$, the complement of A would be

$$A^c = \{\text{annual income is less than or equal to } \$50{,}000\}.$$

Also note that $A^c \cup A = S$.

Probability Law 5

The probability of A^c is given by $P(A^c) = 1 - P(A)$.

Sometimes it is much easier to calculate the probability of the complement of an event than the actual event.

Example 5.5

Consider the event A = {annual income is greater than $50,000}. Suppose the probability of A was .08. Determine the probability of observing someone whose income was less than or equal to $50,000.

Solution

$$P(\text{annual income is less than or equal to } \$50,000) = P(A^c)$$
$$= 1 - P(A)$$
$$= 1 - .08$$
$$= .92$$

Example 5.6

Consider an experiment to see how many tosses of a coin will be required to obtain the first head. The first head could be observed on the first toss or the second toss but there is no upper limit on the number of tosses that could be required. Therefore, the sample space for this experiment is the set of positive integers $\{1, 2, 3, ...\}$. Not only is the sample space infinitely large, but there is another problem: the outcomes are not equally likely. This is a potentially ugly environment in which to compute a probability. But let's make matters slightly worse. Suppose we want to know the probability that it will require at least two tosses to get the first head. That is, we want to know the probability of getting the first head in two or more tosses of the coin. This means that we must compute the probability of 2, the probability of 3, and so on up to infinity and add them up in some way. The problem is rather insidious if approached directly.

Solution

The problem becomes rather trivial by determining the complement of the event and computing its probability. The complement of obtaining the first head in two or more tosses is getting a head on the first toss. The probability of getting a head on the first toss should be about .5, assuming the coin is fair. Therefore,

$$P(\text{two or more tosses to obtain the first head}) = 1 - P(\text{head on the first toss})$$
$$= 1 - .5$$
$$= .5.$$

Often times, when the problem asks you to find the probability of "at least" you want to think **complement,** as in this example.

Another idea that is helpful in determining probabilities is the notion of **mutual exclusivity**.

Definition

Two sets are **mutually exclusive** if they have no points in common.

Mutual exclusivity is also called **disjointedness**. Figure 5.8 represents two disjoint events.

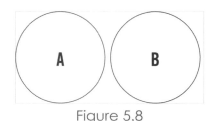

Figure 5.8

Probability Law 6

Union of Mutually Exclusive Events

If the events A and B are mutually exclusive, then

$$P(A \cup B) = P(A) + P(B).$$

Mutually Exclusive

Mutually Exclusive

Two events are mutually exclusive if they cannot occur at the same time. For example, if you were to select one card from a standard deck, the two outcomes:
• The card is a Jack
• The card is a Seven
are mutually exclusive, because you cannot select a card that is both a Jack **and** a Seven. However, the two outcomes
• The card is a Jack
• The card is a Club
are not mutually exclusive, because you can select a card that is both a Jack **and** a Club.

Two People with the Same Birthday

How likely is it that two people in your statistics class will have the same birthday? There is an interesting internet site that will enable you to explore this problem. http://www.hawkeslearning.com/birthday.htm

Probability Law 7

Intersection of Mutually Exclusive Events

If the events A and B are mutually exclusive, then

$$P(A \cap B) = 0.$$

Example 5.7

Suppose $P(A) = .27$ and $P(B) = .19$. If A and B are mutually exclusive, what is the probability of $A \cup B$?

Solution

Since these are mutually exclusive events,

$$P(A \cup B) = P(A) + P(B) = .27 + .19 = .46.$$

There is a more generalized rule that eliminates the assumption of exclusivity between the sets.

Probability Law 8

The Addition Rule

For any two events A and B,

$$P(A \cup B) = P(A) + P(B) - P(A \cap B).$$

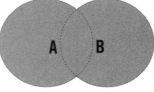

Figure 5.9

This rule is identical to Probability Law 6 when the events are mutually exclusive, since A intersect B will be an empty set whose probability will be zero (i.e. $P(A \cap B) = 0$). In cases where A and B intersect, the probability of the intersection must be subtracted since it is contained once in A and once in B.

Example 5.8

Suppose that the marketing manager mentioned earlier believed that the probability that someone earns more than $50,000 is .2 and the probability that someone will subscribe to more than one sports magazine is .3. If the probability of finding someone in both categories is .08, what is the probability of finding someone who is earning over $50,000 or subscribes to more than one sports magazine, or both?

Solution

The problem involves the union of two events. Using the same event names (A and B) as in previous examples, the desired probability is

$$P(A \cup B) = P(A) + P(B) - P(A \cap B) = .2 + .3 - .08 = .42.$$

Therefore, the probability of finding someone who is earning over $50,000 or subscribes to more than one sports magazine, or both is .42.

5.4 Exercises

Basic Concepts

1. What laws must probability obey, regardless of the methodology used to derive the probabilities?

2. Suppose you are taking a test next week. Interpret each of the following statements. P(receiving an A on the test) = 0, P(receiving an A on the test) = 1, P(receiving an A on the test) = .3.

3. What is a compound event?

4. Define the following set operations: union, intersection, and complement.

5. If you know the probability of two events, what else must you know in order to calculate the probability of *one event or the other*?

6. If events A and B are mutually exclusive, what is $P(A \cap B)$?

Exercises

1. Determine if the following values could be probabilities.

   a. 0

   b. $\dfrac{36}{25}$

   c. $\dfrac{7}{8}$

   d. $-.4$

   e. $.23$

2. Determine if the following values could be probabilities.

   a. 1

   b. $\dfrac{15}{16}$

   c. $\dfrac{4}{3}$

   d. $.99$

   e. $-.05$

3. Interpret the following probabilities with respect to the occurrence of some event.

   a. $P(\text{event}) = 0$

   b. $P(\text{event}) = 1.0$

   c. $P(\text{event}) = .45$

   d. $P(\text{event}) = 65\%$

   e. $P(\text{event}) = -1.0$

4. Find the following probabilities.

   a. The probability of an event that must happen.

   b. The probability of an event that cannot happen.

   c. The probability of having a boy or a girl in a single birth.

   d. The probability of rolling a two and a five in a single toss of a die.

5. The annual premium amounts charged by life insurance companies to their clients are set very carefully. If the amount is too high, the client will take his or her business to another company. If it is too low, the insurance company may not make enough profit to stay in business. In order to properly determine a premium, the company often relies on life tables. These tables allow one to compute the probabilities of death at various ages. They are constructed only after collecting and reviewing extensive data on age at death from a large group of people. A life table is normally constructed assuming that 100,000 people are alive at age 0. This number is simply a reference value used to make comparisons throughout the table. Other numbers could be used. The table then gives the number of people of the original 100,000 that are alive at the beginning of various years of life. In order for the insurance company to optimally set premiums, a separate table should be constructed for the different genders and races. The following abbreviated life table is valid only for females.

Table for Exercise 5 – Life Table								
Year	0	1	5	10	15	20	25	30	35
Number Alive	100,000	99,090	98,912	98,815	98,716	98,477	98,204	97,897	97,500
Year	40	45	50	55	60	65	70	75	80
Number Alive	96,958	96,097	94,766	92,623	89,449	84,565	77,772	68,200	55,535

a. What is the probability that a newborn female lives until the age of 40?

b. What is the probability that a newborn female dies before she reaches the age of 50?

c. What is the probability that a 30 year old female lives until the age of 60?

d. What is the probability that a 20 year old female dies before the age of 70?

6. A mail order company classifies its customers by gender and location of residence. The market research department has gathered data from a random sample of 759 customers.

Table for Exercise 6 – Mail Order Customers		
	Gender	
Location	Male	Female
Suburban	196	298
Urban	92	173

    a. What is the probability that a customer is male?

    b. What is the probability that a customer is female?

    c. What is the probability that a customer is a suburban male?

    d. What is the probability that a customer is an urban female?

    e. What is the probability that a customer is a suburban male or an urban female?

    f. What is the probability that a customer is urban?

    g. What is the probability that a customer is not a suburban female?

    h. What approach to probability did you use to calculate your answers?

    i. Are the events {customer is urban} and {customer is suburban} mutually exclusive? Explain.

7. A large life insurance company is interested in studying the insurance policies held by married couples. In particular, the insurance company is interested in the amount of insurance held by the husbands and the wives. The insurance company collects data for all of its 1000 policies where both the husband and the wife are insured. The results are summarized in the chart below.

Table for Exercise 7 – Life Insurance Coverage		Amount of Life Insurance on Husband ($)			
		0 – 50,000	50,000 – 100,000	100,000 – 150,000	More than 150,000
Amount of Life Insurance on Wife ($)	0 – 50,000	400	200	50	50
	50,000 – 100,000	50	50	30	30
	100,000 – 150,000	20	10	25	25
	More than 150,000	20	10	15	15

a. For a randomly selected policy, what is the probability that the husband will have between $50,000 and $100,000 of insurance?

b. For a randomly selected policy, what is the probability that the husband will have between $100,000 and $150,000 of insurance?

c. For a randomly selected policy, what is the probability that the wife will have more than $150,000 of insurance or the husband will have more than $150,000 of insurance?

d. For a randomly selected policy, what is the probability that the wife will have between $0 and $50,000 of insurance and the husband will have between $0 and $50,000 of insurance?

e. For a randomly selected policy, what is the probability that the wife will not have between $0 and $50,000 of insurance?

f. For a randomly selected policy, what is the probability that the husband will have more than $50,000 of insurance?

g. What approach to probability did you use to calculate your answers?

h. Are the events {the wife has more than $150,000 in insurance} and {the husband has between $50,000 and $100,000 of insurance} mutually exclusive? Explain.

5

5.5   Conditional Probability

Researchers often want to examine a limited portion of the sample space. For example, consider the question of whether cigarette smoking harms those that are indirectly exposed to the smoke. Suppose that 3 percent of women who do not smoke die of cancer. However, if a non-smoking woman is married to a smoking husband (not to be confused with a husband who is on fire), the probability of dying of cancer is .08. This probability is a conditional probability, because the sample space is being limited by some condition – in this case, limited to only wives of smoking husbands. In this instance, the dramatic effect of a smoking husband on cancer rates is readily evident.

P(a non-smoking woman dies of cancer) $\neq$

P(a non-smoking woman dies of cancer given that her husband smokes).

Similarly, the results from a market survey indicate that 39 percent of the customers surveyed believe your product is of high quality. However, if the analysis is limited to only women, 54 percent of women surveyed believe the product is of high quality. Based on the survey, it appears that women have a much higher regard for the company's product than men. The difference in attitude would probably be something that could affect how the company spends its marketing dollars.

The notion of conditional probability is defined below.

Definition

Conditional Probability

The probability that one event will occur given that some other event has occurred is a **conditional probability**.

To compute a conditional probability, apply the following rule:

Probability Law 9

The conditional probability of A, given that B has occurred is

$$P(A|B) = \frac{P(A \cap B)}{P(B)}.$$

The events A and B can be reversed in the preceding rule to compute $P(B|A)$.

The notation $P(A|B)$ is read as *The probability of A given the occurrence of B.* The vertical bar within a probability statement will always mean *given*.

Example 5.9

Suppose a marketing research firm has surveyed a panel of consumers to test a new product and produced the following cross tabulation indicating the number of panelists that liked the product, the number that did not like the product, and the number that were undecided.

Age	Like	Not Like	Undecided	Total
18-35	213	197	103	513
35-50	193	184	67	444
Over 50	144	219	83	446
Total	550	600	253	1403

Table 5.1 – Market Research Survey

If an individual is between 35 and 50 years old, what is the probability he or she will like the product?

Solution

Let the events

A = { like the product },

and

B = { age between 35 and 50 }.

Then the desired probability can be formulated as

$$P(A|B) = \frac{P(A \cap B)}{P(B)}.$$

The $P(A \cap B)$ is called a joint probability since it is the probability of the occurrence of more than one event. To compute $P(A \cap B)$ use the empirical approach; that is,

$$P(A \cap B) = \frac{193}{1403} \approx .138.$$

Let's Make a Deal

A long time ago, back in the 70s, there was a television show called "Let's Make a Deal" starring Monty Hall as the host. A new version of the show premiered in 2009 starring Wayne Brady as the host. The Monty Hall show produced an interesting problem in probability which someone submitted to Marilyn vos Savant which she answered in her column in *Parade* magazine. Incidentally, Ms. Savant is in the Guinness Book of World Records as having the highest recorded IQ (228). Here's the problem that was posed to Ms. Savant.

"Suppose you're on a game show, and you're given a choice of three doors: behind one door is a car: behind the others, goats. You pick a door, say number 1, and the host, who knows what's behind the other doors, opens another door, say number 3, which has a goat. He then says to you, 'Do you want to pick door number 2?' Is it to your advantage to take the switch?"

Continued ...

... Continued

Marilyn vos Savant answered the question in her column saying that it was to your advantage to switch. This set off a firestorm of mail telling Ms. Savant that she was incorrect. Much of this mail came from people with Ph.D.s behind their names. The *New York Times* printed a front page article in 1991 discussing the problem.

What do you think? To find the answer to this problem type "The Monty Hall problem" in your search engine, go to some of the web sites, and try some of the simulations.

Similarly, $P(B)$ can be computed as

$$P(B) = \frac{444}{1403} \approx .316.$$

Consequently, $P(A|B)$ is

$$P(A|B) \approx \frac{.138}{.316} \approx .437.$$

Note that the answer to the previous example could have also been obtained by simply dividing 193 by 444.

 **Exercises**

Basic Concepts

1. Define conditional probability.

2. How do you calculate $P(A|B)$?

Exercises

1. The following table was given in Section 5.4, Exercise 6.

Table for Exercise 1 – Mail Order Customers		
	Gender	
Location	Male	Female
Suburban	196	298
Urban	92	173

   a. Given that the customer is a male, what is the probability that he is urban?

   b. Given that the customer is urban, what is the probability that he is male?

   c. Given that the customer is female, what is the probability that she is suburban?

   d. Given that the customer is suburban, what is the probability that the customer is a woman?

2. The following table was given in Section 5.4, Exercise 7.

Table for Exercise 2 – Life Insurance Coverage		Amount of Life Insurance on Husband ($)			
		0 – 50,000	50,000 – 100,000	100,000 – 150,000	More than 150,000
Amount of Life Insurance on Wife ($)	0 – 50,000	400	200	50	50
	50,000 – 100,000	50	50	30	30
	100,000 – 150,000	20	10	25	25
	More than 150,000	20	10	15	15

a. Given the wife has between $100,000 and $150,000 of insurance, what is the probability that the husband has more than $150,000 of insurance?

b. Given the wife has between $0 and $50,000 of insurance, what is the probability that the husband has between $0 and $150,000 of insurance?

c. Given that the husband has between $0 and $50,000 of insurance, what is the probability that the wife will have more than $150,000 of insurance?

d. Given that the husband has more than $150,000 of insurance, what is the probability that the wife will have more than $150,000 of insurance?

3. A computer software company receives hundreds of support calls each day. There are several common installation problems, call them A, B, C, and D. Several of these problems result in the same symptom, *lock up* after initiation. Suppose that the probability of a caller reporting the symptom *lock up* is .7 and the probability of a caller having problem A and a *lock up* is .6.

a. Given that the caller reports a lock up, what is the probability that the cause is problem A?

b. What is the probability that the cause of the malfunction is not problem A given that the caller is experiencing a lock up?

4. A television advertising representative has determined the following probabilities based on past experience. The probability that an individual will watch an ad during the Super Bowl is .10. Given that the individual watches the ad, the probability that the individual will buy the product is .005. It is also known that the probability that an individual would buy the product is .02. Given that an individual buys the product, find the probability that the individual watched the television ad during the Super Bowl.

5. Medical researchers have determined that there is a 2% chance that an individual will have a gene which gives him a predisposition for heart disease. Given that an individual has the gene, the probability that heart disease will develop is 25%. It is also known that the probability that an individual has heart disease is 12%.

   a. Find the probability that an individual will have the gene and develop heart disease.

   b. Given that a person has heart disease, what is the probability that they have the gene?

5.6 Independence

An extremely important concept in statistical analysis is **independence**. It describes a special kind of relationship between two events. Two events are said to be independent if knowledge of one event does not provide information of the other event's occurrence. In other words, the occurrence of one event does not affect the occurrence of another event if the events are independent.

Example 5.10

Experiment: roll a fair die two times. Consider the two events

A = {rolling a six on the first roll of a fair die}

and

B = {rolling a four on the second roll of a fair die}.

Are these two events independent?

Solution

Since knowledge of the outcome of the first roll does not help one make an inference of the outcome of the second roll, events A and B are independent.

Symbolically the idea of independence is expressed in the following definition.

Definition

Two events, A and B, are **independent** if and only if

Independent Events

$$P(A\mid B) = P(A) \text{ or } P(B\mid A) = P(B).$$

In many cases, regarding the independence of two events, intuition and common sense will lead you to the correct determination. However, there are situations in which independence can only be discovered by formal application of the definition.

What does it mean if two events are not independent? One obvious response is to say that they are **dependent**, a term that is just as much a part of statistical vocabulary as independent. If events are dependent, they are related; the nature of the relationship and whether the relationship can be used for predictive purposes are problems often examined by statisticians.

5

Basketball and Dependence

If we were playing basketball and made a large number of consecutive shots, then there might be a temptation to boast of our skills. Alternatively, someone might suggest that you were on a lucky streak. Two psychologists examined the "lucky streak" phenomenon by analyzing the sequence of made and missed shots by professional basketball players. The selected players made roughly 50 percent of their shots. Their analysis found that there was no evidence of the hot hand – that is, there was no evidence of a dependent relationship between the consecutive shots. They did not find more long streaks of made baskets than would be expected to occur by chance.

During the course of a business negotiation, both negotiators may exhibit numerous types of idiosyncratic behavior. If they have jewelry, they might manipulate it. If they smoke cigarettes, they might play with their lighters or packs of cigarettes. Are their mannerisms independent of the importance of the issue they are negotiating? Does the negotiator tend to smoke a cigarette or play with jewelry when he or she has a strong position? Good negotiators will pick up dependencies and use the information to their advantage. However, the concept of association implied by dependence must not be confused with the idea of causation. It may be that one of the events does indeed cause the other, but the fact that they are not independent (dependent) is not evidence of causation.

Probability Law 10

Multiplication Rule for Independent Events

If two events, A and B, are independent, then

$$P(A \cap B) = P(A) \cdot P(B).$$

If n events, $A_1, A_2, \ldots, A_n$, are independent, then

$$P(A_1 \cap A_2 \cap \ldots \cap A_n) = P(A_1) \cdot P(A_2) \cdot \ldots \cdot P(A_n).$$

The probability law expressed above is sometimes called the **product rule**. The rule simply states that the probability of the joint occurrence of mutually independent events is the product of their probabilities.

Example 5.11

A coin is flipped, a die is rolled, and a card is drawn from a deck of 52 cards. Find the probability of getting tails on the coin, a five on the die, and a Jack of clubs from the deck of cards.

Solution

Since the three events (flipping a coin, rolling a die, and selecting a card) are independent, we can use the **product rule**.

We know the following:

$$P(\text{tails on coin}) = \frac{1}{2},$$

$$P(\text{five on die}) = \frac{1}{6}, \text{ and}$$

$$P(\text{Jack of clubs}) = \frac{1}{52}.$$

Therefore,

$$P(\text{tails on coin} \cap \text{five on die} \cap \text{Jack of clubs})$$
$$= P(\text{tails on coin}) \cdot P(\text{five on die}) \cdot P(\text{Jack of clubs}).$$
$$= \frac{1}{2} \cdot \frac{1}{6} \cdot \frac{1}{52}$$
$$= \frac{1}{624}$$
$$\approx .0016.$$

So the probability of tossing a tail, rolling a five, and then selecting the Jack of clubs is about .0016.

Example 5.12

This is an actual case that stirred up quite a controversy.

People v. Collins (1968)

On June 18, 1964, at about 11:30 A.M., Mrs. Juanita Brooks was assaulted and robbed while walking through an alley in the San Pedro area of Los Angeles. Mrs. Brooks described her assailant as a young woman with a blond pony tail. At about the same time John Bass was watering his lawn and witnessed the assault. He described the assailant as a Caucasian woman with dark-blond hair. As she ran from the alley she jumped into a yellow automobile driven by a black man with a mustache and a beard.

5

Several days later the police arrested two individuals based on the descriptions provided by the assailant and the witness. The two suspects were eventually charged with the crime. During the trial the prosecution called a professor of mathematics to testify. The prosecutor set forth the following probabilities for the characteristics of the assailants:

Table 5.2 – Assailants Data	
Characteristic	**Probability**
Yellow automobile	.10
Man with mustache	.25
Girl with ponytail	.10
Girl with blonde hair	.33
Black man with beard	.10
Interracial couple in a car	.001

How did the prosecution use these probabilities to argue its case?

Solution

If the events are assumed to be independent, then the **product rule** can be used to calculate the likelihood of observing their joint occurrence.

$$P\left(\begin{array}{l} \text{Yellow automobile} \cap \text{Man with} \\ \text{mustache} \cap \text{Girl with ponytail} \cap \text{Girl} \\ \text{with blond hair} \cap \text{Black man with} \\ \text{beard} \cap \text{Interracial couple in car} \end{array}\right) = (.10)(.25)(.10)(.33)(.10)(.001)$$

$$= .0000000825.$$

Based on the product rule, the mathematician testified that there was about a 1 in 12 million chance that a couple selected at random would possess these characteristics. The prosecution added that the probability was the chance that "any other couple possessed the distinctive characteristics of the defendants." The jury convicted the defendants. On appeal, the Supreme Court of California reversed the decision, based on two main points. First there was no proof offered that the probabilities used in the probability calculation were correct and there was no evidence that the events were independent. Second, the prosecution's evidence pertaining to a randomly selected couple was not pertinent to the problem of the existence of any other couple possessing the same characteristics.

Example 5.13

In a production process, a product is assembled by using four independent parts (A, B, C, and D). In order for the part to operate properly, each part must be free of defects. The probability that the parts are defect-free is given by $P(A) = .9$, $P(B) = .7$, $P(C) = .8$, and $P(D) = .9$.

a. What is the probability that all four parts have defects?

b. What is the probability that the product does not work?

Solution

a. Since there are four parts with the probability of each part working (i.e., being defect-free) given to be $P(A) = .9$, $P(B) = .7$, $P(C) = .8$, and $P(D) = .9$, for all parts to have defects, we need the complement of each of the parts. That is,

$$P(\text{all four parts have defects}) = P(A^c \cap B^c \cap C^c \cap D^c).$$

Since each part operates independently of the others, then the probability that all four parts have a defect is the product of the probabilities of each of the part's complement. Thus,

$$P(\text{all four parts have defects}) = P(A^c) \cdot P(B^c) \cdot P(C^c) \cdot P(D^c)$$
$$= (1-.9)(1-.7)(1-.8)(1-.9) = .0006.$$

Thus, the probability that all four parts have defects is .0006, or 0.06%.

b. The probability that the product does not work is the probability that at least one of the parts does not work (since each part must be defect-free for the product to work).

Thus,

$$P(\text{product does not work}) = P(\text{at least one part does not work})$$
$$= 1 - P(\text{all parts work})$$
$$= 1 - P(A \cap B \cap C \cap D)$$
$$= 1 - (.9)(.7)(.8)(.9) = 1 - .4536 = .5464.$$

Thus, given the above probabilities, there is nearly a 55% chance that the product will not work.

Winning the Lottery Twice!

In 1986 a woman won the New Jersey state lottery twice and in 1988 a man in Pennsylvania also won the State lottery twice for a total of 5.4 and 6.8 million dollars respectively. The *New York Times* reported the odds to be 1 in 17 trillion. How is this to be explained?

When millions of people play a lottery daily it can be shown that the odds of winning twice is about 1 in 30 in a 4-month period and the odds are even better in a 7 year period. Thus what appeared to be an almost theoretical impossibility, turns out to be quite a probable event. What one can say is that even when the probability of an event is very small, if there are millions of possibilities, then the rare event rarely remains rare. This is what has been called "The Law of Real Large Numbers" by Diaconis and Mosteller.

Source: Diaconis, P. and Mosteller, F. (1989). Methods for Studying Coincidences," Journal of the American Statistical Association, 84, 853-861.

5.6 Exercises

Basic Concepts

1. Explain the difference between dependent and independent events.

2. Are mutually exclusive events dependent or independent? Explain your answer.

3. If events A and B are independent, what is $P(A|B)$ equal to?

4. What is the product rule?

5. In the case *People v. Collins* an appeals court overturned the conviction. What flaws did the appeals court detect in the case against the accused assailants?

Exercises

1. The following table was given in Section 5.4, Exercise 6.

Table for Exercise 1 – Mail Order Customers		
	Gender	
Location	**Male**	**Female**
Suburban	196	298
Urban	92	173

   Are the events {customer is urban} and {customer is suburban} independent? Explain.

2. The following table was given in Section 5.4, Exercise 7.

Table for Exercise 2 – Life Insurance Coverage				
		Amount of Life Insurance on Husband ($)		
		0 – 50,000	50,000 – 100,000	100,000 – 150,000	More than 150,000
Amount of Life Insurance on Wife ($)	0 – 50,000	400	200	50	50
	50,000 – 100,000	50	50	30	30
	100,000 – 150,000	20	10	25	25
	More than 150,000	20	10	15	15

   Are the events {the husband has more than $150,000 in insurance} and {the wife has more than $50,000 in insurance} independent? Explain.

3. Suppose you were flipping a coin. What is the probability that you would observe a head:

   a. on two consecutive flips?

   b. on three consecutive flips?

   c. on four consecutive flips?

   d. on 100 consecutive flips?

4. Suppose an atomic reactor has two independent cooling systems. The probability that Cooling System A will fail is .01 and the probability that Cooling System B will fail is .01. What is the probability that both systems will fail simultaneously?

5. Mandy is 30, and the probability that she will survive until age 65 is .90. Ashley is 45, and the probability that she will survive until age 65 is .95.

   a. Find the probability that both Mandy and Ashley will survive until age 65.

   b. Find the probability that only Mandy will survive until age 65.

   c. Find the probability that neither Mandy nor Ashley will survive until age 65.

   d. What assumption about the lives of Mandy and Ashley did you make in answering the above questions?

6. An insurance company is considering insuring two large oil tankers against spills. The limit of the liability on the coverage is $10,000,000. The company believes that the probability of an oil spill requiring the maximum liability coverage during the policy period is .001 per tanker.

   a. What is the probability that neither tanker would have a significant spill during the policy period?

   b. What is the probability that only one tanker would have a significant spill during the policy period?

   c. What is the probability that both tankers would have significant spills during the period?

5

7. Coin flipping can be used to model other real life phenomena and aid in certain probability calculations. An example of this would be to compute the probability that the World Series ends in some specified number of games. As many people already know, the World Series is a best of seven game series played at the end of the regular baseball season between the champion of the American League and the champion of the National League. The first team to win four games is declared the champion of baseball for that year. If we assume the probability of either team winning a game is approximately .5 and the games are independent events, the probability that the series ends in either 4, 5, 6, or 7 games can be computed.

   a. What is the probability that the series ends in exactly 4 games? Write the sample space consisting of 16 equally likely simple events similar to the sample space resulting from tossing a coin four times.

   b. What is the probability that the series ends in exactly 5 games?

   c. Assume the probability that the series ends in exactly 6 games is $\frac{5}{16}$. Use this information together with your answers to the first two parts of this problem to compute the probability that the series ends in exactly 7 games.

8. Drug usage in the workplace costs employers incredible amounts of money each year. Drug testing potential employees has become so prevalent that drug users are finding it extremely hard to find jobs. Drug tests, however, are not completely reliable. The most common test used to detect drugs is approximately 98% accurate. To decrease the likelihood of making an error, all potential employees are screened through two tests, which are independent, and each has about 98% accuracy.

   a. If a person were drug free, what is the probability he or she would fail both tests?

   b. If a person were a drug user, what is the probability he or she would pass both tests?

5.7 Bayes' Theorem

We have completed the discussions about conditional probability and independent events in Section 5.5 and Section 5.6. Bayes' theorem (also referred to as Bayes' rule or Bayes' law) is somewhat of an extension of conditional probability in which we calculate probabilities based on new information. You may recall the following formula for conditional probability:

$$P(B \mid A) = \frac{P(A \cap B)}{P(A)} \text{ provided that } P(A) > 0.$$

The notion of conditional probability will be extended to include Bayes' theorem, which is used for revising a probability value based on additional information. Please note and understand that the additional information is obtained for a subsequent event, and the new information is used to revise the initial probability.

Bayes' theorem is developed from extending the definition of conditional probability. That is, to find the conditional probability of B given A, we have

$$P(B \mid A) = \frac{P(A \cap B)}{P(A)} = \frac{P(A \mid B) P(B)}{P(A)}.$$

Recall the Multiplication Rule for Independent Events. That is, we know that if A and B are independent events, then $P(A \cap B) = P(A) \cdot P(B)$. If this rule holds for two events, A and B, then we can generalize the multiplication rule as follows.

$$P(A) = P(A \cap B_1) + P(A \cap B_2) + \cdots + P(A \cap B_k)$$

Using the generalized multiplication rule, we now have

$$P(A) = P(A \mid B_1) \cdot P(B_1) + P(A \mid B_2) \cdot P(B_2) + \cdots + P(A \mid B_k) \cdot P(B_k)$$

where B_1, B_2, ..., B_k are k mutually exclusive and collectively exhaustive events.

Theorem

Bayes' Theorem

Given the above information, we can derive Bayes' theorem as

$$P(B_i \mid A) = \frac{P(A \mid B_i)P(B_i)}{P(A \mid B_1)P(B_1) + P(A \mid B_2)P(B_2) + \cdots + P(A \mid B_k)P(B_k)}$$

where B_i is the ith event out of k mutually exclusive and collectively exhaustive events.

Example 5.14

Of the travelers arriving at a small airport, 60% fly on major airlines, 30% fly on privately owned planes, and the remainder fly on commercially owned planes not belonging to a major airline. Of those traveling on the major airlines, 50% are traveling for business reasons, whereas 60% of those arriving on private planes and 90% of those arriving on the other commercially owned planes are traveling for business reasons. Suppose that we randomly select one person arriving at the airport. What is the probability that the person

a. is traveling on business?

b. is traveling for business on a privately owned plane?

c. arrived on a privately owned plane given that the person is traveling for business reasons?

Solution

First of all, we should define the events associated with this problem. Once we have defined the events, we can then note the probabilities that are given to us.

Let

$$M = \text{Major Airline}$$
$$P = \text{Private Plane}$$
$$C = \text{Commercial Airline}$$
$$B = \text{Travel for Business Reasons.}$$

We know the following:

$$P(M) = .6$$
$$P(P) = .3$$
$$P(C) = .1$$
$$P(B \mid M) = .5$$
$$P(B \mid P) = .6$$
$$P(B \mid C) = .9.$$

a. The first question asks what the probability is that a randomly selected person is traveling on business. We know that a person is travelling on business if they are traveling on business via any of the flight methods. Thus we have

$$
\begin{aligned}
P(B) &= P(B \cap M) + P(B \cap P) + P(B \cap C) \\
&= P(M) \cdot P(B \mid M) + P(P) \cdot P(B \mid P) + P(C) \cdot P(B \mid C) \\
&= (.6)(.5) + (.3)(.6) + (.1)(.9) \\
&= .57.
\end{aligned}
$$

Thus, there is a 57% chance that the randomly selected traveler will be traveling for business.

b. To determine if the traveler is traveling for business on a privately owned plane, we want to find

$$P(B \cap P) = P(P) \cdot P(B \mid P) = (.3)(.6) = .18.$$

So, there is an 18% chance that the traveler will be traveling for business on a privately owned plane.

c. This part of the problem wants us to determine the probability that the person arrived on a privately owned plane given that he or she is traveling for business reasons. We can write this probability statement as $P(P \mid B)$.

By the definition of conditional probability, we can write

$$P(P \mid B) = \frac{P(P \cap B)}{P(B)} = \frac{P(B \mid P) \cdot P(P)}{P(B)}.$$

5

From the items calculated in parts (a) and (b), we know

$$P(P|B) = \frac{P(P \cap B)}{P(B)} = \frac{P(B|P) \cdot P(P)}{P(B)}$$

$$= \frac{P(B|P) \cdot P(P)}{P(M) \cdot P(B|M) + P(P) \cdot P(B|P) + P(C) \cdot P(B|C)}$$

$$= \frac{(.6)(.3)}{.57}$$

$$\approx .3158.$$

Thus, we know that if the passenger is traveling on business, there is about a 32% chance that he or she will be traveling by private plane.

Even though it was fairly subtle (given that we performed the calculations in parts (a) and (b)), please note the use of Bayes' theorem in the calculation above.

 **Exercises**

Basic Concepts

1. Briefly explain the relationship between conditional probability and Bayes' Theorem.

2. Other than conditional probability, which other rule which you previously studied is used in the derivation of Bayes' Theorem?

3. What is Bayes' Theorem?

4. How is Bayes' Theorem used to "revise" a probability based on additional information?

Exercises

1. The issue of Corporate Tax Reform has been cause for much debate in the United States, especially in the House Ways and Means Committee as well as the Senate Finance Committee. Among those in the legislature, 45% are Republicans and 55% are Democrats. It is reported that 30% of the Republicans and 70% of the Democrats favor some type of Corporate Tax Reform to prevent American companies from operating in foreign countries. Suppose a member of Congress is randomly selected and they are found to favor some type of corporate tax reform. What is the probability that this person is a Democrat?

2. Males and females are observed to react differently to sad, emotional movies. It has been observed that 70% of the females tend to cry at some point during those types of movies, whereas only 40% of the males admit to crying during those types of movies. A group of 40 people, of whom 25 are female, was shown a sad, emotional movie and the subjects were asked if they cried. A response picked at random from the 40 indicated that they cried. What is the probability that it was a male?

3. As items come to the end of a production line, an inspector chooses which items are to go through a complete inspection. Eight percent of all items produced are defective. Sixty percent of all defective items go through a complete inspection, and 20% of all good items go through a complete inspection. Given that an item is completely inspected, what is the probability that that it is defective?

4. Two teaching methods for a business statistics class, Online and Face-to-Face, are available during the course of an academic year. The failure rate (students that receive below a C- and thus, will have to repeat the course) is 4% for the online class and 8% for the face-to-face class. However, the online class is more expensive and hence is offered only 25% of the time. (The face-to-face class is offered the other 75% of the time.) A student takes the statistics class via one of the methods of delivery but failed the course. What is the probability that the student took the online class?

5. A personnel director has two lists of applicants for jobs. List 1 contains names of 15 women and 5 men whereas List 2 contains the names of 5 women and 12 men. A name is randomly selected from List 1 and added to List 2. A name is then randomly selected from the augmented List 2. Given that the name selected is that of a man, what is the probability that a woman's name was originally selected from List 1?

5

5.8   Counting

To compute certain probabilities, such as the probability of having winning numbers in the state lottery, requires the ability to count the number of possible outcomes for a given experiment or a sequence of experiments.

However, often it is impractical to list out all the possibilities. Therefore, we will develop some techniques to facilitate our counting.

The Fundamental Counting Principle

Theorem

Fundamental Counting Principle

E_1 is an event with n_1 possible outcomes and E_2 is an event with n_2 possible outcomes. The number of ways the events can occur in sequence is $n_1 \cdot n_2$. This principle can be applied for any number of events occurring in sequence.

Example 5.15

A local bank has three branches. Each branch has four departments and each department has two employees. How many employees does the bank have?

Solution

$$3 \quad \cdot \quad 4 \quad \cdot \quad 2 \quad = \quad 24$$

$$\begin{pmatrix} \text{number of} \\ \text{branches} \end{pmatrix} \quad (\text{departments}) \quad \begin{pmatrix} \text{employees per} \\ \text{department} \end{pmatrix} \quad \begin{pmatrix} \text{total number} \\ \text{of employees} \end{pmatrix}$$

Thus, the bank has 24 total employees.

Example 5.16

Non-personalized license plates in the state of Utah consist of three numbers followed by three letters (excluding I, O, and Q). How many license plates are possible?

Solution

There are ten digits (0-9) possible for each of the first three characters. Likewise, there are 23 letters possible for the last three characters. Therefore, we have:

$$10 \cdot 10 \cdot 10 \cdot 23 \cdot 23 \cdot 23 = 12{,}167{,}000$$

$$(\text{digit}) \ (\text{digit}) \ (\text{digit}) \ (\text{letter}) \ (\text{letter}) \ (\text{letter}) \ \left(\begin{array}{c} \text{possible license} \\ \text{plates} \end{array} \right)$$

Therefore, there are 12,167,000 possible non-personalized license plates in the state of Utah.

Example 5.17

You have a stack of 5 textbooks: English, History, Statistics, Geology, and Psychology. How many ways can you arrange these textbooks on a shelf?

Solution

Because you can put each book on the bookshelf only once, you have five possible choices for the first book. Similarly, there are four possible choices for the second book, three possible choices for the third book, two possible choices for the fourth book, and only one book left for the fifth book. Using the fundamental counting principle, we have

$$(5)(4)(3)(2)(1) = 120 \text{ possible arrangements.}$$

5

Factorials

The product $(5)(4)(3)(2)(1)$ in the previous example is a special type of product called a **factorial**. Factorials occur so frequently that they have their own notation as follows.

Formula

Suppose n is a positive whole number. Then,

$$n! = n(n-1)(n-2)\cdots(3)(2)(1).$$

Note: $0! = 1$ by definition.

$n!$ is read as "n factorial". Note from the previous example that $n!$ represents the number of ways to arrange n items.

Using this notation, $5! = (5)(4)(3)(2)(1) = 120$.

Combinations

We have seen how the fundamental counting principle and factorial notation can help us when counting the number of possible arrangements of items. If we are interested in counting the number of arrangements and order is *not* important, we are dealing with a **combination**.

Definition

A **combination** is a collection or grouping of objects where the order is not important.

The number of combinations of n objects taken k at a time can be found as follows.

Formula

The number of combinations of n unique objects taken k at a time is:

$$C_k^n = \frac{n!}{(n-k)!k!}.$$

Note that some alternate notations for combinations that you may see are $\binom{n}{k}$, ${}_nC_k$, and $C(n,k)$. All of these denote the number of combinations of n objects taken k at a time.

Example 5.18

In the Mega Millions lottery, a player selects five different numbers from 1 to 56 (inclusive) and then another (a sixth number, called the Mega Ball) from 1 to 46 (inclusive). If the first five numbers match the player's numbers in any order along with the Mega Ball number, the player wins.

   a. What is the total number of winning combinations?

   b. What is the probability of winning?

Solution

   a. First, we have to determine the number of ways of selecting 5 numbers from 56. Then, we have to multiply the combination of choosing 5 numbers from 56 by 46, the number of ways you can select the Mega Ball. Thus, we have:

$$C_5^{56} = \frac{56!}{(56-5)!5!} = \frac{56!}{51!5!} = \frac{(56)(55)(54)(53)(52)\,(51!)}{51!5!}$$

$$= \frac{(56)(55)(54)(53)(52)}{(5)(4)(3)(2)(1)} = 3,819,816.$$

So, the total number of winning combinations is

$$46 \cdot 3,819,816 = 175,711,536.$$

   b. The probability of winning with any one combination is

$$\frac{1}{175,711,536},$$

which is approximately 0. The actual probability is .00000000569115.

Permutations

We have just looked at counting where order did not matter. But there are many situations in which the order or arrangement of the objects is important. If we are interested in counting the number of arrangements and order *is* important, we are dealing with **permutations**.

Definition

A **permutation** is a specific order or arrangement of objects in a set. There are $n!$ permutations of n unique objects.

Permutation

5

Example 5.19

To complete your holiday shopping, you need to go to the bakery, department store, grocery store, and toy store. If you are going to visit the stores in sequence, how many different sequences exist?

Solution

This is a permutation problem because order matters. By the permutation definition there are $4! = (4)(3)(2)(1) = 24$ sequences.

There are times when not all objects in a set will be used for a permutation problem. Consider the following.

Example 5.20

At a local fast food restaurant, the door to the kitchen is secured by a five button lock, labeled 1, 2, 3, 4, 5. To open the door, the correct three digit code must be pushed but each button can only be pushed once. How many different codes are possible?

Solution

This is a permutation problem of 5 objects, but we are taking only 3 at a time. There are 5 buttons available for the first character in the code, 4 for the second, and 3 for the third. Therefore, there are

$$(5)(4)(3) = 60 \text{ possible codes.}$$

In the previous example, we had a permutation of 5 objects taken 3 at a time. In general,

Formula

Permutations of n Objects Taken k at a Time

The number of permutations of n unique objects taken k at a time is:

$$P_k^n = \frac{n!}{(n-k)!}.$$

Note that some alterations to this notation that you may see are $n!\binom{n}{k}$, $_nP_k$, and $P(n,k)$. All of these denote the number of permutations of n objects taken k at a time.

Example 5.21

Seven bids are placed for a commercial construction job and three will be selected in order of quality. How many ways can the bids be selected in first, second, and third place?

Solution

Because we have seven bids and the order (first, second, third) is important, we have

$$P_3^7 = \frac{7!}{(7-3)!} = \frac{7!}{4!} = \frac{(7)(6)(5)\,4!}{4!} = 210.$$

There are times when we are interested in finding the number of permutations where some of the objects are duplicates. For instance, consider the word EYE.

If we have interchanged the two E's, the resulting permutation is not distinguishable from the original. To count the number of **distinguishable permutations**, we need the following formula.

Formula

If given n objects, with n_1 alike, n_2 alike, ..., n_k alike, then the number of distinguishable permutations of all n objects is $\dfrac{n!}{(n_1!)(n_2!)(n_3!)\cdots(n_k!)}$.

Distinguishable
Permutations

Example 5.22

How many distinguishable permutations can be made from the word *Mississippi*?

Solution

There are 11 letters in the word *Mississippi*, one M, four I's, four S's, and two P's. So there are,

$$\frac{11!}{(1!)(4!)(4!)(2!)} = 34,650$$

distinguishable permutations of the letters in *Mississippi*.

5

It is important to remember that combinations are used when order is not important, and permutations are used when order is important.

Concept		Formula
Fundamental Counting Principle	If one event has n_1 outcomes and another event has n_2 outcomes, the number of ways the event can occur in sequence is	$n_1 \cdot n_2$
Factorial	$n!$ is the product of each of the positive whole numbers from 1 to n.	$n! = n(n-1)(n-2)\cdots(3)(2)(1)$
Permutation	A specific order or arrangement of objects.	$n!$
	The number of permutations of n unique objects taken k at a time.	$P_k^n = \dfrac{n!}{(n-k)!}$
	Given n objects with n_1 alike, n_2 alike, ..., n_k alike, then the number of distinguishable permutations is	$\dfrac{n!}{(n_1!)(n_2!)(n_3!)\cdots(n_k!)}$
Combination	A collection or grouping of objects where order is not important.	$C_k^n = \dfrac{n!}{(n-k)!k!}$

 **Exercises**

Basic Concepts

1. What is the fundamental counting principle?

2. What is a factorial?

3. Describe the difference between permutations and combinations.

4. Give an example of a situation in which you would need to calculate the number of distinguishable permutations.

Exercises

1. The blue plate lunch at a local cafeteria consists of an entrée, a side item, and a desert. If there are 6 choices for an entrée, 5 choices for a side item, and 4 choices for a dessert, how many different lunches are available?

2. You are interested in buying a home in a new subdivision. The builder offers 3 basic floor plans, each with 4 possible arrangements for the garage, and siding in 6 different colors. How many different homes can be built?

3. Compute each of the following:
   a. 1!
   b. 3!
   c. 5!
   d. 7!

4. Compute each of the following:
   a. 2!
   b. 4!
   c. 6!
   d. 8!

5. A DJ will select 6 songs from a CD containing 12 songs to compose an event's musical lineup. How many different lineups are possible?

6. In how many ways can 11 kids be picked for the 9 positions on a baseball team?

7. How many distinguishable permutations can be made from the word STATISTICS?

8. How many distinguishable permutations can be made from the word SASSAFRAS?

9. A person tosses a coin 11 times. In how many ways can he get 9 heads?

10. How many 5 card hands can be dealt from a deck of 52 cards?

5

Discovering Technology

USING EXCEL

Probability and Independence

A coin is flipped, a die is rolled, and a card is drawn from a deck. Find the probability of getting a head on the coin, a 2 on the die, and drawing a spade from the deck of cards.

1. Fill in the data in a worksheet as shown here.

	A	B	C	D
1		Coin	Die	Card
2	Chance of Success	1	1	13
3	Possible Outcomes	2	6	52
4				

Figure 5.10

2. In cell B4 divide B2 by B3.

3. Copy the formula in cell B4 to C4 and D4.

4. Now we have the probability of success in each event listed in Row 4. In cell E4, multiply cells B4 through D4 using the following formula.

=B4*C4*D4

5. This gives us the result that the probability of getting a head on the coin, a 2 on the die and drawing a spade from the deck of cards is .020833 or about 2.1%.

	A	B	C	D	E
1		Coin	Die	Card	
2	Chance of Success	1	1	13	
3	Possible Outcomes	2	6	52	
4		0.5	0.166667	0.25	0.020833

Figure 5.11

Combinations

For this exercise, use the information from Example 5.18.

1. The first step in this example was to determine the number of ways of selecting 5 numbers from 56. This is equivalent to determining the number of combinations of 56 unique objects taken 5 at a time. In an Excel spreadsheet, enter *n* and *k* in cells A1 and B1, respectively, and **56** and **5** in cells A2 and B2 respectively.

	A	B	C
1	*n*	*k*	
2	56	5	

Figure 5.12

2. Label cell C1 **nCk** to represent the number of combinations of *n* objects taken *k* at a time. The formula to calculate the number of combinations in Microsoft Excel is

COMBIN(number,number_chosen)

where *number* is the number of items and *number_chosen* is the number of items in each combination. In cell C2, enter the formula to calculate the number of combinations of lottery numbers.

=COMBIN(A2,B2)

3. Observe the number of combinations as calculated by Microsoft Excel. Compare this to our solution in part (a) of Example 5.18.

	A	B	C
1	*n*	*k*	*nCk*
2	56	5	3819816

Figure 5.13

Permutations

For this exercise, use the information from Example 5.21.

1. Since order is important and we are interested in finding the number of ways the bids can be selected in first, second, and third place, we need to calculate the number of permutations of 7 unique objects taken 3 at a time. In an Excel spreadsheet, enter **n** and **k** in cells A1 and B1, respectively, and **7** and **3** in cells A2 and B2, respectively.

	A	B
1	*n*	*k*
2	7	3

Figure 5.14

2. Label cell C1 **nPk** to represent the number of permutations of *n* objects taken *k* at a time. The formula to calculate the number of permutations in Microsoft Excel is

PERMUT(number,number_chosen)

3. where *number* is the number of objects and *number_chosen* is the number of objects in each permutation. In cell C2, enter the formula to calculate the number of permutations of bid orders.

=PERMUT(A2,B2)

4. Observe the number of permutations as calculated by Microsoft Excel. Compare this to our solution in Example 5.21.

	A	B	C
1	*n*	*k*	*nPk*
2	7	3	210

Figure 5.15

Chapter 5 Review

Key Terms and Ideas

- Randomness
- Probability
- Random Experiment
- Sample Space
- Outcome
- Event
- Subjective Probability
- Objective Probability
- Relative Frequency
- Statistical Regularity
- Classical Probability
- Statistical Inference
- Probability Law 1
  (Probability of 0)
- Probability Law 2
  (Probability of 1)
- Probability Law 3
  $(0 \leq P(A) \leq 1)$
- Probability Law 4
  $(P(A_1) + P(A_2) + ... + P(A_n) = 1)$
- Compound Event
- Union

- Intersection
- Complement
- Probability Law 5
  $(P(A^c) = 1 - P(A))$
- Mutual Exclusivity
- Probability Law 6
  (Union of Mutually Exclusive Events)
- Probability Law 7
  (Intersection of Mutually Exclusive Events)
- Probability Law 8
  (The Addition Rule)
- Probability Law 9
  (Conditional Probability)
- Independent Events
- Probability Law 10
  (Multiplication Rule for Independent Events)
- Bayes' Theorem
- Fundamental Counting Principle
- Factorial
- Combination
- Permutation
- Distinguishable Permutation

Key Formulas

Concept	Formula	Section
Relative Frequency	If an experiment is performed n times and event A happens k times, the Relative Frequency of $$A = \frac{k}{n}.$$	5.2
Classical Probability	$$P(A) = \frac{\text{number of outcomes in } A}{\text{total number of outcomes in the sample space}}$$	5.2
Probability Law Number 3	$0 \leq P(A) \leq 1$	5.4
Probability Law Number 4	$P(A_1) + P(A_2) + \ldots + P(A_n) = 1$	5.4
Probability Law Number 5	$P(A^c) = 1 - P(A)$	5.4
Union of Mutually Exclusive Events	$P(A \cup B) = P(A) + P(B)$	5.4
Intersection of Mutually Exclusive Events	$P(A \cap B) = 0$	5.4
The Addition Rule	$P(A \cup B) = P(A) + P(B) - P(A \cap B)$	5.4
Conditional Probability	$$P(A \mid B) = \frac{P(A \cap B)}{P(B)}$$	5.5
Independent Events	$P(A \mid B) = P(A)$ or $P(B \mid A) = P(B)$	5.6
Multiplication Rule for Independent Events	$P(A \cap B) = P(A) \cdot P(B)$	5.6
Bayes' Theorem	$$P(B_i \mid A) = \frac{P(A \mid B_i) P(B_i)}{P(A \mid B_1) P(B_1) + P(A \mid B_2) P(B_2) + \cdots + P(A \mid B_k) P(B_k)}$$ where B_i is the ith event out of k mutually exclusive and collectively exhaustive events.	5.7

Fundamental Counting Principle	If E_1 is an event with n_1 possible outcomes and E_2 is an event with n_2 possible outcomes, the number of ways the events can occur in sequence is $n_1 \cdot n_2$.	5.8
n Factorial	$n! = n(n-1)(n-2)...(3)(2)(1)$	5.8
Combination	$C_k^n = \dfrac{n!}{(n-k)!k!}$	5.8
Permutation	$P_k^n = \dfrac{n!}{(n-k)!}$	5.8
Number of Distinguishable Permutations	$\dfrac{n!}{(n_1!)(n_2!)(n_3!)\cdots(n_k!)}$	5.8

5

 **Additional Exercises**

1. A couple plans to have three children.

   a. List all possible outcomes for the sexes of the three children.

   b. Find the probability that the couple will have three girls.

   c. Find the probability that the couple will have at least one boy.

2. 671 registered voters were surveyed and asked their political affiliation and whether or not they favor a national healthcare policy. The results of the survey are displayed in the table below.

Table for Additional Exercise 2 – Survey Results			
Position on National Healthcare	**Democrat**	**Independent**	**Republican**
Favor	161	40	130
Do Not Favor	110	40	190

If one of the surveyed voters is randomly selected,

   a. What is the probability that the voter will be a Republican?

   b. What is the probability that the voter will not favor a national healthcare policy?

   c. What is the probability that the voter will be a Democrat or an Independent?

   d. What is the probability that the voter will be a Democrat and favor a national healthcare policy?

   e. Given that the voter is a Republican, what is the probability that the voter will favor a national healthcare policy?

   f. If the voter does not favor a national healthcare policy, what is the probability that the voter is an Independent?

   g. Are the events {voter is a Democrat} and {voter favors national healthcare policy} independent? Explain.

3. A roulette wheel has 38 outcomes labeled 1 through 36 plus 0 and 00. The wheels are supposed to be designed so that each outcome is equally likely. The numbers 0 and 00 are often referred to as house numbers because the only way that a player can win when these outcomes are observed is by directly betting on the numbers. A great deal of the money wagered on a roulette wheel is wagered on odd or even numbers, or columns or rows of numbers. The numbers 0 and 00 are not in any row or column, nor are they odd or even.

   a. What is the probability of observing an even number (0 and 00 are neither odd nor even)?

   b. What is the probability of observing a number between 1 and 12?

   c. What is the probability of observing 0 or 00?

   d. What is the probability of observing a 4?

   e. What is the probability of not observing 7, 13, or 21?

4. A survey of customers in a particular retail store showed that 10% were dissatisfied with the customer service. Half of the customers who were dissatisfied dealt with Bill, the senior customer service representative. If Bill responds to 40% of the complaints in the retail store, find the following probabilities.

   a. The probability that a customer will be unhappy, given that the representative was Bill.

   b. The probability that the service representative was not Bill, given that the customer complained.

5. A package of documents needs to be sent to a given destination, and it is important that it arrive within one day. To maximize the chances of on-time delivery, three copies of the documents are sent via three different delivery services. Service A is known to have a 90% on-time delivery record, Service B has an 88% on-time delivery record, and Service C has a 91% on-time delivery record. Assuming that the delivery services and their records are independent, what is the probability that at least one copy of the documents will arrive at its destination on time?

6. A boxcar contains six complex electronic systems. Two of the six are to be randomly selected for thorough testing and then classified as defective or not defective. If two of the six systems are actually defective, find the probability that at least one of the two systems tested will be defective. Find the probability that both are defective.

7. *Odds in favor of* and *odds against* are often used to express chances of occurrences. For example, if the odds are 5 to 2 that it will rain tomorrow then we would be wise to carry an umbrella with us. How exactly are odds related to probabilities? If the probability of event A occurring is p, then the odds in favor of A occurring are a to b such that $\dfrac{a}{b} = \dfrac{p}{(1-p)}$. The odds against A occurring are b to a.

   a. What are the odds of rolling a six when a single die is thrown?

   b. What are the odds against getting a head when a coin is tossed?

   c. What are the odds against getting 3 consecutive heads when a coin is tossed 3 times?

   d. Suppose the odds in favor of your favorite athletic team winning this weekend are 8 to 3. What is the probability that they will win?

8. Consider a well-shuffled deck of cards with 13 hearts, 13 spades, 13 clubs, and 13 diamonds.

   a. Find the probability that the first card dealt is a heart.

   b. Find the probability that the first card dealt is a spade.

   c. Find the probability that the first card dealt is not a spade.

   d. If you know that the first card dealt will not be a spade, find the probability that it will be a heart.

   e. Suppose you saw the bottom card, and it was the queen of hearts. What is the probability that the first card dealt will be a heart?

Discrete Probability Distributions: Information about the Future

6

Discovering Technology

Calculating binomial probabilities using Microsoft Excel

Calculating hypergeometric probabilities using Microsoft Excel

Calculating binomial probabilities using Minitab

Calculating Poisson probabilities using Minitab

Introduction

The notions of randomness and uncertainty were introduced in Chapter 5. This chapter extends those ideas by developing concepts to describe a pattern of randomness for an entire set of outcomes produced by some random phenomenon. In the coin tossing experiment the description was rather easy. The totality of outcomes contained only two values, *heads* and *tails*. Probabilities for these events were constructed by assuming a fair coin and by applying the classical definition of probability.

Analyzing more complex random phenomena requires a method of organizing information about random processes and a vocabulary to describe the organizational concepts. Two such descriptive notions will be introduced in this chapter: **random variables** and **probability distributions**.

Random Variable

Definition

A **random variable** is a numerical outcome of a random process.

Probability Distribution

Definition

A **probability distribution** is a model which describes a specific kind of random process.

Probability distributions are the best descriptors of random processes. However, for "real world" random processes they are often difficult to obtain.

6.1 Types of Random Variables

Quantitative random variables are classified as discrete or continuous. This categorization refers to the types of values that outcomes of the random variable can assume. Discrete random variables are analyzed in this chapter, and the next chapter discusses continuous random variables.

In defining random variables, there is a naming convention. Capital letters, such as X, will be used to refer to the random variable, while small letters, such as x will refer to specific values of the random variable. Often the specific values will be subscripted, $x_1, x_2, ..., x_n$.

Discrete Random Variables

With a discrete random variable, you can count the number of outcomes that the random variable might possess.

Definition

A **discrete random variable** is a random variable which has a countable number of possible outcomes.

Discrete Random
Variable

In fact, the values that many discrete random variables assume are the counting numbers from 0 to N, where N depends upon the nature of the variable.

Procedure

When describing a discrete random variable, you should:

1. State the variable.
2. List all of the possible values of the variable.
3. Determine the probabilities of these values.

Example 6.1

Random Phenomenon: Toss a die and observe the outcome of the toss.

1. *Identify the random variable:* X = outcome of the toss of a die.
2. *Range of values*: Integers between 1 and 6.

In this instance, $x_1 = 1$, $x_2 = 2$, ..., $x_6 = 6$. Although the value of the random variable is the same as the subscript in this case, there is usually no relationship between the two.

Table 6.1 – Tossing a Die	
Value of X	Probability
1	$\dfrac{1}{6}$
2	$\dfrac{1}{6}$
3	$\dfrac{1}{6}$
4	$\dfrac{1}{6}$
5	$\dfrac{1}{6}$
6	$\dfrac{1}{6}$

3. *Probability Distribution*: The outcomes of the toss of a die and their probabilities are given in Table 6.1. The probabilities are deduced using the classical method and the assumption of a fair die.

Not all discrete random variables have probability distributions that are easy to determine. In Examples 6.2 and 6.3, neither random variable has an easily determined probability distribution.

Example 6.2

Random Phenomenon: The number of defective integrated circuits received in a batch of 1000. Each outcome of the random variable is a numerical measure whose range of values is given below.

1. *Identify the random variable*:

   $X =$ the number of defective integrated circuits in a batch of 1000.

2. *Range of Values*: Integers between 0 and 1000, where $N = 1000$. If symbols were chosen to represent the values they could be given as $x_1 = 0$, $x_2 = 1$, ..., $x_{N+1} = 1000$.

3. *Probability Distribution*: Unknown.

Example 6.3

Random Phenomenon: A stock market analyst is interested in the number of stocks on the New York Stock Exchange (NYSE) that increased in price on the previous day. She realizes that the number that increases is a random variable. She will have to develop a description of the randomness in order to study the stocks.

1. *Identify the random variable*: X = number of stocks that increased in price.

2. *Range of Values*: Integers between 0 and 2773 (the number of stocks on the NYSE).

3. *Probability Distribution*: Unknown but could be estimated using the relative frequency idea from Section 5.2 in conjunction with historical data of the NYSE.

Continuous Random Variables

Heights, weights, volumes, and time measurements, for example, are usually measured on a continuous scale. These measurements can take on any value in some interval.

Definition

A **continuous random variable** is a random variable whose measurements can assume any one of a countless number of values in a line interval.

Continuous Random Variable

Example 6.4

Random Phenomenon: Sylars Watch Manufacturer has a process that indicates that all watches will be assembled between 20 to 45 minutes. Obviously, the time to assemble a watch will be a function of the style and other accoutrements that are selected by the customer. Since time is measured on a continuous scale and the variability of watch assembly is not predictable due to different workers, the overall time to assemble a watch is considered to be a continuous random variable.

1. *Identify the random variable*: X = time to assemble a watch.

2. *Range of Values*: Between 0 and ∞. Note that X is measured on a continuous scale.

3. *Probability Density*: Unknown, but could be approximated using historical data. (Note that for continuous random variables, we specify probabilities with probability density functions.)

6.1 Exercises

Basic Concepts

1. What is a random variable?

2. What is a probability distribution? Is a probability distribution the same concept as a probability model?

3. Do all random variables have probability distributions? Explain.

4. What are the two types of random variables discussed in the chapter? What distinguishes the two types?

Exercises

1. Classify the following as either a discrete random variable or a continuous random variable.

   a. The number of pages in a standard math textbook.

   b. The amount of electricity used daily in a home.

   c. The number of customers entering a restaurant in one day.

   d. The time spent daily on the phone after supper by a teenager.

   e. Campers at a state park over Labor Day weekend.

2. Classify the following as either a discrete random variable or a continuous random variable.

   a. The speed of a train.

   b. The possible scores on the SAT reasoning test.

   c. The number of pizzas eaten on a college campus each day.

   d. The daily takeoffs at Chicago's O'Hare Airport.

   e. The high temperatures in Maine and Florida tomorrow.

3. Classify the following as either a discrete random variable or a continuous random variable.

   a. The number of emergency phone calls received per day by a local fire department.

   b. The speed of pitches of major league baseball pitchers.

   c. The weight of a lobster caught in Maine.

   d. The number of defective circuits on a computer chip.

   e. The time it takes for a 5-year battery to die.

4. Classify the following as either a discrete random variable or a continuous random variable.

   a. The total points scored per football game for a local high school team.

   b. The daily price of a stock.

   c. The interest rate charged by local banks for 30-year mortgages.

   d. The number of times a backup of the computer network is performed in a month.

   e. The amount of sugar imported by the U.S. in a day.

6.2 Discrete Probability Distributions

So far, the random variable concept is so general that it is not very useful by itself. What would make it useful is to determine what numerical values the random variable could assume and to assess the probabilities of each of these values. That information defines a probability distribution for a discrete random variable.

Definition

Discrete Probability Distribution

A **discrete probability distribution** consists of all possible values of the random variable along with their associated probabilities.

Discrete probability distributions always have three characteristics:

1. The sum of all the probabilities must equal 1. That is,

$$P(X = x_1) + P(X = x_2) + ... + P(X = x_n) = 1.$$

2. The probability of any value must be between 0 and 1, inclusively. That is,

$$0 \leq P(X = x_i) \leq 1.$$

3. The probabilities are additive. That is,

$$P(X = x_i \text{ or } x_j) = P(X = x_i) + P(X = x_j).$$

The association of the possible values with their respective probabilities can be expressed in three different forms: in a table, in a graph, and in an equation.

Fat the Butch

John Scarne, in his book *Scarne's Complete Guide to Gambling*, tells a story about a New York City gambler named Fat the Butch. It seems Fat the Butch lost $49,000 in virtually the same game that led Chevalier de Mere to his famous consultation with Pascal and Fermat. In this particular game another well known gambler offered Fat the chance to bet $1,000 that he would not roll one double six in 21 tosses of the dice. After 12 hours of dice rolling, Fat lost $49,000 and decided to quit. Later, Scarne discussed the fact that Fat needed 24.6 rolls to break even and that he had a significant expected loss on each play. According to Scarne, Fat shrugged his shoulders and said, "Scarne, in gambling you got to pay and learn, but $49,000 was a lot of dough to pay just to learn that."

Example 6.5

Consider the random phenomenon of tossing a coin three times and counting the number of heads. What is the probability distribution for the number of heads observed in three tosses of a coin?

Solution

The random variable is X = the number of heads in three tosses of a coin.

Table 6.2 – Tossing a Coin				
Value of X	**P (X = x)**	**Simple Events**		
0	$\dfrac{1}{8}$	TTT		
1	$\dfrac{3}{8}$	HTT	THT	TTH
2	$\dfrac{3}{8}$	HHT	HTH	THH
3	$\dfrac{1}{8}$	HHH		
	$\sum P(X=x)=1.0$			

The probabilities given above can be deduced using the classical approach to probability.

Example 6.6

K. J. Johnson is a computer salesperson. During the last year he has kept records of his computer sales for the last 200 days. He recognizes that his daily sales constitute a random process and he wishes to determine the probability distribution for daily sales. Then, from the probability distribution, he would like to know what the probability is that he will sell **a.** at least 2 computers each day and **b.** at most two computers each day.

Solution

The random variable is:

X = the number of computers sold each day.

Table 6.3 – Frequency Distribution	
Sales	**Frequency**
0	40
1	20
2	60
3	40
4	40

The probabilities for this random variable are computed in Table 6.4 based upon 200 days of sales data obtained from Mr. Johnson's records using the relative frequency concept.

Table 6.4 – Probability Distribution	
Sales x	Probability P(X = x)
0	$\frac{40}{200} = .2$
1	$\frac{20}{200} = .1$
2	$\frac{60}{200} = .3$
3	$\frac{40}{200} = .2$
4	$\frac{40}{200} = .2$
	$\sum P(X = x) = 1.0$

a. The probability that Mr. Johnson will sell at least 2 computers each day is calculated as follows:

$$P(X \geq 2) = P(X = 2) + P(X = 3) + P(X = 4) = .3 + .2 + .2 = .7.$$

b. To find the probability that Mr. Johnson will sell at most 2 computers each day:

$$P(X \leq 2) = P(X = 0) + P(X = 1) + P(X = 2) = .2 + .1 + .3 = .6.$$

Example 6.7

Phone operators of a TV shopping network usually receive about three calls per minute from interested shoppers. Suppose we are interested in the next three telephone calls and the number of callers that place an order. The probability distribution was created based on historical data. Given the probability distribution, what is the probability that at least one caller will purchase something each minute?

X = the number of callers that place an order.

Table 6.5 – Caller Data	
x	P(X = x)
0	.2
1	.5
2	.1
3	.2

Solution

The probability that at least one caller will purchase something is:

$$P(X \geq 1) = P(X = 1) + P(X = 2) + P(X = 3) = .5 + .1 + .2 = .8$$

or

$$P(X \geq 1) = 1 - P(X = 0) = 1 - .2 = .8.$$

Thus, the probability that at least one caller will purchase an item is 80%.

6.2 Exercises

Basic Concepts

1. Discrete probability distributions always have three characteristics. What are they?

2. What is the value of describing a random variable with a probability distribution?

3. What are three different ways to express possible values of a random variable along with their associated probabilities?

Exercises

1. Tell whether or not the following distribution is a probability distribution. If the distribution is not a probability distribution, give the characteristic which is not satisfied by the distribution.

x	P(X = x)
1	$\frac{1}{3}$
2	$\frac{2}{3}$
3	$\frac{1}{3}$

Table for Exercise 1

2. Tell whether or not the following distribution is a probability distribution. If the distribution is not a probability distribution, give the characteristic which is not satisfied by the distribution.

x	P(X = x)
−2	.25
2	.50
3	.25

Table for Exercise 2

3. Tell whether or not the following distribution is a probability distribution. If the distribution is not a probability distribution, give the characteristic which is not satisfied by the distribution.

x	P(X = x)
2	.30
3	−.50
4	.50
5	.70

Table for Exercise 3

4. Tell whether or not the following distribution is a probability distribution. If the distribution is not a probability distribution, give the characteristic which is not satisfied by the distribution.

x	P(X = x)
5	.46
10	.35
15	.25

Table for Exercise 4

5. Tell whether or not the following distribution is a probability distribution. If the distribution is not a probability distribution, give the characteristic which is not satisfied by the distribution.

Table for Exercise 5	
x	P(X = x)
−10	.18
−5	.39
3	.08
8	.35

6. Tell whether or not the following distribution is a probability distribution. If the distribution is not a probability distribution, give the characteristic which is not satisfied by the distribution.

Table for Exercise 6	
x	P(X = x)
100	−.10
200	.50
300	.50

7. Tell whether or not the following distribution is a probability distribution. If the distribution is not a probability distribution, give the characteristic which is not satisfied by the distribution.

$$P(X = x) = \frac{x}{16}, \text{ for } x = 1, 2, 3, 4, 5$$

8. Tell whether or not the following distribution is a probability distribution. If the distribution is not a probability distribution, give the characteristic which is not satisfied by the distribution.

$$P(X = x) = \frac{x^2}{30}, \text{ for } x = 1, 2, 3, 4$$

6.3	# Expected Value and Variance

The notion of expected value is one of the most important concepts in the analysis of random phenomena. Expected value is important because it is a summary statistic for a probability distribution that can be used as a criterion for comparing alternative decisions in the presence of uncertainty. Conceptually, expected value is closely allied with the notion of mean or average.

The expected value of a random variable should be very close to the average value of a large number of observations from the random process, and the larger the number of observations collected, the more likely the average of the observations will be close to the expected value. It should not be interpreted as the value of the random variable we *expect* to see. In fact, for discrete random variables the expected value is rarely one of the possible outcomes of the random variable.

Formula

Expected Value

The **expected value** of a discrete random variable X is the mean of the random variable X. It is denoted $E(X)$ and is given by computing the expression

$$\mu = E(X) = \sum [xp(x)].$$

where $p(x) = P(X = x)$.

Essentially the expected value is a weighted average, in which each possible value of the random variable is weighted by its probability.

Table 6.6 – Calculating K.J. Johnson's Expected Number of Sales per Day		
x	**p(x)**	**xp(x)**
0	.2	0
1	.1	.1
2	.3	.6
3	.2	.6
4	.2	.8
Total		$E(X) = 2.1$

$$E(X) = \sum [xp(x)] = 0(.2) + 1(.1) + 2(.3) + 3(.2) + 4(.2) = 2.1.$$

The expected value of the probability distribution given in Example 6.6 is computed in Table 6.6. In the long run data from this distribution should average about 2.1. That is, the expected value of a distribution can be considered the long run average of that distribution.

Using Expected Values to Compare Alternatives

Plato believed that happiness was the result of rational behavior. He would appreciate expected value analysis, since it is a rational method of comparing alternatives that involve uncertainty.

Example 6.8

Suppose you are confronted with two investment alternatives that possess uncertain outcomes described by the probability distributions given in Table 6.7.

Solution

Table 6.7 – Expected Value

Option A		Option B	
Profit (Dollars)	Probability	Profit (Dollars)	Probability
−2000	.2	−3000	.2
0	.1	−1000	.1
1000	.3	2000	.2
2000	.3	3000	.3
4000	.1	4000	.2

$$E(X_A) = \sum [x_A p(x_A)]$$
$$= .2(-2000) + .1(0) + .3(1000)$$
$$+ .3(2000) + .1(4000)$$
$$= \$900$$

$$E(X_B) = \sum [x_B p(x_B)]$$
$$= .2(-3000) + .1(-1000)$$
$$+ .2(2000) + .3(3000) + .2(4000)$$
$$= \$1400$$

Because of the randomness of the profit variable, it is difficult to evaluate the investments by merely eyeballing the two distributions. However, by calculating the expected values of the two alternatives the information in each distribution is condensed to a single point. This point characterizes the center of the distribution and facilitates comparison. The expected values of Options A and B are $900 and $1400, respectively. Thus, in the long run Option B would be $500 more profitable. The phrase *in the long run* is a significant qualifier. It means that under repeated investments you would receive an average profit of $1400 from Option B. But on any one investment in Option B, you may lose as much as $3000 or make as much as $4000.

Variance of a Discrete Random Variable

In Example 6.8, while Option B has a greater expected value, it seems to have greater risk than Option A. Option B offers a greater chance of making a substantial gain, but it also has the potential for significant loss. The expected value of a distribution measures only one dimension of the random variable, namely its central value. To gauge the variability of a random variable we need another measure similar to the variance measure previously constructed, but one which accounts for the difference in probabilities of the variable.

Formula

The **variance** of a discrete random variable X is given by

$$\sigma^2 = V(X) = \sum\left[(x-\mu)^2\, p(x)\right].$$

Once again the variance can be considered an average. In this case it is the weighted average of the squared deviations about the mean. This is very similar to the computations for the sample variance (s^2) and population variance (σ^2) given

by $s^2 = \dfrac{\sum(x_i - \bar{x})^2}{n-1}$ and $\sigma^2 = \dfrac{\sum(x_i - \mu)^2}{N}$, respectively. Just as the probability serves as the weights when calculating the expected value for the discrete probability distribution, for s^2 and σ^2, $\dfrac{1}{n-1}$ and $\dfrac{1}{N}$ serve as the weights, respectively. The larger the variance, the more variability in the outcomes.

To manually compute the variance of the random variable, it's often a good idea to construct a table.

Example 6.9

The variance of the random variables described in Example 6.8 are given in Tables 6.8 and 6.9.

Solution

Table 6.8 – Variance of a Random Variable

Option A			
Profit (Dollars)	Probability	$(x-\mu)^2 p(x)$	
−2000	.2	$.2(-2000-900)^2 =$	1,682,000
0	.1	$.1(0-900)^2 =$	81,000
1000	.3	$.3(1000-900)^2 =$	3000
2000	.3	$.3(2000-900)^2 =$	363,000
4000	.1	$.1(4000-900)^2 =$	961,000
		$\sigma^2 = V(X) = 3,090,000$	

The standard deviation is computed by taking the square root of the variance. In this instance, the standard deviation of Option A is given by

$$\sigma = \sqrt{V(X)} = \sqrt{3,090,000} \approx 1757.84.$$

Table 6.9 – Variance of a Random Variable

Option B			
Profit (Dollars)	Probability	$(x-\mu)^2 p(x)$	
−3000	.2	$.2(-3000-1400)^2 =$	3,872,000
−1000	.1	$.1(-1000-1400)^2 =$	576,000
2000	.2	$.2(2000-1400)^2 =$	72,000
3000	.3	$.3(3000-1400)^2 =$	768,000
4000	.2	$.2(4000-1400)^2 =$	1,352,000
		$\sigma^2 = V(X) = 6,640,000$	

The standard deviation of Option B is given by

$$\sigma = \sqrt{6,640,000} \approx 2576.82.$$

A larger standard deviation reflects greater variability in profits and increased risk. When variance is considered, the decision becomes more difficult. The option with the largest expected value (Option B) is also the option with the greatest risk. Hence, the decision maker must subjectively evaluate the trade-off between greater expected return and increased risk.

Example 6.10

EJN Trucking Company is trying to decide which of two trucks to purchase. Each truck costs $125,000 but comes with different features and amenities. EJN's financial advisor estimates that the returns from each truck for the next five years will follow the probability distribution below.

Table 6.10 – Return on Truck Purchase		
Return (Dollars)	Truck 1	Truck 2
−5000	.02	.15
0	.03	.10
5000	.20	.10
10,000	.50	.10
15,000	.20	.30
20,000	.03	.20
25,000	.02	.05

Calculate the expected return, variance, and standard deviation for each truck and determine which truck you would purchase.

Solution

Table 6.11 – Calculations

Return (Dollars)	Truck 1	Truck 2	xp(x) Truck 1	xp(x) Truck 2	$(x-\mu)^2 p(x)$ Truck 1	$(x-\mu)^2 p(x)$ Truck 2
−5000	.02	.15	−100	−750	4,500,000	36,037,500
0	.03	.10	0	0	3,000,000	11,025,000
5000	.20	.10	1000	500	4,000,000	3,025,000
10,000	.50	.10	5000	1000	0	25,000
15,000	.20	.30	3000	4500	5,000,000	6,075,000
20,000	.03	.20	600	4000	3,000,000	18,050,000
25,000	.02	.05	500	1250	4,500,000	10,512,500
		$E(X)=$	$10,000	$10,500		
				$V(X)=\sigma^2 =$	$25,000,000	$84,750,000
				$\sqrt{V(X)}=\sigma =$	$5000	$9206

The expected value, variance, and standard deviation of purchasing Truck 1 are $10,000, $25,000,000, and $5000, respectively. Similarly the expected value, variance, and standard deviation of purchasing Truck 2 are $10,500, $84,750,000, and $9206. Given that the risk (variance) of Truck 2 is more than three times that of Truck 1, it appears that selecting Truck 1 is the best decision, even though the return is slightly less.

6.3 Exercises

Basic Concepts

1. Why is the notion of expected value important in the analysis of random phenomena?

2. True or false: the expected value of a random variable is always one of the possible outcomes of the random variable.

3. Suppose the expected value of a random variable was known to be 6.3. Interpret the meaning of the expected value.

4. Give an example of a situation in which expected value would be useful to compare alternatives.

5. How is the variance of a random variable related to risk?

Exercises

1. Find the expected value, the variance, and the standard deviation for a random variable with the following probability distribution.

Table for Exercise 1 – Probability Distribution				
x	−5	−2	0	2	5
p(x)	.06	.15	.58	.18	.03

2. Find the expected value, the variance, and the standard deviation for a random variable with the following probability distribution.

Table for Exercise 2 – Probability Distribution					
x	400	420	440	460	480	500
p(x)	0	.1	.1	.2	.2	.4

3. A regional hospital is considering the purchase of a helicopter to transport critical patients. The relative frequency of X, the number of times the helicopter is used to transport critical patients each month, is derived for a similarly sized hospital and is given in the following probability distribution.

Table for Exercise 3 – Probability Distribution: Number of Helicopter Transports						
x	0	1	2	3	4	5	6
p(x)	.15	.20	.34	.19	.06	.05	.01

a. Find the average number of times the helicopter is used to transport critical patients each month.

b. Find the variance of the number of times the helicopter is used to transport critical patients.

c. Find the standard deviation of the number of times the helicopter is used to transport critical patients.

d. Find the probability that the helicopter will not be used at all during a month to transport critical patients.

e. Find the probability that the helicopter will be used at least once to transport critical patients.

f. Find the probability that the helicopter will be used at most twice to transport critical patients.

g. Find the probability that the helicopter will be used more than three times to transport critical patients.

4. Based on past experience, an architect has determined a probability distribution for X, the number of times a drawing must be examined by a client before it is accepted.

Table for **Exercise 4** – Probability Distribution: Number of Times Examined					
x	1	2	3	4	5
p(x)	.1	.2	.3	.2	.2

a. Find the average number of times a drawing must be examined by a client before it is accepted.

b. Find the variance of the number of times a drawing must be examined by a client before it is accepted.

c. Find the standard deviation of the number of times a drawing must be examined by a client before it is accepted.

d. What is the probability that a drawing must be examined five times before being accepted by the client?

e. Find the probability that the drawing must be examined at least twice before being accepted by the client.

f. Find the probability that a drawing must be examined at most three times before being accepted by the client.

g. Find the probability that a drawing must be examined less than twice before being accepted by the client.

5. The manager of a retail clothing store has determined the following probability distribution for X, the number of customers who will enter the store on Saturday.

Table for **Exercise 5** – Probability Distribution: Customers on Saturday						
x	10	20	30	40	50	60
p(x)	.10	.20	.30	.20	.10	.10

a. Find the expected number of customers who will enter the store on Saturday.

b. Find the standard deviation of the number of customers who will enter the store on Saturday.

c. Find the variance of the number of customers who will enter the store on Saturday.

d. Find the probability that more than 30 customers will enter the store on Saturday.

e. Find the probability that at most 20 customers will enter the store on Saturday.

f. Find the probability that at least 40 customers will enter the store on Saturday.

g. What is the probability that exactly 10 customers will enter the store on Saturday?

6. An entrepreneur is considering investing in a new venture. If the venture is successful, he will make $50,000. However, if the venture is not successful, he will lose his investment of $10,000. Based on past experience, he believes that there is a 40% chance that the venture will be successful.

   a. Use the information in the problem to determine the probability distribution of the amount of money to be made (or lost) on the venture.

   b. Determine the expected amount of money to be made on the venture.

   c. Determine the standard deviation of the amount of money to be made on the venture.

7. An investor is considering two alternative investment options with the following payoff distributions.

Table for Exercise 7 – Option 1	
Payoff	P(Payoff)
−$100,000	$\frac{1}{3}$
$30,000	$\frac{1}{3}$
$100,000	$\frac{1}{3}$

Table for Exercise 7 – Option 2	
Payoff	P(Payoff)
−$20,000	.25
$0	.50
$20,000	.25

   a. Calculate the expected payoff for each of the investment options.

   b. Calculate the standard deviation of the payoff for each of the investment options.

   c. Which investment option would you choose? Explain.

8. A cereal manufacturer has two new brands of cereal which it would like to produce. Because resources are limited, the cereal manufacturer can only afford to produce one of the new brands. A marketing study produced the following probability distributions for the amount of sales for each of the new brands of cereal.

Table for Exercise 8 – Cereal A	
Sales	P(Sales)
−$150,000	.2
$200,000	.3
$300,000	.2
$400,000	.2

Table for Exercise 8 – Cereal B	
Sales	P(Sales)
−$10,000	.40
$300,000	.40
$600,000	.10
$1,000,000	.10

a. What are the expected sales of each of the new brands of cereal?

b. What is the standard deviation of the sales for each of the brands of cereal?

c. If both of the brands of cereal cost the same amount to produce, which brand of cereal do you think the cereal manufacturer should produce? Explain.

6.4 Where Do Probability Distributions Come From?

In the previous examples, the probability distributions are given. But in the real world there are very few instances in which the probability distribution is conveniently available. Substantial effort is usually required to obtain the probability distribution. Probabilities are determined using the same techniques described in Chapter 5: classical, relative frequency, or subjective.

Sometimes, however, you get lucky. The random variable you wish to analyze either conforms to or can be approximated by an experiment that has a known probability distribution. Four well known discrete distributions will be discussed in this chapter: uniform, binomial, Poisson, and hypergeometric.

Each of the discrete distributions possesses a **probability distribution function**. These functions assign probabilities to each value of the random variable.

Example 6.11

The following function is a discrete probability distribution function:

$$P(X=x)\begin{cases} \dfrac{x^2}{30}, & \text{if } x = 1,2,3,4 \\ 0 & \text{otherwise} \end{cases}$$

Summarize the probability distribution for this function.

Solution

To determine the probability for a value, use the value as the argument to the function. For example, to determine the probability that $X = 3$.

$$P(X=3) = \frac{3^2}{30} = \frac{9}{30},$$

or the probability that $X = 4$

$$P(X=4) = \frac{4^2}{30} = \frac{16}{30}.$$

The resulting probability distribution is summarized in Table 6.12.

Table 6.12 – Probability Distribution	
x	**$P(X = x)$**
1	$\dfrac{1}{30}$
2	$\dfrac{4}{30}$
3	$\dfrac{9}{30}$
4	$\dfrac{16}{30}$
	$\sum P(X = x) = 1$

Note that the distribution possesses the essential properties of all probability distributions; that is, the probabilities sum to one, and all the probabilities are between 0 and 1.

 **Exercises**

Basic Concepts

1. How is a probability distribution created?

2. Identify four discrete probability distributions.

3. What is a probability distribution function?

6.5 The Discrete Uniform Distribution

The discrete uniform distribution is one of the simplest probability distributions. Each value of the random variable is assigned an identical probability. There are many situations in which the discrete uniform distribution arises.

Formula

Mathematically, the function for a **discrete uniform probability distribution** is given by $P(X = x) = \dfrac{1}{n}$ where n = the number of values that the random variable may assume.

Example 6.12

What is the probability distribution for the outcome of the throw of a single die?

Solution

If the die is fair, then each of the outcomes is equally likely and thus we have a uniform distribution in which all probabilities equal $\dfrac{1}{6}$. The probability distribution is given in Table 6.13.

Table 6.13 – Throwing a Die	
x	P(X = x)
1	$\dfrac{1}{6}$
2	$\dfrac{1}{6}$
3	$\dfrac{1}{6}$
4	$\dfrac{1}{6}$
5	$\dfrac{1}{6}$
6	$\dfrac{1}{6}$

Example 6.13

Suppose a purchasing agent has just received a pricing and delivery schedule from a new vendor. The delivery schedule was quoted as 1 to 4 weeks. The agency wishes to construct the probability distribution for the time until delivery.

Solution

The probabilities of the random variable

$$X = \text{the number of weeks until delivery}$$

are given in Table 6.14.

Table 6.14 – Delivery Distribution	
x	**P(X = x)**
1	$\dfrac{1}{4}$
2	$\dfrac{1}{4}$
3	$\dfrac{1}{4}$
4	$\dfrac{1}{4}$

Without any prior information, the agent believes any time frame is as likely as any other. Hence, the number of weeks until delivery will be assumed to have a uniform distribution. Over time the purchasing agent will undoubtedly revise the distribution as more information is gathered about the company's delivery schedule.

Example 6.13 illustrates an important principle in the application of the discrete uniform distribution. That is, when there is little or no information concerning the outcome of a random variable, the discrete uniform distribution may be a reasonable initial alternative.

6.5   Exercises

Basic Concepts

1. What is the most significant property of the uniform distribution?

2. What is the discrete uniform probability distribution function?

3. Explain why the uniform distribution is often used when there is little or no information concerning the outcome of a random variable.

Exercises

1. In the casino game of roulette, a wheel is spun and a ball is set in motion, ultimately coming to rest in one of the 38 slots on the wheel. Any slot is as likely as any other to capture the ball. Of the 38 slots, 18 are red, 18 are black, and 2 are green. Suppose the entry fee to play a single game is $1 and the participant bets on red. If the ball comes to rest in one of the red slots, he wins $1 in addition to getting back the original $1 entry fee. If the ball does not end up in a red slot, the $1 entry fee is lost. Let X denote the monetary gain when betting $1 on red, in a single game of roulette. Gain is defined as the amount won minus the fee to play.

    a. What are the possible values of X?

    b. Is X a discrete or continuous random variable? Explain.

    c. Construct the probability distribution of X.

    d. Find the expected value of X and interpret this number.

    e. Do you feel that in any casino games you would have a positive expected gain? Why?

2. An experiment consists of tossing two coins and a die simultaneously.

    a. List the 24 equally likely outcomes.

    b. Define the random variable X as the sum of the number of heads on the two coins and the number of dots on the die. What are the possible values of X?

    c. Construct the probability distribution of X in the form of a table.

    d. Find the expected value of X.

6.6   The Binomial Distribution

The binomial distribution arises from experiments with repeated two-outcome trials, where only one of the outcomes is counted. Experiments of this kind are rather common in the business world. In market research, a survey respondent (a trial) will either recognize a company's brand or will not. The number that recognize the brand is a count that may be modeled as a binomial random variable. When a customer (a trial) enters a bank for service, he or she may have to wait. If we are counting customers who have to wait, then the count may conform to the binomial model. Experiments are required to meet several conditions in order to qualify as a binomial experiment.

Definition

Binomial Experiment

A **binomial experiment** is a random experiment which satisfies all of the following conditions.

1. There are only two outcomes in each trial of the experiment. (One of the outcomes is usually referred to as a *success*, and the other as a *failure*.)

2. The experiment consists of n identical trials as described in Condition 1.

3. The probability of success on any one trial is denoted by p and does not change from trial to trial. (Note that the probability of a failure is $(1 - p)$ and also does not change from trial to trial.)

4. The trials are independent.

5. The binomial random variable is the count of the number of successes in n trials.

A binomial random variable is formed by counting the number of successes in n trials of an experiment with two outcomes. One of the simplest of binomial random variables is produced by tossing a coin.

Example 6.14

Toss a coin 4 times and record the number of heads. Is the number of heads in 4 tosses a binomial random variable?

Solution

1. There are only two outcomes, heads or tails.

2. The experiment will consist of 4 tosses of a coin. (Hence, $n = 4$.)

3. The probability of getting a head (success) is $\frac{1}{2}$ and does not change from trial to trial. (Hence, $p = \frac{1}{2}$.)

4. The outcome of one toss will not affect other tosses.

5. The variable of interest is the count of the number of heads in 4 tosses.

Table 6.15 – Tossing a Coin		
Events	Number of Heads	Probability
TTTT	0	$\frac{1}{16}$
HTTT THTT TTHT TTTH	1	$\frac{4}{16}$
HHTT HTHT HTTH THHT THTH TTHH	2	$\frac{6}{16}$
THHH HTHH HHTH HHHT	3	$\frac{4}{16}$
HHHH	4	$\frac{1}{16}$

The probability distribution could be derived using the classical method described in the previous chapter. To derive the binomial distribution by listing the simple events is unnecessarily tedious (see Table 6.15). Instead of tossing the coin four times, suppose the coin is tossed 10 times in the experiment. The number of simple events for an experiment with 10 tosses would be 1024, and an experiment with 20 tosses would require listing a staggering 1,048,576 simple events. Fortunately, there is a far simpler method of obtaining the probability distribution. The binomial probability distribution function provides a relatively simple method of calculating binomial probabilities.

Formula

The binomial probability distribution function is

$$P(X = x) = C_x^n p^x (1-p)^{n-x}$$

Where C_x^n represents the number of possible combinations of n objects taken x at a time (without replacement) and is given by

$$C_x^n = \frac{n!}{x!(n-x)!} \text{ where } n! = n(n-1)(n-2)\cdots(2)(1) \text{ and } 0! = 1;$$

n = the number of trials, and

p = the probability of a success.

To calculate a binomial probability, the parameters of the distribution (n and p) as well as the value of the random variable must be specified. For example, to determine the probability that $X = 3$ given that $n = 4$ and $p = \frac{1}{2}$, substitute those values in the probability distribution function as follows:

$$P(X = 3) = C_3^4 \left(\frac{1}{2}\right)^3 \left(1 - \frac{1}{2}\right)^{4-3}.$$

Since $C_3^4 = \frac{4!}{3!(4-3)!} = \frac{(4)(3!)}{(3!)(1!)} = 4$, then

$$P(X = 3) = 4\left(\frac{1}{2}\right)^3 \left(\frac{1}{2}\right) = \frac{4}{16} = \frac{1}{4} = .25.$$

The probability that 2 heads would be tossed would be computed in a similar manner.

$$P(X = 2) = C_2^4 \left(\frac{1}{2}\right)^2 \left(1 - \frac{1}{2}\right)^{4-2}$$

$$= \frac{4!}{(2!)(2!)} \left(\frac{1}{2}\right)^2 \left(\frac{1}{2}\right)^2 = \frac{6}{16} = \frac{3}{8} = .375.$$

The complete distribution can be computed by substituting the remaining values of the random variable into the probability distribution function.

Table 6.16 – Tossing a Coin	
Number of Heads	Probability
0	$\dfrac{1}{16}$
1	$\dfrac{4}{16}$
2	$\dfrac{6}{16}$
3	$\dfrac{4}{16}$
4	$\dfrac{1}{16}$

The coin toss is a classical binomial experiment easily related to the rules of a binomial experiment. In many instances the relationship of an experiment to the binomial definition is not as clear.

Example 6.15

Roll a single die 4 times and record the number of sixes observed. Does the number of sixes rolled in 4 tosses of a die meet the conditions required of a binomial random variable?

Solution

1. The experiment either produces a six or not, and thus satisfies the two outcome requirement. (At first glance, there appears to be a problem. There are six sides to a die and there would appear to be six possible outcomes rather than the two required for a single trial of a binomial experiment.)

2. The experiment is repeated 4 times. (Hence, $n = 4$.)

3. The probability remains constant from trial to trial. (One roll of the die does not affect other rolls.)

4. If X is the number of sixes in 4 rolls, then it has a binomial distribution.

To obtain the probability distribution for X, use the binomial probability distribution function with parameters $n = 4$ and $p = \dfrac{1}{6}$.

$$P(X=0) = C_0^4 \left(\frac{1}{6}\right)^0 \left(1 - \frac{1}{6}\right)^{4-0} = (1)(1)\left(\frac{5}{6}\right)^4 = .4823$$

$$P(X=1) = C_1^4 \left(\frac{1}{6}\right)^1 \left(1 - \frac{1}{6}\right)^{4-1} = (4)\left(\frac{1}{6}\right)\left(\frac{5}{6}\right)^3 = .3858$$

$$P(X=2) = C_2^4 \left(\frac{1}{6}\right)^2 \left(1 - \frac{1}{6}\right)^{4-2} = (6)\left(\frac{1}{6}\right)^2 \left(\frac{5}{6}\right)^2 = .1157$$

$$P(X=3) = C_3^4 \left(\frac{1}{6}\right)^3 \left(1 - \frac{1}{6}\right)^{4-3} = (4)\left(\frac{1}{6}\right)^3 \left(\frac{5}{6}\right) = .0154$$

$$P(X=4) = C_4^4 \left(\frac{1}{6}\right)^4 \left(1 - \frac{1}{6}\right)^{4-4} = (1)\left(\frac{1}{6}\right)^4 (1) = .0008$$

Table 6.17 – Throwing a Die	
x	**Probability**
0	.4823
1	.3858
2	.1157
3	.0154
4	.0008

The calculations required to produce the distribution were reasonably simple in this case. However, if there had been forty cases rather than four, the determination of the probabilities would have been rather burdensome, at best. Binomial tables containing a large collection of binomial distributions have been constructed in order to avoid tedious calculations. These tables are found in Appendix A.

Example 6.16

A department store has decided to interview a random sample of ten customers to determine if they should modify their return policy. The company believes that 70% of the customers will approve the change and 30% will not approve the change. Using the probabilities given, what is the probability that at least three of the ten customers will approve the change in return policy?

Solution

Instead of laboriously computing the distribution, use the binomial tables in Appendix A, Table E. The binomial parameters are $n = 10$ and $p = .7$. Let X equal the number of customers that will approve the change. The table below shows the cumulative binomial distribution for X.

Table 6.18 – Binomial Table $n = 10, p = .7$	
x	$P(X \leq x)$
0	.0000
1	.0001
2	.0016
3	.0106
4	.0473
5	.1503
6	.3504
7	.6172
8	.8507
9	.9718
10	1.0000

The probability that at least three customers will approve the change is equal to $1 - P(X \leq 2) = 1 - .0017 = .9983$. Therefore, it's almost certain that at least three customers will approve the change in return policy.

The Shape of a Binomial Distribution

Binomial Distribution for $n = 12$ and $p = .1$

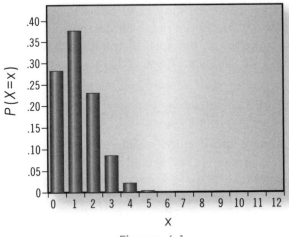

Figure 6.1

Binomial distributions have taken various shapes in the previous problems. The shape of the distribution depends upon the parameters n and p. If p is small the distribution tends to be skewed with a tail on the right as is the case in the previous problem (see Figure 6.1).

Binomial Distribution for $n = 9$ and $p = .5$

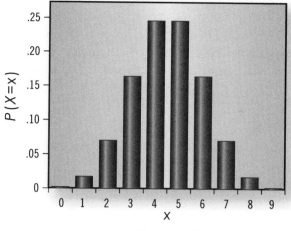

Figure 6.2

If p is near .5 the distribution is symmetrical. The graph in Figure 6.2 displays the probabilities for $n = 9$ and $p = .5$.

Binomial Distribution for $n = 11$ and $p = .7$

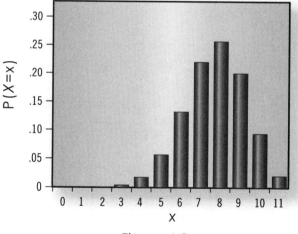

Figure 6.3

If p is large the distribution tends to be skewed with a long tail on the left. The graph in Figure 6.3 displays the binomial probabilities for $n = 11$ and $p = .7$.

The Expected Value and Variance of a Binomial Random Variable

To calculate the expected value of a binomial random variable, such as in Example 6.16, would require a substantial number of arithmetic operations. Fortunately, you can avoid this calculation by utilizing a special characteristic of the binomial distribution.

Formula

Expected Value

The **expected value** of a binomial random variable can be computed using the expression

$$\mu = E(X) = np,$$

where n and p are the parameters of the binomial distribution.

It is important to remember that this formula is only valid for binomial random variables. Also, there is a simple method for obtaining the variance for a binomial random variable.

Formula

Variance and Standard Deviation

To find the **variance** of a binomial random variable, use the expression

$$\sigma^2 = V(X) = np(1-p).$$

Thus, the **standard deviation** of a binomial random variable is given by

$$\sigma = \sqrt{V(X)} = \sqrt{np(1-p)}.$$

Example 6.17

Compute the expected value and the variance of the number of customers that will approve the change in return policy in Example 6.16.

Solution

Since the random variable is binomial, we can use the shortcuts $E(X) = np$ and $V(X) = np(1-p)$. Since $n = 10$ and $p = .7$, the expected value is given by

$$E(X) = np = 10(.7) = 7.$$

The variance is

$$\sigma^2 = V(X) = np(1-p) = 10(.7)(.3) = 2.1$$

which implies that the standard deviation is $\sqrt{2.1} \approx 1.4491$.

Thus, if 10 randomly selected customers are polled, we would expect 7 of the 10 to approve the change in return policy, and the standard deviation would be 1.4491 customers.

6.6 Exercises

Basic Concepts

1. Describe the characteristics of a binomial experiment.

2. What are the parameters of a binomial probability model?

3. Give an example of a binomial experiment in a business context.

4. What is the binomial probability distribution function?

5. Describe the shape of a binomial distribution. Does the shape change? What influences the shape of the distribution?

6. How do you calculate the expected value of a binomial random variable? The variance?

Exercises

1. Calculate C_x^n for each of the following combinations of x and n.

   a. $n = 5, x = 4$

   b. $n = 10, x = 8$

   c. $n = 15, x = 1$

   d. $n = 20, x = 0$

2. Calculate C_x^n for each of the following combinations of x and n.

   a. $n = 4, x = 2$

   b. $n = 12, x = 8$

   c. $n = 18, x = 15$

   d. $n = 23, x = 20$

3. The random variable X is a binomial random variable with $n = 9$ and $p = .1$.

   a. Find the expected value of X.

   b. Find the standard deviation of X.

   c. Find the probability that X equals 2. (Use the formula for $P(X = x)$.)

   d. Find the probability that X is at most 3. (Appendix A, Table E)

   e. Find the probability that X is at least 2. (Appendix A, Table E)

   f. Find the probability that X is less than 5. (Appendix A, Table E)

4. The random variable X is a binomial random variable with $n = 12$ and $p = .8$.

   a. Find the expected value of X.

   b. Find the standard deviation of X.

   c. Find the probability that X equals 7. (Use the formula for $P(X = x)$.)

   d. Find the probability that X is at most 4. (Appendix A, Table E)

   e. Find the probability that X is at least 1. (Appendix A, Table E)

   f. Find the probability that X is more than 10. (Appendix A, Table E)

5. A real estate agent has ten properties that she shows. She feels that there is a ten percent chance of selling any one property during a week. The chance of selling any one property is independent of selling another property.

   a. What probability model would be appropriate for describing the number of properties sold each week?

   b. Compute the expected number of properties to be sold in a week.

   c. Compute the standard deviation of the number of properties sold each week.

   d. Compute the probability of selling one property in one week.

   e. Compute the probability of selling five properties in one week.

   f. Compute the probability of selling at least three properties in one week.

6. A small commuter airline is concerned about reservation no-shows and, correspondingly, how much they should overbook flights to compensate. Assume their commuter planes will hold 15 people. Industry research indicates that 20% of the people making a reservation will not show up for a flight. Whether or not one person takes the flight is considered to be independent of other persons holding reservations.

   a. What probability model would be appropriate for the number of passengers that actually take the flight?

   b. If the airlines decide to book 18 people for each flight, how often will there be at least one person who will not get a seat?

   c. If they book 17 people, how often will there be at least one person who will not get a seat?

   d. If they book 16 people, how often will there be at least one person who will not get a seat?

   e. If they book 18 people for each flight, how often will there be one or more empty seats?

   f. If they book 17 people, how often will there be one or more empty seats?

   g. If they book 16 people, how often will there be one or more empty seats?

   h. Based on the results from parts (b) to (g) above, which booking policy do you prefer?

7. Seven plants are operated by a garment manufacturer. They feel there is a ten percent chance for a strike at any one plant and the risk of a strike at one plant is independent of the risk of a strike at another plant. Let X = number of plants of the garment manufacturer that strike.

   a. Determine the probability distribution for X.

   b. Interpret the results for $P(X = 0)$, $P(X = 4)$, and $P(X = 7)$.

   c. Compute the expected value of X.

   d. Compute the standard deviation for X. Is this value large in relation to the expected value? In what units is the standard deviation expressed?

8. A company that makes traffic signal lights buys switches from a supplier. Out of each shipment of 1000 switches, the company will take a random sample of 10 switches. Let X equal the number of defective switches in the sample.

   a. The company has a policy of rejecting a lot if they find any defective switches in the sample. What is the probability that the shipment will be accepted if, in fact, 2% of the switches are actually defective?

   b. What is the probability that the shipment will be accepted if the percent of defective switches is actually 5%?

   c. The company decides to change their policy and will accept the lot if they find no more than one defective switch. Repeat parts (a) and (b) for this new policy.

9. Parents have always wondered about the sex of a child before it is born. Suppose that the probability of having a male child was .5, and that the sex of one child is independent of the sex of other children.

   a. Determine the probability of having exactly two girls out of four children.

   b. What is the probability of having four boys out of four children?

10. A certain aspirin is advertised as being preferred by 4 out of 5 doctors. If the advertisement is assumed to be true,

    a. What is the probability that at least half of ten doctors chosen at random will prefer this brand of aspirin?

    b. What is the probability that 9 out of 10 of the doctors will prefer this brand?

11. In manufacturing integrated circuits, the yield of the manufacturing process is the percentage of good chips produced by the process. The probability that an integrated circuit manufactured by the Ace Electronics Company will be defective is $p = .05$. If a random sample of 15 circuits is selected for testing,

    a. What is the probability that no more than one integrated circuit will be defective in the sample?

    b. What is the expected number of defective integrated circuits in the sample?

12. The Alvin Secretarial Service procures temporary office personnel for major corporations. They have found that 90% of their invoices are paid within ten working days. If a random sample of 12 invoices is checked,

    a. What is the probability that all of the invoices will be paid within 10 working days?

    b. What is the probability that six or more of the invoices will be paid within 10 working days?

13. An experiment consists of rolling a pair of dice 10 times. On each roll the sum of the dots on the two dice is noted.

    a. Find the probability that on any roll of the 2 dice the sum of the dots is either 7 or 11.

    b. Find the probability that in the 10 rolls of the pair of dice, a 7 or 11 occurs 5 times.

    c. Find the probability that in the 10 rolls of the pair of dice, a 7 or 11 does not occur at all.

    d. Find the mean and variance of the number of times we see a 7 or 11 in the 10 rolls of the dice.

14. *Would you say you eat to live or live to eat?* was asked to each person in a sample of 1001 adults in a Gallup Poll taken in April, 1996. Seventy-four percent of the respondents answered eat to live, 23% answered live to eat, and 3% had no opinion. Assuming these percents are accurate, find the probability, in 12 randomly chosen adults, that the number who would answer "eat to live" is:

    a. Exactly 7.

    b. No more than 10.

    c. At most 11.

    d. At least 3.

6.7 The Poisson Distribution

The binomial random variable requires a fixed number of repetitions of the experiment, where the outcomes are either successes or failures. The **Poisson distribution** is similar to the binomial in that the random variable represents a count of the total number of successes. The major difference between the two distributions is that the Poisson does not have a fixed number of trials. Instead, the Poisson uses a fixed interval of time or space in which the number of successes are recorded. Thus, there is no theoretical upper limit on the number of successes, although large numbers of successes are not very likely. The word *success* in the Poisson context can sometimes take on rather unpleasant connotations. For example, the randomness exhibited by the number of airplane crashes, oil tanker spills, and car accidents in some fixed period of time seem to conform to the randomness described by a Poisson random variable.

In business environments many variables seem to follow a pattern of randomness similar to that described by the Poisson distribution. One of the Poisson's principal areas of use in business is the analysis of waiting lines. Other random phenomena, such as airplane arrivals at an airport, trucks arriving at a loading dock, users logging on to a computer system, or the number of defects in a given surface area, can be modeled with a Poisson distribution. These variables are often of interest in determining personnel requirements, inventories, and quality control.

Poisson Random Variable

Definition

In order to qualify as a **Poisson random variable** an experiment must meet two conditions:

1. Successes occur one at time. (That is, two or more successes cannot occur at exactly the same point in time or exactly at the same point in space.)

2. The occurrence of a success in any interval is independent of the occurrence of a success in any other interval.

If these two conditions are met, it can be proven that the random variable for the number of successes follows the Poisson probability distribution function.

Formula

The Poisson probability distribution function is given by:

$$P(X = x) = \frac{e^{-\lambda}\lambda^x}{x!}, \text{ for } x = 0, 1, 2, \ldots$$

where $e = 2.71828\ldots$, and

λ = mean number of successes.

Poisson Probability
Distribution Function

The Poisson distribution has only one parameter, λ, pronounced *lambda*. One peculiar feature of the distribution is that the variance (lambda) of the distribution is equal to the mean.

The shape of the distribution varies dramatically with the parameter λ. (Tables for the Poisson distribution are found in Appendix A, Table G.) If λ is small, say .3, then the corresponding distribution is found in Table 6.19 and displayed in Figure 6.4.

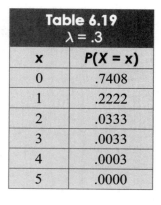

Table 6.19 $\lambda = .3$	
x	P(X = x)
0	.7408
1	.2222
2	.0333
3	.0033
4	.0003
5	.0000

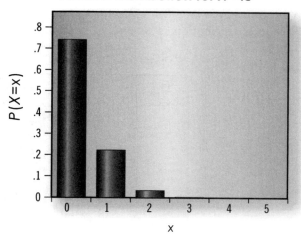

Poisson Distribution for λ =.3

Figure 6.4

As λ increases to 3 (see Table 6.20), the distribution in Figure 6.5 exhibits a mound shape with skewness.

Kicked by Horses

A real world example of the Poisson distribution involves the distribution of Prussian cavalry deaths from getting kicked by horses, in the period 1875-1894. The Prussian military kept meticulous records on horse-kick deaths in each of its army corps, and the data are neatly summarized in a 1963 book called *Lady Luck*, by the late Warren Weaver. There were a total of 196 kicking deaths – these being the successes. The trials were each army corps's observations on the number of kicking deaths sustained during the year. With 14 army corps and data for 20 years, there were 280 trials. The Poisson formula predicts, for example, that there will be 34.1 instances of having exactly two deaths in a year. In fact, there were 32 such cases. Pretty good, eh?

Table 6.20 $\lambda = 3$	
x	**P(X = x)**
0	.0498
1	.1494
2	.2240
3	.2240
4	.1680
5	.1008
6	.0504
7	.0216
8	.0081
9	.0027
10	.0008
11	.0002
12	.0001

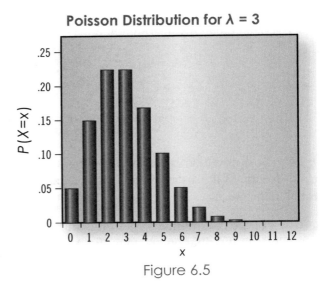

Figure 6.5

As λ becomes even larger, say $\lambda = 12$, the distribution begins to closely resemble a bell-shaped distribution as shown in Figure 6.6.

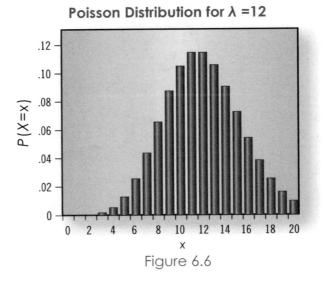

Figure 6.6

Poisson Random Variables for Time Related Variables

Most Poisson applications relate to the number of occurrences of some event in a specific duration of time.

Example 6.18

Suppose a bank has one automatic teller machine. Customers arrive at the machine at a rate of 20 per hour and according to a Poisson pattern.

a. What is the probability that no one will arrive in a 15 minute interval?

b. What is the probability that in a fifteen minute period at least 3 persons will use the automated teller machine?

Solution

a. Let

$$X = \text{number of arrivals in a 15 minute period.}$$

This problem contains one of the standard techniques used in working with Poisson random variables, that is, translating the arrival rate to correspond to the desired time interval. In this problem, the rate is given at 20 per hour which corresponds to a rate of 5 per $\frac{1}{4}$ hour (15 minutes). Thus,

$$\lambda = 5$$

and the desired probability is

$$P(X = 0) = \frac{e^{-5} 5^0}{0!}, \text{ or}$$

$$P(X = 0) = .0067. \text{(Note: 0! Is defined to be 1.)}$$

The probability could also have been found by using the table in the Appendix.

b. To find the probability that in a 15 minute period at least 3 persons will use the automated teller machine, we are interested in $P(X \geq 3)$.

$$
\begin{aligned}
P(X \geq 3) &= 1 - P(X \leq 2) \\
&= 1 - \big(P(X = 0) + P(X = 1) + P(X = 2)\big) \\
&= 1 - (.0067 + .0337 + .0842) \text{ (using the Poisson table)} \\
&= 1 - .1246 = .8754
\end{aligned}
$$

Poisson Random Variables for Length and Space

Instead of counting the number of successes in a time interval, there are a number of applications of the Poisson distribution that measure the number of successes in some area or length. The average number of successes in the area or length will define the parameter of the Poisson random variable.

Example 6.19

The telephone company is considering purchasing optical cable from Optica, Inc. The company wishes to replace approximately 100,000 feet of conventional cable with optical fiber. Since optical fiber is very difficult to repair, it is important that the number of optical cable defects are minimized. Optica claims that on average there is one defect per 200,000 feet of cable. What is the probability that the replaced cable will contain no defects?

Solution

Let $\lambda =$ the number of defects in 100,000 feet of optical cable.

Based on previous experience, we assume that the number of defects is approximated by a Poisson distribution with Poisson parameter

$$\lambda = \frac{100,000}{200,000} = \frac{1}{2} \text{ (average number of defects per 100,000 ft. of cable).}$$

Using the tables provided in the Appendix A,

$$P(X = 0) = .6065.$$

6.7 Exercises

Basic Concepts

1. How is the Poisson distribution similar to the binomial distribution?

2. What are the two conditions that an experiment must meet in order to be considered a Poisson random variable?

3. What are some uses of the Poisson probability model in business?

4. What is the Poisson probability distribution function?

5. What is the parameter of the Poisson probability model?

6. What is the expected value of a Poisson random variable? The variance?

Exercises

1. Suppose that, on average, 5 students enrolled in a small liberal arts college have their automobiles stolen during the semester. What is the probability that exactly 2 students will have their automobiles stolen during the current semester?

2. The number of calls received by an office on Monday morning between 8:00 AM and 9:00 AM has a Poisson distribution with λ equal to 4.0.

   a. Determine the probability of getting no calls between eight and nine in the morning.

   b. Calculate the probability of getting exactly five calls between eight and nine in the morning.

   c. What will be the expected number of calls received by the office during this time period? What is the variance?

   d. Graph the probability distribution of the number of calls using values from the table.

3. The director of a local hospital is studying the occurrence of medication errors. Medication errors are deemed to occur when a patient is given the wrong amount of medication or the wrong medication is given to a patient. Based on past experience, the director believes that medication errors follow a Poisson process with an average rate of 2 per week. (For the following problems, assume that 1 month = 4 weeks.)

   a. What is the probability that there are no medication errors in one week?

   b. What is the probability that there are no medication errors in one month?

   c. Find the average number of medication errors in one week.

   d. Find the average number of medication errors in one month.

   e. Find the standard deviation of the number of medication errors in one month.

   f. How likely is it that at least 4 medication errors will be observed in one month?

4. The number of weaving errors in a twenty foot by ten foot roll of carpet has a Poisson distribution with $\lambda = .1$.

   a. Using Appendix A, Table G, construct the probability distribution for the carpet.

   b. What is the probability of observing less than 2 errors in the carpet?

   c. What is the probability of observing more than 5 errors in the carpet?

6

5. A bank is evaluating their staffing policy to assure they have sufficient staff for their drive up window during the lunch hour. If the number of people who arrive at the window in a 15 minute period has a Poisson distribution with $\lambda = 5$,

   a. How many people are expected to arrive during the lunch hour?

   b. What is the probability that no one will show up during the lunch hour of 12:00 PM to 1:00 PM?

   c. What is the probability that more than 6 people will show up in any fifteen minute period?

6. An aluminum foil manufacturer wants to improve the quality of his product and is trying to develop a probability model for the flaws that occur in a sheet of foil. Assume that X, the number of flaws per square foot, has a Poisson distribution. If flaws occur randomly at an average of one flaw per 50 square feet, what is the probability that a box containing a 200 square foot roll will contain one flaw? More than one flaw?

7. A manufacturing company is concerned about the high rate of accidents that occurred on the production line last week. There were 6 accidents in the last week and this may require a report to be sent to the government agency for safety. Calculate the probability of 6 accidents occurring in a week when the average number of accidents per week has been 3.5.

6.8 The Hypergeometric Distribution

The binomial and the hypergeometric random variables are very similar. Both random variables have only two outcomes in each trial of the experiment. They both count the number of successes in n trials of an experiment. The hypergeometric distribution differs from the binomial distribution in the lack of independence between trials, which also implies that the probability of success will vary between trials. In addition, hypergeometric distributions have finite populations in which the total number of successes and failures are known.

Because the binomial and hypergeometric distributions are closely related, a small change in an experiment can switch the distribution of the random variable. A binomial experiment, such as counting the number of red cards drawn in 8 draws from a deck with replacement, can easily be modified to a hypergeometric by not replacing the cards. Since there are 26 red cards (successes) and 26 black cards (failures), the probability of drawing a red card on the first draw is $\frac{26}{52}$ or $\frac{1}{2}$. If a red card is drawn on the first draw and not replaced, the probability of drawing a red card on the next draw is slightly less $\left(\frac{25}{51}\right)$ since there is one less red card in the deck. If the next card drawn is also red, then the probability of a red card on the third draw will be diminished to $\frac{24}{50}$. The probability distribution function of the hypergeometric distribution is given below.

Formula

The hypergeometric probability distribution function is given by:

$$P(X = x) = \frac{C_x^A C_{n-x}^{N-A}}{C_n^N}, \text{ where } 0 \le x \le \text{ minimum of } (A, n),$$

Hypergeometric Probability Distribution Function

A = the total number of successes possible,

N = the size of the total population, and

n = the size of the sample drawn.

There cannot be more successes than there are successes in the population, nor can there be more successes than the total size of the sample. Thus, the maximum value of X is the smaller of A and n.

Example 6.20

In a volatile stock market, suppose a mutual fund contains 15 stocks. Four of the stocks in the fund have positive gains, while 11 of the stocks are losing money. If two of the stocks from the mutual fund are chosen at random (without replacement), what is the probability distribution for the number of stocks that will have a positive gain?

Solution

The random variable under consideration is given as

X = the number of stocks in the mutual fund that have positive gains.

The parameters of the distribution are

$A = 4$ (a success in this case is a money-making stock)

$N = 15$, and

$n = 2$.

The maximum value of X in this case is 2. Using the hypergeometric distribution function,

$$P(X = 0) = \frac{C_0^4 C_{2-0}^{15-4}}{C_2^{15}} = .5238$$

$$P(X = 1) = \frac{C_1^4 C_{2-1}^{15-4}}{C_2^{15}} = .4190$$

$$P(X = 2) = \frac{C_2^4 C_{2-2}^{15-4}}{C_2^{15}} = .0571.$$

The distribution is summarized in the table below.

Table 6.21 – Probability Distribution	
x	P(X = x)
0	.5238
1	.4190
2	.0571

Expected Value and Variance

It is apparent that the hypergeometric distribution can be rather tedious to calculate, based on the calculations in Example 6.20. Since there are no tables for the distribution, determining an expected value using the definition $\left(\sum \left[xp(x) \right] \right)$ would consume a considerable amount of time. Fortunately, there is a simpler method.

Formula

The **expected value** of a hypergeometric random variable can be obtained using the expression

$$\mu = E(X) = n\frac{A}{N}.$$

Expected Value

Formula

The **variance** of a hypergeometric random variable is given by

$$\sigma^2 = V(X) = n\frac{A}{N}\left(1 - \frac{A}{N}\right)\frac{(N-n)}{(N-1)}.$$

Variance

Example 6.21

Compute the expected value and variance for the random variable defined in Example 6.20.

Solution

$$E(X) = 2\left(\frac{4}{15}\right) = 0.5333$$

$$\sigma^2 = V(X) = 2\left(\frac{4}{15}\right)\left(1 - \frac{4}{15}\right)\frac{(15-2)}{(15-1)} = 0.3632.$$

Thus, if the experiment were repeated many times, the average number of stocks in the mutual fund that had positive gains would be 0.5333. This leads us to believe that this particular fund is not very promising.

6.8 Exercises

Basic Concepts

1. How does the hypergeometric model differ from the binomial model?

2. What is the hypergeometric probability distribution function?

3. What are the parameters of the hypergeometric model?

4. How do you calculate the expected value of a hypergeometric random variable? The variance?

Exercises

1. Suppose a batch of 50 light bulbs contains 3 light bulbs which are defective. Let X = the number of defective light bulbs in a random sample of 10 light bulbs (where the sample is taken without replacement).

   a. What is the probability distribution of X?

   b. Find the expected number of defective bulbs.

   c. Find the standard deviation of the number of defective bulbs.

   d. Find the probability that at least 1 of the bulbs sampled will be defective.

   e. Find the probability that at most 2 of the bulbs sampled will be defective.

   f. Find the probability that more than 3 of the bulbs sampled will be defective.

2. A small electronics firm has 60 employees. Ten of the employees are older than 55. An attorney is investigating a client's claim regarding age discrimination. The attorney randomly selects 15 employees without replacement and records the number of employees over age 55.

   a. What is the probability distribution of X = the number of employees over age 55 in a sample of 15 selected without replacement?

   b. Find the average number of employees over age 55 in the sample.

   c. Find the standard deviation of the number of employees over age 55 in the sample.

   d. Find the probability that at least 2 of the employees selected will be over age 55.

   e. Find the probability that less than 2 of the employees selected will be over age 55.

   f. Find the probability that at most 4 of the employees will be over age 55.

3. A bank has to repossess 100 homes. Fifty of the repossessed homes have market values which are less than the outstanding balance of the mortgage. An auditor randomly selects 10 of the repossessed homes (without replacement) and records the number of homes which have market values less than the outstanding balance of the mortgage.

   a. Find the expected number of homes which the auditor will find with market values less than the outstanding balance of the mortgage.

   b. Find the standard deviation of the number of homes which the auditor will find with market values less than the outstanding balance of the mortgage.

   c. What is the probability that all of the audited homes will have outstanding balances in excess of their mortgage?

   d. What is the probability that none of the audited homes will have outstanding balances in excess of their mortgage?

4. A small liberal arts college in the Northeast has 200 freshmen. Eighty of the freshmen are female. Suppose thirty freshmen are randomly selected (without replacement).

   a. Find the expected number of females in the sample.

   b. Find the standard deviation of the number of females in the sample.

   c. Find the probability that none of the selected students will be female.

   d. Find the probability that all of the selected students will be female.

Discovering Technology

USING EXCEL

Binomial Distribution

For this exercise, use the data from Example 6.16.

$$n = 10, p = .7$$

1. Set up the worksheet as shown below.

	A	B	C	D	E
1	x	p(X=x)		x	P(X<=x)
2	0			0	
3	1			1	
4	2			2	
5	3			3	
6	4			4	
7	5			5	
8	6			6	
9	7			7	
10	8			8	
11	9			9	
12	10			10	

Figure 6.7

2. Using the binomial distribution function in Microsoft Excel, you can calculate both individual and cumulative probabilities for each number of successes. The function in Microsoft Excel which calculates binomial probabilities is

BINOMDIST(number_s,trials,probability_s,cumulative) where

number_s = the number of successes,

trials = the number of trials,

probability_s = the probability of success, and

cumulative = a logical value which is either TRUE (Excel returns the cumulative probability) or FALSE (Excel returns the probability there are **number_s** successes).

3. Begin with the individual probabilities. In cell B2, enter the formula to return the probability that there are 0 successes in 10 trials:

$$=BINOMDIST(0,10,.7,FALSE)$$

Press **Enter**.

4. Continue in Column B by entering the appropriate parameters into the BINOMDIST function for each individual number of successes. Excel will return the probabilities as shown in Figure 6.8.

	A	B	C	D	E
1	x	p (X=x)		x	P (X<=x)
2	0	5.9049E-06		0	
3	1	0.00013778		1	
4	2	0.0014467		2	
5	3	0.00900169		3	
6	4	0.03675691		4	
7	5	0.10291935		5	
8	6	0.20012095		6	
9	7	0.26682793		7	
10	8	0.23347444		8	
11	9	0.12106082		9	
12	10	0.02824752		10	

Figure 6.8

5. Next, calculate the cumulative probabilities. In cell E2, enter the formula to return the cumulative probability that there are no more than 0 successes in 10 trials:

$$=BINOMDIST(0,10,.7,TRUE)$$

Press **Enter**.

6. Continue in Column E by entering the appropriate parameters into the BINOMDIST function for the cumulative probabilities for each number of successes. Excel will return the cumulative probabilities as shown in Figure 6.9. Compare these to the values we found in Example 6.16.

	A	B	C	D	E
1	x	p(X=x)		x	P(X<=x)
2	0	5.9049E-06		0	5.9049E-06
3	1	0.00013778		1	0.00014369
4	2	0.0014467		2	0.00159039
5	3	0.00900169		3	0.01059208
6	4	0.03675691		4	0.04734899
7	5	0.10291935		5	0.15026833
8	6	0.20012095		6	0.35038928
9	7	0.26682793		7	0.61721721
10	8	0.23347444		8	0.85069165
11	9	0.12106082		9	0.97175248
12	10	0.02824752		10	1

Figure 6.9

Hypergeometric Distribution

$$A = 2, n = 16, N = 30$$

1. Set up the worksheet as shown below.

	A	B
1	X	P(X = x)
2	0	
3	1	
4	2	

Figure 6.10

2. The Excel function for the hypergeometric distribution is:

HYPGEOMDIST (sample_s,number_sample,population_s,number_ population) where

sample_s = the number of successes in the sample,

number_sample = the size of the sample,

population_s = the number of successes in the population, and

number_population = the population size.

3. Navigate your cursor to cell B2 and enter the formula as follows:

$$=HYPGEOMDIST(0,16,2,30).$$

Press **Enter**.

4. Cell B2 should now read 0.20915 which is the corresponding probability for 0 successes in this distribution. Apply the same formula to cells B3 and B4, replacing "sample_s" with **1** and **2** respectively. The values for B3 and B4 should read 0.514943 and 0.275862 respectively.

	A	B
1	X	$P(X = x)$
2	0	0.209195
3	1	0.514943
4	2	0.275862

Figure 6.11

USING MINITAB

Binomial Distribution

$$n = 12, p = .1, x = 0,1,2,3,4$$

1. Set up the worksheet in C1 and C2 as shown below.

↓	C1	C2
	x	p(x)
1	0	
2	1	
3	2	
4	3	
5	4	

Figure 6.12

2. Press **Calc**, "Probability Distributions", and **Binomial**.

3. Designate **Probability**. (Alternately, **Cumulative Probability**).

4. Complete the dialog box by entering **12** for "Number of trials", **.1** for "Event probability", **C1** for "Input column", and **C2** for "Optional storage".

5. Press **OK** and read the output in C2.

↓	C1	C2
	x	p(x)
1	0	0.282430
2	1	0.376573
3	2	0.230128
4	3	0.085233
5	4	0.021308

Figure 6.13

Poisson Distribution

$$\lambda = 5, \; x = 0, \; 1, \; 2, \; 3, \; 4$$

1. Set up the worksheet in C1 and C2 as shown below.

↓	C1	C2
	x	p(x)
1	0	
2	1	
3	2	
4	3	
5	4	

Figure 6.14

2. Press **Calc**, "Probability Distributions", and **Poisson**.

3. Designate **Probability**. (Alternately, **Cumulative Probability**).

4. Complete the dialog box by entering **5** for "Mean", **C1** for "Input column", and **C2** for "Optional storage".

5. Press **OK** and read the output in C2.

↓	C1	C2
	x	p(x)
1	0	0.006738
2	1	0.033690
3	2	0.084224
4	3	0.140374
5	4	0.175467

Figure 6.15

Chapter 6 Review

Key Terms and Ideas

- Random Variable

- Probability Distribution

- Discrete Random Variable

- Continuous Random Variable

- Discrete Probability Distribution

- Expected Value of a Discrete Random Variable

- Variance of a Discrete Random Variable

- Probability Distribution Function

- Discrete Uniform Distribution

- Binomial Distribution

- Binomial Experiment

- Binomial Random Variable

- Binomial Probability Distribution Function

- Binomial Tables

- Expected Value of a Binomial Random Variable

- Variance of a Binomial Random Variable

- Poisson Distribution

- Poisson Random Variable

- Lambda

- Poisson Probability Distribution Function

- Hypergeometric Distribution

- Hypergeometric Probability Distribution Function

Key Formulas

Concept	Formula	Section
Expected Value of a Discrete Random Variable X	$\mu = E(X) = \sum[xp(x)]$ where $p(x) = P(X = x)$	6.3
Variance of a Discrete Random Variable X	$\sigma^2 = V(X) = \sum[(x - \mu)^2 p(x)]$	6.3
Discrete Uniform Probability Distribution Function	$P(X = x) = \dfrac{1}{n}$ where $n =$ the number of values that the random variable may assume.	6.5
Binomial Probability Distribution Function	$P(X = x) = C_x^n p^x (1 - p)^{n-x}$ where $C_x^n = \dfrac{n!}{x!(n - x)!}$, $n =$ the number of trials, and $p =$ the probability of a success.	6.6
Expected Value of a Binomial Random Variable	$\mu = E(X) = np$	6.6
Variance and Standard Deviation of a Binomial Random Variable	$\sigma^2 = V(X) = np(1 - p)$ $\sigma = \sqrt{V(X)} = \sqrt{np(1 - p)}$	6.6
Poisson Probability Distribution Function	$P(X = x) = \dfrac{e^{-\lambda}\lambda^x}{x!}$ where $e = 2.71828...$ and $\lambda =$ mean number of successes.	6.7
Expected Value of a Poisson Random Variable	$\mu = E(X) = \lambda$	6.7
Variance and Standard Deviation of a Poisson Random Variable	$\sigma^2 = V(X) = \lambda$ $\sigma = \sqrt{V(X)} = \sqrt{\lambda}$	6.7
Hypergeometric Probability Distribution Function	$P(X = x) = \dfrac{C_x^A C_{n-x}^{N-A}}{C_n^N}$ where $A =$ the total number of successes possible, $N =$ the size of the total population, and $n =$ the size of the sample drawn.	6.8

Expected Value of a Hypergeometric Random Variable	$\mu = E(X) = n\dfrac{A}{N}$	6.8
Variance of a Hypergeometric Random Variable	$\sigma^2 = V(X) = n\dfrac{A}{N}\left(1 - \dfrac{A}{N}\right)\dfrac{(N-n)}{(N-1)}$	6.8

 **Additional Exercises**

1. A statistics professor has determined the following probability distribution for X, the grade which a student will earn in a business statistics class.

Table Exercise 1 – Grade Distribution		
Grade	**x**	**P(X = x)**
A	4.0	.15
B	3.0	.35
C	2.0	.25
D	1.0	.15
F	0.0	.10

  a. What is the average grade which a student will earn in a business statistics class?

  b. Find the variance of the grades which students will earn in a business statistics class?

  c. Find the standard deviation of the grades which students will earn in a business statistics class.

  d. What is the probability that a student will earn a grade of 4.0?

  e. Find the probability that a student will earn a grade of at least 2.0.

  f. Find the probability that a student will earn a grade of at most 1.0.

  g. Find the probability that a student will earn a grade of more than 3.0.

2. The U.S. Department of Labor has issued a new set of guidelines governing certain work practices for employees. They estimate that only 20% of all firms will be subject to the new guidelines. To validate their estimate of the number of firms that will be affected by the new guidelines, they randomly select a sample of twenty firms for a study. Assuming their initial estimate of 20% is correct,

  a. What is the probability that 1 or less of the sampled firms will be subject to the new rules?

  b. What is the probability that between 15 and 25 percent of the sampled firms will be subject to the rules?

  c. One of the directors remarked he thought that ten firms out of the sample would be subject to the rules. If the initial estimate is correct, what is the chance of this occurring?

3. Historically, the probability that a library book will be returned in one week is $p = .50$. The head librarian for the University Staff Hospital library is monitoring a random sample of 10 books to determine if the historical fraction of the books returned within one week, .50, has changed. Assuming the historical return rate is still the same,

   a. What is the probability that between four and six books will be returned in one week?

   b. What is the chance that eight or more books will be returned in one week?

   c. What is the probability that only one book will be returned in one week?

4. The number of fatalities resulting from automobile accidents for a 10 mile stretch of an interstate highway averages 1 per 100,000 automobiles. During a particular holiday weekend, 500,000 automobiles traveled over the 10-mile segment. Using a Poisson distribution, find the probability of:

   a. No fatalities.

   b. 3 fatalities.

   c. At least one fatality.

5. Compute the mean and variance of the following random variables:

   a. The number of sixes obtained in 10 rolls of a single die.

   b. The number of hearts in a 13 card bridge hand.

   c. The number of free throws made by a professional basketball player in his next 10 attempts. (Assume the player makes 88% of his free throws in the long run.)

   d. The number of cracked eggs selected when randomly selecting 5 eggs from a 12 egg carton containing 2 cracked eggs.

   e. The number of dots on the upper face when a single die is thrown.

6. A manufacturer of digital cameras knows that a shipment of 30 cameras sent to a large discount store contains eight defective cameras. The manufacturer also knows that the store will choose two of the cameras at random, test them, and accept the shipment if neither one is defective.

   a. Find the probability that at least one is defective.

   b. What is the probability that the shipment is accepted?

7. In a certain shipment of sixteen radios, four are defective. Eight of the radios are selected at random without replacement. What is the probability that at least one of the eight radios is defective?

8. A box contains eighteen large marbles and ten small marbles. Each marble is either green or white. Twelve of the large marbles are green and four of the small marbles are white. If a marble is randomly selected from the box, what is the probability that it is white or large?

9. User passwords for a certain computer network consist of four letters followed by two numbers. How many different passwords are possible?

10. According to the American Hotel and Lodging Association (AH&LA), women accounted for 31% of business travelers in the year 2009. Suppose that to attract these women business travelers, the AH&LA found that 80% of hotels offer hair dryers in the bathrooms. Consider a random and independent sample of 15 hotels. **Source**: American Hotel & Lodging Association

   a. Based on the information above, how many of the 15 hotels are expected to offer hair dryers in the bathrooms?

   b. Find the probability that all of the hotels in the sample offer hair dryers in the bathroom.

   c. Find the probability that more than 5 but less than 9 of the hotels in the sample offer hair dryers in the bathroom.

11. Hydraulic assemblies for landing coming from an aircraft rework facility are each inspected for defects. Historical records indicate that 8% have defects in shafts only, 6% have defects in bushings only, and 2% have defects in both shafts and bushings. One of the hydraulic assemblies is selected randomly. What is the probability that

   a. The assembly has a bushing defect?

   b. The assembly has a shaft or bushing defect?

   c. The assembly has exactly one of the two types of defects?

   d. The assembly has neither type of defect?

12. A carnival has a game of chance: a fair coin is tossed. If it lands heads, you win $1 and if it lands tails, you lose $0.50. How much should a ticket cost to play this game if the carnival wants to break even?

13. You are working on a multiple choice test which consists of 15 problems. Each of the problems has five answers, only one of which is correct. If you are totally unprepared for the test and are guessing, what is the probability that your first correct answer is within the first fifteen problems?

14. An automobile manufacturer is always trying to improve the quality of their vehicles. Assume that the number of defects per vehicle follows a Poisson distribution. If these defects occur randomly at an average rate of five per vehicle, what is the probability that a randomly selected vehicle will have at least one defect?

15. When proofreading a statistics textbook, one can expect to find a number of errors, whether they are typographical, symbolic, or even incorrect mathematical calculations. On average, a statistics textbook will contain 30 errors. What is the probability that when proofreading a text, one finds at least three errors?

16. While on a shopping spree, you randomly select five portable music players from an electronics store that sells 20 portable music players. Of these 20 music players, 12 will last beyond the 1-year limited warranty and will not need to be replaced or repaired. What is the probability that at least three of the five portable music players selected will not last beyond the limited warranty period without needing to be replaced or repaired?

17. A jeweler was given a collection of twelve diamonds, of which three were synthetic (fake). If the jeweler selected two of these diamonds at random (without replacement), what is the probability that neither jewel is found to be synthetic?

18. L-Mart Inspections is a building inspection company. There were ten new commercial construction buildings completed in the last month and the sites are now available for inspection. L-Mart plans to inspect some of the new constructions for code violations and thinks that half of the homes will have violations. If L-Mart randomly selects four homes to inspect, what is the probability that three of the homes will have violations?

Continuous Random Variables

7

Discovering Technology

Calculating normal probabilities using the TI-84 Plus calculator

Approximating the binomial probabilities using Microsoft Excel

Finding cumulative binomial probabilities using Minitab

Introduction

In the previous chapter random variables were primarily counts of some phenomenon called a *success*. These counts could only take on discrete values, usually starting at zero. In this chapter the focus will be on variables that can take on any value in some continuum, i.e. a range of numbers on the real number line. The range of adult heights, for example, lies on a continuum between 26 and 100 inches.

Observations measured in a continuum can be very close together. For example, two heights could be

68.234175245987149399 inches, and

68.234175245987149398 inches.

As a practical matter, it is hard to imagine a situation that would require the knowledge of a person's height to 18 decimal places. Variables like heights and weights are **continuous random variables** even though heights are usually given to the nearest inch or centimeter and weights to the nearest pound or kilogram. Variables measured in these units give the appearance of being discrete, yet they are continuous.

One of the striking differences in discrete and continuous variables concerns the way probability is defined. In a probability distribution for a discrete random variable, each possible outcome of the random variable is assigned its own probability. However, for continuous random variables, there are infinitely many outcomes, and each has *no* probability. Outcomes of a continuous random variable do not have probability assigned to any one point, because there are simply too many points. If we attempted to assign each value even an infinitesimal probability, the sum of all probabilities would exceed one. Thus, for continuous random variables, probability is only assigned to intervals.

7.1   The Uniform Distribution

There are two types of uniform distributions, discrete and continuous. You already studied the discrete uniform distribution in Chapter 6. Conceptually both uniform distributions distribute probability evenly across a sample space. For the continuous uniform distribution, the probability density is spread out over some range from a to b, as shown in Figure 7.1.

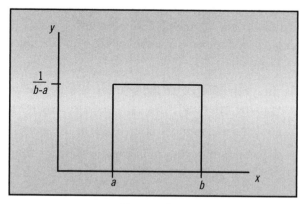

Figure 7.1

Formula

The uniform **probability density function** is given by:

$$f(x) = \begin{cases} \dfrac{1}{b-a} & \text{for } a \leq x \leq b \\ 0 & \text{otherwise} \end{cases}$$

$$\mu = \frac{a+b}{2} \text{ and } \sigma = \frac{b-a}{\sqrt{12}}.$$

Uniform Probability
Density Function

Continuous random variables do not have probability distribution functions. Instead they have **probability density functions**, which are denoted by $f(x)$. The probability density function for the uniform random variable, its expected value (mean), and its standard deviation are given above. The parameters of the probability density function are the minimum and maximum values of the random variable and are referred to as a and b, respectively.

When the uniform probability density function is graphed, it produces a rectangle or square. The probability of observing a random variable in some interval is expressed as the area under the density function associated with the interval. Since the density function for the uniform distribution is a rectangle, calculating the probability of an interval requires uncomplicated geometry.

Example 7.1

The Courier Express Company is interested in the number of arrivals of shipments during the morning hours between 8:00 AM and noon. Suppose the distribution of arrivals follows a uniform distribution with the minimum number of shipments arriving being 6 and the maximum number of shipments being 20.

    a. What is the probability that the courier will get between 10 and 15 shipments in the morning?

    b. What is the expected number of arrivals for the morning hours?

    c. What is the standard deviation of the number of shipment arrivals in the morning hours?

Solution

    a. Let $X =$ the number of shipment orders during the morning hours.

$$\text{Area} = \text{Width} \cdot \text{Height}$$

According to the uniform probability density function $f(x) = \dfrac{1}{b-a}$. Therefore,

$$\text{Height} = \frac{1}{b-a} = \frac{1}{20-6} = \frac{1}{14}.$$

We are interested in the probability that the courier will get between 10 and 15 shipments so,

$$\text{Width} = 15 - 10 = 5, \text{ and}$$

$$\text{Area} = \text{Width} \cdot \text{Height} = 5\left(\frac{1}{14}\right) = \frac{5}{14}.$$

Since the probability of observing a uniform random variable is the area under the density function associated with the interval,

$$P(10 \le X \le 15) = \frac{5}{14}.$$

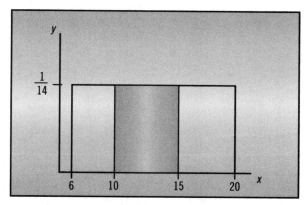

Figure 7.2

b. The expected value of a continuous uniform random variable is given by

$$E(X) = \mu = \frac{a+b}{2} = \frac{(6+20)}{2} = 13.$$

Therefore, the expected number of shipments during the morning hours is 13.

c. The standard deviation of a continuous uniform random variable is given by

$$\sigma = \frac{b-a}{\sqrt{12}} = \frac{20-6}{\sqrt{12}} \approx 4.0415.$$

Therefore, the standard deviation for the number of morning shipment arrivals is 4.0415.

What Does Data From a Uniform Random Variable Look Like?

While the density function for the uniform distribution has a flat top, a histogram of data from a uniformly distributed random process will not be perfectly flat. Suppose that we generated 100 observations from a random process that was uniformly distributed between 2 and 15. Clearly, the frequency of each category is not identical (see Figure 7.3).

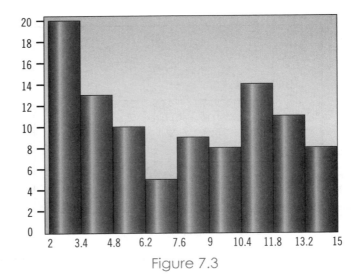

Figure 7.3

However, if we were to generate 1000 observations, the distribution would begin to level (see Figure 7.4).

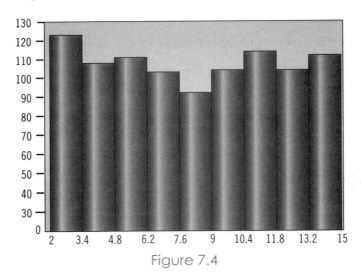

Figure 7.4

7.1 Exercises

Basic Concepts

1. Probability is defined differently for discrete and continuous random variables. Describe this difference.

2. What is a probability density function?

3. How is the continuous uniform distribution different from the discrete uniform distribution?

4. What is the uniform probability density function?

5. Describe the shape of the density function for a uniform distribution.

Exercises

1. Suppose a continuous random variable is uniformly distributed between 10 and 70.

   a. What is the mean of the distribution?

   b. What is the standard deviation of the distribution?

   c. What is the probability that a randomly selected value will be above 45?

   d. What is the probability that a randomly selected value will be less than 30?

   e. What is the probability that a randomly selected value will be between 25 and 50?

   f. Find the probability that a randomly selected value will exactly equal 35?

2. Polar Bear Frozen Foods manufactures frozen French fries for sale to grocery store chains. The final package weight is thought to be a uniformly distributed random variable. Assume X, the weight of French fries has a uniform distribution between 57 ounces and 63 ounces.

   a. What is the average weight for a package?

   b. What is the standard deviation for the weight of a package?

   c. What is the probability that a store will receive a package weighing less than 59 ounces?

   d. What is the probability that a package will contain between 60 and 63 ounces?

   e. What is the probability that a package will contain more than 62 ounces?

   f. Find the probability that a package will contain exactly 60 ounces.

3. The annual growth in height of cedar trees is believed to be distributed uniformly between six and eleven inches.

    a. Draw a picture of the distribution of growth in height of cedar trees.

    b. What is the mean growth per year?

    c. What is the standard deviation of the growth per year?

    d. What is the probability that a randomly selected cedar tree will grow between 9 and 10 inches in a given year?

    e. Find the probability that a randomly selected cedar tree will grow less than 8 inches in a given year.

    f. Find the probability that a randomly selected cedar tree will grow more than 9 inches in a given year.

    g. Find the probability that a randomly selected cedar tree will grow exactly 7 inches in a given year.

4. A particular employee arrives to work sometime between 8:00 AM and 8:30 AM. Based on past experience the company has determined that the employee is equally likely to arrive at any time between 8:00 AM and 8:30 AM.

    a. On average, what time does the employee arrive?

    b. What is the standard deviation of the time at which the employee arrives?

    c. If a call comes in for the employee at 8:10 AM, find the probability that the employee will be there to take the call.

    d. Find the probability that the employee will arrive between 8:20 AM and 8:25 AM.

    e. Find the probability that the employee will arrive after 8:15 AM.

    f. Find the probability that the employee will arrive at exactly 8:10 AM.

7.2 The Normal Distribution

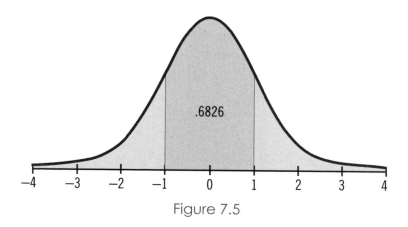

Figure 7.5

The normal distribution, originally called the Gaussian distribution, was named after Karl Gauss who published a work in 1833 describing the mathematical definition of the distribution. Gauss developed this distribution to describe the error in predicting the orbits of planets.

Normal distributions are all bell-shaped, but the bells come in various shapes and sizes. Since all normal distributions are symmetric, the mean, median, and mode are all equal.

Although normally distributed random variables can range in value from negative infinity to positive infinity, values that are a great distance from the mean rarely occur. You may recall that when we discussed box plots, these values were called outliers.

Properties

Properties of the Normal Distribution

1. The normal distribution is symmetric. That is, the curve's shape to the left of the mean is the mirror image of the curve's shape to the right of the mean.

2. The highest point on the normal curve is located at the mean, which is also the location of the median and the mode of the distribution.

3. The area under the curve of the normal distribution equals 1.

4. Due to symmetry, the area to the right of the mean equals the area to the left of the mean, and each of these areas equals .5.

5. The shape of the normal distribution is defined by its two parameters, the mean (μ) and the standard deviation (σ).

The Origins of the Normal Distribution:

Abraham DeMoivre 1667 – 1754

DeMoivre was born in France but lived most of his life in England. In a paper in 1733 DeMoivre published the equation that describes the normal curve. He allegedly was doing calculations using the binomial distribution for gamblers and was looking for a shortcut in very arduous calculations. He discovered the normal distribution as the limit of the binomial distribution. DeMoivre was a highly respected mathematician and friend of Issac Newton.

DeMoivre's discovery received little attention until LaPlace began writing on probability in the 1770s. There are two other mathematicians who discovered the equation of the normal curve, Adrian in 1808 and Gauss in 1809. Even though DeMoivre published the equation for the normal distribution 70 years earlier than Gauss, the normal curve was called the Gaussian distribution for many years. Even now, you will hear the normal curve referred to as the Gaussian distribution.

In Figure 7.5 the shaded area represents the probability of being within ±1σ of the mean. Regardless of the values of the mean and standard deviation of the normal distribution, the area under the curve and the probability of being within one standard deviation (±1σ) of the mean equals .6826.

Figure 7.6 illustrates the area under the curve within two standard deviations of the mean. The probability of being within ±2σ of the mean equals .9544 for every normal distribution.

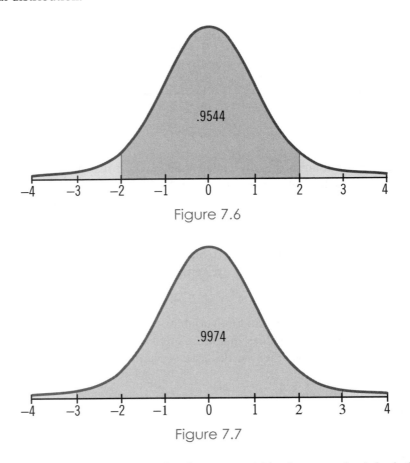

Figure 7.6

Figure 7.7

Figure 7.7 illustrates the area under the curve within three standard deviations of the mean. As you can see, virtually all of the area under the curve is within three standard deviations of the mean. The probability of being within ±3σ of the mean equals .9974.

Since the empirical rule given in Chapter 4 is based on the normal distribution, these results are identical to the empirical rule frequencies.

Although a normal distribution has a bell shape, a bell shape does not imply a normal distribution. A number of non-normal distributions with bell shapes will be introduced in later chapters. In fact the word *normal* can be somewhat misleading. The name suggests that the distribution is a fact of nature. It is not. However, many variables seem to possess a shape that resembles the normal distribution.

The normal distribution is the preeminent distribution used in the statistical theory we will examine. Many statistical inference procedures, either directly or indirectly, have been developed based on the normal distribution. These procedures usually assume that the population from which a random sample is drawn is normally distributed.

Like other theoretical distributions, a normal distribution is completely defined by its probability density function given in the following equation.

Formula

The **normal probability density function** is given by:

$$f(x) = \frac{1}{\sigma\sqrt{2\pi}} e^{-\frac{(x-\mu)^2}{2\sigma^2}}$$

Normal Probability
Density Function

At first glance, this function does not look very *normal*! The distribution has two parameters, μ and σ, which are the mean and standard deviation, respectively. The mean defines the location and the standard deviation determines the dispersion. Figure 7.8 illustrates three normal distributions with identical standard deviations. The only difference in the distributions is the central location, the mean.

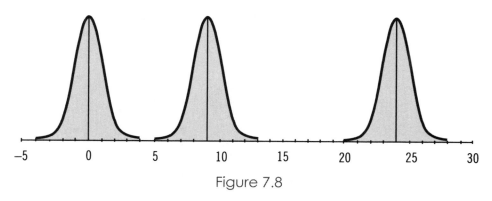

Figure 7.8

In Figure 7.9, there are two distributions with identical means, but with different standard deviations. Changing the standard deviation parameter can have rather significant effects on the shape of the distribution.

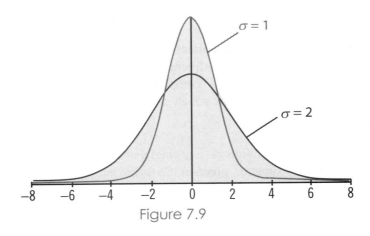

$\sigma = 1$

$\sigma = 2$

Figure 7.9

Looking at Data from Normal Distributions

Astronomy and the Normal Distribution

Although DeMoivre derived the equation of the normal distribution as a consequence of problems involving the binomial distribution, Gauss and LaPlace were inspired by their desire to predict the location of planets, stars, meteors, and comets. Their predictions of the location of celestial bodies produced errors and they needed to describe those errors. In the 19th century the normal distribution was referred to as the astronomers' error law. Much of the early scientific use of the normal distribution was the analysis of errors.

The normal distribution is a theoretical construct with a bell shape. Therefore it would not be unreasonable to expect data drawn from a normal population to exhibit the bell-shaped characteristic. In two small samples taken from a normal population, shown in Figures 7.10 and 7.11, the data do show a faint resemblance of a bell shape. But as you can see, the shapes of the histograms developed from these small samples are somewhat unpredictable, even though the bell-shaped pattern is to some extent apparent.

Sample 1: Histogram of a Small Sample ($n = 25$) from a Normal Population

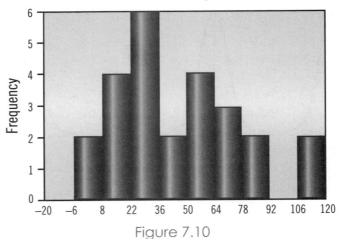

Figure 7.10

Sample 2: Histogram of a Small Sample (*n* = 25) from a Normal Population

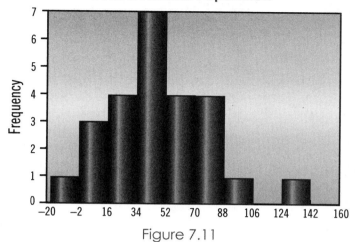

Figure 7.11

For large samples, the representation of the bell curve is usually more visible. While the large sample (*n* = 200) certainly is not a perfect bell curve, it is recognizable (see Figure 7.12).

Histogram of a Large Sample (*n* = 200) from a Normal Population

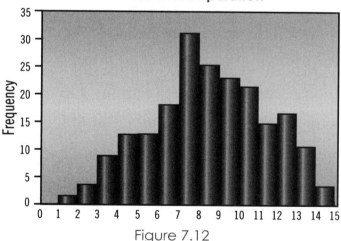

Figure 7.12

Using the probability density function to determine the probability of some interval would be complicated. Fortunately, there is an easier way. A special normal distribution, called the standard normal, can be used to determine probabilities for any normal random variable.

7

7.2 Exercises

Basic Concepts

1. How was the normal distribution developed?

2. Are the normal and uniform distributions probability models?

3. List the properties of the normal distribution.

4. What is the shape of the normal distribution?

5. What are the parameters of the normal distribution?

6. If the variance of a normal distribution is constant, what affect will changes in the mean have on the distribution?

Exercises

1. Sketch a normal curve. Mark the axis corresponding to the parameter μ and the axis corresponding to $\mu + \sigma$ and $\mu - \sigma$.

7.3 The Standard Normal

Given that the normal distribution is a function of two continuous parameters μ and σ, there are an infinite number of combinations for μ and σ, and thus, an infinite number of normal distributions. The **standard normal distribution** in Figure 7.13 is a special version of the normal distribution.

Definition

The **standard normal distribution** is a normal distribution with a mean of zero and a standard deviation of one.

$$\mu = 0 \text{ and } \sigma^2 = \sigma = 1$$

Standard Normal
Distribution

This distribution, called the z-distribution, provides a basis for computing probabilities for all normal distributions. The technique used to convert any normal random variable into a standard normal random variable is called "standardizing" the random variable, and was discussed earlier in Chapter 4.

Appendix A, Tables A, B, and C contain probability calculations for various areas under the standard normal curve. Specifically, Appendix A, Tables A and B provide the probability that a standard normal random variable will be less than a specified value. For example, to compute the probability that a standard normal random variable will be less than 1 (see Figure 7.14), look up the value 1.00 in Table B. The table value of .8413 is the area under the curve between negative infinity and 1, which is also the probability that the random variable will assume a value in that interval.

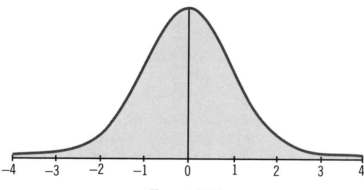

Figure 7.13

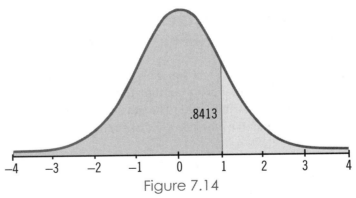

.8413

−4 −3 −2 −1 0 1 2 3 4

Figure 7.14

The z-distribution will be used throughout the remainder of this text. Thus it is important to comprehend the use of the z-tables in the determination of probabilities for a variety of problems. Because of the manner in which the tables are constructed, some types of problems will require manipulation of the table values.

Example 7.2

Compute the probability that a standard normal random variable is less than 1.27.

Solution

Drawing a picture, even when the problem is rather simple, is a good idea.

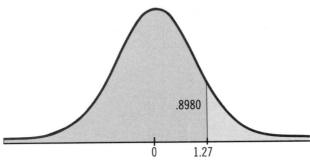

.8980

0   1.27

Figure 7.15

Determining the area under standard normal curve requires little effort. The tables are constructed to give the cumulative probabilities. That is, the table gives probabilities that the random variable z is less than some value (i.e. $P(z < z_0)$ where z_0 is a constant). In this case, the construction of Table B exactly matches the kind of interval you are examining. Thus merely looking up the value corresponding to 1.27 in the table is sufficient to obtain the probability.

$$P(z < 1.27) = .8980.$$

Example 7.3

Determine the probability that a standard normal random variable is between -1.08 and 0.

Solution

First, draw a picture.

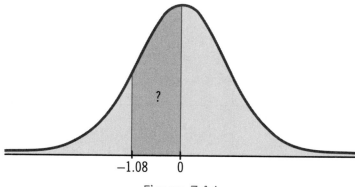

Figure 7.16

In this case we cannot simply look up the value in the table to obtain the probability of interest. Understanding that the table gives us cumulative probabilities, if we find the probability that z is less than 0 and then subtract the probability that z is less than -1.08, we will get the probability that z is between -1.08 and 0.

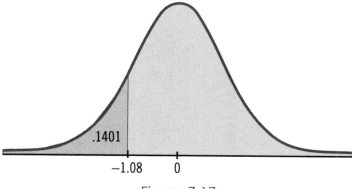

Figure 7.17

Using the standard normal table, the area under the curve less than 0 is $.5$. Similarly we can find $P(z < -1.08)$ to be $.1401$ from looking up -1.08 in Appendix A, Table A. Thus,

$$P(-1.08 < z < 0) = P(z < 0) - P(z < -1.08) = .5 - .1401 = .3599.$$

Example 7.4

What is the probability that a standard normal random variable will be between 1 and 2?

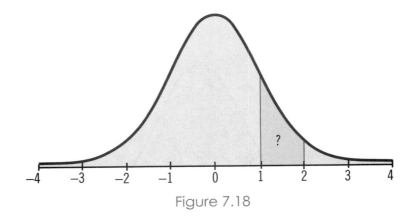

Figure 7.18

Solution

Because the table gives us cumulative probabilities, we can find the probability that z is less than 2 and then subtract the probability that z is less than 1, yielding the probability that z is between 1 and 2. That is,

$$P(1 < z < 2) = P(z < 2) - P(z < 1) = .9772 - .8413 = .1359.$$

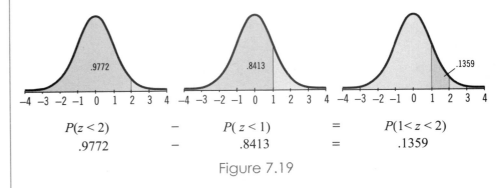

$P(z < 2)$	$-$	$P(z < 1)$	$=$	$P(1 < z < 2)$
.9772	$-$	.8413	$=$	.1359

Figure 7.19

Again, drawing the picture proves to be invaluable in this example.

Example 7.5

Given that z is a standard normal random variable, find the value of z for each situation.

    a. The area to the left of z is .9147.

    b. The area between 0 and z is .3665.

    c. The area to the left of z is .1469.

    d. The area to the right of z is .7967.

Solution

    a. First, draw a picture.

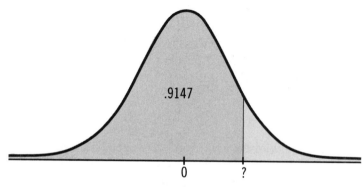

.9147

Figure 7.20

Note that this problem is slightly different from the previous one. In Example 7.4, you were asked to find a probability. In this example, you are given a probability and asked to find the corresponding value of z. Recall that Appendix A, Table B gives you the cumulative probability of the area less than some value of z.

In order to find the value of z, look in the body of Appendix A, Table B and find the probability value .9147. Once you've found the value (the probability), determine the corresponding value of z. In this case, the value of z is 1.37. So,

$$P(z < 1.37) = .9147$$

and the value of z is 1.37 with the area to the left of it being .9147.

b. Again, draw a picture.

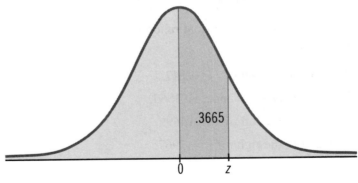

Figure 7.21

Recall that the table gives us cumulative probabilities. Since the area between 0 and z is .3665, if we write this as a cumulative probability, we need to add the area to the left of 0. Thus, the area to the left of z is .8665. This is the probability (less than some value of z) that is provided in the table. Therefore, find .8665 in the body of Table B and locate the corresponding value of z. In this case,

$$P(0 < z < 1.11) = .3665.$$

So, the value of z with the area .3665 between 0 and z is 1.11.

c. Just as in parts (a) and (b), a picture can be helpful.

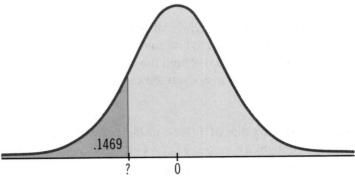

Figure 7.22

Please note that the value of z is to the left of 0. Thus, the value of z is going to be negative. Note that the area to the left of z represents the cumulative probability (in Figure 7.22). So, to find the value of z, we only need to find .1469 in the body of Appendix A Table A. The value of z with the area .1469 to the left of it is -1.05. That is, $P(z < -1.05) = .1469$.

d. Once again, a picture can be very helpful.

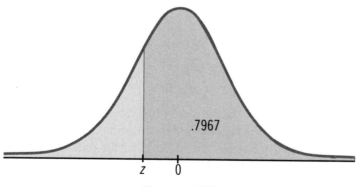

.7967

z 0

Figure 7.23

Note that frm the picture, we have the area to the right of z. However, we know that the total area under the curve is 1. Thus, if the area to the right of z is .7967, then the area to the left of z is $1 - .7967 = .2033$. From the picture, it is clear that if we find .2033 in the body of Appendix A, Table A, the corresponding value of z is -0.83. Therefore, the value of z with the area .7967 to the right is -0.83.

Standardizing Normal Random Variables

Formula

The following formula can transform any normal random variable into a **standard normal random variable**, z.

$$z = \frac{x - \mu}{\sigma}$$

where x is a normal random variable with mean μ and standard deviation σ.

Standardizing a Normal Random Variable

If we look at the individual pieces, exactly how the transformation works is not very mysterious. First, the numerator, $x - \mu$, centers the z-distribution around zero. By subtracting the mean of the random variable from each data value, the mean of the resulting random variable will be zero. A short example illustrates this point. Suppose that a population contained the following data values shown in Table 7.1.

Table 7.1	
Data Set A	**Data Set A − 6**
1	$1 - 6 = -5$
5	$5 - 6 = -1$
6	$6 - 6 = 0$
12	$12 - 6 = 6$

Data Set A has a mean of six. If six is subtracted from each of the data values, the resulting deviations are shown in the second column of the table. The deviations have a mean of zero. Essentially the location of the data set has been shifted to zero. The interrelationship of the data points to one another has not changed. Try this experiment on larger sets of data to convince yourself that subtracting the mean from each value of a data set will produce a data set that always has a mean of zero.

The standard deviation of Data Set A is 3.937. Let's standardize each data value in Data Set A (see Table 7.2). The resulting z-values indicate how far the data values in Table 7.1 are from the mean, measured in standard deviation units. The first value in Table 7.2 indicates that 1 is −1.27 standard deviation units from the mean. The mean and standard deviation of the transformed values in Table 7.2 are zero and one, respectively. You can verify that the mean and standard deviation of the z-scores are actually zero and one. Compute the population standard deviation rather than the sample standard deviation.

Table 7.2 – Standardizing Data Set A		
Data	**Formula**	**Value of z**
1	$\dfrac{1-6}{3.937} =$	−1.27
5	$\dfrac{5-6}{3.937} =$	− 0.254
6	$\dfrac{6-6}{3.937} =$	0
12	$\dfrac{12-6}{3.937} =$	1.524

Now that we have seen how to convert any normal random variable into a standard normal random variable, let's apply it.

Example 7.6

Find the probability that a normal random variable with a mean of 10 and a standard deviation of 20 will lie between 10 and 40.

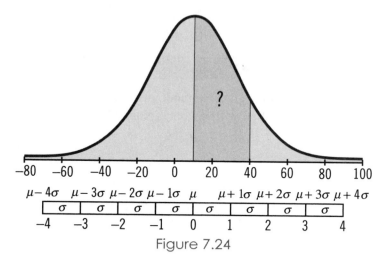

Figure 7.24

Solution

Suppose X is our random variable and X has a mean of 10 and a standard deviation of 20.

Standardizing the random variable X yields

$$P(10 < X < 40) = P\left(\frac{10-10}{20} < \frac{x-\mu}{\sigma} < \frac{40-10}{20}\right) = P(0 < z < 1.5).$$

Note that for each argument in the above probability statement, we subtracted the mean and divided by the standard deviation.

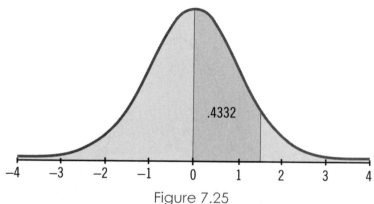

Figure 7.25

Once the problem has been converted to a problem involving z (see Figure 7.25), the appropriate probability can be determined from the standard normal table.

$$P(0<z<1.5)=P(z<1.5)-P(z<0)=.9332-.5=.4332.$$

Example 7.7

Find the probability that a normal random variable with a mean of 10 and a standard deviation of 20 will be greater than 30.

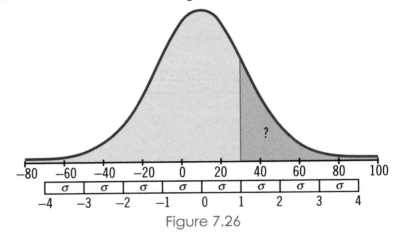

Figure 7.26

Solution

Suppose X is a normal random variable with a mean of 10 and a standard deviation of 20. Standardizing the random variable,

$$P(X>30)=P\left(z>\frac{30-10}{20}\right)$$
$$=P(z>1).$$

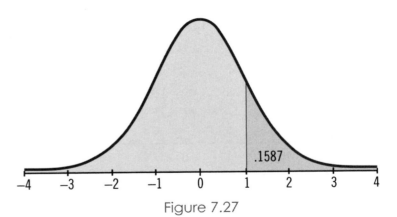

Figure 7.27

$$P(z>1)=1-P(z<1)$$
$$=1-.8413$$
$$=.1587$$

Note that the X value of 30 transformed into the z-value of 1. In other words, 30 is one standard deviation away from the mean.

Example 7.8

Suppose that a national testing service gives a test in which the results are normally distributed with a mean of 400 and a standard deviation of 100. If you score a 644 on the test, what percentage of the students taking the test exceeded your score?

Solution

Let X = a student's score on the test.

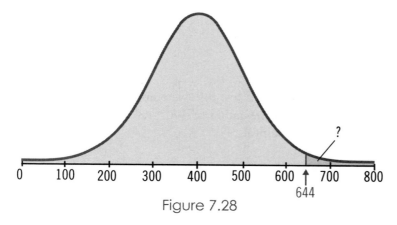

Figure 7.28

The first step is to standardize the random variable.

$$P(X>644)=P\left(z>\frac{644-400}{100}\right)$$
$$=P(z>2.44)$$
$$=1-P(z<2.44)$$
$$=1-.9927=.0073$$

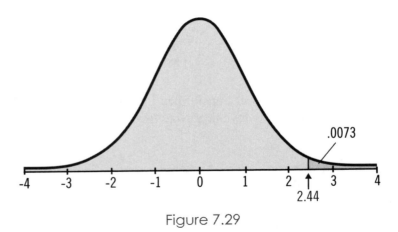

.0073

2.44

Figure 7.29

Thus, only 0.73% of the students scored higher than your score of 644.

Example 7.9

Using the information provided in Example 7.8, what score must a student get to be in the 90th percentile?

Solution

Recall that X = score on a test follows a normal distribution with a mean of 400 and a standard deviation of 100. As with the examples before, a picture can be very helpful.

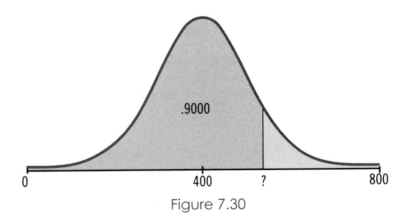

.9000

0   400   ?   800

Figure 7.30

From the picture above, it can be seen that we want to find the values of x (the student's score) that are in the 90th percentile (i.e., the student scored the same or better than 90% of other students taking the test). We would write $P(X \leq x) = .9$.

If we standardize the probability statement, we get

$$P\left(z \leq \frac{x-\mu}{\sigma}\right) = .9.$$

Substituting values for the mean and standard deviation, we get

$$P\left(z < \frac{x-400}{100}\right) = .9.$$

Note that we can rewrite the above probability statement as

$$P(z < z_0) = .9 \text{ where } z_0 = \frac{x-400}{100}.$$

Therefore, we need to find the value of z with the area .9 to the left of it. To do this, we look in the body of the standard normal table for the value 0.9000. It's not often that we can find the exact probability in the body of the table. When this is the case, we find the closest probability along with the corresponding value of z. In this case, the value of $z = 1.28$.

Thus,

$$1.28 = \frac{x-400}{100}.$$

Solving for x, we get $x = 528$.

Therefore, a student who scores 528 on the test will be in the 90th percentile.

Example 7.10

Of the 132 space shuttle missions, the flight duration follows a normal distribution with a mean of 234 hours and a standard deviation of 94 hours. If you just read in the newspaper that a space shuttle will be launched tomorrow, what is the probability that the duration of the flight will be between 100 and 150 hours? **Source:** www.nasa.gov

Solution

Let X = the duration of a space shuttle flight.

$$P(100 < X < 150) = P\left(\frac{100-234}{94} < z < \frac{150-234}{94}\right) = P(-1.43 < z < -0.89)$$

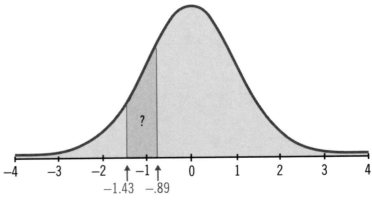

Figure 7.31

Using Table A in Appendix A,

$$P(-1.43 < z < -0.89) = P(z < -0.89) - P(z < -1.43) = .1867 - .0764 = .1103.$$

Thus, there is approximately an 11% chance that the flight will last between 100 and 150 hours.

7.3 Exercises

Basic Concepts

1. What is the standard normal distribution? What are the parameters of the distribution?

2. Why is the standard normal distribution important?

3. Describe the connection between the z-transformation and the standard normal random variable.

Exercises

1. What fraction of the area under the standard normal curve falls between the following z-values?

   a. 0 and .67

   b. 0 and 1.645

   c. 0 and 1.960

   d. 0 and 2.575

2. What fraction of the area under the standard normal curve falls between the following z-values?

   a. 0 and −.67

   b. 0 and −1.645

   c. 0 and −1.960

   d. 0 and −2.575

3. What fraction of the area under the standard normal curve falls between the following z-values?

   a. −.85 and .85

   b. −.55 and .55

   c. −1.56 and 1.98

   d. −2.23 and 2.96

4. What fraction of the area under the standard normal curve falls between the following z-values?

   a. −.97 and .97

   b. −.54 and 1.82

   c. −1.95 and 2.28

   d. −2.89 and 1.59

5. Using the tables for the standard normal distribution (z) in the appendix, determine the probability for each of the events described below. Sketch the associated areas.

   a. $z \leq 0$

   b. $z \geq 0$

   c. $z \leq -1$

   d. $z \leq 1$

   e. $z \geq -1$

   f. $z \geq 1$

6. Using the standard normal tables, determine the probability for each of the following events. Sketch the associated areas.

  a. $z \le -.44$

  b. $z \ge .44$

  c. $-.44 \le z \le .44$

  d. $z \le .67$

  e. $z \ge .67$

  f. $-.67 \le z \le .67$

7. Using the standard normal tables, determine the probability for each of the following events. Sketch the associated areas.

  a. $z \le -1.28$

  b. $z \ge 1.28$

  c. $-1.28 \le z \le 1.28$

  d. $z \le -1.96$

  e. $z \ge 1.96$

  f. $-1.96 \le z \le 1.96$

8. Using the standard normal tables, determine the probability for each of the following events. Sketch the associated areas.

  a. $P(0 \le z \le .79)$

  b. $P(-1.57 \le z \le 2.33)$

  c. $P(z \ge 1.89)$

  d. $P(z \le -2.77)$

9. Using the standard normal tables, determine the probability for each of the following events. Sketch the associated areas.

  a. $P(0 \le z \le 1.24)$

  b. $P(-2.64 \le z \le 3.32)$

  c. $P(z \ge 3.22)$

  d. $P(z \le -3.39)$

10. Find the value of z such that .05 of the area under the curve lies to the right of z.

11. Find the value of z such that .01 of the area under the curve lies to the right of z.

12. Find the value of z such that .10 of the area under the curve lies to the right of z.

13. Find the value of z such that .05 of the area under the curve lies to the left of z.

14. Find the value of z such that .01 of the area under the curve lies to the left of z.

15. Find the value of z such that .10 of the area under the curve lies to the left of z.

16. Find the value of z such that .7458 of the area under the curve lies between $-z$ and z.

17. Find the value of z such that .9505 of the area under the curve lies between $-z$ and z.

18. Find the value of z such that .90 of the area under the curve lies between $-z$ and z.

19. The random variable X has a normal distribution with a mean of 30 and a standard deviation of 5.

    a. Find the probability that X is between 25 and 35.

    b. Find the probability that X is greater than 40.

    c. Find the probability that X is less than 20.

20. The random variable X has a normal distribution with a mean of 200 and a standard deviation of 25.

    a. Find the probability that X is between 160 and 220.

    b. Find the probability that X is greater than 240.

    c. Find the probability that X is less than 150.

21. The Arc Electronic Company had an income of $200,000 last year. Suppose the mean income of firms in the industry for the year is $1,000,000 with a standard deviation of $500,000. If incomes for the industry are distributed normally, what proportion of the firms in the industry earned less than Arc?

22. A certain component for the newly developed electronic diesel engine is considered to be defective if its diameter is less than 8.0 mm or greater than 10.5 mm. The distribution of the diameters of these parts is known to be normal with a mean of 9.0 mm and a standard deviation of 1.5 mm. If a component is randomly selected, what is the probability that it will be defective?

23. A television manufacturer is studying television remote control unit usage. One of the criteria they are measuring is the distance at which people attempt to activate the television set with the remote unit. They have discovered that activation distances are normally distributed with a standard deviation of 3 feet. What average activation distance should the manufacturer advertise if 95% of the televisions are activated from 10 feet?

24. According to the Bureau of Labor Statistics, the median weekly earnings for people working in a sales related profession in 2010 was $631 (Source: www.bls.gov). Assume that the weekly earnings are approximately normally distributed with a standard deviation of $90.

    a. What are the mean weekly earnings for people working in a sales related profession in 2010?

    b. If a salesperson was randomly selected, find the probability that his or her weekly earnings exceed $700.

    c. If a salesperson was randomly selected, find the probability that his or her weekly earnings are at most $525.

    d. If a salesperson was randomly selected, find the probability that his or her weekly earnings are between $400 and $615.

    e. Do you feel that it is reasonable to assume that the weekly earnings have a normal distribution? Why or why not?

25. The repair time for air conditioning units is believed to have a normal distribution with a mean of 38 minutes.

    a. What is the standard deviation of repair time if 40% of the units are repaired between 33 and 43 minutes?

    b. Using the value of the standard deviation that you calculated in (a), what is the probability that a repair will be longer than an hour?

    c. Using the value of the standard deviation that you calculated in (a), what is the probability that the repair time for an air conditioning unit will be less than 25 minutes?

26. VGA monitors manufactured by TSI Electronics have life spans which have a normal distribution with an average life span of 15,000 hours and a standard deviation of 2,000 hours. If a VGA monitor is selected at random, find the following probabilities.

    a. The probability that the life span of the monitor will be less than 12,000 hours.

    b. The probability that the life span of the monitor will be more than 18,000 hours.

    c. The probability that the life span of the monitor will be between 13,000 hours and 17,000 hours.

27. A beer distributor believes the amount of beer in a 12 ounce can of beer has a normal distribution with a mean of 12 ounces and a standard deviation of 1 ounce. If a 12 ounce beer can is randomly selected, find the following probabilities.

    a. The probability that the 12 ounce can of beer will actually contain less than 11 ounces of beer.

    b. The probability that the 12 ounce can of beer will actually contain more than 12.5 ounces of beer.

    c. The probability that the 12 ounce can of beer will actually contain between 10.5 and 11.5 ounces of beer.

28. A statistics teacher believes that the final exam grades for her business statistics class have a normal distribution with a mean of 82 and a standard deviation of 8.

    a. Find the score which separates the top 10% of the scores from the lowest 90% of the scores.

    b. The teacher plans to give all students who score in the top 10% of scores an A. Will a student who scored a 90 on the exam receive an A? Explain.

    c. Find the score which separates the lowest 20% of the scores from the highest 80% of the scores.

    d. The teacher plans to give all students who score in the lowest 10% of scores an F. Will a student who scored a 65 on the exam receive an F? Explain.

29. An investor believes that the yields of his mutual funds have a normal distribution with an average yield of 10% and a standard deviation of 2%. The investor would like to identify the stocks which yield the highest 5% to keep in his portfolio.

    a. Calculate the yield which separates the highest 5% of yields from the lowest 95% of yields.

    b. If a stock yielded 14% would it be kept? Explain.

    c. If a stock yielded 13% would it be kept? Explain.

30. In order for you to become a member of Mensa, a worldwide organization with approximately 100,000 members, your IQ score must be in the top 2%. In 1996, Mensa, which was founded by two British barristers, celebrated its 50th birthday. The word *mensa* is Latin for "table", and was chosen to denote a group or roundtable of people with equal ability. American Mensa Ltd., which was founded in 1960 has almost 50,000 members. Marilyn vos Savant, who is reputed to have the highest recorded IQ, is a member. Assuming that IQ scores have an approximately normal distribution with a mean and standard deviation of 100 and 15, respectively, answer the following.

    a. What IQ must one have in order to become a member of Mensa?

    b. What percent of all Americans have an IQ of at least 145?

    c. What percent of all members of Mensa have an IQ of at least 145?

    d. If Mensa decided to become more exclusive, and accepted only the top 1% instead of the top 2% as members, what IQ would one need in order to become a member of Mensa?

Approximations to Other Distributions

To approximate other distributions, the normal distribution can be very useful. Although it is a continuous distribution, it is used to approximate discrete distributions, specifically the binomial and the Poisson.

The Binomial

Calculating binomial probabilities can be quite time consuming if n is large. For example, suppose that you intend to sample 2000 subjects for a marketing research survey. If 50 percent of the population believes your product is superior to the competition's, what is the probability of obtaining 600 or fewer subjects who believe your company's product is superior?

$$P(X \leq 600) = P(X = 0) + P(X = 1) + P(X = 2) + ... + P(X = 599) + P(X = 600)$$

Determining the appropriate probability using the binomial would require the calculation of 601 individual probabilities, many of which would have extremely large combinations such as

$$C_{400}^{2000} .5^{400} (1 - .5)^{1600}.$$

Computing this and the other 600 similar calculations would be a formidable task. Even if a computer program were used, the programmer must exercise great care in order to obtain reasonably accurate probabilities.

The normal distribution is useful in approximating binomial probabilities. The larger the binomial parameter, n, the more accurate the approximation. Determining the probability described above using the normal approximation is trivial in comparison to calculating the exact probability using the binomial.

Recall that the normal distribution is a function of two parameters, the mean and the standard deviation. Thus, if the normal is to approximate a binomial, it seems reasonable that the mean and standard deviation of the normal should be the same as the mean and standard deviation of the binomial that is being approximated. Specifically, let

$$\mu = E(X) = np, \text{ and}$$

$$\sigma = \sqrt{V(X)} = \sqrt{np(1 - p)}.$$

To approximate a binomial with $n = 20$ and $p = .5$ would require a normal distribution with

$$\mu = (20)(.5) = 10$$

$$\sigma = \sqrt{(20)(.5)(1-.5)} = \sqrt{5} \approx 2.236.$$

In this example, the shapes of the distributions are quite similar and consequently the approximation will be good.

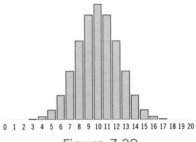

Figure 7.32

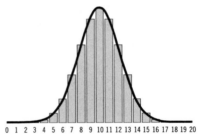

Figure 7.33

So, when should the normal distribution be used to approximate the binomial distribution? Generally, the approximation is reasonable when the mean of the binomial, np, is greater than or equal to 5 and $n(1-p)$ is greater than or equal to 5. The approximation becomes quite good when np is greater than or equal to 10 and $n(1-p)$ is greater than or equal to 10.

Example 7.11

Suppose that 2000 subjects are asked to select whether Pepsi or Coke tastes better. If it is assumed that there is no difference in product preference, what is the probability of observing 960 or fewer subjects who thought Coke was superior?

Solution

Let X = number of subjects that selected Coke as superior. The actual distribution of X is binomial $(n = 2000, p = .5)$, but the desired probability is too difficult to calculate directly. The expected value of X is

$$E(X) = np = 2000(.5) = 1000.$$

The standard deviation of X is

$$\sigma = \sqrt{np(1-p)} = \sqrt{2000(.5)(1-.5)} = \sqrt{500} \approx 22.36.$$

Let Y be a normally distributed random variable with a mean of 1000 and standard deviation of 22.36,

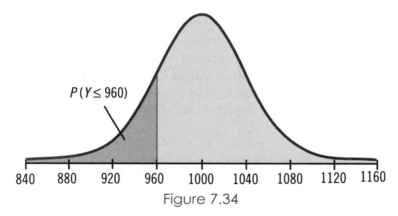

$P(Y \le 960)$

840   880   920   960   1000   1040   1080   1120   1160

Figure 7.34

Then, $P(X \le 960)$ is approximately

$$P(Y \le 960) = P\left(z \le \frac{960 - 1000}{22.36}\right)$$
$$= P(z \le -1.79) = .0367.$$

The exact probability is .0386, so the approximation is quite good.

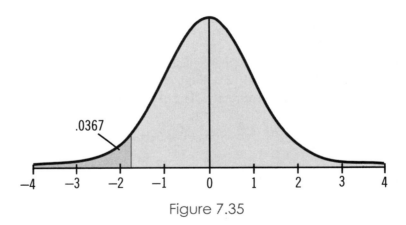

.0367

Figure 7.35

If the assumption of no preference is true, then the probability of observing 960 or fewer out of 2000 that prefer coke is only .0367. If fewer than 960 subjects prefer Coke, what is much more likely is the assumption of no preference is not true and that the population being sampled in fact prefers Pepsi. Based on the observed probability, if only 960 (or fewer) subjects selected Coke, there would be overwhelming evidence that the equal preference hypothesis was not true. Inadvertently, we have used probability theory to develop a method of testing a hypothesis (equal preference). Hypothesis testing is an extremely important topic in statistics and will be formally developed in later chapters.

Example 7.12

An advertising agency hired on behalf of Tech's development office conducted an ad campaign aimed at making alumni aware of their new capital campaign. Upon completion of the new campaign, the agency claimed that 20% of alumni in the state of Virginia were aware of the new campaign. To validate the claim of the agency, the development office surveyed 1000 alumni in the state and found that 150 were aware of the campaign. Assuming that the ad agency's claim is true, what is the probability that no more than 150 of the alumni in the random sample were aware of the new campaign?

Solution

Let X = the number of alumni that were aware of the campaign.

X is a binomial random variable with $n = 1000$ and $p = .20$.

So, $np = 200$ and $n(1 - p) = 800$. Therefore the normal distribution is appropriate to use as an approximation to the binomial distribution.

The mean is $\mu = np = 200$ and the standard deviation is

$$\sigma = \sqrt{np(1-p)} = \sqrt{160} \approx 12.65.$$

Let Y be a normally distributed random variable with a mean of 200 and a standard deviation of 12.65.

So, $P(X \leq 150)$ is approximately

$$P(Y \leq 150) = P\left(z \leq \frac{150 - 200}{12.65}\right) = P(z \leq -3.95) \approx 0.$$

Thus, if the marketing agency's claim is true, the probability that 150 or fewer alumni are aware of the campaign is practically zero. This would lead the development office to believe that the agency's claim is false.

The normal approximation to the binomial can be improved by using a **continuity correction**. Suppose that you wished to determine the probability that a binomial random variable ($n = 20$ and $p = .5$) is equal to 5. Recall that for a continuous random variable X, the probability that X is equal to some specific value is equal to zero since there is no area under the curve for a single point, say $X = 5$. Therefore, to approximate the probability using the normal would be equivalent to approximating the area of the shaded region given in Figure 7.36. To approximate the area of the region using the normal would require finding the area under the curve between 4.5 and 5.5.

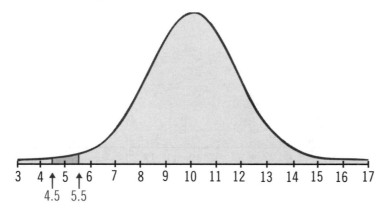

Figure 7.36

Example 7.13

a. Assuming $n = 20$ and $p = .5$, use the normal distribution to approximate the probability that a binomial random variable was 5 or less.

b. Find the probability that the same random variable from part (a) was greater than 4.

Solution

a. This implies finding the area of the rectangles for 0, 1, 2, 3, 4, and 5.

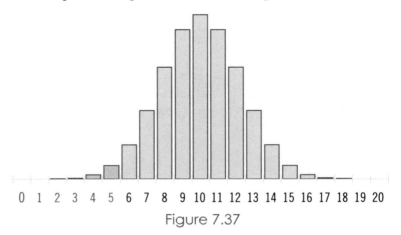

Figure 7.37

Instead of using the normal approximation $P(X \leq 5)$, use the continuity correction $P(X \leq 5.5)$ in order to accumulate all of the probabilities under the normal curve that correspond to the region associated with the point 5.

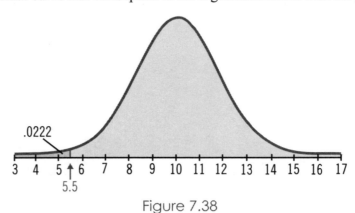

Figure 7.38

To use the normal approximation the mean and standard deviation of the binomial must be calculated.

$$\mu = E(X) = np = (20)(.5) = 10$$

$$\sigma = \sqrt{np(1-p)} = \sqrt{(20)(.5)(1-.5)} = \sqrt{5} \approx 2.236$$

Using the normal distribution, Y, with a mean of 10 and a standard deviation of 2.236 to approximate the binomial using *continuity correction*,

$$P(Y \le 5.5) = P\left(z \le \frac{5.5 - 10}{2.236}\right)$$

$$= P(z \le -2.01)$$

$$= .0222.$$

b.

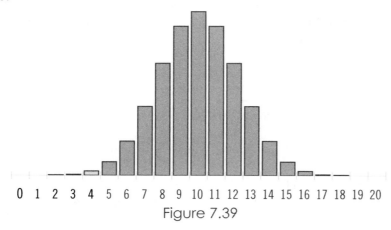

Figure 7.39

The continuity correction for the normal approximation would be $P(X \ge 4.5)$.

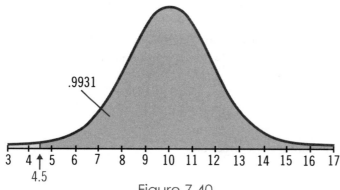

.9931

3   4 ↑ 5   6   7   8   9   10 11 12 13 14 15 16 17
      4.5

Figure 7.40

Using the normal distribution, Y, with a mean of 10 and a standard deviation of 2.236 to approximate the binomial using *continuity correction*,

$$P(Y \geq 4.5) = P\left(z \geq \frac{4.5 - 10}{2.236}\right)$$

$$= P(z \geq -2.46)$$

$$= 1 - P(z \leq -2.46)$$

$$= 1 - .0069$$

$$= .9931.$$

Example 7.14

A popular restaurant near Tech's campus accepts 200 reservations on Saturdays, the day of a Tech football game. Given that many of the reservations are made weeks in advance of game day, the restaurant expects that about eight percent will be no-shows. What is the probability that the restaurant will have no more than 20 no-shows on the next Saturday of a football weekend?

Solution

Let X = the number of no-shows.

X is a binomial random variable with $n = 200$ and $p = .08$.

Since $np = 16$ and $n(1 - p) = 184$ are both greater than 5, the normal distribution can be used to approximate the binomial probability.

For the binomial, $\mu = np = 16$ and

$$\sigma = \sqrt{np(1-p)} = \sqrt{(200)(.08)(1-.08)} = \sqrt{14.72} \approx 3.84.$$

Using the normal distribution, Y, with a mean of 16 and variance of 3.84, to approximate the binomial without continuity correction results in

$$P(Y \leq 20) = P\left(z \leq \frac{20 - 16}{3.84}\right) = P(z \leq 1.04) = .8508.$$

Using the continuity correction,

$$P(Y \leq 20.5) = P\left(z \leq \frac{20.5 - 16}{3.84}\right) = P(z \leq 1.17) = .8790.$$

Notice that the continuity correction has a significant impact on the accuracy of the approximation. Using the binomial distribution, the exact probability is .8775.

Approximating the Poisson Distribution

Approximating the Poisson distribution with the normal distribution is similar to approximating the binomial distribution. To use this approximation, the mean and standard deviation of the normal should be set to the mean and standard deviation of the Poisson. Since the mean and variance of the Poisson are both λ, the appropriate mean, variance, and standard deviation for the normal would be

$$\mu = \lambda, \quad \sigma^2 = \lambda, \quad \sigma = \sqrt{\lambda}.$$

Example 7.15

The manager of a sporting goods store wants to determine the best method of staffing employees without being wasteful. The problem that is often encountered is having too many employees and too few customers, and vice versa. The manager realized that during the initial kick-off of certain sports seasons such as football, baseball, and basketball, the store attracts, on average, 30 customers per hour. On some days, the number is higher, on others, the number is lower. The manager would like to determine the probability of at least 40 customers arriving in a given hour. Use the normal approximation to find the probability.

Solution

Let $X =$ the number of customers that enter the store in a given hour.

Notice that since we are counting the number of customers in a specific time interval, X has a Poisson distribution with

$$\mu = 30 \text{ and } \sigma = \sqrt{30} \approx 5.477.$$

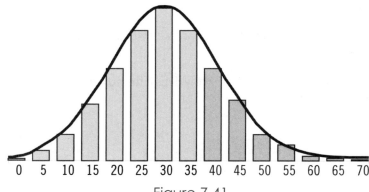

Figure 7.41

If Y represents the normal random variable with a mean of 30 and a standard deviation of 5.477, it should be a good approximation to the Poisson.

$$P(Y > 40) = P\left(z > \frac{40-30}{5.477}\right) = P(z > 1.83) = 1 - P(z < 1.83) = 1 - .9664 = .0336.$$

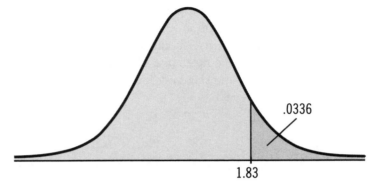

.0336

1.83

Figure 7.42

Just like the binomial, the approximation becomes increasingly accurate as the mean becomes larger. However, it is not very accurate when the mean of the Poisson distribution is less than 5. For small values of λ the continuity correction should be applied.

7.4 Exercises

Basic Concepts

1. Why would you want to use the normal distribution to approximate a binomial distribution or a Poisson distribution?

2. What are the parameters of a normal distribution used to approximate a binomial distribution?

3. What are the parameters of a normal distribution used to approximate a Poisson distribution?

4. What is continuity correction? How does it improve the normal approximation to the binomial?

Exercises

1. Management at a small engineering company is considering the addition of a company cafeteria area. A random sample of 50 persons out of the total number of persons employed by the firm will be surveyed to see if they are in favor of the addition. Assume that the true percentage of persons that favor the addition is 90%. (Hint: Use the normal approximation to the binomial.)

   a. Find the expected number of employees in the sample who will favor the addition of the cafeteria area.

   b. Find the standard deviation of the number of employees in the sample who will favor the addition of the cafeteria area.

   c. Is it advisable to use the continuity correction in calculating probabilities for the above sample? Explain.

   d. What is the probability that between 35 and 37 employees in the sample will favor the cafeteria?

   e. What is the probability that more than 40 of the employees in the sample will favor the cafeteria?

   f. What is the probability that at most 38 of the employees in the sample will favor the cafeteria?

2. The accounting department of a large corporation checks the addition of expense reports submitted by executives before paying them. Historically, they have found that 15% of the reports contain addition errors. An auditor randomly selects 60 expense reports and audits them for addition errors.

   a. Find the expected number of reports in the sample which will have addition errors.

   b. Find the standard deviation of the number of reports sampled which will have addition errors.

   c. Is it advisable to use the continuity correction in calculating probabilities for the above sample? Explain.

   d. Find the probability that fewer than 10 of the sampled expense reports will have addition errors.

   e. Find the probability that at least 30 of the sampled expense reports will have addition errors.

   f. Find the probability that between 5 and 15 of the sampled expense reports will have addition errors.

3. A local video store purchased a market research study which suggests that 60 percent of all homes have video recorders/players. A sample of 200 homes is selected to confirm the study's findings. If the marketing study is correct,

    a. Find the expected number of homes sampled which will have video recorders/players.

    b. Find the standard deviation of the number of homes in the sample which will have video recorders/players.

    c. What is the probability that at most 80 of the sampled homes will have video recorders/players?

    d. What is the probability that between 100 and 120 homes sampled will have video recorders/players?

    e. What is the probability that at least 130 of the sampled homes will have video recorders/players?

4. Suppose a virus is believed to infect two percent of the population. If a sample of 3000 randomly selected subjects are tested,

    a. Find the expected number of subjects sampled that will be infected.

    b. Find the standard deviation of the number of subjects sampled that will be infected.

    c. What is the probability that fewer than 30 of the subjects in the sample will be infected?

    d. What is the probability that between 40 and 80 of the subjects in the sample will be infected?

    e. Find the probability that at least 70 of the subjects in the sample will be infected.

5. A company manufacturing metal sheets believes that the number of defects on a 10' by 10' sheet of metal follows a Poisson distribution with an average defect rate of 5 per sheet.

    a. Find the standard deviation of the number of defects per sheet.

    b. Using the Poisson table in the appendix, find the probability of observing at least 10 defects per sheet.

    c. Using the normal approximation to the binomial, find the probability of observing at least 10 defects per sheet.

    d. How do the answers in parts (b) and (c) compare?

6. Service calls arriving at an electric company follow a Poisson distribution with an average arrival rate of 60 per hour.

    a. Find the average number of service calls in a 30 minute period.

    b. Find the standard deviation of the number of service calls in a 30 minute period.

    c. Find the probability that the electric company receives at least 40 service calls in a 30 minute period.

    d. Find the probability that the electric company receives at most 20 service calls in a 30 minute period.

    e. Find the probability that the electric company receives between 25 and 50 service calls in a 30 minute period.

7. Patients arriving at the emergency room of a local hospital follow a Poisson distribution with an average arrival rate of 15 per half hour.

    a. Find the average number of patients which arrive at the emergency room in one hour.

    b. Find the standard deviation of the number of patients which arrive at the emergency room in one hour.

    c. Find the probability that at least 15 patients will arrive at the emergency room in one hour.

    d. Find the probability that between 30 and 50 patients will arrive at the emergency room in one hour.

    e. Find the probability that at most 35 patients will arrive at the emergency room in one hour.

Discovering Technology

USING THE TI-84 PLUS CALCULATOR

Normal Distribution
(Finding area between an upper and lower bound)

Find the probability that a normal random variable with a mean of 10 and a standard deviation of 20 will lie between −10 and 40.

1. Choose **DISTR** (**2nd** **VARS**), then select option **2:normalcdf**. Press **ENTER**, and then input the (lower bound, upper bound, μ, σ), in this case (−10, 40, 10, 20). Press **ENTER** and observe the results.

Figure 7.43

Normal Distribution (Finding the area under the normal curve above some value)

Find the probability that a normal random variable with a mean of 10 and a standard deviation of 20 will lie above 40.

1. Choose **DISTR** (**2nd** **VARS**), then select option **2:normalcdf**. Press **ENTER**, and then input the (lower bound, upper bound, μ, σ), in this case (40, 999999, 10, 20). Press **ENTER** and observe the results. (**Note**: The upper bound is represented by a large positive number.)

Figure 7.44

Normal Distribution (Finding the area under the normal curve below some value)

Find the probability that a normal random variable with a mean of 10 and a standard deviation of 20 will lie below −10.

1. Choose **DISTR** (2nd VARS), then select option **2:normalcdf.** Press ENTER, and then input the (lower bound, upper bound, μ, σ), in this case (−999999, −10, 10, 20). Press ENTER and observe the results. (Note: The lower bound is represented by a large negative number.)

Figure 7.45

USING EXCEL

Approximating the Binomial

Use the information in Example 7.11 for this exercise.

The problem is about the probability of observing 960 or fewer subjects out of 2000 who thought Coke was superior, assuming that there is no difference in product preference.

1. Enter these values in a new worksheet:

    Cell A1 enter the label *X*.

    Cell B1 enter the value for *X* (the number of people that selected Coke as superior) **960**.

    Cell A2 enter the label *n*.

    Cell B2 enter the value of *n* (people in the sample) **2000**.

    Cell A3 enter the label *p*.

    Cell B3 enter the value for the probability of selecting Coke, **.5**.

    Cell A4 enter the label *E(X)*.

    Cell B4 enter the formula for computing the expected value of *X*, **=B2*B3**.

    Cell A5 enter the label *V(X)*.

    Cell B5 enter the formula for computing the variance of *X*, **=B4*(1−B3)**.

    Cell A6 enter the label **Std Dev**.

    Cell B6 enter the formula for computing standard deviation, **=SQRT(B5)**.

	A	B
1	*X*	960
2	*n*	2000
3	*p*	0.5
4	*E(X)*	1000
5	*V(X)*	500
6	Std Dev	22.36068

Figure 7.46

Now we are ready to find the probability of observing 960 or fewer people selecting Coke as superior.

2. In cell A7 enter the label *P*.

3. The formula for the cumulative normal distribution is

NORMDIST(x,mean,standard_dev,cumulative)

Where *x* is the value of *x*, **mean** is the mean of the random variable (the expected value in this case), **standard_dev** is the standard deviation of the random variable, and **cumulative** = TRUE if we want to calculate the cumulative distribution function or cumulative = FALSE if we want to calculate the probability mass function. For this problem, we want to calculate the probability of observing 960 or less people, so we want to calculate the cumulative distribution function. Therefore, cumulative = TRUE.

4. In cell B7 type the formula for the cumulative distribution function using our parameters:

=NORMDIST(B1,B4,B6,TRUE).

5. The result in cell B7 is .0368.

	A	B
1	*X*	960
2	*n*	2000
3	*p*	0.5
4	*E(X)*	1000
5	*V(X)*	500
6	Std Dev	22.36068
7	*P*	0.036819

Figure 7.47

Thus we have answered the question. If the assumption of no preference is true then the probability of observing 960 or fewer out of 2000 that prefer Coke is only .0368.

USING MINITAB

Binomial Distributions

For a binomial random variable with $n = 20$ and $p = .3$, calculate the probability that X is less than or equal to 4.

1. Enter 0, 1, 2, 3, 4 in the first five rows of C1.
2. Select **Calc**, choose **Probability Distributions**, and then choose **Binomial**.
3. Make sure "Cumulative probability" is selected, then enter **20** as the "Number of trials" and **.3** as the "Event probability".
4. In the "Input" column, select **C1** and press **OK**.
5. The cumulative distribution function is displayed in the Session window. When $x = 4$ the probability that $X \leq 4$ is approximately .2375.

Cumulative Distribution Function

Binomial with n = 20 and p = 0.3

```
x    P( X <= x )
0       0.000798
1       0.007637
2       0.035483
3       0.107087
4       0.237508
```

Figure 7.48

Chapter 7 Review

Key Terms and Ideas

- Continuous Random Variables
- Continuous Uniform Distribution
- Probability Density Function
- Uniform Probability Density Function
- Normal Distribution
- Normal Probability Density Function
- Standard Normal Distribution
- z-Distribution
- z-Score
- Continuity Correction

Key Formulas

Concept	Formula	Section
Uniform Probability Density Function	$f(x) = \begin{cases} \dfrac{1}{b-a} & \text{for } a \le x \le b \\ 0 & \text{otherwise} \end{cases}$	7.1
Expected Value for a Continuous Uniform Random Variable	$\mu = E(x) = \dfrac{a+b}{2}$	7.1
Standard Deviation for a Continuous Uniform Random Variable	$\sigma = \dfrac{b-a}{\sqrt{12}}$	7.1
Normal Probability Density Function	$f(x) = \dfrac{1}{\sigma\sqrt{2\pi}} e^{-\frac{(x-\mu)^2}{2\sigma^2}}$	7.2
Standardizing a Normal Random Variable	$z = \dfrac{x - \mu}{\sigma}$	7.3

Normal Approximation for the Binomial Distribution	If X is a binomial random variable where $np \geq 5$ and $n(1-p) \geq 5$, then X can be approximated by a normal distribution with $\mu = np$ and $\sigma = \sqrt{np(1-p)}$.	7.4
Normal Approximation for the Poisson Distribution	If X has a Poisson distribution, X can be approximated by a normal distribution with $\mu = \lambda$ and $\sigma = \sqrt{\lambda}$.	7.4

 **Additional Exercises**

1. Joe is always between 5 and 35 minutes late for work. Assuming that X, the number of minutes that Joe is late for work, has a continuous uniform distribution, answer the following:

   a. Find the mean of X.

   b. Find the standard deviation of X.

   c. Find the probability that on any randomly selected day, Joe is at least a half hour late for work.

   d. What percent of the time will X fall within one standard deviation of its mean?

   e. Compare this percent to that given by the Empirical Rule of Chapter 4. Why the large discrepancy?

2. Using the standard normal tables, determine the following probabilities. Sketch the associated areas.

   a. $P(0 \leq z \leq 0.85)$ c. $P(z \geq 1.75)$

   b. $P(-1.25 \leq z \leq 2.25)$ d. $P(z \leq -2.75)$

3. Using the standard normal tables, determine the following probabilities. Sketch the associated areas.

   a. $P(0 \leq z \leq 1.00)$ c. $P(z \geq 3.25)$

   b. $P(-2.50 \leq z \leq 3.01)$ d. $P(z \leq -2.50)$

4. Find the value of z such that .99 of the area under the curve lies between $-z$ and z.

5. Find the value of z such that .80 of the area under the curve lies between $-z$ and z.

6. The weights of newborn baby boys born at a local hospital are believed to have a normal distribution with an average weight of 7.25 lb and a standard deviation of 1 lb. If a newborn baby boy, born at the local hospital, is randomly selected, find the following probabilities.

   a. The probability that the weight of the newborn baby boy will be more than 8 lb.

   b. The probability that the weight of the newborn baby boy will be less than 6 lb.

   c. The probability that the weight of the newborn baby boy will be between 6.5 lb. and 8.5 lb.

   d. Find the weight which separates the lowest 10% of the weights from the highest 90% of the weights.

   e. If babies in the lowest 10 percent of weights are kept for observation, would a baby which weighed 5 lb. be kept for observation?

7. Medication errors in a hospital can be dangerous and expensive. Medication errors are defined as giving a patient a non-prescribed medication in any quantity or the improper dosage of a prescribed medication. Suppose the national average for medication errors is one out of every 1000 patients. A hospital believes that their medication error rate is comparable to the national average. If the hospital randomly selects 500 patients,

   a. Find the expected number of patients in the sample that will have had a medication error.

   b. What is the standard deviation of the number of patients in the sample that will have had a medication error?

   c. What is the probability of observing one or more patients who have had medication errors in the sample?

   d. What is the probability of observing two or more patients who have had medication errors in the sample?

   e. If you observed three patients who have had medication errors in the sample, would you believe that the hospital's medication error rate was comparable to the national average? Give reasons for your conclusions.

8. The number of violent crimes committed in a large city follows a Poisson distribution with an average rate of 10 per month.

   a. Find the expected number of violent crimes committed in a 3 month period.

   b. Find the standard deviation of the number of violent crimes committed in a 3 month period.

   c. Find the probability that at least 45 violent crimes will be committed in a 3 month period.

   d. Find the probability that between 25 and 40 violent crimes will be committed in a 3 month period.

e. Find the probability that less than 20 violent crimes will be committed in a 3 month period.

9. According to the 2011 Statistical Abstract of the United States, 20.5% of the scores on the critical reading portion of the SAT Reasoning Test exceeded 600. Approximately 17.4% of the scores were less than 400, according to the same reference. Assuming that scores on the critical reading portion of the SAT are approximately normally distributed, what are the mean and the standard deviation of the scores on the verbal portion of the SAT Reasoning Test? **Source:** U.S. Census Bureau

10. The annual average per capita consumption of red meat in the United States in 2008 was 108.3 pounds, according to the 2011 Statistical Abstract of the United States. This figure was down from a per capita average of 126.4 pounds in 1980. Assume that both in 2008 and 1980 the per capita amount of red meat consumed was a normal random variable with a standard deviation of 15 pounds. **Source:** U.S. Census Bureau

   a. In 1980, what percent of the population consumed at least 100 pounds of red meat?

   b. In 2008, what percent of the population consumed at least 100 pounds of red meat?

   c. In 1980, what percent of the population consumed at most 130 pounds of red meat?

   d. In 2008, what percent of the population consumed at most 130 pounds of red meat?

   e. Do you feel that it is reasonable to assume that the per capita amount of red meat consumed has a normal distribution? Why or why not?

11. A cell phone manufacturer has developed a new type of battery for its phones. Extensive testing indicates that the population battery life (in days) obtained by all batteries of this new type is normally distributed with a mean of 700 days and a standard deviation of 100 days. The manufacturer wishes to offer a guarantee providing a discount on batteries if the original battery purchased does not exceed the days stated in the guarantee. What should the guaranteed battery life be (in days) if the manufacturer desires that no more than 5% of the batteries will fail to meet the guaranteed number of days?

12. The manager of a retail store wants to determine the best method of staffing employees without being wasteful. The problem that is often encountered is having too many employees and too few customers, and vice versa. The manager realized that during the holiday season they attract, on average, 90 customers per hour. On some days, the number is higher, on others, the number is lower. The manager would like to determine the probability of at least 2 customers arriving in a given minute. Use the normal approximation to find the probability.

13. A machine used to regulate the amount of dye dispensed for mixing shades of paint can be set so that it discharges an average of μ milliliters of dye per can of paint. The amount of dye discharged is known to have a normal distribution with a variance equal to 0.0160. If more than 6 milliliters of dye are discharged when making a particular shade of blue paint, the shade is unacceptable. Determine the setting of μ so that no more than 1% of the cans of paint will be unacceptable.

14. The length of time required to complete a college achievement test is found to be normally distributed with a mean of 75 minutes and a standard deviation of 15 minutes. When should the test be terminated if we wish to allow sufficient time for 95% of the students to complete the test?

15. A manufacturing plant utilizes 3000 electric light bulbs that have a length of life that is normally distributed with a mean of 500 hours and a standard deviation of 50 hours. To minimize the number of bulbs that burn out during operation hours, all the bulbs are replaced after a given period of operation. How often should the bulbs be replaced if we want not more than 2% of the bulbs to burn out between replacement periods?

16. Howe's Finance Corporation provides financing for customers at an automotive dealership. The average loan amount is $24,000 with a standard deviation of $8000. Assuming that the loan amount is normally distributed, what is the probability that a randomly selected consumer buying a car will want to finance at least $20,000?

17. Suppose that the income of families in a large community follows a normal distribution. Two families are randomly selected and their incomes are $55,000 and $85,000, respectively. The two incomes correspond to z-scores of -0.5 and 2.0 respectively. Calculate the mean and standard deviation of the income of families in the neighborhood.

18. Suppose that the 30th percentile of a normal distribution is equal to 756 and that the 90th percentile of this normal distribution is 996. Find the mean and standard deviation of the normal distribution.

Samples and Sampling Distributions

8

Discovering the Real World

Holiday Spending

Discovering Technology

Constructing random samples using the TI-84 Plus calculator

Constructing random samples using Microsoft Excel

Constructing random samples using Minitab

Discovery Project

Industry Statistics

 **Discovering the Real World**

Fewer Gift Cards This Holiday Season

The National Retail Federation says shoppers will give fewer gift certificates this season and head to the sale rack instead.

By Catherine Clifford, CNNMoney.com staff writer

November 18, 2008: 4:09 AM ET

NEW YORK (CNNMoney.com) – As consumers try to pinch pennies this holiday season, they are going to spend less money on gift cards than last year, according to a report released Tuesday.

Gift card sales will fall almost 6% this holiday season to $24.9 billion, down from $26.3 billion last year, according to the National Retail Federation's sixth annual Gift Card Survey, conducted by BIGresearch.

Fewer shoppers plan to purchase gift cards this year – 53.5% compared with 56.6% in 2007. And if they do purchase gift cards, shoppers are going to put less cash on them, according to the survey. The average amount that shoppers plan to spend on gift cards in 2008 fell to $147.33 from $156.24 in 2007.

"Since gift cards never go on sale, some price-conscious shoppers will be passing up gift cards in favor of holiday bargains," said NRF President and CEO Tracy Mullin in a written statement.

Nearly 11% of shoppers interviewed for the survey said that the main reason they plan to buy fewer gift cards this holiday season is because they want their holiday shopping dollars to go further by buying gifts from the sale rack.

Of those who will be spending money on gift cards, the biggest spenders will be men and consumers who are a bit older. Men will spend an average of $156.98 on the cards and Americans over age 45 will spend $168.02 on average on gift cards this season.

But the gift card spending pullback comes at a time when a gift certificate is what a majority of consumers want, according to the NRF. The trade group's first holiday spending survey released last month, showed that 54.9% of spenders want to receive a gift card, up from 53.8% last year.

"Most consumers have been holding back on spending for themselves all year long and would love nothing more than receiving a gift card that would let them buy whatever they want," said Phil Rist, Vice President of Strategy for BIGresearch in statement.

The pullback in consumer gift card spending will catch up with retailers in the first months of the coming year, when shoppers hit stores ready to cash in on their holiday gift cards. "Retailers may need to make minor adjustments to holiday plans as fewer people may be hitting the stores in January to redeem gift cards," said Mullin.

The survey was conducted by BIGResearch for the National Retail Federation and polled 8,758 consumers between November 5-11, 2008.

Source: Clifford, Catherine. "Fewer gift cards this holiday season." CNNMoney.com. N.p., 18 Nov. 2008. Web.

A Question to Consider

1. What questions would you have regarding the manner in which the survey data were collected?

An article published in the previous year is given below.

Gift Cards More Popular Than Ever, According to NRF

Consumers to spend a total of $26.3 billion on gift cards this holiday

Kathy Grannis and Scott Krugman

November 13, 2007

WASHINGTON (www.nrf.com) – As gift cards become increasingly convenient, more personalized and more sought after, retailers can expect to see an increase in gift card sales this holiday season. The fifth annual National Retail Federation (NRF) Gift Card Survey, conducted by BIGresearch, found that gift card sales will total $26.3 billion this holiday season, compared to $24.8 billion in 2006. Additionally, the average consumer will spend more on gift cards than they did last year ($122.59 vs. $116.51 in 2006).

"It is no secret why gift cards are the most popular item on consumers' shopping lists," said NRF President and CEO Tracy Mullin. "Many consumers pulled back on spending for themselves this year and are hoping to receive a gift card so they can purchase something they may have had their eye on for months."

According to a recent NRF survey, gift cards will be the one of the most popular gifts this holiday season as 56.6 percent of consumers plan to buy them, compared to other top selling gift items like clothing, toys and books. And with popularity rising among consumers of all ages, 87.7 percent of shoppers said they will purchase two or more gift cards this holiday season.

"As consumers become more strapped for time, they are constantly looking for ways to make holiday shopping easier and less stressful," said Phil Rist, Vice President of Strategy for BIGresearch. "Gift cards allow for a faster and more convenient way to buy gifts for family and friends."

About the Survey

The NRF 2007 Holiday Consumer Intentions and Actions Survey was designed to gauge consumer behavior and shopping trends related to the winter holidays. The survey, which polled 7,982 consumers, was conducted for NRF by BIGresearch from October 31–November 7, 2007. The consumer poll has a margin of error of plus or minus 1.0 percent.

BIGresearch is a consumer market intelligence firm that provides unique consumer insights that are gathered online utilizing very large sample sizes. BIGresearch's syndicated Consumer Intentions and Actions survey monitors the pulse of more than 7,000 consumers each month to empower its clients with unique insights for identifying opportunities in a fragmented and changing marketplace.

The National Retail Federation is the world's largest retail trade association, with membership that comprises all retail formats and channels of distribution including department, specialty, discount, catalog, Internet, independent stores, chain restaurants, drug stores and grocery stores as well as the industry's key trading partners of retail goods and services. NRF represents an industry with more than 1.6 million U.S. retail establishments, more than 24 million employees – about one in five American workers – and 2006 sales of $4.7 trillion. As the industry umbrella group, NRF also represents more than 100 state, national and international retail associations (www.nrf.com).

Questions to Consider

1. What sampling issues are expressed in this article?

2. Does the additional information in the second article make the results of the 2008 article more acceptable?

Source: Grannis, Kathy, and Scott Krugman. "Gift Cards More Popular Than Ever, According to NRF." *National Retail Federation*. N.p., 13 Nov. 2007.

Introduction

When buying or even looking for a new car, one of the features that a customer is most interested in is the miles per gallon rating. Have you ever wondered how these miles per gallon ratings are obtained for vehicles? The miles per gallon ratings are obtained via **sampling** and **sampling distributions**. That is, auto manufacturers randomly sample vehicles, drive them in various conditions (city or highway) and note the mileages obtained under such conditions. This sample provides convincing evidence of the vehicle's average miles per gallon in the city and/or on the highway and thus the manufacturer is able to establish (and eventually publish) these estimates with confidence.

The quality of all statistical analyses and procedures depends on the quality of the sample data. If the sample data are not representative of the population, analyzing the data and drawing conclusions will be unproductive, at best. This is a simple idea, and an important one. It suggests the beginning of any statistical investigation should be focused on the development of representative sample data. Interestingly, obtaining a representative sample requires the introduction of randomness in the sampling procedure.

This chapter begins a bridge from the study of probability to the study of statistical inference. One of the critical links between statistical inference and probability is the **sampling distribution**, which is the probability distribution of a statistic. In the ensuing chapter the language of probability will be used to help define the level of confidence associated with the statistical inferences that are made.

8.1 Random Samples

People do a lot of sampling every day. If someone buys a cup of coffee, that person does not have to drink the whole cup to determine whether the coffee is too hot. He or she takes a sample, a sip or two, then makes a decision. The sampling procedure produces as much information as sampling the entire cup and, if the coffee is too hot, with much less pain. Sampling is a fundamental component of existence. When we cross an intersection, we sample traffic in both directions before making the decision to cross. When driving a car we visually sample traffic conditions, speed, and engine gauges. Sampling is a good idea. It saves time and is less costly than performing a census on the entire population. If the sample is representative of the population, the information it provides can be almost as good as performing a census. The relevant question is, how do you select a sample that is representative of the population?

Drawing samples that are representative of a population is often quite difficult. One "sampling method" that is often seen in the media is **voluntary sampling**. Usually some question is posed to a large audience and people "volunteer" to participate in the sample. The Internet has made this kind of sampling popular. However, this sampling method can often produce misleading results.

For example, the advice columnist Ann Landers once asked her readers, *If you had to do it over again, would you have children?* Over 10,000 readers wrote in; 70% said "No", and many described the misery their children had brought them. Voluntary response of this kind over represents people with strong feelings, especially strong negative feelings. A national random sample on the same issue found that over 90% of parents would choose to have children again. Voluntary response can easily produce 70% "No" in a sample when the truth about the population is close to 90% "Yes". Yet the media continue to conduct voluntary response polls and discuss them as if they provided useful information.

Ann Landers' sample is an extreme example of **selection bias**. Voluntary samples typically are not representative samples of a population.

Biased Sample

Definition

A sample is **biased** if it over represents or under represents some segment(s) of the population.

Choosing a Representative Sample

In order to select a sample, the population must be clearly defined. Otherwise, it is not clear what it represents. A significant portion of the effort required to produce good samples goes into the creation of a **sampling frame**, which is a list containing all the members of the population. Once this list is available, it is possible to construct a **simple random sample**.

Sampling Frame

Definition

A **sampling frame** is a list which identifies all members of the population.

Using Randomness to Remove Sample Bias

One of the more powerful methods of coping with bias is the use of randomness in the sampling process.

Simple Random Sample

Definition

A **simple random sample** from a finite population is one in which each possible random sample has an equal probability of being selected.

This definition implies that each member of the sampling frame has an equal chance of being selected for the sample.

There are a number of ways of selecting a simple random sample. If the sampling frame is small, each member of the list can be assigned a unique number. These numbers can be placed in a hat and drawn randomly. Another technique is to use a **random number table**.

Random number tables are composed of random digits, arranged in groups of 4 or 5 to improve readability. To use the random number table, randomly pick a row and column in the table as a starting point and select the appropriate number of digits. The appropriate number of digits is based on the size of the sampling frame. If the size of the sampling frame is from 1 to 99, then two digits should be selected. If the size of the sampling frame is from 100 to 999, then three digits should be selected. It makes no difference whether the random numbers are selected across the column or down the row. Random numbers which have the correct number of digits, but which are larger than the frame, should be ignored. Once the appropriate random numbers have been selected, sample the items in the frame which correspond to the random numbers. The resulting sample will constitute a simple random sample. Of course, with a computer readily available to nearly everyone, computer software programs are used to generate sets of random numbers. Techniques are shown in the Discovering Technology section at the end of this chapter on using the computer to generate random numbers for sampling.

Example 8.1

Select a simple random sample of 20 customer accounts from a sampling frame that contains 897 accounts.

Solution

If each account is given a number between 1 and 897, then three digits from the table can be used to indicate a specific account. Any consecutive three digits that are greater than 897 should be ignored. We can select the initial starting position as row three and column two, and select three digits across the row. Those accounts colored in red are selected (see Table 8.1).

Literary Digest

For the 1936 presidential election, *Literary Digest* conducted a poll to determine the winner. Over 10 million questionnaires were sent to those who owned automobiles and/or telephones. Over 2.4 million questionnaires were returned, and *Literary Digest* predicted that Alf Landon would defeat Franklin D. Roosevelt with 57% of the vote. George Gallup also conducted a poll of 50,000 random voters and predicted Roosevelt as the winner. Many people laughed at Gallup because *Literary Digest* had been correctly predicting the outcome of the presidential election since 1916 and based its predictions on such a large sample. Gallup was correct and Roosevelt won with 62% of the vote. Where did *Literary Digest* go wrong? First, only those who were rich enough to afford the luxury of a car or phone were sampled. Also, those who were not happy with Roosevelt were more likely to respond. In the end, *Literary Digest* went bankrupt and Gallup started his own company, which still predicts the elections.

Table 8.1 – Random Number Table									
985	201	776	714	905	686	072	210	940	558
609	709	343	350	500	739	981	180	505	431
398	082	773	250	725	682	482	~~940~~	524	201
527	756	785	183	452	~~996~~	340	628	~~898~~	083
137	467	007	818	475	406	106	871	177	817
886	854	020	086	507	584	013	676	667	951
903	476	493	296	091	106	299	594	673	488
751	764	969	918	260	892	893	785	613	682
347	834	113	862	481	176	741	746	850	950
580	477	697	473	039	571	864	021	816	544

Random samples form the basis of almost all inferential statistics. But random sampling is not a haphazard, purposeless selection technique. On the contrary, removing potential selection bias is difficult, and randomness is the only tool for the job.

Suppose you want to obtain a random sample of students at your college. If 8000 students attend the college, deriving the sampling frame would be a formidable task. Fortunately, a college's student population is well-defined, and with the aid of a computer and the registrar's database, a random sample could be selected.

Well-defined populations are the exception, not the rule. Consider the problem of defining the sampling frame for the customer base of a retail shopping mall. Developing a clear definition of the mall's market area would be difficult. Assuming this could be done, developing the list of all potential consumers in the market area would be almost impossible. There would be numerous sources that would have a large segment of the names (utility companies, phone companies, etc.), but however complete these lists may be, there will be people who will be omitted. The principal liability of the simple random sampling technique is the necessity of forming the sampling frame. There are sampling techniques that are designed to overcome this problem, one of which is called cluster sampling. This and other sampling techniques are discussed in Section 8.5.

8.1 Exercises

Basic Concepts

1. Why is the quality of sample data so important?

2. Why is randomness useful in sampling?

3. What is wrong with a voluntary survey?

4. What is a biased sample?

5. What is a sampling frame? Why is this concept important?

6. Discuss how you would draw a simple random sample of the students at your college.

7. What makes drawing a simple random sample from a geographic area a difficult task?

Exercises

1. A magazine reported the results of a survey in which readers were asked to send in their responses to several questions regarding good eating. Consider the reported results to the question, *How often do you eat chocolate?*

Table for Exercise 1 – Survey Responses	
Category	**% of Responses**
Frequently	13
Occasionally	45
Seldom	37
Never	5

   a. What type of sampling technique was used for this survey?

   b. What types of biases may be present in the responses?

   c. Is 13% a reasonable estimate of the proportion of all Americans who eat chocolate frequently? Explain.

2. A magazine reported the results of a survey in which readers were asked to send in their responses to several questions regarding anger. Consider the reported results to the question, *How long do you usually stay angry?*

Table for Exercise 2 – Survey Responses	
Category	**% of Responses**
A few hours or less	48
A day	12
Several days	9
A month	1
I hold a grudge indefinitely	22
It depends on the situation	8

   a. What type of sampling technique was used for this survey?

   b. What types of biases may be present in the responses?

   c. Is 22% a reasonable estimate of the proportion of all Americans who hold a grudge indefinitely? Explain.

3. Students in a marketing class have been asked to perform a survey to determine whether or not there is a demand for an insurance program at a local college. The students decide to randomly select students from the local college and mail them a questionnaire regarding the insurance program. Of the 150 surveys which were mailed, 50 students responded to the following survey item: *Pick the category which best describes your interest in an insurance program.*

Table for Exercise 3 – Survey Responses	
Category	% of Responses
Very Interested	50
Somewhat Interested	15
Interested	10
Not Very Interested	5
Not At All Interested	20

a. What type of sampling technique is used for this survey?

b. What types of biases may be present in the responses?

c. Is 50% a reasonable estimate of the proportion of all students who would be very interested in an insurance program at the local college? Explain.

d. Is 50% a reasonable estimate of the proportion of all business majors who would be very interested in an insurance program at the local college? Explain.

e. What strategies do you think the marketing students could have used to get a less biased response to their survey?

4. Television news programs often conduct opinion surveys by announcing some question on the air and advising listeners to call different numbers for a *yes* or *no* response. National television programs do the same thing except they use 900 numbers and the respondent must pay for the call. Suppose that a news program asks its listeners to phone in a response to the following: *Women should be permitted to assume combat roles in the military.* The results of the particular survey were 34% *yes* and 66% *no*. Is it reasonable to believe that the results of the survey reflect the attitudes of the community on this issue? What biases exist in this sampling method?

5. A local politician wants to know what the residents of his community think about an increase in the local property tax to pay for improvements to the highway. He decides to conduct a survey.

a. What is the population of interest to the politician?

b. Can you think of any good sources for a sampling frame?

c. What are the shortcomings (if any) of the sources you picked for the sampling frame?

8.2 Introduction to Sampling Distributions

The notion of a statistic, such as the sample mean, as a random variable may seem odd. After all, when you studied descriptive statistics in Chapter 4, statistics were numbers, not variables. The focus, however, of Chapter 4 was to demonstrate techniques for summarizing data after they had been collected. When we consider a sampling distribution the "after the data have been collected" condition is dropped. A sampling distribution for the sample mean would describe the means of all possible samples of a particular sample size from a specified population. Since the value of the sample mean for any particular sample depends on the sample we draw, the sample mean is a random variable.

As we studied in Chapter 6, the best way to summarize outcomes of some random phenomena (in this case the sample mean) is with a probability distribution. The probability distribution which describes the distribution of the sample means is called the **sampling distribution of the sample mean**.

Although the discussion has focused on the sample mean, the same arguments could be applied to the sample variance, sample proportion, and sample standard deviation. All of these sample statistics have sampling distributions as well.

Statistics as Random Variables

Statistical inference is the focus of a large portion of the remainder of this text. As we previously discussed, statistical inference uses statistics calculated from samples as the basis of an inference about the population. If the sample is representative, then the sample statistics (which are random variables that depend on which random sample is selected) ought to be close to their population counterparts. In other words, the sample mean ought to be close to the population mean, the sample proportion ought to be close to the population proportion, and the sample standard deviation should be close to the population standard deviation. Since sample statistics will be used as the basis of the statistical inference, we must know how those statistics vary from one sample to another. Once the variability of the sample statistic is understood, we will be able to make probability statements regarding our inferences.

Why Calculate the Sample Mean?

When analyzing ratio data, the first piece of summary information that an analyst wants to determine is the mean. For most populations, performing a census to determine the population mean is impractical. The only alternative is to use sample information. It seems reasonable that the sample mean, $\bar{x}$, would contain an enormous amount of information about the population mean, μ, and would thus be a sensible estimate of the population mean. Generally, if you wish to estimate a population value – be it the mean, standard deviation, or proportion – the corresponding sample value will be a good **estimator**.

Point Estimator

Definition

A **point estimator** is a single-valued estimate, calculated from the sample data, which is intended to be close to the true population value.

Can you be sure that the sample mean will always be close to the population mean? When dealing with random variables, nothing is certain, but there are methods of reducing the probable error. To understand how this is achieved, we must examine how the sample mean varies.

8.2 Exercises

Basic Concepts

1. Is the sample mean always close to the population mean?

2. Under what conditions is the sample mean considered a random variable?

3. What is the sampling distribution of the sample mean?

4. Describe how statistics as random variables are crucial to statistical inference.

5. What is an estimator? Give an example.

The Distribution of the Sample Mean

Sample means vary because sample data vary from sample to sample. As an illustration, suppose that an automobile manufacturer wished to determine the average miles per gallon (mpg) of a specific vehicle model that they manufacture. Since determining the mpg of each vehicle is very time consuming, the manufacturer has decided to select two vehicles from a batch of six. Suppose that the actual mpg of the six vehicles are given in Table 8.2.

Table 8.2 – Miles per Gallon	
Car	**MPG**
A	25
B	27
C	40
D	29
E	28
F	30
Mean	29.83
Variance	23.14
Standard Deviation	4.81

It is important to realize that the above set of data constitutes a population. The mean mpg rating of the population in Table 8.2 is 29.83 and the population standard deviation is 4.81, rounded to two decimal places.

$$\mu = 29.83$$
$$\sigma = 4.81$$

Both of these measures are considered population parameters. The mpg ratings given in Table 8.2 are not known by the manufacturer when the shipment arrives. The manufacturer's job is to estimate the population average using a sample estimate, in this case using the sample mean from a sample of size two.

How many different samples of size two can be drawn? Assuming no replacement, there would be 15 possible samples of size two if order does not matter. A list of all possible samples and the resulting means is given in Table 8.3.

Sample Number	Car 1	Car 2	First Observation	Second Observation	Mean $\bar{x}$
	Table 8.3 – MPG Sample Measurements				
1	A	B	25	27	26.0
2	A	C	25	40	32.5
3	A	D	25	29	27.0
4	A	E	25	28	26.5
5	A	F	25	30	27.5
6	B	C	27	40	33.5
7	B	D	27	29	28.0
8	B	E	27	28	27.5
9	B	F	27	30	28.5
10	C	D	40	29	34.5
11	C	E	40	28	34.0
12	C	F	40	30	35.0
13	D	E	29	28	28.5
14	D	F	29	30	29.5
15	E	F	28	30	29.0

The sample means in Table 8.3 vary and when something varies there are at least three questions to ask:

1. What is the central value of the variable?

2. What is the variability of the variable?

3. Is there a familiar pattern (distribution) to the variability?

What is the Central Value of $\bar{x}$?

Intuitively, you would expect the sample mean to be larger than μ some of the time and smaller than μ some of the time. For large samples, the distribution of $\bar{x}$ will be relatively symmetrical, and consequently $\bar{x}$ should be larger than μ about 50% of the time and smaller than μ about 50% of the time. But for small samples the distribution of the sample mean may not be symmetrical. This is the case for the sample means in Table 8.3. 10 of the 15 means are below 29.83, which is the population mean for the population in Table 8.2. Generally, however, the sample means should be near the population mean, or symbolically $\bar{x}$ should be near μ. It can be shown theoretically that the mean of the $\bar{x}$'s equals μ. In the example, the mean of the sample means is 29.83, which equals the population mean. This is not a coincidence.

Definition

If the average value of an estimator equals the population parameter being estimated, the estimator is said to be **unbiased**.

Estimators are similar to marksmen. When you shoot, you want to hit what you are shooting at. When you estimate, you want to get as close as possible to the population characteristic you are estimating. But, bullets do not always land exactly where the marksman aims. If the gun sights are properly adjusted, then the shots will be dispersed around the middle of the target area.

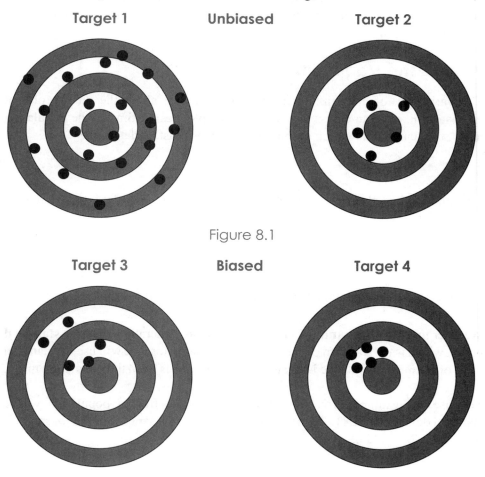

Figure 8.1

Figure 8.2

An estimator which produces estimates centered around the true value is said to be **unbiased**.

Unbiasedness is generally thought to be a good property of an estimator. Just as the ideal target rifle is one that would hit in exactly the same place every shot, the ideal estimator is one that is unbiased and has no variance. Since the mean of $\bar{x}$ equals μ, $\bar{x}$ is an unbiased estimator of μ.

Unbiased Estimators

Definition

The sample mean, $\bar{x}$, is an unbiased estimator of μ.

The sample proportion, $\hat{p}$, is an unbiased estimator of p.

The sample standard deviation, s, is an unbiased estimator of σ.

If an estimator is unbiased, its variability determines its reliability. If an unbiased estimator is extremely variable, then the estimates it produces may not, on average, be as close to the parameter being estimated as a biased estimator with a small standard deviation.

What is the Variability of $\bar{x}$?

The variability of an estimator reveals a great deal about the quality of that estimator. In order to assess how well the sample mean estimates the population mean, the standard deviation of the sample means must be determined.

Standard Deviation of the Sample Mean – Infinite Population

Formula

It can be shown that for a population of infinite size the standard deviation of $\bar{x}$ $(\sigma_{\bar{x}})$ is

$$\sigma_{\bar{x}} = \frac{\sigma}{\sqrt{n}},$$

where σ is the population standard deviation and n is the sample size.

We refer to $\sigma_{\bar{x}}$ as the **standard error of the mean**, generally called the **standard error**, which is the standard deviation of a point estimator. We will use the standard error of the mean to indicate how far the sample mean is from the population mean.

Suppose, for example, you were drawing a sample from a population whose standard deviation is 4.81. The standard deviation of the sample means for samples of size $n = 2$ would be

$$\sigma_{\bar{x}} = \frac{\sigma}{\sqrt{n}} = \frac{4.81}{\sqrt{2}} \approx 3.40.$$

If the population is finite, as in Table 8.2, then the finite population correction factor $\left(\sqrt{\dfrac{N-n}{N-1}}\right)$ must be applied to the calculation of the standard deviation of the sample mean.

Formula

For a finite population the standard deviation of $\bar{x}$ is

$$\sigma_{\bar{x}} = \sqrt{\frac{N-n}{N-1}} \cdot \frac{\sigma}{\sqrt{n}},$$

where N = the size of the population and n = the size of the sample.

Standard Deviation of the Sample Mean – Finite Population

Correcting for the finite population represented in Table 8.2, the standard deviation of the sample means for a sample of size 2 would be

$$\sigma_{\bar{x}} = \sqrt{\frac{N-n}{N-1}} \cdot \frac{\sigma}{\sqrt{n}} = \sqrt{\frac{6-2}{6-1}} \cdot \frac{4.81}{\sqrt{2}} \approx 3.04.$$

Examining the formula for $\sigma_{\bar{x}}$, we notice that as the size of the sample, n, increases, the variability of the sample mean decreases. The possibility of changing the variability of an estimator means the accuracy of the estimator can be manipulated. For example, suppose that instead of using a sample of size two, the manufacturer decides to use a sample of size three. Six items chosen three at a time could produce 20 samples of size three. The samples and means of each sample are shown in Table 8.4. The standard deviation of the sample means for $n=3$ in Table 8.4 is 2.15, using the finite population correction factor.

For both samples ($n=2$ and $n=3$) the mean of the sample means is 29.83 which equals the population mean. But the standard deviation of the sample means for samples of size three is 2.15 which is smaller than the standard deviation for samples of size two (3.04).

$$\text{For } n=2, \quad \sigma_{\bar{x}} = 3.04$$

$$\text{For } n=3, \quad \sigma_{\bar{x}} = 2.15$$

Sample No.	Car 1	Car 2	Car 3	First Observation	Second Observation	Third Observation	Mean $\bar{x}$
				Table 8.4 – MPG Sample Measurements			
1	A	B	C	25	27	40	30.67
2	A	B	D	25	27	29	27.00
3	A	B	E	25	27	28	26.67
4	A	B	F	25	27	30	27.33
5	A	C	D	25	40	29	31.33
6	A	C	E	25	40	28	31.00
7	A	C	F	25	40	30	31.67
8	A	D	E	25	29	28	27.33
9	A	D	F	25	29	30	28.00
10	A	E	F	25	28	30	27.67
11	B	C	D	27	40	29	32.00
12	B	C	E	27	40	28	31.67
13	B	C	F	27	40	30	32.33
14	B	D	E	27	29	28	28.00
15	B	D	F	27	29	30	28.67
16	B	E	F	27	28	30	28.33
17	C	D	E	40	29	28	32.33
18	C	D	F	40	29	30	33.00
19	C	E	F	40	28	30	32.67
20	D	E	F	29	28	30	29.00

Since both estimators are unbiased and are centered around the population mean, the standard deviation of the estimator is a measure of how close the estimator (in this case the sample mean) is to the population mean.

As in many problems, there is an accuracy versus dollars trade off. Greater accuracy can be achieved by taking a larger sample, but larger samples normally cost more to collect and examine.

Suppose a population had a mean of 43,660 and a standard deviation of 2500. The distributions in Figure 8.3 are the distributions of the sample mean for samples of size 25, 100, and 200, respectively from this population. Based on the graphs in Figure 8.3, it seems that the estimator shown for $n = 200$ would be preferred. Because it has less variability, the estimates of μ ($\bar{x}$'s) from samples of $n = 200$ should be closer (on average) to μ.

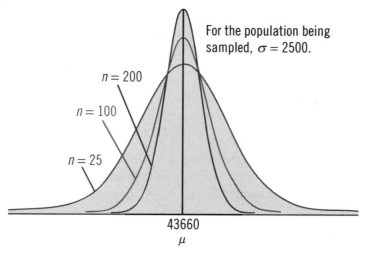

For the population being sampled, $\sigma = 2500$.

$n = 200$

$n = 100$

$n = 25$

43660
μ

Figure 8.3

Properties

If an estimate of the population mean is required, the sample mean possesses two good characteristics:

1. The mean of the sample means is the population mean. Another way of expressing this concept is to say that the expected value of $\bar{x}$ is equal to the population mean. Symbolically, this can be expressed as

$$E(\bar{x}) = \mu \text{ (unbiasedness)}.$$

2. If the sample size is increased, the standard error of the sample mean decreases. This implies that the quality of the estimator tends to improve as the sample size increases.

$$\sigma_{\bar{x}} = \frac{\sigma}{\sqrt{n}}$$

Characteristics of the Sample Mean

The second characteristic has an important consequence for estimating a population parameter. By choosing a sufficiently large sample size, an estimate can be obtained with some specified level of accuracy. Being able to predetermine the accuracy of an estimate is an important topic in statistics and will be discussed in the next chapter.

Is There a Familiar Pattern to the Variability?

The **central limit theorem** is a very important theorem which summarizes the distribution of the sample mean. **The distribution of the sample mean becomes closer to a normal distribution as the sample size becomes larger, regardless of the distribution of the population from which the sample is drawn.**

The most important feature of the central limit theorem is that it can be applied to any population. Because the theorem does not have any distributional assumptions, it is widely applicable and is one of the cornerstones of statistical inference. Many of the statistical techniques discussed in subsequent chapters will have their theoretical basis in this theorem.

Theorem

Central Limit Theorem

If a sufficiently large random sample (i.e. $n \geq 30$) is drawn from a population with mean, μ, and standard deviation, σ, the distribution of the sample mean will have the following characteristics:

1. An approximately normal distribution regardless of the distribution of the underlying population.

2. $\mu_{\bar{x}} = E(\bar{x}) = \mu$ (The mean of the sample means equals the population mean.)

3. $\sigma_{\bar{x}} = \dfrac{\sigma}{\sqrt{n}}$ (The standard deviation of the sample means equals the standard deviation of the population divided by the square root of the sample size.)

The only restrictive feature of the theorem is that the sample size must be sufficiently large for the theorem to be applicable. Even if the distribution of the population deviates substantially from the normal distribution, a sample size of at least 30 will be sufficiently large to produce a sampling distribution for $\bar{x}$ that is approximately normal.

If the population is known to be normally distributed, then the sampling distribution of $\bar{x}$ will be normally distributed for any sample size.

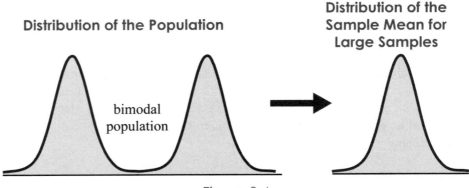

Distribution of the Population

bimodal population

Distribution of the Sample Mean for Large Samples

Figure 8.4

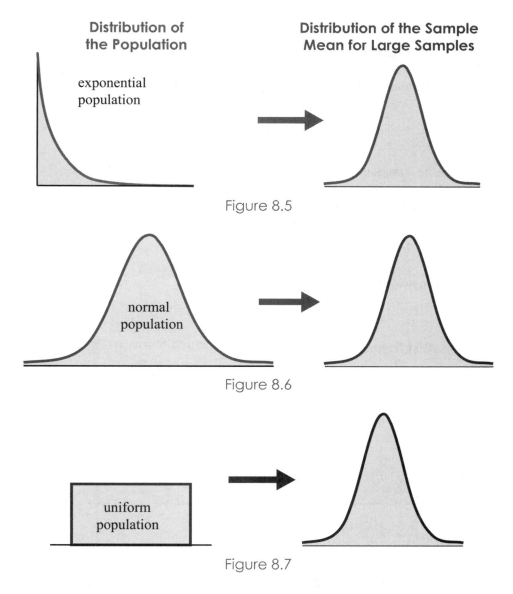

Figure 8.5

Figure 8.6

Figure 8.7

The History of the Central Limit Theorem

Pierre-Simon Laplace is credited with the initial statement of the central limit theorem in 1776. He developed the theorem while working on the probability distribution of the sum of meteor inclination angles.

Although the theorem is stated with respect to the sample mean, it is a more general theorem regarding the sum of random variables. If you add up a sufficiently large number of random variables the sum will be normally distributed.

Using the Central Limit Theorem

Let's look at some examples of the central limit theorem.

Example 8.2

A recycling plant compresses aluminum cans into bales. The weights of the resulting bales are known to have a mean of 100 pounds and a standard deviation of 8 pounds. A simple random sample of 50 bales is taken. What is the probability that the bales will weigh, on average, less than 104 pounds?

Solution

The information provided in the problem is as follows:

$$\mu = 100 \text{ pounds, } \sigma = 8 \text{ pounds, and}$$
$$n = 50.$$

Let X be a random variable that represents the weight of a bale.

By the central limit theorem (since $n \geq 30$), the distribution of $\bar{x}$ will be normal with a mean equal to the population mean, 100, and a standard error given by $\sigma_{\bar{x}} = \dfrac{\sigma}{\sqrt{n}} = \dfrac{8}{\sqrt{50}}$.

Thus, to answer the question,

$$P(\bar{x} < 104) = ?$$

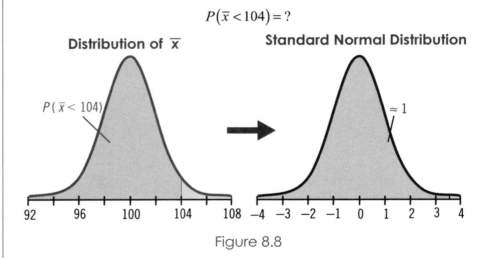

Figure 8.8

Since $\bar{x}$ is a normal random variable, the probability that $\bar{x}$ is less than 104 pounds is determined using a z-transformation.

$$P(\bar{x} < 104) = P\left(z < \frac{104 - 100}{8 / \sqrt{50}} \right) = P(z < 3.54) \approx 1$$

since Table B's largest value is 3.49, yielding a probability of .9998.

Example 8.3

Suppose that a population has an unknown mean and a standard deviation of 5. A sample of size 100 is drawn from the population. If the sample mean is used as an estimate of the population mean, what is the probability that the sample mean will be within one unit of the true mean?

Solution

The concept of using a statistic to estimate a population parameter introduces the concept of the **error of estimation** (also referred to as **sampling error** or **estimation error**). In general, the error of estimation is the difference between a sample statistic and the parameter that it is estimating. In the problem at hand, the error is given by $\mu - \bar{x}$ since we will be using $\bar{x}$ to estimate μ.

However, we are just as interested in negative errors as positive errors. Thus, to satisfy the condition that an error of less than one unit has been made, the condition

$$|\mu - \bar{x}| < 1$$

must be satisfied.

$$P(|\mu - \bar{x}| < 1) = P(-1 < \mu - \bar{x} < 1) = P(\mu - 1 < \bar{x} < \mu + 1)$$

Since for a standard normal random variable, z, $\mu = 0$, the above probability is equal to

$$= P(-1 < z < 1)$$
$$= .3413 + .3413 = .6826.$$

Sampling Distribution of $\bar{x}$

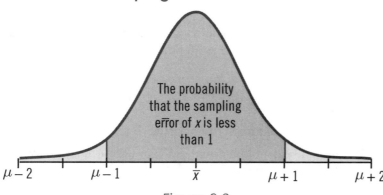

The probability that the sampling error of x is less than 1

$\mu - 2$ $\quad$ $\mu - 1$ $\quad$ $\bar{x}$ $\quad$ $\mu + 1$ $\quad$ $\mu + 2$

Figure 8.9

z-Distribution

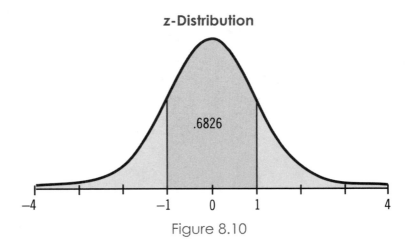

.6826

−4   −1 0 1   4

Figure 8.10

Thus, if a sample size of 100 is drawn from the population given, the probability that the sample mean will be within one unit of the population mean is .6826.

In the previous problem we were able to determine the probability of making an error of less than one unit without knowing the mean of the population. This probability (.6826) tells us a lot about the quality of the estimate $\bar{x}$. The estimate of μ obtained from a sample of size 100 is more than just an estimate now, it is an estimate with a "level of confidence" in its quality.

Example 8.4

The lifetime of a certain type of micro transistor is normally distributed about a mean of 156 hours. It is known that 1.5 percent of the transistors have a lifetime greater than 167 hours.

a. What is the standard deviation of the distribution of the lifetimes of the transistors?

b. Using the standard deviation calculated in part (a), what is the probability that the average lifetime of a sample of 25 transistors is at least 155 hours?

Solution

a. Let X = lifetime of a micro transistor.

X is normally distributed with a mean of 156 hours. We also know that 1.5% of the transistors have a lifetime greater than 167 hours. This can be written as

$$P(X > 167) = .015 \qquad (1)$$

Since σ is unknown, we can find σ using (1) such that

$$P\left(z > \frac{167-156}{\sigma}\right) = .015.$$

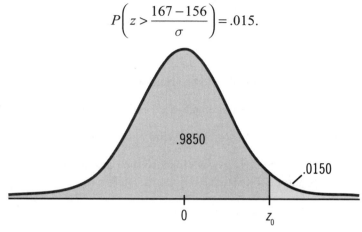

Figure 8.11

$$P(z < z_0) = .9850 \text{ where } z_0 = \frac{167-156}{\sigma}.$$

Finding the value .9850 in Table B, we see that $z_0 = 2.17$.

Thus, $\dfrac{167-156}{\sigma} = 2.17$, and solving for σ, we get

$$\sigma \approx 5.07.$$

b. $P(\bar{x} \geq 155) = ?$

Since X is normally distributed, then $\bar{x}$ is also normally distributed. Thus,

$$P(\bar{x} \geq 155) = P\left(z \geq \frac{155-156}{5.07 / \sqrt{25}}\right)$$
$$= P(z \geq -0.99)$$
$$= 1 - P(z < -0.99)$$
$$= 1 - .1611$$
$$= .8389$$

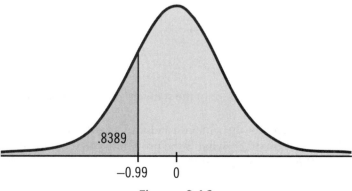

Figure 8.12

8.3 Exercises

Basic Concepts

1. What key three questions should be asked when considering a random variable?

2. Explain the difference between a biased estimator and an unbiased estimator.

3. Give three examples of estimators which are unbiased.

4. Is an unbiased estimator always closer to the parameter being estimated than a biased estimator? Explain.

5. What is the standard error of the mean? What does it indicate?

6. What are two characteristics of the sample mean?

7. Explain the central limit theorem.

8. What effect does increasing the sample size have on the accuracy of an estimate?

9. What is the error of estimation?

Exercises

1. Suppose the random variable X has a mean of 20 and a standard deviation of 5. Calculate the mean and the standard deviation of the sample mean for each of the following sample sizes (assume the population is infinite).

   a. $n = 35$

   b. $n = 50$

   c. $n = 75$

   d. What happens to the size of the standard deviation of the sample mean as the sample size increases?

2. Suppose the random variable X has a mean of 50 and a standard deviation of 10. Calculate the mean and standard error for each of the following sample sizes (assume the population is infinite).

   a. $n = 40$

   b. $n = 55$

   c. $n = 100$

   d. What happens to the size of the standard error as the sample size increases?

3. If there is a normally distributed random variable with a mean of 75 and a standard deviation of 22, what is the probability that the mean of a sample of size 19 will be greater than 80?

4. If a sample of size 40 is drawn from a population that has a mean of 276 and a variance of 81, what is the probability that the mean of the sample will be less than 273?

5. Suppose there is a normally distributed population with a mean of 250 and a standard deviation of 50. If $\bar{x}$ is the average of a sample of 36, find the following probabilities.

   a. $P(\bar{x} \leq 240)$

   b. $P(\bar{x} \geq 255)$

   c. $P(246 \leq \bar{x} \leq 260)$

   d. $P(234 \leq \bar{x} \leq 245)$

6. Suppose there is a normally distributed population with a mean of 100 and a standard deviation of 10. If $\bar{x}$ is the average of a sample of 50, find the following probabilities.

   a. $P(\bar{x} \leq 110)$

   b. $P(\bar{x} \geq 90)$

   c. $P(95 \leq \bar{x} \leq 115)$

   d. $P(85 \leq \bar{x} \leq 98)$

7. A company fills bags with fertilizer for retail sale. The weights of the bags of fertilizer have a normal distribution with a mean weight of 15 lb and standard deviation of 1.70 lb.

   a. What is the probability that a randomly selected bag of fertilizer will weigh between 14 and 16 pounds?

   b. If 35 bags of fertilizer are randomly selected, find the probability that the average weight of the 35 bags will be between 14 and 16 pounds.

8. A travel agency conducted a survey of the prices charged by ocean cruise ship lines and determined they were approximately normally distributed with a mean of $110 per day and a standard deviation of $20 per day.

   a. If an ocean cruise ship line is chosen at random, find the probability that they will charge less than $99 per day.

   b. What is the probability that the average charge for a randomly selected sample of 35 ocean cruise ship lines will be less than $99 per day?

9. The turkeys found in a particular county have an average weight of 15.6 pounds with a standard deviation of 4.00 pounds. Forty-five turkeys are randomly selected for a county fair.

   a. Find the probability that the average weight of the turkeys will be less than 14.5 pounds.

   b. What is the probability that the average weight of the turkeys will be more than 17 pounds?

   c. Find the probability that the average weight of the turkeys will be between 13 and 18 pounds.

10. The average score for a Water Safety Instructor (WSI) exam is 75 with a standard deviation of 12. Fifty scores for the WSI exam are randomly selected.

   a. Find the probability that the average of the fifty scores is at least 80.

   b. Find the probability that the average of the fifty scores is at most 70.

   c. Find the probability that the average of the fifty scores is between 72 and 78.

11. A college food service buys frozen fish in boxes labeled 10 pounds. The true average weight of the boxes is 8 pounds with a standard deviation of 2 pounds. The food service director suspects that the boxes do not contain as much fish as advertised. He decides to inspect 40 boxes from the next shipment. If the average weight is less than 10 pounds he will reject the entire shipment. Find the probability that the food service director will not reject the shipment.

12. The AQI, or the Air Quality Index, is an index used to determine the ozone level in a city. Depending upon the AQI reading, it may not be safe to jog or even to go outside. Readings in the 0-50 range mean that the air quality conditions are considered "good", 51-100 are "moderate", 101-150 means "unhealthy for sensitive groups", 151-200 means "unhealthy", 201-300 means "very unhealthy", and 301-500 means "hazardous". (Source: airnow.gov) Suppose that an industrial region has an average AQI reading of 102 with a standard deviation of 40. Find the probability that for a random sample of 50 days, the average AQI reading is:

   a. at least 105.

   b. at most 90.

   c. between 100 and 115.

8.4 The Distribution of the Sample Proportion

There are many instances in which the variable of interest is a proportion. A manufacturer would be interested in knowing what fraction of his manufacturing components are defective. A market researcher would be interested in knowing what proportion of persons on a mailing list will buy the company's product. A college would be concerned with the fraction of freshmen that may be struggling academically after the first year. Population proportions must be estimated just like population means.

The symbols used to represent the population and sample proportions are

p, the population proportion, and

$\hat{p}$, the sample proportion.

Note: $\hat{p}$ is pronounced *p-hat*.

Determining the Sample Proportion, $\hat{p}$

Suppose you are trying to determine the fraction of manufacturing components that are defective. If you select 120 components at random and 38 components are defective, then

$$\hat{p} = \text{proportion in the sample that are defective} = \frac{38}{120} \approx .317.$$

In general, when calculating a proportion, the number in the sample that possess the characteristic of interest goes in the numerator, and the size of the sample is placed in the denominator.

Formula

The **sample proportion** is given by

$$\hat{p} = \frac{X}{n},$$

where X is the number of observations in the sample possessing the characteristic of interest and n is the total number of observations in the sample.

Sample Proportion

Just as the sample mean was a good estimate of the population mean, the sample proportion is a good estimate of the population proportion. Also, recall that the sample mean varied depending on the sample selected. The sample proportion varies in the same manner.

Since $\hat{p}$ varies, three familiar questions must be examined:

1. What is the central value?
2. What is the variability?
3. Is there a familiar pattern to the variability?

What is the Central Value of $\hat{p}$?

The expected value of the sample proportion, $\hat{p}$, is the population proportion, p. Symbolically, this is expressed as

$$E\left(\hat{p}\right) = p.$$

Since the expected value of the estimator $\hat{p}$ is equal to p, $\hat{p}$ is an unbiased estimator of p.

What is the Variability of $\hat{p}$?

Formula

Standard Deviation of the Sample Proportion

The standard deviation of $\hat{p}$ is given by

$$\sigma_{\hat{p}} = \sqrt{\frac{p(1-p)}{n}}.$$

where p is the population proportion and n is the sample size.

Note that $\sigma_{\hat{p}}$ is affected by the values of p and n.

The standard deviation of $\hat{p}$ decreases as n becomes larger. Also, the numerator reaches a maximum when $p = .5$ and declines as you move away from that figure. So for a fixed value of n, $\hat{p}$ has its greatest standard deviation when the population proportion equals .5. If the population proportion is unknown (which is usually the case), p can be estimated by $\hat{p}$, and the standard deviation of the sample proportion is estimated as

$$\sigma_{\hat{p}} \approx \sqrt{\frac{\hat{p}(1-\hat{p})}{n}}.$$

The sampling distribution of $\hat{p}$ approaches normality as n becomes sufficiently large. The sample size is generally considered "sufficiently large" if $np \geq 5$ and $n(1-p) \geq 5$.

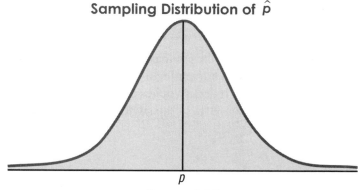

Sampling Distribution of $\hat{p}$

p

Figure 8.13

The sampling distribution of $\hat{p}$ is summarized below, for both finite and infinite populations.

Properties

If the population is infinite and the sample is sufficiently large $(np \geq 5$ and $n(1-p) \geq 5)$, the distribution of $\hat{p}$ has the following characteristics:

1. An approximately normal distribution.
2. $\mu_{\hat{p}} = E\left(\hat{p}\right) = p$. (The mean of the sample proportions equals the population proportion.)
3. $\sigma_{\hat{p}} = \sqrt{\dfrac{p(1-p)}{n}} \approx \sqrt{\dfrac{\hat{p}(1-\hat{p})}{n}}$.

If the population is finite and the sample is sufficiently large, the distribution of $\hat{p}$ has the following characteristics:

1. An approximately normal distribution.
2. $\mu_{\hat{p}} = E\left(\hat{p}\right) = p$.
3. $\sigma_{\hat{p}} = \sqrt{\dfrac{N-n}{N-1}} \cdot \sqrt{\dfrac{p(1-p)}{n}} \approx \sqrt{\dfrac{N-n}{N-1}} \cdot \sqrt{\dfrac{\hat{p}(1-\hat{p})}{n}}$, where N is the size of the population.

Sampling Distribution of the Sample Proportion

Since $\hat{p}$ is a good estimator of p, one of the natural questions to ask is, can limits be established for the error of estimation? Since the sampling distribution of $\hat{p}$ is known, probabilities for various errors of estimation can be determined.

Example 8.5

A series of tests conducted by the company Switches, We Got'em indicates that a particular type of switch manufactured by the company will operate correctly 95% of the time. If 400 switches are selected at random, what is the probability that less than 90% of the switches will operate correctly?

Solution

The information given in the problem is summarized below.

$$p = P\text{ (switch operates correctly)} = .95$$

$$n = 400$$

We want to determine the probability that less than 90% of the switches in the sample will operate correctly. This translates to $P\left(\hat{p} < .90\right)$. Since $np = 400(.95) = 380 \geq 5$ and $n(1-p) = 400(.05) = 20 \geq 5$, the sample size is sufficiently large and we can assume that the sample proportion is approximately normally distributed with $\mu = p = .95$ and

$$\sigma = \sqrt{\frac{p(1-p)}{n}} = \sqrt{\frac{.95(1-.95)}{400}}.$$

Therefore,

$$P\left(\hat{p} < .90\right) = P\left(z < \frac{.90 - .95}{\sqrt{\frac{(.95)(1-.95)}{400}}}\right)$$

$$= P(z < -4.59)$$

$$\approx 0$$

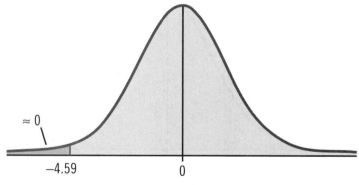

Figure 8.14

Just as in Example 8.2, almost the entire curve is above −4.59 and thus, the probability that $\hat{p} < .90$ is approximately 0.

With the information we have developed thus far, we can begin to draw conclusions (i.e. make inferences about the population proportion). If it is true that this particular type of switch works 95% of the time, then it is extremely unlikely that we would observe a sample proportion of less than 90% in a sample of 400 switches.

Example 8.6

Suppose a sample of 400 persons is used to perform a taste test. If the true proportion of the population that prefers Pepsi is .5, what is the probability that less than 44% of the persons in the sample will prefer Pepsi?

Solution

Assume the population from which the sample is drawn is extremely large and the finite population correction factor is not applicable. The distribution of $\hat{p}$ would then be normal with $\mu = E\left(\hat{p}\right) = p = .5$ and

$$\sigma_{\hat{p}} = \sqrt{\frac{(.5)(1-.5)}{400}} = .025.$$

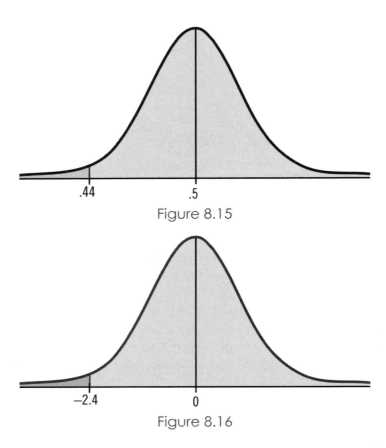

Figure 8.15

Figure 8.16

The probability that the sample proportion is less than .44 is given by

$$P\left(\hat{p} < .44\right) = P\left(z < \frac{(.44 - .5)}{.025}\right)$$
$$= P(z < -2.4) = .0082.$$

If the true proportion of people in the population who prefer Pepsi is .5, it is extremely unlikely (.0082 is less than 1 in 100) to observe a sample proportion as low as .44. Suppose that you had to make a decision as to whether cola drinkers were indifferent between Pepsi and Coke. If they were indifferent, the proportion who prefer Pepsi should be around .5. If you used a sample of 400 people and observed a sample proportion of .438 that preferred Pepsi, which of the conclusions would you believe?

Conclusion A: Cola drinkers are indifferent between Pepsi and Coke. Stated another way, the proportion of persons that favor Pepsi is about .5.

Conclusion B: Cola drinkers are not indifferent between Pepsi and Coke. In other words, people prefer one brand of cola over the other.

The likelihood of observing a sample with $\hat{p}$ less than .44 is very rare (.0082) given that the true proportion who prefer Pepsi is $p = .5$. Most people would doubt Conclusion A, and select Conclusion B. The decision-making problem given above is really a statistical inference problem. Although the procedure for analyzing inference problems will be presented in a subsequent chapter, the problem illustrates the connection between probability and inference. To reach a decision (make the inference) we used the fact that if the true proportion is really .5, a proportion below .44 is highly improbable for a sample of 400.

Example 8.7

Suppose a sample of 400 is used to estimate the proportion of U.S. citizens over 18 that favor expanding government regulation of major financial institutions. If the proportion that favors expanding government regulation is really .6, what is the probability that the error of estimation will be less than five percent?

Solution

Since the true value of the population proportion is .6, the value of $\hat{p}$ must fall between .55 and .65 in order for the error of estimation to be less than .05.

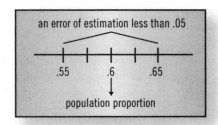

Figure 8.17

In order to determine the probability that $\hat{p}$ will fall in this interval, its distribution must be determined. Since the distribution of $\hat{p}$ is approximately normal for large samples $\left(np \geq 5 \text{ and } n(1-p) \geq 5\right)$, the distribution of $\hat{p}$ will be approximately normal with

$$\mu_{\hat{p}} = p = .6$$

$$\sigma_{\hat{p}} = \sqrt{\frac{\hat{p}\left(1-\hat{p}\right)}{n}} = \sqrt{\frac{.6(1-.6)}{400}} \approx .0245.$$

To find the probability that $\hat{p}$ is within .05 of the true proportion, we must find $P\left(p - .05 < \hat{p} < p + .05\right) = P\left(.55 < \hat{p} < .65\right).$

The Distribution of $\hat{p}$

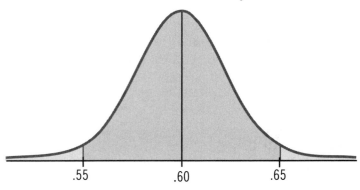

Figure 8.18

Using the z-transformation,

z-Distribution

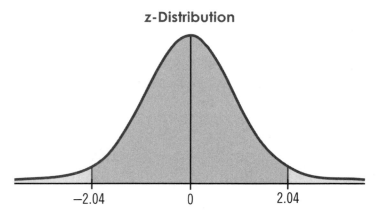

Figure 8.19

$$= P\left(\frac{.55 - .6}{.0245} < z < \frac{.65 - .6}{.0245}\right)$$
$$= P(-2.04 < z < 2.04)$$
$$= P(z < 2.04) - P(z < -2.04)$$
$$= .9793 - .0207$$
$$= .9586.$$

Therefore, for a sample of 400 U.S. citizens over 18 years of age, it is highly likely (.9586) that the error of estimation will be less than five percent.

8.4 Exercises

Basic Concepts

1. What does the symbol $\hat{p}$ represent?

2. What is the connection between $\hat{p}$ and p?

3. Is $\hat{p}$ an unbiased estimator? If so, of what?

4. What are the conditions that make the sample size n "sufficiently large" for a sample proportion?

5. What is the distribution of $\hat{p}$ if n is large?

Exercises

1. A random sample of 40 electronic components has 5 defective components.

    a. Find the sample proportion of components which are defective.

    b. Find the sample proportion of components which are not defective.

2. A random sample of 100 employees of a large steel company has 30 females and 70 males.

    a. Find the sample proportion of female employees.

    b. Find the sample proportion of male employees.

3. Suppose that the true proportion of registered voters who favor the Republican presidential candidate is .45. Find the mean and standard deviation of the sample proportion for samples of the following sizes.

    a. $n = 30$

    b. $n = 45$

    c. $n = 65$

    d. What happens to the size of the standard deviation of the sample proportion as the sample size increases?

4. Suppose that the true proportion of Americans over 25 years old that have a 4 year college degree is .35. Find the mean and the standard deviation of the sample proportion for samples of the following sizes.

    a. $n = 38$

    b. $n = 52$

    c. $n = 75$

    d. What happens to the size of the standard deviation of the sample proportion as the sample size increases?

5. Suppose the true population proportion, $p = .50$. What is the probability that the sample proportion of a sample of size 20 will be greater than .60?

6. Suppose the true population proportion, $p = .30$. What is the probability that the sample proportion of a sample of size 30 will be less than .20?

7. Suppose that the true proportion of Americans who save at least 10% of their income is .15. If $\hat{p}$ is the sample proportion of Americans surveyed who save at least 10% of their income from a sample of size 38, find the following probabilities.

    a. $P\left(\hat{p} > .25\right)$

    b. $P\left(\hat{p} < .09\right)$

    c. $P\left(.10 < \hat{p} < .20\right)$

    d. $P\left(.18 < \hat{p} < .25\right)$

8. Suppose that the true proportion of airline pilots between the ages of 35 and 45 is .60. If $\hat{p}$ is the sample proportion of airline pilots between the ages of 35 and 45 from a sample of size 100, find the following probabilities.

    a. $P\left(\hat{p} > .55\right)$

    b. $P\left(\hat{p} < .45\right)$

    c. $P\left(.50 < \hat{p} < .60\right)$

    d. $P\left(.60 < \hat{p} < .75\right)$

9. The director of a radio station in a large metropolitan area believes that the proportion of young professionals (his target market) in the area who prefer rock 'n' roll music has increased from 25% to 35%. The director randomly decides to select 50 young professionals and ask them if they prefer rock 'n' roll to any other type of music. If the sample proportion is greater than .35, he will switch to a new format emphasizing rock 'n' roll.

    a. If the true proportion of young professionals who prefer rock 'n' roll has not changed, find the probability that the radio director will switch to the new format.

    b. If the true proportion of young professionals who prefer rock 'n' roll has changed as the director suspects, find the probability that the radio director will switch to the new format.

10. The property manager of a large office building would like to make the building smoke free; however, he does not want to upset too many of his customers. He decides to randomly select 50 of the workers in the building and ask them whether or not they smoke. If the sample proportion of workers who smoke is less than .30, the property manager will make the building smoke free.

    a. Find the probability that the property manager will make the building smoke free when the true proportion of smokers is .5.

    b. Find the probability that the property manager will not make the building smoke free when the true proportion of smokers is .2.

11. Eighty percent of the flights arriving in Atlanta for a large U.S. airline are on time. If the FAA randomly selects 50 of the airline's flights, find the following probabilities.

    a. Find the probability that at least 85% of the sampled flights will be on time.

    b. Find the probability that at most 70% of the sampled flights will be on time.

    c. Find the probability that between 75% and 85% of the sampled flights will be on time.

12. Approximately 7% of the nation's public school children in grades 2 through 5 took medication in 2003 for attention deficit hyperactivity disorder (ADHD), a developmental disorder characterized by impulsiveness or difficulty concentrating or sitting still. The main treatment prescribed for ADHD is Ritalin, a relatively safe drug with few side effects. Assume that a suburban elementary school had an enrollment of 286 students in 2003.

    a. Find the probability that at least 4% of the school children took medication for ADHD.

    b. Find the probability that between 5% and 8% of the school children took medication for ADHD.

8.5 Other Forms of Sampling

Random sampling is an effective means of obtaining a sample that is representative of the population. As we discussed previously, acquiring an exact sampling frame for the population under consideration is a requirement for simple random sampling, a requirement which can be time-consuming and expensive. There are other sampling strategies that are designed to reduce the cost of sampling or add control to the sampling procedure. These techniques can be categorized as probability samples or non-probability samples.

Probability samples enable an analyst to determine the probable errors that an estimator might generate. Essentially, they allow the analyst a known degree of confidence in their estimation. All of statistical inference relies on probability sampling. **Non-probability samples** are convenient means of obtaining sample data. If data from a non-probability sample are used to estimate a population parameter, there is no statistical theory that helps define the potential error of the estimate, and hence no statement about the estimate's reliability can be made.

Non-Probability Samples

Non-probability samples come in several forms. A **judgment sample** is a sample in which sample values are selected by an expert in the field. One of the common uses of judgment samples is in auditing. When auditing a company's accounts receivables, an auditor may use a judgment sample to verify the accounts outstanding. The quality of the sample data is related to the competence of the expert. If the expert is good at what he or she does, this type of sampling can produce reasonable representations of the population and correspondingly good estimates of the population parameters.

Another type of non-probability sample is the **convenience sample**. As the name implies, a convenience sample is nothing more than a convenient group of observations. For example, the students in your statistics class would be a convenience sample of students at your college. Although convenience samples could be representative of the population, they tend to possess more bias than other forms of sampling. Consider your statistics class. It is likely that the class is dominated by some particular group of majors and has a disproportionate number of sophomores and juniors. Despite their shortcomings, convenience samples are convenient, and certainly a convenient sample is often better than no sample at all. There are two disadvantages to using a convenience sample. First, it's difficult to determine how representative the sample is of the population, or if it is representative at all. Secondly, even though the convenience sample may not be representative of the population, statistical methods are often applied. Since it's not a probability sample, the results will lack validity and are questionable.

Convenience Sampling

Figure 8.20

The worst forms of non-probability samples are voluntary or self-selected samples. Those samples were discussed in Section 8.1.

Systematic Sampling

One type of sampling technique, the **systematic sample**, does not belong to the probability or non-probability sample categories.

Definition

Systematic sampling involves including every k^{th} member of the population in the sample.

Systematic Sampling

Systematic Sampling

Figure 8.21

For example, suppose a sample of 1000 names is to be selected from a mailing list that contains 80,000 names. If every 80th person in the mailing list is selected for inclusion in the sample, the result will be a sample of 1000 names. If the names are in random order, then the systematic sample will produce a random sample. Unfortunately, it is difficult to be sure that the list does not possess some pattern that would bias the sample. Still systematic samples are regularly used in sampling mailing lists. They are also used in controlling production quality. Production-oriented quality control plans frequently call for the inspection (sample) of every k^{th} item on an assembly line. Conceptually, inspection of every k^{th} item is no different from sampling every k^{th} item from a mailing list. A sample using this technique is often called an "almost random sample."

Systematic samples are generally good samples. But if there is some pattern in the sampling frame that corresponds to the sampling pattern, an unrepresentative sample can result. For example, suppose you wished to sample a list containing total daily sales. If you sampled every 7th item, the result would be a sample that contained sales from only one day of the week.

Cluster Sampling

Although simple random sampling may be feasible, the traveling cost required to obtain the sample information may be prohibitive. Suppose McDonald's wishes to perform quality control inspection on its franchises. If a random sample of 500 is drawn from the 31,000 McDonald's scattered throughout the world, the quality inspection team could be in for quite a bit of traveling. Instead of selecting the stores individually, suppose we divide the world into 200 regions. Then we could select 20 of these regions and inspect every store in the region. This technique is called **cluster sampling**. Using this technique, an inspector would be required to travel much less and a substantial reduction in cost would result.

Clusters are not always geographic. Suppose you were interested in soliciting student opinion regarding book store prices. If everyone in the college had a 9:00 AM class, one reasonable method of clustering would be to use each class as a cluster. Randomly select a set of clusters (classes) and interview each member of the selected cluster. The selection of clusters depends greatly on the population and variables of interest.

Cluster Sampling

Definition

Cluster Sampling involves dividing the population into clusters, and randomly selecting a sample of clusters to represent the population.

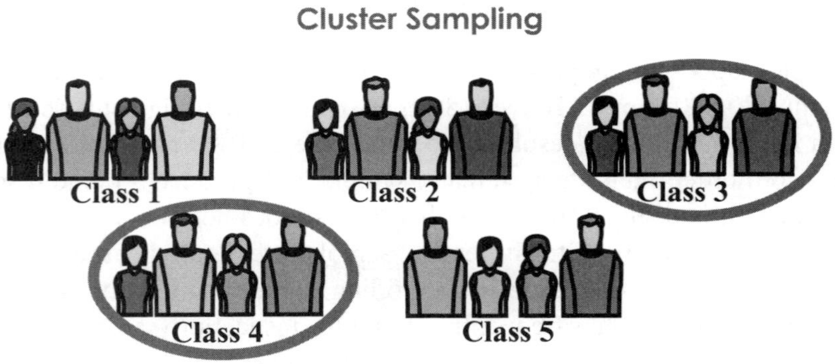

Cluster Sampling

Figure 8.22

Cluster sampling can be as effective as simple random sampling if the clusters are as heterogeneous as the population. Unfortunately clusters are almost never as diverse as the population. If the clusters are geographic, people in the same geographic area tend to be less diverse than the population. If the clusters are not heterogeneous, cluster sampling is less efficient than simple random sampling for a given sample size. Generally, smaller cluster sizes will result in more representative samples.

In simple random sampling, constructing the sampling frame is frequently cumbersome. Cluster sampling simplifies the task, since the initial frame is composed only of clusters. Only those clusters selected as part of the sample must be completely enumerated and sampled.

Cluster sampling is a good alternative to simple random sampling when the population's geographic area is spread out over a large area or when the sampling frame for a simple random sample is difficult to construct.

Stratified Sampling

The fundamental goal of sampling is to obtain a sample that is representative of the population. *Representative* means that characteristics of the population are proportionally represented in the sample. For example, if a population contained 60% females and 30% with blood type A, then it would be desirable for the sample to have 60% females and 30% with blood type A. Simple random samples make no guarantees regarding the constituency of the sample. If a random sample could be taken such that it was assured that population characteristics were properly represented, the resulting samples would tend to be more representative of the population. This is precisely the objective of **stratified sampling**.

Definition

In **stratified sampling**, the population is divided into strata, which are sub-populations. A stratum can be any identifiable characteristic that can be used to classify the population. If the population consists of people, then strata could be sex, income, political party, religion, education, race, and location.

Stratified Sampling

Stratified Sampling

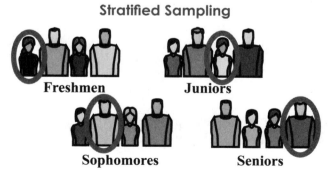

Figure 8.23

Suppose you wished to estimate the average profit of companies on the New York Stock Exchange (NYSE). Given that all companies are not the same size, it would be best to stratify the companies by some characteristic such as market cap or number of employees. For example, if companies were classified in intervals based on market cap, stratification would mean that a fixed percentage of the companies would come from each interval (stratum), thus, giving us a representative sample of the population of companies on the NYSE. The mean and standard deviation from each stratum would be calculated separately and combined to form an estimate of the population parameters. The standard deviation of each subgroup should be smaller than the standard deviation of the population. When these standard deviations are combined to form an estimate of the population standard deviation, the resulting standard deviation will be smaller than if a simple random sample had been used.

In summary, stratified sampling can provide greater accuracy if the population is heterogeneous, and sub-populations of the population can be identified that are relatively homogeneous.

 **Exercises**

Basic Concepts

1. What are advantages and disadvantages of non-probability samples?

2. What is a judgment sample? Give an example of when a judgment sample would be appropriate.

3. What is a convenience sample? Are these samples usually representative of the population?

4. What are the worst forms of non-probability samples?

5. Explain the idea of systematic sampling. What are the advantages and disadvantages of this sampling procedure?

6. Explain the idea of cluster sampling. What are the advantages and disadvantages of this sampling procedure?

7. Explain the idea of stratified sampling. What are the advantages and disadvantages of this sampling procedure?

Exercises

1. An employee owned company has 6000 female employees and 2000 male employees. The personnel department decides to develop a survey on several different benefit plans, including child care and retirement benefits, they may offer employees in the future. The results of the survey are to be presented to the board of directors for consideration. Because the personnel department wants to be sure of equal representation of the sexes, it has decided to randomly select 500 females and 500 males. What kind of sampling method is the personnel department using? If the sample is used to make inferences regarding the desirability of various benefits package for all employees, discuss any deficiencies in the sampling procedure.

2. Explain why a systematic sample is not a random sample.

3. Suppose you were instructed to draw a simple random sample from a metropolitan area in order to gain information on the citizens' view on a proposed amendment to the state constitution. To create a simple random sample, you must create a sampling frame. You have decided to use the telephone directory as your frame for the metropolitan area.

   a. Identify the population under consideration.

   b. What kinds of people will be omitted from your frame?

   c. What kinds of biases will be introduced in your sample as a consequence of the omission you described in part (b)? Can you think of ways of compensating for the bias?

4. A social researcher in Florida wants to determine the average number of children per family in the state.

   a. What is the population of interest?

   b. What variable will be measured?

   c. What level of measurement is the variable of interest?

   d. Discuss the steps that would be necessary for each of the following sampling methods:

      i. Simple random sampling

      ii. Cluster sampling

      iii. Stratified sampling

   e. What sampling method do you believe would be the most cost effective?

5. A stock analyst wants to estimate the average yearly earnings of stocks on the New York Stock Exchange.

   a. What is the population of interest?

   b. Discuss the steps necessary to apply each of the following sampling methods:

      i. Simple random sampling

      ii. Cluster sampling

      iii. Stratified sampling

6. A news reporter in Orlando, Florida wants to conduct a survey to determine how local residents feel about the institution of a state income tax. Since there will be a lot of people from which to choose, he goes to Disney World and randomly selects individuals entering the complex. He asks the selected people whether or not they favor a state income tax in Florida. The responses to the survey are as follows:

Table for Exercise 6 – Survey Responses	
Category	% of Responses
Favor a Florida State Income Tax	50
Do Not Favor a Florida State Income Tax	50

   a. What type of sampling technique was used for this survey?

   b. What type of biases may be present in the responses?

   c. Is 50% a reasonable point estimate of the proportion of Orlando residents who favor the state income tax? Explain.

 **Discovering Technology**

USING THE TI-84 PLUS CALCULATOR

Random Samples

Select a simple random sample of 20 customer accounts from a sampling frame that contains 897 accounts.

Choose **MATH**, then select **PRB** and option **5:randInt.** Press **ENTER**, and then input the (minimum number, maximum number, random numbers desired), in this case **(1, 897, 20)**. Press **ENTER**, and the random numbers are listed on the screen.

Figure 8.24

USING EXCEL

Random Samples

Select a simple random sample of 20 customer accounts from a sampling frame that contains 897 accounts.

1. Click on cell A1.

2. The function in Microsoft Excel for generating a random number in a certain range is

$$\text{RANDBETWEEN(bottom,top)}$$

where *bottom* is the lower limit of the sampling frame and *top* is the upper limit of the sampling frame.

3. In cell A1 enter the function with the parameters for this problem:

$$\text{=RANDBETWEEN(1,897).}$$

Press **Enter**. A random customer account has been chosen.

4. Place the cursor over the bottom right-hand corner of cell A1, click and drag the box down to cell A20. Twenty random numbers are shown in those cells.

	A
1	757
2	97
3	133
4	353
5	680
6	661
7	897
8	551
9	441
10	323
11	136
12	716
13	264
14	512
15	199
16	39
17	789
18	698
19	433
20	382

Figure 8.25

USING MINITAB

Random Samples

Select a random sample of 20 customer accounts from a sampling frame that contains 897 accounts.

1. Press **Calc**, select "Random Data", and then choose **Integer**.

2. Complete the dialog box (Figure 8.26) with **20** for "Number of rows of data to generate", **C1** for "Store in column", **1** for "Minimum value", and **897** for "Maximum value". Press **OK**.

3. Observe the 20 random numbers in column C1.

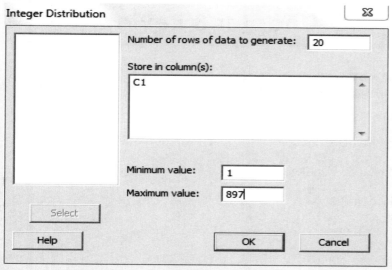

Figure 8.26

↓	C1
1	595
2	240
3	5
4	841
5	889
6	456
7	574
8	255
9	183
10	328
11	886
12	548
13	756
14	77
15	400
16	516
17	500
18	603
19	657
20	790

Figure 8.27

Chapter 8 Review

Key Terms and Ideas

- Sampling
- Sampling Distribution
- Voluntary Sampling
- Selection Bias
- Biased Sample
- Sampling Frame
- Simple Random Sample
- Random Number Table
- Sampling Distribution of the Sample Mean
- Unbiased Estimator
- Standard Error of the Mean
- Central Limit Theorem
- Population Proportion
- Sample Proportion
- Sampling Distribution of the Sample Proportion
- Error of Estimation
- Probability Samples
- Non-Probability Samples
- Judgment Sample
- Convenience Sample
- Systematic Sampling
- Cluster Sampling
- Stratified Sampling

Key Formulas

Concept	Formula	Section
Standard Deviation of the Sample Mean: Infinite Population	$$\sigma_{\bar{x}} = \frac{\sigma}{\sqrt{n}}$$ where σ is the population standard deviation and n is the sample size.	8.3
Standard Deviation of the Sample Mean: Finite Population	$$\sigma_{\bar{x}} = \sqrt{\frac{N-n}{N-1}} \cdot \frac{\sigma}{\sqrt{n}}$$ where N = the size of the population and n = the size of the sample.	8.3
Characteristics of the Sample Mean	1. $E(\bar{x}) = \mu$ 2. $\sigma_{\bar{x}} = \frac{\sigma}{\sqrt{n}}$	8.3
Central Limit Theorem	If a sufficiently large random sample $(n \geq 30)$ is drawn from a population with mean μ and standard deviation σ, the distribution of the sample mean will have the following characteristics: 1. An approximately normal distribution regardless of the distribution of the underlying population. 2. $\mu_{\bar{x}} = E(\bar{x}) = \mu$ 3. $\sigma_{\bar{x}} = \frac{\sigma}{\sqrt{n}}$	8.4
Sample Proportion	$$\hat{p} = \frac{X}{n}$$ where X is the number of observations in the sample possessing the characteristic of interest and n is the total number of observations in the sample.	8.4
Standard Deviation of the Sample Proportion: Infinite Population	$$\sigma_{\hat{p}} = \sqrt{\frac{p(1-p)}{n}} \approx \sqrt{\frac{\hat{p}(1-\hat{p})}{n}}$$ where p is the population proportion and n is the sample size.	8.4
Standard Deviation of the Sample Proportion: Finite Population	$$\sigma_{\hat{p}} = \sqrt{\frac{N-n}{N-1}} \cdot \sqrt{\frac{p(1-p)}{n}} \approx \sqrt{\frac{N-n}{N-1}} \cdot \sqrt{\frac{\hat{p}(1-\hat{p})}{n}}$$ where N is the size of the population.	8.4

8

 **Additional Exercises**

1. A national news network is interested in the opinion which Americans have regarding a national healthcare policy. During the evening news they display a 900 telephone number and ask their viewers to call in and respond to the question: *Do you favor a national healthcare policy in the U.S.?*

Table for Exercise 1 – Survey Responses	
Category	% of Responses
Yes	45
No	45
Do not have enough information to decide	10

   a. What type of sampling technique was used for this survey?

   b. What types of biases may be present in the responses?

   c. Is 45% a reasonable estimate of the proportion of all Americans who favor a national healthcare policy? Explain.

2. An entrepreneur wants to open a new Indian restaurant in a resort community. To determine if there is a market for the new restaurant, the entrepreneur decides to conduct a survey.

   a. What is the population of interest to the entrepreneur?

   b. Can you think of any good sources for a sampling frame?

   c. What are the shortcomings (if any) of the sources you picked for the sampling frame?

3. A paint manufacturer is developing a new type of paint. Test panels were exposed to various corrosive conditions to measure the protective ability of the paint. Based on the results of the test, the manufacturer has concluded that the mean life before corrosive failure for the new paint is 168 hours with a standard deviation of 30 hours. If the manufacturer's conclusions are correct, find the probability that the paint on a sample of 60 test panels will have a mean life before corrosive failure of less than 150 hours.

4. Seventy-five percent of the students graduating from high school in a small Iowa farm town attend college. The town's Chamber of Commerce randomly selects 30 recent graduates and determines whether or not they will attend college.

   a. Find the probability that at least 80% of the surveyed students will be attending college.

   b. Find the probability that at most 70% of the surveyed students will be attending college.

   c. Find the probability that between 65% and 85% of the surveyed students will be attending college.

5. A biology professor is interested in the proportion of students at his college who are pre-med majors. In his next class he asks for the students who are pre-med majors to raise their hands. Fifty percent of the students raised their hands.

   a. What type of sampling technique was used for this survey?

   b. What types of biases may be present in the responses?

   c. Is 50% a reasonable point estimate of the proportion of students at the college who are pre-med majors? Explain.

6. A report released by the U.S. Census Bureau in November of 2001 stated that fewer families fit the traditional family makeup in 2000 as compared with 1970. The report stated that in 1970, 5.6 million families were headed by women with no husband present, and 16.6% of the households consisted of people living alone. In 2000 these figures increased to 16.2 million and 26.7% respectively. The report also stated that in 1970, 40% of the households consisted of married couples with no children while in the year 2000 this decreased to 25%. Suppose that a random sample of 150 households is chosen in 2000 and the percent of these that consist of people living alone is determined.

   a. Find the probability that at least 30% of those households sampled consist of people living alone.

   b. Find the probability that at most 28% of those sampled households consist of people living alone.

   c. Find the probability that between 26% and 36% of those households consist of people living alone.

7. It is known that the percentage return for a group of stocks in the technology sector is normally distributed with a mean of 15 percent and a standard deviation of 22 percent. Suppose you selected a random sample of 10 stocks from this sector.

   a. What is the mean and standard deviation of $\bar{x}$?

   b. Find the interval containing 68.26% of all possible sample mean returns.

8. A restaurant wants to determine the average time to prepare meals for its customers. To aid in this process, the restaurant randomly selects the meal preparation time of 150 of its customers and finds that the average preparation time is 18 minutes with a standard deviation of eight minutes. Describe the distribution of the sample mean of preparation time for its customers.

9. With such a large number of people using text messages as a means of communication, a company is interested in determining the number of work hours lost due to text messaging. Based on a survey of 30 randomly selected employees (anonymously, of course), the company has determined that the average amount of time spent texting over a one-month period is 180 minutes with a standard deviation of 60 minutes.

   a. What is the probability that the average amount of time spent using text messages is more than 210 minutes in this one-month period?

   b. Thinking that it's practically impossible for her employees to spend, on average, three hours a month texting while at work, the manager conducts another survey. She randomly samples 45 employees and finds that the average amount of time spent texting while at work over a one-month period is less than 180 minutes. Is it reasonable to conclude that the average amount of time spent using text messaging has decreased since the initial survey? Justify your answer.

10. Suppose that a random sample of size 64 was selected and found that the mean was 30 and the standard deviation was 4.

   a. What is the probability that the sample mean is more than 31.25?

   b. What assumptions were made in part (a)?

11. A town is considering building a high school football stadium approximately one-half mile from a well-established housing development. The residents of the development opposed the stadium construction due to the noise coming from the stadium during games. In presenting their argument, the residents indicated that any noise more than 103 decibels would be unacceptable. Using a sample of 35 games previously played in the old arena, the town found that the average decibels were 100 with a standard deviation of eight decibels.

   a. What is the probability that a randomly selected game will generate noise in excess of the 103 decibels at the stadium?

   b. What is the probability that a randomly selected game will generate a noise level of exactly 103 decibels?

   c. Suppose a compromise was made that required the noise level to be lower than 103 decibels 95% of the time. Will the mean level of the noise have to be lowered to comply with the new regulation? If so, by how much? Assume that the standard deviation remains at eight decibels.

12. The town manager believes that 60% of the residents will approve the construction of the proposed high school football stadium. A random sample of 100 residents will be used to estimate the proportion of residents that will approve the construction.

    a. Assuming that the town manager is correct and that $p = 6$ what is the sampling distribution of $\hat{p}$?

    b. What is the probability that between 50% and 70% of the residents will approve the stadium construction?

13. It is believed that 90% of all adults and 85% of all kids between the ages of 12 and 17 have cellular phones. Suppose a sample of 500 adults and 400 kids was taken.

    a. Describe the sampling distribution of the proportion of adults that have cellular phones. Assume that the stated probabilities above are true.

    b. Describe the sampling distribution of the proportion of kids that have cellular phones. Assume that the stated probabilities above are true.

    c. What is the probability that the sample proportion of adults having cell phones will be within 2% of the true proportion?

    d. What is the probability that the sample proportion of kids having cell phones will be within 4% of the true proportion?

14. A survey of college students was conducted to learn about their attitudes toward alcohol abuse on college campuses. Sixty-two percent of student respondents indicated that they believe there was a high rate of alcohol abuse on college campuses. Suppose that a sample of 250 college students was taken. What is the probability that more than seventy percent believed that there was a high rate of alcohol abuse on college campuses?

15. A credit card issuer believes that 75% of college students between the ages of 18 and 22 years old have more than $5000 of credit card debt. The credit card issuer conducted a survey of 500 college students between the ages of 18 and 22.

    a. What is the probability that at least 70% of college students between the ages of 18 and 22 have credit card debt in excess of $5000?

    b. Assuming that the credit card issuer is correct, what is the probability that the proportion will be within three percent of the population proportion?

16. A marketing firm conducts a survey by mail with a 20% response rate. If the firm mailed 1000 surveys for a new study, what is the probability that at least 220 individuals will respond?

Discovery Project

Pick an industry (software companies, computer manufacturers, oil, etc.) and research the financial information about companies in that industry. The Internet, your library, the prospectus from the companies, etc., may be useful resources to help you with your research. Also, select a statistic to track or follow about the companies such as sales, profit, revenue, etc. Using the information that you gather about the companies, answer the following questions.

1. Identify the population of interest.

2. Select a random sample of 10 companies in the industry that you've selected and record the variable of interest for each of the companies.

3. Compute the average and standard error of the variable of interest.

4. What is the error of estimation using the 10 companies selected?

5. Discuss what you have learned about statistics and companies in your population.

Estimating Means and Proportions: Single Samples

9

 **Discovering the Real World**

Each year, the U.S. Bureau of Labor Statistics (BLS) makes forecasts on travel. They forecast the times when people will travel the most, the lengths of the vacations, the method of transportation, and many other factors that interest travelers and the travel industry. The travel industry depends on travelers to support its businesses, and travelers rely on the travel industry to provide them with services such as transportation, lodging, food and beverage, and entertainment. Businesses rely on forecasts from the BLS to give them insight on travel-related expenditures, employment expectations within the industry, and earnings of various travel-related occupations. Of course, regardless of which branch of the government (or other entity in the travel industry) is making the predictions, these forecasts are evaluated based on their validity and reliability.

In 2008, U.S. households spent, on average, a total of $1415 on transportation, lodging, food and beverage, entertainment, and gifts while on vacation. This dollar amount represents three percent of total household expenditures. The largest travel expense was transportation, which represented 44 percent of the total amount spent. Households spent the least amount on the most discretionary travel-related expense, entertainment, which represented 10 percent of all travel-related expenses. **Source:** U.S. Bureau of Labor Statistics

The estimates provided by the BLS are viewed as the "best possible" information available. That is, they don't know the true population mean amount that households spend on travel. However, they took a random sample of households that vacationed and estimated the mean from that sample. These forecasts (or estimates) can be later validated when the actual outcomes become available, giving the analysts an idea of the accuracy of their predictions.

Many estimates are *subjective*; that is, a person with experience in the field estimates an unknown population value. If the expert is experienced with the population or process, then formal statistical methods may add very little quality to the resulting forecast. These types of predictions are called **judgment estimates**.

The problem with judgment estimates is that their degree of accuracy or reliability cannot be determined. If a decision has important consequences, standard statistical methods should be applied, especially if there is no expert to rely upon. Even if an expert is available, statistics can offer estimates with known reliability. In this chapter, we will discuss estimation techniques to estimate the population mean, standard deviation, and population proportion.

Introduction

The importance of the statistical measures to a decision-making process depends on the confidence the decision maker has in the estimated values. How much faith can be placed in the accuracy of the estimate? Statistical inference permits the estimation of statistical measures (means, proportions, etc.) with a known degree of confidence. This ability to assess the quality of estimates is one of the significant benefits statistics brings to decision making and problem solving.

Applications of statistics are usually concerned with learning about populations or processes. Populations are described using summary measures called parameters, such as the mean, the standard deviation, and the proportion. Processes are also described with summary measures and with various models. Unfortunately, determining the exact mean and standard deviation of a population is seldom an easy task and often is not feasible. Statistical methods rely upon samples of the population to obtain information about the population's parameters. Whether the sample data will produce reliable information about a process or population depends on the methods used to collect the data.

Definition

Using properly drawn sample data to draw conclusions about the population is called **statistical inference**.

Statistical Inference

The previous chapter concentrated on sampling and how the practice of drawing samples produces a statistic (e.g. the sample mean) that is a random variable. This chapter marks the beginning of statistical inference. It discusses the properties of sample summary statistics (sample means, sample proportions, etc.) as well as methods for assessing the reliability of those estimates.

All forms of statistical inference are tarnished with a degree of uncertainty. If samples are selected randomly, the uncertainty of the inference is measurable. Drawing random samples allows us to measure the level of confidence associated with an estimate. If samples are not selected randomly, there will be no known relationship between the sample estimates and the population parameters they purport to estimate. Henceforth, if a statistical technique requires a sample, assume the sample will be a random sample from a population or process.

This chapter is devoted to the one-sample problem. That is, a sample consisting of n measurements, $x_1, x_2, ..., x_n$, of some population will be analyzed with the objective of making inferences about the population. Inference will be introduced with the one-sample problem, not because it is the most common, but because the procedures and basic principles of inference are easier to understand.

9.1   What is an Estimator?

What is meant by the terms **estimator** and **estimate**?

Estimator

> ### Definition
>
> An **estimator** is a strategy or rule that is used to estimate a population parameter. If the rule is applied to a specific set of data, the result is an **estimate**.

The sample mean is an *estimator* of the population mean. A specific sample mean, $\bar{x}$, such as 103.4, is an *estimate* of the population mean (μ).

In this chapter we will study two different kinds of estimators, point and interval. A **point estimator** uses a single point to estimate a population parameter. For example, $\bar{x}$ is a *point estimator* of a population mean ($\bar{x} = 12.7$ is a *point estimate* of a population mean.)

Table 9.1 – Point Estimators		
Point Estimator	**Parameter Being Estimated**	**Point Estimate**
$\bar{x}$	μ	$\bar{x} = 12.7$
$\hat{p}$	p	$\hat{p} = .37$
s	σ	$s = 6.4$

An **interval estimate** defines an upper and lower boundary for an interval that will hopefully contain the population parameter. Often times, the interval estimate for a parameter is a function of the point estimate of that parameter.

9.1 Exercises

Basic Concepts

1. What is statistical inference?

2. What is an estimator?

3. What is a judgment estimate? What are some drawbacks of judgment estimates?

4. Explain, in your own words, the difference between the terms *estimator* and *estimate*.

5. What is the difference between a point estimate and an interval estimate?

6. Give three examples of point estimators. Identify the parameters being estimated by these estimators.

7. Describe the advantages of random sampling procedures.

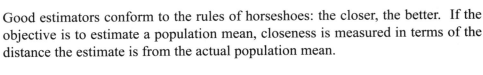

9.2 Point Estimation of the Population Mean

Like other statistical inference methods, estimation begins with the collection of data. Two important questions come to mind.

1. How should the data be used to estimate the population mean?

2. How can you tell a good estimator from a bad one?

Good estimators conform to the rules of horseshoes: the closer, the better. If the objective is to estimate a population mean, closeness is measured in terms of the distance the estimate is from the actual population mean.

One of the more puzzling questions is, *how can you judge the accuracy of your estimate without knowing the true value of the population parameter?* It's like shooting an arrow at a bull's-eye without being able to see it. If you can't see the bull's-eye, how do you know how close you are?

Mean Squared Error

> ### Definition
>
> An estimator's average squared distance from the true parameter is referred to as its **mean squared error** (MSE). The mean squared error for the sample mean is given by:
>
> $$\mathrm{MSE}(\bar{x}) = E(\bar{x} - \mu)^2.$$

A perfect estimator would have a mean squared error of zero, but there is no such thing as a perfect estimator. Since statistical estimators depend on data which is randomly drawn, estimates are random variables and will seldom be equal to the true population characteristic. The goal is to find an estimator whose average squared error is the smallest. Unfortunately, there are a number of different estimators, and without restricting the kinds of estimators that will be considered, very little progress can be made.

One desirable restriction is **unbiasedness**. As was discussed in Chapter 8, to be an unbiased estimator, the expected value of the estimator must be equal to the parameter that is being estimated. For example, $\bar{x}$ is an unbiased estimator of the population mean since

$$E(\bar{x}) = \mu.$$

Unfortunately, there are a number of estimators that are unbiased estimators of the population mean including the sample mean, sample median, or any single sample value. **Among unbiased estimators of the population mean, the sample mean**

has the smallest mean squared error. There is no other unbiased estimator that can consistently do a better job of estimating the population mean.

The fact that the sample mean is a good estimator of the population mean should not be surprising, since you would expect most sample statistics to be reasonably good estimators of their population counterparts. One of the exceptions is the sample range, which is a poor estimate of the population range. In short, the best estimate is the one that is unbiased with the smallest mean squared error.

 **Exercises**

Basic Concepts

1. What are two important questions to consider when estimating a population mean?

2. What is mean squared error?

3. What is an unbiased estimator? Give an example.

4. Why is the sample mean considered the best point estimate of the population mean?

5. Are all estimators unbiased? Explain.

6. Generally we expect most sample statistics to be good estimators of their population counterparts. Which statistic is the exception to this idea?

7. What are two characteristics of the best available estimate for a parameter?

<table>
<tr><td>**9.3**</td><td># Interval Estimation of the Population Mean</td></tr>
</table>

Rarely will a point estimate of the population mean result in a value which exactly matches the population mean, μ. In fact, the probability that a point estimate for the population mean exactly equals the population mean is zero for data drawn from continuous distributions. Yet, if an estimate is used for decision making, it is desirable that there be some indication of its potential error. One of the significant limitations of simply reporting a point estimate is the lack of information concerning the estimator's accuracy.

Interval estimates, however, are constructed to provide additional information about the precision of the estimate. An **interval estimator** is made by developing an upper and lower boundary for an interval that will hopefully contain the population parameter. It would be easy to construct an interval estimator that would always contain the population parameter: for example, the interval from negative infinity to positive infinity. But this particular estimator would not contain any useful information about the location of the population parameter. In interval estimation, the smaller the interval for a given level of confidence, the better the estimator.

The seeds of a good interval estimator for the population mean can be found in Chapter 8, which defined how $\bar{x}$ should vary. Recall that if the sample size is reasonably large ($n \geq 30$), the central limit theorem ensures that $\bar{x}$ has an approximately normal distribution with mean, μ, and standard deviation, $\dfrac{\sigma}{\sqrt{n}}$.

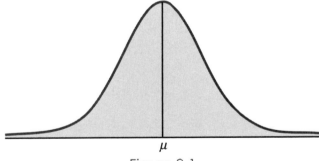

μ

Figure 9.1

The sampling distribution can be used to develop an interval estimator. For the standard normal random variable, we know that

$$P(-1.96 < z < 1.96) = .95.$$

Since $\bar{x}$ can be transformed into a standard normal random variable by using the z-transformation, $z = \dfrac{\bar{x} - \mu}{\sigma_{\bar{x}}}$, then by substitution,

$$P\left(-1.96 < \frac{\overline{x} - \mu}{\sigma_{\overline{x}}} < 1.96\right) = .95,$$

and with some algebraic manipulation we obtain

$$P\left(\overline{x} - 1.96\sigma_{\overline{x}} < \mu < \overline{x} + 1.96\sigma_{\overline{x}}\right) = .95.$$

If the sample size is greater than or equal to 30, then by the central limit theorem there is a .95 probability that the sample mean will be within 1.96 standard deviations of the population mean **before a particular sample is selected**.

Sampling Distribution of $\overline{x}$

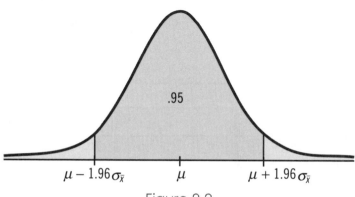

Figure 9.2

Since we discussed the sampling distribution of the sample mean in Chapter 8, the idea of defining the probability that the sample mean should fall within some specified distance of the population mean is not a new one. The expression above does suggest a specific form for the interval since it provides an interval and the associated probability that the population mean will fall within the interval:

$$\overline{x} \pm 1.96\sigma_{\overline{x}}.$$

However, the provision *before a particular sample is selected* modifies the interpretation of the interval for a specific sample. After the sample is selected, the sample mean is no longer a random variable. Suppose a sample has been drawn from a population with a standard deviation of 200, and the following characteristics have been observed:

$\sigma = 200,$ (given)

$n = 100,$ (chosen by researcher)

$\overline{x} = 150,$ (obtained from the sample)

The Father of Confidence Intervals:

Jerzy Neyman

1894 – 1981

Jerzy Neyman grew up in Poland. However, a significant part of Poland was under Russian control during his youth and Neyman received his training in mathematics in Russia.

In her book *Neyman – from Life,* Constance Reid attributes the development of the confidence interval to Jerzy Neyman. "During the years 1934-38 Neyman made four fundamental contributions to the science of statistics. Each of them would have been sufficient to establish an international reputation, both for their immediate effect and for the impetus which the new ideas and methods had on the thinking of young and old alike. He put forward the theory of confidence intervals, the importance of which in statistical theory and analysis of data cannot be overemphasized. His contribution to the theory of contagious distributions is still of great utility in the interpretation of biological data. Continued ...

... Continued
His paper on sampling
stratified populations
paved the way for
a statistical theory
which, among other
things, gave us the
Gallup poll. His work,
and that of Fisher,
each with a different
model for randomized
experiments, led to
the whole new field
of experimentation
so much used in
agriculture, biology,
medicine, and
physical sciences."

Remember,

$$\sigma_{\bar{x}} = \frac{\sigma}{\sqrt{n}} = \frac{200}{\sqrt{100}} = \frac{200}{10} = 20.$$

The resulting interval would be

$$150 \pm 1.96(20).$$

That is,

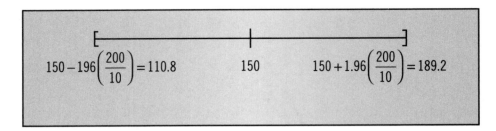

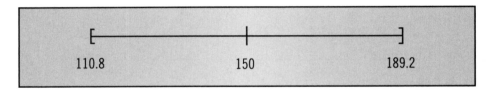

Is the population mean, μ, inside this interval? If not, what fraction of the time will μ be inside the interval? Even though the interval is calculated using a technique that captures the population mean 95% of the time, it would not be appropriate from a relative frequency point of view, to state that

$$P(110.8 < \mu < 189.2) = .95$$

since the population mean is an unknown but constant quantity. Either μ will always be inside the interval or will always be outside the interval. Then what information do we have about the interval? We say that this interval was constructed with a **confidence level** of 95% (i.e., $100(1-\alpha)\%$) or a **confidence coefficient** of .95 (i.e. $1-\alpha$). Hence, the term **confidence interval** is used to describe the method of construction rather than a particular interval.

In summary, a 95% confidence interval can be interpreted to mean that if all possible samples of a given size are taken from a population, 95% of the samples would produce intervals that captured the true population mean and 5% would not. In Figure 9.3 we have plotted, as line segments, the confidence intervals from 20 random samples. All but one of the intervals, number 5, capture the mean, μ.

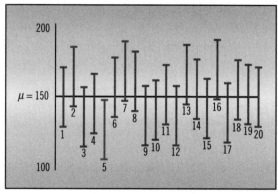

Figure 9.3

So far we have examined only the 95% confidence interval, yet the idea is a general one and can be extended to any specified degree of confidence.

In a practical sense, the selection of the degree of confidence depends upon the importance of the decision for which the confidence interval will be utilized. If we are launching a space vehicle, we would want to be very certain that the vehicle would have sufficient fuel to return safely. For other decisions, we might be willing to accept an 80% confidence of correctly estimating the population mean, especially if the cost of gathering additional data is large.

Formula

A $100(1-\alpha)\%$ **confidence interval** for the population mean is given by

$$\bar{x} \pm z_{\alpha/2} \frac{\sigma}{\sqrt{n}}$$

Confidence Interval for the Population Mean

if either of the following conditions are true:

1. $n \geq 30$ (use s as an approximation for σ), or

2. if σ is known and the population being studied is normally distributed.

The expression $\bar{x} \pm z_{\alpha/2} \frac{\sigma}{\sqrt{n}}$ creates the "generalized" confidence interval shown below.

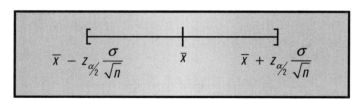

The term $z_{\alpha/2}$ represents the z-value required to obtain an area of $\alpha/2$ in the right tail under the standard normal curve. The z-values for obtaining various $(1-\alpha)$ areas centered under the standard normal curve are given in Table 9.2 and graphed in Figure 9.4.

Table 9.2	
Confidence $(1-\alpha)$	$z_{\alpha/2}$
.80	1.28
.90	1.645
.95	1.96
.99	2.575

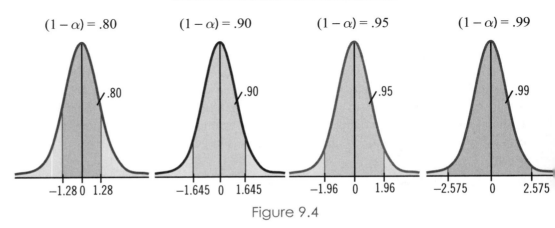

Figure 9.4

Example 9.1

Construct 80%, 90%, 95%, and 99% confidence intervals for the population mean if the standard deviation of the population is 900. Use the following sample data.

$$n = 100$$
$$\bar{x} = 425$$

Solution

80% Confidence Interval:

$$425 \pm 1.28 \cdot \frac{900}{\sqrt{100}} \quad \text{or} \quad 309.8 \text{ to } 540.2$$

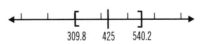

90% Confidence Interval:

$$425 \pm 1.645 \cdot \frac{900}{\sqrt{100}} \text{ or } 276.95 \text{ to } 573.05$$

276.95   425   573.05

95% Confidence Interval:

$$425 \pm 1.96 \cdot \frac{900}{\sqrt{100}} \text{ or } 248.6 \text{ to } 601.4$$

248.6   425   601.4

99% Confidence Interval:

$$425 \pm 2.575 \cdot \frac{900}{\sqrt{100}} \text{ or } 193.25 \text{ to } 656.75$$

193.25   425   656.75

The intervals in Example 9.1 illustrate that to achieve more confidence we must pay a price. For a given sample size the only way to achieve greater confidence is to widen the interval. However, the resulting information provides a less precise location of the population mean.

Example 9.2

Given the rapid rate of technological innovation, SWN Management Company wants to study the number of new products introduced by top technology firms in the United States. Suppose a random sample of 150 companies is selected and each company is asked to report the number of new products that it has introduced in the last 12 months. It is also known from past experience that the population standard deviation of the new products introduced is 7.85. The sample mean is found to be 8.56 products. Calculate a 98 percent confidence interval for the population mean number of new products introduced in the last 12 months.

Solution

From the information given above, we know that

$$n = 150 \text{ and } \sigma = 7.85.$$

Since we want a 98% confidence interval, we need to find the value of $z_{\alpha/2}$. Remember that $z_{\alpha/2}$ represents the z-value required to obtain an area of $(1-\alpha)$ centered under the standard normal curve. Therefore, for a 98% confidence interval, $\alpha = .02$.

$$\text{For } \alpha = .02,\ z_{\alpha/2} = z_{.01} = 2.33.$$

Similar to finding the values in Table 9.2 we can use Table A to find the corresponding value of z. That is, if we are to use Table A, we look up .01 in the body of the standard normal table. Since the exact value of .01 is not in the table, we use the value that is closest. In this case, we can see that 0.0099 corresponds to a z-value of -2.33. Since the standard normal is symmetrical, $z_{\alpha/2}$ capturing an area of .01 in the upper tail of the distribution will be 2.33.

A 98% confidence interval is calculated as

$$\bar{x} \pm z_{\alpha/2} \frac{\sigma}{\sqrt{n}}$$

$$8.56 \pm 2.33 \frac{7.85}{\sqrt{150}}$$

$$8.56 \pm 1.49$$

$$\text{or } 7.07 \text{ to } 10.05.$$

```
┌──────────────┼──────────────┐
7.07          8.56          10.05
```

Thus, we are 98% confident that the true mean number of new products introduced in the last 12 months will be contained in the above interval.

So far, the confidence interval has been discussed as a way of placing bounds on the location of a parameter with a specific degree of confidence. But we can also think about the confidence interval as a means of describing the quality of a point estimate. Let's look at the expression for the confidence interval for the population mean.

$$\underbrace{\bar{x}}_{\text{point estimate}} \quad \pm \quad \underbrace{z_{\alpha/2} \frac{\sigma}{\sqrt{n}}}_{\substack{\text{maximum error of} \\ \text{estimation with a} \\ \text{specific level of} \\ \text{confidence}}} \qquad \text{(confidence interval for } \mu\text{)}$$

Another interpretation of the confidence interval is given below the expression of the confidence interval for μ. The part of the expression that is added and subtracted to the point estimate, $z_{\alpha/2}\dfrac{\sigma}{\sqrt{n}}$, can be thought of as the **maximum error of estimation** (also known as the **margin of error**) using the point estimate $\bar{x}$ with a specified level of confidence. For example, the 95% confidence interval in Example 9.1 was given as

$$425 \pm 1.96 \cdot \frac{900}{\sqrt{100}}$$
$$= 425 \pm 176.4.$$

We could say that we are 95% confident that the point estimate of μ, $\bar{x} = 425$, has an error of estimation no larger than 176.4. Being able to assess the error of an estimate is one of the most useful applications of statistical methods.

 **Exercises**

Basic Concepts

1. What is an interval estimator?

2. What is the distinction between probability and confidence?

3. What is the role of the z-value in the confidence interval expression?

4. Describe in words the ideas behind the construction of a confidence interval.

5. Consider the following statement: *If the sample size is greater than 30, then by the central limit theorem there is a .95 probability that the sample mean will be within 1.96 standard deviations of the population mean before a particular sample is selected.* Explain why the phrase "before a particular sample is selected" is important here.

6. Explain what is wrong with the following expression:
   $P(110.8 < \mu < 189.2) = .95$.

7. Distinguish between the following terms: confidence level, confidence coefficient, confidence interval.

8. What are the conditions required in order to construct a $100(1-\alpha)\%$ confidence interval using the expression $\bar{x} \pm z_{\alpha/2}\dfrac{\sigma}{\sqrt{n}}$?

9. Describe the effect on the width of a confidence interval as each of the following increases:

    a. n

    b. $1 - \alpha$

    c. α

    d. $\bar{x}$

10. What expression indicates the maximum error of estimation? Is this the same as the margin of error?

Exercises

1. Find $z_{\alpha/2}$ for the following levels of α:

    a. $\alpha = .05$

    b. $\alpha = .01$

    c. $\alpha = .10$

2. Find $z_{\alpha/2}$ for the following levels of α:

    a. $\alpha = .04$

    b. $\alpha = .02$

    c. $\alpha = .08$

3. Find $z_{\alpha/2}$ for the following confidence levels:

    a. 98%

    b. 94%

    c. 92%

4. Find $z_{\alpha/2}$ for the following confidence levels:

    a. 96%

    b. 88%

    c. 85%

5. Consider a normally distributed population with a standard deviation of 64. If a random sample of size 90 from the population produces a sample mean of 250, construct a 95% confidence interval for the true mean of the population.

6. Construct a 90% confidence interval for the mean of a normal population if a random sample of size 40 from the population yields a sample mean of 75 and the population has a standard deviation of 5.

7. A psychologist is studying learning in rats. The psychologist wants to determine the average time required for rats to learn to traverse a maze. She randomly selects 40 rats and records the time it takes for the rats to traverse the maze in minutes. The sample average time required for the rats to traverse the maze is 5 minutes with a standard deviation of 1 minute. Estimate the average time required for rats to learn to traverse the maze with a 90% confidence interval.

8. A paint manufacturer is developing a new type of paint. Thirty panels were exposed to various corrosive conditions to measure the protective ability of the paint. The mean life for the samples was 168 hours before corrosive failure. The life of paint samples is assumed to be normally distributed with a population standard deviation of 30 hours. Find the 95% confidence interval for the mean life of the paint.

9. The chief purchaser for the State Education Commission is reviewing test data for a metal link chain which will be used on children's swing sets in elementary school playgrounds. The average breaking strength for a sample of 50 pieces of chain is 5000 pounds. Based on past experience, the breaking strength of metal chains is known to be normally distributed with a standard deviation of 100 pounds. Estimate the actual mean breaking strength of the metal link chain with 99% confidence.

10. Tomatoes are grown in Florida for shipment to other parts of the country by the Anderson Produce Company. A random sample of 40 boxes is selected at one warehouse for weighing. The average weight for the sample is 33.5 pounds per box with a standard deviation of 2.1 pounds. Find a 90% confidence interval for the true average weight of the boxes of tomatoes.

11. Thirty-five strands of piano wire were selected at random from a recent shipment by the Quality Control Department at Elkins Piano Company. The strands of piano wire were tested to failure in tests of tensile strength. The average tensile strength of the sample was 30,000 pounds per square inch (psi) with a sample standard deviation of 1950 psi. Find the 98% confidence interval for the mean tensile strength.

12. When preparing a standardized test to be given to all the sixth graders, the Standard Test Company gave a version of the test to a random sample of 45 sixth graders and timed how long it took them to finish the test. The average time required to finish the test for the sample was 2 hours and 15 minutes with a standard deviation of 30 minutes. Estimate the true average time required to finish the test with 95% confidence.

13. According to the 2009 College Senior Survey administered by the Higher Education Research Institute at UCLA, 56.4% of college seniors spend 10 hours or less studying or doing homework in a typical week. Suppose a random sample of 50 college seniors was selected from all the college seniors in the Southeast region to determine the homework habits of college seniors in the Southeast region of the United States. Each student in the sample is asked approximately how many hours per week he or she spends studying or doing homework. If the mean and standard deviation of the sample are 9.6 hours and 3.1 hours, respectively, construct a 99% confidence interval for the average number of hours a week that a college senior in the region spends studying or doing homework per week. **Source**: Cooperative Institutional Research Program at the Higher Education Research Institute at UCLA

9.4 Interval Estimation of the Population Mean, Small Samples, σ Unknown

In the last section we assumed that the population standard deviation was known. In practice this assumption is not very realistic, since the standard deviation describes variability about the mean. If the population standard deviation is known, the mean is usually also known, and there is no need to create an interval estimate for it. Why estimate something we already know?

If σ is not known and $n < 30$, the derivation of the confidence interval must be changed slightly. Provided the population from which the sample is drawn is normally distributed, the distribution of the quantity

$$t = \frac{\bar{x} - \mu}{s/\sqrt{n}} \text{ where } s \text{ is the standard deviation of the sample,}$$

has a **Student's t-distribution**. The t-distribution was discovered by W.S. Gossett in 1908. Gossett published the result under the pen name of Student while working as an employee of the Guinness Brewery in Dublin.

The t-distribution is very much like the normal distribution (see Figure 9.5). It is a symmetrical, bell-shaped distribution with slightly thicker tails than a normal distribution. The shape of the t-distribution approaches the normal distribution as the sample size, n, and thus the degrees of freedom become larger.

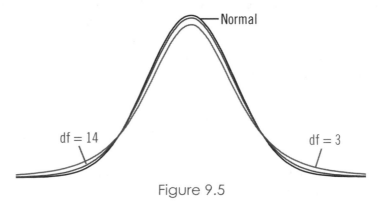

Figure 9.5

The t-distribution has one parameter, **degrees of freedom**.

Formula

The **degrees of freedom** for any t-distribution are computed in the following manner:

$$df = \text{number of sample observations} - 1 = n - 1.$$

Formula

If σ is unknown and the sample is drawn from a normal population, a $100(1-\alpha)\%$ confidence interval for the population mean is given by

$$\bar{x} \pm t_{\alpha/2,n-1} \frac{s}{\sqrt{n}},$$

where $t_{\alpha/2,n-1}$ is the critical value for a t-distribution with $n-1$ degrees of freedom which captures an area of $\alpha/2$ in the right tail of the distribution.

The form of the confidence interval is identical to the previous confidence interval for the mean of a population except that the z has been replaced by a t and σ has been replaced by s. The interpretation of the confidence interval is identical to the previous interval.

Example 9.3

Given the following data drawn from a normal population with unknown mean and variance, construct a 95% confidence interval for the population mean.

Seven values have been selected randomly from the population.

$$25, 19, 37, 29, 40, 28, 31$$

Solution

The sample mean and standard deviation are $\bar{x} \approx 29.86$ and $s \approx 7.08$, respectively. The degrees of freedom associated with the problem is

$$df = n - 1 = 7 - 1 = 6.$$

The t-value corresponding to 6 degrees of freedom and 95% confidence $(\alpha = .05)$ is given in Table D of Appendix A as $t_{.025,6} = 2.447$. The corresponding confidence interval is

$$29.86 \pm 2.447\left(\frac{7.08}{\sqrt{7}}\right)$$

$$29.86 \pm 6.55.$$

Thus, we are 95 percent confident that the interval

$$23.31 \text{ to } 36.41$$

will contain the population mean.

An alternate interpretation would be that we are 95% confident that the point estimate (29.86) has a maximum error of estimation of 6.55.

Example 9.4

A manufacturing company is interested in the amount of time it takes to complete a certain stage of the production process. The project manager randomly samples 10 products as they come from the production line and notes the time of completion. The average completion time is 23.45 minutes with a sample standard deviation of 4.32 minutes. Based on this sample, construct a 95% confidence interval for the mean completion time for that stage in the production process.

Solution

Since the company wants to calculate a 95% confidence interval for the average completion time, μ, we know that $\alpha = .05$. We also have a sample size of $n = 10$ and thus, $n - 1 = 10 - 1 = 9$ degrees of freedom. Therefore, we use $t_{\alpha/2, df} = t_{.025, 9} = 2.262$ from Table D in the Appendix.

We also know that the general form of the confidence interval for the population mean when σ is unknown and $n < 30$ is given by

$$\bar{x} \pm t_{\alpha/2, n-1} \frac{s}{\sqrt{n}}$$

$$23.45 \pm 2.262 \frac{4.32}{\sqrt{10}}$$

$$23.45 \pm 3.09$$

or 20.36 to 26.54 minutes.

Thus, we are 95% confident that the interval above will contain the true population mean (which is the average completion time of a product in that stage of the process).

Interval Estimation of the Population Mean: A Summary

In Sections 9.3 and 9.4 we have outlined two procedures for determining an interval estimate for the population mean. In Section 9.3 we used the interval $\bar{x} \pm z_{\alpha/2} \dfrac{\sigma}{\sqrt{n}}$ for normally distributed populations in which the population standard deviation, σ, is known. We also stated that if the population standard deviation is unknown and the sample size is sufficiently large $(n \geq 30)$, we may use the sample standard deviation, s, as an approximation for σ. For these sufficiently large sample sizes, the t-distribution very closely resembles the z-distribution, so using the critical value $z_{\alpha/2}$ when constructing the confidence interval is acceptable. In Section 9.4 we introduced the t-distribution with $n-1$ degrees of freedom and used the interval $\bar{x} \pm t_{\alpha/2,n-1} \dfrac{s}{\sqrt{n}}$ to find an interval estimate for the population mean for a normally distributed population where σ is unknown and $n < 30$. The following flow chart is useful when deciding how to construct an interval estimate for the population mean.

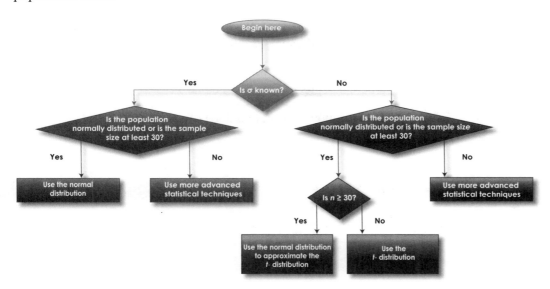

 **Exercises**

Basic Concepts

1. Why is the assumption that the population standard deviation is known when estimating the population mean not very realistic?

2. What effect does knowing the standard deviation of the population have on the construction of the confidence interval?

3. What is the Student's t-distribution?

4. What are the conditions in which the t-distribution is used in interval estimation of the population mean?

5. What is the parameter of the t-distribution? How is it calculated?

Exercises

1. Find the t-value such that .025 of the area under the curve is to the right of the t-value. Assume the degrees of freedom equal 13.

2. Find the t-value such that .01 of the area under the curve is to the right of the t-value. Assume the degrees of freedom equal 21.

3. Find $t_{\alpha/2,n-1}$ for the following combinations of α and n.
   a. $\alpha = .05, n = 15$
   b. $\alpha = .01, n = 20$
   c. $\alpha = .10, n = 8$

4. Find $t_{\alpha/2,n-1}$ for the following combinations of α and n.
   a. $\alpha = .05, n = 12$
   b. $\alpha = .01, n = 18$
   c. $\alpha = .10, n = 22$

5. A random sample, consisting of the values listed below, was taken from a normally distributed population. Assuming the standard deviation of the population is unknown, construct a 99% confidence interval for the population mean.

27.4	26.5	25.7	31.4
28.2	21.9	16.3	22.7
18.8	34.4	29.2	20.5

6. Construct an 80% confidence interval for the mean of a normal population assuming that the values listed below comprise a random sample taken from the population. The population standard deviation is unknown.

83.9	87.4	65.2	86.0	73.1
80.3	92.7	87.5	69.3	77.5
91.9	71.1	79.1	72.4	88.2

7. An FDA representative randomly selects 8 packages of ground chuck from a grocery store and measures the fat content (as a percent) of each package. The resulting measurements are given below:

13%	12%
15%	16%
14%	17%
18%	15%

a. Calculate the sample mean and the sample standard deviation of the fat contents.

b. Construct a 90% confidence interval for the average fat content of all the packages of ground beef.

c. What assumption did you make about the fat content in constructing your interval?

8. A hospital would like to determine the average length of stay for its patients having abdominal surgery. A sample of 15 patients revealed a sample mean of 6.4 days and a sample standard deviation of 1.4 days.

a. Find a 95% confidence interval for the mean stay for patients with abdominal surgery.

b. Interpret this interval and state any assumptions that were made in the construction of the interval.

9. An independent group of food service personnel conducted a survey on tipping practices in a large metropolitan area. They collected information on the percentage of the bill left as a tip for 25 randomly selected bills. The average tip was 12.3% of the bill with a standard deviation of 2.7%.

a. Construct an interval to estimate the true average tip (as a percent of the bill) with 99% confidence.

b. Interpret the interval and state any assumptions that were made in the construction of the interval.

10. A travel agent is interested in the average price of a hotel during the summer in a resort community. The agent randomly selects 15 hotels from the community and determines the price of a regular room with a king size bed. The average price of the room for the sample was $115 with a standard deviation of $30.

    a. Construct an interval to estimate the true average price of a regular room with a king size bed in the resort community with 90% confidence.

    b. Interpret the interval and state any assumptions that were made in the construction of the interval.

11. In 2010 the median home price in all regions of the United States was $221,800. It is commonly thought that better schools are found in wealthier areas. In *Forbes* magazine's list of the "Best Schools for your Real Estate Buck," the top 10 cities in America were identified where your housing dollar will go the furthest in getting your children a great education. 17,589 towns and cities were analyzed using results from the most recent National Assessment for Educational Progress data, and the top 10 school districts were identified. The list counteracted the idea that more money equals better schools, as Falmouth, Maine topped the list beating out high-dollar school districts like Manhattan Beach, California. The top 10 cities are given below, along with the median home price for each city. **Source:** *Forbes* magazine

Table for Exercise 10 Best Schools for your Real Estate Buck		
Education Rank	City	Median Home Price ($)
1	Falmouth, Maine	351,550
2	Mercer Island, Washington	708,740
3	Pella, Iowa	148,200
4	Barrington, Rhode Island	296,010
5	Bedford, New Hampshire	293,730
6	Manhattan Beach, California	1,278,980
7	Moraga, California	722,010
8	Parkland, Florida	426,390
9	St. Johns, Florida	181,700
10	Southlake, Texas	476,880

    a. Construct a 90% confidence interval for the median home price of cities on the top 10 list.

    b. Is the median price for these cities higher than the U.S. as a whole?

    c. What population assumption needs to be made here?

Precision and Sample Size: Means

The more accurate an estimate, the greater its potential value in decision making. The only way to accurately determine an unknown population parameter is to perform a census, though this is usually impractical because of cost or time considerations. Realistically, the best interval estimates a decision maker could hope for would be an interval with a small width possessing a large amount of confidence. The width of the confidence interval defines the precision with which the population mean is estimated; the smaller the interval, the greater the precision. If the width of a confidence interval could be controlled, we could achieve estimates with a level of accuracy that is appropriate for the decision at hand.

Determining the Sample Size, σ Known

There are three components which affect the width of the confidence interval for the population mean:

$z_{\alpha/2}$	Represents the distance the confidence interval boundary is from the estimated mean $\bar{x}$ in standard deviation units. The distance is related to the specific level of confidence.
σ	Represents the population standard deviation.
n	Represents the sample size.

As discussed in Section 9.3, the level of confidence will affect confidence interval width. That is, the higher the level of confidence, the wider the confidence interval. The population standard deviation, σ, is a constant, and does not change. The sample size, however, is selected by the decision maker. The larger the sample, the smaller the width of the resulting confidence interval for some given level of confidence. Since the sample size can be increased, which reduces the width of the confidence interval, how large should the sample be? Taking too large a sample wastes money, while taking too small a sample produces an estimator that does not possess sufficient reliability.

The sample size should be selected in relation to the size of the maximum positive or negative error (also called the **margin of error**) the decision maker is willing to accept. This can be achieved by setting the error equal to one-half the confidence interval width.

$$E = error = z_{\alpha/2} \frac{\sigma}{\sqrt{n}}$$

Six Degrees of Separation: A Law of Small Worlds

What is the number of people a randomly chosen person in Omaha, Nebraska needs to contact before she can find a connection with a randomly chosen housewife in New England? How many intervening people do you think separates you from the President of the United States? Unsuspecting readers might very well guess very large numbers but the actual numbers are quite small. The answer to both of these questions may very well be less than 6! Psychologists have done very ingenuous experiments and have actually calculated this *degree of separation*, on the average to be six. What is amazing about this degree of separation is that it is equally true for the President of the United States and a sweet vendor in Bangladesh. Continued ...

... Continued
The degree of separation for the number of clicks that you will need to make to get to a website that interests you, as well as the analysis of terrorist networks turn out to be of similar nature. The new science of networks can shed useful light and help to derive general laws applicable to many of these types of questions.

The preceding equation can be solved for the sample size, n.

$$E = z_{\alpha/2} \frac{\sigma}{\sqrt{n}}$$

$$\sqrt{n} = z_{\alpha/2} \frac{\sigma}{E}$$

$$n = \left(\frac{z_{\alpha/2}\sigma}{E} \right)^2$$

By selecting a level of confidence and the maximum error, the relationship can be used to determine the sample size necessary to estimate the sample mean with the desired accuracy. **In order to assure the desired level of confidence, always round the value obtained for the sample size up to the next integer.**

Example 9.5

Consider a population having a standard deviation of 15. We want to estimate the mean of the population. How large of a sample is needed to construct a 95% confidence interval for the mean of this population if the margin of error is equal to 1.5?

Solution

$$n = \left(\frac{z_{\alpha/2}\sigma}{E} \right)^2 = \left(\frac{1.96 \cdot 15}{1.5} \right)^2 = 384.16$$

Rounding up, we have to have a sample size of 385 to ensure that we get at least a 95% confidence interval with a margin of error equal to 1.5.

Example 9.6

Suppose that a quality control manager at Argon Chemical Company wishes to measure the average amount of cleaning fluid the company is placing in their 12 ounce bottles. From previous samples, they believe that the standard deviation is 0.3 ounces. How large a sample must be taken in order to be 95% confident of estimating the mean amount of cleaning fluid in a 12 ounce bottle to within 0.05 ounces?

Solution

$$n = \left(\frac{z_{\alpha/2}\sigma}{E}\right)^2 = \left(\frac{1.96 \cdot 0.3}{0.05}\right)^2 \approx 138.30$$

To be assured of finding the desired level of confidence, always round up. Thus, we are 95% confident that a sample of $n = 139$ observations would produce an estimate of the mean cleaning fluid in a 12 ounce bottle to within 0.05 ounces. Being able to know the accuracy of your estimate is one of the significant benefits of inferential statistics. In this case, if 139 bottles are measured, we will be 95% confident that the resulting sample mean is within five one-hundredths of an ounce of the true mean. That's close.

Determining the Sample Size, σ Unknown

In the previous discussion of sample size determination, σ was assumed to be known. This assumption is usually unreasonable in most problem-solving environments.

The most obvious method for obtaining an estimate of σ is to take a small sample and use the sample standard deviation as an estimate of the population standard deviation. Replacing σ with s in the sample size determination relationship will provide an initial estimate of the required sample size. Another alternative is to use the value of the sample standard deviation obtained in a previous study, sometimes called a **pilot study**.

Example 9.7

An airline's maintenance manager desires to estimate the average time (in hours) required to replace a jet engine in a Boeing 767. How large a sample would be necessary if the manager wishes to be 95% confident of estimating the mean to within one-quarter of an hour ($E = 0.25$)? Assume a preliminary sample of size $n = 30$ has an average replacement time of 16.7 hours with a standard deviation of 4.3 hours.

Solution

Using the results from the initial sample,

$$n = \left(\frac{z_{\alpha/2} \cdot s}{E}\right)^2 = \left(\frac{1.96 \cdot 4.3}{0.25}\right)^2 \approx 1136.50$$

$n = 1137$. (Always round up to assure required confidence.)

Notice that while the sample data values are being collected they can be used to improve the estimate of the population standard deviation. For example, suppose the sample standard deviation after sampling the first 1000 observations was 4.1. Using this estimate of s instead of 4.3 results in a sample size of 1034 compared to the original specification of 1137. The notion of modifying the sample size estimate as additional data are observed can be applied at regular intervals during the sampling process until the estimate of the standard deviation stabilizes.

9.5 Exercises

Basic Concepts

1. What is the value of having a confidence interval with a small width?

2. Can a confidence interval be constructed with a width of your choice? Explain.

3. What are the three components which affect the width of the confidence interval for the population mean?

4. What is the margin of error? What is the connection between the expression for the margin of error and the equation to determine the sample size?

5. What is the rounding rule regarding the determination of the sample size?

6. What is the difference between the method of determining the sample size when σ is known versus when σ is unknown?

7. What is a pilot study?

Exercises

1. A technician working for the Chase-National Food Additive Company would like to estimate the preserving ability of a new additive. This additive will be used for Auntie's brand preserves. Based on past tests, it is believed that the time to spoilage for this additive will have a standard deviation of 6 days. To be 90% confident of the average time to spoilage, what sample size will be needed to estimate mean time to spoilage with an accuracy of one day?

2. A computer software company would like to estimate how long it will take a beginner to become proficient at creating a graph using their new spreadsheet package. Past experience has indicated that the time required for a beginner to become proficient with a particular function of the new software product has an approximately normal distribution with a standard deviation of 15 minutes. Find the sample size necessary to estimate the average time required for a beginner to become proficient at creating a graph with the new spreadsheet package to within 5 minutes with 95% confidence.

3. A hot-dog vendor is evaluating a downtown location by counting the number of people who walk past the prospective location on a particular day during lunch time (i.e. 11:00AM to 2:00PM). A preliminary study has indicated a standard deviation of about 30 people per lunch period. How many lunch periods will be needed to estimate the true number of people who walk past the prospective location during the lunch period to within 9 people with 90% confidence?

Estimating the Population Proportion

An attribute is a characteristic that members of a population either possess or do not possess. Attributes are almost always measured as the **proportion** of the population that possesses the characteristic.

Many decisions require a measure of a population attribute. Television and radio stations base their advertising charges on ratings reflecting the *percentage of television viewers who are watching a particular program.* A political analyst wants to know the *fraction of voters who favor a particular candidate.* A social researcher needs the *fraction of teachers who believe group learning is a beneficial instructional method.* An insurance company is interested in estimating the *fraction of their policies that will result in claims.* A quality control engineer requires the *percentage defective in a lot of goods.* A marketing researcher demands the *fraction of persons on a mailing list that will purchase the product as a result of a direct mail marketing campaign.* The items in italics are measures of attributes of some population. Researchers estimate the proportion of population members possessing those characteristics.

Estimating the proportion of the population that possesses an attribute is straightforward. A random sample is selected and the sample proportion is computed as follows:

X = number in the sample that possesses the attribute,

n = sample size, and

$$\hat{p} = \frac{X}{n}.$$

The symbol above the p indicates an estimate of the quantity specified. Since $\hat{p}$ is computed from a random sample, $\hat{p}$ is a random variable whose value depends on which random sample is selected.

Example 9.8

Estimate the fraction of defective transistors in a lot containing 100,000 transistors. Suppose a sample of size 800 is drawn from the lot, and 5 transistors were found to be defective.

Solution

X = number in the sample that possesses the attribute = 5

n = sample size = 800

Then,

$$\hat{p} = \frac{5}{800} = .00625,$$

which is an estimate of the proportion of defective transistors in the lot of 100,000.

A natural question to ask is, *How good is the estimate of the fraction of defective transistors?* The answer to this question naturally arises in the discussion of interval estimation for proportions.

Interval Estimation of the Population Proportion

The concept of confidence intervals, used to apprise a decision maker of the reliability of estimates of a population mean, can also be applied to estimating proportions. In order to develop the confidence interval for a population proportion, the sampling distribution of the point estimate must be developed. (See Section 8.4 for review.)

The random variable, $\hat{p}$, has a binomial distribution which is approximated with a normal random variable.

Thus, the sample proportion, $\hat{p}$, is normally distributed with mean, p, and variance,

$$\sigma_{\hat{p}}^2 = \frac{p(1-p)}{n}.$$

The standard deviation of the sample proportion, $\hat{p}$, is denoted symbolically as $\sigma_{\hat{p}}$ and is given by

$$\sigma_{\hat{p}} = \sqrt{\frac{p(1-p)}{n}} \approx \sqrt{\frac{\hat{p}(1-\hat{p})}{n}},$$

where $\hat{p}$ is used as an estimate of p.

As before,

$$P(-1.96 < z < 1.96) = .95.$$

Substituting

$$z = \frac{\hat{p} - p}{\sigma_{\hat{p}}}$$

results in

$$P\left(-1.96 < \frac{\hat{p} - p}{\sigma_{\hat{p}}} < 1.96\right) = .95.$$

Manipulating the inequalities results in

$$P\left(\hat{p} - 1.96\sigma_{\hat{p}} < p < \hat{p} + 1.96\sigma_{\hat{p}}\right) = .95,$$

which suggests that the interval

$$\hat{p} \pm 1.96\sigma_{\hat{p}}$$

would be a good choice for a 95% confidence interval for the population proportion. As before, the probability that the interval will contain the true population proportion is .95 *before a specific sample is drawn*. After a specific sample is drawn, the only available information about the interval is that the technique which generated it will bound the true proportion 95% of the time.

Formula

If the sample size is sufficiently large, i.e. $np \geq 5$ and $n(1-p) \geq 5$, the $100(1-\alpha)\%$ confidence interval for the population proportion is given by the expression

$$\hat{p} \pm z_{\alpha/2}\sigma_{\hat{p}},$$

where $z_{\alpha/2}$ is the value of z which captures an area of $\alpha/2$ in the right tail of the standard normal distribution, and $\sigma_{\hat{p}}$ is the standard deviation of $\hat{p}$.

Example 9.9

Suppose a sample of 410 randomly selected radio listeners revealed that 48 listened to WJLN.

$$\hat{p} = \frac{48}{410} \approx .117$$

This is a point estimate of the proportion that listen to WJLN.

To obtain an interval estimate, the amount of confidence to be placed in the interval must be specified. Suppose we desire 95% confidence.

Solution

$$z_{\alpha/2} = z_{.05/2} = z_{.025} = 1.96, \text{ and } \sigma_{\hat{p}} \approx \sqrt{\frac{\hat{p}(1-\hat{p})}{n}} = \sqrt{\frac{.117(1-.117)}{410}} \approx .0159.$$

Note that the sample proportion $\hat{p}$ is used in place of p in the computation of $\sigma_{\hat{p}}$. For any realistic problem, this will always be the case. Fortunately, unless $\hat{p}$ and p are far apart, the value of $\sigma_{\hat{p}}$ will not be greatly affected.

Computing the confidence interval $\hat{p} \pm z_{\alpha/2}\sigma_{\hat{p}}$ results in

$$.117 \pm 1.96(.0159)$$
$$= .117 \pm .0312$$

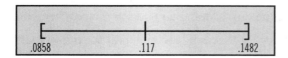

creating the interval .0858 to .1482. We are 95% confident in the procedure that created this interval. Another interpretation would be that we are 95% confident that the point estimate, .117, has a maximum error of estimation of .0312. A maximum error of only .0312 with 95% confidence suggests a rather high level of accuracy in the estimation of the proportion.

9.6   Exercises

Basic Concepts

1. What is a proportion? What type of information does it give us about the population?

2. How is the sample proportion found?

3. Describe how a confidence interval is constructed for a population proportion.

Exercises

1. Acid rain accumulations in lakes and streams in the northeastern part of the United States are a major environmental concern. A researcher wants to know what fraction of lakes contain hazardous pollution levels. He randomly selects 200 lakes and determines that 45 of the selected lakes have an unsafe concentration of acid rain pollution.

   a. Calculate the best point estimate of the population proportion of lakes that have unsafe concentrations of acid rain pollution.

   b. Determine a 95% confidence interval for the population proportion.

   c. If a local politician states that only 20% of the lakes are contaminated, does the study provide overwhelming evidence to contradict his views?

2. *The Richland Gazette*, a local newspaper, conducted a poll of 1000 randomly selected readers to determine their views concerning the city's handling of snow removal. The paper found that 650 people in the sample felt the city did a good job.

   a. Compute the best point estimate for the percentage of readers who believe the city is doing a good job of snow removal.

   b. Construct a 90% confidence interval for this percentage.

3. The clinical testing of drugs involves many factors. For example, patients that have been given placebos, which are harmless compounds that have no effect on the patient, often will still report that they feel better. Assume that in a study of 500 random subjects conducted by the Poppins Sucre Drug Company, the percentage of patients reporting improvement when given a placebo was 37%.

   a. What would be a 95% confidence interval for the true proportion of patients who exhibit the placebo effect?

   b. What would the 99% confidence interval be?

   c. To gain the additional 4% of confidence how much wider did the interval become?

4. The Peacock Cable Television Company thinks that 40% of their customers have more outlets wired than they are paying for. A random sample of 400 houses reveals that 110 of the houses have excessive outlets.

   a. Construct a 99% confidence interval for the true proportion of houses having too many outlets.

   b. Do you feel the company is accurate in its belief about the proportion of customers who have more outlets wired than they are paying for?

5. Jogging continues to be a very popular sport in America. At a major race, like the Peachtree Road Race in Atlanta, there may be over 10,000 people entered to run. The race promoters for a road race in the Pacific Northwest took a random sample of 750 runners out of the 5000 runners entered to estimate the number of runners who will need hotel accommodations. Five hundred runners indicated they would need hotel accommodations.

   a. Construct a 90% confidence interval for the true proportion of runners who will need hotel accommodations.

   b. Is the confidence interval obtained sufficiently narrow to be of help in planning the number of hotel rooms which will be necessary to accommodate the runners?

6. In the fourth quarter of 2010 the homeowner vacancy rate was 66.5%. This rate is 2.7 percentage points lower than the 2004 peak of 69.2%, and the lowest rate since 1998. (Source: U.S. Census Bureau) Home ownership fell at an alarming pace in the fourth quarter of the year, and despite the fact that home prices fell, affordability was much improved and inventories of new and existing homes were running quite high. Suppose that a random sample of 120 was selected from an area in the Midwest that is particularly economically depressed. Suppose that 57 of the households sampled were owned by the residents of the homes.

   a. Construct a 95% confidence interval for the proportion of households in the area sampled that are owned by the residents of the homes.

   b. Is there evidence that the proportion of the households in the area sampled that are owned by residents is less than the national rate?

7. In the *Gallup Poll Monthly*, it was reported that 31% of the people surveyed in a recent poll claimed that vegetables were their least favorite food. Surprisingly, only 14% responded with liver, and 10% of those surveyed did not submit a response because they claimed that they liked everything. The poll was based upon a sample of 1001 people. Assuming that a random sample was chosen, construct a 90% confidence interval for the percent of all Americans who say that vegetables are their least favorite food.

8. The Federal Trade Commission (FTC) conducted a study investigating the accuracy of bar-code scanners. It was concluded that these computer scanners, used mainly at grocery, department store, and drugstore checkout counters, ring up the wrong price about 5% of the time. In most instances, however, the error was in favor of the shopper, according to the FTC. Suppose that your local grocery store conducts a study to determine the accuracy of its scanners. Assume a total of 200 shoppers are randomly chosen and their bills as indicated by the scanner are checked against the correct bill, computed by conventional means. Suppose that in 21 of the cases an error is detected.

   a. Construct a 95% confidence interval for the proportion of customers whose bills are in error.

   b. Does it appear that the local grocery store has a larger error rate than 5%?

Precision and Sample Size: Proportions

Just as for the population mean, a specific level of accuracy in estimating a population proportion is desirable. Suppose, for example, that a direct-mail marketer would like to estimate the fraction of a mailing list that will purchase the company's product. To be profitable, a purchase response of at least .008 is required. Because the proportion to be estimated is of such a small magnitude, a high degree of precision in estimating the proportion is necessary. How large a sample would be required if the population proportion (the actual proportion of persons on the mailing list that will buy the product) is to be estimated with an accuracy of .002? We are saying that we want our maximum error to be less than two one-thousandths. That would seem to be a highly precise estimate. But, the quantity we are trying to estimate (the proportion of people on the list that will buy the product) could easily be near .008. The maximum error is about 25% as large as the value we are trying to estimate. When we estimate extremely small quantities, highly precise estimates are necessary.

The technique for deriving the sample size parallels the discussion of precision and sample size for the sample mean (Section 9.5). Setting one-half the entire width of the confidence interval equal to the maximum allowable error yields

$$E = error = z_{\alpha/2}\sigma_{\hat{p}} = z_{\alpha/2}\sqrt{\frac{p(1-p)}{n}}.$$

Solving for n yields

$$n = \frac{z_{\alpha/2}^2 p(1-p)}{E^2}.$$

Generally the population proportion is unknown and is estimated from a pilot study. In this case the sample size necessary to estimate the population proportion to within a particular error with a certain level of confidence is given by

$$n \approx \frac{z_{\alpha/2}^2 \hat{p}(1-\hat{p})}{E^2}$$

where $\hat{p}$ is the estimate of the population proportion obtained from the pilot study.

If an estimate of the population proportion is not available, then the population proportion is set equal to .5. The value .5 maximizes the quantity $p(1-p)$ and thus provides the most conservative estimate of the sample size possible. Hence if no estimate of the population proportion is available, the sample size necessary to estimate the population proportion to within a particular error with a certain level of confidence is given by

$$n = \frac{z_{\alpha/2}^2 (.5)(1-.5)}{E^2} = \frac{z_{\alpha/2}^2 (.25)}{E^2}.$$

By selecting a level of confidence and an error, a sample size can be determined that will likely (at the level of confidence) produce an estimate with at least the desired accuracy. Remember to always round the sample size to the next largest integer to assure the desired level of accuracy.

Example 9.10

How large a sample would be required to estimate the proportion of buyers on a mailing list that will buy the product with an accuracy of .002 with a 95% degree of confidence, if the true proportion is approximately .008?

Solution

$$p \approx .008,$$
$$z_{\alpha/2} = 1.96 \text{ for 95\% confidence, and}$$
$$E = .002$$

Using the sample size determination expression yields

$$n = \frac{z_{\alpha/2}^2 p(1-p)}{E^2}$$
$$= \frac{1.96^2 (.008)(1-.008)}{.002^2}$$
$$= 7621.7344 \approx 7622 \text{ (always round up)}.$$

Thus, to be 95% confident that the proportion is estimated with an error of at most .002 requires a sample size of 7622.

Example 9.11

Using Example 9.9, suppose that the radio station WJLN desires to estimate the proportion of the market they hold with a maximum error of .01 and a confidence coefficient of .95. How large a sample would be required to estimate the fraction of listeners to within the desired level of accuracy? Since we don't know the true population proportion, let's assume the previous point estimate of .117 is the true proportion.

Solution

$$p \approx .117,$$
$$z_{\alpha/2} = 1.96 \text{ for } 95\% \text{ confidence, and}$$
$$E = .01$$

Using the sample size determination expression yields

$$n = \frac{z_{\alpha/2}^2 \, p(1-p)}{E^2} = \frac{1.96^2 (.117)(1-.117)}{.01^2} \approx 3968.8 = 3969 \text{ (always round up).}$$

Thus to be 95% confident that the proportion of listeners is estimated with an accuracy of at least .01 would require a sample size of 3969.

Suppose we did not have a previous estimate of the population proportion in Example 9.11. In this case we would estimate p with .5. The sample size necessary to estimate the true proportion of listeners to within 1% with 95% confidence is given by

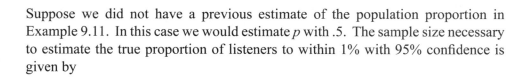

$$n = \frac{z_{\alpha/2}^2 (.5)(1-.5)}{E^2} = \frac{1.96^2 (.5)(1-.5)}{.01^2} = 9604.$$

Notice that the required sample size is significantly larger when an estimate of the population proportion is not available.

The value of drawing random samples resides in the ability to assess the reliability of sample inference. Reliability is expressed in probability. That is why so much of the text has been devoted to probabilistic ideas.

9.7 Exercises

Basic Concepts

1. It seems that estimating proportions produces estimates which are much more precise than those for means. Explain why this is the case.

2. The population proportion is often unknown. How is this issue dealt with when determining sample size?

3. What is the guideline to follow when there is no estimate available for the population proportion? Why is this done?

4. How do the resulting required sample sizes differ when there is an estimate available versus when there is no estimate available for the population proportion?

Exercises

1. The Big Green Poster Company wants to estimate the fraction of poster sites controlled by their competition, Bird's Billboard Service. What sample size would be necessary to estimate this to within 3% of the poster sites with 95% confidence? (They think Bird controls about 33 percent of the boards.)

2. Researchers working in a remote area of Africa feel that 40% of families in the area are without adequate drinking water either through contamination or unavailability. What sample size will be necessary to estimate the percentage without adequate water to within 5% with 95% confidence?

3. Companies that provide environmental cleanup for hazardous waste and toxic chemicals are growing rapidly. W.R. Gross is thinking about entering this field with a subsidiary called Saf-t-Soil. They wish to estimate the proportion of U.S. corporations that produce hazardous waste as a by-product of their manufacturing process to within 10% with 80% confidence. What sample size will be needed?

4. The public relations manager for a political candidate would like to determine if the registered voters in the candidate's district agree with the politician's view on a particular issue. Find the sample size necessary for the public relations manager to estimate the true proportion to within 5% with 95% confidence.

Discovering Technology

USING THE TI-84 PLUS CALCULATOR

Confidence Intervals

Construct the 90% confidence interval for the population mean of a normal population if the sample standard deviation is 900, the sample mean is 425, and the sample size is 100.

1. Choose **STAT**, then select **TESTS** and choose option **7:ZInterval**.

2. Press **ENTER** and choose **Stats**. Input "900" for σ (or s in this case), "425" for $\bar{x}$, "100" for n, and ".90" for the Confidence Level. Press **Calculate**, and the confidence interval, (276.96, 573.04) is listed on the screen.

Figure 9.6

Figure 9.7

USING EXCEL

Confidence Intervals

Construct a 90% confidence interval for the population mean of a normal population if the sample standard deviation is 900, the sample mean is 425, and the sample size is 100.

1. The function which returns the error of estimation in Microsoft Excel is

    CONFIDENCE(alpha,standard_dev,size)

    Where *standard_dev* is the standard deviation, *size* is the sample size, and *alpha* is the significance level where the confidence level is $100(1 - alpha)\%$. Therefore, for this example alpha = .10.

2. Enter the confidence function in cell A1 as follows to reflect the parameters of the given problem:

    =CONFIDENCE(.10,900,100)

3. Press **Enter**. The result is 148.0368, the error of estimation. Subtract and add this value to the sample mean, 425, to find the confidence interval, (276.9632, 573.0368).

	A	B
1	148.0368	Error of Estimation
2		
3	276.9632	Lower Confidence Interval
4	573.0368	Upper Confidence Interval

Figure 9.8

USING MINITAB

One Proportion

Use the information in Example 9.9 to construct the 95% confidence interval.

1. Choose **Stat**, select **Basic Statistics**, and then choose **1 Proportion**.

2. Select **Summarized data** and enter **48** as "Number of events" and **410** as "Number of trials".

3. Click on the **Options** button. Make sure the "Confidence level" is 95.0 and check the box **Use test and interval based on normal distribution**.

4. Press **OK**, and then **OK** again.

5. The 95% confidence interval is (0.085953, 0.148194).

Test and CI for One Proportion

```
Sample   X    N   Sample p        95% CI
1       48  410   0.117073   (0.085953, 0.148194)

Using the normal approximation.
```

Figure 9.9

 **Chapter 9 Review**

Key Terms and Ideas

- Statistical Inference
- Judgment Estimates
- Estimator
- Estimate
- Point Estimator
- Point Estimate
- Interval Estimate
- Mean Squared Error
- Unbiasedness
- Unbiased Estimator
- Confidence Interval
- Confidence Level
- Confidence Coefficient
- Confidence Interval for the Population Mean
- Critical Values
- Maximum Error of Estimation
- Student's t-Distribution
- Degrees of Freedom
- Margin of Error
- Pilot Study
- Proportion
- Sample Proportion
- Confidence Interval for the Population Proportion

Key Formulas

Concept	Formula	Section
Mean Squared Error for the Sample Mean	$\text{MSE}(\bar{x}) = E(\bar{x} - \mu)^2$	9.2
$100(1-\alpha)\%$ Confidence Interval for the Population Mean for Normal Populations, σ Known or $n \geq 30$	$\bar{x} \pm z_{\alpha/2} \dfrac{\sigma}{\sqrt{n}}$ where $\bar{x}$ is the sample mean, $z_{\alpha/2}$ is the critical value for a z-distribution which captures an area of $\alpha/2$ in the right tail of the distribution, σ is the population standard deviation (approximated by s if σ is unknown and $n \geq 30$), and n is the sample size.	9.3
Student's t-Distribution	$t = \dfrac{\bar{x} - \mu}{s/\sqrt{n}}$ where $\bar{x}$ is the sample mean, s is the sample standard deviation, and n is the sample size.	9.4
Degrees of Freedom	$df = $ number of sample observations $- 1$ $= n - 1$	9.4
$100(1-\alpha)\%$ Confidence Interval for the Population Mean for Normal Populations, σ Unknown, $n < 30$	$\bar{x} \pm t_{\alpha/2,n-1} \dfrac{s}{\sqrt{n}}$ where $t_{\alpha/2,n-1}$ is the critical value for a t-distribution with $n-1$ degrees of freedom which captures an area of $\alpha/2$ in the right tail of the distribution.	9.4
Margin of Error for the Population Mean (Maximum Error)	$E = z_{\alpha/2} \dfrac{\sigma}{\sqrt{n}}$	9.5
Determining the Sample Size for the Population Mean, σ Known	$n = \left(\dfrac{z_{\alpha/2} \cdot \sigma}{E}\right)^2$	9.5
Determining the Sample Size for the Population Mean, σ Unknown	$n = \left(\dfrac{z_{\alpha/2} \cdot s}{E}\right)^2$	9.5

Point Estimate of the Population Proportion	$$\hat{p} = \frac{X}{n}$$ where X is the number in the sample that possesses the attribute and n is the sample size.	9.6
$100(1-\alpha)\%$ Confidence Interval for the Population Proportion, $np \geq 5$ and $n(1-p) \geq 5$	$$\hat{p} \pm z_{\alpha/2}\sigma_{\hat{p}}$$ where $z_{\alpha/2}$ is the critical value for a z-distribution which captures an area of $\alpha/2$ in the right tail of the distribution, and $\sigma_{\hat{p}}$ is the standard deviation of $\hat{p}$.	9.6
Margin of Error for the Population Proportion (Maximum Error)	$$E = z_{\alpha/2}\sigma_{\hat{p}} = z_{\alpha/2}\sqrt{\frac{p(1-p)}{n}}$$ where $z_{\alpha/2}$ is the critical value for a z-distribution which captures an area of $\alpha/2$ in the right tail of the distribution, p is the population proportion, and n is the sample size.	9.7
Determining the Sample Size for the Population Proportion	$$n = \frac{z_{\alpha/2}^2 p(1-p)}{E^2} \approx \frac{z_{\alpha/2}^2 \hat{p}(1-\hat{p})}{E^2}$$ where $z_{\alpha/2}$ is the critical value for a z-distribution which captures an area of $\alpha/2$ in the right tail of the distribution, p is the population proportion, and $\hat{p}$ is the sample proportion.	9.7
Determining the Sample Size for the Population Proportion, No Estimate $(\hat{p})$ Available	$$n = \frac{z_{\alpha/2}^2 (.5)(1-.5)}{E^2} \approx \frac{z_{\alpha/2}^2 (.25)}{E^2}$$	9.7

 **Additional Exercises**

1. The owner of Sloppy Jack's bar is thinking about installing some video game machines. To estimate the profitability of the machines, he measures the number of times a competitor's machines are played over a randomly selected sample of days. The preliminary sample showed that the standard deviation of the number of times the machines are played is 10 times per day. Find the sample size (in days) necessary to estimate the average number of times the machines will be played in a day to within 5 plays with 99% confidence.

2. A random sample of fifteen eleven-year-old boys is selected in order to estimate the average height for boys belonging to that age group. The resulting measurements in inches are given below.

55	58	52
57	56	54
52	59	55
58	61	56
58	54	57

   a. Calculate the sample mean and the sample standard deviation of the heights.

   b. Construct a 95% confidence interval for the mean height of all eleven-year-old boys.

   c. What assumption did you make about the heights in constructing your interval?

3. R. Cramden, chief development officer for Fontana Area Transport bus company, is concerned about the declining use of the bus system. He wishes to estimate the percentage of Fontana residents who consider safety a significant factor in their decision about whether or not to ride a bus. This will be a preliminary study so he is willing to develop an estimate with an error of 10% at a confidence level of 90%.

   a. What sample size will be needed?

   b. If 150 residents in a random sample of 500 Fontana residents say that they consider safety a significant factor in their decision about whether or not to ride a bus, estimate the true proportion of Fontana residents who think safety is a significant factor in their decision about whether or not to ride a bus with 95% confidence.

4. According to a 2001 study conducted by the American Stock Exchange, 87% of 500 young Americans surveyed said that they can't count on Social Security as a source of income when they retire. Construct a 90% confidence interval for the proportion of young Americans who feel they can't count on Social Security as a source of income when they retire.

5. The State Bureau of Standards must inspect gasoline station pumps on a regular basis to be sure they are operating properly. A recent survey of a randomly selected group of 61 pumps produced a sample mean of 9.75 gallons dispensed for a pump reading ten gallons. If the sample had a standard deviation of 1.12 gallons, find the 80% confidence interval for the average amount of gas dispensed when a gas pump reads ten gallons.

6. In a population of non-unionized employees, 55% are sympathetic toward unionization. The American Federation of Labor has drawn a random sample of 250 persons selected from this population to investigate union interest. Construct a 90% confidence interval for the proportion of the sample that will be sympathetic to unionization.

7. Suppose a study designed to collect the data on smokers and nonsmokers uses a preliminary estimate of the proportion that smoke of twenty-two percent. How large a sample should be taken to estimate the proportion of smokers in the population with a margin of error of 0.02 with 88% confidence?

8. Suppose that it has been reported by a group of researchers that the average number of hours of TV viewing per household per week in the United States is 50.4 hours. Suppose the standard deviation is 11.8 hours, and a random sample of 42 U.S. households is taken.

   a. What is the probability that the sample average is more than 35 hours? If the sample average is actually more than 35 hours, what would it mean in terms of the figures presented by the researchers?

   b. Suppose the population standard deviation is unknown. If 71% of all sample means are greater than 49 hours and the population mean is still 50.4 hours, what is the value of the population standard deviation? Use a sample size of 42.

9. As part of an annual review of its accounts, a discount brokerage selects a random sample of 15 customers. Their accounts are reviewed for a total account valuation, which showed a mean of $32,000 with a sample standard deviation of $8200. What is a 99% confidence interval for the mean account valuation of the population of customers? Interpret the interval in terms of the problem.

10. Direct Music has 250 retail outlets throughout the United States. The firm is evaluating a potential location for a new outlet, based in part, on the mean annual income of the individuals in the marketing area of the new location. A sample of size 36 was taken; the sample mean income is $31,100. The population standard deviation is estimated to be $4500. Construct a confidence interval using a confidence coefficient of .95.

11. Suppose we want to determine the sample size required to give us a 95% confidence interval that estimates, to within $500, mean for the average salary of a Virginia Tech employee. Also, suppose that from a previous experiment, we know that $s = \$6300$.

12. A reporter for a student newspaper is writing an article on the cost of off-campus housing. A sample of 16 efficiency apartments within a half-mile of campus resulted in a sample mean of $650 per month and a sample standard deviation of $55. Let us provide a 95% confidence interval estimate of the mean rent per month for the population of efficiency apartments within a half-mile of campus. We will assume that this population is normally distributed.

13. A stock market analyst wants to estimate the average return on a certain stock. A random sample of 15 days yields an average return of 10.37% and a standard deviation of 3.5%. Give a 90% confidence interval for the average return on the stock.

14. Voting, Inc. specializes in voter polls and surveys designed to keep political office seekers informed of their position in a race. Using telephone surveys interviewers ask registered voters who they would vote for if the election were held that day. In a current election campaign, Voting, Inc. has found that 220 registered voters, out of 500 contacted, favor a particular candidate. Voting, Inc. wants to develop a 95% confidence interval estimate for the proportion of the population of registered voters that favor the candidate.

15. Before beginning a pension program for its workers, a corporation wishes to estimate the proportion of its workers who have been employed at the company for at least 20 years. A random sample of 138 employees yielded 16 who have been with the corporation for at least 20 years. Construct a 92.2% confidence interval for the proportion of employees who have worked for this corporation for at least 20 years. Interpret your results.

Discovery Project

The article below was taken from the monthly newsletter of the National Association of Realtors®. The article presents common examples of the use of statistics in the media. Answer the questions at the end of the article. **Source**: National Association of Realtors – realtor.org

Existing-Home Sales Slow in June but Remain Above Year-Ago Levels

WASHINGTON – July 22, 2010

With the scheduled closing deadline for the home buyer tax credits, existing-home sales slowed in June but remained at relatively elevated levels, according to the National Association of Realtors®.

Existing-home sales, which are completed transactions that include single-family, townhomes, condominiums, and co-ops, fell 5.1 percent to a seasonally adjusted annual rate of 5.37 million units in June from 5.66 million in May, but are 9.8 percent higher than the 4.89 million-unit pace in June 2009.

Lawrence Yun, NAR chief economist, said the market shows uncharacteristic yet understandable swings as buyers responded to the tax credits. "June home sales still reflect a tax credit impact with some sales not closed due to delays, which will show up in the next two months," he said.

"Broadly speaking, sales closed after the home buyer tax credit will be significantly lower compared to the credit-induced spring surge. Only when jobs are created at a sufficient pace will home sales return to sustainable healthy levels."

According to Freddie Mac, the national average commitment rate for a 30-year, conventional, fixed-rate mortgage fell to a record low 4.74 percent in June from 4.89 percent in May; the rate was 5.42 percent in June 2009.

The national median existing-home price for all housing types was $183,700 in June, which is 1.0 percent higher than a year ago. Distressed homes were at 32 percent of sales last month, compared with 31 percent in May; it was also 31 percent in June 2009.

NAR president Vicki Cox Golder, owner of Vicki L. Cox & Associates in Tucson, Ariz., said softer home sales expected this summer don't tell the whole story. "Despite these market swings, total annual home sales are rising above 2009 and we're looking for overall gains again this year as well as in 2011," she said.

"Conditions have become more balanced in much of the country, which is good for both buyers and sellers. However, consumers find it even more challenging to navigate the transaction process, especially for distressed properties, which only underscores the value Realtors bring to buyers and sellers in this market."

A parallel NAR practitioner survey shows first-time buyers purchased 43 percent of homes in June, down from 46 percent in May. Investors accounted for 13 percent of sales in June, little changed from 14 percent in May; the remaining purchases were by repeat buyers. All-cash sales were at 24 percent in June compared with 25 percent in May.

Total housing inventory at the end of June rose 2.5 percent to 3.99 million existing homes available for sale, which represents an 8.9-month supply at the current sales pace, up from an 8.3-month supply in May.

"The supply of homes on the market is higher than we'd like to see. But home prices are still holding their ground because prices had already over-corrected in many local markets," Yun said. Raw unsold inventory remains 12.7 percent below the record of 4.58 million in July 2008.

Single-family home sales fell 5.6 percent to a seasonally adjusted annual rate of 4.70 million in June from a level of 4.98 million in May, but are 8.5 percent above the 4.33 million pace in June 2009. The median existing single-family home price was $184,200 in June, up 1.3 percent from a year ago.

Single-family median existing-home prices were higher in 10 out of 19 metropolitan statistical areas reported in June in comparison with June 2009. In addition, existing single-family home sales rose in 12 of the 19 areas from a year ago while two were unchanged.

Existing condominium and co-op sales slipped 1.5 percent to a seasonally adjusted annual rate of 670,000 in June from 680,000 in May, but are 20.5 percent higher than the 556,000-unit pace in June 2009. The median existing condo price was $180,000 in June which is 1.4 percent below a year ago.

Regionally, existing-home sales in the Northeast rose 7.9 percent to an annual level of 960,000 in June and are 17.1 percent above June 2009. The median price in the Northeast was $244,300, down 1.2 percent from a year ago.

Existing-home sales in the Midwest dropped 7.5 percent in June to a pace of 1.23 million but are 11.8 percent higher than a year ago. The median price in the Midwest was $155,900, down 0.1 percent from June 2009.

In the South, existing-home sales fell 6.5 percent to an annual level of 2.01 million in June but are 11.0 percent above June 2009. The median price in the South was $163,600, unchanged from a year ago.

Existing-home sales in the West dropped 9.3 percent to an annual pace of 1.17 million in June but are 0.9 percent higher than a year ago. The median price in the West was $221,800, up 1.5 percent from June 2009.

Questions to Consider:

1. What type of statistical measure is used throughout the article?

2. Are point and interval estimates used in the article?

3. What is the population from which the sample is drawn?

4. What sampling method is used to obtain the data?

5. Are margins of error presented?

6. Overall, do you believe the statistics used in this article are reasonably good estimates of the population? Justify your answer.

Hypothesis Testing: Single Samples

10

Discovering Technology

Performing a large sample hypothesis test for μ using the TI-84 Plus calculator

Performing a small sample hypothesis test for μ using the TI-84 Plus calculator

Calculating the z test statistic using Microsoft Excel

Performing a large sample hypothesis test for μ using Minitab

Performing a small sample hypothesis test for μ using Minitab

Introduction

Given the recent economic crisis – with rising gas/oil prices, the decline of the banking industry and financial markets, as well as many other companies and corporations – one would think that the travel industry would also face a significant decrease in the amount of money spent on vacations (or the number of vacations taken). As part of the domino effect, one would also expect the number of jobs available in the travel industry to be limited. If we wanted to determine if the previous assumptions were valid, we would be interested in making inferences about the average amount of money spent on vacations in the last year versus the amount of money spent on vacations five years ago. Similarly, we would also want to make inferences about the number of jobs available in the travel industry last year versus five years ago. In both cases, we are interested in testing how the value of a parameter relates to (i.e. whether it is less than, equal to, or greater than) some specific numerical value. This type of inference is called **hypothesis testing**, which is the subject of this chapter.

Like the above example, we perform some type of hypothesis test on a daily basis. Whether it's trying to determine if the shower temperature is reasonable (acceptable, too hot, or too cold) or if we want to confirm if the day's weather forecast is accurate (will it be too hot to wear a sweater, adequate, or if you'll be underdressed), this type of subjective decision making is always a part of our lives. We rely on personally accumulated data to help us make informed decisions. What distinguishes statistical hypothesis testing from the everyday variety is the use of statistical measures in the statement of the hypotheses, the collection of the sample data, and the use of the sample data in a well-defined decision-making process.

10.1 Developing a Hypothesis

It should come as no surprise that the first step in all statistical hypothesis testing is a statement of hypothesis, regardless of the nature of the problem. Further, if the hypothesis test is conducted using statistical methods, the hypotheses must be stated in terms of statistical measures such as the population mean, population proportion, or population variance.

Example 10.1

Tech Travel, which is a travel agency managed by C. Dubya, is interested in determining how much money people are spending on travel and entertainment during the economic downturn. From previous data, the agency knows that in 2008, U.S. households spent, on average, a total of $1,415 on transportation, food, lodging, and pleasure trips. However, the agency believes that in spite of economic woes, people will spend more in 2010 on travel than they did two years ago. The agency's question can be investigated with two hypotheses:

- Travel expenses have not increased since 2008.
- Travel expenses have increased since 2008.

To apply statistical methodology to answer the question, the preceding hypotheses must be translated into a problem statement concerning a statistical measure (e.g. mean, proportion, or variance). The statistical measure will be used in the definition of a criterion to decide the issue. There is a great deal of variability in the amount of money one spends on vacations, depending on the location, whether they are flying or driving, etc. Comparing the mean amount spent per family with that which was spent previously is a reasonable method of evaluating the differences. The average amount spent in 2008 is known to be $1,415. However, the average amount spent in 2010 is currently unknown, and that uncertainty is what makes the problem difficult. If μ is defined as

$$\mu = \text{average amount spent on travel expenses in 2010,}$$

then the two claims can be written in the following manner.

$$H_0 : \mu \le \$1415 \quad \begin{pmatrix} \text{Money spent on 2010 travel expenses is} \\ \text{less than or equal to that spent in 2008.} \end{pmatrix}$$

$$H_a : \mu > \$1415 \quad \begin{pmatrix} \text{More money is spent on travel expenses} \\ \text{in 2010 than in 2008.} \end{pmatrix}$$

H_0 is called the **null hypothesis**, and contends that the mean amount spent on travel expenses in 2010 is less than or equal to that spent in 2008. This would contradict the agency's assertion. H_a, called the **alternative hypothesis** and sometimes denoted by H_1, declares that the mean amount spent in 2010 is more than that spent in 2008. Once the problem statement is formulated in terms of the population parameter (in this case, the parameter is μ), sample data can be developed to help determine which hypothesis is more reasonable.

This example illustrates another important component of a hypothesis test, namely, deciding whether H_a should be one-sided or two-sided. In Example 10.1, H_a involves a **one-sided alternative**, since the agency is only interested in whether travelers spent *more* money. If the agency was interested in whether travelers spent *less* money in 2010, then H_a would also have been one-sided, but the inequality would have been in the other direction $\left(H_a: \mu < \$1415\right)$. A **two-sided alternative** $\left(H_a: \mu \neq \$1415\right)$ would indicate that the agency is concerned with expenditures that are *above or below* the average in 2008. One-sided alternatives require a one-tailed hypothesis test and two-sided alternatives require a two-tailed hypothesis test.

The hypothesis testing procedure is a method for choosing between two competing hypotheses. Although the procedure will change for different kinds of hypotheses, there are common elements among all tests.

Common Elements and Comments about Hypothesis Testing

Properties

- The null hypothesis is presumed to be true unless sample data produces overwhelming evidence to the contrary. That is, the test statistic is calculated under the assumption that the null hypothesis is true.

- Sample data is used to calculate a **test statistic**. The form of the test statistic will change depending upon the statistical measure used in the hypothesis statement, μ, p, or σ^2, as well as with the assumptions about knowledge of the population. The test statistic is a component of the criteria used to evaluate the hypothesis. If the test statistic falls into a **rejection region**, the null hypothesis, H_0, will be rejected in favor of the alternative hypothesis, H_a.

- The test statistic is usually designed so that if the null hypothesis is true, the value of the test statistic will "probably" be close to zero. (The notion of *close* is arbitrary. Developing a formal test of a hypothesis will draw upon the theory of sampling distributions and the language of probability to more precisely define the meaning of *close*.)

- The conclusion of the hypothesis test results in a decision to either **reject** or **fail to reject** the null hypothesis. Note that we do not accept the null hypothesis; we only conclude that there is insufficient evidence to support the alternative.

- There is no way to be absolutely certain your decision is correct, no matter which hypothesis is selected.

Roles of the Null and Alternative Hypotheses

In the previous example, we treated the null and alternative hypotheses equally. In the practice of statistical inference, this is not the case. In a statistical test of a hypothesis, the null hypothesis, H_0, is a statement that is presumed to be true unless there is overwhelming evidence in favor of the alternative. In other words, the null hypothesis is given the benefit of the doubt.

A familiar example of the disparate treatment of H_0 and H_a is found in our judicial system.

H_0: defendant is not guilty   (null hypothesis)

H_a: defendant is guilty   (alternative hypothesis)

A jury must believe that the evidence (data) demonstrates guilt "beyond a reasonable doubt" in order to convict a defendant (H_a). However, the defendant only has to demonstrate there is insufficient evidence of guilt in order to be acquitted (H_0). In other words, the null hypothesis $(H_0$: defendant is not guilty$)$ is presumed to be true unless there is overwhelming evidence to the contrary. The defendant is innocent until proven guilty.

In Example 10.1 the hypotheses were formulated as:

Correct		Incorrect
$H_0: \mu \le \$1415$	instead of	~~$H_0: \mu > \$1415$~~
$H_a: \mu > \$1415$		~~$H_a: \mu \le \$1415$~~

The statement $H_0: \mu > \$1415$ says that the average travel expenditures, μ, are greater than they were in 2008. The essence of the problem at hand is whether the statement $\mu > \$1415$ is true or untrue.

The <u>Incorrect</u> Formulation: $H_0: \mu > \$1415$

The incorrect formulation states in the null hypothesis, H_0, that travel expenditures in 2010 were greater than those in 2008. By placing this statement in H_0, the statement is presumed to be true unless there is overwhelming evidence to the contrary. This does not make sense! Why would the agency trying to prove that travel expenditures are greater in 2010 start out by assuming that expenditures in 2010 are greater?

The <u>Correct</u> Formulation: $H_0: \mu \le \$1415$

The agency must demonstrate overwhelming evidence that travel expenditures are greater in 2010 than in 2008 in order to be correct. To achieve this goal, the statement $H_0: \mu > \$1415$ must be placed in the alternative hypothesis. In the correct version, the null hypothesis, $H_0: \mu \le \$1415$, states that we believe that travel expenditures are no greater in 2010 than they were in 2008. Because the null hypothesis is presumed to be true, this hypothesis is not rejected unless there is overwhelming evidence to the contrary. If $H_0: \mu \le \$1415$ is rejected in favor of

$H_a: \mu > \$1415$, then there is overwhelming evidence that households spent more on travel in 2010 than in 2008.

To summarize, the agency wants to know if the travel expenditures are greater in 2010 than in 2008. If the agency is correct, the null hypothesis will be rejected in favor of the alternative. Rejecting the null in favor of the alternative means the sample data overwhelmingly support the idea that expenditures in 2010 are greater than those in 2008. Failing to reject the null hypothesis would mean that there is insufficient evidence to warrant concluding that people spent more on travel in 2010 than they did in 2008.

This type of formulation is typical of a test of a hypothesis in a research environment (testing a new theory or idea against an established one). In many research hypothesis tests, the investigator hopes to reject the null hypothesis in order to demonstrate the significance of a new idea. It is often the case that if there is a standard value for a population parameter, the null hypothesis states that the population parameter is equal to the **standard value**.

Example 10.2

Suppose a potato chip manufacturer is concerned that the bagging equipment is not functioning properly when filling 10 ounce bags. He wants to test a hypothesis that will help determine if there is a problem with the bagging equipment. What are the correct hypotheses?

$$H_0: \mu = 10 \text{ oz} \qquad \qquad H_0: \mu \neq 10 \text{ oz}$$
$$\text{or}$$
$$H_a: \mu \neq 10 \text{ oz} \qquad \qquad H_a: \mu = 10 \text{ oz}$$

Solution

Since the standard value in this problem is 10 ounces, the null hypothesis is $H_0: \mu = 10$ oz. The bagging equipment ordinarily functions properly; thus the manufacturer requires overwhelming evidence that the machine is overfilling or underfilling the bags before shutting down the equipment.

When the alternative hypothesis allows values above and below the standard value, it is called a **two-sided alternative**. In this case, the manufacturer hopes that he *fails to reject* the null hypothesis, since that would suggest that his equipment is putting the right amount in the bags. This type of hypothesis is quite common in quality control and other kinds of system monitoring.

Example 10.3

Analysts at JBN Technologies want to assess the use of Macintoshes and Windows computers in their line of work. With the rise in popularity of Apple and the Mac OS X operating system, analysts believe that businesses are more likely to allow their employees to deploy Macintoshes as their enterprise desktops. How should JBN Technologies analysts formulate an appropriate hypothesis to determine if more businesses will deploy Macintoshes as their enterprise desktops?

Solution

The correct formulation of the hypotheses is

$$H_0 : p \leq .5 \qquad \left(\begin{array}{l} \text{There is not sufficient evidence to believe} \\ \text{enterprises will support Macs.} \end{array} \right)$$

$$H_a : p > .5 \qquad \left(\begin{array}{l} \text{There is sufficient evidence to believe} \\ \text{enterprises will support Macs.} \end{array} \right)$$

Where p is the fraction of enterprises that would support the use of Macintoshes as their desktops.

The problem's formulation requires the use of a different statistical measure, p, the population proportion. The crucial value of the proportion is .5, since in order to believe that more businesses will support Macs, this proportion has to be at least 50%. The null hypothesis contends that there is not sufficient evidence that businesses will support the use of Macs. If the null hypothesis is rejected in favor of the alternative, $H_a : p > .5$, then there is overwhelming evidence that businesses are prepared to adopt Mac computers.

The alternative is one-sided, since the intent of the study is to learn if Macs are more popular in the workplace. (A two-sided alternative would imply interest in finding out if more companies or fewer companies are willing to accept Macs in the workplace, a rather useless idea.) The analysts hope the conclusion of the test will be to *reject* the null hypothesis, since that would support the analysts' claim.

Procedure

Formulating Hypothesis Testing Problems

To be successful at formulating hypothesis testing problems you must be able to:

- determine the appropriate statistical measure to test the desired hypothesis (population mean, proportion, variance, etc.).

- determine the appropriate value to use in the null hypothesis. (This may be stated in the problem as a standard value or may need to be deduced from the information at hand.)

- decide whether the alternative should be one-sided or two-sided.

10.1 Exercises

Basic Concepts

1. What is a hypothesis?

2. What is the first step in the test of a hypothesis?

3. Describe the common elements present in all hypothesis tests.

4. Summarize the difference between the null and alternative hypotheses.

5. Define and give an example of a one-sided alternative. How does this differ from a two-sided alternative?

6. What is the connection between one and two-sided alternatives and one and two-tailed tests?

7. Is there a way to be absolutely certain your decision is correct when performing a hypothesis test? Explain.

8. What is a rejection region?

9. What are the three important things you must be able to do in order to be successful at formulating hypothesis testing problems?

10.2 Reaching a Conclusion

The point of a hypothesis test is to select one of the competing hypotheses $(H_0 \text{ or } H_a)$ as the *correct* decision. Once you have reached a conclusion, there will remain a possibility that the inference (decision) is incorrect. The idea of performing the correct statistical test, exactly following the procedure, and still possibly making an incorrect decision may be bothersome. Uncertainty, however, is a part of every statistical inference.

How Uncertain Are Our Conclusions?

Errors can happen in two ways. In statistical terminology, we call these Type I errors and Type II errors.

Definition

Rejecting H_0 when in fact H_0 is the correct choice is called a **Type I error**.

Type I Error

In a statistical test of hypothesis, we can only control for Type I errors. This fact often influences how we construct hypotheses.

Definition

Failing to reject H_0 when in fact H_a is the correct choice is called a **Type II error**.

Type II Error

Example 10.4

Carmen is the President and CEO of a regional healthcare organization. She has set a target that the average waiting time for non-emergency patients will not exceed 20 minutes. In a random sample (taken over numerous days), she finds the waiting time for 25 patients. Assuming that the population standard deviation of waiting times is eight minutes, how should Carmen formulate the hypotheses as she examines the waiting times?

	True State of Nature	
Decision	H_0 is true	H_0 is false
Reject H_0	Type I Error (rejecting a true H_0) α	Correct Decision
Do Not Reject H_0	Correct Decision	Type II Error (Failing to reject a false H_0) β

Solution

Formulation A

H_0 : Average waiting time does not exceed 20 minutes.

H_a : Average waiting time is more than 20 minutes.

Type I error using Formulation A

To have an error, you must make a mistake. Suppose this is what happened.

Truth: H_0: Average waiting time does not exceed 20 minutes.

Carmen's Decision: H_a: Average waiting time is more than 20 minutes.

To have Type I error, we must reject the null hypothesis when the null hypothesis is true. In this case, Carmen believes that the average waiting time is more than 20 minutes when it is not.

Consequence: Given that the average wait time is not more than 20 minutes, Carmen might spend an unnecessary amount of time and resources changing policies and practices in order to reduce the average wait time.

Type II error using Formulation A

Carmen's Decision: H_0: Average waiting time does not exceed 20 minutes.

Truth: H_a: Average waiting time is more than 20 minutes.

A Type II error means that we fail to reject the null hypothesis when the alternative hypothesis is true.

Consequence: In this case, Carmen believes that the average wait time is not more than 20 minutes, but it is actually more than 20 minutes. In this situation, Carmen doesn't make changes to any policies and practices to make things better, leaving patients unhappy.

Let's examine another formulation.

Formulation B

H_0: Average waiting time is 20 minutes or more.
H_a: Average waiting time is less than 20 minutes.

Type I error using Formulation B

Truth: H_0: Average waiting time is 20 minutes or more.

Carmen's Decision: H_a: Average waiting time is less than 20 minutes.

Carmen believes that the average wait time is less than 20 minutes when, in fact, the average wait time is 20 minutes or more.

Consequence: Carmen believes that the average wait time is adequate (less than 20 minutes) when in fact the average wait time is more than 20 minutes. In this situation, Carmen doesn't make any changes to improve the services being provided risking the potential loss of customers.

Type II error using Formulation B

Carmen's Decision: H_0 : Average waiting time is 20 minutes or more.

Truth: H_a : Average waiting time is less than 20 minutes.

Carmen believes that the average wait time is 20 minutes or more when in fact the average wait time is less than 20 minutes.

Consequence: Since Carmen believes that the average wait time is more than 20 minutes, she will likely change policies and procedures to reduce the waiting time. However, since the true average waiting time is less than 20 minutes, Carmen will have wasted time and resources to improve a service that currently doesn't need to be improved.

For Carmen, the most serious consequence is wasting time and resources to improve a process that doesn't need to be improved. She has decided that she would rather risk a loss of customers than implement changes to a functional process. Therefore, given the two formulations, A and B, Formulation A is the correct formulation of the problem, since the most serious consequence is the result of a Type I error. That's good because the probability of a Type I error can be controlled in the hypothesis testing procedure.

Given the two formulations, A and B, Formulation A is the correct formulation of the problem, since the most serious consequence is the result of a Type I error. That's good because the probability of a Type I error can be controlled in the hypothesis testing procedure.

The last example demonstrates an important consideration when formulating hypotheses that is worth repeating. **Formulate the hypotheses so that the most serious consequence of a mistaken decision is associated with a Type I error**.

Definition

The probability of a Type I error is denoted by α (the Greek letter alpha), and is referred to as the **level of the test**, or **significance level of the test**.

Level of the Test, α

It is up to the researcher to select alpha prior to the start of the hypothesis test.

β

> ### Definition
>
> The probability of a Type II error is denoted by β (the Greek letter beta). Unfortunately, the value of β depends on the actual value of the population parameter and thus cannot be determined unless the actual value of the population parameter is known, which is rarely the case.

In examining the relationship between α and β, a natural question which might arise is:

Why not make both α and β as small as possible?

Unfortunately, the probability of making a Type I error, α, and the probability of making a Type II error, β, are inversely related. Thus, the smaller we make the probability of making a Type I error, the more likely we are to make a Type II error. Choose the largest level of α which is tolerable to avoid unnecessarily increasing the probability of making a Type II error.

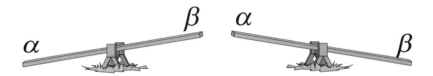

10.2 Exercises

Basic Concepts

1. Describe a Type I error.

2. Describe a Type II error.

3. Explain how Type I and Type II errors influence the construction of a hypothesis.

4. Can both Type I and Type II errors be controlled in the hypothesis testing procedure? Explain.

5. What is the level of the test?

6. Why is a Type II error difficult to express numerically?

Exercises

1. For the following situations, develop the appropriate H_0 and H_a and state what the consequences would be for Type I and Type II errors.

   a. The Standard Tire Company has introduced a new tire in Europe that will be guaranteed to last at least 30,000 kilometers. Standard Tire has hired an independent agency to determine if there is overwhelming evidence that their tires will last through the warranty period.

   b. Mrs. Russell, head product tester for Hathaway Tool Corporation, is testing a newly designed series of bar hooks. The hooks have been designed to give way if they get too hot. The previous design gave way at 240 degrees. Develop a test to determine if the newly designed hooks give way at a higher temperature than the previous design.

   c. The regional manager of a large grocery store chain believes that a checkout person using a new scanner can process a full basket of groceries in less than seven minutes. Develop a test to determine if there is overwhelming evidence to support the manager's belief.

2. For the following situations, develop the appropriate H_0 and H_a and state what the consequences would be for Type I and Type II errors.

   a. A company that manufactures one-half inch bolts selects a random sample of bolts to determine if the diameter of the bolts differs significantly from the required one-half inch.

   b. A company that manufactures safety flares randomly selects 100 flares to determine if the flares last at least three hours on average.

   c. A consumer group believes that a new sports coupe gets significantly fewer miles to the gallon than advertised on the sales sticker. To confirm this belief, they randomly select several of the new coupes and measure the miles per gallon.

10.3 A Procedure for Testing Hypothesis

A procedure for testing a hypothesis is given below. In examining this procedure, you will notice we have already discussed the first five steps. The next two steps define a decision rule, which is a criterion used to determine whether the null or the alternative hypothesis will be chosen. As you look over these steps, do not be overly concerned if you do not understand everything. You will learn by following the examples.

Procedure

Steps in the Test of a Hypothesis

Step 1:

Define the hypothesis to be tested in plain English.

↓

Step 2:

Select the appropriate statistical measure, such as the mean, proportion, or variance, to restate the hypothesis.

↓

Step 3:

Determine whether the hypotheses should be one-sided or two-sided.

↓

Step 4:

State the hypotheses using the statistical measure found in Step 2.

↓

Step 5:

Specify α, the level of the test.

↓

Step 6:

Select the appropriate test statistic based on the information at hand and the assumptions you are willing to make.

Step 7:

Determine the critical value of the test statistic. Three factors must be considered:

1. The type of alternative hypothesis: two-sided, one-sided left, one-sided right.
2. The specification of α, the level of the test.
3. The distribution of the test statistic.

Step 8:

Collect sample data and compute the value of the test statistic.

Step 9:

Make the decision:

- If the value of the test statistic is in the rejection region, reject the null hypothesis in favor of the alternative.
- If the value of the test statistic is not in the rejection region, do not reject the null hypothesis.

Step 10:

State the conclusion in terms of the original question.

10.3 Exercises

Basic Concepts

1. State the 10 steps of a hypothesis test.

10.4 Testing a Hypothesis about a Population Mean

The following example will be used to illustrate the hypothesis testing procedure. The example goes through all the steps and contains detailed explanations of several new concepts.

Example 10.6

Suppose that the average amount of money a student spends on textbooks per semester at college campuses in the U.S. is $500 with a standard deviation of $100. A local university wants to know if their students are spending that amount on textbooks. The level of the test is to be set at .05. A random sample of 75 college students has been selected and the resulting average is $540 spent per semester on textbooks.

Solution

Step 1: Define the hypotheses in plain English.

The hypotheses are fairly straightforward.

- The local university's students are spending an average of $500 per semester on textbooks.

- The students are not spending an average of $500 per semester on textbooks.

Step 2: Select the appropriate statistical measure.

Since the problem states that the university wants to know how much their students are spending on textbooks per semester in relation to the national average, the hypotheses will concern the population mean. Let

μ = average amount spent on textbooks per semester by college students at the local university.

Step 3: Determine whether the hypotheses should be one-sided or two-sided.

Nothing is mentioned in the problem to indicate that the university is interested in learning if their students are spending more than the national average per semester on textbooks, nor is there anything mentioned that the university is interested in learning if their students are spending less than the national average per semester on textbooks. Thus, it is assumed that the university is interested in determining if there is any departure from the national average. Consequently, the problem needs to be formulated as a two-sided alternative.

Step 4: State the hypotheses using the appropriate statistical measure.

$$H_0: \mu = \$500$$
$$H_a: \mu \neq \$500$$

The null hypothesis states that the average amount spent per semester on textbooks at the local university is equal to the national average (the standard value). The alternative states that it is not. This is an application of testing against the standard value.

Step 5: Specify the level of the test.

The level of the test has been defined in the problem statement as the $\alpha = .05$ level. If it were not specified in the problem statement, then it would be necessary to select the value. Typical values for the level of the test are .10, .05, and .01. It is important to remember that the level of the test specifies the probability of a Type I error.

Step 6: Select the appropriate test statistic.

What we know about the population will affect the methods used to perform the test of the hypothesis. There are three key questions:

1. Is the variance of the population known?
2. Is the distribution of the population normal?
3. Is the sample size large?

Is the variance of the population known?

In most instances, the variance of the population will not be known.

Is the distribution of the population normal?

If we have a large sample size $(n \geq 30)$, we will not have to be concerned about the distribution of the population. If the sample size is small $(n < 30)$, then the distribution of the population will need to be normally distributed. When the population is normal, then the histogram of the sample data should be bell-shaped. However, should the frequency distribution show substantial deviation from normality, a nonparametric procedure may be warranted. These methods are discussed in Chapter 16.

Is the sample size large?

Fortunately, the central limit theorem enables us to define the following rule to make this decision.

Formula

If $n \geq 30$ or if the standard deviation of the population, σ, is known and the sample is drawn from a normal population, then by the central limit theorem the test statistic is approximately given by

$$z = \frac{\bar{x} - \mu_0}{\sigma_{\bar{x}}}, \text{ where } \sigma_{\bar{x}} = \frac{\sigma}{\sqrt{n}}$$

where z has a standard normal distribution.

If σ is unknown and n is greater than or equal to 30, s can be used as an approximation of σ.

The symbol for the hypothesized mean is μ_0. In this example, $\mu_0 = \$500$. The difference between the symbols μ and μ_0 is that μ_0 is a specific claim about the value of μ. The actual value of μ is unknown since it is a population parameter.

In this example, the symbol μ refers to the mean amount spent per semester on textbooks at the local university. If this value were known, then it would be easy to decide which of the two claims

$$H_0: \mu = \$500 \quad \text{(null hypothesis)}$$
$$H_a: \mu \neq \$500 \quad \text{(alternative hypothesis)}$$

is correct.

What is the Rationale for the Test Statistic?

Although the true population mean is unknown, the central limit theorem implies that the sample mean, $\bar{x}$, is usually close to the population mean, μ, if the sample data is representative of the population. **If the null hypothesis is true**, the value of the population mean is specified in the null hypothesis, $H_0: \mu = \$500$. **If the null is true**, the sample mean $\bar{x}$ should be close to 500 (μ_0).

$$\mu_0 \quad \bar{x}$$

Another way of expressing this idea of closeness is to measure the difference between the sample mean and the hypothesized mean, $\bar{x} - \mu_0$. The difference should be close to zero, *if the null is true*.

Conversely, a large distance between $\bar{x}$ and μ_0

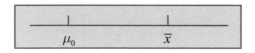

$$\mu_0 \qquad\qquad \bar{x}$$

would indicate either an improbable value of $\bar{x}$ has been observed given that the null hypothesis is true; or that the null hypothesis is false and μ_0 is not the actual value of the population mean.

Although this approach has intuitive appeal, the notion of *close* is too ambiguous to have practical value. Changing the unit of measure from inches to miles may affect one's perception of closeness. What is needed is a statistic that will be the same regardless of the scale of measurement the sample data possesses.

Measuring Closeness

Converting the distance, $\bar{x} - \mu_0$, into standard deviation units using the z-transformation eliminates the problems caused by differing measurement scales, since the value of the z-transformation will be the same regardless of the unit of measure.

Recall that the z-transformation is $z = \dfrac{x - \mu}{\sigma_{\bar{x}}}$. The variable x represents the random variable that will be transformed. In this case, the random variable to be transformed is $\bar{x}$. The symbol μ in the z-transformation stands for the mean of the random variable being transformed $(\bar{x})$. In Example 10.6, the null hypothesis states that $\mu_0 = \$500$. **If the null hypothesis is true**, μ_0 is the mean of the population and thus the mean of the sample means.

Using the data provided in Example 10.6 and substituting $\bar{x}$, σ, n, and μ_0 into the formula for the z-transformation yields

$$z = \frac{\bar{x} - \mu_0}{\sigma_{\bar{x}}} = \frac{540 - 500}{100 / \sqrt{75}} \approx 3.4641$$

$$\text{where } \sigma_{\bar{x}} = \frac{\sigma}{\sqrt{n}} = \frac{100}{\sqrt{75}} \approx 11.5470.$$

The resulting z-value, 3.46, is the number of standard deviations that the sample mean (540) is from the hypothesized value of the mean, 500 (μ_0). If $\bar{x}$ is close to the hypothesized value, then the z-value is close to zero. If $\bar{x}$ is far away from the hypothesized value, the z-value will be large in absolute value. The larger z grows, the more difficult it becomes to believe H_0 is true. In this example, $\bar{x}$ is 3.46 standard deviation units from the hypothesized mean. How far does the hypothesized value of the null hypothesis, μ_0, need to be from $\bar{x}$ before we would be willing to believe that the deviation was not caused by ordinary sampling variability? If $\bar{x}$ is an improbable event given H_0 is true, then we have two choices. We could believe H_0 is true, and we have witnessed a rare event caused by sampling variability, or we say that we doubt that we have witnessed a rare event and believe H_a is true.

Modern Hypothesis Testing

Many of the concepts in modern hypothesis testing were first proposed by Jerzy Neyman and Egon Pearson.

They were the first to recognize the need for an alternative hypothesis.

They developed and named the notions of Type I and Type II errors.

They proposed a term, "critical region," to denote a set of sample statistical values leading to the rejection of the hypothesis being tested.

Is an $\bar{x}$ that is 3.46 standard deviation units from the mean a rare occurrence? When we study P-values later in this chapter this question will be answered quite specifically. But to answer that question, an understanding of the sampling variability of the z-value will be essential in judging the likelihood that any difference between $\bar{x}$ and μ_0 is due to ordinary sampling variability.

The original motivation for using the z-transformation was that it provided a reasonable method of measuring how close the sample mean was to the hypothesized mean. While this is true, it suggests concern only with the results of one sample. However, to develop a theory which can be applied to all possible samples, we must broaden the discussion to all potential values of $\bar{x}$ and z. In other words, we must concern ourselves with the sampling distribution of $\bar{x}$.

Fortunately, the central limit theorem provides a great deal of information about the variability of $\bar{x}$. Namely, that it is normally distributed and has the same mean as the population from which the sample is drawn. The standard deviation of $\bar{x}$ is known to be $\dfrac{\sigma}{\sqrt{n}}$, the standard deviation of the population being sampled divided by the square root of the sample size.

The test statistic, z, is a random variable because $\bar{x}$ is a random variable. It will be normally distributed because $\bar{x}$ has a normal distribution.

In addition to measuring the distance between $\bar{x}$ and μ_0, the numerator of the z-transformation $(\bar{x} - \mu_0)$ also centers the distribution of the transformed random variable $\bar{x}$ around zero. If the null hypothesis is true, then the mean of $\bar{x}$ will be correctly specified in the null hypothesis, and the centering will work. If the null hypothesis is false, the mean of z will not be centered at 0. By using the z-transformation, we have shifted the focus of the problem. Instead of focusing our attention directly on $\bar{x}$ and its relation to the hypothesized value of μ, the crux of the hypothesis test will be to decide whether the z-value is near zero, or not. In our case the question is whether 3.46 is close to 0 or not.

This question will be addressed when the decision rule is constructed.

If the null hypothesis is true, the z-test statistic has a normal distribution with a mean of 0 and a standard deviation of 1.

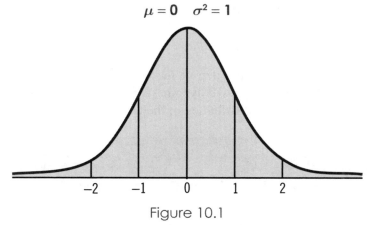

z-The Standard Normal Random Variable

$\mu = 0 \quad \sigma^2 = 1$

Figure 10.1

If the null is true, the distribution of the z-test statistic is known (normal with mean 0 and standard deviation 1), and a plan can be developed for defining ordinary variability of the test statistic. Since the test statistic has a z-distribution, we know that 95% of the time the value of z should be within ±1.96 standard deviations of the mean.

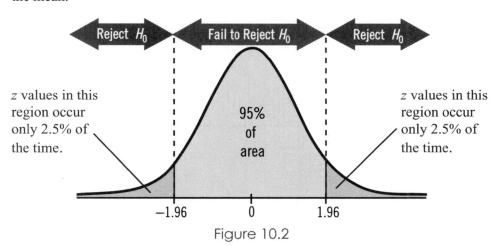

Figure 10.2

A Decision Strategy

Suppose we claim that any value of the z-test statistic less than 1.96 in absolute value represents ordinary sampling variability of $\bar{x}$. Any value of $|z|$ greater than or equal to 1.96 is attributed to a false null hypothesis.

It is important to recognize that this strategy attempts to define the notion of *close* (for $\alpha = .05$) as being within 1.96 standard deviation units. Using this definition of closeness, if $\bar{x}$ is within 1.96 standard deviations of the hypothesized value, it is close enough to the hypothesized value in the null to have occurred from ordinary sampling variability; otherwise it is too far to have happened by chance, and we reject the null. In our example, 1.96 is a **critical value** of z.

Continuing Example 10.6

Step 7: Determine the critical value.

In determining the critical value of the test statistic, we must take into account whether the alternative hypothesis is one-sided or two-sided, the level of the test, and the distribution of the test statistic.

Table 10.1 – Critical Values of the z-Test Statistic for Two-Sided Alternatives		
Level of Test	**Definition of Ordinary Variability**	**z**
.20	80% interval around hypothesized mean	1.28
.10	90% interval around hypothesized mean	1.645
.05	95% interval around hypothesized mean	1.96
.01	99% interval around hypothesized mean	2.575

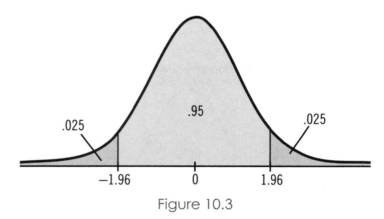

Figure 10.3

Notice that the **rejection region** is divided into two parts. The right hand rejection region indicates above average amounts of money spent on textbooks per semester and, conversely, the left hand rejection region indicates below average amounts of money spent on textbooks per semester. Also observe that the probability associated with the level of the test is divided equally between the two rejection regions, each region receiving .025. If the probabilities in these two regions are added together, .025 + .025 = .05, the sum equals the level of the test (α).

The level of the test can be thought of as a tolerance for rareness. The level of the test defines a rejection region which can be thought of as an intolerance zone. If the test statistic falls in this "intolerance" region, then the data have produced a sample mean that has in turn produced a test statistic that is too rare to have occurred by chance if the null were true.

Essentially, we lose faith in the null hypothesis; the data has cast too much doubt. Consequently, the null hypothesis is rejected. The "fail to reject" zone can be interpreted as a zone of ordinary sampling variation given the null is true. For two-tailed tests with the level of the test set to $\alpha = .05$, the investigator is stating that any value of the test statistic which falls in a 95% interval around the hypothesized mean represents ordinary sampling variability. For the z-test statistic, this corresponds to a critical value of 1.96 standard deviation units (see Table 10.1). If the test statistic falls into the ordinary sampling variation zone, the null hypothesis will not be rejected.

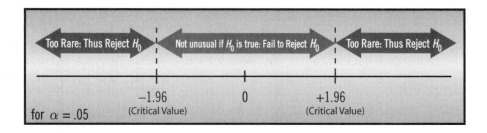

Step 8: Compute the test statistic.

A random sample of 75 students revealed a mean of $540 per semester spent on textbooks at the local university. As discussed earlier, the z-statistic is given by

$$z = \frac{\bar{x} - \mu_0}{\sigma_{\bar{x}}} = \frac{540 - 500}{100 / \sqrt{75}} \approx 3.46.$$

The sample mean is 3.46 standard deviations from the hypothesized value. Is the sample mean too far away from the value of the mean specified in the null hypothesis for us to believe that the null is true?

Step 9: Make the decision.

The critical values of the test statistic are ±1.96. If the null were true, observing a value of z larger in absolute value than 1.96 would occur only 5% of the time.

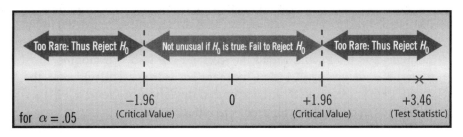

The test statistic $z = 3.46$ implies $\bar{x}$ is 3.46 standard deviation units from the mean which is substantially more than 1.96 standard deviations from the hypothesized value. The decision must be to reject H_0. The sample mean is too far from the hypothesized value for us to believe the difference is caused by ordinary sampling variation. Essentially, $\bar{x}$ exceeds the tolerance for rareness that we have imposed by setting $\alpha = .05$.

Step 10: State the conclusion in terms of the original question.

There is significant evidence at the .05 level that the students at the local university do not spend, on average, $500 per semester on textbooks. It would be tempting to conclude that the students at the local university spend more since the sample mean is greater than the national average. However, we did not test a hypothesis for spending more; we tested whether the students at the local university were spending *more or less* than the national average, and the conclusion must be consistent with the hypothesis tested.

Stating a Conclusion

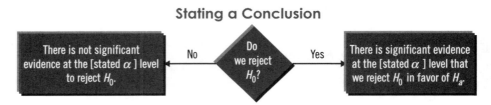

One temptation might be to reformulate the hypothesis and test to see if the students are spending more on textbooks with the same data. This would be practically unethical. If you already know the z-value for a given set of data, you should not formulate a hypothesis and use the data to "support" that hypothesis.

Part of every hypothesis test is arbitrary. The level of the test, α, is arbitrarily defined by the researcher. As you have seen (e.g. Table 10.1) in the last example, the level of the test affects the decision rule. Since the level of the test is arbitrarily set, the decision rule inherits the arbitrariness.

Example 10.7

The manufacturer of a portable music player (PMP) has shown that the average life of the product is 72 months with a standard deviation of 12 months. The manufacturer is considering using a new parts supplier for the PMPs and wants to test that the new hard drives will increase the life of the PMP. Before manufacturing the PMPs on a large scale, the manufacturer sampled 200 PMPs and found the average life to be 78 months. Test the hypothesis using $\alpha = .01$ that the new hard drives will increase the life of the PMPs. Assume that the standard deviation of the new PMPs is the same as the standard deviation of the older model.

Solution

Step 1: Define the hypotheses in plain English.

The hypotheses are fairly straightforward:

- The new hard drives do not increase the life of the PMPs.
- The new hard drives increase the life of the PMPs.

Step 2: Select the appropriate statistical measure.

Once again, the population mean is the parameter of interest. If the average life of the new PMP is greater than the average life of the older model, all other things being equal, the new PMP will be better. Let

$$\mu = \text{mean life of the new PMP.}$$

Step 3: Determine whether the hypotheses should be one-sided or two-sided.

The goal is to determine if there is sufficient evidence to conclude that the new PMPs will last longer, on average, than the older model. The hypotheses will be one-sided.

Step 4: State the hypotheses using the appropriate statistical measure.

In the formulation of the hypotheses, we will be comparing the life of the new PMP model to that of the older model. Comparing a new model or design against an older model (or "standard value") is very common in hypothesis testing.

$$H_0 : \mu \leq 72$$
$$H_a : \mu > 72$$

Remember, if the purpose is to demonstrate that there is overwhelming evidence in support of a hypothesis, that hypothesis should be the alternative hypothesis. In this example, the aim is to determine if there is sufficient evidence to conclude that the new PMP model will last longer.

Step 5: Specify the level of the test.

The level of the test is given in the problem to be $\alpha = .01$. If it were not given, the investigator would choose the level.

Step 6: Select the appropriate test statistic.

The problem states that the standard deviation of the new model is equivalent to the standard deviation of the older model, which is known. Therefore, the standard deviation of the new PMP's life is assumed to be known. Since the sample is relatively large, the central limit theorem asserts the distribution of $\bar{x}$ should be approximately normal. Because the standard deviation is known and the sample is a sufficient size, the z-test statistic can be used.

Step 7: Determine the critical value.

Since the alternative hypothesis is one-sided, we want to know if there is evidence that μ (the mean life of the new PMP model) is greater than the hypothesized value μ_0 (72 months – the standard life of the existing PMP model). If $\bar{x}$ (the mean life of the 200 PMP sample) is much larger than μ_0, that would suggest that H_a is a more reasonable choice than H_0. Of course, through ordinary sampling variation, $\bar{x}$ could be larger than μ_0. How much greater than μ_0 does $\bar{x}$ have to be in order for us to believe that the mean life of the new PMP is greater than 72 months (H_a)?

Table 10.2 – Critical Values of the z-Test Statistic for One-Sided (Greater Than) Alternatives		
Level of Test	**Definition of Ordinary Variability**	**z**
.20	Lower 80% of the distribution	0.84
.10	Lower 90% of the distribution	1.28
.05	Lower 95% of the distribution	1.645
.01	Lower 99% of the distribution	2.33

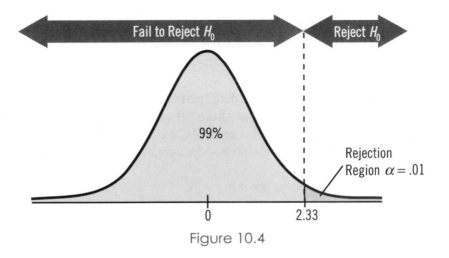

Figure 10.4

The z-test statistic has a standard normal distribution; so critical values are determined from the probability distribution of the standard normal distribution. The alternative hypothesis is one-sided $\left(H_a : \mu > 72\right)$ and $\alpha = .01$. From Table 10.2, we find that the appropriate critical value for the test is 2.33. This critical value means that if $\bar{x}$ is 2.33 standard deviations larger than μ_0, then H_0 should be rejected in favor of H_a. However, if H_0 is true, ordinary variation would cause $\bar{x}$ to be greater than 2.33 about 1% of the time. Thus, 1% of the time H_0 will be rejected when it is true, a Type I error. To locate the critical value of z for a one-sided "greater than" alternative, find the value of z that cuts off α worth of probability in the right hand tail of the distribution. The critical values for "greater than" alternative hypotheses are given in Table 10.2 for typical values of α.

Procedure

One-sided "Less Than" Alternatives

For tests which are based on a test statistic which has a standard normal distribution and "less than" alternatives, find the value of z that cuts off α worth of probability in the left hand tail of the distribution. The critical values for "less than" alternative hypotheses are given in Table 10.3 for typical values of α.

Table 10.3 – Critical Values of the z-Test Statistic for One-Sided (Less Than) Alternatives		
Level of Test	**Definition of Ordinary Variability**	**z**
.20	Upper 80% of the distribution	−0.84
.10	Upper 90% of the distribution	−1.28
.05	Upper 95% of the distribution	−1.645
.01	Upper 99% of the distribution	−2.33

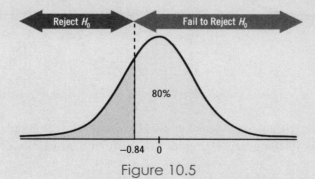

Figure 10.5

The figure above shows the rejection region for a test with a one-sided "less than" alternative hypothesis, and a significance level of .20. For this test, the null hypothesis will be rejected if the calculated value of the test statistic is less than or equal to −0.84.

Step 8: Compute the test statistic.

Suppose a random sample of 200 PMPs revealed a mean life of 78 months. The resulting z-test statistic is

$$z = \frac{\bar{x} - \mu_0}{\sigma_{\bar{x}}} = \frac{78 - 72}{12 \Big/ \sqrt{200}} \approx 7.07$$

indicating that the sample mean life of the new PMP model is more than 7 standard deviations larger than the life of the current PMP model. It is quite unlikely that ordinary sampling variation could have caused the sample mean to be more than 7 standard deviations from the hypothesized value.

Step 9: Make the decision.

Since the test statistic is larger than the critical value, the conclusion is to reject H_0 in favor of H_a.

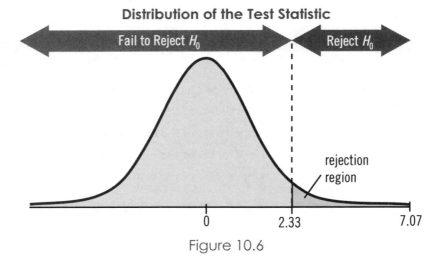

Distribution of the Test Statistic

Figure 10.6

Step 10: State the conclusion in terms of the original question

There is sufficient evidence at the $\alpha = .01$ level to conclude that the life of the new PMP model is superior to the life of the older model.

Small Sample Hypothesis Tests, σ Unknown

The previous hypothesis testing strategy assumes that the sample size is greater than or equal to 30 or the standard deviation of the population is known and the population is normal. However, in most instances, the population standard deviation is just as unknown as the population mean, and sometimes a sample size of at least 30 is not feasible from either a cost or a time perspective. Despite the added uncertainty, the general approach to testing a hypothesis is the same provided that it is reasonable to assume that the population from which you are sampling is normal. Some of the technical details concerning the distribution of the test statistic change, since the sample standard deviation, s, will be used in place of the population standard deviation, σ, and $n < 30$. This modification will cause a change in the distribution of the test statistic.

Formula

If the standard deviation of the population is unknown, but the distribution of the population is normal, then the test statistic is given by

$$t = \frac{\overline{x} - \mu_0}{s_{\overline{x}}}, \text{ where } s_{\overline{x}} = \frac{s}{\sqrt{n}}.$$

t-Test Statistic

The test statistic has a t-distribution with $n - 1$ degrees of freedom.

If we assume the population we are sampling from is normally distributed, the test statistic has a t-distribution. Consequently, the test statistic will be called a t-test statistic. The fundamental notion embodied in the test statistic has not changed. It measures how far the sample mean is from the hypothesized mean in standard deviation units.

In the previous chapter, we discussed the t-distribution in conjunction with estimating the population mean. Steps 6 and 7 in our hypothesis testing procedure must be modified to reflect the change in distribution of the test statistic.

Example 10.8

A website developer has indicated to potential clients that for the sites he has developed, visitors spend an average of 45 minutes per day on the sites. One of his potential clients conducted a survey of 20 visitors to several of his sites and found that the average time spent on the sites was 35 minutes with a standard deviation of 7 minutes. Determine if there is sufficient evidence to conclude that the average time spent on his sites is different from what he has indicated. Conduct the test at the .05 level.

Solution

Step 1: Define the hypotheses in plain English.

- The average time spent on the sites is 45 minutes.

- The average time spent on the sites is not 45 minutes.

Step 2: Select the appropriate statistical measure.

In this case, the population consists of the time spent per visitor on all of the sites created by the web developer. Since the test is specified as having an average amount of time spent on the sites of 45 minutes, the parameter of interest will be the population mean. Let

μ = mean time spent on sites created by the web developer.

Step 3: Determine whether the hypotheses should be one-sided or two-sided.

From the information given, we must assume that the client is interested in learning if the time spent on the sites is either significantly longer than 45 minutes or significantly less than 45 minutes. Thus the hypotheses will be two-sided.

Step 4: State the hypotheses using the appropriate statistical measure.

The resulting hypotheses would be

$$H_0 : \mu = 45$$
$$H_a : \mu \neq 45$$

Step 5: Specify the level of the test.

The level of the test is specified as .05.

Step 6: Select the appropriate test statistic.

Since the standard deviation of the population is not known and the sample size is less than 30, the t-test statistic is utilized. However, to know that the test statistic possesses a t-distribution, we must be willing to make the assumption that the population possesses a reasonably normal distribution. At this state, we will have to assume normality of the population since there is not enough data available to provide much assistance.

Step 7: Determine the critical value.

The *t*-distribution has a parameter called degrees of freedom, which must be defined in order to utilize the distribution. Since 20 employees were sampled, the degrees of freedom are

$$df = n - 1 = 20 - 1 = 19.$$

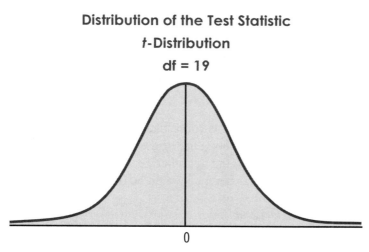

Distribution of the Test Statistic
t-Distribution
df = 19

0

Figure 10.7

Since the alternative hypothesis (H_a) is two-sided, two tails of the distribution must be cut off as rejection regions. Each tail will receive half of the allotted level of the test. The value of *t* which begins the right hand side rejection region is $t_{.025,19}$, which corresponds to a value of 2.093. Since the *t*-distribution is symmetrical, the left hand side rejection region begins at −2.093.

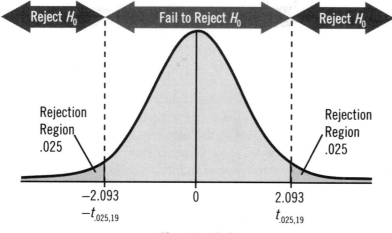

Reject H_0 Fail to Reject H_0 Reject H_0

Rejection
Region
.025

Rejection
Region
.025

−2.093   0   2.093
$-t_{.025,19}$ $t_{.025,19}$

Figure 10.8

What the picture says is that it is unlikely (only occurs 5% of the time) that ordinary sampling variability will cause $\bar{x}$ to differ as much as 2.093 standard deviation units from the hypothesized mean of 45.

Step 8: Compute the test statistic.

Since 20 visitors were sampled and the mean time spent on the sites was 35 minutes with a standard deviation of 7 minutes, the computed value of the test statistic is

$$t = \frac{\bar{x} - \mu_0}{s_{\bar{x}}} = \frac{35 - 45}{7/\sqrt{20}} \approx -6.39.$$

The observed sample mean is more than 6 standard deviations less than the hypothesized mean. The value of the test statistic signifies a striking difference between $\bar{x}$ and the hypothesized value, μ_0. It is very unlikely that the cause of such a difference would be ordinary sampling variation.

Step 9: Make the decision.

Since the test statistic falls in the rejection region, we must reject H_0 in favor of H_a.

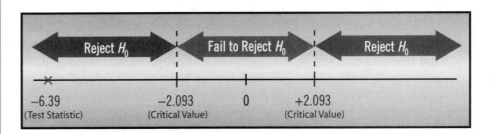

Step 10: State the conclusion in terms of the original question.

There is sufficient evidence at the $\alpha = .05$ level to conclude that the average time spent on the developer's sites is different from 45 minutes. Since the sample mean is much less than the indicated 45 minutes, it is tempting to conclude that the time spent on the sites is less than 45 minutes. However, we did not test the one-sided hypothesis. If the potential client would like to demonstrate that visitors spend significantly less time on the developer's sites, then they must start over by testing a one-sided hypothesis and obtaining new sample data.

Example 10.9

The Alexander Bolt Company produces half-inch A-class stainless steel bolts. The specified quality standard is that they have a mean tensile strength of more than 4000 pounds. These bolts are primarily used in the manufacturing of farm implements. The company is very concerned about quality and wants to be sure that its A-class product does not fall below the standard. A sample of 25 bolts is to be randomly selected from stock and tested for tensile strength. Design a test of hypothesis to determine if there is overwhelming evidence that the bolts meet the specified quality standard.

Solution

Step 1: State the hypotheses in plain English.

- The half-inch A-class stainless steel bolts have a mean tensile strength of no more than 4000 pounds.

- The half-inch A-class stainless steel bolts have a mean tensile strength of more than 4000 pounds.

Step 2: Select the appropriate statistical measure.

Although there is nothing in the problem that specifically defines the population parameter of interest, there is mention of a "standard value". By comparing the mean breaking strength of the population to the **standard value**, 4000 pounds, a conclusion about the quality can be drawn. Let

μ = mean tensile strength of the half-inch A-class stainless steel bolts.

Step 3: Determine whether the hypotheses should be one-sided or two-sided.

If the population mean is significantly above the standard, then there would be evidence that the desired quality is being produced. Thus, the hypotheses will be one-sided.

Step 4: State the hypotheses using the appropriate statistical measure.

The resulting hypotheses would be:

$H_0: \mu \leq 4000$ Mean tensile strength is below the quality standard of 4000 pounds. The bolt production system is flawed.

$H_a: \mu > 4000$ Mean tensile strength is above 4000 pounds. The bolt production system is working well.

This is another problem in which we are comparing something to a standard value. In this case, the **standard value** is 4000 pounds.

Step 5: Specify the level of the test.

The level of the test is not stated in the problem, and thus the selection is left to the researcher. This is a typical predicament and, unfortunately, leaves us with what appears to be an arbitrary decision regarding the level of the test. What is a reasonable value for the level of the test?

In this problem, making a Type I error (rejecting the null hypothesis when it is true) means that management believes that the bolt production system is not flawed, when it is. If we set α too high, management will too frequently believe the quality level is being met, when it is not and poor quality bolts will not be readily detected. After all is said and done, the decision remains arbitrary. A Type I error could be calamitous, so a small level of alpha would be desirable. Let's use $\alpha = .01$.

Step 6: Select the appropriate test statistic.

The population standard deviation is unknown and will be estimated with the sample standard deviation, and the sample size is less than 30. Assuming the distribution of the tensile strengths is reasonably normal, the t-statistic is appropriate.

Step 7: Determine the critical value.

Since the alternative hypothesis implies that we are interested in discovering if the mean is above the standard value, the rejection region will only be on the right hand side of the sampling distribution. Because the level of the test has been chosen to be .01, the interval encompassing .01 of the area on the right hand side of the curve will define the rejection region. The test statistic has a t-distribution.

To obtain the critical value, first determine the degrees of freedom.

$$d.f. = n - 1 = 25 - 1 = 24$$

Large negative values of t indicate that the sample mean is substantially smaller than the hypothesized population mean. If the observed t-value is greater than 2.492 $\left(\text{using Table D in the Appendix, } t_{.010,24} = 2.492\right)$ then the observed mean is presumed to be too far from the hypothesized value to have occurred from ordinary sample variation. If $t > 2.492$, the presumption will be that the mean tensile strength is greater than 4000 pounds per square inch.

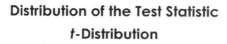

Distribution of the Test Statistic
t-Distribution
df = 24

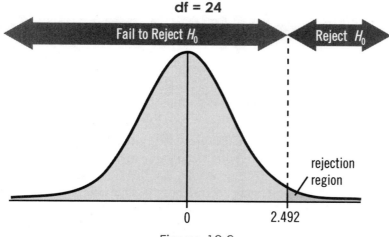

Figure 10.9

Step 8: Compute the test statistic:

Suppose that after randomly selecting and testing 25 bolts, the average tensile strength is 4014 pounds per square inch, with a standard deviation of 20 pounds per square inch. Symbolically this is expressed as

$$\bar{x} = 4014, \ s = 20, \text{ and } n = 25.$$

The resulting test statistic is

$$t = \frac{\bar{x} - \mu_0}{s_{\bar{x}}} = \frac{4014 - 4000}{20 / \sqrt{25}} = 3.5.$$

The sample mean is 3.5 standard deviations more than the hypothesized value of the mean. Is this difference caused by ordinary sampling variation, or is this evidence of a false null hypothesis? Keep in mind that rejecting the null hypothesis (H_0) will be a desirable outcome since the null states that the bolts are below quality standards.

Step 9: Make the decision.

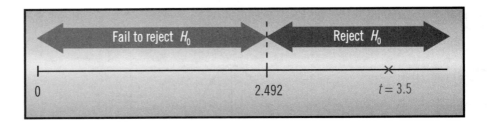

Since the test statistic falls in the rejection region, it indicates that the sample mean is too far from the hypothesized value to believe it is due to ordinary sampling variation. (In other words, $\bar{x} = 4014$ is a rare observation and has exceeded our tolerance for rareness.) The null hypothesis must be rejected in favor of the alternative hypothesis.

Step 10: State the conclusion in terms of the original question.

There is sufficient evidence to conclude that the bolt tensile strength is above 4000 pounds.

This conclusion is stated in a rather absolute manner. However, there is always a degree of subjectivity in any statistical conclusion. In this instance, we arbitrarily selected the value of α, and we assumed that the distribution of the population was normal.

P-Values

We have been examining the classical approach to hypothesis testing. This approach results in a conclusion to reject or fail to reject the null hypothesis. What is missing from this type of conclusion is the degree to which the data confirm the inference. For example, suppose we are testing a hypothesis with the following rejection region.

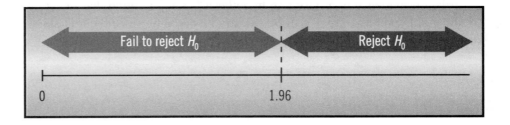

If the test statistic were $z = 2.03$, it would fall into the rejection region (but just barely), and the null hypothesis would be rejected.

Compare this to a test statistic of $z = 3.09$, which falls far into the rejection region and results in the same conclusion, rejecting the null hypothesis. Clearly, the sample data which produced a test statistic of 3.09 provides much stronger evidence against the null hypothesis than the sample which produced a test statistic of 2.03. Expressing the difference in the strength of our conclusion is accomplished using P-values.

Definition

A **P-value** is the probability of observing a value of a test statistic as extreme or more extreme than the one observed, assuming the null hypothesis is true.

P-value

The following graph displays the application of the definition to the test statistics $z = 2.03$ and $z = 3.09$.

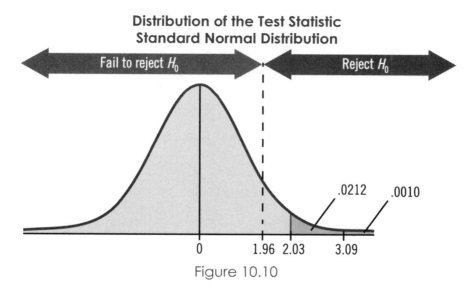

Distribution of the Test Statistic
Standard Normal Distribution

Fail to reject H_0 Reject H_0

.0212   .0010

0   1.96 2.03   3.09

Figure 10.10

If the null hypothesis is true, the probability of observing a test statistic greater than or equal to 2.03 is .0212, which is the P-value. One interpretation of the P-value is that if 10,000 researchers were to draw similar size samples, assuming the null hypothesis is true, ordinary sampling variation would cause roughly 212 researchers to obtain samples that would produce test statistics as large or larger than 2.03.

Compare this to the test statistic 3.09. If the null hypothesis is true, the chance of sampling variation causing a test statistic greater than or equal to 3.09 is .0010, which is the P-value. If 10,000 researchers drew similar size samples, ordinary sampling variation would cause only about 10 of the researchers to observe test statistics as large or larger than 3.09. The further the test statistic penetrates the rejection region, the more confidence the researcher can place in the conclusions.

Many statistical computer programs provide P-values in their output. It is a fairly easy task to utilize these values to perform a classical hypothesis test.

10

Procedure

Performing a Hypothesis Test Using P-Values

- If the computed P-value is smaller than α, reject the null hypothesis in favor of the alternative.
- If the computed P-value is greater than α, fail to reject the null hypothesis.

The rationale for this approach is that if the P-value is smaller than alpha, we have observed a test statistic that is more unusual than the level of the test, which defines how rare an event we must observe in order to reject the null hypothesis. Conversely, if the P-value is larger than α, the test statistic is not sufficiently rare (it could have been caused by ordinary sampling variation) to reject the null hypothesis.

P-values for a Two-Sided Hypothesis

So far, we have only discussed calculating a P-value for a one-tailed hypothesis test. To compute the P-value for a two-tailed test, simply double the tail probability of the test statistic. For example, suppose that we are testing the following hypotheses:

$$H_0 : \mu = 5 \qquad \text{(null hypothesis)}$$
$$H_a : \mu \neq 5 \qquad \text{(alternative hypothesis)}$$

Further, suppose the computed test statistic is $z = 2.31$.

For an upper one-tailed test (i.e. $H_a : \mu > 5$), we would calculate the P-value as P-value $= P(z > 2.31) = .0104$. However, for a two-tailed test, the P-value is calculated as P-value $= 2P(z > |\text{Test Statistic}|)$. Thus, to compute the P-value for a two-tailed test, we double the tail area.

P-value $= .0104 + .0104 = .0208$

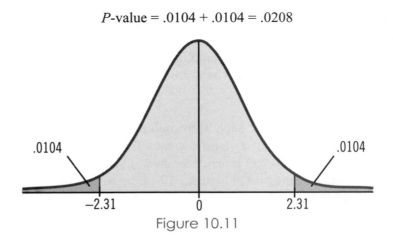

Figure 10.11

The P-value of .0208 is the likelihood of observing a value of the test statistic greater than 2.31 or less than −2.31 given the null hypothesis is true.

P-values for t-Test Statistics

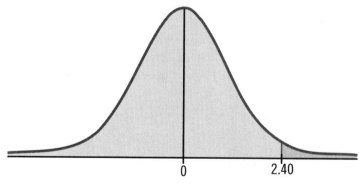

Figure 10.12

Because there are numerous *t*-distributions, one for each different degree of freedom, the *t*-tables are constructed differently from the *z*-table. The *t*-table only provides *t*-values for frequently used tail probabilities. Note in the *t*-table (Table D) that we only have five tail areas. Because of this limitation, in most instances the exact value of the *t*-test statistic will not be in the table. When this circumstance arises, find the closest *t*-values with the appropriate degrees of freedom which surround the test statistic. For example, suppose the value of the test statistic was

$$t = 2.40 \text{ with } 17 \text{ degrees of freedom.}$$

The value of the test statistic falls between 2.110, which corresponds to $\alpha = .025$ on the distribution, and 2.567, which corresponds to $\alpha = .01$ on the distribution.

		Area in One Tail			
		$t_{.100}$	$t_{.050}$	$t_{.025}$	$t_{.010}$
Degrees of Freedom	1	3.078	6.314	12.706	31.821
	2	1.886	2.920	4.303	6.965
	3	1.638	2.353	3.182	4.541
	⋮				
	17	1.333	1.740	2.110	2.567
	18	1.330	1.734	2.101	2.552
	⋮				

Thus, we report a bound for the *P*-value. In this case, the *P*-value is $.01 < P\text{-value} < .025$. That is, the *P*-value falls between .01 and .025. If a value of alpha is given that is greater than .025, then our test is significant at the .025 level. Thus, the *P*-value would be reported as being significant at the .025 level, but not significant at the .01 level.

Because of the arbitrariness of assigning the level of the test, researchers will often

10

report the significance of their findings as *P*-values. Determining the significance of the results is left to the researcher. There are few universal standards when it comes to evaluating the significance of a *P*-value. However, most researchers would view a *P*-value of less than .01 as significant and a *P*-value of greater than .10 as insignificant. Interpreting *P*-values between .01 and .10 will depend on the circumstances. However, once the *P*-value gets above .05, the conclusion starts to become unconvincing.

10.4 Exercises

Basic Concepts

1. What is the rationale for the z-statistic?

2. What are the three key questions to be asked in the hypothesis testing procedure to determine which test statistic is appropriate?

3. Describe the distribution of the z-test statistic.

4. If the variance for a population is not known, how is the test statistic affected?

5. What are critical values? How do critical values influence the decision rule in the hypothesis testing procedure?

6. What is a *P*-value?

7. Discuss how *P*-values are used in the test of a hypothesis.

Exercises

1. Determine the critical value(s) of the test statistic for each of the following large sample tests for the population mean.

   a. Left-tailed test, $\alpha = .01$

   b. Right-tailed test, $\alpha = .10$

   c. Two-tailed test, $\alpha = .05$

2. Determine the critical value(s) of the test statistic for each of the following large sample tests for the population mean.

   a. Left-tailed test, $\alpha = .05$

   b. Right-tailed test, $\alpha = .02$

   c. Two-tailed test, $\alpha = .08$

3. A random sample of 1000 observations produces a sample mean of 53.5 with a standard deviation of 5.3. Test the hypothesis that the mean is not equal to 55 at $\alpha = .05$.

4. A random sample of 200 observations indicate a sample mean of 4117 with a standard deviation of 300. Test the hypothesis that the mean is greater than 4100 at $\alpha = .01$.

5. The head of the Veterans Administration has been receiving complaints from a Vietnam veterans' organization concerning disability checks. The organization claims that checks are continually late. The checks are supposed to arrive no later than the tenth of each month. The administrator randomly selects 100 disabled veterans and measures the arrival time in relation to the tenth of the month for each check. If the check arrives early, it receives a negative value. For example, if the check arrives on the eighth of the month, it is measured as –2. If the check arrives on the twelfth of the month, it is measured as a +2.

   a. What statistical measure should you use in your statement of hypothesis?

   b. Formulate a hypothesis to test the veterans' organization's claim.

   c. Suppose in the sample of 100 disabled veterans receiving checks, the average number of days late was 1.2 with a standard deviation of 1.4. Calculate the test statistic for your hypothesis.

   d. If the test is conducted at the .05 level, construct the decision rule for the test statistic.

   e. Is there overwhelming evidence that the checks arrive late?

   f. If you are the head of the Veterans Administration, what is your conclusion?

6. Hurricane Andrew swept through southern Florida causing billions of dollars of damage. Because of the severity of the storm and the type of residential construction used in this semitropical area, there was some concern that the average claim size would be greater than the historical average hurricane claim of $24,000. Several insurance companies collaborated in a data gathering experiment. They randomly selected 84 homes and sent adjusters to settle the claims. In the sample of 84 homes, the average claim was $27,500 with a standard deviation of $2400.

   a. What is the population being studied?

   b. What statistical measure should you use in your hypothesis?

   c. State your hypothesis.

   d. Test the hypothesis at the .01 level.

   e. Is there overwhelming evidence (at the .01 level) that home damage is greater than the historical average?

7. A retail computer store is considering offering a two year service warranty, instead of their current one year plan. In order to do this, they must determine the average service costs for their systems in the second year of operation. A committee of technicians, sales, and management staff believe that the average repair cost in the second year should be approximately $50. Seventy-five customers who purchased machines between two and four years earlier are randomly selected. Tracking the service needs of these customers reveals an average service cost of $38 with a standard deviation of $10.

   a. What is the population being studied?

   b. What variable is being measured in this problem?

   c. What level of measurement does the variable possess?

   d. Test the committee's claim at the .10 level.

   e. What concerns might you have about the data that were collected?

8. In preparation for upcoming wage negotiations with the union, the managers for the Bevel Hardware Company want to establish the time required to assemble a kitchen cabinet. A first line supervisor believes that the job should take 45 minutes on average to complete. A random sample of 125 cabinets has an average assembly time of 47 minutes with a standard deviation of 10 minutes. Is there overwhelming evidence to contradict the first line supervisor's belief at a .05 significance level?

9. The Better Business Bureau has received several complaints that a flour company is underfilling their five pound bags of flour. The Bureau randomly selects 750 bags of flour and determines the weight of each bag. The sample average weight of the bags is 4.80 pounds with a standard deviation of 0.15 pounds. Is there overwhelming evidence at the .01 level that the bags are underfilled?

10. A horticulturist working for a large plant nursery is conducting experiments on the growth rate of a new shrub. Based on previous research, the horticulturist feels the average daily growth rate of the new shrub is 1 cm per day. A random sample of 45 shrubs has an average growth of 0.90 cm per day with a standard deviation of 0.30 cm. Will a test of hypothesis at the .05 significance level support the claim that the growth rate is less than 1 cm per day?

11. Del Valley Foods requires that corn supplied for canning must weigh more than 5 ounces per ear. South Valley Farms claims that the corn they supply meets the required specifications. Two hundred ears of corn are selected at random from a delivery. The sample has a mean of 5.01 ounces and a standard deviation of 0.30 ounce. Will a test of hypothesis at $\alpha = .10$ support South Valley Farms' claim?

12. Government regulations restrict the amount of pollutants that can be released to the atmosphere through industrial smokestacks. To demonstrate that their smokestacks are releasing pollutants below the mandated limit of 5 parts per billion pollutants, REM Industries collects a random sample of 300 readings. The mean pollutant level for the sample is 4.85 parts per billion with a standard deviation of 0.3 parts per billion. Does the data support the claim that the average pollutants produced by REM Industries are below the mandated level at a .01 significance level?

13. The director of the IRS has been flooded with complaints that people must wait more than 45 minutes before seeing an IRS representative. To determine the validity of these complaints, the IRS randomly selects 400 people entering IRS offices across the country and records the times which they must wait before seeing an IRS representative. The average waiting time for the sample is 55 minutes with a standard deviation of 15 minutes.

   a. What is the population being studied?

   b. Are the complaints substantiated by the data at $\alpha = .10$?

14. The manufacturer of Brand X floor polish is developing a new polish that they hope will dry faster than their competition's polish. The competition's polish is advertised to have an average drying time of 10 minutes. A random sample of 1000 Brand X polishes has an average drying time of 9.3 minutes with a standard deviation of 0.5 minute. Based on the data, can the manufacturer conclude that drying time for Brand X is faster than the competition's brand at a .05 significance level?

15. Determine the critical value(s) of the test statistic for each of the following small sample tests for the population mean where the assumption of normality is satisfied.

   a. Left-tailed test, $\alpha = .01$, $n = 15$

   b. Right-tailed test, $\alpha = .10$, $n = 20$

   c. Two-tailed test, $\alpha = .05$, $n = 8$

16. Determine the critical value(s) of the test statistic for each of the following small sample tests for the population mean where the assumption of normality is satisfied.

   a. Left-tailed test, $\alpha = .005$, $n = 12$

   b. Right-tailed test, $\alpha = .025$, $n = 5$

   c. Two-tailed test, $\alpha = .10$, $n = 25$

17. Consider the following random sample of size six from a normal population. Based on the sample, perform a hypothesis test to test the claim that the mean of the population is not equal to 10 at $\alpha = .05$.

10	15	12	9	11	10

18. Consider the following random sample of size eight from a normal population. Based on the sample, perform a hypothesis test to test the claim that the mean of the population is greater than 100 at $\alpha = .05$.

100	150	120	90	95	110	100	80

19. Consider the following random sample of size seven from a normal population. Based on the sample, perform a hypothesis test to test the claim that the mean of the population is less than 0.5 at $\alpha = .10$.

0.3	0.5	0.4	0.6	0.5	0.4	0.4

20. NarStor, a computer disk drive manufacturer, claims that the average time to failure for their hard drives is 14,400 hours. You work for a consumer group that has decided to examine this claim. Technicians ran 16 drives continuously for three years. Recently the last drive failed. The time to failure (in hours) are given below.

330	620	1870	2410	4620	6396	7822	8102
8309	12882	14419	16092	18384	20916	23812	25814

    a. What is the population being studied?

    b. What is the variable being measured?

    c. What level of measurement does the variable possess?

    d. Conduct a hypothesis test to determine whether there is overwhelming evidence that the average time to failure is less than the manufacturer's claim. Use $\alpha = .01$.

    e. What assumption did you make in performing the test in part (d)?

21. The admitting office at Sisters of Mercy Hospital wants to be able to inform patients of the average level of expenses they can expect per day. Historically, the average has been approximately $1240. The office would like to know if there is evidence of an increase in the average daily billing. Twenty randomly selected patients have an average daily charge of $1491 with a standard deviation of $342.

    a. What is the population being studied?

    b. Conduct a hypothesis test to determine whether there is evidence that average daily charges have increased at $\alpha = .10$.

    c. What assumption did you make in performing the test in part (b)?

22. A supplier has agreed to provide the manager of a large hospital with light bulbs that he claims will last more than 1000 hours. Twenty-five bulbs are randomly selected and tested by the hospital's maintenance department. The sample has an average life of 1099 hours with a standard deviation of 99 hours.

    a. Perform a hypothesis test to determine whether the data support the supplier's claim at $\alpha = .05$.

    b. What assumption did you make in performing the test in part (a)?

23. The managers of a large department store wish to test reactions of shoppers to a new in-store video screen which will broadcast continuous information about the store and the items currently on sale. The video production company claims that the average shopper will watch for five or more minutes. The managers randomly select 17 shoppers and determine how long they watch the video. The average time is 4.5 minutes with a standard deviation of 2.5 minutes.

    a. Perform a hypothesis test to determine whether there is overwhelming evidence that the average time spent watching the in-store video screen is less than 5 minutes. Use $\alpha = .01$.

    b. What assumption did you make in performing the test in part (a)?

24. A group of local businessmen is thinking about developing land into a shopping mall. To evaluate the desirability of the location, they count the number of shoppers who visit the neighboring shopping center each day. A random sample of 25 days reveals a daily average of 107 shoppers with a standard deviation of 23 shoppers. The businessmen will develop the land if the average number of shoppers per day is more than 100.

    a. Based on the sample data, should the businessmen develop the land? Perform a hypothesis test and use $\alpha = .10$.

    b. What assumption did you make in performing the test in part (a)?

25. The Dodge Reports are used by many companies in the construction field to estimate the time required to complete various jobs. The company has received several complaints that the time required to install 130 square feet of bathroom tile is greater than the eight hours reported in the current manual. A researcher for Dodge randomly selects 10 construction workers and determines the time required to install 130 square feet of bath tile. The average time required to install the tile for the sample is 8.5 hours with a standard deviation of 1 hour.

    a. Use a hypothesis test to determine whether the customers' complaints are substantiated by the data. Use $\alpha = .05$.

    b. What assumption did you make in performing the test in part (a)?

26. Officials in charge of televising an international chess competition in South America want to determine if the average time per move for the top players has remained under five minutes over the last two years. Video tapes of matches which have been played over the two year period are reviewed and a random sample of 50 moves are timed. The sample mean is 3.5 minutes with a standard deviation of 1.5 minutes.

    a. What is the population under study?

    b. Can the officials conclude at $\alpha = .05$ that the time per move is still under five minutes?

    c. What assumption did you make in performing the test in part (b)?

27. Buckshot Heaven is developing a new shotgun shell which they hope will have a significantly tighter pellet pattern than their competition. Twenty-five shells are tested at fifty yards. The average pellet pattern of the sample was 8.7 inches in diameter with a standard deviation of 2.0 inches. Their competitor advertises that the average pellet pattern of their shells is nine inches.

    a. Does the test completed by Buckshot Heaven support their claim that their shell pattern is tighter than the competition at a level of significance of .10?

    b. What assumption did you make in performing the test in part (a)?

28. For each of the following combinations of the P-value and α, decide whether you would reject or fail to reject the null hypothesis.

    a. P-value = .09 $\alpha = .10$

    b. P-value = .03 $\alpha = .05$

    c. P-value = .05 $\alpha = .01$

    d. P-value = .04 $\alpha = .05$

29. For each of the following combinations of the P-value and α, decide whether you would reject or fail to reject the null hypothesis.

    a. P-value = .08 $\alpha = .05$

    b. P-value = .01 $\alpha = .02$

    c. P-value = .04 $\alpha = .10$

    d. P-value = .03 $\alpha = .01$

30. Consider the following large sample hypothesis tests for the population mean. Compute the P-value for each test and decide whether you would reject or fail to reject the null hypothesis at $\alpha = .05$.

    a. $H_0 : \mu \leq 15$ vs $H_a : \mu > 15$, $z = 1.58$

    b. $H_0 : \mu \geq 1.9$ vs $H_a : \mu < 1.9$, $z = -2.25$

    c. $H_0 : \mu = 100$ vs $H_a : \mu \neq 100$, $z = 1.90$

31. Consider the following large sample hypothesis tests for the population mean. Compute the P-value for each test and decide whether you would reject or fail to reject the null hypothesis at $\alpha = .01$.

    a. $H_0: \mu \leq 10$ vs $H_a: \mu > 10$, $z = 2.00$

    b. $H_0: \mu \geq 82$ vs $H_a: \mu < 82$, $z = -2.45$

    c. $H_0: \mu = 100$ vs $H_a: \mu \neq 100$, $z = 2.70$

32. Consider the following small sample hypothesis tests for the population mean. Compute the P-value for each test and decide whether you would reject or fail to reject the null hypothesis at $\alpha = .01$.

    a. $H_0: \mu \leq 25$ vs $H_a: \mu > 25$, $t = 2.7$, $n = 15$

    b. $H_0: \mu \geq 0.85$ vs $H_a: \mu < 0.85$, $t = -2.5$, $n = 7$

    c. $H_0: \mu = 1000$ vs $H_a: \mu \neq 1000$, $t = 2.0$, $n = 15$

Hint: The TI-84 Plus has a function *tcdf* that will help calculate the P-values exactly. Excel also has a function called *tdist* that also is useful in calculating the P-values exactly.

33. Consider the following small sample hypothesis tests for the population mean. Compute the P-value for each test and decide whether you would reject or fail to reject the null hypothesis at $\alpha = .05$.

    a. $H_0: \mu \leq 120$ vs $H_a: \mu > 120$, $t = 1.5$, $n = 20$

    b. $H_0: \mu \geq 0.2$ vs $H_a: \mu < 0.2$, $t = -2.75$, $n = 18$

    c. $H_0: \mu = 50$ vs $H_a: \mu \neq 50$, $t = 2.4$, $n = 5$

34. A.C. Bone has developed a duck hunting boot which they claim can remain immersed for more than 12 hours without leaking. Five hundred pairs of the boots are tested and the time until first leakage is measured. The average time until first leakage for the sample is 12.25 hours with a standard deviation of 3.0 hours.

    a. Find the P-value to test the claim that the average time until first leakage for the hunting boot is at least 12 hours.

    b. Does this sample support A.C. Bone's claim at $\alpha = .10$?

Practical Significance versus Statistical Significance

A hypothesis is rarely exactly true. As the sample size becomes larger, the likelihood of rejecting the null becomes greater.

Example 10.10

Suppose that Fife Police Department was concerned about speeds in the town school zone, especially during the beginning and end of the school day. The posted speed limit is 25 mph and the deputy officer, Benny, believes that the speed is being exceeded. To test his assumption, Benny randomly samples (via radar) 2000 vehicles in the school zone over a 30-day period and finds that the average speed is 25.01 mph with a standard deviation of .10 mph.

Solution

To test Benny's claim, the hypothesis test is carried out with

$$H_0 : \mu \leq 25 \text{ mph}$$
$$H_a : \mu > 25 \text{ mph}$$

The resulting test statistic is

$$z = \frac{\bar{x} - \mu_0}{s/\sqrt{n}} = \frac{25.01 - 25}{.10/\sqrt{2000}} = 4.47.$$

The *P*-value for this test is .000004 and suggests that the test statistic is extremely rare, if the null hypothesis is true. Considering that a test statistic this large would result from ordinary sampling variation in only about 4 in a million samples, we should reject the null hypothesis $(H_0 : \mu \leq 25 \text{ mph})$ in favor of the alternative. With Benny being a "strictly by the book" officer, he would conclude that the speeds are significantly higher than 25 mph in the school zone and the department should allocate extra resources in that area to reduce speeds. However, from a practical perspective, there isn't much difference (other than random variation) between 25 mph and 25.01 mph, and it isn't likely to be detected by radar. So, despite the "statistical significance" of the test, the practical significance is negligible.

10.5 Exercises

Basic Concepts

1. Describe the difference between statistical significance and practical significance.

2. Give an example of a situation in which results could be statistically significant but not practically significant.

Exercises

1. Consider Exercise 8 in Section 10.4:

   In preparation for upcoming wage negotiations with the union, the managers for the Bevel Hardware Company want to establish the time required to assemble a kitchen cabinet. A first line supervisor believes that the job should take 45 minutes on average to complete. A random sample of 125 cabinets has an average assembly time of 47 minutes with a standard deviation of 10 minutes. Is there overwhelming evidence to contradict the first line supervisor's belief at a .05 significance level?

   Discuss the statistical and practical significance for this problem.

2. Consider Exercise 10 in Section 10.4:

   A horticulturist working for a large plant nursery is conducting experiments on the growth rate of a new shrub. Based on previous research, the horticulturist feels the average daily growth rate of the new shrub is 1 cm per day. A random sample of 45 shrubs has an average growth of 0.90 cm per day with a standard deviation of 0.30 cm. Will a test of hypothesis at the .05 significance level support the claim that the growth rate is less than 1 cm per day?

   Discuss the statistical and practical significance for this problem.

3. Consider Exercise 13 in Section 10.4:

   The director of the IRS has been flooded with complaints that people must wait more than 45 minutes before seeing an IRS representative. To determine the validity of these complaints, the IRS randomly selects 400 people entering IRS offices across the country and records the times which they must wait before seeing an IRS representative. The average waiting time for the sample is 55 minutes with a standard deviation of 15 minutes.

   a. What is the population being studied?

   b. Are the complaints substantiated by the data at $\alpha = .10$?

   Discuss the statistical and practical significance for this problem.

4. Consider Exercise 23 in Section 10.4:

The managers of a large department store wish to test reactions of shoppers to a new in-store video screen which will broadcast continuous information about the store and the items currently on sale. The video production company claims that the average shopper will watch for five or more minutes. The managers randomly select 17 shoppers and determine how long they watch the video. The average time is 4.5 minutes with a standard deviation of 2.5 minutes.

a. Perform a hypothesis test to determine whether there is overwhelming evidence that the average time spent watching the in-store video screen is less than 5 minutes. Use $\alpha = .01$.

b. What assumption did you make in performing the test in part (a)?

Discuss the statistical and practical significance for this problem.

The Relationship between Confidence Interval Estimation and Hypothesis Testing

Previously, we discussed interval estimation for the population mean and the population proportion. We know that when estimating the population mean, a $100(1-\alpha)\%$ confidence interval for μ is given by

$$\bar{x} \pm z_{\alpha/2} \frac{\sigma}{\sqrt{n}}.$$

In this chapter, we have shown that the two-sided hypothesis test about the population mean μ is

$$H_0 : \mu = \mu_0$$
$$H_a : \mu \neq \mu_0$$

where μ_0 is some specific value of the population mean.

From the previous chapter, we know that $100(1-\alpha)\%$ of the confidence intervals will contain μ. Therefore, if we reject the null hypothesis when the confidence interval does not contain the value of μ_0, we will reject the null hypothesis when it is true with probability of α. You may recall that α represents the probability of committing a Type I error (i.e., we reject the null hypothesis when the null hypothesis is true). So, when we construct a $100(1-\alpha)\%$ confidence interval and reject the null hypothesis when the interval does not contain μ_0, this is equivalent to performing a two-tailed hypothesis test using α as the level of the test.

Procedure

Using a Confidence Interval to Test a Hypothesis

Step 1: If the hypothesis test is of the form

$$H_0 : \mu = \mu_0$$
$$H_a : \mu \neq \mu_0$$

Step 2: calculate the $100(1-\alpha)\%$ two-sided confidence interval given by

$$\bar{x} \pm z_{\alpha/2} \frac{\sigma}{\sqrt{n}}.$$

Step 3: If μ_0 falls within the interval, then we fail to reject the null hypothesis; however, if μ_0 falls outside the calculated interval, then reject the null hypothesis in favor of the alternative.

10

Let's look at Example 10.6. Recall that the hypotheses were

$$H_0 : \mu = 500$$
$$H_a : \mu \neq 500.$$

The test statistic for this example was $z = 3.46$ and the test was rejected at the .05 level.

Note that the value $z_{.025} = 1.96$. Calculating a 95% confidence interval for μ, we get

$$\bar{x} \pm z_{\alpha/2} \frac{\sigma}{\sqrt{n}}$$
$$540 \pm 1.96 \frac{100}{\sqrt{75}}$$
$$540 \pm 22.63$$
$$517.37 \text{ to } 562.63.$$

Because the hypothesized value (500) does not fall in this interval, we reject the null hypothesis, which is consistent with the earlier conclusion. Although we presented this demonstration using the confidence interval for the population mean, the same relationship exists for other population parameters.

10.6 Exercises

Basic Concepts

1. How can a confidence interval be used to test a hypothesis?

Exercises

1. AAA Controls makes a switch that is advertised to activate a warning light if the power supplied to a machine reaches 100 volts. A random sample of 250 switches is tested and the mean voltage at which warning occurs is 98 volts with a sample standard deviation of 3 volts. Using the confidence interval approach, test the hypothesis that the mean voltage activation is different from AAA Controls' claim at the .05 level.

2. Researchers studying the effects of diet on growth would like to know if a vegetarian diet affects the height of a child. The researchers randomly selected 12 vegetarian children that were six years old. The average height of the children is 42.5 inches with a standard deviation of 3.8 inches. The average height for all six year old children is 45.75 inches. Using confidence intervals, test to determine whether there is overwhelming evidence at $\alpha = .05$ that six year old vegetarian children are not the same height as other six year old children.

3. High power experimental engines are being developed by the Stevens Motor Company for use in their new sports coupe. The engineers have calculated the maximum horsepower for the engine to be 600 HP. Sixteen engines are randomly selected for horsepower testing. The sample has an average maximum HP of 620 with a standard deviation of 50 HP.

   a. Use the confidence interval approach to determine whether the data suggest that the average maximum HP for the experimental engine is significantly different than the maximum horsepower calculated by the engineers. Use a significance level of $\alpha = .01$.

   b. What assumption did you make in performing the test?

4. The nutrition label for Oriental Spice Sauce states that one package of sauce has 1190 milligrams of sodium. To determine if the label is accurate the FDA randomly selects two hundred packages of Oriental Spice Sauce and determines the sodium content. The sample has an average of 1167.34 milligrams of sodium per package with a sample standard deviation of 252.94 milligrams.

   a. Calculate a 99% confidence interval for the mean sodium content in Oriental Spice Sauce.

   b. Using the confidence interval approach, is there evidence that the sodium content is different than the nutrition label states?

10.7 ## Testing a Hypothesis about a Population Proportion

The topic that we will develop in this section will be a hypothesis testing approach for categorical values (nominal data). The inferences that we will make with these data will concern one population. We will use the information in the sample proportion $\left(\hat{p}\right)$ to test hypotheses about the population proportion, p.

Testing hypotheses about a population proportion could involve a variety of problems.

- What fraction of a student's grades will be A's?
- What fraction of graduating seniors obtain jobs with starting salaries in excess of $38,000?
- What fraction of products that a company produces are defective?
- What fraction of the voters favor the incumbent in the next election?
- What fraction of the customers who purchase a Ford Focus are extremely satisfied?
- What fraction of the time will a baseball player get a hit?
- What fraction of the time will a drug be successful in treating a specific disorder?

Developing the Test

Testing a hypothesis concerning a population proportion is nearly identical to testing a hypothesis about a population mean. The major changes in the procedure include the use of the population proportion $\left(p\right)$ in the formulation of the hypotheses rather than the population mean $\left(\mu\right)$, and the calculation of the test statistic. Let's try an example.

Example 10.11

Sir is a novice at trading stocks and feels that if the Dow Jones Industrial Average (DJIA) is up on a given day, then it's likely that his portfolio will also be up, regardless of the stocks in his portfolio. Sir would like to know if there is sufficient evidence to conclude that more than 60% of stocks in the New York Stock Exchange (NYSE) increase on days that the DJIA increases.

Solution

Step 1: State the hypotheses in plain English.

- At most 60% of the stocks on the NYSE increase on days when the DJIA increases.

- More than 60% of the stocks increase on days when the DJIA increases.

Step 2: Select the appropriate statistical measure.

Since the problem concerns the fraction of stocks on the NYSE that will increase on days that the DJIA increases, the appropriate statistical measure will be a proportion.

Let p = fraction of the stocks on the NYSE that will increase on days when the DJIA increases.

Step 3: Determine whether the hypotheses should be one-sided or two-sided.

Since the problem is concerned with finding evidence that the percentage is greater than 60%, the formation of the hypothesis will be one-sided.

Step 4: Specify the hypotheses using the appropriate statistical measure.

$$H_0: p \leq .60 \quad \left(\begin{array}{l} \text{At most 60\% of stocks on the NYSE} \\ \text{increase when the DJIA increases.} \end{array} \right)$$

$$H_a: p > .60 \quad \left(\begin{array}{l} \text{More than 60\% of the stocks on the NYSE} \\ \text{increase when the DJIA increases.} \end{array} \right)$$

Step 5: Specify the level of the test.

Since the level of the test is not specified in the problem, let's use $\alpha = .05$.

Step 6: Select the appropriate test statistic.

If $np \geq 5$ and $n(1-p) \geq 5$, the appropriate test statistic is given by

$$z = \frac{\hat{p} - p}{\sigma_{\hat{p}}}, \text{ where } \sigma_{\hat{p}} = \sqrt{\frac{p(1-p)}{n}}.$$

The test statistic measures how far the sample proportion, $\hat{p}$ is from the unknown population proportion, p, measured in standard deviation units. This is exactly the same concept used in testing hypotheses about a population mean.

There is one interesting aspect to the calculation of the standard deviation of $\hat{p}$ $\left(\sigma_{\hat{p}}\right)$; it requires knowledge of p. This may seem odd, since the entire purpose of the hypothesis test is to make an inference about the unknown value of p. If p is unknown, how can it be used to compute $\sigma_{\hat{p}}$?

The answer to this riddle lies in the hypothesis testing procedure. The null hypothesis is assumed to be true, unless there is overwhelming evidence to the contrary. Since the null is presumed to be true, let p equal the value hypothesized in the null hypothesis.

Step 7: Determine the critical value.

The test statistic, z, has a normal distribution with a mean of zero and a standard deviation of one. So designating the decision rule is exactly like what has been done in previous problems. The test is a one-tailed test, and in Step 5 we decided to set the level of the test at .05.

The decision rule will be to reject $H_0: p \leq .6$ if the value of z is greater than 1.645. In essence, we are saying that ordinary sampling variation might account for a $\hat{p}$ up to 1.645 standard deviations larger than the hypothesized value. But if a z-value is observed that is larger than 1.645, then we will lose faith in the null hypothesis because we have observed something that is too rare by the standards we have set for the level of the test.

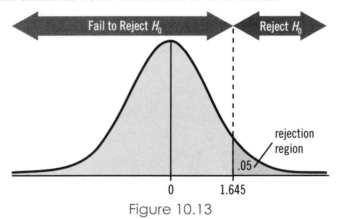

Figure 10.13

Step 8: Compute the test statistic.

In a random sample of 520 stocks on the NYSE, 350 increased on days that the DJIA increased. The value of $\hat{p}$ is given by

$$\hat{p} = \frac{350}{520} \approx .6731, \text{ and } z = \frac{\hat{p} - p}{\sqrt{\dfrac{p(1-p)}{n}}} = \frac{.6731 - .6}{\sqrt{\dfrac{.6(1-.6)}{520}}} \approx 3.40.$$

In this case, the sample proportion favoring Sir's assumption is 3.40 standard deviation units larger than the hypothesized proportion. If H_0 is true, would we expect a sample proportion that is 3.40 standard deviation units larger than the hypothesized proportion? Or, is this test statistic $(z = 3.40)$ overwhelming evidence in favor of the alternative hypothesis?

Step 9: Make the decision.

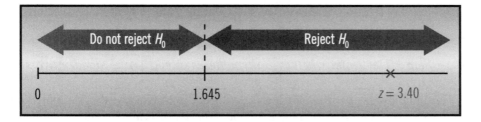

The value of the test statistic, $z = 3.40$, falls in the rejection region. According to the standard of rareness established in Step 5, the z-value is too rare to believe the null hypothesis $(H_0 : p \leq .6)$ is true. The sample evidence contradicts the null hypothesis, and it will be rejected in favor of the alternative hypothesis,

$$H_a : p > .6.$$

Step 10: State the conclusion in terms of the original question.

At a significance level of .05, there is overwhelming evidence that over 60% of the stocks on the NYSE increase when the DJIA increases.

Example 10.12

A consulting firm believes that at least 39% of online shoppers have bad experiences on websites and do not purchase anything because sites are too complicated and do not possess good user interfaces. Out of a random sample of 60 online shoppers, only 15 reported frustration with the sites and thus, didn't make a purchase. Do the data provide sufficient evidence to reject the claim made by the consulting firm? Test using a significance level of .01.

Solution

Step 1: State the hypotheses in plain English.

- At least 39% of online shoppers do not purchase anything due to a bad website experience.

- Less than 39% of online shoppers do not purchase anything due to a bad website experience.

Step 2: Select the appropriate statistical measure.

Since the problem concerns the fraction of online shoppers that had a good experience, the appropriate statistical measure will be a proportion.

Let p = fraction of the online shoppers that did not purchase anything due to a bad experience on the website.

Step 3: Determine whether the hypotheses should be one-sided or two-sided.

Since the problem is concerned with finding evidence that the percentage of online shoppers that have a good experience is at least 39%, it should be a one-sided alternative.

Step 4: State the hypotheses using the appropriate statistical measure.

$$H_0: p \geq .39 \quad \left(\begin{array}{l} \text{At least 39\% of online shoppers have a} \\ \text{bad experience and do not purchase anything.} \end{array} \right)$$

$$H_a: p < .39 \quad \left(\begin{array}{l} \text{Less than 39\% of online shoppers have a} \\ \text{bad experience and do not purchase anything.} \end{array} \right)$$

Step 5: Specify the level of the test.

The significance level of .01 is given in the problem.

Step 6: Select the appropriate test statistic.

The appropriate test statistic is given by

$$z = \frac{\hat{p} - p}{\sigma_{\hat{p}}}, \text{ where } \sigma_{\hat{p}} = \sqrt{\frac{p(1-p)}{n}}.$$

Step 7: Determine the critical value.

The null hypothesis should only be rejected if there is overwhelming evidence that the population proportion is less than .39. Since the test is one-sided, the entire probability associated with the level of the test $(\alpha = .01)$ will be placed in the left-hand tail of the distribution.

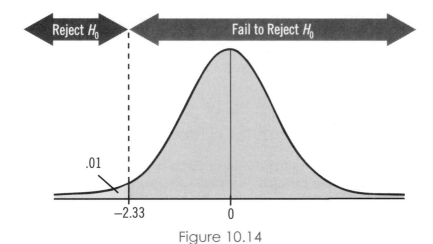

Figure 10.14

From Table 10.3, we know that the critical value of the test statistic is −2.33 (because it's a lower one-sided alternative hypothesis). The rejection region is the shaded area in the above graph. The decision will be to reject the null hypothesis if the value of the test statistic is less than −2.33.

Step 8: Compute the test statistic.

In a random sample of 60 online shoppers to the retailer's site, 15 indicated that they did not have a good experience on the site and thus, did not purchase anything. The value of $\hat{p}$ is given by

$$\hat{p} = \frac{15}{60} = .25, \text{ and}$$

$$z = \frac{\hat{p} - p}{\sqrt{\dfrac{p(1-p)}{n}}} = \frac{.25 - .39}{\sqrt{\dfrac{.39(1-.39)}{60}}} \approx -2.22.$$

The z-value indicates that the sample proportion is 2.22 standard deviation units below the hypothesized proportion. Could this have happened by ordinary sampling variation, or is this overwhelming evidence that the null hypothesis is not true and the alternative should be selected?

Step 9: Make the decision.

Note that the value of z does not fall in the rejection region. Thus, we fail to reject $H_0: p \geq .39$. There is not sufficient evidence (at the .01 level) to reject the null hypothesis. Another way of thinking about this is that the sample proportion was not sufficiently rare to reject $H_0: p \geq .39$.

Step 10: State the conclusion in terms of the original question.

At the .01 level of significance, there was not overwhelming evidence to conclude that shoppers' experience during online shopping deterred them from making a purchase.

Calculating a *P*-value for a Proportion

Note:

In order to assure approximate normality of the test statistic in Example 10.12, we need to verify whether $np \geq 5$ and $n(1-p) \geq 5$. $np = 60(.39) = 23.4$ and $n(1-p) = 60(1-.39) = 36.6$ so we can use the z-test statistic.

We can use exactly the same idea in determining a *P*-value for a test about a proportion as we did in calculating *P*-values for the test statistic of a hypothesis concerning a population mean. Let's calculate the *P*-value using the test statistic we computed in Step 8 of the previous problem. If the null is true, how rare is the sample proportion that produced a *z*-value of −2.22?

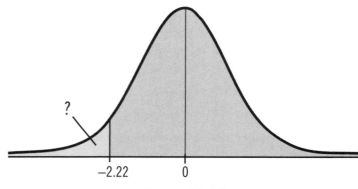

Figure 10.15

Assuming the null is true, $\hat{p}$ has a normal distribution which is centered around .39. If the null is really true, a *z*-value of −2.22 is uncommon. The probability of observing a value as small or smaller than −2.22 is the *P*-value. Using Table A in the Appendix,

$$P\text{-value} = P(z \leq -2.22) = .0132.$$

Table 10.4 – If *P*-value = .0132	
Level of the Test	Reject or Fail to Reject
.10	Reject
.05	Reject
.01	Fail to Reject
.005	Fail to Reject

If the null is true, the *P*-value measures the rareness of the test statistic under ordinary sampling variation. In other words, how often would we see a test statistic as small or smaller than the test statistic we have observed. Presuming the null is true, ordinary sampling variation produces a test statistic smaller than

−2.22 about 1 time out of every 100. Should H_0 be rejected? Have we observed a test statistic that is too "rare" for H_0 to be true? The level of the test defines an unacceptable level of rareness for the test statistic. In the previous example $\alpha = .01$. Setting $\alpha = .01$ implies we are only willing to make a Type I error (reject the null hypothesis when it was true) once in every 100 trials of the experiment. Since the P-value of our test statistic, .0132 is greater than .01, the null hypothesis was not rejected.

If the level of the test had been .05, then to reject H_0 in favor of H_a requires a test statistic whose rareness under ordinary sampling variation is less than .05. For $\alpha = .05$, the null hypothesis is rejected in favor of the alternative, since the test statistic has a P-value (.0132) less than α. In general, if the P-value is smaller than the level of the test, α, H_0 is rejected in favor of H_a. If the level of the test is less than the P-value, then H_0 is not rejected.

Note, if H_a had required a two-tailed test we would double the single tail area. Thus, for a test statistic of −2.33 and a two-tailed H_a the resulting P-value would be $2(.0132) = .0264$.

 **Exercises**

Basic Concepts

1. How does testing a hypothesis about a proportion differ from testing a hypothesis about a mean?

2. What is the appropriate test statistic to be used in hypothesis testing of a population proportion?

3. What conditions must be met in order to perform a hypothesis test about a population proportion?

4. How are P-values determined for a proportion?

Exercises

1. Determine the critical value(s) of the test statistic for each of the following large sample tests for the population proportion.

   a. Left-tailed test, $\alpha = .05$

   b. Right-tailed test, $\alpha = .01$

   c. Two-tailed test, $\alpha = .10$

2. Determine the critical value(s) of the test statistic for each of the following large sample tests for the population proportion.

   a. Left-tailed test, $\alpha = .07$

   b. Right-tailed test, $\alpha = .04$

   c. Two-tailed test, $\alpha = .09$

3. A commercial airline is concerned about the increase in usage of carry-on luggage. For years the percentage of passengers with one or more pieces of carry-on luggage has been stable at approximately 38%. The airline recently selected 300 passengers at random and determined that 148 possessed carry-on luggage. Is there overwhelming evidence of an increase in carry-on luggage at a significance level of .01?

4. Ordinarily, when a company recruits a technical staff member, about 25% of the applicants are qualified. However, based on the information in 120 recently received resumes 18 appear to be technically qualified.

   a. Is there overwhelming evidence that the percentage of qualified applicants is less than 25%? Test at the .05 level.

   b. What concerns might you have about the data in this problem?

5. The National Center for Drug Abuse is conducting a study to determine if heroin usage among teenagers has changed. Historically, about 1.3 percent of teenagers between the ages of 15 and 19 have used heroin one or more times. In a recent survey of 1824 teenagers, 37 indicated they had used heroin one or more times.

   a. Is there overwhelming evidence of a change in heroin usage among teenagers? Test at the .05 level.

   b. What concerns might you have about the data in this problem?

6. Paper International, Inc. has a large staff of salespeople nationwide. Top officials of the company believe that 75% of their salespeople have met their monthly sales goals by the end of the third week of each month. To investigate this, they randomly select 250 salespeople and examine their sales records at the end of the third week of the current month. One-hundred and seventy-five of the 250 salespeople surveyed had already met their monthly sales goals.

   a. Does this sample support the belief of the top officials at the company at $\alpha = .10$?

   b. What concerns might you have about the manner in which the data were collected?

7. Ships arriving in U.S. ports are inspected by customs officials for contaminated cargo. Assume, for a certain port, that 20% of the ships arriving in the previous year contained cargo that was contaminated. A random selection of 50 ships in the current year included five that had contaminated cargo.

   a. Does the data suggest that the proportion of ships arriving in the port with contaminated cargoes has decreased in the current year at $\alpha = .01$?

   b. Do you have any concerns about the sample size? Explain.

8. Grain elevators store hundreds of thousands of bushels of grain each year that are waiting to be processed. It is critical to control the amount of moisture in the grain so that it does not spoil. A large storage facility is deemed to be "in control" if less than 1% of the grain elevators have a moisture content which exceeds 10%. One-hundred and fifty grain elevators are randomly selected and the moisture content is measured. Two of the grain elevators sampled have a moisture content in excess of 10%.

   a. Is there sufficient evidence for the manager to conclude that the storage facility is "out of control"? Use $\alpha = .05$.

   b. Do you have any concerns about the sample size? Explain.

9. Electronic circuit boards are randomly selected each day to determine if any of the boards are defective. A random sample of 100 boards from one day's production has four boards which are defective.

   a. Based on the data, is there overwhelming evidence that more than 5% of the circuit boards are defective? Test at the $\alpha = .10$ level.

   b. Do you have any concerns about the sample size? Explain.

10. Loch Ness Fish Farm breeds fish for commercial sale. The fish are kept in breeder tanks until at least 70% of the fish are five inches long at which time they are transferred to outdoor ponds. To determine if it is the appropriate time to transfer the fish, 50 fish are randomly selected and measured. If 33 of the fish are found to be over five inches long, does the sample data suggest that it is the appropriate time to transfer the fish at $\alpha = .05$?

11. Digger and Digger, a precious metals mining company, is considering the development of a new mining area. They have a lease on an area which they believe contains gypsum. The area will be profitable to mine if at least 15% of the rocks contain more than trace amounts of the mineral. Eighty rocks are randomly selected and the amount of gypsum is measured. Thirteen rocks in the sample are observed to have more than trace amounts of the mineral. Based on the sample data, should Digger and Digger conclude that the area will be profitable to mine? Use $\alpha = .01$.

12. A socially conscious corporation wants to relocate their headquarters to another part of town. One concern expressed by workers is that their commuting distance will increase. The corporation has decided that if more than 50% of the employees will have to drive farther to the proposed new location, they will cancel the move. In a random sample of 398 employees, 201 indicated that their commuting distance to the new office will be longer. Based on the sample data, should the corporation cancel the move? Use a significance level of .01.

13. A production process will normally produce defective parts 0.2% of the time. In a random sample of 1400 parts, three defectives are observed.

    a. Is this overwhelming evidence at the .05 level to indicate that the defective rate of the process has increased?

    b. Compute the P-value for the test statistic.

    c. Based on the P-value, would the decision change at $\alpha = .01$?

14. Bombay Charlie's, a fast food Indian restaurant, is thinking about adding a certain spice to their chicken curry dish to attract more customers. The restaurant manager has decided to add the spice if more than 80% of their customers prefer the taste of the chicken curry with the spice added. Sixty-five customers are randomly selected to participate in a blind taste test. Fifty-four of these customers prefer the chicken curry with the added spice.

    a. Find the P-value for the hypothesis test which the manager will perform to decide if more than 80% of the customers prefer the taste of the chicken curry with the added spice.

    b. Do the data suggest that more than 80% of the customers prefer the curry with the new spice at $\alpha = .05$?

15. The news program for KOPE, the local television station, claims to have 40% of the market. A random sample of 500 viewers conducted by an independent testing agency found 192 who claim to watch the KOPE news program on a regular basis.

    a. Find the P-value for testing the hypothesis that the news program for KOPE does not have at least 40% of the market as it claims.

    b. Is there sufficient evidence to reject the hypothesis that KOPE does not have at least 40% of the market at a significance level of .05?

16. The length of time that a storm window will last before beginning to leak is of interest to a window manufacturer who wishes to guarantee his windows. He believes that 50% of the windows will last at least four years. To research this, 931 windows, which were installed at least four years ago, are randomly selected and checked for leakage. Five hundred of the windows are found to still be leak-free.

a. Find the *P*-value for testing the hypothesis that at least 50% of the windows will be leak-free in four years.

b. Does the sample support the hypothesis that at least 50% of the windows will be leak-free in four years at $\alpha = .05$?

17. In order to discourage soldiers from smoking, the Pentagon raised the price of cigarettes by $4 a carton in October of 1996. This increased the average price of a carton of brand-name cigarettes to $17.50, an increase of about 30%. Prior to the price increase, about 32% of military personnel smoked, as opposed to 25% of all adult Americans. Suppose that following the price increase, a random sample of military personnel is selected to determine smoking habits. With $\alpha = .05$, can we conclude that the price increase was effective in decreasing the percentage of smokers if 50 of the 200 military personnel sampled smoke?

18. Wearing bright or fluorescent orange colored clothing clearly reduces the risk of being shot or killed by hunting. According to an October 1996 article appearing in *The Augusta Chronicle* (Georgia), about two-thirds of the hunters shot in Georgia and South Carolina during the preceding five years were not wearing bright clothes. Of the 52 that were killed, only 19 wore orange. Suppose that a random sample of 100 hunters in Georgia are surveyed and it is determined that of the 100, 62 routinely wear fluorescent orange colored clothing while hunting. With $\alpha = .10$, can it be concluded that over half the hunters in Georgia routinely wear fluorescent orange colored clothing while hunting?

19. According to the Federal Communications Commission, about 49% of the households in the United States had cable television in 1985. Suppose that a sample of 200 households is selected in 2003 and it is determined that 125 of them have cable television. With $\alpha = .05$, can it be concluded that a higher proportion of households in 2003 have cable television as compared with 1985?

20. Selling autographed sports memorabilia has become a multimillion dollar industry in the United States. But just how does the purchaser of an autographed football jersey or an autographed baseball know that the autograph is indeed authentic? Unfortunately, the sports memorabilia market is teeming with con artists who prey upon the trusting nature of sports fans. In 1996, the FBI said that 70% of all autographed sports memorabilia is fraudulent. Assume that 50 pieces of autographed sports memorabilia are sampled at a large memorabilia show and that 40 of them are determined to be fraudulent. With $\alpha = .05$, can it be concluded that the proportion of fraudulent autographed sports memorabilia at the show differs from the FBI claim?

10.8 Testing a Hypothesis about a Population Variance

In this section we want to adapt the hypothesis testing procedure to test a hypothesis concerning a population variance. Before we can perform the test about the population variance, we need to review a few topics that were discussed earlier in the text.

Recall that the sample variance is

$$s^2 = \frac{\sum (x_i - \bar{x})^2}{n-1}$$

and it serves as the point estimate of the population variance, σ^2. As with the other tests developed for the population mean and the population proportion, we first need to develop a sampling distribution for

$$\frac{(n-1)s^2}{\sigma^2}$$

which will allow us to calculate a confidence interval as well as perform hypothesis testing about the population variance.

Note that if we have a random sample of size n, taken from a normal population, then the sampling distribution of $\frac{(n-1)s^2}{\sigma^2}$ follows a **chi-square distribution** with $n-1$ degrees of freedom.

The chi-square distribution is a positively skewed (or skewed to the right) distribution. Like the t-distribution, the shape of the distribution is a function of its degrees of freedom. See Figure 10.16 which illustrates the chi-square distributions with 4 and 10 degrees of freedom.

χ^2 Distribution with 4 and 10 Degrees of Freedom

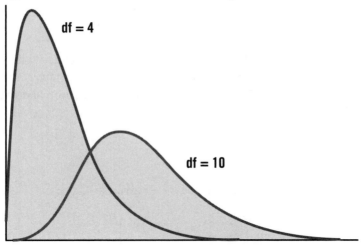

Figure 10.16

To use the chi-square distribution, we need a chi-square point, denoted by χ_α^2 (the Greek letter chi, pronounced *Ki*). We'll later call this our critical value for the chi-square distribution. As is shown in Figure 10.17 below, χ_α^2 is the point on the horizontal axis under the curve with an area of α to the right of it. The value of χ_α^2 depends on the right-hand tail area, α, and the number of degrees of freedom of the chi-square distribution. The values are tabulated in Table H in Appendix A. Looking at the chi-square table, the rows correspond to the appropriate number of degrees of freedom (the first column listed down the left side of the table), while the columns represent the right-hand tail area.

Chi-square distribution

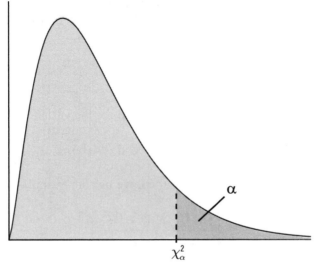

Figure 10.17

Using Table H in Appendix A, suppose we want to find the chi-square value that gives us a right-hand tail area of .05 with 5 degrees of freedom. To do this, we would look down the left-most column for 5 degrees of freedom and then the column labeled $\chi^2_{.05}$. Doing so, we find that $\chi^2_{.05}$ is 11.0705.

Now that we've established the sampling distribution associated with the sample variance, we can make inferences about the population variance. Suppose we have a random sample of size n taken from a normal population and that s^2 is the estimate of the population variance, σ^2.

Formula

A $100(1-\alpha)\%$ confidence interval for σ^2 is given by

$$\left(\frac{(n-1)s^2}{\chi^2_{\alpha/2}}, \frac{(n-1)s^2}{\chi^2_{1-\alpha/2}} \right)$$

where $\chi^2_{\alpha/2}$ and $\chi^2_{1-\alpha/2}$ are points under the curve of the chi-square distribution with $n-1$ degrees of freedom.

Example 10.13

The quality control supervisor of a bottling plant is concerned about the variance of fill per bottle. Regulatory agencies specify that the standard deviation of the amount of fill should be less than 0.1 ounce. To determine whether the process is meeting this specification, the supervisor randomly selects ten bottles, weighs the contents of each, and finds that the sample standard deviation of these measurements is 0.04. Compute a 95% confidence interval for the standard deviation of ounces of fill for the bottling plant.

Solution

We want to find a 95% confidence interval for the variance. We are given that

$$n = 10, \ s = 0.04, \text{ and } \alpha = .05.$$

To calculate a 95% confidence interval, we use the formula

$$\left(\frac{(n-1)s^2}{\chi^2_{\alpha/2}}, \frac{(n-1)s^2}{\chi^2_{1-\alpha/2}} \right).$$

Thus, we need to find the values of $\chi^2_{.025}$ and $\chi^2_{.975}$ for $n-1 = 10 - 1 = 9$ degrees of freedom.

Using Table H in Appendix A, at 9 degrees of freedom,

$$\chi^2_{.025} = 19.0228$$
$$\chi^2_{.975} = 2.7004.$$

Substituting the values in the formula above, we have

$$\left(\frac{(10-1)(0.04)^2}{19.0228}, \frac{(10-1)(0.04)^2}{2.7004} \right)$$
$$(0.000757, 0.00533)$$
$$(0.0275, 0.0730).$$

So, a 95% confidence interval for the variance of fill of the bottles is between 0.000757 and 0.00533 ounce. However, the statement above mentions the tolerance for the standard deviation of fill. So, to ensure that we make our interpretation in terms of the problem, to find a 95% confidence interval for the standard deviation, we take the square root of the confidence interval for the variance, yielding

$$(0.0275, 0.0730).$$

The 95% confidence interval for the standard deviation of fill for the bottles is between 0.0275 and 0.0730 ounce, indicating that the process is meeting the specifications of being less than 0.1 ounce.

To adapt the hypothesis testing procedure to test a hypothesis concerning a population variance, let's look at the following example.

Example 10.14

A drug manufacturer believes that the manufacturing process is in control if the standard deviation of the dosage in each tablet is at most 0.10 milligram. The quality control manager is willing to shut down the manufacturing process if there is overwhelming evidence that the process has an excessive variation. Use $\alpha = .01$.

Solution

Step 1: State the hypotheses in plain English.

- The tablet manufacturing process does not have excessive variation.
- The tablet manufacturing process does have excessive variation.

Step 2: Select the appropriate statistical measure.

Since the issue in this example is variation, the hypothesis can be stated in terms of the standard deviation or the variance.

Step 3: Determine whether the hypotheses should be one-sided or two-sided.

Most hypothesis tests concerning a variance will be one-sided. Small variation is desirable, while too much variation is undesirable. Because we are interested in determining if there is evidence that the process has excessive variation, the test will be one-sided.

Step 4: State the hypotheses using the appropriate statistical measure.

$$H_0: \sigma \leq 0.10 \quad \text{(the variation of the process is acceptable)}$$
$$H_a: \sigma > 0.10 \quad \text{(the variation of the process is excessive)}$$

Step 5: Specify the level of the test.

The level of the test is specified in the problem as $\alpha = .01$.

Step 6: Select the appropriate test statistic.

The test statistic will change rather dramatically. In the previous test statistics, the goal was to measure how far the sample statistic, $\bar{x}$ or $\hat{p}$, was from the hypothesized value. The test statistic for a population variance is given by

$$\chi^2 = \frac{(n-1)s^2}{\sigma_0^2} \quad \text{with } n-1 \text{ degrees of freedom.}$$

Let's look at the pieces of this statistic. The term σ_0^2 refers to the hypothesized value of the variance. In this sample, $\sigma_0 = 0.10$. which implies $\sigma_0^2 = 0.01$. The actual variance of the population is unknown. But the sample variance, s^2, should be reasonably close to the unknown population variance, σ^2. If the null is true, then $\sigma_0^2 = 0.01$ and the ratio $\frac{s^2}{\sigma_0^2}$ should be near 1, since s^2 should be close to σ_0^2. Assuming the null is true, multiplying this ratio by $(n-1)$ should produce a result near $(n-1)$. If the χ^2 expression is a great deal larger than $(n-1)$, then s^2 will be a great deal larger than σ_0^2. Such an event would cast doubt on the validity of the null hypothesis.

Sampling Distribution of the χ^2 Test Statistic

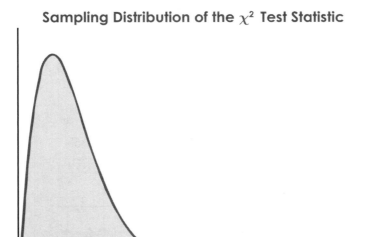

Figure 10.18

Step 7: Determine the critical value.

The role of the critical value in this test is no different from other hypothesis tests discussed earlier. It defines a range of values for the test statistic, the rejection region, that will be too rare to have likely occurred from ordinary sampling variability. From a probabilistic standpoint, the level of the test defines the size of the rejection region. Should the value of the test statistic fall in this region, the null hypothesis will be rejected. Determining the critical value will require knowledge of the sample size. Suppose the company intends to draw a sample size of 30 tablets. Since the level of the test is .01 and there are $d.f = 30 - 1 = 29$ degrees of freedom, the critical value is 49.5878 (see Table H). The test statistic will exceed this value because of ordinary variation only 1% of the time.

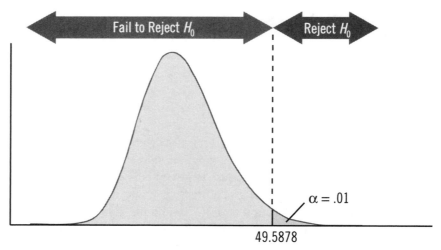

DF	...	$\chi^2_{.025}$	$\chi^2_{.010}$	$\chi^2_{.005}$
1		5.0239	6.6349	7.8794
2		7.3778	9.2104	10.5965
3		9.3484	11.3449	12.8381
⋮				
29		45.7223	49.5878	52.3355
30		46.9792	50.8922	53.6719
⋮				

Fail to Reject H_0 Reject H_0

$\alpha = .01$

49.5878

Figure 10.19

Step 8: Compute the test statistic.

Suppose a sample of 30 tablets are evaluated, and the sample standard deviation is found to be 0.14 milligram.

$$\chi^2 = \frac{(n-1)s^2}{\sigma_0^2} = \frac{(30-1)(0.14)^2}{(0.10)^2} = 56.84$$

Step 9: Make the decision.

Since the test statistic, $\chi^2 = 56.84$, exceeds the critical value, 49.5878, we will conclude the test statistic is too rare to have been caused by ordinary sampling variation. The null hypothesis is rejected in favor of the alternative hypothesis.

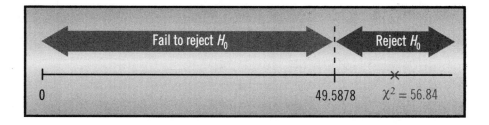

Step 10: State the conclusion in terms of the original question.

There is overwhelming evidence that the process variation exceeds the desired level.

10.8 Exercises

Basic Concepts

1. How does testing a hypothesis about a variance differ from testing a hypothesis about a mean?

2. What is the sampling distribution for $\dfrac{(n-1)s^2}{\sigma^2}$?

3. What assumption must hold to use the chi-square distribution to make inferences about the population variance?

4. True or false: the chi-square distribution is skewed to the right.

5. What is the symbol for a critical value for the chi-square distribution? Describe the meaning of this critical value.

6. Give an example where we would want to calculate a confidence interval for σ^2.

Exercises

1. Determine the critical value(s) of the test statistic for each of the following tests for a population variance where the assumption of normality is satisfied.

    a. Right-tailed test, $\alpha = .01$, $n = 20$

    b. Right-tailed test, $\alpha = .05$, $n = 24$

    c. Right-tailed test, $\alpha = .005$, $n = 24$

2. Determine the critical value(s) of the test statistic for each of the following tests for a population variance where the assumption of normality is satisfied.

   a. Right-tailed test, $\alpha = .025$, $n = 18$

   b. Right-tailed test, $\alpha = .10$, $n = 24$

   c. Right-tailed test, $\alpha = .05$, $n = 41$

3. A bolt manufacturer is very concerned about the consistency with which his machines produce bolts that are $\frac{3}{4}$ inch in diameter. Wxhen the manufacturing process is working normally the standard deviation of the bolt diameter is 0.05 inch. A random sample of 30 bolts has an average diameter of 0.25 inch with a standard deviation of 0.07 inch.

   a. Construct a 95% confidence interval for the standard deviation of the bolt diameter. Interpret the interval

   b. Can the manufacturer conclude that the standard deviation of bolt diameters is greater than 0.05 inches at $\alpha = .05$?

   c. What assumption did you make about the diameter of the bolts in constructing the confidence interval in part (a) and performing the test in part (b)?

4. A drug which is used for treating cancer has potentially dangerous side effects if it is taken in doses which are larger than the required dosage for the treatment. The pharmaceutical company which manufactures the drug must be certain that the standard deviation of the drug content in the tablet is not more than 0.1 mg. Twenty-five tablets are randomly selected and the amount of drug in each tablet is measured. The sample has a mean of 20 mg and a variance of 0.015 mg.

   a. Do the data suggest at $\alpha = .01$ that the standard deviation of drug content in the tablets is greater than 0.1 mg?

   b. Construct a 99% confidence interval for the variance of the amount of drug in each tablet. Interpret the interval.

   c. What assumption did you make about the amount of drug contained in the tablets in performing the test in part (a) and constructing the confidence interval in part (b)?

5. A conservative investor would like to invest some money in a bond fund. The investor is concerned about the safety of her principal (the original money invested). Colonial Funds claims to have a bond fund which has maintained a consistent share price of $7. They claim that this share price has not varied by more than 0.25 on average since its inception. To test this claim, the investor randomly selects 25 days during the last year and determines the share price for the bond fund. The average share price of the sample is $7 with a standard deviation of 0.35.

   a. Can the investor conclude that the standard deviation of share price of the bond fund is greater than 0.25? Test at the .01 level.

   b. Construct a 90% confidence interval for the standard deviation of the share price of the bond fund. Interpret the interval.

   c. What assumption did you make about the share price of the bond fund in your test in part (a) and constructing the confidence interval in part (b)?

Discovering Technology

USING THE TI-84 PLUS CALCULATOR

Hypothesis Testing, Large Sample Test for μ

$$z = \frac{\bar{x} - \mu_0}{\sigma_{\bar{x}}}, \quad \text{where } \sigma_{\bar{x}} = \frac{\sigma}{\sqrt{n}}$$

$$H_0: \mu \leq 16,000 \qquad n = 1000 \qquad \bar{x} = 16,500$$
$$H_a: \mu > 16,000 \qquad \sigma = 2500$$

1. Choose **STAT**, then select **TESTS** and **1:Z-Test**. Press **ENTER**, choose **Stats**. Input **16000** for μ_0, **2500** for σ, **16500** for $\bar{x}$, **1000** for n, and select $>\mu_0$. Press **Calculate**.

Figures 10.20   Figure 10.21

Hypothesis Testing, Small Sample Test for μ

$$t = \frac{\bar{x} - \mu_0}{s_{\bar{x}}}, \quad \text{where } s_{\bar{x}} = \frac{s}{\sqrt{n}}$$

$$H_0: \mu = 35 \qquad n = 20 \qquad \bar{x} = 27$$
$$H_a: \mu \neq 35 \qquad s = 4$$

2. Choose **STAT**, then select **TESTS** and **2:T-Test**. Press **ENTER**, choose **Stats**. Input **35** for μ_0, **27** for $\bar{x}$, **4** for s (designated on calculator as $s_{\bar{x}}$), **20** for n, and select $\neq \mu_0$. Press **Calculate**.

Figures 10.22

Figure 10.23

USING EXCEL

Hypothesis Testing, z-Test Statistic

Finding the z-test statistic can be one of the more laborious steps in hypothesis testing. Use Excel to compute the z-score for Example 10.10.

1. Create a worksheet with these labels.

	A
1	Hypothesized mean
2	Sample mean
3	Sample Standard Deviation
4	Sample Size

Figure 10.24

2. Referring to the example, we see that the null hypothesized mean is 25. Enter **25** in cell B1. Enter the sample mean, **25.01** in cell B2. Enter the sample standard deviation, **0.1** in cell B3. Enter the sample size, **2000** in cell B4.

3. Given these values, we have enough data to compute the z-test statistic. In cell B5 construct the following formula for the z-test statistic.

$$=(B2-B1)/(B3/(SQRT(B4))$$

4. Press **Enter**. The resulting z-test statistic, 4.472136, should now appear in cell B5.

	A	B
1	Hypothesized mean	25
2	Sample mean	25.01
3	Sample Standard Deviation	0.1
4	Sample Size	2000
5		4.472136

Figure 10.25

You can use this worksheet to compute z for other hypothesis testing questions by changing the values for the hypothesized mean and sample statistics.

USING MINITAB

Hypothesis Testing, Large Sample Test for μ

Minitab will compute the z-test statistic for a set of sample data.

Sample data:

95	110	60	75	85	90	110	90	115	100	90	100
90	50	60	110	90	90	55	100	40	115	50	100
70	70	80	95	90	70	95	80	105	90	55	65

$$H_0 : \mu \geq 80 \qquad \alpha = .05$$
$$H_a : \mu < 80 \qquad \sigma = 20.15$$

1. Enter the sample data into column C1.
2. Choose **Stat**, **Basic Statistics**, and **1-Sample Z**. Select **Options** to enter the alternative of **less than** and press **OK**.
3. Enter **C1** for "Samples in columns", enter **20.15** for "Standard deviation", check the box next to "Perform hypothesis test" and enter **80** for "Hypothesized mean". Press **OK**.
4. Observe the output screen for the results. The z-test statistic for this sample data is 1.28.

One-Sample Z: C1

```
Test of mu = 80 vs < 80
The assumed standard deviation = 20.15


                                          95% Upper
Variable   N    Mean  StDev  SE Mean        Bound      Z      P
C1        36   84.31  20.15     3.36        89.83   1.28  0.900
```

Figure 10.26

Hypothesis Testing, Small Sample Test for μ

Sample data:

24.9	26.8	27.2	34.1	28.9	25.9	25.1	23.9	23.0	30.9
31.9	35.1	27.4	25.9	19.1	23.7	22.0	25.9	29.0	29.3

$$H_0: \mu = 35 \qquad\qquad \alpha = .05$$
$$H_a: \mu \neq 35$$

1. Enter the sample data into column C1.

2. Choose **Stat**, **Basic Statistics**, and **1-Sample t**. Select Options to enter the alternative of **not equal** and press **OK**.

3. Enter **C1** for "Samples in columns", check the box next to "Perform hypothesis test", and enter **35** for "Hypothesized mean". Press **OK**.

4. Observe the output screen for the results. The *t*-test statistic for these sample data is −8.95.

One-Sample T: C1

Test of mu = 35 vs not = 35

Variable	N	Mean	StDev	SE Mean	95% CI	T	P
C3	20	27.000	4.000	0.894	(25.128, 28.872)	−8.95	0.000

Figure 10.27

R Chapter 10 Review

Key Terms and Ideas

- Hypothesis Testing
- Null Hypothesis
- Alternative Hypothesis
- One-Sided Alternative
- Two-Sided Alternative
- One-Tailed Test
- Two-Tailed Test
- Test Statistic
- Rejection Region
- Reject
- Fail To Reject
- Decision Rule
- Standard Value
- Type I Error
- Type II Error
- Level of the Test (Significance Level of the Test)
- z-Test Statistic
- Critical Value
- t-Test Statistic
- P-Value
- Practical vs. Statistical Significance
- Chi-Square Distribution
- Confidence Interval for σ^2

Key Formulas

Concept	Formula	Section
z-Test Statistic for a Population Mean	$z = \dfrac{\bar{x} - \mu_0}{\sigma_{\bar{x}}}$, where $\sigma_{\bar{x}} = \dfrac{\sigma}{\sqrt{n}}$	10.4
t-Test Statistic	$t = \dfrac{\bar{x} - \mu_0}{s_{\bar{x}}}$, where $s_{\bar{x}} = \dfrac{s}{\sqrt{n}}$	10.4
Using a Confidence Interval to Test a Hypothesis	**Step 1**: If the hypothesis test is of the form $$H_0 : \mu = \mu_0$$ $$H_a : \mu \neq \mu_0,$$ **Step 2**: calculate the $100(1-\alpha)\%$ two-sided confidence interval given by $$\bar{x} \pm z_{\alpha/2}\frac{\sigma}{\sqrt{n}}.$$ **Step 3**: If μ_0 falls within the interval, then we fail to reject the null hypothesis; however, if μ_0 falls outside the calculated interval, then reject the null hypothesis in favor of the alternative.	10.6
z-Test Statistic for a Population Proportion	If $np \geq 5$ and $n(1-p) \geq 5$, the appropriate test statistic is given by $$z = \frac{\hat{p} - p}{\sigma_{\hat{p}}}, \text{ where } \sigma_{\hat{p}} = \sqrt{\frac{p(1-p)}{n}}.$$	10.7
$100(1-\alpha)\%$ Confidence Interval for the Population Variance	A $100(1-\alpha)\%$ confidence interval for σ^2 is given by $$\left(\frac{(n-1)s^2}{\chi^2_{\alpha/2}}, \frac{(n-1)s^2}{\chi^2_{1-\alpha/2}} \right)$$ where $\chi^2_{\alpha/2}$ and $\chi^2_{1-\alpha/2}$ are points under the curve of the chi-square distribution with $n-1$ degrees of freedom.	10.8
Test Statistic for a Population Variance	$\chi^2 = \dfrac{(n-1)s^2}{\sigma^2_0}$ with $n-1$ degrees of freedom	10.8

AE   Additional Exercises

1. A tire company has found that the mean time required for a mechanic to replace a set of four tires is 18 minutes. After instituting a new installation procedure, the company unfortunately believes that the expected time required to replace the set of four tires remains unchanged. A test of the company's belief will be performed.

    a. What are the null and alternative hypotheses for the test of the company's belief?

    b. Describe, in terms of the problem, how a Type I error could occur.

    c. Describe, in terms of the problem, how a Type II error could occur.

2. Tech Transit wishes to test whether the mean number of passenger miles on a particular route exceeds 66,000 passenger miles, the number of passenger miles the company needs on that route to cover all allocated costs. A random sample of 25 trips on the route yields a mean of 70,250 and a standard deviation of 9,000. It is desired to control the significance level at 1%.

    a. State the appropriate hypotheses for this problem.

    b. Describe, in terms of the problem, how a Type I error could occur.

    c. Describe, in terms of the problem, how a Type II error could occur.

3. A pain reliever currently being used in a hospital is known to bring relief to patients in a mean time of 3.5 minutes. To compare a new pain reliever with the one currently being used, the new drug is administered to a random sample of 50 patients. The mean time to relief for the sample of patients is 2.8 minutes and the standard deviation is 1.14 minutes. Do the data provide sufficient evidence to conclude that the new drug was effective in reducing the mean time until a patient receives relief from pain? Test using $\alpha = .10$.

4. Tech uses thousands of fluorescent light bulbs each year. The brand of bulb it currently uses has a mean life of 900 hours. A manufacturer claims that its new brand of bulbs, which cost the same as the brand the university currently uses, has a mean life of more than 900 hours. The university has decided to purchase the new brand if, when tested, the test evidence supports the manufacturer's claim at the .05 significance level. Suppose 64 bulbs were tested and they were found to have an average life of 920 hours with a standard deviation of 80 hours. Will the university purchase the new brand of fluorescent bulbs?

5. The daily wages in a particular industry are normally distributed with a mean of $13.20 and a standard deviation of $2.50. If a company in this industry employing 40 workers pays these workers, on average, $12.20, can this company be accused of paying inferior wages? Use the P-value approach with a significance level of 1%.

6. A coin-operated soft drink machine was designed to discharge, on average, 12 ounces of beverage per cup. In a test of the machine, ten cupfuls of beverage were drawn from the machine and measured. The mean and standard deviation of the ten measurements were 12.1 ounces and 0.12 ounce, respectively. Do these data present sufficient evidence to indicate that the mean discharge differs from 12 ounces? Test using $\alpha = .10$.

7. Techside Real Estate, Inc. is a research firm that tracks the cost of apartment rentals in Southwest Virginia. In mid-2002, the regional average apartment rental rate was $895 per month. Assume that, based on the historical quarterly surveys, it is reasonable to assume that the population standard deviation is $225. In a current study of apartment rental rates, a sample of 180 apartments in the region provided the apartment rental rates. Do the sample data enable Techside Real Estate, Inc. to conclude that the population mean apartment rental rate now exceeds the level reported in 2002? The sample mean is $915 and the sample standard deviation is $227.50. Make your decision based on $\alpha = .10$.

8. Suppose that the national average price for used cars is $10,192. A manager of a local used car dealership reviewed a sample of 25 recent used car sales at the dealership in an attempt to determine whether the population mean price for the used cars at this particular dealership differed from the national mean. The prices for the sample of 25 cars are given in the data with a mean of $9750 and standard deviation of $1400. Test using $\alpha = .05$ whether a difference exists in the mean price for used cars at the dealership.

9. Suppose you are responsible for auditing invoices. Historically, about .003 of the invoices possessed material errors. During the last audit cycle a number of suggestions were made and implemented, and you hope that the next audit will provide evidence of improvement in the error rate. An audit of 6000 recent invoices reveals 12 material errors.

   a. Do the data suggest an improvement in the invoice error rate at $\alpha = .05$?

   b. Compute the P-value of the test statistic.

   c. Based on the P-value, would the decision change at $\alpha = .10$?

10. After completing Chemistry 101, Tommy Walker decides to conduct an experiment on his favorite brand of whiskey to determine if the proof rating on the bottle is accurate. He selects eight small eighty-proof bottles from different stores around town and measures the percent of alcohol in each bottle. (Note: 80 proof alcohol contains 40% alcohol.)

The resulting measurements are:

38%	40%	42%	41%	39%	38%	40%	38%

   a. What is the population being studied?
   b. What is the variable being measured?
   c. What level of measurement does the data possess?
   d. Can Tommy conclude that the actual proof of whiskey is not equal to 80 at $\alpha = .05$?
   e. What assumption did Tommy make in performing the test in part (d)?

11. You have decided to become a professional gambler specializing in roulette. If the roulette wheel is fair (each number has a $\frac{1}{38}$ chance) then you will lose in the long run. However, you plan to locate wheels that are not balanced properly. An unbalanced wheel will produce some numbers more often than expected. You believe that you have found such a wheel and have started keeping track of the number 29. After 420 spins of the wheel, the number 29 has been observed 14 times. Is this overwhelming evidence at the $\alpha = .05$ level that you should start betting heavily on the number 29?

12. A commercial airline is concerned over the increase in weight of a carry-on luggage. In the past the airline has estimated that the average piece of carry-on luggage will weigh 12 pounds. A random selection of 148 pieces of carry-on luggage has an average weight of 14.2 pounds with a standard deviation of 3.4 pounds. Do you think that the airline's concern is justified? Use $\alpha = .01$.

13. Consider the following large sample hypothesis tests for the population mean. Compute the P-value for each test and decide whether you would reject or fail to reject the null hypothesis at $\alpha = .01$.

   a. $H_0 : \mu = 15$ vs $H_a : \mu > 15$, $z = 2.50$
   b. $H_0 : \mu = 80$ vs $H_a : \mu < 80$, $z = -1.95$
   c. $H_0 : \mu = 1200$ vs $H_a : \mu \neq 1200$, $z = 3.70$

14. Deli Delivery delivers sandwiches to neighboring office buildings during lunch time in New York City. The deli claims that the sandwiches will be delivered within 20 minutes from receiving the order. Given the hectic schedules of their customers, consistent delivery time is a must. The owner has decided that the standard deviation of delivery times should be at most 4 minutes. To determine how consistently the sandwiches are being delivered, the manager randomly selects 27 orders and measures the time from receiving the order to delivery of the sandwich. The average time to delivery of the sample was 20 minutes with a standard deviation of 4.5 minutes.

    a. Will the manager conclude at $\alpha = .10$ that the delivery times vary more than the owner desires?

    b. What assumption did you make about the delivery times in performing the test in part (a)?

15. Consider the following small sample hypothesis tests for the population mean. Compute the P-value for each of the tests and decide whether you would reject or fail to reject the null hypothesis at $\alpha = .05$.

    a. $H_0: \mu = 12$ vs $H_a: \mu > 12$, $t = 1.75$, $n = 25$

    b. $H_0: \mu = .12$ vs $H_a: \mu < .12$, $t = -2.95$, $n = 16$

    c. $H_0: \mu = 55$ vs $H_a: \mu \neq 55$, $t = 2.35$, $n = 8$

16. In each of the following experimental situations give the appropriate null and alternative hypotheses to be tested. Define all terms that appear in these hypotheses.

    a. A random sample of 100 customers in a bank are selected and their times to be served are noted. The bank has recently retrained its tellers to be more efficient with the hope of decreasing its average time in servicing its customers, which has been 4 minutes in the past.

    b. A local driver training school claims that at least 75% of its pupils pass the driving test on their first attempt. A sample of 60 students from the school are selected, and their performances on the driving test are noted. Based upon the data collected, we would like to refute the claim of the school.

    c. A spokesperson for a popular diet claims that the average weight lost for someone on the diet will be at least 15 pounds over a two-month period. The amount of weight lost for each person in a sample of 10 people on the diet is determined in order to try to refute the claim of the diet spokesperson.

    d. A tire company tests 68 of its new premium tires to determine if the average lifespan of the tire is more than the average lifespan of its major competitor's best tire. The average lifespan of the competitor's tire is 63,000 miles.

    e. An elementary statistics student conducts an experiment in order to show that a coin from a magic kit is biased. The student flips the coin 500 times.

17. It is essential in the manufacture of machinery to utilize parts that conform to specifications. In the past, diameters of the ball-bearings produced by a certain manufacturer had a variance of 0.00156. To cut costs, the manufacturer instituted a less expensive production method. The variance of the diameters of 101 randomly sampled bearings produced by the new process was 0.0021. Do the data provide sufficient evidence to indicate that the diameters of ball-bearings produced by the new process are more variable than those produced by the old process? Test using $\alpha = .10$.

18. A national news magazine is interested in the proportion of counties in which the cost of living has decreased in the past 24 months. The news magazine believes that the true proportion is less than 30%. In a random sample of 100 counties, 20 counties had cost of living decreases.

    a. Test the news magazine's claim at $\alpha = .08$.

    b. Find the P-value for this test.

19. An increasing number of businesses are offering child-care benefits for their workers. However, one union claims that at least 90% of firms in the manufacturing sector still do not offer any child-care benefits to their workers. A random sample of 350 manufacturing firms is selected, and only 28 of them offer child-care benefits.

    a. Does this sample result support the claim of the union? Test using $\alpha = .10$.

    b. Calculate the P-value associated with this test.

20. During the holiday season, law enforcement officials estimated that 500 people would be killed and 25,000 injured on the nation's roads. They claimed that at least 50% of the accidents would be caused by drunk driving. A sample of 120 accidents showed that 67 were caused by drunk driving. Use these data to test their claim with $\alpha = .05$.

21. The quality control supervisor of a cannery is concerned about the variance of fill per can. Regulatory agencies specify that the standard deviation of the amount of fill should be less than 0.1 ounce. To determine whether the process is meeting this specification, the supervisor randomly selects ten cans, weighs the contents of each, and finds that the sample standard deviation of these measurements is 0.04.

    a. Do these data provide sufficient evidence to indicate that the variability is as small as desired? Test using $\alpha = .05$.

    b. Compute a 95% confidence interval for the variance of ounces of fill for the cannery.

Inferences about Means and Proportions: Two Samples

11

Introduction

Basic concepts of hypothesis testing were introduced in Chapter 10. In this chapter we will continue to follow the same basic hypothesis testing procedure developed in the previous chapter.

We have focused on problems in which variables were measured on the ratio level of measurement (dollars, grams, pounds, miles, etc.). The inferential methods that we previously developed concerned one population and the value of its mean, proportion, or variance. We use the information in the sample statistics $\bar{x}$, $\hat{p}$, and s^2 to test hypotheses about the population parameters.

There are many instances in which we wish to compare two population means or two population proportions. For example, in Chapter 2 we discussed controlled experiments in which we tried to develop data that would be used to efficiently test hypotheses about two or more proportions. In this chapter, we will begin to explore methods for testing population parameters of this type.

In particular, we will develop methods for comparing two population means,

and try to answer questions like:

- Is $\mu_1 > \mu_2$?
- Is $\mu_1 < \mu_2$?
- Is $\mu_1 \neq \mu_2$?

Similarly, we will develop methods for comparing two population proportions,

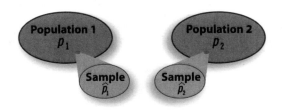

and try to answer questions like:

- Is $p_1 > p_2$?
- Is $p_1 \neq p_2$?
- Is $p_1 < p_2$?

Comparing Two Population Means

We developed procedures for testing a hypothesis about a single population mean in Section 10.4. In this section, a procedure is developed for comparing two population means when large independent samples are available. Section 11.2 will develop a procedure that is used when the independent samples are small (but have been drawn from normal populations).

There are many situations where our interest is in comparing two population means or the average response of experimental units to two different treatments. For example, a marketing professor may be interested in students' grades when using slides as a delivery method during lecture as opposed to when using the blackboard. A fleet manager may be interested in comparing the average gas mileage for two different makes of cars. An economist may be interested in the cost of living between industrialized and non-industrialized countries.

In each of the above situations, an experiment can be designed for sampling from two separate populations (two different makes of cars or groups of students), or the experiment can be designed for randomly assigning experimental units to two different treatments (students receiving lecture via slides and students receiving lecture via the blackboard).

When a large number of observations are randomly selected from two independent populations or a large number of experimental units are randomly assigned to two different treatments where the variation between experimental units is small, the sampling design is called an **independent experimental design** or a **completely randomized design**.

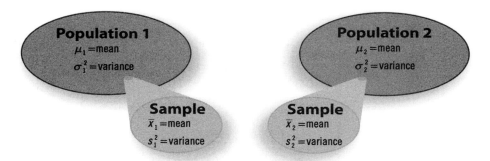

We will use the sample means $\bar{x}_1$ and $\bar{x}_2$ to compare the means of two populations. The sampling distribution for the difference between two sample means, $\bar{x}_1 - \bar{x}_2$, has an approximately normal distribution (when an independent experimental design is used to make comparisons between two population means and the samples drawn from each population, n_1 and n_2, are "large").

The properties of the sampling distribution for the difference between sample means are given below.

Properties

Properties of the Sampling Distribution of $\bar{x}_1 - \bar{x}_2$

1. If $n_1 \geq 30$ and $n_2 \geq 30$, the sampling distribution of $\bar{x}_1 - \bar{x}_2$ has an approximately normal distribution.

2. $\mu_{\bar{x}_1 - \bar{x}_2} = \mu_1 - \mu_2$

3. $\sigma_{\bar{x}_1 - \bar{x}_2} = \sqrt{\dfrac{\sigma_1^2}{n_1} + \dfrac{\sigma_2^2}{n_2}}$ if the two samples are independent. σ_1^2 and σ_2^2 can be approximated with s_1^2 and s_2^2, respectively, if $n_1 \geq 30$ and $n_2 \geq 30$.

The sampling distribution of $\bar{x}_1 - \bar{x}_2$ will be used in the development of the confidence interval and test statistic for comparing two population means.

Interval Estimation of $\mu_1 - \mu_2$

Given the sampling distribution of $\bar{x}_1 - \bar{x}_2$, we can develop the confidence interval estimate of the difference between two population means.

100 (1−α) %
Confidence Interval
for $\mu_1 - \mu_2$

Formula

The $100\,(1-\alpha)\,\%$ **confidence interval** estimate for the difference in the two population means of two independent populations is given by

$$(\bar{x}_1 - \bar{x}_2) \pm z_{\alpha/2} \sqrt{\frac{\sigma_1^2}{n_1} + \frac{\sigma_2^2}{n_2}}$$

where $z_{\alpha/2}$ is the critical value of the standard normal distribution with an area of $\alpha/2$ in the upper tail. σ_1^2 and σ_2^2 can be approximated with s_1^2 and s_2^2, respectively, if the independent samples are large, i.e. $n_1 \geq 30$ and $n_2 \geq 30$.

Hypothesis Testing about $\mu_1 - \mu_2$

You may recall that when comparing the means of two independent populations, you take a random sample of size n_1 from the first population and a random sample of size n_2 from the second population. If both n_1 and n_2 are greater than or equal to 30, then the following test statistic is valid. If one or both of the sample sizes are less than 30, the test is also valid if we assume that the standard deviation of each population $(\sigma_1$ and $\sigma_2)$ is known, and the samples are taken from normal populations.

Formula

The test statistic for a hypothesis test about $\mu_1 - \mu_2$ is given by

$$z = \frac{(\bar{x}_1 - \bar{x}_2) - (\mu_1 - \mu_2)}{\sqrt{\dfrac{\sigma_1^2}{n_1} + \dfrac{\sigma_2^2}{n_2}}}$$

where $\bar{x}_1$ is the sample mean taken from population 1, n_1 is the sample size taken from population 1, σ_1^2 is the variance of population 1, $\bar{x}_2$ is the sample mean taken from population 2, n_2 is the sample size taken from population 2, and σ_2^2 is the variance of population 2. If n_1 and n_2 are greater than or equal to 30, s_1 and s_2 can be used as approximations for σ_1 and σ_2.

Note that $(\mu_1 - \mu_2)$ represents the hypothesized difference between the two population means and that the z-statistic follows the standard normal distribution.

Test Statistic for a Hypothesis Test about $\mu_1 - \mu_2$

The hypothesis test for comparing two population means will be developed in Example 11.1.

Example 11.1

A telecommunications analyst is interested in knowing if there is a significant difference in the average quality of service (QOS) between cable television subscribers and satellite television subscribers. She randomly selects 50 cable subscribers and 50 satellite subscribers for the study. She gives each subscriber a survey and asks them to complete it. She tallies the results of the survey and calculates an average QOS for each service. The QOS is ranked on a scale of 1–10, with the higher value implying that subscribers are more satisfied with their service. The results of the study are shown in Table 11.1.

Table 11.1 – QOS Scores for Subscribers

	n	$\bar{x}$	s
Cable	50	8.8	3
Satellite	50	9.5	2

a. Calculate a 95% confidence interval for the mean difference in average QOS between cable and satellite subscribers.

b. Is there persuasive evidence for the analyst to conclude at $\alpha = .05$ that there is a difference in average QOS between cable and satellite subscribers?

Solution

a. From the information given in the problem, we know that

$$n_1 = 50, \ n_2 = 50, \ s_1 = 3, \ s_2 = 2, \ \bar{x}_1 = 8.8, \ \text{and} \ \bar{x}_2 = 9.5.$$

Since both sample sizes are at least 30, we can invoke the Central Limit Theorem and assume that the sample means are approximately normally distributed. In addition, we can use the sample standard deviations to estimate the population standard deviations.

Since we want a 95% confidence interval, we need to find the value of $z_{\alpha/2}$. Remember that $z_{\alpha/2}$ represents the z-value required to obtain an area of $(1-\alpha)$ centered under the standard normal curve. Therefore, for a 95% confidence interval, $\alpha = .05$.

$$\text{For } \alpha = .05, \ z_{\alpha/2} = z_{.025} = 1.96.$$

A 95% confidence interval for the difference in the average QOS between cable and satellite providers is given by

$$\left(\bar{x}_1 - \bar{x}_2 \right) \pm z_{\alpha/2} \sqrt{\frac{s_1^2}{n_1} + \frac{s_2^2}{n_2}},$$

since both n_1 and n_2 are greater than or equal to 30.

This gives,

$$(8.8 - 9.5) \pm 1.96 \sqrt{\frac{3^2}{50} + \frac{2^2}{50}}$$

$$-0.7 \pm 1.96 \sqrt{\frac{13}{50}}$$

$$-0.7 \pm 1.0$$

$$-1.7 \text{ to } 0.3.$$

Thus, we are 95% confident that the true mean difference in QOS between cable and satellite subscribers is between −1.7 and 0.3. Another way to interpret this interval in terms of the problem is that the average QOS for satellite subscribers is between 1.7 rating points higher and 0.3 rating points lower than cable subscribers. This indicates that satellite subscribers appear to be more satisfied.

b. *Step 1: State the hypotheses in plain English.*

- There is no difference in average QOS between cable and satellite subscribers.

- There is a difference in average QOS between cable and satellite subscribers.

Step 2: Select the appropriate statistical measure.

Since the analyst is interested in comparing the average QOS between cable and satellite subscribers, the appropriate statistical measures are:

μ_1 = the true average QOS for cable subscribers

μ_2 = the true average QOS for satellite subscribers.

Step 3: Determine whether the hypotheses should be one-sided or two-sided.

The analyst is interested in whether or not there is a difference in the QOS between cable and satellite subscribers. Thus, the hypotheses are two-sided and the test is two-tailed.

Step 4: State the hypotheses using the appropriate statistical measure.

Since the analyst is interested in comparing the two population means, a natural way to make this comparison is to look at the difference between the two population means. Hence the null and alternative hypotheses are formulated as follows:

$H_0 : \mu_1 - \mu_2 = 0$ (There is no difference in average QOS.)

$H_a : \mu_1 - \mu_2 \neq 0$ (There is a difference in average QOS.).

In this situation, the hypothesized difference in average QOS is 0. However, it is possible to be interested in non-zero differences. For example, if the analyst had been interested in testing if the difference in average QOS was one unit, the hypothesized difference would have been one.

Step 5: Specify the level of the test.

The level of the test is specified in the problem as $\alpha = .05$.

Step 6: Select the appropriate test statistic.

The difference in sample means, $\bar{x}_1 - \bar{x}_2$, is an unbiased point estimate of the difference in population means, $\mu_1 - \mu_2$. The sampling distribution for the point estimate, $\bar{x}_1 - \bar{x}_2$, provides essential information for determining the test statistic. If $n_1 \geq 30$ and $n_2 \geq 30$ and an independent experimental design is used, the sampling distribution of $\bar{x}_1 - \bar{x}_2$ has an approximately normal distribution with mean, $\mu_1 - \mu_2$, and standard deviation,

$$\sigma_{\bar{x}_1 - \bar{x}_2} = \sqrt{\frac{\sigma_1^2}{n_1} + \frac{\sigma_2^2}{n_2}}.$$

Thus, the test statistic is a standard normal random variable which is calculated by using the familiar z-transformation. The test statistic is given by

$$z = \frac{(\bar{x}_1 - \bar{x}_2) - \mu_{\bar{x}_1 - \bar{x}_2}}{\sigma_{\bar{x}_1 - \bar{x}_2}} = \frac{(\bar{x}_1 - \bar{x}_2) - \overbrace{(\mu_1 - \mu_2)}^{\substack{\text{Hypothesized} \\ \text{Difference} \\ \text{in Means}}}}{\sqrt{\dfrac{\sigma_1^2}{n_1} + \dfrac{\sigma_2^2}{n_2}}},$$

where σ_1^2 and σ_2^2 can be approximated by s_1^2 and s_2^2 when $n_1 \geq 30$ and $n_2 \geq 30$.

If the null hypothesis is true, z has an approximately normal distribution. If the observed value of $\bar{x}_1 - \bar{x}_2$ is significantly larger or smaller than $\mu_1 - \mu_2$, the hypothesized value of the difference, this will produce a large or small value of the test statistic causing us to doubt whether or not the null hypothesis is in fact true. How large is "large"? This is answered by the critical value of the test statistic specified in Step 7.

Step 7: Determine the critical value.

The role of the critical value(s) in this test is exactly the same as for all of the hypothesis tests discussed earlier. It defines a range of values for the test statistic, the rejection region, that will be so rare that it is unlikely that the test statistic occurred from ordinary sampling variability assuming the null is true. The level of the test defines the size of the rejection region. Should the computed value of the test statistic fall within the rejection region, the null hypothesis will be rejected.

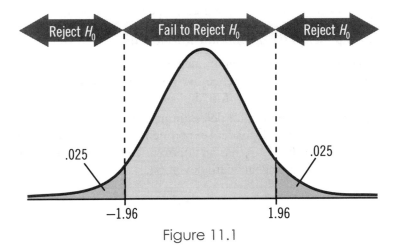

Figure 11.1

If the null hypothesis is true, the test statistic has an approximately normal distribution. Thus the critical value is determined in the same way as for the other tests of hypothesis in which the test statistic had an approximately normal distribution. The rejection region for a two-tailed test with level of significance, $\alpha = .05$, is displayed in Figure 11.1.

The null hypothesis will be rejected if the computed value of the test statistic is larger than 1.96 or smaller than −1.96. In other words, we will reject the null hypothesis if the observed difference in the average QOS scores is at least 1.96 standard deviations above or below the hypothesized value of 0 (no difference in QOS between cable and satellite).

Step 8: Compute the test statistic.

Based on the data in Table 11.1, the computed value of the test statistic is given by

$$z = \frac{(8.8 - 9.5) - 0}{\sqrt{\dfrac{3^2}{50} + \dfrac{2^2}{50}}} \approx -1.37.$$

Step 9: Make the decision.

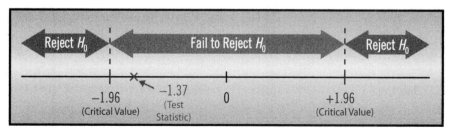

Figure 11.2

As shown in Figure 11.2, the calculated value of the test statistic does not fall in the rejection region because −1.37 falls between the critical values −1.96 and 1.96. There is insufficient evidence to conclude that the difference between the observed value and the hypothesized value is due to anything other than ordinary sampling variation. Thus we fail to reject the null hypothesis at $\alpha = .05$.

Step 10: State the conclusion in terms of the original question.

There is not sufficient evidence at the .05 level to conclude that the average QOS is significantly different between cable and satellite television subscribers.

Hypothesis Testing is Not Loved by All Statisticians

The view is expressed in an article by Marks R. Nester entitled "An Applied Statistician's Creed," *Applied Statistics*, 45: 401-410.

"I contend that the general acceptance of statistical hypothesis testing is one of the most unfortunate aspects of 20th century applied science. Tests for the identity of population distributions, for equality of treatment means, for presence of interactions, for the nullity of a correlation coefficient, and so on, have been responsible for much bad science, much lazy science, and much silly science. A good scientist can manage with, and will not be misled by, parameter estimates and their associated standard errors or confidence limits. A theory dealing with the statistical behavior of populations should be supported by rational argument as well as data. In such cases, accurate statistical evaluation of the data is hindered by null hypothesis testing. The scientist must always give due thought to the statistical analysis, but must never let statistical analysis be a substitute for thinking!"

11

 **Exercises**

Basic Concepts

1. What questions are we interested in answering when comparing two population means?

2. What is an independent experimental design?

3. Which sampling distribution do we use in the formulation of the test statistic when comparing two population means with large samples? What are the properties of this distribution?

4. Does the determination of the critical value(s) for two-sample hypothesis tests differ from one-sample hypothesis tests?

5. What conditions are necessary to perform a large sample test for the difference between two population means?

Exercises

1. Determine the critical value(s) of the test statistic for each of the following large sample tests for the comparison of two population means.

   a. Left-tailed test, $\alpha = .05$

   b. Right-tailed test, $\alpha = .10$

   c. Two-tailed test, $\alpha = .01$

2. Determine the critical value(s) of the test statistic for each of the following large sample tests for the comparison of two population means.

   a. Left-tailed test, $\alpha = .04$

   b. Right-tailed test, $\alpha = .08$

   c. Two-tailed test, $\alpha = .02$

3. A luxury car dealer is considering two possible locations for a new auto mall. The rent on the south side of town is cheaper. However, the dealer believes that the average household income is significantly higher on the north side of town. The dealer has decided that he will locate the new auto mall on the north side of town if the results of a study which he commissioned show that the average household income is significantly higher on the north side of town. The results of the study are as follows.

Table for Exercise 3 – Income (Thousands of Dollars)			
	n	Average Income $\bar{x}$	s
North Side	35	50	10
South Side	40	43	5

a. Calculate a 90% confidence interval for the difference in average income between the north and south sides of town. Interpret the interval.

b. Based on the study, will the auto dealer decide to locate the new auto mall on the north side of town? Use $\alpha = .05$.

4. An internal auditor for Tiger Enterprises has been asked to determine if there is a difference in the average amount charged for daily expenses by two top salesmen, Mr. Ellis and Mr. Ford. The auditor randomly selects 45 days and determines the daily expenses for each of the salesmen.

Table for Exercise 4 – Expenses			
	n	Average Expenses $\bar{x}$	s
Mr. Ellis	45	$55	$8
Mr. Ford	45	$60	$3

a. Calculate a 95% confidence interval for the difference in average expenses between Mr. Ellis and Mr. Ford. Interpret the interval.

b. Based on the survey, can the auditor conclude that there is a difference in the average amount charged for daily expenses by two top salesmen? Use $\alpha = .05$.

c. Explain how the 95% confidence interval in part (a) would lead you to make the same decision that was made in part (b).

5. The military has two different programs for training aircraft personnel. A government regulatory agency has been commissioned to evaluate any differences which may exist between the two programs. The agency administers standardized tests to randomly selected groups of students from the two programs. The results of the tests for the students in each of the programs are as follows.

Table for Exercise 5 – Military Training Programs			
	n	Average Score $\bar{x}$	s
Program A	50	85	10
Program B	55	87	9

a. Calculate a 99% confidence interval for the difference between the average score of the two military programs. Interpret the interval.

b. Can the agency conclude that there is a difference in the average test scores of students in the two programs? Use $\alpha = .01$.

6. Tom Sealack, a supply clerk with the Navy, has been asked to determine if a new battery which has been offered to the Navy (at a reduced price) has a shorter average life than the battery which they are currently using. He randomly selects batteries of each type and allows them to run continuously so that he can measure the time until failure for each battery. The results of the test are as follows.

Table for Exercise 6 – Battery Life (Hours)			
	n	Average $\bar{x}$	s
New Battery	35	700	30
Old Battery	35	710	35

   a. Do the data suggest at $\alpha = .10$ that the time until failure for the new battery is significantly less than the time until failure for the old battery?

   b. Calculate the P-value for the test in (a).

   c. Based on the P-value, would the decision change at $\alpha = .05$?

7. The City Bank believes that checking account balances are significantly larger for customers who are aged 40 to 49 than those who are aged 30 to 39. To investigate this belief, they randomly select customers from each age group and determine the average daily account balance for each customer for the current month. The results of the study are as follows.

Table for Exercise 7 – Checking Account Balances			
Age Group	n	Average $\bar{x}$	s
30 – 39	200	$2500	$550
40 – 49	150	$3500	$950

   a. Do the data suggest at $\alpha = .05$ that the average daily account balances are significantly higher for the 40 to 49 age group than the 30 to 39 age group?

   b. Calculate the P-value for the test in (a).

   c. Based on the P-value, would the decision change at $\alpha = .10$?

Comparing Two Population Means, Small Samples, σ_1 and σ_2 Unknown

Is it still possible to make comparisons between two population means if we do not have "large samples"? There are many situations where it is not practical from either a monetary or time perspective to take such samples.

It is still possible to compare the two population means even if large samples are not available. But in order for the confidence interval or hypothesis test to be valid, there are several assumptions which must be met. These assumptions are outlined below.

Assumptions

Assumptions for Small Sample Inferences about $\mu_1 - \mu_2$

1. An independent experimental design is used.

2. Both populations of interest are approximately normal.

3. Both of the populations have approximately equal (but unknown) variances, $\sigma_1^2 = \sigma_2^2 = \sigma^2$.

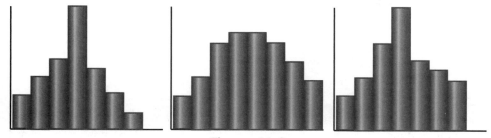

Figure 11.3

In order to determine if both populations of interest are approximately normal, it is helpful to draw histograms of the sample observations from each population. If these histograms appear to be approximately normal, then it is reasonable to infer this assumption is satisfied. With limited data, it is sometimes difficult to determine if the sample data are from a normal population. In these situations, you may have to assume normality and recognize that your inferences are predicated on the validity of the assumption. Figure 11.3 shows three histograms of sample data drawn from normal populations.

11

To examine the equal variance assumption, we can compare the variances of the samples drawn from the populations. In addition to comparing the sample variances we can draw box plots of the data from each of the distributions and compare the spread of the box plots. If the box plots look approximately the same, it is reasonable to assume that the variances of the two distributions are approximately equal. Figure 11.4 displays two box plots of sample data from populations with approximately equal variances, but with slightly different means.

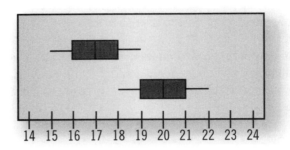

14 15 16 17 18 19 20 21 22 23 24

Figure 11.4

Small Sample Interval Estimation of $\mu_1 - \mu_2$ (σ_1 and σ_2 Unknown)

We can use an interval estimate to determine the difference in two independent population means. In Section 11.1 we used the following interval estimate for the case when samples were drawn from normal populations and σ_1 and σ_2 were known or when the sample sizes n_1 and n_2 were greater than or equal to 30.

$$\left(\bar{x}_1 - \bar{x}_2\right) \pm z_{\alpha/2} \sqrt{\frac{\sigma_1^2}{n_1} + \frac{\sigma_2^2}{n_2}}$$

Assuming that the standard deviations, σ_1 and σ_2 are unknown, we will use the sample standard deviations, s_1 and s_2 to estimate the population standard deviations. However, since we are assuming that the variances are equal, we can estimate the standard error by

$$\sqrt{s_p^2 \left(\frac{1}{n_1} + \frac{1}{n_2}\right)}$$

where $s_p^2 = \dfrac{(n_1 - 1)s_1^2 + (n_2 - 1)s_2^2}{n_1 + n_2 - 2}$, and is called the **pooled variance**. In addition, we will assume that the data follows a normal distribution and thus, replace $z_{\alpha/2}$ with $t_{\alpha/2, df}$ since the samples are not sufficiently large.

Formula

Assuming equal variances, the $100\,(1-\alpha)\,\%$ interval estimate for the difference between two population means if sample sizes are small and σ_1 and σ_2 are unknown is given by

$$\left(\bar{x}_1 - \bar{x}_2\right) \pm t_{\alpha/2,df} \sqrt{s_p^2\left(\frac{1}{n_1} + \frac{1}{n_2}\right)}$$

where $s_p^2 = \dfrac{\left(n_1 - 1\right)s_1^2 + \left(n_2 - 1\right)s_2^2}{n_1 + n_2 - 2}$, the pooled variance, and $t_{\alpha/2,df}$ is the critical value of the t-distribution with $n_1 + n_2 - 2$ degrees of freedom capturing an area of $\alpha/2$ in the upper tail.

Small Sample Hypothesis Test for $\mu_1 - \mu_2$ (σ_1 and σ_2 Unknown)

Providing the assumptions previously outlined for small sample inferences have been met, the test procedure developed in Example 11.2 may be used for making comparisons between two population means.

Example 11.2

For a consumer product, the mean dollar sales per retail outlet last year in a sample of 15 stores were $3425 with a standard deviation of $200. For a second product, the mean dollar sales per outlet in a sample of 16 stores were $3250 with a standard deviation of $175. The sales amounts per outlet are assumed to be approximately normally distributed for both products.

Table 11.2 – Retail Sales for Each Product

	n	$\bar{x}$	s
Product 1	15	$3425	200
Product 2	16	$3250	175

a. Calculate a 95% confidence interval for the difference in average dollar sales between the two products.

b. Test to see if the Product 1 has a higher mean dollar sales record than Product 2. Use $\alpha = .01$.

Solution

a. From the information given in the problem, we know that

$$n_1 = 15,\ n_2 = 16,\ s_1 = 200,\ s_2 = 175,\ \bar{x}_1 = \$3425,\ \text{and}\ \bar{x}_2 = \$3250.$$

With σ_1 and σ_2 unknown and small samples (both n_1 and n_2 are less than 30), we assume that the data follows a normal distribution and that the population variances are equal, and estimate the population standard deviation with the sample standard deviations. Since we want a 95% confidence interval, we need to find the value of $t_{\alpha/2,df}$. Note that $df = n_1 + n_2 - 2 = 16 + 15 - 2 = 29$. Thus, $t_{.025,29} = 2.045$.

A 95% confidence interval for the difference in average dollar sales between the two products is given by

$$\left(\bar{x}_1 - \bar{x}_2\right) \pm t_{\alpha/2,df} \sqrt{s_p^2\left(\frac{1}{n_1} + \frac{1}{n_2}\right)} \quad \text{where } s_p^2 = \frac{\left(n_1 - 1\right)s_1^2 + \left(n_2 - 1\right)s_2^2}{n_1 + n_2 - 2}.$$

First we need to calculate s_p^2.

$$s_p^2 = \frac{\left(15 - 1\right)200^2 + \left(16 - 1\right)175^2}{15 + 16 - 2} \approx 35{,}150.86$$

The confidence interval is then

$$\left(3425 - 3250\right) \pm 2.045 \sqrt{35150.86\left(\frac{1}{15} + \frac{1}{16}\right)}$$

$$175 \pm 137.80$$

$$37.20 \text{ to } 312.80.$$

Thus, we are 95% confident that the true mean difference in dollar sales between Product 1 and Product 2 is between $37.20 and $312.80. That is, on average, Product 1 generates between $37.20 and $312.80 more dollar sales than Product 2.

b. *Step 1: Define the hypotheses in plain English.*

- There is no difference in average retail sales between Product 1 and Product 2.

- The average retail sales for Product 1 are greater than the average retail sales for Product 2.

Step 2: Select the appropriate statistical measure.

Since the analyst is interested in comparing the average retail sales between the two products, the appropriate statistical measures are:

μ_1 = the true average retail sales of Product 1

μ_2 = the true average retail sales of Product 2.

Step 3: Determine whether the hypotheses should be one-sided or two-sided.

The retailer is interested in whether the average sales of Product 1 are higher than the average sales of Product 2. Thus, the hypotheses are one-sided and the test is one-tailed.

Step 4: State the hypotheses using the appropriate statistical measure.

The retailer is interested in determining if the average sales for Product 1 are higher than that of Product 2. One way to state this in terms of the statistical measures in Step 2 is $\mu_1 > \mu_2$. But in order to perform the hypothesis test, this statement must be rewritten in a form for which we have a point estimate, or $\mu_1 - \mu_2 > 0$. The resulting hypotheses are:

$H_0 : \mu_1 - \mu_2 \leq 0$ (There is no difference in average sales.)

$H_a : \mu_1 - \mu_2 > 0$ $\left(\begin{array}{l}\text{Average sales of Product 1 are higher than} \\ \text{average sales of Product 2.}\end{array}\right)$

Step 5: Specify the level of the test.

The level of the test is specified in the problem as $\alpha = .01$.

Step 6: Select the appropriate test statistic.

To develop the appropriate test statistic, a random variable whose value will be used to make the decision to reject or fail to reject H_0 must be found. The sampling distribution $\bar{x}_1 - \bar{x}_2$ provides essential information in assessing the rareness of the test statistic. If $n_1 < 30$ or $n_2 < 30$ and the assumptions previously outlined are satisfied, the sampling distribution of $\bar{x}_1 - \bar{x}_2$ has a t-distribution. The t-test statistic is given by

$$t = \frac{(\bar{x}_1 - \bar{x}_2) - (\mu_1 - \mu_2)}{\sqrt{s_p^2\left(\dfrac{1}{n_1} + \dfrac{1}{n_2}\right)}},$$

where $s_p^2 = \dfrac{(n_1 - 1)s_1^2 + (n_2 - 1)s_2^2}{n_1 + n_2 - 2}$, and is called the pooled variance.

In this hypothesis test, the population variances are assumed to be equal. Thus s_p^2, which is the weighted average of the two sample variances, is used to approximate the unknown population variance.

Note

$\mu_1 - \mu_2$ in the t-test statistic is the hypothesized difference in means. In most problems this difference is hypothesized to be 0.

If the null hypothesis is true, t has a t-distribution with $n_1 + n_2 - 2$ degrees of freedom. If the observed value of $\bar{x}_1 - \bar{x}_2$ is significantly larger than the hypothesized value of the difference $(H_0 : \mu_1 - \mu_2 \leq 0)$, this will produce a large value of the test statistic, causing us to doubt whether the null hypothesis is in fact true. How large is "large"? The critical value of the test statistic specified in Step 7 will implicitly define the notion of "large".

Step 7: Determine the critical value.

The role of the critical value in this test is exactly the same as for all of the hypothesis tests discussed earlier. It defines a range of values for the test statistic, the rejection region, that will be so rare that it is unlikely that it occurred from ordinary sampling variability if the null hypothesis is true. The level of the test defines the size of the rejection region. Should the computed value of the test statistic fall in the rejection region, we will presume that the value of the test statistic is too large to have occurred from ordinary sampling variation, and the null hypothesis will be rejected.

If the null hypothesis is true, the test statistic has a t-distribution. Thus, the critical value is determined in the same way as for the other tests of hypothesis where the test statistic had a t-distribution, except that the degrees of freedom are $n_1 + n_2 - 2$, or $(15 + 16 - 2) = 29$. The rejection region corresponding to the alternative hypothesis, $H_a : \mu_1 - \mu_2 > 0$, with $\alpha = .01$ for a t-test statistic with 29 degrees of freedom is given in Figure 11.5.

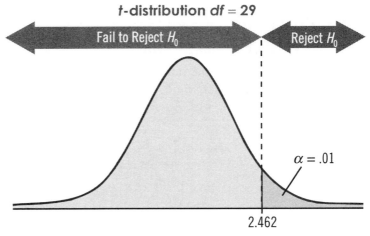

t-distribution df = 29

Figure 11.5

We will reject the null hypothesis if the computed value of the test statistic is larger than 2.462.

Step 8: Compute the test statistic.

Based on the data in Table 11.2, the computed value of the test statistic is given by

$$t = \frac{(3425 - 3250) - 0}{\sqrt{(35,150.86)\left(\dfrac{1}{15} + \dfrac{1}{16}\right)}} \approx 2.597$$

where $s_p^2 = \dfrac{(14)(200)^2 + (15)(175)^2}{15 + 16 - 2} \approx 35,150.86.$

Step 9: Make the decision.

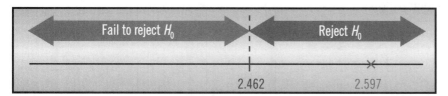

Figure 11.6

As displayed in Figure 11.6, the value of the test statistic does fall in the rejection region. In fact, a test statistic of 2.597 says that the observed difference between the means is about 2.6 standard deviations higher than the hypothesized difference of zero. It is highly unlikely that the difference between the observed value and the hypothesized value is due to ordinary sampling variation. Thus, we reject the null hypothesis at $\alpha = .01$.

Step 10: State the conclusion in terms of the original question.

There is sufficient evidence at the .01 level to conclude that the average sales for Product 1 are significantly higher than the average sales of Product 2.

t-Test for $\mu_1 - \mu_2$ Assuming Unequal Variances

Recall that one of the assumptions when performing the two-sample *t*-test is that the population variances are unknown but equal $\left(\text{that is, } \sigma_1^2 = \sigma_2^2 = \sigma^2\right)$. If you cannot make the assumption that the variances are equal, then it is not appropriate to pool the two sample variances into one common variance, s_p^2. Instead, you must use a separate variance test developed by Satterthwaite (Satterthwaite, F.E., "An Approximate Distribution for Estimates of Variance Components," *Biometrics Bulletin*, 2 (1946): 110-114.). Satterthwaite's test procedure uses a series of computations that involve using the two separate sample variances to calculate the degrees of freedom for the test statistic. The computations for the $100(1 - \alpha)\%$ confidence interval and test statistic are as follows:

Formula

Confidence Interval:

$$\left(\bar{x}_1 - \bar{x}_2\right) \pm t_{\alpha/2, df} \sqrt{\frac{s_1^2}{n_1} + \frac{s_2^2}{n_2}}$$

Test Statistic:

$$t = \frac{\left(\bar{x}_1 - \bar{x}_2\right) - \left(\mu_1 - \mu_2\right)}{\sqrt{\frac{s_1^2}{n_1} + \frac{s_2^2}{n_2}}},$$

which follows a *t*-distribution with degrees of freedom equal to:

$$df = \frac{\left(\frac{s_1^2}{n_1} + \frac{s_2^2}{n_2}\right)^2}{\frac{1}{n_1 - 1}\left(\frac{s_1^2}{n_1}\right)^2 + \frac{1}{n_2 - 1}\left(\frac{s_2^2}{n_2}\right)^2}.$$

Remember, these formulas should only be used if σ_1 and σ_2 are unknown, the sample sizes n_1 and n_2 are less than 30 and drawn from normal populations, and the population variances are assumed to be unequal.

11.2 Exercises

Basic Concepts

1. Why might large samples not be available when attempting to make inferences about two population means?

2. What assumptions are necessary to perform a small sample test for the difference between two population means?

3. What constitutes a "small sample"?

4. What is the test statistic for a small sample hypothesis test about two population means? How does this statistic differ from the test statistic used for large samples?

5. What is a pooled variance? Why is it used?

Exercises

1. Determine the critical value(s) of the test statistic for each of the following small sample tests for the comparison of two population means where the assumptions of normality and equal variance have been satisfied.

    a. Left-tailed test, $\alpha = .05$, $n_1 = 10$, $n_2 = 15$

    b. Right-tailed test, $\alpha = .10$, $n_1 = 8$, $n_2 = 12$

    c. Two-tailed test, $\alpha = .01$, $n_1 = 5$, $n_2 = 7$

2. Determine the critical value(s) of the test statistic for each of the following small sample tests for the comparison of two population means where the assumptions of normality and equal variance have been satisfied.

    a. Left-tailed test, $\alpha = .025$, $n_1 = 13$, $n_2 = 25$

    b. Right-tailed test, $\alpha = .005$, $n_1 = 7$, $n_2 = 18$

    c. Two-tailed test, $\alpha = .10$, $n_1 = 15$, $n_2 = 15$

3. *Popular Science* (Vol. 242, No. 3) reported the results of a comparison of several popular minivans. One of the features which they compared was the time required to accelerate from 0 to 60 miles per hour in seconds. The Dodge Grand Caravan ES was able to accelerate from 0 to 60 mph in 11.3 seconds on average. The Volkswagen Eurovan took 16.5 seconds on average to accelerate from 0 to 60 mph. Suppose that 15 minivans of each type were tested and that the sample standard deviation of the times required to accelerate from 0 to 60 for each minivan was 4 seconds.

    a. Calculate a 95% confidence interval for the difference in average acceleration time between the two types of minivans. Interpret the interval.

    b. Do the data suggest that there is a significant difference in the time required to accelerate from 0 to 60 between the two types of minivans at $\alpha = .05$?

    c. What assumptions did you make about the time required to accelerate from 0 to 60 mph in calculating the confidence interval in part (a) and for performing the test in part (b)?

4. A cereal manufacturer has advertised that its product, Fiber Oat Flakes, has a lower fat content than its competitor, Bran Flakes Plus. Because of complaints from the manufacturers of Bran Flakes Plus, the FDA has decided to test the claim that Fiber Oat Flakes has a lower average fat content than Bran Flakes Plus. Several boxes of each cereal are selected and the fat content per serving is measured. The results of the study are as follows.

Table for Exercise 4 – Fat Content (Grams)			
	n	Average Fat Content x̄	s
Fiber Oat Flakes	16	5	1
Bran Flakes Plus	15	6	2

a. Calculate a 90% confidence interval for the difference in average fat content between Fiber Oat Flakes and Bran Flakes Plus. Interpret the interval.

b. Does the study performed by the FDA substantiate the claim made by the manufacturer of Fiber Oat Flakes at $\alpha = .10$?

c. What assumptions must be made in order to calculate the confidence interval in part (a) and perform the hypothesis test in part (b)?

5. A large construction company would like to expand its operations into a new geographic area. The company has narrowed the choice of locations down to two cities. A major consideration in deciding between the two cities will be the average hourly wage which they must pay for general laborers. The company randomly selects laborers from each city and determines their hourly wage with the following results.

Table for Exercise 5 – Wages			
	n	Average Hourly Wage x̄	s
City A	20	$7	$3
City B	20	$8	$2

a. Calculate a 99% confidence interval for the difference in average hourly wage between City A and City B. Interpret the interval.

b. Do the data indicate that there is a significant difference in hourly wages at $\alpha = .05$?

c. Calculate the P-value for the test performed in part (b).

d. What assumptions must be made in order to calculate the confidence interval in part (a) and perform the hypothesis test in part (b)?

6. A Hollywood studio believes that a movie which is considered a drama will draw a larger crowd on average than a movie which is a comedy. To test this theory, the studio randomly selects several movies which are classified as dramas and several movies which are classified as comedies and determines the box office revenue for each movie. The results of the survey are as follows.

Table for Exercise 6 – Box Office Revenues (Millions of Dollars)			
	n	Average Revenue $\bar{x}$	s
Drama	15	$180	$50
Comedy	13	$150	$30

a. Calculate a 95% confidence interval for the difference in average revenue at the box office between drama and comedy movies. Interpret the interval.

b. Do the data substantiate the studio's belief that dramas will draw a larger crowd on average than comedies at $\alpha = .01$?

c. Calculate the P-value for the test you conducted in part (b).

d. What assumptions must be made in order to calculate the confidence interval in part (a) and to perform the hypothesis test in part (b)?

7. *Consumer Magazine* is reviewing the top of the line amplifiers produced by two major stereo manufacturers. One of the most important qualities of the amplifiers is the maximum power output. Brand A has redone their internal design and claims to have a higher maximum power level than Brand B. To test this claim, *Consumer Magazine* randomly selects amplifiers from each brand and determines the maximum power output. The results of the test are as follows.

Table for Exercise 7 – Amplifier Power Output (Watts)			
	n	Average Max Power Output $\bar{x}$	s
Brand A	12	800	25
Brand B	10	780	25

a. What assumptions must be made in order to perform the hypothesis test?

b. Do the data substantiate the claim that the Brand A amplifier has a higher average maximum power output than Brand B at $\alpha = .05$?

8. The State Environmental Board wants to compare pollution levels in two of its major cities. Sunshine City thrives on the tourist industry and Service City thrives on the service industry. The Environmental Board randomly selects several areas within the cities and measures the pollution levels in parts per million with the following results:

Table for Exercise 8 – Pollution Levels (ppm)			
	n	Average Pollution Level $\bar{x}$	s
Sunshine City	15	8.5	0.57
Service City	10	7.9	0.50

a. What assumptions must be made in order to perform the hypothesis test?

b. Will the State Environmental Board conclude at $\alpha = .01$ that Service City has a lower pollution level on average than Sunshine City?

c. Repeat part (b), assuming that the population variances are not equal.

d. Compare the results of part (b) and part (c).

9. In 2009 U.S. charitable giving fell 3.6 percent to $303.75 billion for the year. Total charitable contributions from American individuals, corporations, and foundations fell to $303.75 billion from $315.08 billion for 2008. The largest share of contributions went to religious organizations, representing 33 percent of total giving. The next largest shares went to educational organizations, receiving an estimated 13 percent of the total, and foundations, which received 10 percent of the total. (**Source**: Giving USA Foundation, the Center on Philanthropy at Indiana University.) Suppose a sample of 6 employees is randomly chosen from a large corporation and their charitable contributions in 2008 and 2009 are determined. The following table gives these amounts (in dollars).

Table for Exercise 9 – Charitable Contributions ($)	
Giving in 2008	**Giving in 2009**
232	215
150	125
50	50
400	350
325	210
175	150

a. Can we conclude with $\alpha = .01$ that the average contribution to charity has decreased in this corporation from 2008 to 2009?

b. Give the assumptions for your test.

c. Repeat part (a), assuming that the population variances are not equal.

d. Compare the results of part (a) and part (c).

11.3 Paired Difference

Suppose we are interested in comparing the durability of the soles of two brands of tennis shoes, Spikes and Kickers. One approach to making this comparison is the independent experimental design discussed in Section 11.1. Using this design one may randomly select 10 people to wear the Spikes brand of shoes for six months and then randomly select 10 other people to wear the Kickers brand of shoes for six months. After the six month period, the average wear for the 10 pairs of Spikes shoes is measured and compared to the average wear for the 10 pairs of Kickers tennis shoes.

While this is a perfectly reasonable approach, it does have shortcomings. For example, what if one of the people selected to wear the Spikes brand of shoes is a cross-country runner? Certainly the wear on the runner's pair of shoes will be much greater than the wear on the shoes for someone who just wears the shoes in the evenings after work. Certainly many factors could have a large effect on the observed wear of the tennis shoes.

What can we do to help reduce the effect of factors that cloud the issue of tennis shoe durability? One approach is to have each person wear a Spikes brand of shoe on one foot and a Kickers brand of shoe on the other foot, where the feet are randomly selected. After six months, the wear on the Spikes shoe would be compared to the wear on the Kickers shoe for each person. By designing the experiment in this fashion, the external effects of weight, amount of use, and so forth have been significantly reduced when comparing the two brands of tennis shoes. This type of design is an example of a **paired difference experimental design**.

In a paired design, experimental units are paired such that units within a pair are much more alike than in the population as a whole. If we have been successful at significantly reducing the variation among the sample observations by pairing, we will create very potent data to make decisions.

The paired difference design is frequently used in experiments where we are interested in the average response of an experimental unit before and after some treatment. For example a physician might be interested in comparing a patient's heart rate before and after treatment with some drug. A state legislator may be interested in comparing a person's reaction time before and after drinking one ounce of 100-proof alcohol. An instructor may be interested in comparing a student's math skills before and after being taught a particular course. A company may be interested in a customer's response to a product before and after a particular marketing campaign.

Generally, the sample size for a paired difference experimental design is small, and we must make several assumptions for the test to be valid.

Assumptions

Assumptions for the Paired Difference Experimental Design

1. Experimental units can be paired such that they are more alike within the pair than within the population as a whole.

2. The differences have an approximately normal distribution.

To test the mean difference between two related population means, we treat the difference scores, denoted by d_i, as values from a single sample. The general data setup is shown in Table 11.3.

Table 11.3 – General Setup for the Difference between Paired Samples			
	Sample		
Observation	1	2	Difference
1	x_{11}	x_{21}	$d_1 = x_{11} - x_{21}$
2	x_{12}	x_{22}	$d_2 = x_{12} - x_{22}$
3	x_{13}	x_{23}	$d_3 = x_{13} - x_{23}$
$\vdots$	$\vdots$	$\vdots$	$\vdots$
$\vdots$	$\vdots$	$\vdots$	$\vdots$
i	x_{1i}	x_{2i}	$d_i = x_{1i} - x_{2i}$
$\vdots$	$\vdots$	$\vdots$	$\vdots$
$\vdots$	$\vdots$	$\vdots$	$\vdots$
n	x_{1n}	x_{2n}	$d_n = x_{1n} - x_{2n}$

Note that d_i is the difference between the ith observations in each sample.

We can use an interval estimate to determine the difference in two related population means. Given the differences, we can use the sample standard deviation of the difference to estimate the population standard deviation of the difference. We can construct a $100(1-\alpha)\%$ confidence interval for the mean difference using the following formula.

Formula

100 (1–α) %
Confidence Interval
for Paired Differences

A $100(1-\alpha)\%$ confidence interval for the mean difference is given by

$$\bar{x}_d \pm t_{\alpha/2,df} \frac{s_d}{\sqrt{n_d}}$$

where $\bar{x}_d$ is the sample mean of the differences, n_d is the number of

differences, $\bar{x}_d = \dfrac{\displaystyle\sum_{i=1}^{n} d_i}{n_d}$, $s_d = \sqrt{\dfrac{\displaystyle\sum_{i=1}^{n} (d_i - \bar{x}_d)^2}{n_d - 1}}$, and $t_{\alpha/2,df}$ is the critical value

of the t-distribution with an area of $\alpha/2$ in the upper tail with $n_d - 1$ degrees of freedom (df).

The methodology for the paired difference test of hypothesis and the calculation of the confidence interval for the paired difference will be presented in Example 11.3.

Example 11.3

Bull & Bones Brewhaus is a microbrewery that has two restaurants located within 15 miles of each other. The owner of the microbrewery wants to compare average daily food sales of the two restaurants. To do so, the owner randomly selects 10 days over a five-month period (college football season) and records the daily food sales. The results are recorded in Table 11.4.

a. Calculate a 95% confidence interval for the mean difference in restaurant sales.

b. The owner wants to know if there is evidence of a difference between the average daily food sales of the two restaurants. Test using $\alpha = .01$.

	Table 11.4 – Daily Food Sales for Two Restaurants		
Day	Restaurant 1	Restaurant 2	Difference = Restaurant 1 – Restaurant 2
1	$5828	$7894	−$2066
2	$9836	$11,573	−$1737
3	$3984	$5319	−$1335
4	$5845	$6389	−$544
5	$5210	$6055	−$845
6	$9668	$10,631	−$963
7	$6768	$7866	−$1098
8	$6726	$7976	−$1250
9	$4399	$5652	−$1253
10	$6692	$8083	−$1391

Solution

a. From the information given, we know that $n = 10$ and $\alpha = .05$. We now need to calculate the mean and standard deviation of the differences, $\bar{x}_d$ and s_d, respectively.

$$\bar{x}_d = \frac{\sum_{i=1}^{n} d_i}{n_d} = \frac{(-2066)+(-1737)+\cdots+(-1253)+(-1391)}{10} = -1248.20$$

$$s_d = \sqrt{\frac{\sum_{i=1}^{n}(d_i - \bar{x}_d)^2}{n_d - 1}}$$

$$= \sqrt{\frac{\begin{array}{l}(-2066-(-1248.2))^2 +(-1737-(-1248.2))^2 + \cdots \\ +(-1253-(-1248.2))^2 +(-1391-(-1248.2))^2\end{array}}{10-1}}$$

$$\approx 434.36$$

Since we want a 95% confidence interval, we need to find the value of $t_{\alpha/2,df}$. Note that $df = n_d - 1 = 9$. Thus, $t_{\alpha/2,df} = t_{.025,9} = 2.262$.

A 95% confidence interval for the average difference in sales record between the two restaurants is given by

$$\bar{x}_d \pm t_{\alpha/2,df}\frac{s_d}{\sqrt{n_d}}$$

$$-1248.20 \pm 2.262\left(\frac{434.36}{\sqrt{10}}\right)$$

$$-1248.20 \pm 310.70$$

$$-1558.90 \text{ to } -937.50.$$

We are 95% confident that the true mean difference in sales between Restaurant 1 and Restaurant 2 is between −$1558.90 and −$937.50. That is, on average, Restaurant 2 averages between $937.50 and $1558.90 more in sales.

b. Before performing the hypothesis test, we need to ensure that the assumption that the differences have a normal distribution is reasonable for the sales data. A histogram of differences is provided in Figure 11.7. Based on this histogram, it appears that the differences are approximately normal and it is safe to proceed with the paired difference test.

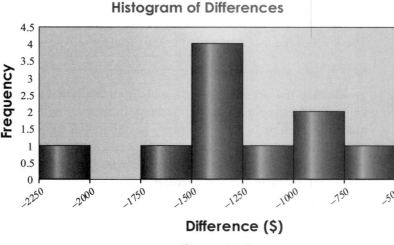

Histogram of Differences

Figure 11.7

Step 1: Define the hypotheses in plain English.

- There is no difference in the average sales between the two restaurants on a given day.

- There is a difference in the average sales between the two restaurants on a given day.

Step 2: Select the appropriate statistical measure.

In a paired difference experimental design, the population parameter of interest is the population mean of the differences. Thus, the appropriate statistical measure is given by

μ_d = the average of the differences in daily sales between the two restaurants.

Step 3: Determine whether the hypotheses should be one-sided or two-sided.

Since the owner is interested in whether or not the average daily sales are different between the two restaurants, the hypotheses will be two-sided and this will be a two-tailed test.

Step 4: State the hypotheses using the appropriate statistical measure.

The statistical measure being used is the average difference in daily sales between the two restaurants. Since we have a two-tailed test, the hypotheses will be as follows:

$H_0 : \mu_d = 0$ $\left(\begin{array}{l}\text{There is no difference in average daily sales between}\\ \text{the two restaurants.}\end{array}\right)$

$H_a : \mu_d \neq 0$ $\left(\begin{array}{l}\text{There is a difference in average daily sales between}\\ \text{the two restaurants.}\end{array}\right)$.

Step 5: Specify the level of the test.

The level of the test is specified in the problem to be $\alpha = .01$.

Step 6: Select the appropriate test statistic.

To develop the appropriate test statistic, a random variable whose value will be used to make the decision to reject or fail to reject H_0 must be developed. It is interesting to notice that by evaluating the differences of the paired data, we have effectively reduced the two-sample problem into a small, one-sample t-test for a population mean. The point estimate for the population mean of the differences, μ_d is $\bar{x}_d$, the sample average of the differences. Hence, the sampling distribution for $\bar{x}_d$ provides essential information for testing the hypothesis. If the differences are normally distributed and the null hypothesis is assumed to be true, the sampling distribution of $\bar{x}_d$ has a t-distribution with $n_d - 1$ degrees of freedom. Note that n_d represents the number of differences. The t-test statistic is given by

$$t = \frac{\bar{x}_d - \mu_d}{s_d \big/ \sqrt{n_d}},$$

where s_d is the sample standard deviation of the differences.

If the observed value of $\bar{x}_d$ is significantly smaller or larger than μ_d, this will produce a large negative (or positive) value of the test statistic, causing us to question whether the null hypothesis is in fact true. How large is "large"? This is answered by the critical value of the test statistic specified in Step 7.

Step 7: Determine the critical value.

The role of the critical value in this test is exactly the same as for all of the hypothesis tests discussed earlier. It defines a range of values for the test statistic, the rejection region, that will be so rare that it is unlikely that it occurred from ordinary sampling variability. The level of the test defines the size of the rejection region. Should the computed value of the test statistic fall in the rejection region, its value will be presumed to be too rare to have occurred because of ordinary sampling variation, and the null hypothesis will be rejected.

If the null hypothesis is true, the test statistic has a t-distribution with $n_d - 1$ degrees of freedom. Thus, the critical value is determined in the same way as for the other tests of hypothesis where the test statistic had a t-distribution, except that the degrees of freedom are $n_d - 1 = 10 - 1 = 9$. The rejection region for the alternative hypothesis, $H_a : \mu_d \neq 0$, with $\alpha = .01$ and 9 degrees of freedom is displayed in Figure 11.8. Because we have a two-sided hypothesis, we reject H_0 if the test statistic is less than -3.250 or if it is more than 3.250.

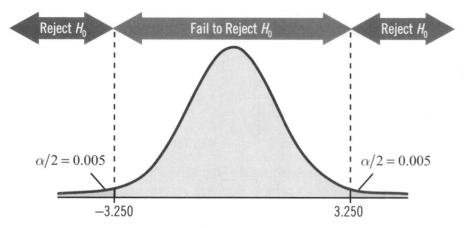

Figure 11.8

Step 8: Compute the test statistic.

Based on the data in Table 11.4, the computed value of the test statistic is given by

$$t = \frac{x_d - \mu_d}{s_d / \sqrt{n}} = \frac{-1248.2 - 0}{434.36 / \sqrt{10}} \approx -9.087.$$

Step 9: Make the decision.

As shown in Figure 11.9, the value of the test statistic falls in the rejection region to the left. The test statistic indicates that the observed average daily sales are more than 9 standard deviations below the hypothesized value of 0. It is highly unlikely that the difference between the observed value and the hypothesized value is due to ordinary sampling variation. Thus, the null hypothesis is rejected at $\alpha = .01$.

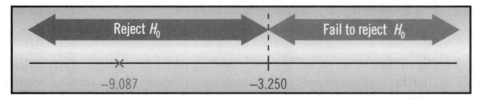

Figure 11.9

Step 10: State the conclusion in terms of the original question.

There is sufficient evidence for the owner to conclude at the $\alpha = .01$ level that the average daily sales between the two restaurants are significantly different.

11.3 Exercises

Basic Concepts

1. Describe the differences between an independent experimental design and a paired design.

2. What are the assumptions for a paired difference experimental design?

3. What is the appropriate statistical measure to use when performing a hypothesis test about a paired difference experiment?

4. How does the hypothesis testing procedure for a paired difference experiment differ from that of a two-sample t-test?

5. What is the test statistic used in a paired difference hypothesis test?

Exercises

1. Determine the critical value(s) of the test statistic for each of the following small sample paired difference tests (assume the differences have an approximately normal distribution).

   a. Left-tailed test, $\alpha = .01$, $n_d = 15$

   b. Right-tailed test, $\alpha = .10$, $n_d = 20$

   c. Two-tailed test, $\alpha = .05$, $n_d = 8$

2. Determine the critical value(s) of the test statistic for each of the following small sample paired difference tests (assume the differences have an approximately normal distribution).

   a. Left-tailed test, $\alpha = .005$, $n_d = 12$

   b. Right-tailed test, $\alpha = .025$, $n_d = 5$

   c. Two-tailed test, $\alpha = .10$, $n_d = 25$

3. Given that most textbooks can now be purchased online, one wonders if students can save money by comparison shopping for textbooks at online retailers and at their local bookstores. To investigate, students at Tech University randomly sampled 25 textbooks on the shelves of their local bookstores. The students then found the "best" available price for the same textbooks via online retailers. The prices for the textbooks are listed in the following table.

Table for Exercise 3 – Textbook Prices		
	Price ($)	
Textbook	Bookstore	Online Retailer
1	70	60
2	38	36
3	88	89
4	165	149
5	80	136
6	103	95
7	42	50
8	98	111
9	89	65
10	97	86
11	140	130
12	40	30
13	175	150
14	85	75
15	100	85
16	68	62
17	67	69
18	140	142
19	49	40
20	149	127
21	126	130
22	92	93
23	144	129
24	98	84
25	40	52

a. Is a paired design appropriate for the above study? Explain.

b. What assumption must be made in order to perform the test of hypothesis?

c. Do the data appear to satisfy the assumption described in part (b)? Why or why not?

d. Based on the data, is it less expensive for the students to purchase textbooks from the online retailers than from local bookstores? Use $\alpha = .01$.

e. Calculate a 99% confidence interval for the average difference in cost between the bookstores and the online retailers. Interpret the interval.

4. The management for a large grocery store chain would like to determine if a new cash register will enable cashiers to process a larger number of items on average than the cash register which they are currently using. Seven cashiers are randomly selected, and the number of grocery items which they can process in three minutes is measured for both the old cash register and the new cash register. The results of the test are as follows.

Table for Exercise 4 – Number of Grocery Items Processed in Three Minutes							
Cashier	1	2	3	4	5	6	7
Old Cash Register	60	70	55	75	62	52	58
New Cash Register	65	71	55	75	65	57	57

a. Is a paired design appropriate for the above experiment? Explain.

b. What assumption must be made in order to perform the test of hypothesis?

c. Does the data appear to satisfy the assumption described in part (b)? Why or why not?

d. Calculate a 95% confidence interval for the average difference between the number of items processed on the old cash register and the new cash register. Interpret this interval.

e. Can the management conclude that the new cash register will allow cashiers to process a significantly larger number of items on average than the old cash register at $\alpha = .05$?

5. An auto dealer is marketing two different models of a high-end sedan. Since customers are particularly interested in the safety features of the sedans, the dealer would like to determine if there is a difference in the braking distance (the number of feet required to go from 60 mph to 0 mph) of the two sedans. Six drivers are randomly selected and asked to participate in a test to measure the braking distance for both models. Each driver is asked to drive both models and brake once they have reached exactly 60 mph. The distance required to come to a complete halt is then measured in feet. The results of the test are as follows.

Table for Exercise 5 – Braking Distance of High-End Sedans (in Feet)						
Driver	1	2	3	4	5	6
Model A	150	145	160	155	152	153
Model B	152	146	160	157	154	155

a. Is a paired design appropriate for the above experiment? Explain.

b. What assumption must be made in order to perform the test of hypothesis?

c. Do the data appear to satisfy the assumption described in part (b)? Why or why not?

d. Calculate a 90% confidence interval for the average difference between braking distances for Model A and Model B. Interpret the interval.

e. Can the auto dealer conclude that there is a significant difference in the braking distance of the two models of high end sedans? Use $\alpha = .10$.

11.4 Comparing Two Population Proportions

Techniques are developed in this section for comparing two population proportions. A methodology for comparing two population proportions is particularly useful because proportions are among the few measures which can be used for summarizing categorical data. For a more extensive treatment of comparisons for categorical data, the reader is referred to Chapter 15.

There are many situations where comparing two population proportions may be of interest. For example, a sociologist may be interested in comparing the proportion of females who believe it is okay to cry in public to the proportion of males who think it is okay to cry in public. A marketing manager may be interested in comparing the proportion of customers who favor Product A to the proportion of customers who favor Product B.

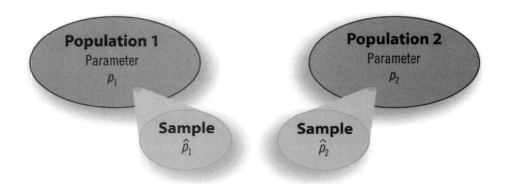

In order to perform a comparison of two population proportions, the assumptions outlined below must be met.

Assumptions

Assumptions for Comparing Two Population Proportions

1. An independent experimental design.
2. The samples are large enough such that $n_1 \hat{p}_1 \geq 5$, $n_1\left(1-\hat{p}_1\right) \geq 5$, $n_2 \hat{p}_2 \geq 5$, and $n_2\left(1-\hat{p}_2\right) \geq 5$ where $\hat{p}_1$ and n_1 are the sample proportion and sample size, respectively, from the first population and $\hat{p}_2$ and n_2 are the sample proportion and sample size, respectively, from the second population.

Interval Estimation Comparing Two Population Proportions, $p_1 - p_2$

Formula

We can construct a 100 $(1-\alpha)$ % confidence interval estimate for the difference between two population proportions using the following:

$$\hat{p}_1 - \hat{p}_2 \pm z_{\alpha/2}\sqrt{\frac{\hat{p}_1\left(1-\hat{p}_1\right)}{n_1} + \frac{\hat{p}_2\left(1-\hat{p}_2\right)}{n_2}}$$

where $\hat{p}_1$ and n_1 are the sample proportion and sample size, respectively, from the first population, $\hat{p}_2$ and n_2 are the sample proportion and sample size, respectively, from the second population, $n_1\hat{p}_1 \geq 5$, $n_1\left(1-\hat{p}_1\right) \geq 5$, $n_2\hat{p}_2 \geq 5$, and $n_2\left(1-\hat{p}_2\right) \geq 5$, and $z_{\alpha/2}$ is the critical value for the z-distribution that captures an area of $\alpha/2$ in the upper tail.

Hypothesis Test Comparing Two Population Proportions, $p_1 - p_2$

The hypothesis test procedure for comparing two population proportions is developed in Example 11.4.

Example 11.4

A telephone executive has recently been bombarded with complaints from his customers about defective phones. He has two plants which produce the telephones, and he is not sure where the defective phones are coming from. In the past, the plants have had good control over the number of defective phones produced. Because of the recent flurry of complaints, he thinks that one of the plants may have lost control over its production process. To test this theory, he randomly selects 200 phones from each of the plants and counts the number of defective phones. The results of the survey are displayed in Table 11.5.

Table 11.5 – Telephone Survey Data		
	Number Sampled	**Number of Defectives**
Plant A	200	8
Plant B	200	10

a. Calculate a 95% confidence interval for the difference between the proportions of defective phones from Plant A and Plant B.

b. Is there sufficient evidence for the telephone executive to conclude that there is a difference in the proportion of defective telephones produced by the two plants at $\alpha = .10$?

Solution

a. Let

$p_1 = $ the proportion of defective phones produced in Plant A

$p_2 = $ the proportion of defective phones produced in Plant B

$X_1 = $ the number of defective phones produced in Plant A

$X_2 = $ the number of defective phones produced in Plant B.

We know that $n_1 = n_2 = 200$, $X_1 = 8$, and $X_2 = 10$. With the information given, we can calculate

$$\hat{p}_1 = \frac{X_1}{n_1} = \frac{8}{200} = .04$$

$$\hat{p}_2 = \frac{X_2}{n_2} = \frac{10}{200} = .05.$$

For a 95% confidence interval, $\alpha = .05$, $z_{\alpha/2} = z_{.025} = 1.96$.

Therefore, the 95% confidence interval is given by

$$\left(\hat{p}_1 - \hat{p}_2\right) \pm z_{\alpha/2} \sqrt{\frac{\hat{p}_1\left(1 - \hat{p}_1\right)}{n_1} + \frac{\hat{p}_2\left(1 - \hat{p}_2\right)}{n_2}}$$

$$(.04 - .05) \pm 1.96 \sqrt{\frac{.04(1 - .04)}{200} + \frac{.05(1 - .05)}{200}}$$

$$-.01 \pm .04$$

$$-.05 \text{ to } .03.$$

Thus, we are 95% confident that the true difference in the proportion of defectives between Plant A and Plant B is between −.05 and .03.

b. *Step 1: Define the hypotheses in plain English.*

- There is no difference in the proportion of defective telephones produced at the two plants.

- There is a difference in the proportion of defective telephones produced at the two plants.

Step 2: Select the appropriate statistical measure.

Since the executive is interested in comparing the proportion of defective phones produced at Plant A to the proportion of defective phones produced at Plant B, the appropriate statistical measures are

p_1 = the true proportion of defective phones produced at Plant A

p_2 = the true proportion of defective phones produced at Plant B.

Step 3: Determine whether the hypotheses should be one-sided or two-sided.

The executive's interest is in whether or not there is a difference in the proportion of defective phones produced by the two plants. Thus, the hypotheses are two-sided and this is a two-tailed test.

Step 4: State the hypotheses using the appropriate statistical measure.

Since the executive is interested in comparing the two population proportions, a natural way to perform this comparison is to look at the difference between the two population proportions. Hence, the null and alternative hypotheses are as follows:

$$H_0 : p_1 - p_2 = 0 \quad \left(\begin{array}{l} \text{There is no difference in the proportion of} \\ \text{defective phones produced at the two plants.} \end{array} \right)$$

$$H_a : p_1 - p_2 \neq 0 \quad \left(\begin{array}{l} \text{There is a difference in the proportion of} \\ \text{defective phones produced at the two plants.} \end{array} \right).$$

In order for the following hypothesis testing procedure to be valid, the hypothesized difference in the null hypothesis between the two population proportions must be 0.

Step 5: Specify the level of the test.

The level of the test is specified in the problem to be $\alpha = .10$.

Step 6: Select the appropriate test statistic.

To develop the appropriate test statistic, a random variable whose value will be used to help make the decision to reject or fail to reject H_0 must be found. The point estimate of $p_1 - p_2$ is $\hat{p}_1 - \hat{p}_2$. The sampling distribution of $\hat{p}_1 - \hat{p}_2$ will be used in determining the critical values of the test statistic. If the assumptions previously outlined are met, and we assume the null hypothesis is true, the sampling distribution of $\hat{p}_1 - \hat{p}_2$ has an approximately normal distribution with mean, 0, and standard deviation,

$$\sigma_{\hat{p}_1 - \hat{p}_2} = \sqrt{\frac{p_c(1 - p_c)}{n_1} + \frac{p_c(1 - p_c)}{n_2}},$$

$$\text{where } p_c = \frac{n_1}{n_1 + n_2}\hat{p}_1 + \frac{n_2}{n_1 + n_2}\hat{p}_2.$$

Note that p_c is the weighted average of the two sample proportion estimates, $\hat{p}_1$ and $\hat{p}_2$. In hypothesis tests comparing two population proportions, we will always assume that the hypothesized difference between the two proportions is zero.

If the null hypothesis is assumed to be true, then $p_1 - p_2 = 0$, which implies that $p_1 = p_2$. Thus $\hat{p}_1$ and $\hat{p}_2$ are estimating the same quantity. Therefore, $\hat{p}_1$ and $\hat{p}_2$ are pooled to derive a better estimate of the population proportion. The test statistic is a standard normal random variable given by

$$z = \frac{\left(\hat{p}_1 - \hat{p}_2\right) - 0}{\sqrt{\dfrac{p_c\left(1 - p_c\right)}{n_1} + \dfrac{p_c\left(1 - p_c\right)}{n_2}}}.$$

If the null hypothesis is true, z has an approximately normal distribution. If the observed value of $\hat{p}_1 - \hat{p}_2$ is significantly larger or smaller than 0, this will produce a large or small value of the test statistic, causing us to question whether the null hypothesis is true. How large is "large"? This is answered by the critical value of the test statistic specified in Step 7.

Step 7: Determine the critical value.

The role of the critical value in this test is exactly the same as for all of the hypothesis tests discussed earlier. It defines a range of values for the test statistic, the rejection region, that will be so rare that it is unlikely that it occurred from ordinary sampling variability assuming H_0 is true. The level of the test defines the size of the rejection region. Should the computed value of the test statistic fall in the rejection region, the null hypothesis will be rejected.

The Distribution of the z-Test Statistic (assumes H_0 is true)

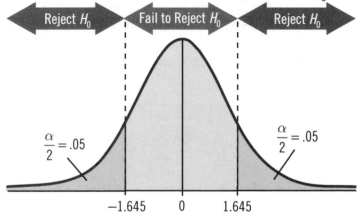

Reject H_0 Fail to Reject H_0 Reject H_0

$\dfrac{\alpha}{2} = .05$ $\dfrac{\alpha}{2} = .05$

−1.645   0   1.645

Figure 11.10

If the null hypothesis is true, the test statistic has an approximately standard normal distribution. Thus the critical value is determined in the same way as for other tests of hypothesis where the test statistic had an approximately standard normal distribution. The rejection region for a two-tailed test with $\alpha = .10$ is displayed in Figure 11.10.

Reject the null hypothesis if the computed value of the test statistic is larger than 1.645 or smaller than −1.645.

Step 8: Compute the test statistic.

Based on the data in Table 11.5, the computed value of the test statistic is given by

$$z = \frac{\dfrac{8}{200} - \dfrac{10}{200} - 0}{\sqrt{\dfrac{.045(1-.045)}{200} + \dfrac{.045(1-.045)}{200}}} \approx -0.4824$$

$$\text{where } p_c = \frac{200}{200+200}\left(\frac{8}{200}\right) + \frac{200}{200+200}\left(\frac{10}{200}\right) = .045.$$

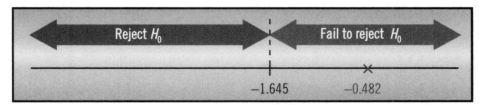

Figure 11.11

Step 9: Make the decision.

As displayed in Figure 11.11, the value of the test statistic does not fall in the rejection region because $-1.645 < -0.482 < 1.645$. Thus, the difference between the observed value and the hypothesized value is likely due to ordinary sampling variation. Thus, we fail to reject the null hypothesis at $\alpha = .10$.

Step 10: State the conclusion in terms of the original question.

There is insufficient evidence at $\alpha = .10$ for the telephone executive to conclude that the proportion of defective phones produced differs between the two plants.

 **Exercises**

Basic Concepts

1. Why is comparing two population proportions particularly useful?

2. Give two examples of situations in which someone would be interested in comparing population proportions.

3. What assumptions are necessary to perform a hypothesis test for the difference between two population proportions?

4. Which sampling distribution is used in a two-sample test of hypothesis about population proportions? What are the characteristics of this sampling distribution?

5. What is the test statistic that is used when comparing two population proportions?

6. True or false: in order to use the specified test statistic, the hypothesized difference in the null hypothesis between the two population proportions must be zero.

Exercises

1. Determine the critical value(s) of the test statistic for each of the following large sample tests for the comparison of two population proportions.

   a. Left-tailed test, $\alpha = .01$

   b. Right-tailed test, $\alpha = .05$

   c. Two-tailed test, $\alpha = .10$

2. Determine the critical value(s) of the test statistic for each of the following large sample tests for the comparison of two population proportions.

   a. Left-tailed test, $\alpha = .025$

   b. Right-tailed test, $\alpha = .02$

   c. Two-tailed test, $\alpha = .04$

3. A fund-raiser believes that women are more likely to say "Yes" when asked to donate to a worthy cause than men. To test this theory, she randomly selects 100 men and 95 women and asks for donations to the same cause. The results of the survey are as follows.

Table for Exercise 3 – Fund-Raiser Survey		
	Number Surveyed	# of Yes Responses
Men	100	6
Women	95	9

a. Does the data substantiate the fund-raiser's theory at $\alpha = .10$?

b. Calculate the P-value for the test and interpret its meaning.

c. Calculate a 95% confidence interval for the difference in the proportion of men and women who would most likely donate to a worthy cause. Interpret the interval.

4. A poll is conducted to determine if U.S. citizens think that there should be a national health care system in the U.S. 69% of the 300 women surveyed and 63% of the 250 men surveyed think that there should be a national health care system in the U.S. Is there sufficient evidence to conclude at $\alpha = .05$ that men and women feel differently about this issue?

5. Major television networks have never seemed to have issues showing commercials for beer and other alcoholic beverages. Even though adult viewers tend to enjoy the commercials, most adults seem to think that the commercials target teenagers and young adults (those under 21 years old). To study this belief, the networks conducted a joint poll of viewers and asked them if they felt that beer and other alcoholic beverage commercials targeted teenagers and young adults. The results of the survey are as follows.

Table for Exercise 5 – Network Advertising Survey		
Age Group	Number Surveyed	Number of "Yes" Responses
30 or Younger	1000	450
Older than 30	1000	655

a. Calculate a 99% confidence interval for the difference in the proportions of those older than 30 and those 30 and younger that believe alcoholic beverage commercials targeted teenagers and young adults. Interpret the interval.

b. Based on the data, can the networks conclude that the percentage of viewers who believe beer and alcoholic beverage commercials target teenagers and young adults is significantly higher in the over 30 age group than in the 30 or younger age group at $\alpha = .01$?

6. A manufacturer is comparing shipments of machine parts from two suppliers. The parts from Supplier A are less expensive; however, the manufacturer is concerned that the parts may be of a lower quality than those from Supplier B. The manufacturer has decided that he will purchase his supplies from Supplier A unless he can show that the proportion of defective parts is significantly higher for Supplier A than for Supplier B. He randomly selects parts from each supplier and inspects them for defects. The results are as follows.

Table for Exercise 6 – Number of Defective Parts		
	Number Surveyed	Number of Defective Parts
Supplier A	400	8
Supplier B	300	5

Which supplier will the manufacturer choose at $\alpha = .05$? Explain.

Discovering Technology

USING EXCEL

When using these data analysis tools in Excel, the raw data must be available and you will not be able to plug in summary statistics. You will be asked to select a range of data to compute the answer.

Table 11.6 – Excel Data Analysis Tools for this Chapter		
Section	Topic	Excel Data Analysis Tool
11.1	Comparing Two Population Means: Large Samples	z-Test: Two Sample for Means
11.2	Comparing Two Population Means: Small Samples (σ_1 and σ_2 Unknown and $\sigma_1 = \sigma_2$)	t-Test: Two-Sample Assuming Equal Variances
11.3	Paired Difference	t-Test: Paired Two Sample for Means

Paired Difference

For this exercise, use the data from Example 11.3.

1. Enter the daily food sales for each restaurant found in Table 11.3 into Column A and Column B in an Excel worksheet.

	A	B
1	5828	7894
2	9836	11573
3	3984	5319
4	5845	6389
5	5210	6055
6	9668	10631
7	6768	7866
8	6726	7976
9	4399	5652
10	6692	8083

Figure 11.12

2. The data analysis tool in Excel which performs the hypothesis test for paired difference experiments is *t*-Test: Paired Two Sample for Means. Select this option from the data analysis tools window.

3. Input the range **$A$1:$A$10** as the "Variable 1 Range" or click and drag in the worksheet to select the sales for Restaurant 1 as the first variable. Input the range **$B$1:$B:10** as the "Variable 2 Range" or click and drag in the worksheet to select the sales for Restaurant 2 as the second variable.

4. Enter **0** for the "Hypothesized Mean Difference".

5. Specify the level of the test by entering **0.01** for "Alpha".

6. Press **OK**. The results of the test are displayed. Notice that the test statistic (t Stat) and the critical values for one tailed (t Critical one-tail) and two tailed (t Critical two-tail) tests are displayed. Compare the test statistic to that which we obtained in Example 11.3.

	A	B	C
1	t-Test: Paired Two Sample for Means		
2			
3		Variable 1	Variable 2
4	Mean	6495.6	7743.8
5	Variance	3845984	4238664
6	Observations	10	10
7	Pearson Correlation	0.9778171	
8	Hypothesized Mean Difference	0	
9	df	9	
10	t Stat	-9.087225	
11	P(T<=t) one-tail	3.945E-06	
12	t Critical one-tail	1.8331129	
13	P(T<=t) two-tail	7.89E-06	
14	t Critical two-tail	2.2621572	

Figure 11.13

USING MINITAB

Table 11.7 – Minitab Functions for this Chapter		
Section	**Topic**	**Minitab Function**
11.1 – 11.2	Comparing Two Population Means	2-Sample *t*
11.3	Paired Difference	Paired *t*
11.4	Comparing Two Population Proportions	2 Proportions

Comparing Two Population Means

For this exercise, use the data from Example 11.2.

$n_1 = 15$	$n_2 = 16$	$\bar{x}_1 = 3425$	$\bar{x}_2 = 3250$	$s_1 = 200$	$s_2 = 175$

1. The Minitab function for a two sample hypothesis test is **2-Sample t**. Select **Stat**, then **Basic Statistics**, then **2-Sample t**.

2. Select the button next to **Summarized data**.

3. Enter the parameters from Table 11.2. In the "First" row, enter **15** for "Sample size", **3425** for "Mean" and **200** for "Standard deviation". In the "Second" row, enter **16** for "Sample size", **3250** for "Mean", and **175** for "Standard deviation".

4. Check the box next to **Assume equal variances**.

5. Press **OK**. The results are displayed in the session window. Notice that the confidence interval is displayed along with the results of the hypothesis test. Compare the value of the test statistic to the one we determined in Example 11.2.

```
Two-Sample T-Test and CI

                       SE
Sample   N   Mean   StDev   Mean
1       15   3425    200     52
2       16   3250    175     44


Difference = mu (1) - mu (2)
Estimate for difference:  175.0
95% CI for difference:   (37.2, 312.8)
T-Test of difference = 0 (vs not =): T-Value = 2.60  P-Value = 0.015  DF = 29
Both use Pooled StDev = 187.4856
```

Figure 11.14

Comparing Two Population Proportions

For this exercise, use the data from Example 11.4.

1. The Minitab function for a hypothesis test about two population proportions is **2 Proportions**. Select **Stat**, **Basic Statistics**, and **2 Proportions**.

2. Choose the button next to **Summarized data**. Enter the data from Table 11.4. In the "First" row, enter **8** for "Events" and **200** for "Trials". In the "Second" row, enter **10** for "Events" and **200** for "Trials".

3. Click **OK**. The results of the hypothesis test are displayed in the session window. Compare the Z statistic to the one which we found in Example 11.4.

Test and CI for Two Proportions

```
Sample    X    N    Sample p
1         8   200   0.040000
2        10   200   0.050000


Difference = p (1) - p (2)
Estimate for difference:  -0.01
95% CI for difference:  (-0.0506190, 0.0306190)
Test for difference = 0 (vs not = 0):  Z = -0.48  P-Value = 0.629

Fisher's exact test: P-Value = 0.810
```

Figure 11.15

Chapter 11 Review

Key Terms and Ideas

- Large Independent Samples

- Independent Experimental Design

- Completely Randomized Design

- Sampling Distribution of $\bar{x}_1 - \bar{x}_2$

- Interval Estimation Comparing Two Population Means

- Hypothesized Difference

- Hypothesis Test about $\mu_1 - \mu_2$

- Assumptions for Small Sample Inferences

- Small Sample Interval Estimation Comparing Two Population Means

- Small Sample Hypothesis Test about $\mu_1 - \mu_2$ (σ_1 and σ_2 Unknown)

- t-Test for Differences between Means Assuming Unequal Variances

- Paired Differences

- Paired Difference Experimental Design

- Assumptions for the Paired Difference Experimental Design

- Mean of the Differences

- Assumptions for Comparing Two Population Proportions

- Interval Estimation Comparing Two Population Proportions

- Hypothesis Test for Comparing Two Population Proportions, $p_1 - p_2$

Key Formulas

Concept	Formula	Section
Sampling Distribution of $\bar{x}_1 - \bar{x}_2$	$$\mu_{\bar{x}_1 - \bar{x}_2} = \mu_1 - \mu_2$$ $$\sigma_{\bar{x}_1 - \bar{x}_2} = \sqrt{\frac{\sigma_1^2}{n_1} + \frac{\sigma_2^2}{n_2}}$$ σ_1^2 and σ_2^2 can be approximated with s_1^2 and s_2^2, respectively, if $n_1 \geq 30$ and $n_2 \geq 30$.	11.1
$100(1-\alpha)\%$ Confidence Interval for $\mu_1 - \mu_2$	$$\left(\bar{x}_1 - \bar{x}_2 \right) \pm z_{\alpha/2} \sqrt{\frac{\sigma_1^2}{n_1} + \frac{\sigma_2^2}{n_2}}$$ where n_1 and n_2 are greater than or equal to 30 or σ_1 and σ_2 are known and the samples are drawn from a normal population.	11.1
Test Statistic for a Large Sample Hypothesis Test for $\mu_1 - \mu_2$	$$z = \frac{\left(\bar{x}_1 - \bar{x}_2 \right) - \mu_{\bar{x}_1 - \bar{x}_2}}{\sigma_{\bar{x}_1 - \bar{x}_2}} = \frac{\left(\bar{x}_1 - \bar{x}_2 \right) - \left(\mu_1 - \mu_2 \right)}{\sqrt{\frac{\sigma_1^2}{n_1} + \frac{\sigma_2^2}{n_2}}}$$	11.1
Small Sample $100(1-\alpha)\%$ Confidence Interval for $\mu_1 - \mu_2$ (σ_1 and σ_2 Unknown and $\sigma_1 = \sigma_2$)	$$\left(\bar{x}_1 - \bar{x}_2 \right) \pm t_{\alpha/2,df} \sqrt{s_p^2 \left(\frac{1}{n_1} + \frac{1}{n_2} \right)}$$ where $s_p^2 = \dfrac{\left(n_1 - 1 \right) s_1^2 + \left(n_2 - 1 \right) s_2^2}{n_1 + n_2 - 2}$, the pooled variance, and $t_{\alpha/2,df}$ is the critical value of the t-distribution with $n_1 + n_2 - 2$ degrees of freedom capturing an area of $\alpha/2$ in the upper tail.	11.2
Test Statistic for a Small Sample Hypothesis Test for $\mu_1 - \mu_2$	$$t = \frac{\left(\bar{x}_1 - \bar{x}_2 \right) - \left(\mu_1 - \mu_2 \right)}{\sqrt{s_p^2 \left(\frac{1}{n_1} + \frac{1}{n_2} \right)}}$$ where $s_p^2 = \dfrac{\left(n_1 - 1 \right) s_1^2 + \left(n_2 - 1 \right) s_2^2}{n_1 + n_2 - 2}$	11.2

Small Sample $100(1-\alpha)\%$ Confidence Interval for $\mu_1 - \mu_2$ (σ_1 and σ_2 Unknown and $\sigma_1 \neq \sigma_2$)	$$\left(\overline{x}_1 - \overline{x}_2\right) \pm t_{\alpha/2,df}\sqrt{\frac{s_1^2}{n_1} + \frac{s_2^2}{n_2}},$$ where $t_{\alpha/2,df}$ is the critical value capturing an area of $\alpha/2$ in the upper tail of t-distribution with degrees of freedom equal to: $$df = \frac{\left(\dfrac{s_1^2}{n_1} + \dfrac{s_2^2}{n_2}\right)^2}{\dfrac{1}{n_1 - 1}\left(\dfrac{s_1^2}{n_1}\right)^2 + \dfrac{1}{n_2 - 1}\left(\dfrac{s_2^2}{n_2}\right)^2}.$$	11.2
Test Statistic for a Small Sample Hypothesis Test for $\mu_1 - \mu_2$ (σ_1 and σ_2 Unknown and $\sigma_1 \neq \sigma_2$)	$$t = \frac{\left(\overline{x}_1 - \overline{x}_2\right)}{\sqrt{\dfrac{s_1^2}{n_1} + \dfrac{s_2^2}{n_2}}},$$ which follows a t-distribution with degrees of freedom equal to: $$df = \frac{\left(\dfrac{s_1^2}{n_1} + \dfrac{s_2^2}{n_2}\right)^2}{\dfrac{1}{n_1 - 1}\left(\dfrac{s_1^2}{n_1}\right)^2 + \dfrac{1}{n_2 - 1}\left(\dfrac{s_2^2}{n_2}\right)^2}.$$	11.2
$100(1-\alpha)\%$ Confidence Interval for μ_d	$$\overline{x}_d \pm t_{\alpha/2,df}\frac{s_d}{\sqrt{n_d}},$$ where $\overline{x}_d$ is the sample mean of the differences, s_d is the sample standard deviation of the differences, n_d is the number of differences, and $t_{\alpha/2,df}$ is the critical value of the t-distribution with an area of $\alpha/2$ in the upper tail with $n_d - 1$ degrees of freedom (df).	11.3
Test Statistic for a Paired Difference Hypothesis Test	$$t = \frac{\overline{x}_d - \mu_d}{s_d\big/\sqrt{n_d}},$$ where $\overline{x}_d$ is the mean of the sample differences, μ_d is the hypothesized mean of the differences, s_d is the standard deviation of the sample differences, and n_d is the number of differences.	11.3

11

Sampling Distribution of $\hat{p}_1 - \hat{p}_2$	$\mu_{\hat{p}_1 - \hat{p}_2} = p_1 - p_2$ $$\sigma_{\hat{p}_1 - \hat{p}_2} = \sqrt{\frac{p_c(1-p_c)}{n_1} + \frac{p_c(1-p_c)}{n_2}}$$ where $p_c = \dfrac{n_1}{n_1+n_2}\hat{p}_1 + \dfrac{n_2}{n_1+n_2}\hat{p}_2$	11.4
$100(1-\alpha)\%$ Confidence Interval for $p_1 - p_2$	$$\hat{p}_1 - \hat{p}_2 \pm z_{\alpha/2}\sqrt{\frac{\hat{p}_1(1-\hat{p}_1)}{n_1} + \frac{\hat{p}_2(1-\hat{p}_2)}{n_2}}$$ where $n_1\hat{p}_1 \geq 5$, $n_1(1-\hat{p}_1) \geq 5$, $n_2\hat{p}_2 \geq 5$, and $n_2(1-\hat{p}_2) \geq 5$ and $z_{\alpha/2}$ is the critical value for the z-distribution that captures an area of $\alpha/2$ in the upper tail.	11.4
Test Statistic for $p_1 - p_2$	$$z = \frac{\left(\hat{p}_1 - \hat{p}_2\right)}{\sqrt{\dfrac{p_c(1-p_c)}{n_1} + \dfrac{p_c(1-p_c)}{n_2}}}$$ where $n_1\hat{p}_1 \geq 5$, $n_1(1-\hat{p}_1) \geq 5$, $n_2\hat{p}_2 \geq 5$, and $n_2(1-\hat{p}_2) \geq 5$.	11.4

Additional Exercises

1. Black Bark, a Colorado based company, makes wood burning stoves. They are interested in comparing two designs to determine which design will produce a stove with a greater average burning time. Several prototypes of each design are tested and the time required to burn 15 pounds of wood, the burning time, is measured in hours. The results of the test are as follows.

Table for Exercise 1 – Burning Time for Stoves (in Hours)			
	n	Average Burning Time $\bar{x}$	s
Stove A	32	9.35	.50
Stove B	35	9.75	.75

Is there sufficient evidence at $\alpha = .05$ for Black Bark to conclude that the mean burning time for Stove B is greater than for Stove A?

2. In each of the following experimental situations give the appropriate null and alternative hypotheses to be tested. Define all terms that appear in these hypotheses.

   a. Independent random samples of 50 male nurses and 50 female nurses are selected from the hospitals in a Southern state. Each nurse is asked whether he or she is satisfied with the working conditions in the hospital. It is of interest to see if there is a difference between male nurses and female nurses on satisfaction with working conditions.

   b. A group of 45 high school seniors take the SAT reasoning test both before and after a 3-month training course, which is designed to improve SAT scores. We wish to determine if the training course is effective.

   c. Starting salaries are determined for 40 female and 40 male electrical engineers. It is of interest to determine if female electrical engineers tend to have higher starting salaries than their male counterparts. Does the evidence support the idea that female engineers start at higher salaries than the male engineers?

   d. Random and independent samples of younger (age $\leq$ 30) and older (age > 30) automobile drivers are chosen and asked whether they have had a speeding ticket in the past 12 months. It is intended to show that younger drivers are more likely than older drivers to have had a speeding ticket in the past 12 months.

   e. Do women have a shorter reaction time than men when exposed to a certain stimulus? Random and independent samples of 10 men and 10 women are included in an experiment that measures reaction time to the stimulus.

3. A nutritionist is interested in determining the decrease in cholesterol level which a person can achieve by following a particular diet which is low in fat and high in fiber. Seven subjects are randomly selected to try the diet for six months, and their cholesterol level is measured both before and after the diet. The results of the study are as follows.

Table for Exercise 3 – Cholesterol Levels							
Subject	1	2	3	4	5	6	7
Before Diet	155	170	145	200	162	180	160
After Diet	152	168	148	195	162	178	157

a. Is a paired design appropriate for the above experiment? Explain.

b. What assumption must be made in order to perform the test of hypothesis?

c. Do the data appear to satisfy the assumption described in part (b)? Why or why not?

d. Can the nutritionist conclude that there is a significant decrease in average cholesterol level when the diet is used? Use $\alpha = .01$.

4. The design group for a monofilament cord manufacturer is testing two possible compositions of the cord for tensile strength. Composition A is more difficult to manufacture than Composition B, so the design group has decided that it will recommend Composition A only if the mean tensile strength for Composition A is shown to be significantly greater than the mean tensile strength for Composition B. Several monofilament cords of each sample are tested and the tensile strengths are measured in pounds per square inch.

Table for Exercise 4 – Tensile Strength (in Pounds per Square Inch)			
	n	Average Tensile Strength $\bar{x}$	s
Composition A	20	52,907	2575
Composition B	20	50,219	1210

a. What assumptions must be made in order to perform the hypothesis test?

b. Will the design group recommend Composition A or Composition B for the monofilament cord at $\alpha = .10$?

5. Consider Example 11.3. If you were to perform a two-sample t-test, you would find that you would fail to reject the null hypothesis and conclude that there is no difference in average daily sales between the two restaurants. Of course, it would be difficult to believe such a test given that if we examine the data in Table 11.3, we see that each of the daily sales figures from Restaurant 2 is more than that from Restaurant 1. From this observation, it is clear that the average daily sales between the restaurants are different.

Why, then, would the *t*-test be unable to detect this difference? The answer: **an independent samples *t*-test is not a valid procedure to use with paired data**. The *t*-test is inappropriate because the assumption of independent samples is invalid since the dependence between restaurants is a function of the days. Perform the two-sample *t*-test to verify that the independent samples test would lead the owner to fail to reject the null hypothesis and conclude that there is not a significant difference between average daily sales. The data from Table 11.3 are replicated below for your convenience. Use $\alpha = .01$.

Table 11.3 – Daily Food Sales for Two Restaurants			
Day	Restaurant 1	Restaurant 2	Difference = Restaurant 1 – Restaurant 2
1	$5828	$7894	−$2066
2	$9836	$11,573	−$1737
3	$3984	$5319	−$1335
4	$5845	$6389	−$544
5	$5210	$6055	−$845
6	$9668	$10,631	−$963
7	$6768	$7866	−$1098
8	$6726	$7976	−$1250
9	$4399	$5652	−$1253
10	$6692	$8083	−$1391

6. Two independent random samples have been selected, 100 from Population 1 and 150 from Population 2. The sample mean and standard deviation from the first population is 1025 and 10, respectively. For the second sample, the mean is 1039 with a standard deviation of 12.

   a. Test that there is no difference between the groups using $\alpha = .01$.

   b. Construct a 95% confidence interval for the true mean difference between Population 1 and Population 2.

7. The manufacturer of Brand 1 cigarettes claims that his cigarettes are no more harmful to health than Brand 2 (filtered) cigarettes. Assuming harmfulness is to be associated with nicotine content, the FDA took random samples of 125 cigarettes from Brand 1 and 180 cigarettes from Brand 2. The average nicotine content in the sample of Brand 1 was 24.6 mg with a standard deviation of 1.4 mg; the average nicotine content in the sample of Brand 2 was 24.3 mg with a standard deviation of 1.1 mg.

   a. Is there evidence to refute the manufacturer's claim at $\alpha = .05$?

   b. Construct an 85% confidence interval for the true mean difference in nicotine content between Brand 1 and Brand 2.

8. A team of organizational behavior managers investigated the effects of an orientation program on "first day of work" anxiety levels of new employees. 72 new employees were randomly assigned to receive or not to receive a two-day company orientation program prior to their first day at work. Two hours after beginning work, each employee was given a test to measure his or her level of anxiety. The mean score was 1002 for the 37 receiving orientation and 1018 for the 35 who did not receive the orientation. Scores of employees who attended similar orientation programs in the past have had a standard deviation of 142. Scores of employees that did not attend the orientation program had this same standard deviation.

   a. Test to see if there is evidence of a difference in the mean test scores between those who participate in an orientation program and those who do not. Use a level of significance equal to .05.

   b. Calculate the observed significance level (*P*-value) of this test.

9. A property manager of thousands of apartments wants to test the difference in the mean net annual income between two types of leasing arrangements. Arrangement A is to charge a lower rent but to require the tenants to make repairs. Arrangement B is to charge a higher rent and to state that the landlord will make the repairs. A sample of 25 apartments using Arrangement A had a mean net annual income of $1532.50 with a standard deviation of $400. A sample of 22 apartments using Arrangement B had a mean net annual income of $1489.20 with a standard deviation of $100. Test at $\alpha = .025$ that Arrangement B will have a lower mean net annual income by **at least $10** than Arrangement A. Assume that the incomes are normally distributed and that the population variances are equal.

10. For a consumer product, the mean dollar sales per retail outlet last year in a sample of 25 stores were $3425 with a variance of $400. For a second product, the mean dollar sales per outlet in a sample of 16 stores were $3250 with a standard deviation of $175. The sales amounts per outlet are assumed to be approximately normally distributed for both products. Test to see if the first product has a better mean dollar sales record than the second product. Use the *P*-value approach and base your decision on a significance level of .01. Assume that the population variances are not equal.

11. A random sample of 10 filled sports drink bottles is taken in one bottling plant, and the mean weight of the bottles is found to be 22 ounces with a variance of 0.09 ounces squared. At another plant, 10 randomly selected bottles have a mean weight of 21 ounces with a variance of 0.04 ounces squared. Assuming the weights in both populations are normally distributed and the population variances are equal, test to see that there is no difference between the average weights of the bottles being filled at the two plants. Use $\alpha = .05$.

Appendix A:
Statistical Tables

A

Table A – **Standard Normal Distribution**

Numerical entries represent the probability that a standard normal random variable is between $-\infty$ and z where $z = \dfrac{x - \mu}{\sigma}$.

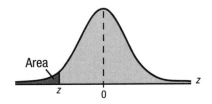

Area

z

0

z

z	0.09	0.08	0.07	0.06	0.05	0.04	0.03	0.02	0.01	0.00
-3.4	.0002	.0003	.0003	.0003	.0003	.0003	.0003	.0003	.0003	.0003
-3.3	.0003	.0004	.0004	.0004	.0004	.0004	.0004	.0005	.0005	.0005
-3.2	.0005	.0005	.0005	.0006	.0006	.0006	.0006	.0006	.0007	.0007
-3.1	.0007	.0007	.0008	.0008	.0008	.0008	.0009	.0009	.0009	.0010
-3.0	.0010	.0010	.0011	.0011	.0011	.0012	.0012	.0013	.0013	.0013
-2.9	.0014	.0014	.0015	.0015	.0016	.0016	.0017	.0018	.0018	.0019
-2.8	.0019	.0020	.0021	.0021	.0022	.0023	.0023	.0024	.0025	.0026
-2.7	.0026	.0027	.0028	.0029	.0030	.0031	.0032	.0033	.0034	.0035
-2.6	.0036	.0037	.0038	.0039	.0040	.0041	.0043	.0044	.0045	.0047
-2.5	.0048	.0049	.0051	.0052	.0054	.0055	.0057	.0059	.0060	.0062
-2.4	.0064	.0066	.0068	.0069	.0071	.0073	.0075	.0078	.0080	.0082
-2.3	.0084	.0087	.0089	.0091	.0094	.0096	.0099	.0102	.0104	.0107
-2.2	.0110	.0113	.0116	.0119	.0122	.0125	.0129	.0132	.0136	.0139
-2.1	.0143	.0146	.0150	.0154	.0158	.0162	.0166	.0170	.0174	.0179
-2.0	.0183	.0188	.0192	.0197	.0202	.0207	.0212	.0217	.0222	.0228
-1.9	.0233	.0239	.0244	.0250	.0256	.0262	.0268	.0274	.0281	.0287
-1.8	.0294	.0301	.0307	.0314	.0322	.0329	.0336	.0344	.0351	.0359
-1.7	.0367	.0375	.0384	.0392	.0401	.0409	.0418	.0427	.0436	.0446
-1.6	.0455	.0465	.0475	.0485	.0495	.0505	.0516	.0526	.0537	.0548
-1.5	.0559	.0571	.0582	.0594	.0606	.0618	.0630	.0643	.0655	.0668
-1.4	.0681	.0694	.0708	.0721	.0735	.0749	.0764	.0778	.0793	.0808
-1.3	.0823	.0838	.0853	.0869	.0885	.0901	.0918	.0934	.0951	.0968
-1.2	.0985	.1003	.1020	.1038	.1056	.1075	.1093	.1112	.1131	.1151
-1.1	.1170	.1190	.1210	.1230	.1251	.1271	.1292	.1314	.1335	.1357
-1.0	.1379	.1401	.1423	.1446	.1469	.1492	.1515	.1539	.1562	.1587
-0.9	.1611	.1635	.1660	.1685	.1711	.1736	.1762	.1788	.1814	.1841
-0.8	.1867	.1894	.1922	.1949	.1977	.2005	.2033	.2061	.2090	.2119
-0.7	.2148	.2177	.2206	.2236	.2266	.2296	.2327	.2358	.2389	.2420
-0.6	.2451	.2483	.2514	.2546	.2578	.2611	.2643	.2676	.2709	.2743
-0.5	.2776	.2810	.2843	.2877	.2912	.2946	.2981	.3015	.3050	.3085
-0.4	.3121	.3156	.3192	.3228	.3264	.3300	.3336	.3372	.3409	.3446
-0.3	.3483	.3520	.3557	.3594	.3632	.3669	.3707	.3745	.3783	.3821
-0.2	.3859	.3897	.3936	.3974	.4013	.4052	.4090	.4129	.4168	.4207
-0.1	.4247	.4286	.4325	.4364	.4404	.4443	.4483	.4522	.4562	.4602
-0.0	.4641	.4681	.4721	.4761	.4801	.4840	.4880	.4920	.4960	.5000

Table B – **Standard Normal Distribution**

Numerical entries represent the probability that a standard normal random variable is between $-\infty$ and z where $z = \dfrac{x - \mu}{\sigma}$.

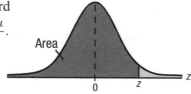

z	0.00	0.01	0.02	0.03	0.04	0.05	0.06	0.07	0.08	0.09
0.0	.5000	.5040	.5080	.5120	.5160	.5199	.5239	.5279	.5319	.5359
0.1	.5398	.5438	.5478	.5517	.5557	.5596	.5636	.5675	.5714	.5753
0.2	.5793	.5832	.5871	.5910	.5948	.5987	.6026	.6064	.6103	.6141
0.3	.6179	.6217	.6255	.6293	.6331	.6368	.6406	.6443	.6480	.6517
0.4	.6554	.6591	.6628	.6664	.6700	.6736	.6772	.6808	.6844	.6879
0.5	.6915	.6950	.6985	.7019	.7054	.7088	.7123	.7157	.7190	.7224
0.6	.7257	.7291	.7324	.7357	.7389	.7422	.7454	.7486	.7517	.7549
0.7	.7580	.7611	.7642	.7673	.7704	.7734	.7764	.7794	.7823	.7852
0.8	.7881	.7910	.7939	.7967	.7995	.8023	.8051	.8078	.8106	.8133
0.9	.8159	.8186	.8212	.8238	.8264	.8289	.8315	.8340	.8365	.8389
1.0	.8413	.8438	.8461	.8485	.8508	.8531	.8554	.8577	.8599	.8621
1.1	.8643	.8665	.8686	.8708	.8729	.8749	.8770	.8790	.8810	.8830
1.2	.8849	.8869	.8888	.8907	.8925	.8944	.8962	.8980	.8997	.9015
1.3	.9032	.9049	.9066	.9082	.9099	.9115	.9131	.9147	.9162	.9177
1.4	.9192	.9207	.9222	.9236	.9251	.9265	.9279	.9292	.9306	.9319
1.5	.9332	.9345	.9357	.9370	.9382	.9394	.9406	.9418	.9429	.9441
1.6	.9452	.9463	.9474	.9484	.9495	.9505	.9515	.9525	.9535	.9545
1.7	.9554	.9564	.9573	.9582	.9591	.9599	.9608	.9616	.9625	.9633
1.8	.9641	.9649	.9656	.9664	.9671	.9678	.9686	.9693	.9699	.9706
1.9	.9713	.9719	.9726	.9732	.9738	.9744	.9750	.9756	.9761	.9767
2.0	.9772	.9778	.9783	.9788	.9793	.9798	.9803	.9808	.9812	.9817
2.1	.9821	.9826	.9830	.9834	.9838	.9842	.9846	.9850	.9854	.9857
2.2	.9861	.9864	.9868	.9871	.9875	.9878	.9881	.9884	.9887	.9890
2.3	.9893	.9896	.9898	.9901	.9904	.9906	.9909	.9911	.9913	.9916
2.4	.9918	.9920	.9922	.9925	.9927	.9929	.9931	.9932	.9934	.9936
2.5	.9938	.9940	.9941	.9943	.9945	.9946	.9948	.9949	.9951	.9952
2.6	.9953	.9955	.9956	.9957	.9959	.9960	.9961	.9962	.9963	.9964
2.7	.9965	.9966	.9967	.9968	.9969	.9970	.9971	.9972	.9973	.9974
2.8	.9974	.9975	.9976	.9977	.9977	.9978	.9979	.9979	.9980	.9981
2.9	.9981	.9982	.9982	.9983	.9984	.9984	.9985	.9985	.9986	.9986
3.0	.9987	.9987	.9987	.9988	.9988	.9989	.9989	.9989	.9990	.9990
3.1	.9990	.9991	.9991	.9991	.9992	.9992	.9992	.9992	.9993	.9993
3.2	.9993	.9993	.9994	.9994	.9994	.9994	.9994	.9995	.9995	.9995
3.3	.9995	.9995	.9995	.9996	.9996	.9996	.9996	.9996	.9996	.9997
3.4	.9997	.9997	.9997	.9997	.9997	.9997	.9997	.9997	.9997	.9998

Table C – **Standard Normal Distribution**

Numerical entries represent the probability that a standard normal random variable is between 0 and z where $z = \dfrac{x - \mu}{\sigma}$.

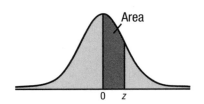

z	0.00	0.01	0.02	0.03	0.04	0.05	0.06	0.07	0.08	0.09
0.0	.0000	.0040	.0080	.0120	.0160	.0199	.0239	.0279	.0319	.0359
0.1	.0398	.0438	.0478	.0517	.0557	.0596	.0636	.0675	.0714	.0753
0.2	.0793	.0832	.0871	.0910	.0948	.0987	.1026	.1064	.1103	.1141
0.3	.1179	.1217	.1255	.1293	.1331	.1368	.1406	.1443	.1480	.1517
0.4	.1554	.1591	.1628	.1664	.1700	.1736	.1772	.1808	.1844	.1879
0.5	.1915	.1950	.1985	.2019	.2054	.2088	.2123	.2157	.2190	.2224
0.6	.2257	.2291	.2324	.2357	.2389	.2422	.2454	.2486	.2517	.2549
0.7	.2580	.2611	.2642	.2673	.2704	.2734	.2764	.2794	.2823	.2852
0.8	.2881	.2910	.2939	.2967	.2995	.3023	.3051	.3078	.3106	.3133
0.9	.3159	.3186	.3212	.3238	.3264	.3289	.3315	.3340	.3365	.3389
1.0	.3413	.3438	.3461	.3485	.3508	.3531	.3554	.3577	.3599	.3621
1.1	.3643	.3665	.3686	.3708	.3729	.3749	.3770	.3790	.3810	.3830
1.2	.3849	.3869	.3888	.3907	.3925	.3944	.3962	.3980	.3997	.4015
1.3	.4032	.4049	.4066	.4082	.4099	.4115	.4131	.4147	.4162	.4177
1.4	.4192	.4207	.4222	.4236	.4251	.4265	.4279	.4292	.4306	.4319
1.5	.4332	.4345	.4357	.4370	.4382	.4394	.4406	.4418	.4429	.4441
1.6	.4452	.4463	.4474	.4484	.4495	.4505	.4515	.4525	.4535	.4545
1.7	.4554	.4564	.4573	.4582	.4591	.4599	.4608	.4616	.4625	.4633
1.8	.4641	.4649	.4656	.4664	.4671	.4678	.4686	.4693	.4699	.4706
1.9	.4713	.4719	.4726	.4732	.4738	.4744	.4750	.4756	.4761	.4767
2.0	.4772	.4778	.4783	.4788	.4793	.4798	.4803	.4808	.4812	.4817
2.1	.4821	.4826	.4830	.4834	.4838	.4842	.4846	.4850	.4854	.4857
2.2	.4861	.4864	.4868	.4871	.4875	.4878	.4881	.4884	.4887	.4890
2.3	.4893	.4896	.4898	.4901	.4904	.4906	.4909	.4911	.4913	.4916
2.4	.4918	.4920	.4922	.4925	.4927	.4929	.4931	.4932	.4934	.4936
2.5	.4938	.4940	.4941	.4943	.4945	.4946	.4948	.4949	.4951	.4952
2.6	.4953	.4955	.4956	.4957	.4959	.4960	.4961	.4962	.4963	.4964
2.7	.4965	.4966	.4967	.4968	.4969	.4970	.4971	.4972	.4973	.4974
2.8	.4974	.4975	.4976	.4977	.4977	.4978	.4979	.4979	.4980	.4981
2.9	.4981	.4982	.4982	.4983	.4984	.4984	.4985	.4985	.4986	.4986
3.0	.4987	.4987	.4987	.4988	.4988	.4989	.4989	.4989	.4990	.4990
3.1	.4990	.4991	.4991	.4991	.4992	.4992	.4992	.4992	.4993	.4993
3.2	.4993	.4993	.4994	.4994	.4994	.4994	.4994	.4995	.4995	.4995
3.3	.4995	.4995	.4995	.4996	.4996	.4996	.4996	.4996	.4996	.4997
3.4	.4997	.4997	.4997	.4997	.4997	.4997	.4997	.4997	.4997	.4998

Table D – **Critical Values of *t***

	Area in One Tail				
	$t_{.100}$	$t_{.050}$	$t_{.025}$	$t_{.010}$	$t_{.005}$
	Area in Two Tails				
df	$t_{.200}$	$t_{.100}$	$t_{.050}$	$t_{.025}$	$t_{.010}$
1	3.078	6.314	12.706	31.821	63.657
2	1.886	2.920	4.303	6.965	9.925
3	1.638	2.353	3.182	4.541	5.841
4	1.533	2.132	2.776	3.747	4.604
5	1.476	2.015	2.571	3.365	4.032
6	1.440	1.943	2.447	3.143	3.707
7	1.415	1.895	2.365	2.998	3.499
8	1.397	1.860	2.306	2.896	3.355
9	1.383	1.833	2.262	2.821	3.250
10	1.372	1.812	2.228	2.764	3.169
11	1.363	1.796	2.201	2.718	3.106
12	1.356	1.782	2.179	2.681	3.055
13	1.350	1.771	2.160	2.650	3.012
14	1.345	1.761	2.145	2.624	2.977
15	1.341	1.753	2.131	2.602	2.947
16	1.337	1.746	2.120	2.583	2.921
17	1.333	1.740	2.110	2.567	2.898
18	1.330	1.734	2.101	2.552	2.878
19	1.328	1.729	2.093	2.539	2.861
20	1.325	1.725	2.086	2.528	2.845
21	1.323	1.721	2.080	2.518	2.831
22	1.321	1.717	2.074	2.508	2.819
23	1.319	1.714	2.069	2.500	2.807
24	1.318	1.711	2.064	2.492	2.797
25	1.316	1.708	2.060	2.485	2.787
26	1.315	1.706	2.056	2.479	2.779
27	1.314	1.703	2.052	2.473	2.771
28	1.313	1.701	2.048	2.467	2.763
29	1.311	1.699	2.045	2.462	2.756
30	1.310	1.697	2.042	2.457	2.750
40	1.303	1.684	2.021	2.423	2.704
60	1.296	1.671	2.000	2.390	2.660
120	1.289	1.658	1.980	2.358	2.617
∞	1.282	1.645	1.960	2.326	2.576

Left Tail

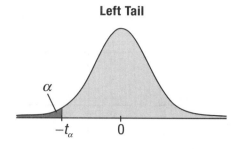

Right Tail

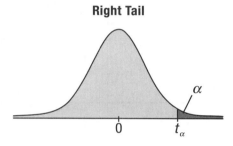

Two Tails

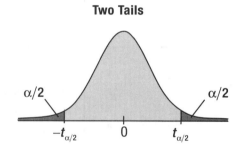

Critical Values of z

Level of Confidence	$z_{\alpha/2}$
.80	1.28
.90	1.645
.95	1.96
.99	2.575

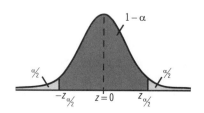

Table E – **Binominal Probabilities**

n	x	.1	.2	.3	.4	.5	.6	.7	.8	.9
1	0	.9000	.8000	.7000	.6000	.5000	.4000	.3000	.2000	.1000
	1	.1000	.2000	.3000	.4000	.5000	.6000	.7000	.8000	.9000
2	0	.8100	.6400	.4900	.3600	.2500	.1600	.0900	.0400	.0100
	1	.1800	.3200	.4200	.4800	.5000	.4800	.4200	.3200	.1800
	2	.0100	.0400	.0900	.1600	.2500	.3600	.4900	.6400	.8100
3	0	.7290	.5120	.3430	.2160	.1250	.0640	.0270	.0080	.0010
	1	.2430	.3840	.4410	.4320	.3750	.2880	.1890	.0960	.0270
	2	.0270	.0960	.1890	.2880	.3750	.4320	.4410	.3840	.2430
	3	.0010	.0080	.0270	.0640	.1250	.2160	.3430	.5120	.7290
4	0	.6561	.4096	.2401	.1296	.0625	.0256	.0081	.0016	.0001
	1	.2916	.4096	.4116	.3456	.2500	.1536	.0756	.0256	.0036
	2	.0486	.1536	.2646	.3456	.3750	.3456	.2646	.1536	.0486
	3	.0036	.0256	.0756	.1536	.2500	.3456	.4116	.4096	.2916
	4	.0001	.0016	.0081	.0256	.0625	.1296	.2401	.4096	.6561
5	0	.5905	.3277	.1681	.0778	.0313	.0102	.0024	.0003	.0000
	1	.3281	.4096	.3602	.2592	.1563	.0768	.0284	.0064	.0005
	2	.0729	.2048	.3087	.3456	.3125	.2304	.1323	.0512	.0081
	3	.0081	.0512	.1323	.2304	.3125	.3456	.3087	.2048	.0729
	4	.0005	.0064	.0284	.0768	.1563	.2592	.3602	.4096	.3281
	5	.0000	.0003	.0024	.0102	.0313	.0778	.1681	.3277	.5905
6	0	.5314	.2621	.1176	.0467	.0156	.0041	.0007	.0001	.0000
	1	.3543	.3932	.3025	.1866	.0938	.0369	.0102	.0015	.0001
	2	.0984	.2458	.3241	.3110	.2344	.1382	.0595	.0154	.0012
	3	.0146	.0819	.1852	.2765	.3125	.2765	.1852	.0819	.0146
	4	.0012	.0154	.0595	.1382	.2344	.3110	.3241	.2458	.0984
	5	.0001	.0015	.0102	.0369	.0938	.1866	.3025	.3932	.3543
	6	.0000	.0001	.0007	.0041	.0156	.0467	.1176	.2621	.5314
7	0	.4783	.2097	.0824	.0280	.0078	.0016	.0002	.0000	.0000
	1	.3720	.3670	.2471	.1306	.0547	.0172	.0036	.0004	.0000
	2	.1240	.2753	.3177	.2613	.1641	.0774	.0250	.0043	.0002
	3	.0230	.1147	.2269	.2903	.2734	.1935	.0972	.0287	.0026
	4	.0026	.0287	.0972	.1935	.2734	.2903	.2269	.1147	.0230
	5	.0002	.0043	.0250	.0774	.1641	.2613	.3177	.2753	.1240
	6	.0000	.0004	.0036	.0172	.0547	.1306	.2471	.3670	.3720
	7	.0000	.0000	.0002	.0016	.0078	.0280	.0824	.2097	.4783

Binominal Probabilities (continued)

		p								
n	x	.1	.2	.3	.4	.5	.6	.7	.8	.9
8	0	.4305	.1678	.0576	.0168	.0039	.0007	.0001	.0000	.0000
	1	.3826	.3355	.1977	.0896	.0313	.0079	.0012	.0001	.0000
	2	.1488	.2936	.2965	.2090	.1094	.0413	.0100	.0011	.0000
	3	.0331	.1468	.2541	.2787	.2188	.1239	.0467	.0092	.0004
	4	.0046	.0459	.1361	.2322	.2734	.2322	.1361	.0459	.0046
	5	.0004	.0092	.0467	.1239	.2188	.2787	.2541	.1468	.0331
	6	.0000	.0011	.0100	.0413	.1094	.2090	.2965	.2936	.1488
	7	.0000	.0001	.0012	.0079	.0313	.0896	.1977	.3355	.3826
	8	.0000	.0000	.0001	.0007	.0039	.0168	.0576	.1678	.4305
9	0	.3874	.1342	.0404	.0101	.0020	.0003	.0000	.0000	.0000
	1	.3874	.3020	.1556	.0605	.0176	.0035	.0004	.0000	.0000
	2	.1722	.3020	.2668	.1612	.0703	.0212	.0039	.0003	.0000
	3	.0446	.1762	.2668	.2508	.1641	.0743	.0210	.0028	.0001
	4	.0074	.0661	.1715	.2508	.2461	.1672	.0735	.0165	.0008
	5	.0008	.0165	.0735	.1672	.2461	.2508	.1715	.0661	.0074
	6	.0001	.0028	.0210	.0743	.1641	.2508	.2668	.1762	.0446
	7	.0000	.0003	.0039	.0212	.0703	.1612	.2668	.3020	.1722
	8	.0000	.0000	.0004	.0035	.0176	.0605	.1556	.3020	.3874
	9	.0000	.0000	.0000	.0003	.0020	.0101	.0404	.1342	.3874
10	0	.3487	.1074	.0282	.0060	.0010	.0001	.0000	.0000	.0000
	1	.3874	.2684	.1211	.0403	.0098	.0016	.0001	.0000	.0000
	2	.1937	.3020	.2335	.1209	.0439	.0106	.0014	.0001	.0000
	3	.0574	.2013	.2668	.2150	.1172	.0425	.0090	.0008	.0000
	4	.0112	.0881	.2001	.2508	.2051	.1115	.0368	.0055	.0001
	5	.0015	.0264	.1029	.2007	.2461	.2007	.1029	.0264	.0015
	6	.0001	.0055	.0368	.1115	.2051	.2508	.2001	.0881	.0112
	7	.0000	.0008	.0090	.0425	.1172	.2150	.2668	.2013	.0574
	8	.0000	.0001	.0014	.0106	.0439	.1209	.2335	.3020	.1937
	9	.0000	.0000	.0001	.0016	.0098	.0403	.1211	.2684	.3874
	10	.0000	.0000	.0000	.0001	.0010	.0060	.0282	.1074	.3487
11	0	.3138	.0859	.0198	.0036	.0005	.0000	.0000	.0000	.0000
	1	.3835	.2362	.0932	.0266	.0054	.0007	.0000	.0000	.0000
	2	.2131	.2953	.1998	.0887	.0269	.0052	.0005	.0000	.0000
	3	.0710	.2215	.2568	.1774	.0806	.0234	.0037	.0002	.0000
	4	.0158	.1107	.2201	.2365	.1611	.0701	.0173	.0017	.0000
	5	.0025	.0388	.1321	.2207	.2256	.1471	.0566	.0097	.0003
	6	.0003	.0097	.0566	.1471	.2256	.2207	.1321	.0388	.0025
	7	.0000	.0017	.0173	.0701	.1611	.2365	.2201	.1107	.0158
	8	.0000	.0002	.0037	.0234	.0806	.1774	.2568	.2215	.0710
	9	.0000	.0000	.0005	.0052	.0269	.0887	.1998	.2953	.2131
	10	.0000	.0000	.0000	.0007	.0054	.0266	.0932	.2362	.3835
	11	.0000	.0000	.0000	.0000	.0005	.0036	.0198	.0859	.3138

Binominal Probabilities (continued)

p

n	x	.1	.2	.3	.4	.5	.6	.7	.8	.9
12	0	.2824	.0687	.0138	.0022	.0002	.0000	.0000	.0000	.0000
	1	.3766	.2062	.0712	.0174	.0029	.0003	.0000	.0000	.0000
	2	.2301	.2835	.1678	.0639	.0161	.0025	.0002	.0000	.0000
	3	.0852	.2362	.2397	.1419	.0537	.0125	.0015	.0001	.0000
	4	.0213	.1329	.2311	.2128	.1208	.0420	.0078	.0005	.0000
	5	.0038	.0532	.1585	.2270	.1934	.1009	.0291	.0033	.0000
	6	.0005	.0155	.0792	.1766	.2256	.1766	.0792	.0155	.0005
	7	.0000	.0033	.0291	.1009	.1934	.2270	.1585	.0532	.0038
	8	.0000	.0005	.0078	.0420	.1208	.2128	.2311	.1329	.0213
	9	.0000	.0001	.0015	.0125	.0537	.1419	.2397	.2362	.0852
	10	.0000	.0000	.0002	.0025	.0161	.0639	.1678	.2835	.2301
	11	.0000	.0000	.0000	.0003	.0029	.0174	.0712	.2062	.3766
	12	.0000	.0000	.0000	.0000	.0002	.0022	.0138	.0687	.2824
13	0	.2542	.0550	.0097	.0013	.0001	.0000	.0000	.0000	.0000
	1	.3672	.1787	.0540	.0113	.0016	.0001	.0000	.0000	.0000
	2	.2448	.2680	.1388	.0453	.0095	.0012	.0001	.0000	.0000
	3	.0997	.2457	.2181	.1107	.0349	.0065	.0006	.0000	.0000
	4	.0277	.1535	.2337	.1845	.0873	.0243	.0034	.0001	.0000
	5	.0055	.0691	.1803	.2214	.1571	.0656	.0142	.0011	.0000
	6	.0008	.0230	.1030	.1968	.2095	.1312	.0442	.0058	.0001
	7	.0001	.0058	.0442	.1312	.2095	.1968	.1030	.0230	.0008
	8	.0000	.0011	.0142	.0656	.1571	.2214	.1803	.0691	.0055
	9	.0000	.0001	.0034	.0243	.0873	.1845	.2337	.1535	.0277
	10	.0000	.0000	.0006	.0065	.0349	.1107	.2181	.2457	.0997
	11	.0000	.0000	.0001	.0012	.0095	.0453	.1388	.2680	.2448
	12	.0000	.0000	.0000	.0001	.0016	.0113	.0540	.1787	.3672
	13	.0000	.0000	.0000	.0000	.0001	.0013	.0097	.0550	.2542
14	0	.2288	.0440	.0068	.0008	.0001	.0000	.0000	.0000	.0000
	1	.3559	.1539	.0407	.0073	.0009	.0001	.0000	.0000	.0000
	2	.2570	.2501	.1134	.0317	.0056	.0005	.0000	.0000	.0000
	3	.1142	.2501	.1943	.0845	.0222	.0033	.0002	.0000	.0000
	4	.0349	.1720	.2290	.1549	.0611	.0136	.0014	.0000	.0000
	5	.0078	.0860	.1963	.2066	.1222	.0408	.0066	.0003	.0000
	6	.0013	.0322	.1262	.2066	.1833	.0918	.0232	.0020	.0000
	7	.0002	.0092	.0618	.1574	.2095	.1574	.0618	.0092	.0002
	8	.0000	.0020	.0232	.0918	.1833	.2066	.1262	.0322	.0013
	9	.0000	.0003	.0066	.0408	.1222	.2066	.1963	.0860	.0078
	10	.0000	.0000	.0014	.0136	.0611	.1549	.2290	.1720	.0349
	11	.0000	.0000	.0002	.0033	.0222	.0845	.1943	.2501	.1142
	12	.0000	.0000	.0000	.0005	.0056	.0317	.1134	.2501	.2570
	13	.0000	.0000	.0000	.0001	.0009	.0073	.0407	.1539	.3559
	14	.0000	.0000	.0000	.0000	.0001	.0008	.0068	.0440	.2288

Binominal Probabilities (continued)

n	x	.1	.2	.3	.4	.5	.6	.7	.8	.9
15	0	.2059	.0352	.0047	.0005	.0000	.0000	.0000	.0000	.0000
	1	.3432	.1319	.0305	.0047	.0005	.0000	.0000	.0000	.0000
	2	.2669	.2309	.0916	.0219	.0032	.0003	.0000	.0000	.0000
	3	.1285	.2501	.1700	.0634	.0139	.0016	.0001	.0000	.0000
	4	.0428	.1876	.2186	.1268	.0417	.0074	.0006	.0000	.0000
	5	.0105	.1032	.2061	.1859	.0916	.0245	.0030	.0001	.0000
	6	.0019	.0430	.1472	.2066	.1527	.0612	.0116	.0007	.0000
	7	.0003	.0138	.0811	.1771	.1964	.1181	.0348	.0035	.0000
	8	.0000	.0035	.0348	.1181	.1964	.1771	.0811	.0138	.0003
	9	.0000	.0007	.0116	.0612	.1527	.2066	.1472	.0430	.0019
	10	.0000	.0001	.0030	.0245	.0916	.1859	.2061	.1032	.0105
	11	.0000	.0000	.0006	.0074	.0417	.1268	.2186	.1876	.0428
	12	.0000	.0000	.0001	.0016	.0139	.0634	.1700	.2501	.1285
	13	.0000	.0000	.0000	.0003	.0032	.0219	.0916	.2309	.2669
	14	.0000	.0000	.0000	.0000	.0005	.0047	.0305	.1319	.3432
	15	.0000	.0000	.0000	.0000	.0000	.0005	.0047	.0352	.2059
16	0	.1853	.0281	.0033	.0003	.0000	.0000	.0000	.0000	.0000
	1	.3294	.1126	.0228	.0030	.0002	.0000	.0000	.0000	.0000
	2	.2745	.2111	.0732	.0150	.0018	.0001	.0000	.0000	.0000
	3	.1423	.2463	.1465	.0468	.0085	.0008	.0000	.0000	.0000
	4	.0514	.2001	.2040	.1014	.0278	.0040	.0002	.0000	.0000
	5	.0137	.1201	.2099	.1623	.0667	.0142	.0013	.0000	.0000
	6	.0028	.0550	.1649	.1983	.1222	.0392	.0056	.0002	.0000
	7	.0004	.0197	.1010	.1889	.1746	.0840	.0185	.0012	.0000
	8	.0001	.0055	.0487	.1417	.1964	.1417	.0487	.0055	.0001
	9	.0000	.0012	.0185	.0840	.1746	.1889	.1010	.0197	.0004
	10	.0000	.0002	.0056	.0392	.1222	.1983	.1649	.0550	.0028
	11	.0000	.0000	.0013	.0142	.0667	.1623	.2099	.1201	.0137
	12	.0000	.0000	.0002	.0040	.0278	.1014	.2040	.2001	.0514
	13	.0000	.0000	.0000	.0008	.0085	.0468	.1465	.2463	.1423
	14	.0000	.0000	.0000	.0001	.0018	.0150	.0732	.2111	.2745
	15	.0000	.0000	.0000	.0000	.0002	.0030	.0228	.1126	.3294
	16	.0000	.0000	.0000	.0000	.0000	.0003	.0033	.0281	.1853

Binominal Probabilities (continued)

						p				
n	x	.1	.2	.3	.4	.5	.6	.7	.8	.9
17	0	.1668	.0225	.0023	.0002	.0000	.0000	.0000	.0000	.0000
	1	.3150	.0957	.0169	.0019	.0001	.0000	.0000	.0000	.0000
	2	.2800	.1914	.0581	.0102	.0010	.0001	.0000	.0000	.0000
	3	.1556	.2393	.1245	.0341	.0052	.0004	.0000	.0000	.0000
	4	.0605	.2093	.1868	.0796	.0182	.0021	.0001	.0000	.0000
	5	.0175	.1361	.2081	.1379	.0472	.0081	.0006	.0000	.0000
	6	.0039	.0680	.1784	.1839	.0944	.0242	.0026	.0001	.0000
	7	.0007	.0267	.1201	.1927	.1484	.0571	.0095	.0004	.0000
	8	.0001	.0084	.0644	.1606	.1855	.1070	.0276	.0021	.0000
	9	.0000	.0021	.0276	.1070	.1855	.1606	.0644	.0084	.0001
	10	.0000	.0004	.0095	.0571	.1484	.1927	.1201	.0267	.0007
	11	.0000	.0001	.0026	.0242	.0944	.1839	.1784	.0680	.0039
	12	.0000	.0000	.0006	.0081	.0472	.1379	.2081	.1361	.0175
	13	.0000	.0000	.0001	.0021	.0182	.0796	.1868	.2093	.0605
	14	.0000	.0000	.0000	.0004	.0052	.0341	.1245	.2393	.1556
	15	.0000	.0000	.0000	.0001	.0010	.0102	.0581	.1914	.2800
	16	.0000	.0000	.0000	.0000	.0001	.0019	.0169	.0957	.3150
	17	.0000	.0000	.0000	.0000	.0000	.0002	.0023	.0225	.1668
18	0	.1501	.0180	.0016	.0001	.0000	.0000	.0000	.0000	.0000
	1	.3002	.0811	.0126	.0012	.0001	.0000	.0000	.0000	.0000
	2	.2835	.1723	.0458	.0069	.0006	.0000	.0000	.0000	.0000
	3	.1680	.2297	.1046	.0246	.0031	.0002	.0000	.0000	.0000
	4	.0700	.2153	.1681	.0614	.0117	.0011	.0000	.0000	.0000
	5	.0218	.1507	.2017	.1146	.0327	.0045	.0002	.0000	.0000
	6	.0052	.0816	.1873	.1655	.0708	.0145	.0012	.0000	.0000
	7	.0010	.0350	.1376	.1892	.1214	.0374	.0046	.0001	.0000
	8	.0002	.0120	.0811	.1734	.1669	.0771	.0149	.0008	.0000
	9	.0000	.0033	.0386	.1284	.1855	.1284	.0386	.0033	.0000
	10	.0000	.0008	.0149	.0771	.1669	.1734	.0811	.0120	.0002
	11	.0000	.0001	.0046	.0374	.1214	.1892	.1376	.0350	.0010
	12	.0000	.0000	.0012	.0145	.0708	.1655	.1873	.0816	.0052
	13	.0000	.0000	.0002	.0045	.0327	.1146	.2017	.1507	.0218
	14	.0000	.0000	.0000	.0011	.0117	.0614	.1681	.2153	.0700
	15	.0000	.0000	.0000	.0002	.0031	.0246	.1046	.2297	.1680
	16	.0000	.0000	.0000	.0000	.0006	.0069	.0458	.1723	.2835
	17	.0000	.0000	.0000	.0000	.0001	.0012	.0126	.0811	.3002
	18	.0000	.0000	.0000	.0000	.0000	.0001	.0016	.0180	.1501

Binominal Probabilities (continued)

						p				
n	x	.1	.2	.3	.4	.5	.6	.7	.8	.9
19	0	.1351	.0144	.0011	.0001	.0000	.0000	.0000	.0000	.0000
	1	.2852	.0685	.0093	.0008	.0000	.0000	.0000	.0000	.0000
	2	.2852	.1540	.0358	.0046	.0003	.0000	.0000	.0000	.0000
	3	.1796	.2182	.0869	.0175	.0018	.0001	.0000	.0000	.0000
	4	.0798	.2182	.1491	.0467	.0074	.0005	.0000	.0000	.0000
	5	.0266	.1636	.1916	.0933	.0222	.0024	.0001	.0000	.0000
	6	.0069	.0955	.1916	.1451	.0518	.0085	.0005	.0000	.0000
	7	.0014	.0443	.1525	.1797	.0961	.0237	.0022	.0000	.0000
	8	.0002	.0166	.0981	.1797	.1442	.0532	.0077	.0003	.0000
	9	.0000	.0051	.0514	.1464	.1762	.0976	.0220	.0013	.0000
	10	.0000	.0013	.0220	.0976	.1762	.1464	.0514	.0051	.0000
	11	.0000	.0003	.0077	.0532	.1442	.1797	.0981	.0166	.0002
	12	.0000	.0000	.0022	.0237	.0961	.1797	.1525	.0443	.0014
	13	.0000	.0000	.0005	.0085	.0518	.1451	.1916	.0955	.0069
	14	.0000	.0000	.0001	.0024	.0222	.0933	.1916	.1636	.0266
	15	.0000	.0000	.0000	.0005	.0074	.0467	.1491	.2182	.0798
	16	.0000	.0000	.0000	.0001	.0018	.0175	.0869	.2182	.1796
	17	.0000	.0000	.0000	.0000	.0003	.0046	.0358	.1540	.2852
	18	.0000	.0000	.0000	.0000	.0000	.0008	.0093	.0685	.2852
	19	.0000	.0000	.0000	.0000	.0000	.0001	.0011	.0144	.1351
20	0	.1216	.0115	.0008	.0000	.0000	.0000	.0000	.0000	.0000
	1	.2702	.0576	.0068	.0005	.0000	.0000	.0000	.0000	.0000
	2	.2852	.1369	.0278	.0031	.0002	.0000	.0000	.0000	.0000
	3	.1901	.2054	.0716	.0123	.0011	.0000	.0000	.0000	.0000
	4	.0898	.2182	.1304	.0350	.0046	.0003	.0000	.0000	.0000
	5	.0319	.1746	.1789	.0746	.0148	.0013	.0000	.0000	.0000
	6	.0089	.1091	.1916	.1244	.0370	.0049	.0002	.0000	.0000
	7	.0020	.0545	.1643	.1659	.0739	.0146	.0010	.0000	.0000
	8	.0004	.0222	.1144	.1797	.1201	.0355	.0039	.0001	.0000
	9	.0001	.0074	.0654	.1597	.1602	.0710	.0120	.0005	.0000
	10	.0000	.0020	.0308	.1171	.1762	.1171	.0308	.0020	.0000
	11	.0000	.0005	.0120	.0710	.1602	.1597	.0654	.0074	.0001
	12	.0000	.0001	.0039	.0355	.1201	.1797	.1144	.0222	.0004
	13	.0000	.0000	.0010	.0146	.0739	.1659	.1643	.0545	.0020
	14	.0000	.0000	.0002	.0049	.0370	.1244	.1916	.1091	.0089
	15	.0000	.0000	.0000	.0013	.0148	.0746	.1789	.1746	.0319
	16	.0000	.0000	.0000	.0003	.0046	.0350	.1304	.2182	.0898
	17	.0000	.0000	.0000	.0000	.0011	.0123	.0716	.2054	.1901
	18	.0000	.0000	.0000	.0000	.0002	.0031	.0278	.1369	.2852
	19	.0000	.0000	.0000	.0000	.0000	.0005	.0068	.0576	.2702
	20	.0000	.0000	.0000	.0000	.0000	.0000	.0008	.0115	.1216

Table F – **Cumulative Binominal Probabilities**

p

n	x	.1	.2	.3	.4	.5	.6	.7	.8	.9
1	0	.900	.800	.700	.600	.500	.400	.300	.200	.100
	1	1.000	1.000	1.000	1.000	1.000	1.000	1.000	1.000	1.000
2	0	.810	.640	.490	.360	.250	.160	.090	.040	.010
	1	.990	.960	.910	.840	.750	.640	.510	.360	.190
	2	1.000	1.000	1.000	1.000	1.000	1.000	1.000	1.000	1.000
3	0	.729	.512	.343	.216	.125	.064	.027	.008	.001
	1	.972	.896	.784	.648	.500	.352	.216	.104	.028
	2	.999	.992	.973	.936	.875	.784	.657	.488	.271
	3	1.000	1.000	1.000	1.000	1.000	1.000	1.000	1.000	1.000
4	0	.656	.410	.240	.130	.063	.026	.008	.002	.000
	1	.948	.819	.652	.475	.313	.179	.084	.027	.004
	2	.996	.973	.916	.821	.688	.525	.348	.181	.052
	3	1.000	.998	.992	.974	.938	.870	.760	.590	.344
	4	1.000	1.000	1.000	1.000	1.000	1.000	1.000	1.000	1.000
5	0	.590	.328	.168	.078	.031	.010	.002	.000	.000
	1	.919	.737	.528	.337	.188	.087	.031	.007	.000
	2	.991	.942	.837	.683	.500	.317	.163	.058	.009
	3	1.000	.993	.969	.913	.813	.663	.472	.263	.081
	4	1.000	1.000	.998	.990	.969	.922	.832	.672	.410
	5	1.000	1.000	1.000	1.000	1.000	1.000	1.000	1.000	1.000
6	0	.531	.262	.118	.047	.016	.004	.001	.000	.000
	1	.886	.655	.420	.233	.109	.041	.011	.002	.000
	2	.984	.901	.744	.544	.344	.179	.070	.017	.001
	3	.999	.983	.930	.821	.656	.456	.256	.099	.016
	4	1.000	.998	.989	.959	.891	.767	.580	.345	.114
	5	1.000	1.000	.999	.996	.984	.953	.882	.738	.469
	6	1.000	1.000	1.000	1.000	1.000	1.000	1.000	1.000	1.000
7	0	.478	.210	.082	.028	.008	.002	.000	.000	.000
	1	.850	.577	.329	.159	.063	.019	.004	.000	.000
	2	.974	.852	.647	.420	.227	.096	.029	.005	.000
	3	.997	.967	.874	.710	.500	.290	.126	.033	.003
	4	1.000	.995	.971	.904	.773	.580	.353	.148	.026
	5	1.000	1.000	.996	.981	.938	.841	.671	.423	.150
	6	1.000	1.000	1.000	.998	.992	.972	.918	.790	.522
	7	1.000	1.000	1.000	1.000	1.000	1.000	1.000	1.000	1.000

Cumulative Binominal Probabilities (continued)

n	x	.1	.2	.3	.4	.5	.6	.7	.8	.9
8	0	.430	.168	.058	.017	.004	.001	.000	.000	.000
	1	.813	.503	.255	.106	.035	.009	.001	.000	.000
	2	.962	.797	.552	.315	.145	.050	.011	.001	.000
	3	.995	.944	.806	.594	.363	.174	.058	.010	.000
	4	1.000	.990	.942	.826	.637	.406	.194	.056	.005
	5	1.000	.999	.989	.950	.855	.685	.448	.203	.038
	6	1.000	1.000	.999	.991	.965	.894	.745	.497	.187
	7	1.000	1.000	1.000	.999	.996	.983	.942	.832	.570
	8	1.000	1.000	1.000	1.000	1.000	1.000	1.000	1.000	1.000
9	0	.387	.134	.040	.010	.002	.000	.000	.000	.000
	1	.775	.436	.196	.071	.020	.004	.000	.000	.000
	2	.947	.738	.463	.232	.090	.025	.004	.000	.000
	3	.992	.914	.730	.483	.254	.099	.025	.003	.000
	4	.999	.980	.901	.733	.500	.267	.099	.020	.001
	5	1.000	.997	.975	.901	.746	.517	.270	.086	.008
	6	1.000	1.000	.996	.975	.910	.768	.537	.262	.053
	7	1.000	1.000	1.000	.996	.980	.929	.804	.564	.225
	8	1.000	1.000	1.000	1.000	.998	.990	.960	.866	.613
	9	1.000	1.000	1.000	1.000	1.000	1.000	1.000	1.000	1.000
10	0	.349	.107	.028	.006	.001	.000	.000	.000	.000
	1	.736	.376	.149	.046	.011	.002	.000	.000	.000
	2	.930	.678	.383	.167	.055	.012	.002	.000	.000
	3	.987	.879	.650	.382	.172	.055	.011	.001	.000
	4	.998	.967	.850	.633	.377	.166	.047	.006	.000
	5	1.000	.994	.953	.834	.623	.367	.150	.033	.002
	6	1.000	.999	.989	.945	.828	.618	.350	.121	.013
	7	1.000	1.000	.998	.988	.945	.833	.617	.322	.070
	8	1.000	1.000	1.000	.998	.989	.954	.851	.624	.264
	9	1.000	1.000	1.000	1.000	.999	.994	.972	.893	.651
	10	1.000	1.000	1.000	1.000	1.000	1.000	1.000	1.000	1.000
11	0	.314	.086	.020	.004	.000	.000	.000	.000	.000
	1	.697	.322	.113	.030	.006	.001	.000	.000	.000
	2	.910	.617	.313	.119	.033	.006	.001	.000	.000
	3	.981	.839	.570	.296	.113	.029	.004	.000	.000
	4	.997	.950	.790	.533	.274	.099	.022	.002	.000
	5	1.000	.988	.922	.753	.500	.247	.078	.012	.000
	6	1.000	.998	.978	.901	.726	.467	.210	.050	.003
	7	1.000	1.000	.996	.971	.887	.704	.430	.161	.019
	8	1.000	1.000	.999	.994	.967	.881	.687	.383	.090
	9	1.000	1.000	1.000	.999	.994	.970	.887	.678	.303
	10	1.000	1.000	1.000	1.000	1.000	.996	.980	.914	.686
	11	1.000	1.000	1.000	1.000	1.000	1.000	1.000	1.000	1.000

Cumulative Binominal Probabilities (continued)

						p				
n	x	.1	.2	.3	.4	.5	.6	.7	.8	.9
12	0	.282	.069	.014	.002	.000	.000	.000	.000	.000
	1	.659	.275	.085	.020	.003	.000	.000	.000	.000
	2	.889	.558	.253	.083	.019	.003	.000	.000	.000
	3	.974	.795	.493	.225	.073	.015	.002	.000	.000
	4	.996	.927	.724	.438	.194	.057	.009	.001	.000
	5	.999	.981	.882	.665	.387	.158	.039	.004	.000
	6	1.000	.996	.961	.842	.613	.335	.118	.019	.001
	7	1.000	.999	.991	.943	.806	.562	.276	.073	.004
	8	1.000	1.000	.998	.985	.927	.775	.507	.205	.026
	9	1.000	1.000	1.000	.997	.981	.917	.747	.442	.111
	10	1.000	1.000	1.000	1.000	.997	.980	.915	.725	.341
	11	1.000	1.000	1.000	1.000	1.000	.998	.986	.931	.718
	12	1.000	1.000	1.000	1.000	1.000	1.000	1.000	1.000	1.000
13	0	.254	.055	.010	.001	.000	.000	.000	.000	.000
	1	.621	.234	.064	.013	.002	.000	.000	.000	.000
	2	.866	.502	.202	.058	.011	.001	.000	.000	.000
	3	.966	.747	.421	.169	.046	.008	.001	.000	.000
	4	.994	.901	.654	.353	.133	.032	.004	.000	.000
	5	.999	.970	.835	.574	.291	.098	.018	.001	.000
	6	1.000	.993	.938	.771	.500	.229	.062	.007	.000
	7	1.000	.999	.982	.902	.709	.426	.165	.030	.001
	8	1.000	1.000	.996	.968	.867	.647	.346	.099	.006
	9	1.000	1.000	.999	.992	.954	.831	.579	.253	.034
	10	1.000	1.000	1.000	.999	.989	.942	.798	.498	.134
	11	1.000	1.000	1.000	1.000	.998	.987	.936	.766	.379
	12	1.000	1.000	1.000	1.000	1.000	.999	.990	.945	.746
	13	1.000	1.000	1.000	1.000	1.000	1.000	1.000	1.000	1.000
14	0	.229	.044	.007	.001	.000	.000	.000	.000	.000
	1	.585	.198	.047	.008	.001	.000	.000	.000	.000
	2	.842	.448	.161	.040	.006	.001	.000	.000	.000
	3	.956	.698	.355	.124	.029	.004	.000	.000	.000
	4	.991	.870	.584	.279	.090	.018	.002	.000	.000
	5	.999	.956	.781	.486	.212	.058	.008	.000	.000
	6	1.000	.988	.907	.692	.395	.150	.031	.002	.000
	7	1.000	.998	.969	.850	.605	.308	.093	.012	.000
	8	1.000	1.000	.992	.942	.788	.514	.219	.044	.001
	9	1.000	1.000	.998	.982	.910	.721	.416	.130	.009
	10	1.000	1.000	1.000	.996	.971	.876	.645	.302	.044
	11	1.000	1.000	1.000	.999	.994	.960	.839	.552	.158
	12	1.000	1.000	1.000	1.000	.999	.992	.953	.802	.415
	13	1.000	1.000	1.000	1.000	1.000	.999	.993	.956	.771
	14	1.000	1.000	1.000	1.000	1.000	1.000	1.000	1.000	1.000

Cumulative Binominal Probabilities (continued)

						p				
n	x	.1	.2	.3	.4	.5	.6	.7	.8	.9
15	0	.206	.035	.005	.000	.000	.000	.000	.000	.000
	1	.549	.167	.035	.005	.000	.000	.000	.000	.000
	2	.816	.398	.127	.027	.004	.000	.000	.000	.000
	3	.944	.648	.297	.091	.018	.002	.000	.000	.000
	4	.987	.836	.515	.217	.059	.009	.001	.000	.000
	5	.998	.939	.722	.403	.151	.034	.004	.000	.000
	6	1.000	.982	.869	.610	.304	.095	.015	.001	.000
	7	1.000	.996	.950	.787	.500	.213	.050	.004	.000
	8	1.000	.999	.985	.905	.696	.390	.131	.018	.000
	9	1.000	1.000	.996	.966	.849	.597	.278	.061	.002
	10	1.000	1.000	.999	.991	.941	.783	.485	.164	.013
	11	1.000	1.000	1.000	.998	.982	.909	.703	.352	.056
	12	1.000	1.000	1.000	1.000	.996	.973	.873	.602	.184
	13	1.000	1.000	1.000	1.000	1.000	.995	.965	.833	.451
	14	1.000	1.000	1.000	1.000	1.000	1.000	.995	.965	.794
	15	1.000	1.000	1.000	1.000	1.000	1.000	1.000	1.000	1.000
16	0	.185	.028	.003	.000	.000	.000	.000	.000	.000
	1	.515	.141	.026	.003	.000	.000	.000	.000	.000
	2	.789	.352	.099	.018	.002	.000	.000	.000	.000
	3	.932	.598	.246	.065	.011	.001	.000	.000	.000
	4	.983	.798	.450	.167	.038	.005	.000	.000	.000
	5	.997	.918	.660	.329	.105	.019	.002	.000	.000
	6	.999	.973	.825	.527	.227	.058	.007	.000	.000
	7	1.000	.993	.926	.716	.402	.142	.026	.001	.000
	8	1.000	.999	.974	.858	.598	.284	.074	.007	.000
	9	1.000	1.000	.993	.942	.773	.473	.175	.027	.001
	10	1.000	1.000	.998	.981	.895	.671	.340	.082	.003
	11	1.000	1.000	1.000	.995	.962	.833	.550	.202	.017
	12	1.000	1.000	1.000	.999	.989	.935	.754	.402	.068
	13	1.000	1.000	1.000	1.000	.998	.982	.901	.648	.211
	14	1.000	1.000	1.000	1.000	1.000	.997	.974	.859	.485
	15	1.000	1.000	1.000	1.000	1.000	1.000	.997	.972	.815
	16	1.000	1.000	1.000	1.000	1.000	1.000	1.000	1.000	1.000

Cumulative Binominal Probabilities (continued)

p

n	x	.1	.2	.3	.4	.5	.6	.7	.8	.9
17	0	.167	.023	.002	.000	.000	.000	.000	.000	.000
	1	.482	.118	.019	.002	.000	.000	.000	.000	.000
	2	.762	.310	.077	.012	.001	.000	.000	.000	.000
	3	.917	.549	.202	.046	.006	.000	.000	.000	.000
	4	.978	.758	.389	.126	.025	.003	.000	.000	.000
	5	.995	.894	.597	.264	.072	.011	.001	.000	.000
	6	.999	.962	.775	.448	.166	.035	.003	.000	.000
	7	1.000	.989	.895	.641	.315	.092	.013	.000	.000
	8	1.000	.997	.960	.801	.500	.199	.040	.003	.000
	9	1.000	1.000	.987	.908	.685	.359	.105	.011	.000
	10	1.000	1.000	.997	.965	.834	.552	.225	.038	.001
	11	1.000	1.000	.999	.989	.928	.736	.403	.106	.005
	12	1.000	1.000	1.000	.997	.975	.874	.611	.242	.022
	13	1.000	1.000	1.000	1.000	.994	.954	.798	.451	.083
	14	1.000	1.000	1.000	1.000	.999	.988	.923	.690	.238
	15	1.000	1.000	1.000	1.000	1.000	.998	.981	.882	.518
	16	1.000	1.000	1.000	1.000	1.000	1.000	.998	.977	.833
	17	1.000	1.000	1.000	1.000	1.000	1.000	1.000	1.000	1.000
18	0	.150	.018	.002	.000	.000	.000	.000	.000	.000
	1	.450	.099	.014	.001	.000	.000	.000	.000	.000
	2	.734	.271	.060	.008	.001	.000	.000	.000	.000
	3	.902	.501	.165	.033	.004	.000	.000	.000	.000
	4	.972	.716	.333	.094	.015	.001	.000	.000	.000
	5	.994	.867	.534	.209	.048	.006	.000	.000	.000
	6	.999	.949	.722	.374	.119	.020	.001	.000	.000
	7	1.000	.984	.859	.563	.240	.058	.006	.000	.000
	8	1.000	.996	.940	.737	.407	.135	.021	.001	.000
	9	1.000	.999	.979	.865	.593	.263	.060	.004	.000
	10	1.000	1.000	.994	.942	.760	.437	.141	.016	.000
	11	1.000	1.000	.999	.980	.881	.626	.278	.051	.001
	12	1.000	1.000	1.000	.994	.952	.791	.466	.133	.006
	13	1.000	1.000	1.000	.999	.985	.906	.667	.284	.028
	14	1.000	1.000	1.000	1.000	.996	.967	.835	.499	.098
	15	1.000	1.000	1.000	1.000	.999	.992	.940	.729	.266
	16	1.000	1.000	1.000	1.000	1.000	.999	.986	.901	.550
	17	1.000	1.000	1.000	1.000	1.000	1.000	.998	.982	.850
	18	1.000	1.000	1.000	1.000	1.000	1.000	1.000	1.000	1.000

Cumulative Binominal Probabilities (continued)

		p								
n	x	.1	.2	.3	.4	.5	.6	.7	.8	.9
19	0	.135	.014	.001	.000	.000	.000	.000	.000	.000
	1	.420	.083	.010	.001	.000	.000	.000	.000	.000
	2	.705	.237	.046	.005	.000	.000	.000	.000	.000
	3	.885	.455	.133	.023	.002	.000	.000	.000	.000
	4	.965	.673	.282	.070	.010	.001	.000	.000	.000
	5	.991	.837	.474	.163	.032	.003	.000	.000	.000
	6	.998	.932	.666	.308	.084	.012	.001	.000	.000
	7	1.000	.977	.818	.488	.180	.035	.003	.000	.000
	8	1.000	.993	.916	.667	.324	.088	.011	.000	.000
	9	1.000	.998	.967	.814	.500	.186	.033	.002	.000
	10	1.000	1.000	.989	.912	.676	.333	.084	.007	.000
	11	1.000	1.000	.997	.965	.820	.512	.182	.023	.000
	12	1.000	1.000	.999	.988	.916	.692	.334	.068	.002
	13	1.000	1.000	1.000	.997	.968	.837	.526	.163	.009
	14	1.000	1.000	1.000	.999	.990	.930	.718	.327	.035
	15	1.000	1.000	1.000	1.000	.998	.977	.867	.545	.115
	16	1.000	1.000	1.000	1.000	1.000	.995	.954	.763	.295
	17	1.000	1.000	1.000	1.000	1.000	.999	.990	.917	.580
	18	1.000	1.000	1.000	1.000	1.000	1.000	.999	.986	.865
	19	1.000	1.000	1.000	1.000	1.000	1.000	1.000	1.000	1.000
20	0	.122	.012	.001	.000	.000	.000	.000	.000	.000
	1	.392	.069	.008	.001	.000	.000	.000	.000	.000
	2	.677	.206	.035	.004	.000	.000	.000	.000	.000
	3	.867	.411	.107	.016	.001	.000	.000	.000	.000
	4	.957	.630	.238	.051	.006	.000	.000	.000	.000
	5	.989	.804	.416	.126	.021	.002	.000	.000	.000
	6	.998	.913	.608	.250	.058	.006	.000	.000	.000
	7	1.000	.968	.772	.416	.132	.021	.001	.000	.000
	8	1.000	.990	.887	.596	.252	.057	.005	.000	.000
	9	1.000	.997	.952	.755	.412	.128	.017	.001	.000
	10	1.000	.999	.983	.872	.588	.245	.048	.003	.000
	11	1.000	1.000	.995	.943	.748	.404	.113	.010	.000
	12	1.000	1.000	.999	.979	.868	.584	.228	.032	.000
	13	1.000	1.000	1.000	.994	.942	.750	.392	.087	.002
	14	1.000	1.000	1.000	.998	.979	.874	.584	.196	.011
	15	1.000	1.000	1.000	1.000	.994	.949	.762	.370	.043
	16	1.000	1.000	1.000	1.000	.999	.984	.893	.589	.133
	17	1.000	1.000	1.000	1.000	1.000	.996	.965	.794	.323
	18	1.000	1.000	1.000	1.000	1.000	.999	.992	.931	.608
	19	1.000	1.000	1.000	1.000	1.000	1.000	.999	.988	.878
	20	1.000	1.000	1.000	1.000	1.000	1.000	1.000	1.000	1.000

Table G – **Poisson Probabilities**

λ

x	0.02	0.03	0.04	0.05	0.06	0.07	0.08	0.09	0.10	0.20	0.30
0	.9802	.9704	.9608	.9512	.9418	.9324	.9231	.9139	.9048	.8187	.7408
1	.0196	.0291	.0384	.0476	.0565	.0653	.0738	.0823	.0905	.1637	.2222
2	.0002	.0004	.0008	.0012	.0017	.0023	.0030	.0037	.0045	.0164	.0333
3	.0000	.0000	.0000	.0000	.0000	.0001	.0001	.0001	.0002	.0011	.0033
4	.0000	.0000	.0000	.0000	.0000	.0000	.0000	.0000	.0000	.0001	.0003

x	0.40	0.50	0.60	0.70	0.80	0.90	1.00	1.10	1.20	1.30	1.40
0	.6703	.6065	.5488	.4966	.4493	.4066	.3679	.3329	.3012	.2725	.2466
1	.2681	.3033	.3293	.3476	.3595	.3659	.3679	.3662	.3614	.3543	.3452
2	.0536	.0758	.0988	.1217	.1438	.1647	.1839	.2014	.2169	.2303	.2417
3	.0072	.0126	.0198	.0284	.0383	.0494	.0613	.0738	.0867	.0998	.1128
4	.0007	.0016	.0030	.0050	.0077	.0111	.0153	.0203	.0260	.0324	.0395
5	.0001	.0002	.0004	.0007	.0012	.0020	.0031	.0045	.0062	.0084	.0111
6	.0000	.0000	.0000	.0001	.0002	.0003	.0005	.0008	.0012	.0018	.0026
7	.0000	.0000	.0000	.0000	.0000	.0000	.0001	.0001	.0002	.0003	.0005
8	.0000	.0000	.0000	.0000	.0000	.0000	.0000	.0000	.0000	.0001	.0001

x	1.50	1.60	1.70	1.80	1.90	2.00	2.10	2.20	2.30	2.40	2.50
0	.2231	.2019	.1827	.1653	.1496	.1353	.1225	.1108	.1003	.0907	.0821
1	.3347	.3230	.3106	.2975	.2842	.2707	.2572	.2438	.2306	.2177	.2052
2	.2510	.2584	.2640	.2678	.2700	.2707	.2700	.2681	.2652	.2613	.2565
3	.1255	.1378	.1496	.1607	.1710	.1804	.1890	.1966	.2033	.2090	.2138
4	.0471	.0551	.0636	.0723	.0812	.0902	.0992	.1082	.1169	.1254	.1336
5	.0141	.0176	.0216	.0260	.0309	.0361	.0417	.0476	.0538	.0602	.0668
6	.0035	.0047	.0061	.0078	.0098	.0120	.0146	.0174	.0206	.0241	.0278
7	.0008	.0011	.0015	.0020	.0027	.0034	.0044	.0055	.0068	.0083	.0099
8	.0001	.0002	.0003	.0005	.0006	.0009	.0011	.0015	.0019	.0025	.0031
9	.0000	.0000	.0001	.0001	.0001	.0002	.0003	.0004	.0005	.0007	.0009
10	.0000	.0000	.0000	.0000	.0000	.0000	.0001	.0001	.0001	.0002	.0002

x	2.60	2.70	2.80	2.90	3.00	3.10	3.20	3.30	3.40	3.50	3.60
0	.0743	.0672	.0608	.0550	.0498	.0450	.0408	.0369	.0334	.0302	.0273
1	.1931	.1815	.1703	.1596	.1494	.1397	.1304	.1217	.1135	.1057	.0984
2	.2510	.2450	.2384	.2314	.2240	.2165	.2087	.2008	.1929	.1850	.1771
3	.2176	.2205	.2225	.2237	.2240	.2237	.2226	.2209	.2186	.2158	.2125
4	.1414	.1488	.1557	.1622	.1680	.1733	.1781	.1823	.1858	.1888	.1912
5	.0735	.0804	.0872	.0940	.1008	.1075	.1140	.1203	.1264	.1322	.1377
6	.0319	.0362	.0407	.0455	.0504	.0555	.0608	.0662	.0716	.0771	.0826
7	.0118	.0139	.0163	.0188	.0216	.0246	.0278	.0312	.0348	.0385	.0425
8	.0038	.0047	.0057	.0068	.0081	.0095	.0111	.0129	.0148	.0169	.0191
9	.0011	.0014	.0018	.0022	.0027	.0033	.0040	.0047	.0056	.0066	.0076
10	.0003	.0004	.0005	.0006	.0008	.0010	.0013	.0016	.0019	.0023	.0028
11	.0001	.0001	.0001	.0002	.0002	.0003	.0004	.0005	.0006	.0007	.0009
12	.0000	.0000	.0000	.0000	.0001	.0001	.0001	.0001	.0002	.0002	.0003
13	.0000	.0000	.0000	.0000	.0000	.0000	.0000	.0000	.0000	.0001	.0001

Poisson Probabilities (continued)

λ

x	3.70	3.80	3.90	4.00	4.10	4.20	4.30	4.40	4.50	4.60	4.70
0	.0247	.0224	.0202	.0183	.0166	.0150	.0136	.0123	.0111	.0101	.0091
1	.0915	.0850	.0789	.0733	.0679	.0630	.0583	.0540	.0500	.0462	.0427
2	.1692	.1615	.1539	.1465	.1393	.1323	.1254	.1188	.1125	.1063	.1005
3	.2087	.2046	.2001	.1954	.1904	.1852	.1798	.1743	.1687	.1631	.1574
4	.1931	.1944	.1951	.1954	.1951	.1944	.1933	.1917	.1898	.1875	.1849
5	.1429	.1477	.1522	.1563	.1600	.1633	.1662	.1687	.1708	.1725	.1738
6	.0881	.0936	.0989	.1042	.1093	.1143	.1191	.1237	.1281	.1323	.1362
7	.0466	.0508	.0551	.0595	.0640	.0686	.0732	.0778	.0824	.0869	.0914
8	.0215	.0241	.0269	.0298	.0328	.0360	.0393	.0428	.0463	.0500	.0537
9	.0089	.0102	.0116	.0132	.0150	.0168	.0188	.0209	.0232	.0255	.0281
10	.0033	.0039	.0045	.0053	.0061	.0071	.0081	.0092	.0104	.0118	.0132
11	.0011	.0013	.0016	.0019	.0023	.0027	.0032	.0037	.0043	.0049	.0056
12	.0003	.0004	.0005	.0006	.0008	.0009	.0011	.0013	.0016	.0019	.0022
13	.0001	.0001	.0002	.0002	.0002	.0003	.0004	.0005	.0006	.0007	.0008
14	.0000	.0000	.0000	.0001	.0001	.0001	.0001	.0001	.0002	.0002	.0003
15	.0000	.0000	.0000	.0000	.0000	.0000	.0000	.0000	.0001	.0001	.0001

x	4.80	4.90	5.00	5.10	5.20	5.30	5.40	5.50	5.60	5.70	5.80
0	.0082	.0074	.0067	.0061	.0055	.0050	.0045	.0041	.0037	.0033	.0030
1	.0395	.0365	.0337	.0311	.0287	.0265	.0244	.0225	.0207	.0191	.0176
2	.0948	.0894	.0842	.0793	.0746	.0701	.0659	.0618	.0580	.0544	.0509
3	.1517	.1460	.1404	.1348	.1293	.1239	.1185	.1133	.1082	.1033	.0985
4	.1820	.1789	.1755	.1719	.1681	.1641	.1600	.1558	.1515	.1472	.1428
5	.1747	.1753	.1755	.1753	.1748	.1740	.1728	.1714	.1697	.1678	.1656
6	.1398	.1432	.1462	.1490	.1515	.1537	.1555	.1571	.1584	.1594	.1601
7	.0959	.1002	.1044	.1086	.1125	.1163	.1200	.1234	.1267	.1298	.1326
8	.0575	.0614	.0653	.0692	.0731	.0771	.0810	.0849	.0887	.0925	.0962
9	.0307	.0334	.0363	.0392	.0423	.0454	.0486	.0519	.0552	.0586	.0620
10	.0147	.0164	.0181	.0200	.0220	.0241	.0262	.0285	.0309	.0334	.0359
11	.0064	.0073	.0082	.0093	.0104	.0116	.0129	.0143	.0157	.0173	.0190
12	.0026	.0030	.0034	.0039	.0045	.0051	.0058	.0065	.0073	.0082	.0092
13	.0009	.0011	.0013	.0015	.0018	.0021	.0024	.0028	.0032	.0036	.0041
14	.0003	.0004	.0005	.0006	.0007	.0008	.0009	.0011	.0013	.0015	.0017
15	.0001	.0001	.0002	.0002	.0002	.0003	.0003	.0004	.0005	.0006	.0007
16	.0000	.0000	.0000	.0001	.0001	.0001	.0001	.0001	.0002	.0002	.0002
17	.0000	.0000	.0000	.0000	.0000	.0000	.0000	.0000	.0001	.0001	.0001

x	5.90	6.00	6.10	6.20	6.30	6.40	6.50	6.60	6.70	6.80	6.90
0	.0027	.0025	.0022	.0020	.0018	.0017	.0015	.0014	.0012	.0011	.0010
1	.0162	.0149	.0137	.0126	.0116	.0106	.0098	.0090	.0082	.0076	.0070
2	.0477	.0446	.0417	.0390	.0364	.0340	.0318	.0296	.0276	.0258	.0240
3	.0938	.0892	.0848	.0806	.0765	.0726	.0688	.0652	.0617	.0584	.0552
4	.1383	.1339	.1294	.1249	.1205	.1162	.1118	.1076	.1034	.0992	.0952
5	.1632	.1606	.1579	.1549	.1519	.1487	.1454	.1420	.1385	.1349	.1314

Poisson Probabilities (continued)

λ

x	5.90	6.00	6.10	6.20	6.30	6.40	6.50	6.60	6.70	6.80	6.90
6	.1605	.1606	.1605	.1601	.1595	.1586	.1575	.1562	.1546	.1529	.1511
7	.1353	.1377	.1399	.1418	.1435	.1450	.1462	.1472	.1480	.1486	.1489
8	.0998	.1033	.1066	.1099	.1130	.1160	.1188	.1215	.1240	.1263	.1284
9	.0654	.0688	.0723	.0757	.0791	.0825	.0858	.0891	.0923	.0954	.0985
10	.0386	.0413	.0441	.0469	.0498	.0528	.0558	.0588	.0618	.0649	.0679
11	.0207	.0225	.0244	.0265	.0285	.0307	.0330	.0353	.0377	.0401	.0426
12	.0102	.0113	.0124	.0137	.0150	.0164	.0179	.0194	.0210	.0227	.0245
13	.0046	.0052	.0058	.0065	.0073	.0081	.0089	.0099	.0108	.0119	.0130
14	.0019	.0022	.0025	.0029	.0033	.0037	.0041	.0046	.0052	.0058	.0064
15	.0008	.0009	.0010	.0012	.0014	.0016	.0018	.0020	.0023	.0026	.0029
16	.0003	.0003	.0004	.0005	.0005	.0006	.0007	.0008	.0010	.0011	.0013
17	.0001	.0001	.0001	.0002	.0002	.0002	.0003	.0003	.0004	.0004	.0005
18	.0000	.0000	.0000	.0001	.0001	.0001	.0001	.0001	.0001	.0002	.0002
19	.0000	.0000	.0000	.0000	.0000	.0000	.0000	.0000	.0001	.0001	.0001

x	7.00	7.10	7.20	7.30	7.40	7.50	7.60	7.70	7.80	7.90	8.00
0	.0009	.0008	.0007	.0007	.0006	.0006	.0005	.0005	.0004	.0004	.0003
1	.0064	.0059	.0054	.0049	.0045	.0041	.0038	.0035	.0032	.0029	.0027
2	.0223	.0208	.0194	.0180	.0167	.0156	.0145	.0134	.0125	.0116	.0107
3	.0521	.0492	.0464	.0438	.0413	.0389	.0366	.0345	.0324	.0305	.0286
4	.0912	.0874	.0836	.0799	.0764	.0729	.0696	.0663	.0632	.0602	.0573
5	.1277	.1241	.1204	.1167	.1130	.1094	.1057	.1021	.0986	.0951	.0916
6	.1490	.1468	.1445	.1420	.1394	.1367	.1339	.1311	.1282	.1252	.1221
7	.1490	.1489	.1486	.1481	.1474	.1465	.1454	.1442	.1428	.1413	.1396
8	.1304	.1321	.1337	.1351	.1363	.1373	.1381	.1388	.1392	.1395	.1396
9	.1014	.1042	.1070	.1096	.1121	.1144	.1167	.1187	.1207	.1224	.1241
10	.0710	.0740	.0770	.0800	.0829	.0858	.0887	.0914	.0941	.0967	.0993
11	.0452	.0478	.0504	.0531	.0558	.0585	.0613	.0640	.0667	.0695	.0722
12	.0263	.0283	.0303	.0323	.0344	.0366	.0388	.0411	.0434	.0457	.0481
13	.0142	.0154	.0168	.0181	.0196	.0211	.0227	.0243	.0260	.0278	.0296
14	.0071	.0078	.0086	.0095	.0104	.0113	.0123	.0134	.0145	.0157	.0169
15	.0033	.0037	.0041	.0046	.0051	.0057	.0062	.0069	.0075	.0083	.0090
16	.0014	.0016	.0019	.0021	.0024	.0026	.0030	.0033	.0037	.0041	.0045
17	.0006	.0007	.0008	.0009	.0010	.0012	.0013	.0015	.0017	.0019	.0021
18	.0002	.0003	.0003	.0004	.0004	.0005	.0006	.0006	.0007	.0008	.0009
19	.0001	.0001	.0001	.0001	.0002	.0002	.0002	.0003	.0003	.0003	.0004
20	.0000	.0000	.0000	.0001	.0001	.0001	.0001	.0001	.0001	.0001	.0002
21	.0000	.0000	.0000	.0000	.0000	.0000	.0000	.0000	.0000	.0001	.0001

x	8.10	8.20	8.30	8.40	8.50	8.60	8.70	8.80	8.90	9.00	9.10
0	.0003	.0003	.0002	.0002	.0002	.0002	.0002	.0002	.0001	.0001	.0001
1	.0025	.0023	.0021	.0019	.0017	.0016	.0014	.0013	.0012	.0011	.0010
2	.0100	.0092	.0086	.0079	.0074	.0068	.0063	.0058	.0054	.0050	.0046
3	.0269	.0252	.0237	.0222	.0208	.0195	.0183	.0171	.0160	.0150	.0140
4	.0544	.0517	.0491	.0466	.0443	.0420	.0398	.0377	.0357	.0337	.0319

Poisson Probabilities (continued)

λ

x	8.10	8.20	8.30	8.40	8.50	8.60	8.70	8.80	8.90	9.00	9.10
5	.0882	.0849	.0816	.0784	.0752	.0722	.0692	.0663	.0635	.0607	.0581
6	.1191	.1160	.1128	.1097	.1066	.1034	.1003	.0972	.0941	.0911	.0881
7	.1378	.1358	.1338	.1317	.1294	.1271	.1247	.1222	.1197	.1171	.1145
8	.1395	.1392	.1388	.1382	.1375	.1366	.1356	.1344	.1332	.1318	.1302
9	.1256	.1269	.1280	.1290	.1299	.1306	.1311	.1315	.1317	.1318	.1317
10	.1017	.1040	.1063	.1084	.1104	.1123	.1140	.1157	.1172	.1186	.1198
11	.0749	.0776	.0802	.0828	.0853	.0878	.0902	.0925	.0948	.0970	.0991
12	.0505	.0530	.0555	.0579	.0604	.0629	.0654	.0679	.0703	.0728	.0752
13	.0315	.0334	.0354	.0374	.0395	.0416	.0438	.0459	.0481	.0504	.0526
14	.0182	.0196	.0210	.0225	.0240	.0256	.0272	.0289	.0306	.0324	.0342
15	.0098	.0107	.0116	.0126	.0136	.0147	.0158	.0169	.0182	.0194	.0208
16	.0050	.0055	.0060	.0066	.0072	.0079	.0086	.0093	.0101	.0109	.0118
17	.0024	.0026	.0029	.0033	.0036	.0040	.0044	.0048	.0053	.0058	.0063
18	.0011	.0012	.0014	.0015	.0017	.0019	.0021	.0024	.0026	.0029	.0032
19	.0005	.0005	.0006	.0007	.0008	.0009	.0010	.0011	.0012	.0014	.0015
20	.0002	.0002	.0002	.0003	.0003	.0004	.0004	.0005	.0005	.0006	.0007
21	.0001	.0001	.0001	.0001	.0001	.0002	.0002	.0002	.0002	.0002	.0003
22	.0000	.0000	.0000	.0000	.0001	.0001	.0001	.0001	.0001	.0001	.0001

x	9.20	9.30	9.40	9.50	9.60	9.70	9.80	9.90	10.00	11.00	12.00
0	.0001	.0001	.0001	.0001	.0001	.0001	.0001	.0001	.0000	.0000	.0000
1	.0009	.0009	.0008	.0007	.0007	.0006	.0005	.0005	.0005	.0002	.0001
2	.0043	.0040	.0037	.0034	.0031	.0029	.0027	.0025	.0023	.0010	.0004
3	.0131	.0123	.0115	.0107	.0100	.0093	.0087	.0081	.0076	.0037	.0018
4	.0302	.0285	.0269	.0254	.0240	.0226	.0213	.0201	.0189	.0102	.0053
5	.0555	.0530	.0506	.0483	.0460	.0439	.0418	.0398	.0378	.0224	.0127
6	.0851	.0822	.0793	.0764	.0736	.0709	.0682	.0656	.0631	.0411	.0255
7	.1118	.1091	.1064	.1037	.1010	.0982	.0955	.0928	.0901	.0646	.0437
8	.1286	.1269	.1251	.1232	.1212	.1191	.1170	.1148	.1126	.0888	.0655
9	.1315	.1311	.1306	.1300	.1293	.1284	.1274	.1263	.1251	.1085	.0874
10	.1210	.1219	.1228	.1235	.1241	.1245	.1249	.1250	.1251	.1194	.1048
11	.1012	.1031	.1049	.1067	.1083	.1098	.1112	.1125	.1137	.1194	.1144
12	.0776	.0799	.0822	.0844	.0866	.0888	.0908	.0928	.0948	.1094	.1144
13	.0549	.0572	.0594	.0617	.0640	.0662	.0685	.0707	.0729	.0926	.1056
14	.0361	.0380	.0399	.0419	.0439	.0459	.0479	.0500	.0521	.0728	.0905
15	.0221	.0235	.0250	.0265	.0281	.0297	.0313	.0330	.0347	.0534	.0724
16	.0127	.0137	.0147	.0157	.0168	.0180	.0192	.0204	.0217	.0367	.0543
17	.0069	.0075	.0081	.0088	.0095	.0103	.0111	.0119	.0128	.0237	.0383
18	.0035	.0039	.0042	.0046	.0051	.0055	.0060	.0065	.0071	.0145	.0255
19	.0017	.0019	.0021	.0023	.0026	.0028	.0031	.0034	.0037	.0084	.0161
20	.0008	.0009	.0010	.0011	.0012	.0014	.0015	.0017	.0019	.0046	.0097
21	.0003	.0004	.0004	.0005	.0006	.0006	.0007	.0008	.0009	.0024	.0055
22	.0001	.0002	.0002	.0002	.0002	.0003	.0003	.0004	.0004	.0012	.0030
23	.0001	.0001	.0001	.0001	.0001	.0001	.0001	.0002	.0002	.0006	.0016
24	.0000	.0000	.0000	.0000	.0000	.0000	.0001	.0001	.0001	.0003	.0008

Poisson Probabilities (continued)

x	λ 13.00	14.00	15.00	16.00	17.00	18.00	19.00	20.00	21.00	22.00	23.00
0	.0000	.0000	.0000	.0000	.0000	.0000	.0000	.0000	.0000	.0000	.0000
1	.0000	.0000	.0000	.0000	.0000	.0000	.0000	.0000	.0000	.0000	.0000
2	.0002	.0001	.0000	.0000	.0000	.0000	.0000	.0000	.0000	.0000	.0000
3	.0008	.0004	.0002	.0001	.0000	.0000	.0000	.0000	.0000	.0000	.0000
4	.0027	.0013	.0006	.0003	.0001	.0001	.0000	.0000	.0000	.0000	.0000
5	.0070	.0037	.0019	.0010	.0005	.0002	.0001	.0001	.0000	.0000	.0000
6	.0152	.0087	.0048	.0026	.0014	.0007	.0004	.0002	.0001	.0000	.0000
7	.0281	.0174	.0104	.0060	.0034	.0019	.0010	.0005	.0003	.0001	.0001
8	.0457	.0304	.0194	.0120	.0072	.0042	.0024	.0013	.0007	.0004	.0002
9	.0661	.0473	.0324	.0213	.0135	.0083	.0050	.0029	.0017	.0009	.0005
10	.0859	.0663	.0486	.0341	.0230	.0150	.0095	.0058	.0035	.0020	.0012
11	.1015	.0844	.0663	.0496	.0355	.0245	.0164	.0106	.0067	.0041	.0024
12	.1099	.0984	.0829	.0661	.0504	.0368	.0259	.0176	.0116	.0075	.0047
13	.1099	.1060	.0956	.0814	.0658	.0509	.0378	.0271	.0188	.0127	.0083
14	.1021	.1060	.1024	.0930	.0800	.0655	.0514	.0387	.0282	.0199	.0136
15	.0885	.0989	.1024	.0992	.0906	.0786	.0650	.0516	.0395	.0292	.0209
16	.0719	.0866	.0960	.0992	.0963	.0884	.0772	.0646	.0518	.0401	.0301
17	.0550	.0713	.0847	.0934	.0963	.0936	.0863	.0760	.0640	.0520	.0407
18	.0397	.0554	.0706	.0830	.0909	.0936	.0911	.0844	.0747	.0635	.0520
19	.0272	.0409	.0557	.0699	.0814	.0887	.0911	.0888	.0826	.0735	.0629
20	.0177	.0286	.0418	.0559	.0692	.0798	.0866	.0888	.0867	.0809	.0724
21	.0109	.0191	.0299	.0426	.0560	.0684	.0783	.0846	.0867	.0847	.0793
22	.0065	.0121	.0204	.0310	.0433	.0560	.0676	.0769	.0828	.0847	.0829
23	.0037	.0074	.0133	.0216	.0320	.0438	.0559	.0669	.0756	.0810	.0829
24	.0020	.0043	.0083	.0144	.0226	.0328	.0442	.0557	.0661	.0743	.0794
25	.0010	.0024	.0050	.0092	.0154	.0237	.0336	.0446	.0555	.0654	.0731
26	.0005	.0013	.0029	.0057	.0101	.0164	.0246	.0343	.0449	.0553	.0646
27	.0002	.0007	.0016	.0034	.0063	.0109	.0173	.0254	.0349	.0451	.0551
28	.0001	.0003	.0009	.0019	.0038	.0070	.0117	.0181	.0262	.0354	.0452
29	.0001	.0002	.0004	.0011	.0023	.0044	.0077	.0125	.0190	.0269	.0359
30	.0000	.0001	.0002	.0006	.0013	.0026	.0049	.0083	.0133	.0197	.0275
31	.0000	.0000	.0001	.0003	.0007	.0015	.0030	.0054	.0090	.0140	.0204
32	.0000	.0000	.0001	.0001	.0004	.0009	.0018	.0034	.0059	.0096	.0147
33	.0000	.0000	.0000	.0001	.0002	.0005	.0010	.0020	.0038	.0064	.0102
34	.0000	.0000	.0000	.0000	.0001	.0002	.0006	.0012	.0023	.0041	.0069
35	.0000	.0000	.0000	.0000	.0000	.0001	.0003	.0007	.0014	.0026	.0045
36	.0000	.0000	.0000	.0000	.0000	.0001	.0002	.0004	.0008	.0016	.0029
37	.0000	.0000	.0000	.0000	.0000	.0000	.0001	.0002	.0005	.0009	.0018
38	.0000	.0000	.0000	.0000	.0000	.0000	.0000	.0001	.0003	.0005	.0011
39	.0000	.0000	.0000	.0000	.0000	.0000	.0000	.0001	.0001	.0003	.0006
40	.0000	.0000	.0000	.0000	.0000	.0000	.0000	.0000	.0001	.0002	.0004
41	.0000	.0000	.0000	.0000	.0000	.0000	.0000	.0000	.0000	.0001	.0002
42	.0000	.0000	.0000	.0000	.0000	.0000	.0000	.0000	.0000	.0000	.0001
43	.0000	.0000	.0000	.0000	.0000	.0000	.0000	.0000	.0000	.0000	.0001

Table H – **Critical Values of** χ^2

Numerical entries represent the area to the right of the critical value.

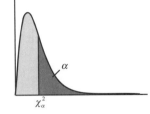

df	$\chi^2_{.995}$	$\chi^2_{.990}$	$\chi^2_{.975}$	$\chi^2_{.950}$	$\chi^2_{.900}$	$\chi^2_{.100}$	$\chi^2_{.050}$	$\chi^2_{.025}$	$\chi^2_{.010}$	$\chi^2_{.005}$
1	0.000	0.000	0.001	0.004	0.016	2.706	3.841	5.024	6.635	7.879
2	0.010	0.020	0.051	0.103	0.211	4.605	5.991	7.378	9.210	10.597
3	0.072	0.115	0.216	0.352	0.584	6.251	7.815	9.348	11.345	12.838
4	0.207	0.297	0.484	0.711	1.064	7.779	9.488	11.143	13.277	14.860
5	0.412	0.554	0.831	1.145	1.610	9.236	11.070	12.833	15.086	16.750
6	0.676	0.872	1.237	1.635	2.204	10.645	12.592	14.449	16.812	18.548
7	0.989	1.239	1.690	2.167	2.833	12.017	14.067	16.013	18.475	20.278
8	1.344	1.646	2.180	2.733	3.490	13.362	15.507	17.535	20.090	21.955
9	1.735	2.088	2.700	3.325	4.168	14.684	16.919	19.023	21.666	23.589
10	2.156	2.558	3.247	3.940	4.865	15.987	18.307	20.483	23.209	25.188
11	2.603	3.053	3.816	4.575	5.578	17.275	19.675	21.920	24.725	26.757
12	3.074	3.571	4.404	5.226	6.304	18.549	21.026	23.337	26.217	28.300
13	3.565	4.107	5.009	5.892	7.042	19.812	22.362	24.736	27.688	29.819
14	4.075	4.660	5.629	6.571	7.790	21.064	23.685	26.119	29.141	31.319
15	4.601	5.229	6.262	7.261	8.547	22.307	24.996	27.488	30.578	32.801
16	5.142	5.812	6.908	7.962	9.312	23.542	26.296	28.845	32.000	34.267
17	5.697	6.408	7.564	8.672	10.085	24.769	27.587	30.191	33.409	35.718
18	6.265	7.015	8.231	9.390	10.865	25.989	28.869	31.526	34.805	37.156
19	6.844	7.633	8.907	10.117	11.651	27.204	30.144	32.852	36.191	38.582
20	7.434	8.260	9.591	10.851	12.443	28.412	31.410	34.170	37.566	39.997
21	8.034	8.897	10.283	11.591	13.240	29.615	32.671	35.479	38.932	41.401
22	8.643	9.542	10.982	12.338	14.041	30.813	33.924	36.781	40.289	42.796
23	9.260	10.196	11.689	13.091	14.848	32.007	35.172	38.076	41.638	44.181
24	9.886	10.856	12.401	13.848	15.659	33.196	36.415	39.364	42.980	45.559
25	10.520	11.524	13.120	14.611	16.473	34.382	37.652	40.646	44.314	46.928
26	11.160	12.198	13.844	15.379	17.292	35.563	38.885	41.923	45.642	48.290
27	11.808	12.878	14.573	16.151	18.114	36.741	40.113	43.195	46.963	49.645
28	12.461	13.565	15.308	16.928	18.939	37.916	41.337	44.461	48.278	50.993
29	13.121	14.256	16.047	17.708	19.768	39.087	42.557	45.722	49.588	52.336
30	13.787	14.953	16.791	18.493	20.599	40.256	43.773	46.979	50.892	53.672
40	20.707	22.164	24.433	26.509	29.051	51.805	55.758	59.342	63.691	66.766
50	27.991	29.707	32.357	34.764	37.689	63.167	67.505	71.420	76.154	79.490
60	35.534	37.485	40.482	43.188	46.459	74.397	79.082	83.298	88.379	91.952
70	43.275	45.442	48.758	51.739	55.329	85.527	90.531	95.023	100.425	104.215
80	51.172	53.540	57.153	60.391	64.278	96.578	101.879	106.629	112.329	116.321
90	59.196	61.754	65.647	69.126	73.291	107.565	113.145	118.136	124.116	128.299
100	67.328	70.065	74.222	77.929	82.358	118.498	124.342	129.561	135.807	140.169